TELECOMMUNICATIONS
for Business

Eleanor Hollis Tedesco

University of Maryland

 PWS-KENT PUBLISHING COMPANY, BOSTON

PWS-KENT
Publishing Company

Sponsoring Editor: Rolf Janke
Editorial Assistant: Maureen A. Brooks
Production Editor: Eve B. Mendelsohn
Production: Technical Texts
Manufacturing Coordinator: Margaret Sullivan Higgins
Interior Designer: George McLean
Cover Designer: Eve B. Mendelsohn
Cover Photographer: Kenneth Scallon/The Image Bank
Compositor: Thompson Type
Cover Printer: John P. Pow Company, Inc.
Text Printer and Binder: Arcata Graphics/Halliday

PWS-KENT Publishing Company is a division of Wadsworth, Inc.

Copyright © 1990 by PWS-KENT Publishing Company. All rights reserved. No part of this book may be reproduced, stored in a retrieval system, or transcribed, in any form or by any means, electronic, mechanical, photocopying, recording, or otherwise, without the prior written permission of the publisher, PWS-KENT Publishing Company, 20 Park Plaza, Boston, Massachusetts 02116.

Printed in the United States of America.
1 2 3 4 5 6 7 — 94 93 92 91 90

Library of Congress Cataloging-in-Publication Data

Tedesco, Eleanor Hollis.
    Telecommunications for business / Eleanor Hollis Tedesco.
      p. cm.
    Includes bibliographical references.
    ISBN 0-534-92001-2
    1. Business—Communication systems.   2. Telecommunication systems.
  3. Computer networks.   4. Data transmission systems. I. Title.
HF5541.T4T43   1990   89-23082
651.7—dc20   CIP

Kent Series in Business Education

Arntson, **Word/Information Processing: Concepts, Procedures, and Systems,** Second Edition

Arntson/Auvil, **MS/PC DOS on the IBM PC and Compatibles: Concepts, Exercises, and Applications**

Arntson/Todesco, **Word/Information Processing: Exercises, Applications, and Procedures,** Second Edition

Carbone, **Modern Business English: A Systems Approach**

Clark/Clark, **HOW5: A Handbook for Office Workers,** Fifth Edition

Clark/Clark, **Universal Transcription**

Guffey, **Business English,** Third Edition

Guffey, **Essentials of Business Communication**

Himstreet/Baty, **Business Communications: Principles and Methods,** Ninth Edition

Kupsh/Rhodes, **Automated Office Systems for Managers and Professionals**

Lee, **Self-Paced Business Mathematics,** Fourth Edition

Lundgren/Lundgren, **Records Management in the Computer Age**

McCready, **Business Mathematics,** Sixth Edition

McCready, **Office Machines: Electronic Calculators,** Seventh Edition

Penrose/Rasberry/Myers, **Advanced Business Communication**

Quinn/Arntson, **WordPerfect 5.0**

Ruch/Crawford, **Business Reports: Written and Oral**

Swindle, **Business Math Basics,** Fourth Edition

Tedesco, **Telecommunications for Business**

Wells, **Communications in Business,** Fifth Edition

PREFACE

"Impressive as technological changes have been in other fields, there is no more striking example than in communications of how they operate to instigate social change, modifying the material environment, creating new and perplexing problems of adjustment and changing manners and morals."

Recent Social Trends in the United States, 1933.

Telecommunications has become the infrastructure of the information age. For business people to exchange information and succeed in the workplace today, they must know how to communicate and perform their tasks in an environment that is telecommunications-oriented, including working with and often managing people with extensive technical expertise. This book gives the nontechnical reader a basic foundation of the knowledge and concepts of telecommunications and, at the same time, provides the reader with a working knowledge of telecommunications technology, applications, and management.

■ Overview

Each chapter begins with an outline that provides an overview of the topics that will be covered in the chapter. The performance-based objectives identify the purpose of the chapter and primary learning goals. To arouse interest and give relevance to what is to be read or studied, a diagram and brief scenario follow the objectives and describe actual technological applications occurring in the workplace. Each chapter contains many diagrams and photographs that illustrate concepts and applications to help the reader apply, analyze, synthesize, and evaluate the material presented in the text.

Abundant end-of-chapter material helps enhance the reader's learning and understanding. A summary serves as a snapshot or quick overview of the chapter; it can be read before and/or after reading the chapter. A list of important terms follows the summary; definitions can be found within the chapter or in the glossary at the end of the book. A self-quiz on chapter terms and concepts gives immediate feedback on chapter basics (answers can be found in Appendix E). Review questions provide another opportunity for self-checking and learning reinforcement. Activities/projects offer an opportunity for more in-depth work with chapter concepts and applications. A chapter case provides a situation similar to what a person might face in the workplace. Finally a list of readings and resources provides suggestions for further study.

The book is divided into four parts. Part I presents the reader with an overview of the telecommunications industry. Part II presents the technological concepts necessary to understand how communication systems operate. Chapter 2 introduces the basic terms and concepts of voice transmission, analog and digital transmissions, and the various types of transmission media and their impairments. Chapter 3 tells how a telephone works, how calls are handled, and what services are available and describes the telecommunications network and its components and features. In Chapter 4, the reader is given an overview of the transition of AT&T from a regulated monopoly to a number of fully competitive businesses and a description of the options now available to long-distance users. Chapter 5 covers the interconnect industry and the basic business telephone systems (key telephone, PBX, and Centrex). Chapter 6 describes the basic network configurations and accompanying hardware used for communicating data over public and private networks while Chapter 7 presents the basics about wide- and local-area networks and how companies manage and utilize them. Chapter 8 discusses the technologies, operations, and applications of microwave and satellite communications including teleports.

Part III describes the various telecommunications applications: electronic mail including telex, computer-based message systems, electronic document interchange, voice processing, and facsimile (Chapters 9–11); videotex and teletext (Chapter 12); teleconferencing (Chapter 13); and mobile communications (Chapter 14). Each one of these applications is discussed in terms of its technology, operations, and applications in the workplace in order to assist the reader in selection and management.

In Part IV the reader learns how to manage a telephone/telecommunications system including the basic concepts of traffic management and the available tools for managing telephone networks. Telecommunication trends are also identified.

Five appendices present (A) a quick review of the evolution of telecommunications, (B) a history of telecommunications regulations, (C) a list of the major standard-setting organizations, (D) a list of commercial videotex systems and services, and (E) answers to chapter self-quizzes.

■ Instructor's Manual

The Instructor's Manual assists both the instructor and the student by providing the following:

Pretest. A pretest to be administered at the opening of the course gives the instructor information about how much students already know and gives the students a glimpse of what they'll be learning in the course.

Course Schedules. Suggested teaching plans are included to assist in planning the course.

Test Bank. Multiple choice and true/false questions are provided for each chapter. A final examination is also included.

Answers to the Test Bank. Answers to the Test Bank are included with page/source references.

Answers to Activities/Projects. Answers to the textbook review questions are also included with page number references.

Teaching Suggestions. Ideas are offered for implementing class presentations and evaluating learning. Also included are suggestions for obtaining more information for additional activities, particularly resources offered by companies for implementing chapter concepts (such as providing actual hands-on experience).

Transparencies. Transparency masters of key concepts are included for each chapter.

■ Acknowledgments and Dedication

I am indebted to the many individuals, companies, and professional organizations who contributed to the preparation of this book. I also am especially thankful to the following professors for their suggestions and recommendations given during the development of the book: Ron Kapper (College of DuPage), James Koerlin (Golden Gate University), Fred Lovgren (Ferris State University), Rhonda Rhodes (California State Polytechnic University), Elaine Schmittke (Nassau Community College), and Kay Wagoner (Ball State University).

I am particularly grateful to Sara T. Tagget of Dialcom and James B. Tedesco of Data General for their technical assistance. A special word of thanks goes to Paul H. Tedesco, my husband, for his encouragement during the book's preparation.

I also appreciate the outstanding assistance of many PWS-KENT employees—especially Read Wickham, Rolf Janke, Maureen Brooks, Eve Mendelsohn—and Sylvia Dovner at Technical Texts.

This book is dedicated to my father, Earl A. Hollis, a former purchasing manager and 36-year employee of AT&T Bell Laboratories. His remarkable knowledge of telecommunications and enthusiasm for developments in the industry have provided me with a rare source of information and understanding of a field that has become an integral part of our existence.

Eleanor Hollis Tedesco

CONTENTS

I Introduction to Telecommunications 1

1 Telecommunications Overview 2

Telecommunications Defined 4

A Sampling of Telecommunications Technologies and Applications 4
  Telecommunications Technologies 4; Telecommunications Applications 5

Major Issues in the Telecommunications Industry 10
  The Regulatory Environment 10; Equipment and Network Standards 12; Privacy/Security 13

The Changing Role of the Telecommunications Manager 14
  Increased Internal Visibility 14; New Career Paths 15; New Responsibilities 15; Job Qualifications 15

Summary 16
  Key Terms 16; Self-Quiz 16; Review Questions 17; Activities/Projects 18; Notes 18; Additional Readings 18

II Principles of Telecommunications 19

2 Transmission Basics 20

Principles of Voice Transmission 22
  Sound Waves 22; Electrical Waves 24; Bandwidth 24

Signal Conversion 27
  Analog Signals and Circuits 29; Digital Signals and Circuits 29; Converting the Signals 34

Transmission 36
  The Transmission Circuit 37; Signal Direction 37; Telephone Transmission Links 38; Modulation 39; Multiplexing 39

Transmission Impairments and Media 43
  Transmission Impairments 44; Transmission Media 49

Summary 57
  Key Terms 57; Self-Quiz 58; Review Questions 59; Activities/Projects 59; Additional Readings 60

3 Telephone Basics 62

Telephone Components 64

The Transmitter and the Receiver 64; The Switchhook 67; The Rotary Dial or Pushbutton Keypad 67; The Ringer 67

Basic Telephone Operations 68

The Central Office 68; Local Telephone Calls 71; The Numbering Plan—Domestic and International 73

Exchange Services 76

Basic Exchange Services 76; Custom Calling Services 78; Class Calling Services 79; Business Exchange Services—Centrex Services 80

The Telecommunications Network 82

Telecommunications Network Defined 82; Physical Facilities of the Telecommunications Network 82

Summary 87

Key Terms 88; Self-Quiz 88; Review Questions 89; Activities/Projects 90; Case: Selecting Exchange Services 90; Additional Readings 91

4 The Public Telephone System 92

The Bell System in 1982 94

The American Telephone and Telegraph Company 94; Independent Telephone Companies 96

The Bell System After Divestiture 96

The New AT&T 96; The Twenty-Two Bell Operating Companies 98; Regional Bell Operating Companies 98; Independent Telephone Companies 99; Long-Distance Competitors 99

The Public Switched Telephone Network 100

PSTN Defined 100; Hierarchy of Switching 100; Dynamic Nonhierarchical Routing 103

Local Access and Transport Areas or Market Service Areas 103

IntraLATA and InterLATA Calls 103; Regulatory Agencies 105

Long-Distance Carriers 106

Equal Access 106; How an OCC Operates 106; Resellers 107; Bypassing the PSTN 108

Long-Distance Services 109

AT&T Communications 109; MCI Communications 110; Wide-Area/Bulk-Rate Services 110

Private Lines 113

Tie Lines 114; Foreign Exchange 114; Remote Call Forwarding 115; T-1 Lines 116

Selecting a Long-Distance Carrier *116*

    Cost of Using a Carrier for Long-Distance Calling *116;* Other Factors to Consider *117;* Application *118*

Summary *118*

    Key Terms *119;* Self-Quiz *119;* Review Questions *120;* Activities/Projects *121;* Case: Should This Company Use WATS for Long-Distance Calling? *121;* Notes *123;* Additional Readings *123*

5 *Business Telephone Systems* *124*

The Interconnect Industry *126*

    The Carterfone Decision *126;* Computer Inquiry II *127*

Key Telephone Systems *127*

    Evolution of Key System Technology *129;* 1A2 Key Telephone System—An Electromechanical System *130;* Electronic Key Telephone System *132;* Hybrid Key Telephone System *133;* KTS Functions/Features *135;* KTS Costs *136;* The Key System Market *136*

Private Branch Exchanges *137*

    Evolution of PBX Technology *138;* PBX Components and Operation *139;* PBX Features *144;* PBX Architecture—Centralized or Distributed *150;* The PBX Market *151*

Centrex Services *151*

    Evolution of Centrex Services Technology *153;* Centrex Services Operation *153;* Centrex Services Features *154;* Centrex Services Rates *155;* Centrex Services Market *155*

Comparison of PBX Systems and Centrex Services *155*

Selecting a Business Telephone System *157*

    Phase 1: Analyze the Current Telephone System *157;* Phase 2: Specify the Requirements of the New Telephone System *158;* Phase 3: Select the New Telephone System *158*

Summary *160*

    Key Terms *160;* Self-Quiz *160;* Review Questions *161;* Activities/Projects *162;* Case: Should a Company Replace Its Key System? *162;* Notes *163;* Additional Readings *163*

6 *Data Communication Networks and Hardware* *164*

Terminals *166*

    Types of Terminals *166;* Selecting a Terminal *169*

Buffers *169*

Modems *169*

    Modem Defined *170;* Modem Configuration *172;* Types of Modems *175;* Modem Features *182;* Selecting a Modem *183*

Point-To-Point and Multipoint Networks   *185*

    Point-To-Point Network *185*;   Multipoint Network *187*;   Multiplexing Networks *190*

Front-End Processors   *197*

Packet-Switching Networks   *199*

    Packet-Switching Routes *202*;   Types of Packet-Switching Networks *202*; X.25 Standard *204*;   Advantages of Packet-Switching Networks *204*; Selecting a Packet-Switching Network *204*

Summary   *205*

    Key Terms *206*;   Self-Quiz *206*;   Review Questions *207*;   Activities/ Projects *208*;   Case: Comparing Costs of Network Operations *209*; Additional Readings *210*

7 *Networks: Local- and Wide-Area Networks*   *212*

Local-Area Networks and Wide-Area Networks   *214*

    Local-Area Network Defined *214*;   Wide-Area Network Defined *215*;   Why LANs and WANs? *216*

LAN Technology   *217*

    LAN Hardware Components *217*;   LAN Software Components *219*;   LAN Topologies *221*;   LAN Access Methods *225*;   LAN Transmission Media *228*; LAN Transmission Methods *230*

LAN Standards   *231*

    The OSI Model *232*;   IEEE 800 Standard for LAN *234*;   De Facto Standards *235*

Commecial LANs—The Hardware Configuration   *237*

LANs to LANs to WANs   *237*

    LAN Hierarchy *237*;   Span Technology *239*

Alternatives to LANs   *247*

    Floppy-Disk Exchange *247*;   Data Switches *248*;   SubLANs *250*; Data PBX *252*;   Multiuser Systems *254*;   Central Office Local-Area Network *256*

Selecting and Managing a LAN   *256*

    Do You Need a LAN? *256*;   Selecting a LAN *256*;   Managing a LAN *256*

Integrated Services Digital Network   *257*

    ISDN Technology and Operation *258*;   Comparison of ISDNs and LANs *260*;   Benefits of ISDN *260*

Summary   *260*

    Key Terms *261*;   Self-Quiz *261*;   Review Questions *263*;   Activities/ Projects *263*;   Case: Increasing Productivity with LANs *264*; References *265*;   Additional Readings *265*

8 Microwave and Satellite Communications 268

Microwave Radio 270

Microwave Radio Defined *271;* Microwave Radio Evolution *272;* Microwave Radio Technology and Operation *272;* Comparison of Fiber-Optic Cable, Leased Lines, and Microwave Radio *280;* Planning a Microwave Radio System *280*

Satellite Communications 282

Satellite Communications Defined *285;* Satellite Communications Evolution *285;* Satellite Technology and Operation *287;* Comparison of Satellite Communications with Fiber-Optic Networks *299*

Selecting a VSAT System 300

Planning a VSAT System *300;* Selecting a VSAT System *301*

Teleports 302

Teleport Defined *302;* Types of Teleports *303;* Teleport Operation *304;* Profile of a Teleport *305;* Teleport Issues and Trends *307*

Summary 308

Key Terms *308;* Self-Quiz *308;* Review Questions *309;* Activities/Projects *310;* Notes *310;* Additional Readings *311*

III Telecommunications Applications 313

9 Electronic Mail 314

Electronic Mail Defined 316
Evolution of Electronic Mail 317
Telex 317

Origin *318;* How Telex Operates *318;* Domestic Telex *319;* International Telex *320;* Benefits and Drawbacks *320*

Computer-Based Message Systems 321

CBMS Defined *321;* How Electronic Mail Operates *322;* Types of CBMSs *327;* Benefits and Drawbacks of CBMSs *332*

Electronic Mail Standards 332

The X.400 Standard *332;* The X.500 Standard *334*

Electronic Data Interchange 337

EDI Defined *337;* How EDI Operates *338;* EDI Standards *342;* Benefits and Drawbacks of EDI *344*

Selecting an E-Mail System 345
Summary 346

Key Terms *348;* Self-Quiz *348;* Review Questions *349;* Activities/Projects *350;* Case: Which Public E-Mail Service Provider Should It Be? *351;* Notes *351;* Additional Readings *351*

10 *Voice Processing* 352

Voice Processing Defined 355
Voice Processing Evolution 355
How to Use Voice Processing 356
Operating a Voice Processing System 356; Voice Processing System Features 358

Voice Processing Technology 360
Digitized Speech 361; Text-to-Speech Conversion 369; Voice-to-Text Conversion 371

Types of Voice Processing Systems 373
Stand-Alone Voice Processing Systems 373; Integrated Voice Processing Systems 374; Automated Office Systems 375; Service Bureaus 376

Voice Processing Functions and Applications 376
Telephone Answering 376; Caller Routing 377; Interactive Messaging 378; Information Providing 378; Transaction Processing 379

Benefits and Drawbacks of Voice Processing 379
Benefits of Voice Processing 379; Drawbacks of Voice Processing 381

Selecting a Voice Processing System 382
Summary 384
Key Terms 384; Self-Quiz 384; Review Questions 385; Activities/Projects 386; Case: A Paper Nightmare 386; Notes 387; Additional Readings 387

11 *Facsimile* 388

Facsimile Defined 390
Facsimile Evolution 390
Facsimile Technology 392
Fax System Components 392; Sending and Receiving 393; Printing 395; Transmission Facility 395

Facsimile Equipment Standards 396
Classification of Fax Machines 396; Machine Protocol and Transmission 397

Facsimile Equipment 399
Types of Equipment 399; Placement of Equipment 401; Equipment Features 402; Special Fax Equipment 404

Public Facsimile Services 408
Users of Public Fax Services 408; Companies Offering Public Fax Services 408; Services Available to Fax Owners 410

Facsimile Applications 411

Benefits and Drawbacks of Facsimile 412

Benefits of Facsimile *412;* Drawbacks of Facsimile *414*

Selecting a Fax System 415

Phase 1: Evaluate Your Current Delivery System *415;* Phase 2: Select a Fax System *415*

Summary 418

Key Terms *418;* Self-Quiz *419;* Review Questions *420;* Activities/Projects *421;* Case: Facsimile versus Telex *422;* Notes *423;* Additional Readings *423*

12 *Videotex and Teletext* 424

Evolution of Videotex and Teletext 426

Videotex 427

Videotex Defined *427;* How Videotex Operates *427;* Videotex Equipment Components *430;* Ways of Accessing a Videotex System *432*

Teletext 433

Teletext Defined *433;* How Teletext Operates *433;* Teletext Equipment Components *434*

Comparison of Videotex and Teletext Systems 436

Videotex Standards 437

Major Videotex Standards *437;* Other Standards *438*

Applications—Types 439

Information Retrieval *439;* Computation *440;* Transaction *440;* Messaging *441;* Downline Loading *441*

Applications—Ways of Using Videotex 442

Business Videotex *442;* Home or Consumer-Oriented Videotex *443;* Public Access Videotex *444*

Commercial Videotex Systems 448

General-Purpose Commercial Videotex Systems *448;* Specialized Commercial Videotex Systems *449;* Commercial Videotex—Revenue and Fees *450;* Selecting a Commercial Videotex System *452*

Videotex and Teletext Issues 454

Standards *454;* Information Reliability *455;* Information Privacy and Confidentiality *455;* Legal Issues *455*

Summary 456

Key Terms *456;* Self-Quiz *457;* Review Questions *458;* Activities/Projects *458;* Case: Costing a Videotex System/Service *459;* Notes *460;* Additional Readings *460*

13 *Teleconferencing* 462

Teleconferencing Defined 464

Types of Teleconferencing Systems 465; Applications 465

Teleconferencing Evolution 466

Audio Conferencing 468

Audio-Conferencing Transmission 468; Audio-Conferencing Bridges 469; Audio-Conferencing Equipment and Facilities 473; Benefits and Drawbacks of Audio Conferencing 476; Audio-Conferencing Applications 476

Enhanced Audio Conferencing 476

Telewriters 477; Facsimile 477; Freeze-Frame Video 478; Enhanced Audio-Conferencing Applications 479

Two-Way Videoconferencing 480

Two-Way Videoconferencing Defined 480; Videoconferencing Operation, Technology, and Equipment 480; Videoconferencing Applications 485

Business Television 485

Business Television Defined 486; Business Television Operation, Technology, and Equipment 486; Business Television Networks 487; Business Television Applications 488

Computer Conferencing 491

Computer Conferencing Defined 491; Computer Conferencing Operation 492; Computer Conferencing Applications 492; Administering Computer Conferencing 493; A Computer Conferencing System—VAX Notes 493; Benefits and Drawbacks of Computer Conferencing 494; Comparison of Electronic Mail, Bulletin Boards, and Computer Conferencing 495

Benefits and Drawbacks of Teleconferencing 496

Planning, Conducting, and Evaluating a Teleconference 498

Summary 500

Key Terms 500; Self-Quiz 501; Review Questions 502; Activities/Projects 502; Case: Traditional Training versus Teletraining 504; Notes 504; Additional Readings 505

14 *Mobile Communications* 506

Mobile Communication Services 508

Types of Mobile Communication Services 508; Evolution of Mobile Communication Services 508; Channel Availability 510

Radio Paging 510

Radio Paging Operation 511; Types of Pagers 511; Cost of Paging 512

Two-Way Radio 512

Two-Way Radio Operation 513; Conventional Two-Way Radio 514; Trunked Radio 514

Mobile Telephone Service 514

    Conventional Mobile Telephone Service *514*; Cellular Mobile Telephone Service *515*

Selecting a Cellular Telephone 522

Summary 527

    Key Terms *528*; Self-Quiz *528*; Review Questions *529*; Activities/Projects *529*; Case: Two-Way Radio System Savings Analysis *530*; Notes *531*; Additional Readings *531*

IV Telecommunications Management 533

15 *Managing Your Telephone/Telecommunications System* 534

Ten Steps to Telecommunications Management 536

Basic Traffic Concepts 537

    Traffic Defined *538*; Traffic Engineering *538*; Traffic Load *538*

Tariffs 546

Active Cost Control Methods 546

    Automatic Route Selection/Least-Cost Routing *546*; Calling Restrictions *549*; Authorization Codes and Levels of Services *549*; Timed Signals *550*

Telephone Management Systems 550

    Telephone Management Systems Defined *551*; TMS Configurations *551*; TMS Features *555*; TMS Reports *564*; Benefits of Telephone Management Systems *564*

Selecting a Telephone Management System 568

Managing Telecommunications in the Next Decade 569

    Technology Trends *569*; Regulatory Trends *570*; Organizational and Management Trends *570*

Summary 572

    Key Terms *572*; Self-Quiz *573*; Review Questions *574*; Activities/Projects *575*; Case: Analyzing a Company's Telephone Usage *576*; Notes *576*; Additional Readings *578*

Appendix A 579

The Evolution of Telecommunications: A Brief Review 579

    Telegraph *579*; Telephone *580*; Wireless Telegraphy *581*; Microwave Radio *581*; Satellite *581*; Computer Communication *581*; Telecommunications Network *582*

Appendix B   *583*

History of Telecommunications Regulations   *583*

Appendix C   *585*

Major Standard-Setting Organizations   *585*

    International Standard Setting *585;*   U.S. Standard Setting *586;*   Major Organizations *586*

Appendix D   *588*

Selected Commercial Videotex Systems/Services—System Operators   *588*

Appendix E   *591*

Answers to Chapter Self-Quizzes   *591*

Glossary   *597*

Index   *618*

PART I

Introduction to Telecommunications

CHAPTER 1

Telecommunications Overview

Telecommunications Defined

A Sampling of Telecommunications Technologies and Applications
Telecommunications Technologies
Telecommunications Applications

Major Issues in the Telecommunications Industry
The Regulatory Environment
Equipment and Network Standards
Privacy/Security

The Changing Role of the Telecommunications Manager
Increased Internal Visibility
New Career Paths
New Responsibilities
Job Qualifications

CHAPTER OBJECTIVES

After studying this chapter, you should be able to

1. Define telecommunications.
2. Give examples of telecommunications technologies and applications.
3. Describe major issues in telecommunications.
4. Discuss the changing role of the telecommunications manager.

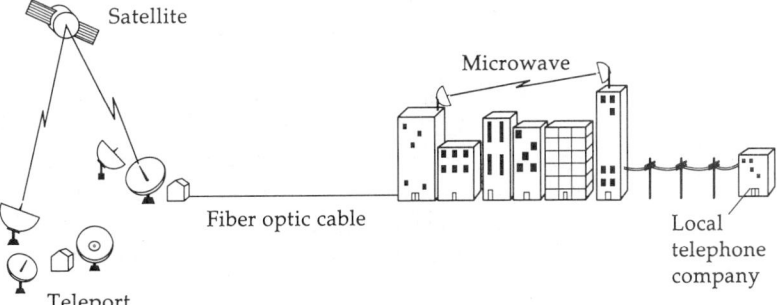

Throughout the world, telecommunications including computer technologies are changing the way businesses operate, the way we go about our daily activities, and even the way we think about our future. Technologies are being harnessed to provide efficient telecommunications in the most innovative and productive ways. They are creating new and better ways to communicate, increasing business productivity, and reducing costs.

By the year 2001, worldwide annual spending on telecommunication products and services is expected to reach $1 trillion.[1] Private and public organizations are investing heavily in telecommunications in order to deal with a world economy that is becoming increasingly dependent on moving information. At the same time, profound changes are taking place within our nation's telecommunications industry. The changes, resulting from the breakup of AT&T and deregulation, are leading to a restructuring of the marketplace.

This chapter introduces the reader to telecommunications by defining the term, giving examples of technologies and applications, identifying major issues, and discussing the changing role of the telecommunications (telecom) manager.

Telecommunications Defined

What is telecommunications? The Greek meaning for *tele* is "far off." *Communications* is the transfer of meaningful information from one location to a second location—from a sender to a receiver. The basic components include the sender or transmitter, the receiver, and the transmission link over which information flows.

More specifically, **telecommunications** is "any process that permits the passage of information from a sender to one or more receivers in any usable form (printed copy, fixed or moving pictures, visible or audible signals, etc.) by means of any electromagnetic system (electrical transmission by wire, radio, optical transmission, waveguides, etc.). Includes telegraphy, telephony,* video-telephony, data transmission, etc."[2] For a review of the evolution of telecommunications, refer to Appendix A.

A Sampling of Telecommunications Technologies and Applications

Some of the telecommunications technologies and applications that are changing how people in business communicate with each other and how they conduct business are described in this section.

■ Telecommunications Technologies

Transmission Media. Voice, data, and video can be transmitted by the use of many types of technology, such as twisted pair wire, coaxial cable, fiber-optic cable, microwave radio, and satellite communication. Microwave radio is used for communicating among several sites within a city, and satellite communication is used for transmitting over longer distances.

For example, when a company's managers in Manchester, New Hampshire, wanted to set up a communications line between two of its buildings separated by a highway, the managers selected a microwave radio system rather than trying to have the highway dug up to lay cable. The microwave system also allows the company to bypass the local telephone company, since radio signals can be transmitted from one building rooftop to another. Companies are also using fiber-optic links and microwave radio to link directly to *teleports*, from which the signals travel via satellite to another teleport or a private satellite antenna.

Local Area Networks. A local area network, commonly called a LAN, consists of high-speed cables that let such devices as computers, terminals,

---

*The engineering science of converting voices and other sounds into electrical signals that can be transmitted by wire, fiber, or radio and reconverted to audible sound upon receipt.

FIGURE 1-1   **A Local Area Network (LAN)**

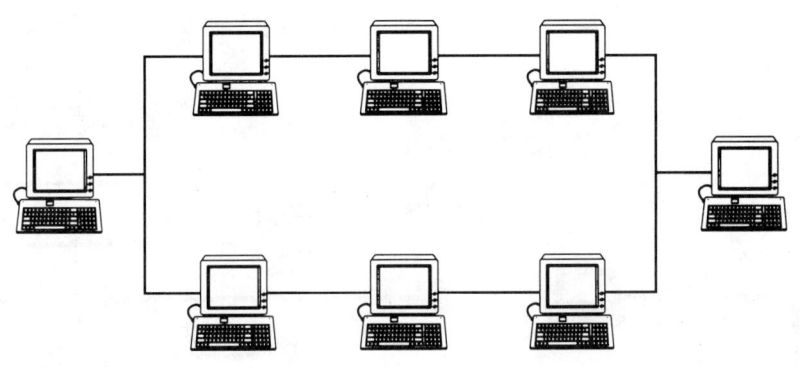

and printers "talk" to each other in a local setting, typically within an office or a factory. With a personal computer connected to a LAN, shown in Figure 1-1, an employee can transfer documents from one computer to another, access company databases for customer information, or chart monthly sales on the printer in the adjoining room—all without leaving his or her desk. A LAN can connect to another LAN, a mainframe computer, or a minicomputer within the same or another office building.

Integrated Services Digital Network (ISDN). An integrated services digital network (ISDN) is an all-digital system that allows voice, data, and video to be simultaneously transmitted by sharing high-speed digital transmission facilities. With ISDN, users conveniently access all communication services from a single entry point—a common wall-plug interface—that allows all types and makes of equipment, including telephones, computers, and facsimile machines, to exchange information worldwide. ISDN not only uses existing communication lines, which avoids having to rewire offices, but also eliminates the need to have separate wiring for different tasks. For example, a user can conduct a voice conversation with one person while simultaneously transmitting data to another person's computer. Refer to Figure 1-2 to compare communicating without ISDN and with ISDN.

■ **Telecommunications Applications**

Electronic Mail. Electronic mail comes in the form of computer-based message systems, electronic data interchange, voice processing, and facsimile. A *computer-based message system,* such as the one shown in Figure 1-3, allows the user to type a message on a computer terminal, where the message is stored for future use or forwarded to the recipient's computer. The key to the success of electronic mail is its ease of use. A user has only to

FIGURE 1-2   Comparison of Communicating With and Without ISDN

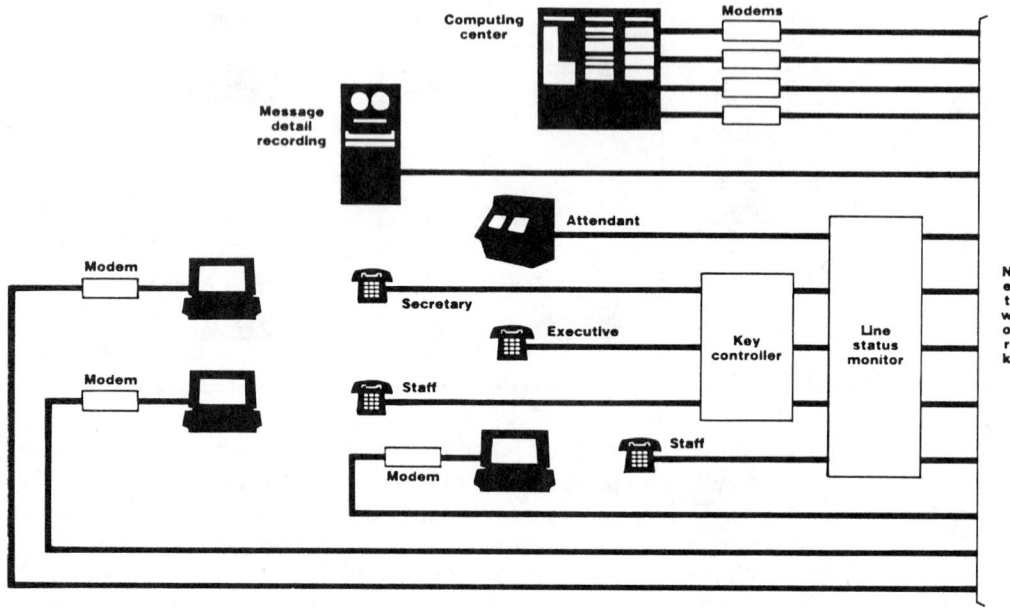

(a) Headquarters Location Without ISDN

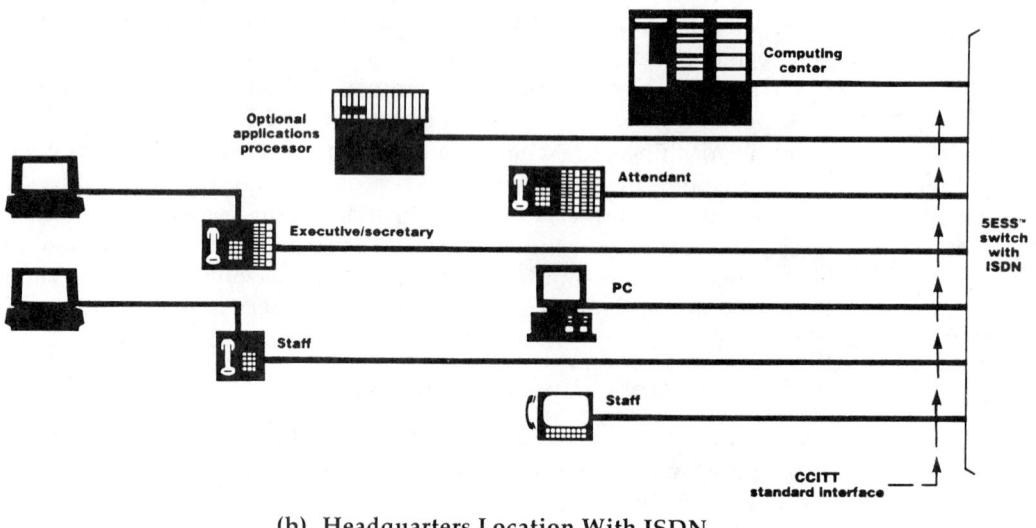

(b) Headquarters Location With ISDN

Copyright, 1985, AT&T Bell Laboratories, reprinted by permission.

FIGURE 1-3 Using Electronic Mail

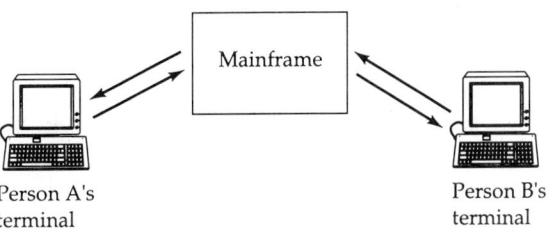

turn on a personal computer or terminal to be instantly notified of any waiting mail.

Electronic data interchange (EDI) is replacing paper as a means of exchanging standard business documents, such as purchase orders and invoices, between companies. EDI is a set of standards stipulating how common business documents can be electronically transmitted between various companies' computer systems. For example, Super Valu Stores, a grocery chain with over 3000 stores in the Midwest, no longer telephones orders to its approximately 1800 suppliers. Instead, the company uses a third-party provider, McDonnell Douglas's EDI*Net, to electronically transmit a purchase order to each supplier. Transmitting purchase orders instead of telephoning them saves the company $1.20 to $1.30 per purchase order. This figure becomes quite impressive when multiplied by the 6500 orders that are placed weekly. An additional annual savings of $600,000 through reduced labor costs will be realized when the company uses EDI for processing invoices from 100 vendors.[3]

By replacing a computer keyboard with a touch-tone telephone, *voice processing* technology allows a caller to route a message to the desired extension by keying the appropriate button. If the person does not answer the telephone, the caller can leave a voice message in the person's voice mailbox. Or the voice processing system can either direct the caller to a voice bulletin board that provides prerecorded information or ask the caller a series of prerecorded questions. In the latter situation the system, responding to the caller's keyed responses, gives the requested information by converting textual machine-readable code in a database into synthesized human speech.

Just a few years ago, the overnight delivery business (e.g., Federal Express) introduced a new kind of entrepreneurial thinking by moving business operations into a more time-sensitive, competitive realm. Facsimile is on its way to becoming the Federal Express of the 1990s. The *facsimile machine*, which sends and receives copies of documents over telephone lines, is creating significant new ways for companies to do their business. The increasingly widespread acceptance of facsimile points toward more significant and cost-effective ways of conducting business. "What is your fax number?" has become a common business query. "Faxing" a one-page document takes less than a minute and costs the same as a telephone call. The same document sent by overnight service typically costs $8.75 (U.S. Postal Service Express Mail) and $15.00 (Federal Express)* and delivery is not until the next day.

Videotex. *Videotex* is another application of telecommunications. It is an interactive electronic service that allows easy accessing of textual or graphics information services on a personal computer or terminal. With home or business videotex systems, such as Dow Jones News/Retrieval, GEnie, and CompuServe, users can retrieve information such as news, weather, and databases of summaries of business articles; conduct transactions such as shopping and banking; perform tasks related to work and/or personal business such as calculating loan payments; and/or send and receive messages. The general public can access videotex by using kiosks (electronic terminals) that are placed in public places like airports, shopping malls, and hotels. Travelers at an airport, for example, can use kiosks to identify places to stay and eat and local transportation services.

Teleconferencing. Meetings are an everyday occurrence in business. Many companies are replacing their conventional type of meetings with electronic ones; for example, audio only teleconferencing, two-way videoconferencing, and business television. Electronic meetings can be scheduled more easily than conventional ones and eliminate travel expenses as well as unproductive time spent traveling to and from meetings. With *two-way videoconferencing*, all participants use conference rooms, such as the one in Figure 1-4, that transmit and receive both video and audio signals. With *business television*, companies transmit video and audio to a number of locations while the receiving locations can transmit only audio.

Domino's Pizza, which had over 4000 locations in 1988, uses business television to inform and train staff. The company uses a satellite network to broadcast audio and video to one or more of its thirty receiving sites located throughout the country. Its transmission equipment is housed in a transportable truck, shown in Figure 1-5, making it possible for the company to broadcast from any of its franchise sites. Receiving stations can receive video and audio and transmit only audio, which allows for following up on a presentation with questions and answers.

Workstations that include a computer with a camera combined with a speakerphone and a high-resolution color video graphics display screen are making *desktop videoconferencing* possible. Without leaving the office, conferees can confer with other users in the office or at different locations. These workstations permit users to shift between the videoconferencing mode and the normal personal computer mode with a touch of a button.

---

*1989 rates.

FIGURE 1-4   A Videoconference

Courtesy of AT&T Archives.

FIGURE 1-5   Business Television

Courtesy of Pro-Vision, Inc./Domino's Pizza Satellite Network.

Another type of teleconferencing, probably the least expensive form, is *computer conferencing*. Wherever conferees are located, they can use their computers to interact simultaneously or whenever they choose to communicate. When a message is sent, it is stored on a host computer. Conferees can then use their computers to access and respond to the message at any time. The main advantage of this type of conference is that conferees do not have to interact simultaneously. A conferee can sign on at any time of the day and night wherever a computer can be connected to a telephone.

Mobile Communications. Work is no longer being performed only in the traditional office. Two types of mobile communication that are important for business and personal communications are pagers and cellular telephones. Both rely on radio transmission and the telephone network. *Pagers* provide relatively inexpensive one-way communications, while *cellular telephones*—hand-held, battery-powered units that are used in cars or on foot—offer the same telephone capabilities as business or home telephones. Users can combine both paging and cellular telephone technologies in their work. A cellular subscriber, for example, can avoid answering unnecessary incoming calls by directing calls to an accompanying paging receiver and then screening them to decide whether they require immediate attention.

Cellular car phones enable users to turn hours that had been wasted commuting to and from the office into productive time. Calls and appointments that formerly could be handled only at the office can now be taken care of by using a cellular telephone when away from the office—in the car, on a boat, on an airborne jetliner with telephone service, or in the field. As shown in Figure 1-6, a cellular telephone can also be connected to a battery-powered facsimile machine, allowing documents to be exchanged with other facsimile machines. With a laptop computer, a cellular telephone, and a modem (a device that allows signals to be transmitted over telephone lines), the user can access and receive information from virtually any computer, and by attaching a printer to the laptop computer, the user can print hard copies. Real estate sales agents away from the office, for example, use portable terminals connected to cellular car phones to access multiple listings or retrieve copies of contracts. During office visits, salespeople use their terminals and cellular phones to access customer contracts and policies.

Major Issues in the Telecommunications Industry

Major issues in the telecommunications industry include the regulatory environment, equipment and network standards, and privacy/security.

- **The Regulatory Environment**

In the United States, federal and state governments intervene in the marketplace when free competition does not adequately regulate the supply, price,

FIGURE 1-6   Sending and Receiving Documents Using a Portable Fax and a Car Telephone

Courtesy of Nissei Electric USA, Inc.

and distribution of goods or services. The federal government derives its regulatory power of commerce from Article 1, Section 8, of the U.S. Constitution, while the states derive their power from the Tenth Amendment of the Constitution. The nature of the telephone industry has made government intervention necessary to ensure fair business practices and to guarantee uninterrupted service to the public. For example, the Justice Department's 1982 Consent Decree resulted in the breakup of AT&T.

Public Utility Classification.   The telephone industry is still thought of as a public utility, even though advances in technology have changed the telecommunications market. A **public utility** is defined as a legal monopoly consisting of a privately owned company that provides an essential public service and is subject to government regulation. The government grants the company monopoly status because it believes that competition would be harmful to the public interest. The government also imposes regulations to ensure that a monopoly does exist and that the company be permitted to operate as a monopoly offering services at reasonable rates. Otherwise, the company could set any price it chooses regardless of demand. The operation of the telephone industry continues to be in the public interest, although the breakup of AT&T has changed the industry's monopolistic structure.

As the telephone industry developed in the United States, no benefit would have been gained by having two or more companies competing in the same geographical areas. Duplication of telephone facilities and services would have resulted in wasted resources as well as confusion to users. Although these reasons still apply to local telephone service, long-distance service is now open to competition.

Regulatory Commissions. The nation's telephone industry is regulated by the *Federal Communications Commission* (FCC) and by public utility commissions (PUCs) in each of the fifty states. The FCC, created by the Communications Act of 1934, regulates interstate communications (crossing state lines), while state public utility commissions regulate intrastate (within a state) communications services. The FCC is responsible for regulating the rates and conditions of interstate, international, and marine communications, while the state commissions function similarly to the FCC but are independent of it. **Regulatory commissions** are endowed by law with legislative, executive, and judicial powers. To help in understanding the present regulatory situation, refer to Appendix B, which outlines the history of telecommunications regulations.

One of the controversial issues affecting telecommunications regulations in the United States is the issue of FCC preemption of state regulation. The supremacy clause in the Constitution authorizes Congress or a congressionally delegated authority to preempt state regulations to bring about greater competition in the telecommunications market. In May 1986 the Supreme Court's ruling in the *Louisiana Public Service Commission v. FCC* did not uphold the preemptive powers of the FCC. This ruling has significantly weakened these preemptive powers, causing the FCC to become more cautious in taking actions to preempt state regulations.

AT&T and the Regional Bell Operating Companies. Another area of regulatory controversy concerns waiver of the consent decree restrictions that bar AT&T and the regional Bell operating companies from fully competing in the telecommunications market. No consensus exists among the regulators, policymakers, and industry representatives concerning the appropriate degree of competition versus regulation that should exist in the United States. These groups, with their differing interests, are battling over regulatory issues when they should be focusing on the critical task of building tomorrow's network infrastructure.*

■ Equipment and Network Standards

Each time we insert a plug into a socket, we rely on standards. The companies that manufacture appliances and the electricians who wire our buildings and houses are all following the same guidelines. Several national and

---

*Infrastructure refers to the essential elements of a structure or a system such as a communications facility.

international organizations provide standards in telecommunications. See Appendix C for information on the major standards-setting organizations.

Standards, or sets of procedures, govern the interaction of equipment and networks, allowing diverse equipment to communicate. They permit different manufacturers' devices, such as telephones and computer terminals, to communicate successfully with one another. Equipment can connect to the public telephone network or have an interface between the station and the network to allow them to be compatible. Without standards, users are limited in creating, expanding, or linking their networks.

The advantages of standards are as follows:

- Standards foster a competitive environment among vendors and users.
- Standards simplify manufacturing and maintenance procedures. Vendors can concentrate their efforts on developing more advanced technologies.
- Standards allow equipment from different vendors to be compatible.

On the other hand, standard setting can freeze technology. After a standard has been developed, reviewed, and approved, more advanced techniques may not be possible. Also, while standards are being set, a large base of installed equipment designed to meet *proprietary (company) standards* is already in place. After standards are adopted, equipment may exist that does not conform to the standards.

■ Privacy/Security

How can users of public and private telecommunications networks protect against electronic theft of intellectual property and electronic invasion of privacy? A difficult challenge is to find a way for individuals and companies to interact electronically and still keep their property and privacy intact.

When does data (text, audio, video) that is being transmitted over a network cease to be the copyrighted property of its creator and become instead the newly copyright property of the receiver? Legislative proposals and special-interest groups are trying to address this problem.

Users of both private company networks and public telephone networks are becoming increasingly vulnerable to electronic eavesdropping. How can users of these networks protect their privacy? For example, telephone companies have the potential ability to collect statistics about callers. They know who is placing a call whether or not the called party does. Furthermore, the Bell operating companies are now allowed to handle billing for third-party services accessed via the public network. As a result, these companies are able to collect statistics about individual callers and companies and construct detailed profiles of them. Such profiles can include information about their calling patterns that can be compiled into databases* and sold to third

---

*A database is a set of logically related files stored in a computer and organized in such a way that data access is improved and duplication is minimized.

parties without the callers' knowledge or their consent. The economic incentives to conduct these activities will be extremely inviting. The resolution of these issues will affect how networks are used and managed in the 1990s.[4]

The Changing Role of the Telecommunications Manager

The "good old days," when the telephone company handled everything, ended in 1984 when the Bell system broke up. However, even before 1984, deregulation was increasing competition, and rapidly advancing technology was making it possible for companies to select their own long-distance carriers and telephone systems. Yet for many users the breakup of the Bell system—the divestiture—has brought forth a confusing array of technologies and choices. Most users favor the new choices, even though they also face new risks and responsibilities. As shown in Figure 1-7, these changes have also affected the job descriptions of telecommunications personnel, particularly the telecom manager.

■ Increased Internal Visibility

Advances in technology, deregulation, and the increasing costs of telecommunications have escalated the importance of telecommunications within the company and its visibility to upper-level executives. Companies are increasingly recognizing that new technology can provide them with a strategic advantage, such as serving as a business vehicle for competing in the marketplace. For example, the large networks of major organizations like Citicorp and the Bank of America not only deliver products and services, but also serve as strategic resources that can increase a company's competi-

FIGURE 1-7 The Role of Telecommunications Managers

Traditional Responsibilities	Evolving Responsibilities
Voice-only technologies	Voice, data, and image technologies
Low-level administrative duties	Complex business/technical functions
Utility (expense item)	Competitive factor (revenue and cost-related)
Limited staff	Increased staff with multiple skill requirements
Single-vendor environment	Multiple-vendor environment
Vendor-supplied expertise	In-house, contracted, and vendor-supplied expertise

Source: Courtesy of David E. Harper, "The Future of Telecommunications: Part II," *Telecommunications*, February 1989. Reprinted courtesy of *Telecommunications* Magazine.

tive position in the marketplace. These networks also generate revenue by offering their services to other organizations.

■ New Career Paths

Advances in technology, deregulation, and increased in-company visibility have created opportunities in telecommunications that previously were unimagined for telecommunications personnel. No longer are telecommunications personnel reporting to the company's administrative manager or to the facilities manager. After divestiture, as telecommunications began to have a growing influence in the company, telecommunications personnel in many large organizations were moved to the Management Information Systems Department, the Data Processing Department, or the Communications Department. Their career paths now extend beyond being manager of a telecommunications (or communications) department to becoming company vice-president. Increasing job responsibilities have also resulted in appropriate salary increases.

■ New Responsibilities

Telecom managers no longer fit the traditional image of telephone supervisors, technicians, or installers. Their responsibilities now include designing, installing, and operating telecommunications networks; merging voice, data, and video systems; dealing with problems associated with interconnecting telecommunications systems that are not compatible, and managing both technical and nontechnical people.

Telecom/communication managers view their job not as managing voice and data operations managers but identifying and implementing voice, data, and video applications. A network is no longer thought of as just an end-to-end system connecting a collection of communication devices such as telephones and computers; instead, the network concept must now be expanded to include applications. As a result, managers must be knowledgeable about the company's functions such as finance, sales, and marketing. They must tailor technology to suit the company's objectives; be able to handle large budgets; and hire, train, and manage an operations staff that is growing in number. Telecom managers may also act as clearinghouses for the company's telecommunications problems, including being responsible for solving them.

■ Job Qualifications

The job responsibilities of telecom managers, which now include increased technical challenges and choices, require not only technical training but also business and strategic planning skills as well. Telecom managers must become adept at understanding the needs of their companies—a challenge that they cannot ignore.

Unfortunately, accelerating technological change in the telecommunications industry has made it difficult for many managers to be adequately informed and trained in applying many of the new technologies. Keeping up to date on the latest telecommunications regulations and legislation has added to their dilemma. Such knowledge is necessary, for example, when managers must decide whether to buy and install a product or service now or wait a while so that they can better judge its effectiveness. Continued education is necessary for managers and their staff. Telecom managers often concentrate on technical training and lack an opportunity to study business subjects such as marketing, management, accounting, finance, and economics. Knowledge of these areas is crucial for managers, particularly as they interact with other segments of the company. The success of a company's telecommunications operations depends to a large extent on the telecommunications manager's skills and how he or she uses them.

Summary

Telecommunications is the science and technology of communicating by electronic transmission of impulses, as by telegraphy, cable, telephony, radio, or television. Issues of concern to the telecommunications industry deal with regulatory control, setting equipment standards, and security/privacy (electronic theft of intellectual property and electronic invasion of privacy). In the United States, federal and state governments intervene in the operation of the telephone industry to ensure fair business practices and to guarantee uninterrupted service to the public. For example, the Justice Department's 1982 Consent Decree resulted in the breakup of AT&T. National and international standards-setting organizations develop and set telecommunications standards to allow equipment and networks from different vendors to communicate with each other. Advances in technology, deregulation, and increased internal visibility have changed the role of the telecommunications manager to include greater responsibilities and challenges.

■ *Key Terms*

Federal Communications Commission
Public utility
Public utility commission
Regulatory commissions
Standards
Telecommunications

■ *Self-Quiz*

Indicate whether the statement is true or false.

1. The tenth amendment to the Constitution is the basis for state government regulation of commerce.   T/F

2. Microwave radio can provide communication among several sites within a city and at the same time bypass the local telephone company.   T/F
3. Computer conferencing is a type of electronic mail.   T/F
4. Standards set by international standards-setting organizations are the same as proprietary standards.   T/F
5. Standards allow diverse equipment to communicate.   T/F
6. When the telephone industry was being established, telephone subscribers would have benefited by having two or more different companies competing in the same geographical areas.   T/F

Complete each of the following statements.

1. The basic components of telecommunications include _____ .
2. An all-digital system that allows voice, data, and video to be transmitted simultaneously by sharing high-speed digital transmission facilities is called _____ .
3. A set of standards stipulating how common business documents can be electronically transmitted between various companies' computer systems is called _____ .
4. The breakup of AT&T is referred to as the _____ .
5. The Federal Communications Commission was created by the _____ .
6. The nation's telephone industry is regulated by _____ .

Match Column A with Column B (based on Appendix C and Chapter 1).

Column A
(a) ANSI
(b) CCIR
(c) CCITT
(d) FCC
(e) ITU
(f) PUC

Column B
___ 1. Suggests equipment standards for common carriers.
___ 2. Addresses issues related to broadcasting, the radio spectrum, and the geostationary orbit.
___ 3. Represents the United States in its dealings with ISO.
___ 4. Regulates interstate communications.
___ 5. An intergovernmental body established by treaty.
___ 6. Regulates intrastate telephone services.

■ *Review Questions*

1. How would you define telecommunications?
2. How does a public utility differ from a privately owned business?
3. (a) Who regulates the telephone industry?
   (b) What is the responsibility of the Federal Communications Commission?
4. Describe how three telecommunications applications can change the way tasks are performed in an office.
5. (a) Give examples of how equipment standards allow you to communicate with others.
   (b) Give examples of how the lack of equipment standards prevents you from communicating with others.

6. (a) What are some of the issues facing the telecommunications industry?
   (b) How do they affect the industry?
7. How has the role of the telecommunications manager changed in the past decade?

Activities/Projects

1. Discuss one of the following with a small group:
   (a) Is the telecommunications industry controlled by the U.S. government? Should the government interfere in the operation of the telecommunications industry?
   (b) Are telecommunications standards necessary?
   (c) Should vendors and/or manufacturers be allowed to develop their own telecommunications standards to encourage competition and technology advancements?
   (d) How important are privacy/security issues to the operation of a company's telecommunications system?
2. Refer to Appendix A, "The Evolution of Telecommunications." What do you consider to be the key inventions in telecommunications? Why?
3. Obtain definitions of telecommunications from four or more sources. Discuss the differences and similarities of the definitions. Develop a working definition of telecommunications.
4. Prepare a short written or oral report on the following:
   (a) Discuss the telecommunications applications that you have experienced.
   (b) Will any of these applications change how business operations are being performed? Explain.

Notes

1. David E. Harper, "The Future of Telecommunications: Part I," *Telecommunications*, January 1989, p. 27.
2. *Glossary of Communications Terminology* (Delran, N.J.: Datapro Research Corporation, 1987).
3. Information courtesy of George Klima, Director of Accounting Procedures, SuperValu Stores, Eden Prairie, Minneapolis, Minn.
4. "You Still Own the Right to Remain Silent," *Network World*, March 6, 1989, p. 22.

Additional Readings

H. M. Boettinger, *The Telephone Book: Bell, Watson, Vail and American Life, 1876–1983* (New York: Stearns Publishers Ltd., 1983).
Prescott C. Mabon, *Mission Communications: The Story of Bell Laboratories* (Murray Hill, N.J.: Bell Telephone Laboratories, Inc., 1975).
James Martin, *The Wired Society* (Englewood Cliffs, N.J.: Prentice-Hall, Inc., 1978).
James Martin, *An Information Systems Manifesto* (Englewood Cliffs, N.J.: Prentice-Hall, Inc., 1984).

PART II

Principles of Telecommunications

CHAPTER 2

Transmission Basics

Principles of Voice Transmission
    Sound Waves
    Electrical Waves
    Bandwidth

Signal Conversion
    Analog Signals and Circuits
    Digital Signals and Circuits
    Converting the Signals

Transmission
    The Transmission Circuit
    Signal Direction
    Telephone Transmission Links
    Modulation
    Multiplexing

Transmission Impairments and Media
    Transmission Impairments
    Transmission Media

CHAPTER OBJECTIVES

After studying this chapter, you should be able to

1. Describe how voice sounds are transmitted over a telephone circuit.
2. Explain how analog signals and digital signals are transmitted over analog transmission.
3. Explain how analog and digital signals are transmitted over digital transmission.
4. Specify the different types of transmission impairments.
5. Describe the different kinds of transmission media.

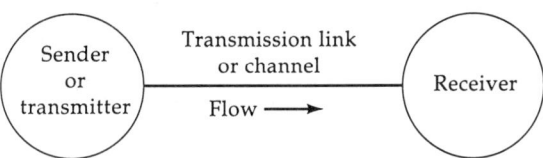

While away from the office, field representatives want to obtain information from the company's computer. All they need to do is connect their computers to a device, called a *modem*, so that they can use the telephone line as shown in the opening diagram. The modem converts the computer's signals to ones that the telephone line recognizes.

Employees in another company are using a digital transmission line that requires their voice signals to be in digital form when transmitted. They must use a device, called a *codec*, that will change their voice signals to digital ones for transmission over the line.

In one company, telephone conversations are plagued with talker echo, and in another company, they are experiencing voice fading. Talker echo is being corrected with echo suppressors, while voice fading is being resolved with line amplifiers.

The fundamental purpose of a communications system is to transfer meaningful information from one location to another. The three basic elements of a communications system are the *sender* or *transmitter*, the *transmission link* or *channel*, and the *receiver*. The sender encodes the message, enabling it to travel over the transmission link to the receiver, who then decodes it. The originating input is typically called the source, the sender, the transmitter, or the originator, while the terminating end is referred to as the receiver or the destination.

The purpose of this chapter is to provide the reader with the basic terms and concepts of transmission—telephony, as it is sometimes called—necessary to understanding telecommunication operations and applications. This chapter discusses how voices and other sounds are converted into electrical signals that can be transmitted by wire, fiber, fiber optics, microwave radio, or satellite communications.

Principles of Voice Transmission

The invention of the telephone made it possible for electrical waves (also called signals) to transmit speech over wires. To be transmitted over a wire, a human voice must first be converted into electrical waves. The conversion is accomplished by a **transducer**—a generic term for any device that converts energy from one form to another. The electrical waves are passed to their destination by a medium such as a wire or a cable link. At their destination a second transducer converts the electrical waves back into their original form. Figure 2-1 shows the basic components of a typical telecommunications system that can transmit voice, television, data, teletypewriter, and facsimile signals. In more complex systems, other items are required. For example, *amplifiers* might be needed at appropriate points in the system to increase the power level to prevent any loss in signal strength as the signal is being transmitted. Before learning how sound can be changed into electrical waves, you should first understand what sound is.

■ Sound Waves

Sound can be viewed as a system involving a source, a transmission path, and a receiver. Sound originates with the vibration of a source. As the source vibrates, its movement creates a disturbance of air molecules. For example, as we speak, our voices set the air in motion. As shown in Figure 2-2, air molecules alternately compress and depress hundreds or even thousands of times a second and result in a series of high- and low-pressure waves moving away from the source. When these waves reach the human ear, they cause the eardrum to vibrate and produce the sensation of hearing. The vibrations or waves are actually what we hear.

FIGURE 2-1   Basic Components of a Communications System

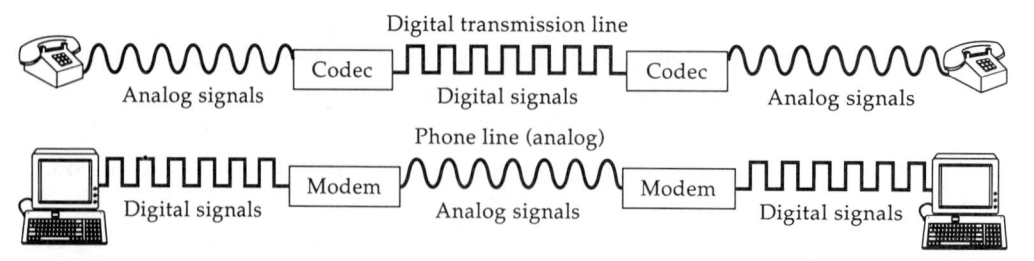

Principles of Voice Transmission

A **sound wave** is one complete cycle or vibration—from normal pressure through high pressure back to normal through low pressure and back to normal pressure again to complete the entire sound wave cycle. The number of times a complete cycle occurs in one second is the *frequency of the wave*. Frequency is expressed in cycles per second or the unit hertz (Hz). For example, if a train whistle completes 344 cycles each second, then its frequency is 344 Hz, and 344 separate high-low pressure combinations will strike the eardrum each second. Every sound that you hear has a specific frequency—a number of complete vibrations that occur in one second.

Sound that reaches our ears consists of a continuous band of frequencies moving through the air together. The ear detects these frequencies of sound as pitch. A piano has frequencies ranging from the lowest key of 50 Hz to its highest of 4000 Hz. We say that the piano has a bandwidth of 3950 Hz (4000 Hz minus 50 Hz), each piano key having its own frequency. For example, middle C has a frequency of 261 Hz.

The voice sounds we make as we talk also reflect a combination of different frequencies. The frequency range from 20 to 20,000 Hz is audible to most people. Sounds with frequencies near 20,000 Hz are very high in pitch, while those at the other end of the scale are very low in pitch.

The *wavelength of a sound wave* is the distance between the same point in two consecutive waves, as shown in Figure 2-2. The frequency of the sound and the speed of travel determine the wavelength. The composition of the conductor, such as air, steel, or wood, affects travel speed. But since the speed of sound in any particular conductor is constant, frequency becomes the only variable. A wave can be described in terms of its frequency in hertz or its wavelength in meters.

The *amplitude of the sound wave* is the distance the air particles are displaced from their original undisturbed position. Figure 2-2 shows the amplitude as the vertical dimension between a wave's trough and its crest. Amplitude represents the loudness of the sound.

FIGURE 2-2 **Characteristics of Sound Waves**

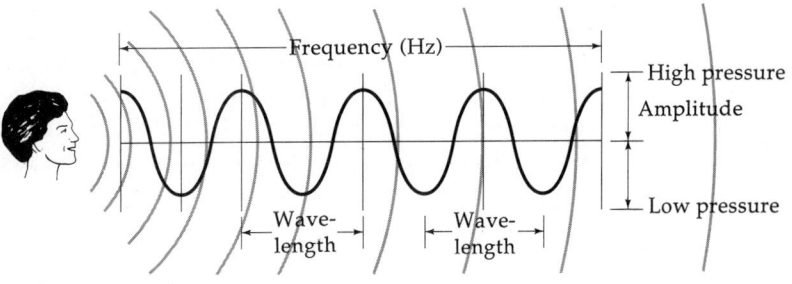

■ Electrical Waves

In a telephone system the transmission path is an electrical circuit—a closed path in which current flows. A telephone sends a voice along this path by converting the pattern of sound waves into a matching pattern of electrical waves. At the other end of the line, the telephone reverses the process by changing the electrical pattern to a matching sound pattern.

Sine Wave. The basic shape of an electrical wave is represented by what is called a **sine wave**.

Frequency. Like sound waves, sine waves that travel along an electrical circuit are described in terms of frequencies. A sine wave is current alternating or reversing direction in a circuit with one sine wave equal to one complete up/down cycle, as shown in Figure 2-3. The number of times this cycle occurs in one second is the *frequency of the sine wave*. One up/down cycle per second equals 1 hertz (Hz), 100 cycles per second equal 1 kilohertz (kHz),* one million cycles per second equal 1 megahertz (MHz), and one billion cycles per second equal 1 gigahertz (GHz). As with a sound wave, the wavelength of a sine wave is the distance between the same point in two consecutive waves.

When the human voice is transmitted through the telephone system, the sound waves are converted into electrical waves of the same frequency as the original sound. As the telephone system was developed, the transmission of the entire range of the human voice, from 20 to 20,000 Hz, was found to be impractical. Frequencies between 200 and 3500 Hz were deemed adequate for making a person's voice recognizable and intelligible. Transmission paths of telephone systems are designed to transmit voice waves in this range of frequencies. However, as will be discussed in the next section, these human voice frequencies may be changed into higher or lower frequencies for transmission purposes and then changed back to their original frequencies at the receiving end.

■ Bandwidth

Electromagnetic Spectrum. The entire range of available signal frequencies, as shown in Figure 2-4, is referred to as the *electromagnetic spectrum*. A spectrum consists of a continuous range of frequencies from very low ones, such as radio waves of a few kilohertz, to extremely high ones, such as cosmic rays of more than 10 million trillion hertz. Any portion of this

---

*Rather than writing many zeros before or after the decimal point in expressing very large or very small numbers, a preferred practice is to indicate positive or negative multiples by prefixes such as k, M, and G.

FIGURE 2-3 **Frequency of Sine Waves**

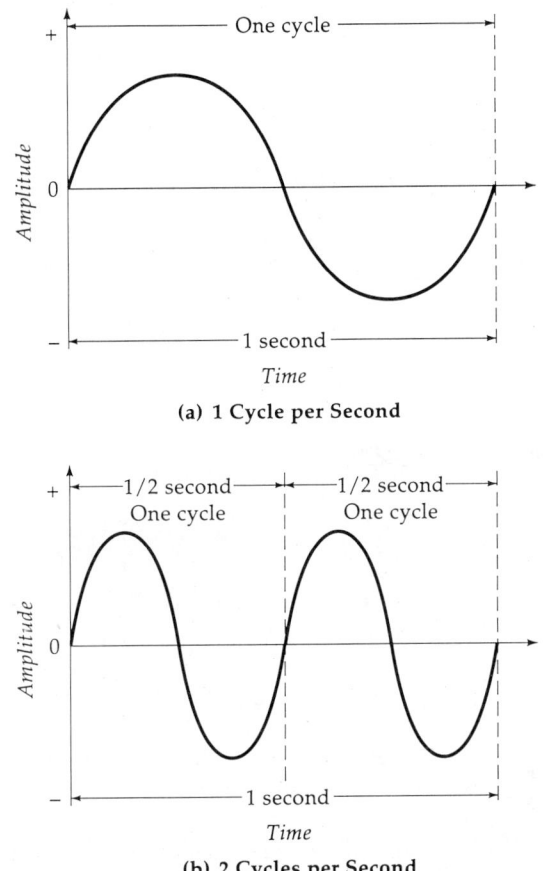

(a) 1 Cycle per Second

(b) 2 Cycles per Second

spectrum is called a *band*. The **bandwidth** is the difference between the upper and lower limits or between the highest and lowest frequency in a band of frequencies.

The Federal Communications Commission. In the United States the Federal Communications Commission (FCC) is responsible for determining how the electromagnetic spectrum will be used. The FCC assigns frequencies, licenses stations, and oversees the spectrum's use. The FCC sets its regulations in conjunction with international agreements on the spectrum's use.

FIGURE 2-4 Electromagnetic Spectrum

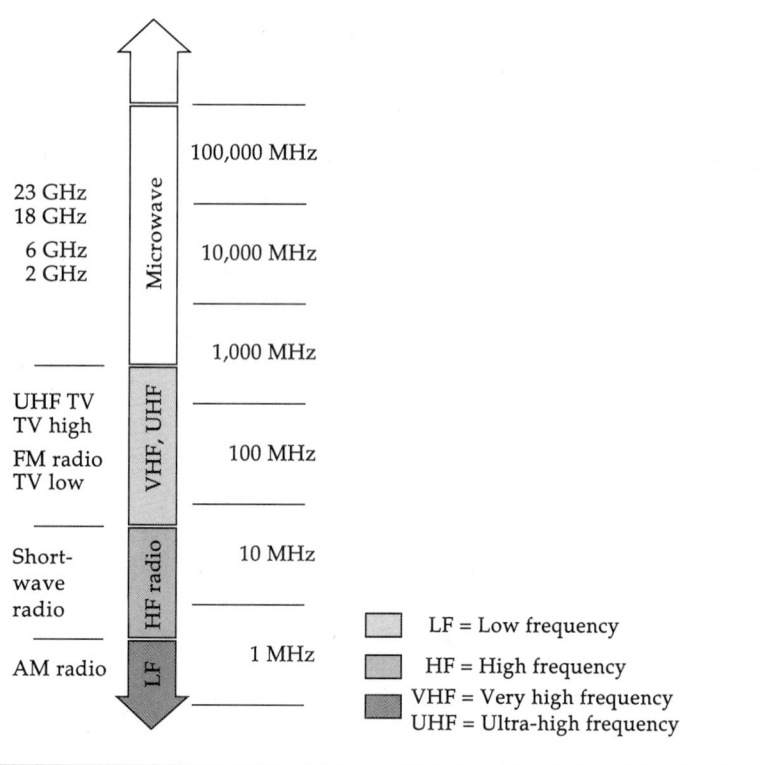

Redrawn courtesy of *Communications News*.

National and international allocations are divided according to general categories of users. Within each of these categories the FCC defines specific categories of users for the spectrum, as shown in Figure 2-5.

For example, within the general category of broadcasting, the AM broadcast band in the United States is assigned frequencies that range from 535 to 1605 kHz, while the FM band occupies frequencies from 88 to 108 MHz. In any given geographical area, the bandwidth for each AM or FM station must be adequate so that it does not interfere with other stations. Thus the number of stations that can be licensed within the AM or FM band in a particular geographical area depends on the bandwidth required for each station. VHF television band occupies the range of frequencies from 54 to 72 MHz and from 76 to 88 MHz, and UHF television occupies the range from 470 to 806 MHz.

Voice Bandwidth. Telephone waves can be packed together so that one circuit can carry a number of waves simultaneously. Although the terms *circuit* and *channel* are often used interchangeably, a distinction can be made.

FIGURE 2-5 **Examples of FCC Spectrum Categories**

General Category	Specific Category of User
Broadcasting	AM, FM, TV, common carriers
Citizen's radio	Amateur, CB
Government and industrial communications	Armed services; governmental departments; public safety; industrial communication; meteorological services; telemetry; industrial, scientific, and medical equipment
Commercial transportation communications	Paging services and radiotelephones; mobile land vehicles; aeronautical control; aviation, maritime, navigational beacons

When a circuit is divided into more than one transmission path, each path can be called a channel.

As has been mentioned, transmission of voice waves requires frequencies ranging from a low of 200 Hz to a high of 3500 Hz. The difference between these two frequencies is a bandwidth of 3300 Hz, also expressed as 3.3 kHz. A circuit with more than one channel may be able to transmit waves ranging from 30,000 to 33,300 Hz; its bandwidth is 3.3 kHz. A bandwidth tells the range of frequencies being used; it does not specify which ones.

By using different ranges, voice waves can travel together without interfering with one another. Your voice may be raised in frequency from a range of 200–3500 Hz to a range of 30,000–33,300 Hz. Another person's voice might be raised to a range of 60,000–63,300 Hz. Although voice waves are band-limited from 200 Hz to 3.5 kHz, a voice circuit requires 4 kHz. The additional bandwidth, referred to as a **guardband**, allows a separation between channels that prevents signals from interfering with adjacent channels (see Figure 2-6).

Circuit Capacity. An open-wire medium uses a frequency up to 150 kHz. A carrier system may occupy frequencies that range from 40 to 88 kHz for one direction and from 100 to 148 kHz for the other direction. Since the total bandwidth required for a voice channel is 4 kHz, this carrier system would have a capacity of twelve voice channels.

Signal Conversion

A circuit or channel is the means by which information in the form of signals is transmitted from sender to receiver. Before voice waves can be transmitted along an electrical circuit or any kind of transmission facility to a receiver, the voice waves must be converted into electrical waves that can carry these frequencies.

FIGURE 2-6 **Voice Bandwidth**

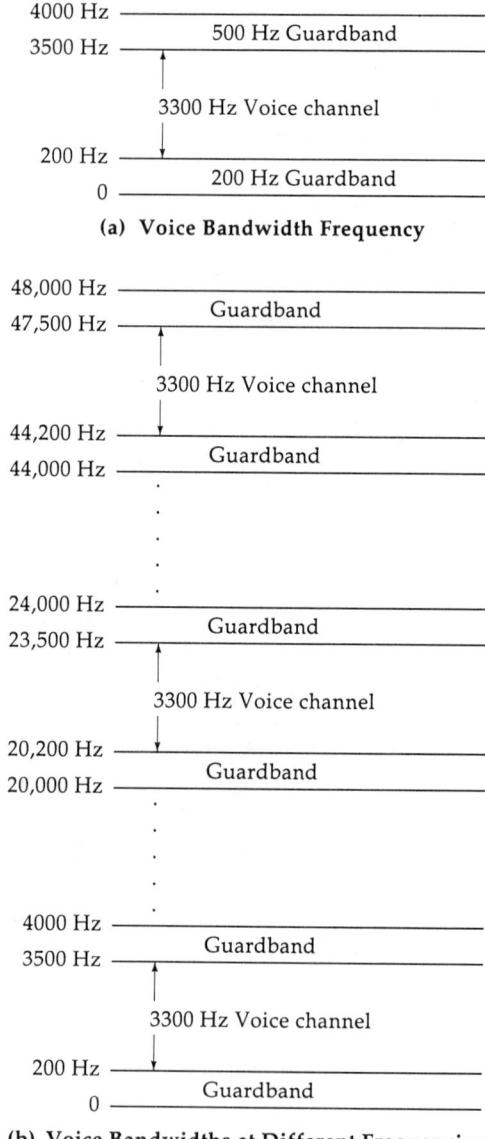

FIGURE 2-7 **Analog Signals or Waves**

- ### Analog Signals and Circuits

    The two basic forms of electrical signals are analog and digital. The characteristics of the transmission circuit used to transmit the signals determine which form to use. These signals may originate in one form but may be converted to the other form to make them compatible with the transmission path over which they will travel. The two types of transmission circuits are analog and digital.

    Analog Signals. An **analog signal** is a continuously varying electromagnetic wave whose pattern varies to represent the message being transmitted. These electromagnetic waves look like voice waves. Figure 2-7 shows variations in the amplitude and the frequencies of analog signals. These variations convey loudness and pitch as in speech and in music.

    Analog Circuit An *analog circuit* accepts a band of frequencies and carries analog signals. The capacity of an analog circuit is indicated by its bandwidth, such as the bandwidth of a voiceband channel being 4 kHz. A narrowband channel may be 100 Hz or 200 Hz, while a broadband channel may be 48 kHz or 240 kHz. Analog transmission carries voice patterns in almost the same format as they were generated. As was discussed earlier, sound waves generated at the sending end are copied onto analog electromagnetic waves, which are converted back to sound waves when they arrive at the receiving end.

- ### Digital Signals and Circuits

    Digital Signals. A **digital signal** is a series of discrete, discontinuous voltage pulses, a stream of "on-off" pulses, as shown in Figure 2-8. The pattern created by the pulses indicates the message. An example of digital signals is those produced by computers.

FIGURE 2-8 Example Digital Signal: Representation of Binary Number 101100

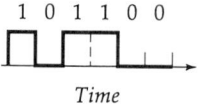

Time

Binary System. The simplest kind of signal for transmitting messages is the binary signal consisting of only two states, such as the dot-dash of the Morse code, an on-off signal in teletype, and 1 or 0 in binary. Computer messages use some kind of a binary system. A *binary system* codes messages into the numerals 1 and 0.* A 1 represents a tiny pulse of current (on), and a 0 represents a lack of current (off). Each 1 or 0—each on-off pulse—is called a *bit*, which is a contraction of "binary digit." The signals to be transmitted are coded as distinct and separate pulses (1's or 0's).

A number of codes have been devised to represent characters by bits. The most commonly used code in the United States is the *ASCII (American Standard Code for Information Interchange) Code*, as shown in Figure 2-9. Each character in the code is represented by a unique seven-bit pattern. The code provides 128 unique patterns to represent letters, numbers, special characters, punctuation marks, and characters that deal with printing and communication procedures. Code compatibility between the sender's and the receiver's equipment is essential.

ASCII encoded characters are stored and transmitted using eight bits per character. A block of eight bits is referred to as a *byte*, as shown in Figure 2-10. The eighth bit is a parity bit that is used for error detection. The bit is set so that the total number of binary 1's in each byte is always odd (odd parity) or always even (even parity). Parity makes it possible to detect any transmission error that changes a single bit. For example, for even parity, to make the 1 bits add up to an even number, the parity bit is either a 1 or a 0, as shown in Figure 2-11.

Digital Circuits. A *digital circuit* accepts a series of pulses and carries signals in digital form. An electromagnetic pulse of a given voltage represents a binary 1, and another pulse of weaker voltage represents a binary 0.

---

*Binary is a numbering system with a base of 2, whereas a decimal system has a base of 10. For example, in binary, 0001 represents decimal value 1, 0010 represents decimal value 2, 0100 represents decimal value 4, and 1000 represents decimal value 8. In binary, each move to the left multiples the number by 2, which is similar to changing from decimal 10 to decimal 100. In the decimal system the number has been multiplied by 10.

FIGURE 2-9 U.S. ASCII Code

b7 b6 b5				0 0 0	0 0 1	0 1 0	0 1 1	1 0 0	1 0 1	1 1 0	1 1 1
b4 b3 b2 b1				0	1	2	3	4	5	6	7
0	0	0	0	0	NUL	DLE	SP	0	@	P	`	p
0	0	0	1	1	SOH	DC1	!	1	A	Q	a	q
0	0	1	0	2	STX	DC2	"	2	B	R	b	r
0	0	1	1	3	ETX	DC3	#	3	C	S	c	s
0	1	0	0	4	EOT	DC4	$	4	D	T	d	t
0	1	0	1	5	ENQ	NAK	%	5	E	U	e	u
0	1	1	0	6	ACK	SYN	&	6	F	V	f	v
0	1	1	1	7	BEL	ETB	'	7	G	W	g	w
1	0	0	0	8	BS	CAN	(	8	H	X	h	x
1	0	0	1	9	HT	EM	)	9	I	Y	i	y
1	0	1	0	10	LF	SUB	*	:	J	Z	j	z
1	0	1	1	11	VT	ESC	+	;	K	[	k	{
1	1	0	0	12	FF	FS	,	<	L	\	l	|
1	1	0	1	13	CR	GS	-	=	M	]	m	}
1	1	1	0	14	SO	RS	.	>	N	^	n	~
1	1	1	1	15	SI	US	/	?	O	_	o	DEL

This material is reproduced with permission from the American National Standards, ANSI × 3.4–1986. Copyrighted 1986 by the American National Standards Institute. Copies of this standard may be purchased from American National Standards Institute, Inc., 1430 Broadway, New York, NY 10018.

FIGURE 2-10 Electronic Pulses for Binary Digits: Bit and Byte

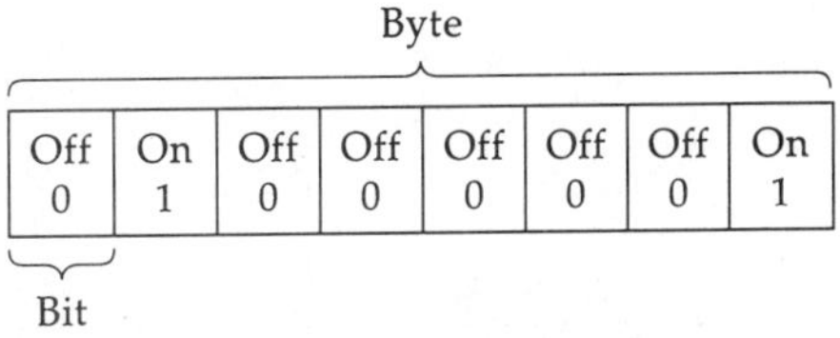

Off	On	Off	Off	Off	Off	Off	On
0	1	0	0	0	0	0	1

Byte (entire row); Bit (single cell)

FIGURE 2-11   Even Parity

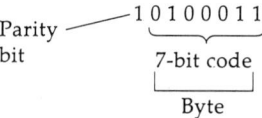

(a) No Error: Bits Add to an Even Number

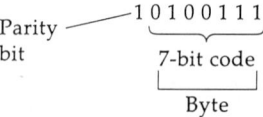

(b) Error: Bits Add to an Odd Number

For example, in Figure 2-12, binary 1's are represented by 5 volts, and binary zeros are represented by 0 volts. The capacity of a digital circuit is indicated by pulse rate or bit rate. Circuits can accept signals at such rates as 300, 1200, 2400, 4800, 9600, 56,000, and 64,000 bits per second (bps). The 64,000 bps (64 kbps) rate is often used in telephone systems.

Asynchronous/Synchronous.   Digital circuits require synchronization to keep the sending and receiving ends in step with each other. *Synchronization* enables the receiving end to determine which pulse is the first bit of a character.

The simplest synchronizing method is *asynchronous*, also called stop-start synchronization. Characters are separated and transmission is synchronized by a start bit and a stop bit at each end of the individual eight-bit character. An asynchronous signal has ten bits per character. Figure 2-13(a) shows asynchronous transmission of three ASCII characters. The distance between characters will vary depending, for example, on whether they are transmitted as they are typed or held in a buffer and then transmitted all at once.

FIGURE 2-12   Digital Signals

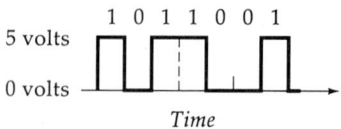

Signal Conversion

FIGURE 2-13 **Data Transmission**

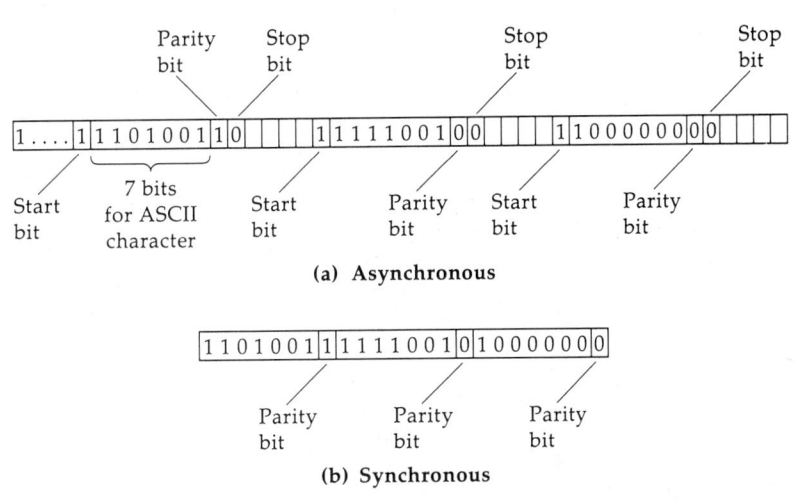

(a) Asynchronous

(b) Synchronous

Data can also be transmitted in blocks in a *synchronous mode*, as shown in Figure 2-13(b). Synchronous transmission is used for high-speed transmission of a block of characters. Both the sending and receiving devices are operated simultaneously and are resynchronized for each block of data. Start and stop bits are not required. If you transmit 100 characters using an eight-bit ASCII code structure, the message part of the block of data would be 800 bits long.

Types of Transmission Currently Used. Historically, telephone systems have been analog circuits. Today, the majority of telephone circuits still carry the human voice as an analog signal, many being used to carry computer-generated digital information. With advances in technologies and decreasing costs of digital transmission, tomorrow's systems will be specifically designed for digital traffic. Analog voice signals will then have to be converted to binary digit codes for transmission and decoded at the receiving end.

Benefits of Digital Transmission. Compared to analog signals, digital signals can be transmitted over less costly equipment. They also transmit without noise and are less subject to error over long distance. Analog signals are subject to deviations in amplitude or frequency that change the signal pattern and thus distort the message. In digital pulses, deviations are more easily detected.

FIGURE 2-14   Converting Analog Signals for Digital Transmission

- ### Converting the Signals

    Converting from Analog to Digital. As companies convert their communication systems from analog to digital, they still must transmit the human voice, which is in analog form. Before voice signals can be transmitted over a digital path, they must be transformed into discrete pulses to be sent digitally. The transducer for making this transformation is called a *codec*.* As Figure 2-14 shows, a codec codes an analog signal into digital form at the sending end, and another codec decodes it at the receiving end.

    The codec accomplishes its task in three stages. Since the analog signals from a telephone conversation vary (Figure 2-15(a)), the first step in converting the analog signals to digital ones is *sampling the amplitude* (the voltage) of the analog signals at very short intervals by measuring their amplitude at discrete intervals (see Figure 2-15(b)). In the second step, called *quantizing*, the value of each voltage sample is assigned a specific measurement, as shown by the bars in Figure 2-15(c). The result is called *pulse-amplitude modulation* (PAM). In the last step, called *pulse-code modulation* (PCM), the voltage values are converted, or coded, into 1's and 0's of binary numbers for digital transmission, as shown in Figure 2-15(d). When the signals are received at their destination, the three steps of the conversion process are reversed.

    To ensure that speech remains intelligible, a large number of samples, called the Nyquist interval,** must be taken. The sampling rate must be twice that of the highest significant frequency to be transmitted. A voice signal with an upper frequency limit of 4 kHz over the telephone system requires the codec to take 8000 samples per second (8000 samples per second × 8 bits per second = 64,000 bits per second). Speech lost between samples is undetected when the signal is decoded at the receiving end.

    Converting from Digital to Analog. Suppose that you want to use your computer to access a distant database or exchange information by screen

---

*The name codec is derived from its function of *coding* an analog signal into digital form at the sending end and then *decoding* it back to analog form at the receiving end.

**The Nyquist interval was developed by Harry Nyquist at Bell Laboratories.

FIGURE 2-15   Steps to Convert Analog Signals for Digital Transmission

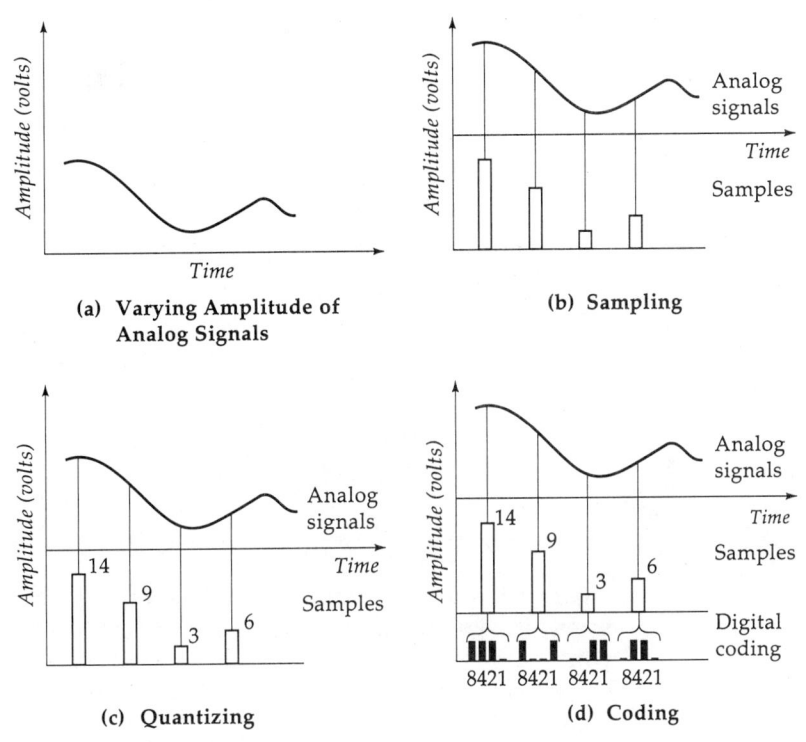

with another computer user. (A *database* is a collection of information of technical or commercial importance to an organization. Database information stored in a computer-accessed memory is usually subdivided into pages, each page being accessible to all users unless it belongs to a closed user group.) To access a database, you could use your telephone system to make the electrical connection with other computers. However, most telephone systems are designed for transmitting analog signals over analog circuits. Such circuits distort digital signals, causing the signals to become garbled after traveling a short distance. This problem is resolved by using a transducer, which in this situation is referred to as a modulator-demodulator—*modem* for short—to change digital signals to correspond with analog signal characteristics for transmission, as shown in Figure 2-16.

At the transmitting end, a modem changes the digital signals to correspond with analog signal characteristics through a process called modulation. An example of a popular modulation method is the **frequency-shift keying method**. In this method the modem generates two different frequencies, a higher frequency for a binary 1 and a lower frequency for a binary 0.

FIGURE 2-16   Converting Digital Signals for Analog Transmission

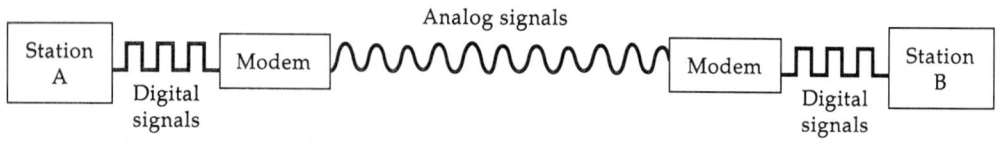

FIGURE 2-17   Frequency-Shift Keying Method

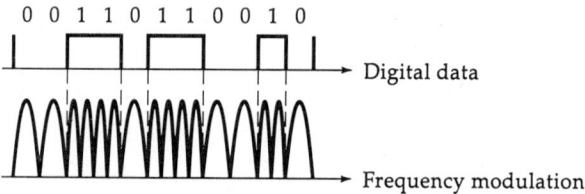

Figure 2-17 shows a frequency modulation of a bit stream of 1's and 0's. The transmitted frequency is shifted back and forth between higher frequencies, which correspond to the presence of a pulse or a binary 1, and lower frequencies, which correspond to the absence of a pulse or a binary 0. Transmission speed is limited to 1.8 kpbs. A bandwidth wider than that provided by the telephone voice channel (of 4 kHz) is required for higher speeds. Another method, called differential phase-shift keying, uses bandwidth more efficiently by putting more information in each transmitted sample pulse. This method has become the worldwide standard for 2.4 kbps data transmission over voiceband channels. At the receiving end, the analog signal is demodulated, or changed back into a form that the computer understands, which is an on-off binary code.

Before transmission can be established, the sending and receiving units must be compatible. The system must transmit and receive data at the same rate. For example, if the sending rate is 1200 bps, then the receiving modem must be able to receive at this rate.

Transmission

This section discusses the transmission circuit in terms of signal direction, using different frequencies to send voice signals, and using one circuit to send more than one message at the same time. The following section will discuss the transmission impairments that can occur and the types of transmission media.

Transmission

■ The Transmission Circuit

As was previously mentioned, the transmission path between the transmitter and the receiver is referred to as a circuit, a link, or even a channel, with the smallest subdivision of a circuit or route dedicated to transmitting messages being called a channel. Within a circuit a channel may be a voice channel, a data channel, or a teletypewriter channel.

Several voice channels can be sent over one circuit by modulating the carrier wave at different frequencies and then restoring the signals to their original form at the receiving end. This system is referred to as a *carrier system*. In the 1930s a two-wire circuit could carry twelve voice channels. Today, the transmission medium makes it possible for one circuit to carry hundreds of thousands of voices simultaneously.

■ Signal Direction

A transmission circuit or channel or transmission medium can be simplex, half-duplex, or full-duplex, as shown in Figure 2-18.

In **simplex transmission**, signals are transmitted in only one direction. One station is the transmitter, and the other is the receiver. Simplex transmission is used by doorbells and radio and television broadcasting. For example, a home radio can only receive signals transmitted from a radio station. The listener cannot reverse the communication and talk to the radio station.

Half-duplex transmission allows signals to be transmitted in only one direction at a time. When transmission in one direction is completed, transmission in the other direction is possible. Walkie-talkies and CB radios, with their send and receive buttons, are examples of half-duplex transmission.

FIGURE 2-18 Types of Signal Direction

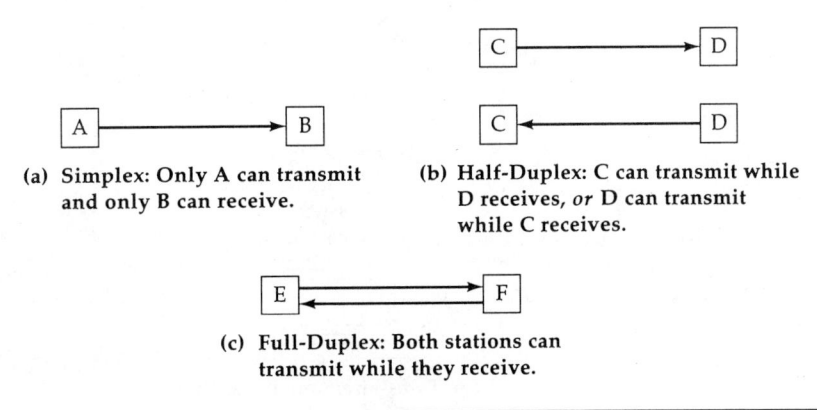

(a) Simplex: Only A can transmit and only B can receive.

(b) Half-Duplex: C can transmit while D receives, *or* D can transmit while C receives.

(c) Full-Duplex: Both stations can transmit while they receive.

In **full-duplex transmission**, signals are transmitted in both directions simultaneously. A telephone conversation, for example, is easily carried out on multiwire lines. Each wire is transmitting in simplex mode.

■ Telephone Transmission Links

The transmission links of telephone systems are two-wire or four-wire circuits. The terms "two-wire" and "four-wire" specify the number of wires used to carry the signals in both directions. Figure 2-19 illustrates sending signals by two- and four-wire circuits. A *hybrid*—transmission device—serves as an interface between two-wire and four-wire circuits.

Two-Wire Circuit. In most telephone systems the local loop or line (the line connecting your telephone to the telephone company's central office) is a two-wire circuit consisting of two insulated wires and usually a two-way amplifier. Conversations in the form of signals are sent in both directions, using the same pair of wires.

Four-Wire Circuit. In a four-wire (two pairs) circuit, one pair carries signals in one direction, while the other pair carries them in the opposite direction. However, a pair of wires may physically be two wires or may be the same pair of wires using a different signal frequency for each direction. Long-distance lines generally use four-wire circuits because they can carry many conversations simultaneously and generally require one-way amplifiers for each direction.

FIGURE 2-19 Sending Signals

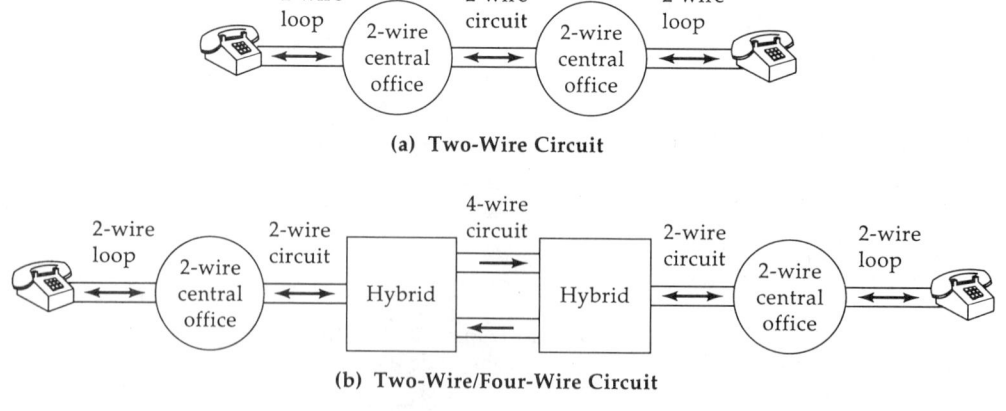

Transmission

■ Modulation

Modulation converts an electrical signal from one form to another more appropriate form for transmission over a circuit between two locations. *Demodulation* restores the signal to the original form at the receiving end. Signal conversion—from analog to digital or from digital to analog—as discussed in the previous section is one reason for modulating a signal before transmission. Another reason, as explained below, is to enable a number of signals to be combined and transmitted simultaneously over the same medium, which also reduces the per-channel transmission cost.

When sound is converted into analog signals for transmission, the converted signals are sent or carried by high-frequency sine waves. Since the frequency of voice, music, or data often is lower than the frequency of sine waves, the frequency of the sine wave must be changed for transmission. A sine wave is called a **carrier wave** when it can be varied by using a second wave to carry information.

The frequency of information signals—voice, music, or data signals—is superimposed on the single frequency of the carrier wave for transmission. Varying or changing the carrier wave so that it contains the information signals to be transmitted is the process of modulation. In this case, modulation is putting intelligence on a carrier wave, the sine wave. The most common forms of modulation are amplitude modulation (AM) and frequency modulation (FM).

Amplitude modulation is a method of modifying a sine wave in order to make it carry information (see Figure 2-20). The sine wave, or carrier, has its amplitude modified in accordance with the information to be transmitted. AM varies with the voltage or amplitude. The amplitude of the higher-frequency carrier wave is modulated by the amplitude of the lower-frequency signal wave.

Frequency modulation is another way of modulating a sine wave to make it carry information (see Figure 2-21). The sine wave, or carrier, has its *frequency* modified in accordance with information transmitted (voice, data, or video). The frequency function of the modulated wave may be continuous or discontinuous. By changing the frequency to lower or higher values, information can be transmitted.

■ Multiplexing

If each circuit was assigned exclusively to transmit a single message, communications would be hopelessly slow and expensive. But if circuits can be shared, message transmission can be speeded and transmission cost decreased. Such sharing is accomplished by **multiplexing**, which allows multiple streams of electronic messages or signals to be transmitted over the same circuit in the time otherwise required for one message. With multiplexing, from several to several thousand users may each occupy a portion of a particular circuit.

FIGURE 2-20 **Amplitude Modulation**

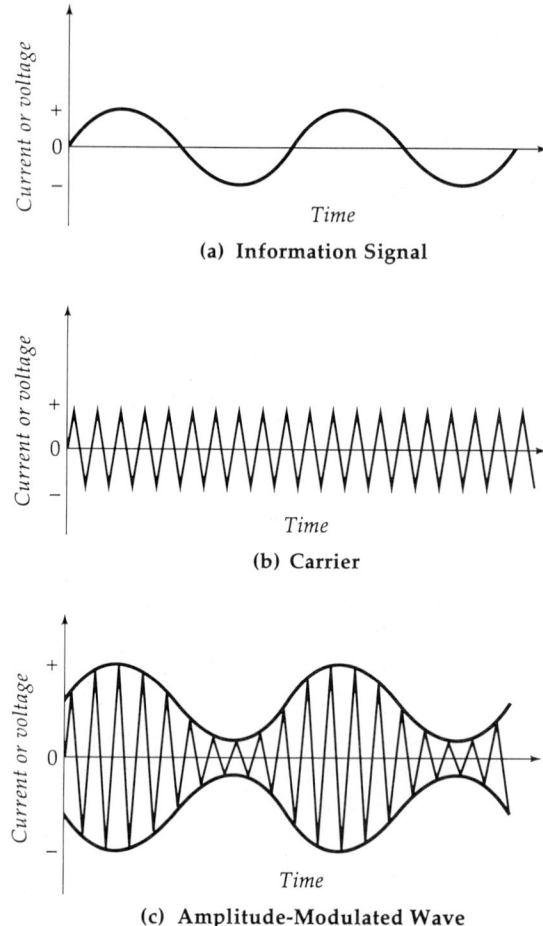

(a) Information Signal

(b) Carrier

(c) Amplitude-Modulated Wave

A circuit is most frequently divided among users by frequency or time. The two basic multiplexing methods are frequency-division multiplexing (FDM) and time-division multiplexing (TDM). FDM is used with analog transmission; TDM is used with digital transmission.

Frequency-Division Multiplexing. Frequency-division multiplexing (FDM) is often used in long-distance telephone transmission. This multiplexing method makes it possible for analog signals of many transmissions to travel simultaneously over a single circuit but at different frequencies. It

FIGURE 2-21 Frequency Modulation

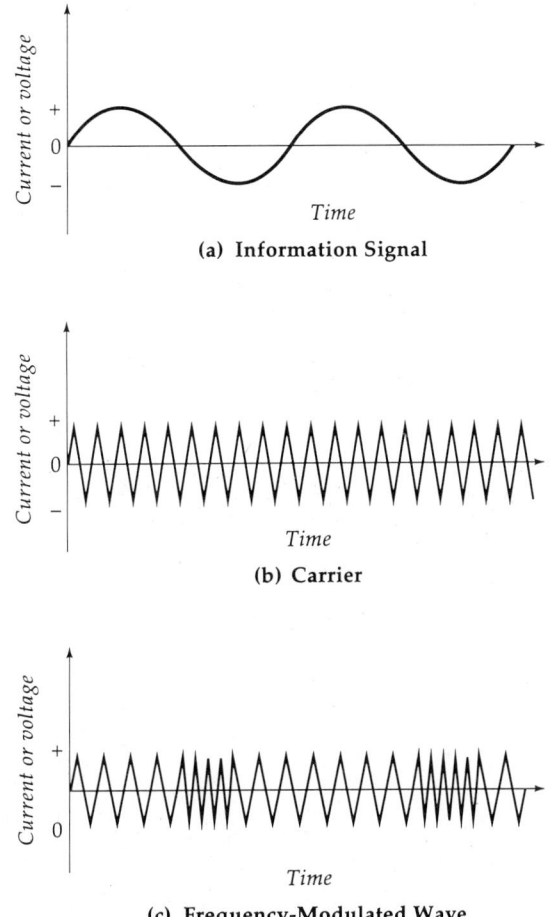

(a) Information Signal

(b) Carrier

(c) Frequency-Modulated Wave

uses the bandwidth of a single-voice-grade circuit and divides it into multiple subchannels so that each user's frequencies are transmitted over a separate channel, as shown in Figure 2-22. Since each channel occupies a different bandwidth, all channels can transmit signals simultaneously. Guardbands prevent signals of adjacent channels from interfering with each other.

Operation of FDM. Because the bandwidth of a telephone circuit is wider than is needed for a single speech, each voiceband channel can be

FIGURE 2-22 **Frequency-Division Multiplexing (FDM)**

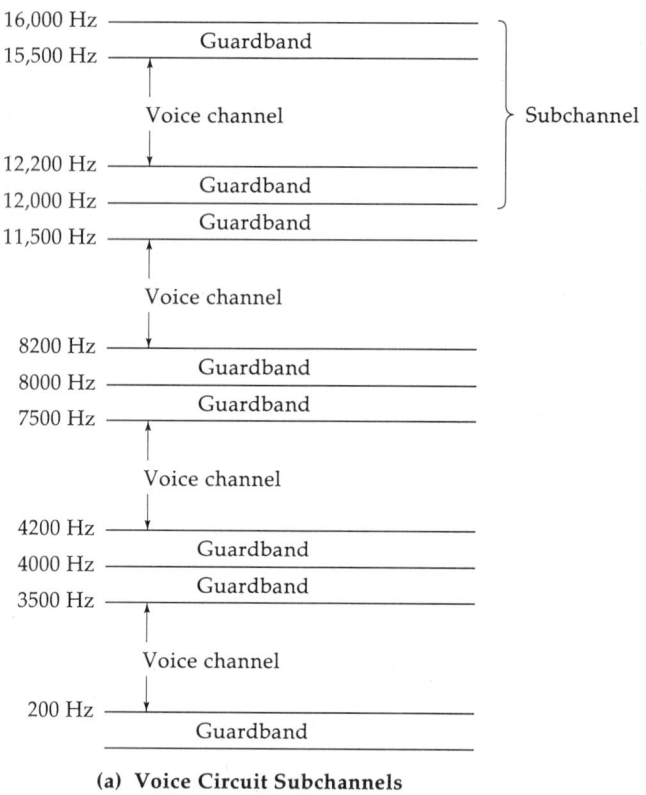

(a) Voice Circuit Subchannels

modulated at different frequencies, allowing several telephone conversations to be sent at the same time. As shown in Figure 2-23, a transmitting multiplex terminal shifts each voiceband channel to a different frequency using amplitude modulation. At the receiving demultiplex terminal, demultiplexing of the circuit separates and recovers the original channels. *Demultiplexing* is actually the reverse of multiplexing. The greater the medium's bandwidth, the more carriers it can transmit, and the more messages it can handle simultaneously. Review Figure 2-22(b).

Time-Division Multiplexing. Time-division multiplexing (TDM) is designed for transmitting digital signals over a single digital circuit. A device scans individual channels in rotation by taking a byte from each channel and transmitting the bytes in a string according to a prearranged plan over a single circuit, as shown in Figure 2-24. To allow many bytes to be sent during the time ordinarily required for one, each byte is condensed.

FIGURE 2-22 Continued

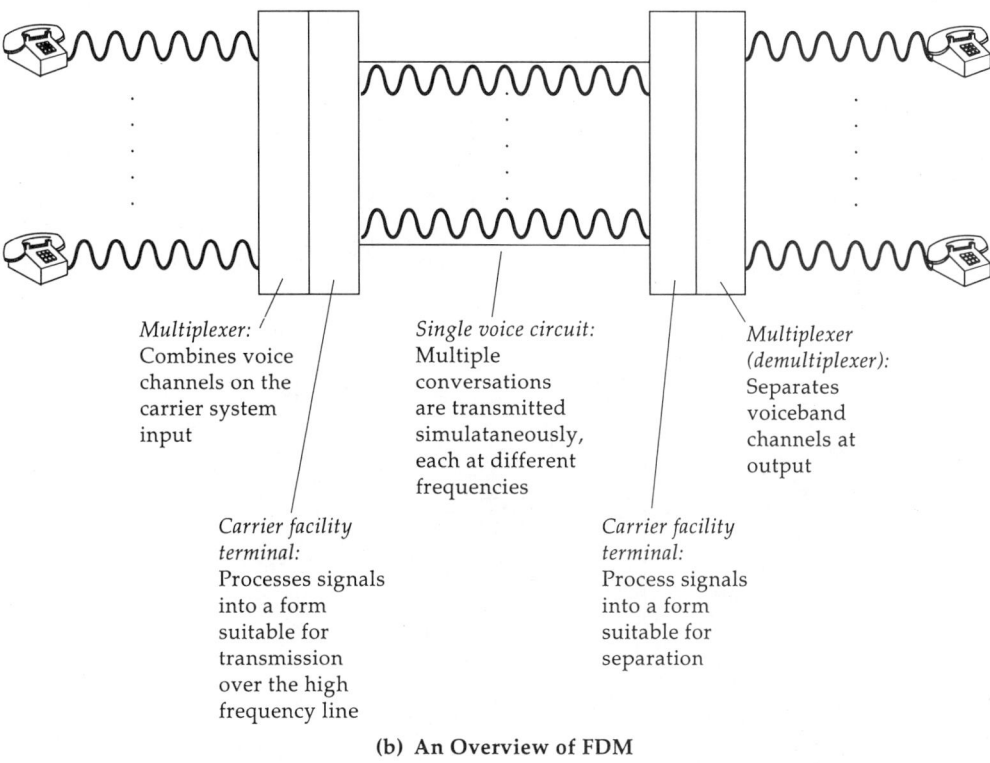

(b) An Overview of FDM

Operation of TDM. In TDM the transmission circuit is divided into time slots into which signals are assigned and removed. Only one signal occupies the channel at a given instant, with guard times separating the signals. If analog signals are to be sent, they must first be converted to digital form.

Transmission Impairments and Media

The first telephone calls were transmitted by metal wire, a medium that is still in use today. Telephone wires continue to be strung on poles; others are buried underground, bundled together in heavy, well-protected cables. Cables are laid on lake and river bottoms; there are even cables on ocean floors for carrying calls between continents.

However, many of our long-distance telephone calls travel only part of the way by wire or cable. They may also be carried through the air on radio

FIGURE 2-23 Modulation of a Voiceband Channel

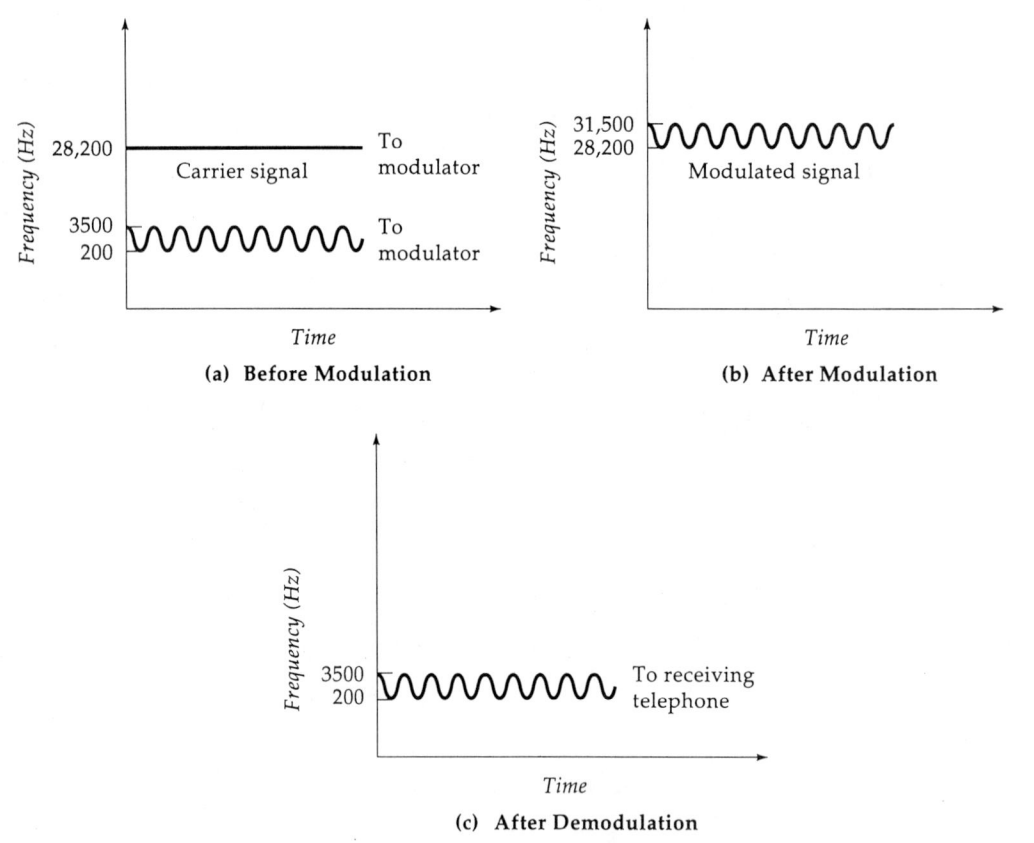

waves to cross large land areas and great expanses of water. For example, radio relay systems use radio waves called microwaves. They communicate by line-of-sight paths from tower to tower. Short-wave radio signals are used for radiotelephone calls to many parts of the world. Communication satellites—towers in space—receive and rebroadcast microwave messages.

■ Transmission Impairments

Successful transmission depends on the quality of the signal being transmitted and the characteristics of the transmission media. Figure 2-25 is a diagram of a typical long-distance circuit with multiple links that connect two telephone stations. As signals are being transmitted, they are subject to certain impairments over distance. Each link can also introduce impairments

FIGURE 2-24   Time-Division Multiplexing

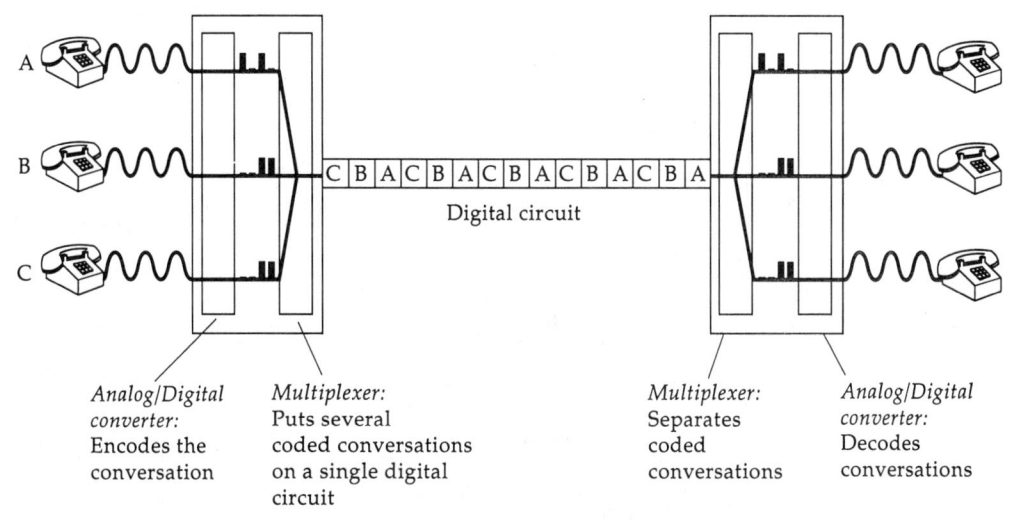

Analog/Digital converter: Encodes the conversation

Multiplexer: Puts several coded conversations on a single digital circuit

Multiplexer: Separates coded conversations

Analog/Digital converter: Decodes conversations

FIGURE 2-25   Typical Long-Distance Circuit with Multiple Links

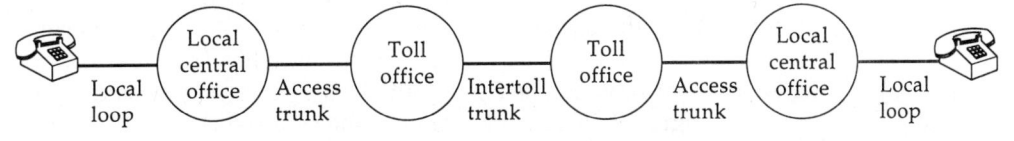

into the system. To ensure quality transmission and user satisfaction, impairments such as attenuation, delay distortion, noise, crosstalk, and echo must be controlled.

Attenuation.   All transmission links between the sender and receiver have a common characteristic: **attenuation**. As a signal travels from the sender to the receiver, its strength decreases or weakens. The decrease in signal strength during transmission is called attenuation.

Decibels.   In telecommunications, a signal's strength is expressed in terms of the **decibel** (dB), a measure first used to refer to sound. The unit measures differences in signal strength, not the absolute value. For example, the intensities of common sounds are measured in decibels relative to the

FIGURE 2-26 **Decibel Power Ratios**

Decibels	Losses	Gains
1	0.8	1.25
2	0.63	1.6
3	0.5	2.0
4	0.4	2.5
5	0.32	3.2
6	0.25	4.0
7	0.2	5.0
8	0.16	6.3
9	0.125	8.0
10	0.1	10.0

threshold of human hearing. A decibel level of 0 represents the faintest sound audible to the average person, while conversation level for most people is about 50–70 dB. Sounds become physically painful and damaging above 150 dB.

The use of decibels makes it easy to calculate losses or gains of signal strength between two transmission points. Signal strength is measured by determining the loss or gain between the sending point and the receiving point. In other words, the difference between power input and power output is calculated and expressed as a ratio in decibels.

When power output is the same as power input, no increase or decrease in signal strength has occurred: The ratio is 1:1 or 0 dB. When power output is less than power input, a loss of signal strength has occurred. For example, when a power ratio equals 0.8, or 80% loss, the decibel measure is 1 dB, as shown in Figure 2-26. A 1 dB change is the smallest change that the human ear can detect. The decibel values in Figure 2-26 have been calculated by using logarithms.

Suppose the difference in a signal's strength from the sending station (power input) to the receiving station (power output) shows a 0.50 loss. According to Figure 2-26, a loss of 50 percent indicates that the signal at the receiving station has a loss of 3 dB, referred to as being "down 3 dB." In fact, any decrease in signal strength that halves the signal is a 3 dB reduction, a change that is noticeable to most listeners. The original signal can be restored to its original strength by installing amplifiers, also called repeaters, at intervals along the transmission path, as shown in Figure 2-27. The spacing between amplifiers depends on the amount of power lost for each unit length of transmission medium.

If the power output is more than the power input, a signal gain has been experienced. When a signal is too loud, an artificial loss can be achieved by inserting a specially designed device into the circuit.

FIGURE 2-27 **Attenuation**

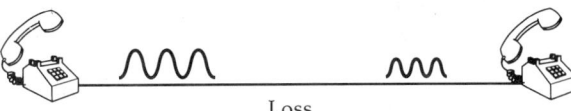
Loss
(a) Signal Strength Decreasing During Transmission

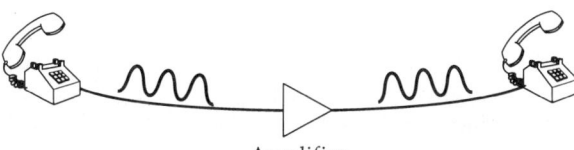
Amplifier
(b) Correcting Signal Loss During Transmission

Decibels also specify the *overall signal gain or loss during part of the transmission*. For example, suppose a transmission line connecting a sender and a receiver has one amplifier about halfway along the line. Suppose the loss on the first part of the line is 8 dB, the gain of the amplifier is 20 dB, and the loss on the second part of the line is 30 dB. In this case the overall loss would be 18 dB ($-8 + 20 - 30 = -18$ dB).

Specific Power Level. It is customary to represent attenuation in terms of a specific power level, such 0 dBm. Power in a telephone circuit can be represented by milliwatts (1 milliwatt (mW) equals 0.001 watt or one-thousandth of a watt). For example, for 1 mW a value of 0 dBm means no gain or loss in power strength from the 1 mW reference. Thus while "dB" refers to a ratio of power, "dBm" refers to a specific power level based on the 1 mW reference value. For example, +3 dBm specifies a power level 3 dB above the reference. As shown in Figure 2-26, a gain of 3 dB represents a doubling of power or signal strength, which means that 3 dBm doubles its original level of power, in this case "m," to 2 mW. Conversely, a loss of 3 dBm means losing one half of the signal power, in this case, 0.5 mW. A value of -10 dBm (a loss) is equal to 10 dB below the level of power or 0.1 mW. When the expression "dB" is followed by one or more other letters, it represents a gain or a loss relative to a known value and becomes an absolute quantity, rather than merely a ratio.

Delay Distortion. The term *propagation* is used to describe an electrical wave moving along a transmission medium. Propagation does not occur at a uniform rate of speed. The type of medium, such as wires, cable, or microwave, and the frequency being used for transmission affect a signal's movement. Unequal signal delays at different frequencies result in **delay distortion**. Such delay usually has little effect on voice communication but is of concern to high-speed data transmission.

Noise. *Noise* is any unwanted signal in a transmission path. Most people have experienced noise while talking on the phone. The two kinds of noise inherent to terrestrial (ground) transmission are white noise and impulse noise.

White Noise. **White noise**, also called *thermal noise*, is the familiar background hiss or static on radio and telephones. The noise is caused by the thermal agitation of electrons that results from the transmission of extraneous electrical signals over lines.

White noise is always present in terrestrial transmission, although we usually do not notice it. But it can become annoying when it is louder than a normal level and interferes with our conversation. White noise is usually not a problem with local calls. However, as the distance between the caller and the called party increases, the noise becomes louder. The amplifiers that strengthen voice signals along the transmission path also increase the noise, as shown in Figure 2-28.

Impulse Noise. The second type of noise, **impulse noise**, causes voice transmission to be corrupted by short clicks or crackles but without loss of intelligibility. It can also cause large blocks of data to be obliterated. Impulse noise is caused by intermittent disturbances such as interference from nearby electrical sources, the effects of electrical storms in the atmosphere, and poorly operating electromechanical transmission equipment and circuits. The replacement of electromechanical transmission with computerized equipment helps to diminish impulse noise.

Signal-to-Noise Ratio. Decibels are also used to express the quality or performance of a transmission system. A signal-to-noise ratio is usually measured at a receiver, since it is at this point that an attempt would be made

FIGURE 2-28 White Noise

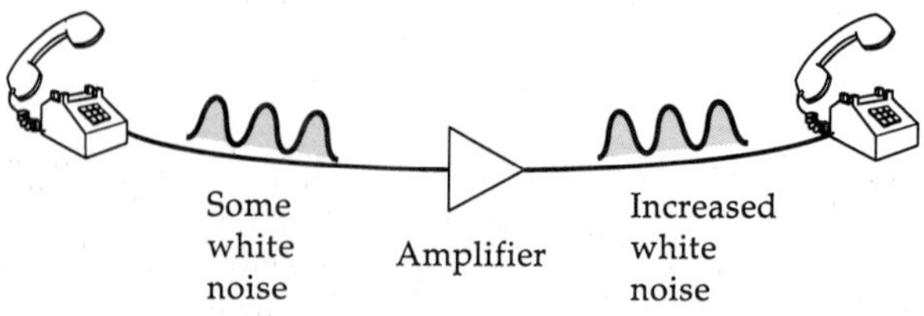

FIGURE 2-29   Crosstalk

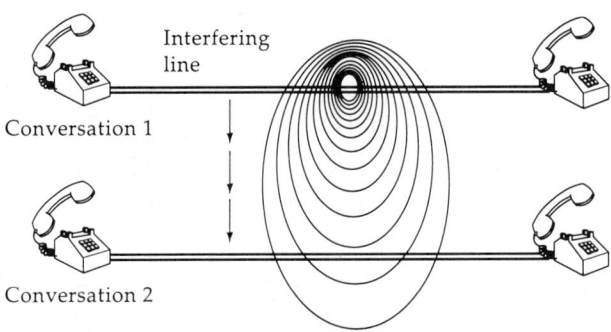

to eliminate unwanted noise. The ratio is signal plus noise divided by noise; the answer is expressed in decibels.

Crosstalk.   When you hear faint fragments of somebody else's conversation while conversing on the telephone, you are experiencing **crosstalk**. If crosstalk is intelligible, you may doubt the privacy of the connection. What is happening is that one channel is picking up some of the signals that are traveling on another person's channel or microwave antennas are picking up unwanted signals.

Crosstalk is more likely to take place on long-distance calls than on local calls. Crosstalk occurs when space or insulation between the links or wires is insufficient to prevent electromagnetic interference between signals, as shown in Figure 2-29. One way to reduce the effect of crosstalk when using cable is to separate adjacent channels from each other by distance or insulation.

Echo.   Echo is the reflection of a signal back to its source. For example, talker echo results when an electrical signal travels a distance and a portion of it is reflected back toward the speaker. The size of an echo can occasionally be so large that speaking becomes almost impossible. In voice telephone, echoes of the speaker's voice become annoying when they are heard with a time delay measured in tens of milliseconds. In data transmission, delays of a fraction of a millisecond are significant, causing errors in the transmitted data. Electronic devices such as echo suppressors or echo cancellers help to minimize the effects of this kind of noise.

■ Transmission Media

A transmission medium may physically constrain and guide signals, or it may permit them to be transmitted without guiding them. Types of *guided media* include open-wire lines, twisted-wire, coaxial cable, and fiber-optic

FIGURE 2-30 **Open-Wire Lines**

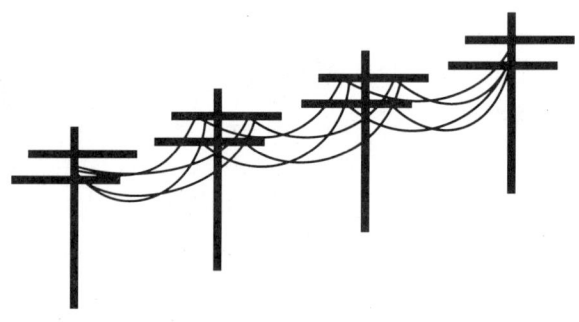

cable. The atmosphere and outer space are *unguided media* for transmitting terrestrial microwave radio and satellite communications, respectively. Each type of transmission medium has unique characteristics and capabilities.

Open-Wire Lines. The first telephone systems that carried conversations were uninsulated *open pairs of wire*. **Open-wire lines** were strung between telephone poles that were spaced about 125 feet apart, as shown in Figure 2-30. Five open-wire pairs are mounted on a single crossarm on a pole with wires separated by a foot of space to prevent short circuits in high winds. Wires are made of copper, copper-clad steel, or galvanized steel. Although open-wire lines are still used in many places, particularly rural areas, they are being replaced by other transmission media.

Paired Cable. Another type of two-wire line, **paired cable**, uses wood pulp or plastic insulated wires twisted together into pairs. Twisting these pairs of wires minimizes electromagnetic interference between the pairs, which causes crosstalk. Many twisted pairs can be formed into a ropelike *binder group*. Several binder groups are bundled together into a cable by wrapping them in a protective sheath. For long distances, cables may contain hundreds of pairs. Figure 2-31 shows a typical paired cable.

Paired cable is manufactured in standard sizes containing from 6 to 3600 wire pairs. Paired cable may be increased from two to four wires. It also may be strung on poles, installed in underground conduits, or buried directly in the ground. Paired cable is primarily used by local telephone systems. Individual telephone sets are connected to the local exchange by twisted-pair cable. Within an office building, twisted wire often connects telephones to private branch exchanges (PBXs) (see Chapter 5).

Coaxial Cable. A coaxial cable is suitable for transmission at much higher frequencies than open-wire lines or paired cable. **Coaxial cable** contains

FIGURE 2-31   Paired Cable

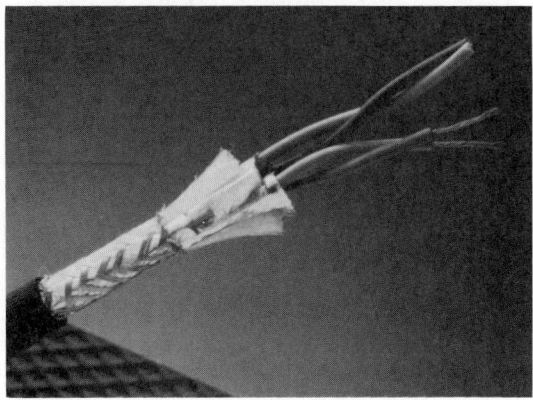

Courtesy of Siecor Corporation, Hickory, N.C.

from four to twenty-two coaxial units called *tubes*. Each tube consists of a hollow cylinder, usually copper, that surrounds a single wire conductor. The space between the cylinder shell and the inner conductor is filled with an insulator of plastic or air. Supports separating the shield and the inner conductor are placed about every inch or so. Coaxial tubes are bound together in one large cable. Figure 2-32 shows a coaxial cable. Twisted-wire pairs are packed in among the coaxial tubes for control purposes.

FIGURE 2-32   Coaxial Cable

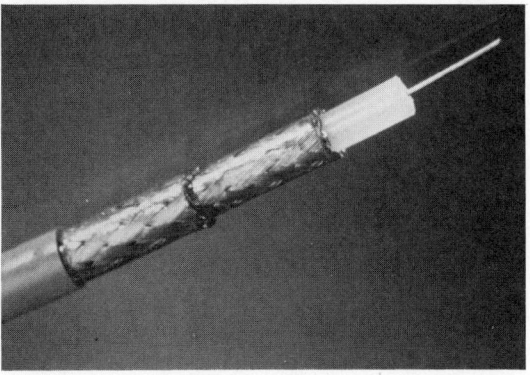

Photo courtesy of AT&T Network Systems.

A coaxial cable system allows a large number of separate telephone calls to be transmitted together. A single wire pair can carry twelve or twenty-four voice channels. While one single coaxial tube typically carries 3600 channels, some carry as many as 10,000 channels.

Coaxial cable is less susceptible to crosstalk than is paired cable, although attenuation and thermal noise are problems. Coaxial cable is primarily used for long-distance networks. Other uses include television transmission, cable television, local area networks (see Chapter 6), short-range connections such as connecting computer devices, and undersea cable systems.

Fiber-Optic Cable. **Fiber-optic cable**, also referred to as *lightguide cable*, replaces electricity with light and copper wires with hair-thin strands of glass. An electrical signal is converted to a light signal by a light source, such as a laser, and then coupled into a glass fiber.

Very fine transparent fibers composed of silicon and other materials such as germanium are bundled together into a flexible cable and act as a guide for the light frequencies, as shown in Figure 2-33. Currently, one company manufactures a cable that has 192 fibers and is aiming for a 600-strand version. An optical fiber cable is nothing more than a passive medium through which signals flow. Most of the work is performed by the transmitting and receiving devices, such as a laser, at each end.

The two types of lightguide cable are *ribbon-fiber cable* and *stranded cable*. A ribbon fiber cable may consist of one to twelve flat ribbons, each containing twelve glass fibers. Such a cable provides up to 144 one-way paths for light signals. Single-unit stranded cable consists of up to 16 fibers woven

FIGURE 2-33 **Fiber-Optic Cable**

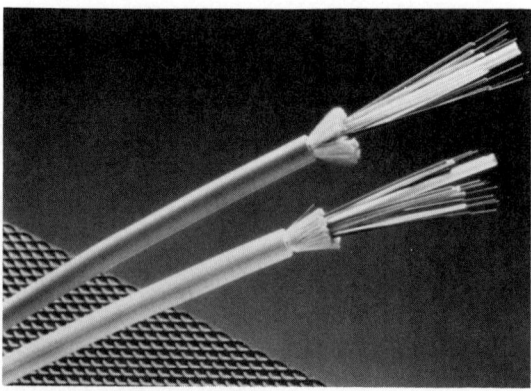

Courtesy of Siecor Corporation, Hickory, N.C.

around a central strength member. A 72-fiber multiunit cable contains six single units, each with twelve fibers.

The two types of optical fibers are *single mode* and *multimode*, as shown in Figure 2-34. Single-mode fiber, introduced in 1983, is replacing multimode fiber because it offers increased capacity and covers longer distances without repeaters.

The main advantages of fiber-optic cables are

- High communication capacity. A 144-fiber cable accommodates 250,000 voice channels.
- Being immune to electrical noises, such as impulse noise and crosstalk, and interference generated by surrounding equipment.
- Small size (0.5-inch outer diameter) and light weight (80 pounds per 1000 feet of cable). It weighs substantially less than coaxial cable and wire. Its small size is advantageous for use in buildings and for use underground along public rights-of-way. Its light weight reduces structural support requirements.
- Wide bandwidth. Single-mode fiber can transmit information at rates of 100 GHz and higher. By increasing speed, long-distance carriers boost transmission capacity and can pack more revenue-generating traffic onto circuits.
- No electromagnetic radiation leaks, making it more secure than other media.
- Optical signals that cannot be tapped without detection.

FIGURE 2-34 **Types of Fiber Optic Cable**

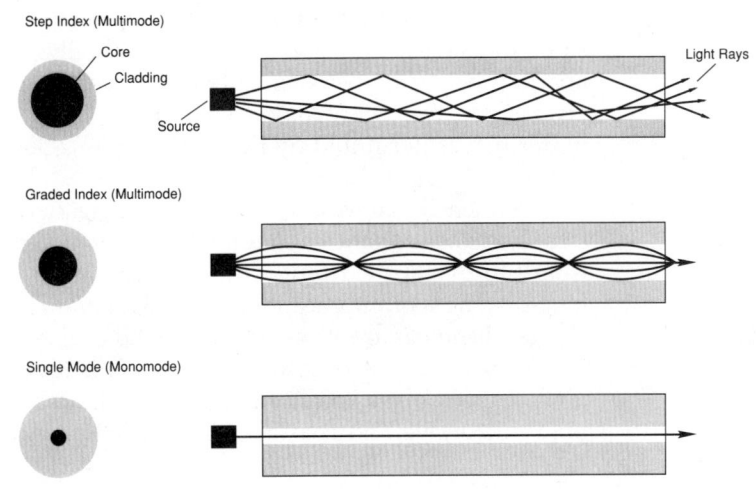

Courtesy of Belden Wire and Cable.

- Fewer repeaters required. For example, systems can now operate at nearly 1 Gbps* over a distance of about 25 miles without any signal amplification. Copper wires are limited to less than 100 Mbps* and require a repeater every 4–6 miles.
- Inexpensive maintenance once fiber-optic cable has been installed.

Over the past decade, fiber-optic cable has been used mainly by long-distance carriers such as AT&T, MCI Communications, and U.S. Sprint. It is now being used increasingly by local telephone companies to replace the copper wire that goes to a customer's premises and by other companies for in-company use.

Yet fiber-optic cable does require right-of-way and sufficient conduit space. Microwave, coaxial cable, or some other medium may still be a better solution. For example, microwave might be more advantageous when rights-of-way for fiber lines are impossible or very expensive to obtain. Satellite transmission might be preferable for covering rural areas that would be costly to reach by fiber optics.

Terrestrial Microwave Radio. Microwave radio is a point-to-point medium. *Microwaves* travel in a narrow beam as they are transmitted from and received by parabolic (bowl-shaped) antennas (see Figure 2-35). The sending antenna focuses a narrow beam to achieve *line-of-sight* transmission to the receiving antenna; the transmitter and receiver must be within visual sight of each other. Signals are broadcast through the air to the receiving antenna, which in turn retransmits them to the next antenna. No physical transmission facility is required to guide the microwaves between antennas.

Microwave antennas are usually located at substantial heights above ground level to extend the range between antennas and to enable **terrestrial microwave radio transmission** over intervening obstacles. To allow line-of-sight transmission, relay stations are usually spaced about 20–30 miles apart. The spacing between antennas is determined by the geography of a given route, the technology used in the terminal equipment, and the transmitter power permitted by the FCC. Figure 2-36 shows a microwave radio station.

Frequencies above one billion hertz (1 gigahertz or 1 GHz) are microwave frequencies. Frequencies commonly used for microwave transmission range from 1 to 23 GHz. Currently, the most commonly used frequency bands for long-distance communication are the 4, 6, and 11 GHz bands, and those for shorter distances are 18 and 23 GHz bands, as authorized by the FCC.

A major use of terrestrial microwave is long-distance telecommunications, especially as an alternative to coaxial cable for voice and television. Both microwave and coaxial cable can carry thousands of voice channels,

---

*bps (bits per second) is the unit for measuring the speed of transmission of digital signals. Gbps (Gigabits per second) is equal to a transmission speed of one billion bits per second. Mbps (Megabits per second) is equal to a transmission speed of one million bits per second.

Transmission Impairments and Media

FIGURE 2-35 Terrestrial Microwave Radio Transmission

FIGURE 2-36 A Microwave Radio Station

Courtesy of AT&T Archives.

but microwave requires fewer repeaters or amplifiers over the same amount of distance. However, microwave does require line-of-sight transmission.

Microwave transmission has certain drawbacks. Attenuation increases with rainfall. With overlapping areas, microwave signals can interfere with radio signals. A number of the nation's cities, such as New York City, have become so congested with microwave beams that it is difficult or impossible to add more microwave systems.

Radio. The primary difference between radio and microwave is that radio is omnidirectional (the signal propagating in all directions from the antenna), while microwave is focused. Thus radio does not require either dish-shaped antennas or antennas mounted in precise alignment with each other. Radio uses the range of frequencies from 30 MHz to 1 GHz. Radio waves are less sensitive to attenuation from rainfall. Applications include teletext, cellular radio, and citizen's band radio, which are discussed in the chapters on applications of telecommunications.

Satellite Communication. Satellite communication is actually a form of microwave radio; information is transmitted by microwaves. A satellite, placed in orbit about 22,300 miles above the earth, relays signals over long distances that would not be possible to cover by using a single link on the earth's surface. As shown in Figure 2-37, the satellite links two or more ground-based microwave transmitters/receivers, known as *earth stations*. Many stations can transmit to a satellite, and a transmission from a satellite can be received by many stations, also shown in Figure 2-37.

The satellite receives transmission from an earth station on one frequency band, amplifies or repeats the signal, and then transmits it to another earth station on another frequency. So that the satellite is always within line of sight of its earth stations, it is positioned above the equator and travels around the earth in exactly the same time as the earth takes to rotate. Thus a satellite appears to be stationary above the equator.

Like terrestrial microwave, satellites can transmit several thousand voice channels simultaneously. This medium competes with terrestrial microwave and coaxial cable for long-distance transmission. It has the advantage of being able to send large amounts of information to nearly any place on earth, regardless of its location or distance. Another advantage is that, in contrast to other media, satellite transmission costs are independent of the distance between the transmitting and receiving locations. Still another is that each satellite system requires only one repeater, while a similar terrestrial micro-

FIGURE 2-37 Satellite Communications

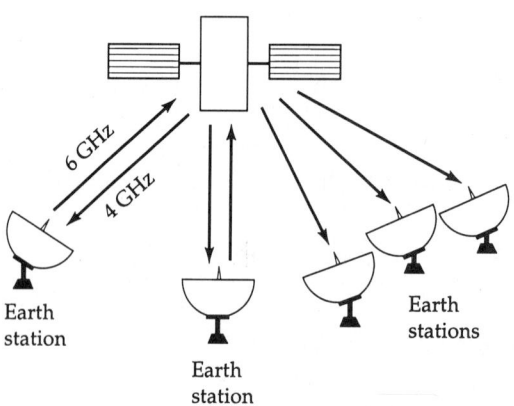

wave system requires many repeaters because the curvature of the earth interferes with its line-of-sight transmission path.

Satellites typically use a frequency bandwidth ranging from 5.925 to 6.425 GHz for transmission from earth to satellite (referred to as uplink) and a bandwidth ranging from 3.7 to 4.2 GHz for transmission from satellite to earth (downlink). This combination is referred to as the 6/4 GHz band pair. Note that the uplink and downlink frequencies must differ for continuous operation without interference. Another commonly used band pair is 14/12 GHz.

Satellite transmission can produce greater attenuation and longer delays (a 0.25-second delay for the uplink and a 0.25-second delay for the downlink) than transmission using terrestrial systems. Delays can impair the quality of voice transmissions and seriously affect data transmission. Eliminating these delays requires the careful design and use of equipment. Rain attenuation can also be a problem on satellite paths.

Summary

A telephone sends the human voice along a wire by converting the sound pattern into a matching electrical pattern—analog or digital. At the receiving end, the telephone reverses the process. The voice that is heard on the telephone is really not the caller's voice; it is a reproduction of that voice, a reconstruction of the tone and personality of his or her voice. Multiplexing allows a transmission circuit to be shared without forcing a caller to wait on others to complete their telephone calls. But as signals are transmitted, they can be subject to various impairments such as attenuation, delay distortion, noise, crosstalk, and echo. The particular transmission medium that is selected determines whether signals will suffer any type of impairment and to what extent.

Key Terms

Amplitude
Bandwidth
Carrier wave
Decibel
Frequency
Frequency-shift keying method
Guardband
Modulation:
    Amplitude modulation
    Frequency modulation

Multiplexing:
    Frequency-division multiplexing
    Time-division multiplexing
Signal direction:
    Simplex transmission
    Half-duplex transmission
    Full-duplex transmission

Signals:
    Analog
    Digital
Sine wave
Sound wave
Transducer
Transmission impairments:
    Attenuation
    Crosstalk
    Delay distortion

Echo
Impulse noise
White noise
Transmission media:
   Coaxial cable
   Fiber-optic cable
   Open-wire lines
   Paired cable
   Satellite communication
   Terrestrial microwave radio
   Wavelength

■ Self-Quiz

Indicate whether the statement is true or false.

1. The telephone system transmits the entire range of the human voice.   T/F
2. A bandwidth tells the range of frequencies being used; it does not tell which ones.   T/F
3. The capacity of a digital circuit is indicated by bit rate.   T/F
4. Both a modem and a codec are transducers.   T/F
5. The primary difference between radio and microwave is that radio is focused while microwave is omnidirectional.   T/F
6. A satellite transmits information by microwaves.   T/F

Complete each of the following statements.

1. The organization responsible for assigning frequencies for commercial transportation communication in the United States is _____ .
2. A voice circuit requires a band of _____ .
3. The type of transmission in which signals are transmitted in only one direction is called _____ .
4. When sine waves are varied by using a second wave to carry information, they are called _____ .
5. The technique of providing a transmission circuit with the capability of handling several separate, individual signals simultaneously is called _____ .
6. When the loss of a signal is 3 dB, the output signal power is _____ of the input signal power.

Match Column A with Column B.

Column A
(a) Attenuation
(b) Crosstalk
(c) Delay distortion
(d) Echo
(e) Noise
(f) Propagation

Column B
____ 1. Describes an electrical wave moving along a transmission medium.
____ 2. Reflection of a signal back to its source.
____ 3. Occurs when space between the wires is insufficient to prevent electromagnetic interference between signals.
____ 4. Unequal delays of signal movements at different frequencies.
____ 5. Signal strength decreases as it is being transmitted.
____ 6. Any unwanted signal in a transmission path.

Review Questions

1. (a) What are the characteristics of a sound wave?
   (b) How does a sound wave differ from a sine wave?
2. How are voice sounds transmitted over a telephone system to their destination?
3. (a) What is the total bandwidth of a voice channel?
   (b) How can voices travel on the same circuit without interfering with each other?
4. (a) What is the difference between analog signals and digital signals?
   (b) What is the difference between an analog circuit and a digital circuit?
5. (a) How are voice signals transmitted over a digital transmission facility?
   (b) How does a codec convert analog signals to digital ones?
6. How can a computer transmit data to another computer using an analog transmission facility?
7. (a) What is the difference between half-duplex and full-duplex transmission?
   (b) Identify at least three applications for which a simplex line might be used.
8. (a) What is the difference between modulation and demodulation?
   (b) What is the difference between amplitude modulation and frequency modulation?
9. (a) What is multiplexing?
   (b) What is the difference between frequency-division multiplexing and time-division multiplexing?
10. (a) What does it mean when we learn that a signal is "down 3 dB"?
    (b) Explain the meaning of the following: signal gain of 2 dB and signal loss of 2 dB.
    (c) Convert the following power ratios to decibels by referring to Figure 2.26: 0.50 loss and 2.00 gain.
11. (a) What is the difference between 3 dB and 3 dBm?
    (b) A transmission line connecting a sender and a receiver has one amplifier about midway along the line. The signal loss on the first part of the line is −4 dB, the gain from the amplifier is 10 dB, and the loss on the second part of the line is −3 dB. What is the signal gain or loss at the receiving end?
12. Describe at least three transmission impairments.
13. (a) What is the difference between guided media and unguided media?
    (b) Give examples of each type.
14. Give brief examples of where each transmission medium is used.

Activities/Projects

1. Investigate and discuss with a small group some aspect of the Federal Communications Commission, such as:
   (a) History of FCC

(b) Organizational structure of the FCC
  (c) Authorities and responsibilities of the FCC
  (d) FCC licensing procedures for users of the spectrum
  (e) Rules and regulations for frequency allocation
  (f) Impact of the FCC on others
  (g) Frequency requirements of a particular communication system commonly used in your vicinity
2. Perform the following experiment to demonstrate that when a person speaks, his or her voice sets the air in motion. The air waves or vibrations are what we hear.
  (a) *Obtain the following materials*: A cardboard tube at least 5 inches long, a small sheet of thin paper such as tissue paper, a rubber band to fit around the cardboard tube, and some grains of rice or sand.
  (b) *Prepare for the experiment*: Cut a hole in the side of the tube. Then stretch the paper across one end of the tube. Hold it in place with a rubber band. With the tube in an upright position, place the rice or sand on the paper.
  (c) *Conduct the experiment*: Shout into the hole in the tube wall. Notice how the grains bounce on the paper. Why are they vibrating?
3. With a telephone, a microcomputer, and a modem, demonstrate how information stored in another computer is accessed. Explain why the modem modulates and demodulates signals for transmission.

Additional Readings

Herb Brody, "The Rewiring of America," *High Technology Business*, February 1988, pp. 34–38.

J. H. Green, "Transmission Basics in Voice Transmission," *Communication Age*, January 1985, pp. 20–24.

J. H. Green, *The Dow Jones–Irwin Handbook of Telecommunications* (Homewood, Ill.: Dow Jones–Irwin, 1986).

Edward A. Lacy, *Fiber Optics* (Englewood Cliffs, N.J.: Prentice-Hall, Inc., 1982).

Graham Langley, *Telecommunications Primer* (London, England: Pitman Publishing Ltd., 1984).

James Martin, *Telecommunications and the Computer*, 2nd edition (Englewood Cliffs, N.J.: Prentice-Hall, Inc., 1976).

Information Seeker's Guide: How to Find Information at the Federal Communications Commission, prepared by Consumer Assistance and Small Business Division Office of Congressional and Public Affairs Federal Communications Commission, Washington, D.C.

CHAPTER 3

Telephone Basics

Telephone Components
    The Transmitter and the Receiver
    The Switchhook
    The Dial
    The Ringer

Basic Telephone Operations
    The Central Office
    Local Telephone Calls
    The Numbering Plan—Domestic and International

Exchange Services
    Basic Exchange Services
    Custom Calling Services
    Class Calling Services
    Business Exchange Services—Centrex Services

The Telecommunications Network
    Telecommunications Network Defined
    Physical Facilities of the Telecommunications Network

CHAPTER OBJECTIVES

After completing this chapter, you should be able to

1. Explain how a telephone operates.
2. Describe how a local call is completed using a central office switch.
3. Give examples of exchange services provided through a central office switch.
4. Discuss the telecommunications network, its components, and functions.

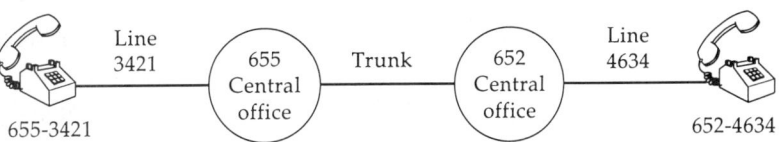

What calling service options would you add to your present local telephone service to solve each of the following business problems?

a. You would like to stop worrying about missed calls from customers when you are talking on the telephone to friends.
b. You frequently call the same customers in other states, and each call requires that you dial eleven digits. You would like to be able to use fewer digits to dial each number.
c. You would like to talk with two people by telephone on the same call at the same time without having to ask the operator to arrange the call.
d. You would like to be able to answer your calls when working in another office.
e. When you are working on certain projects, you do not want to answer telephone calls from anyone other than your supervisor, one of your customers, and your family.
f. You would like to prevent a persistent advertiser from calling you.
g. You will be working in another office for two or three hours. You would like to forward only your supervisor's and a friend's calls to this office.
h. You would like to know who is calling you before answering the telephone.
i. Often you are unable to reach the telephone before it stops ringing.
j. You spend a great deal of time trying to get through busy lines.

These problems can be solved easily by adding the following calling service options offered by your local telephone company: (a) *Call Waiting* allows you to engage in a call and still be reached by another caller; (b) *Speed Dialing* uses one or two digits for dialing frequently called numbers; (c) *Three-Way Calling* lets you add a third party to your existing conversation without operator assistance; (d) *Call Forwarding* transfers your calls to another office; (e) *Priority Ring* assigns a distinct ring to each of several callers; (f) *Call Block* prevents certain people from reaching you; (g) *Number Identification* displays the number calling you on your telephone screen before you answer the telephone; (i) *Return Call* allows you to call back the last number that called you, whether or not you answered the ring; and (j) *Repeat Call* redials the last number you dialed, even if it was not busy. These calling service options are described in this chapter.

Telephone systems have become an integral part of modern telecommunications systems. The telephone makes it possible for speech and other sounds to be reproduced at a remote location through the medium of electric currents. Speech is transmitted over distances by converting sound waves to electric currents and sending these currents to a remote location. There they are converted back into sound waves that reproduce the caller's original voice. The conversion of sound waves to electric currents and back to sound is accomplished by three elements within the telephone system: the transmitter, the receiver, and the transmission network.

The basic functions of a telephone system are

- Transmitting the voice signals between the two telephones.
- Switching circuits (a transmission path) to set up a unique path for the call.
- Using signaling circuits for telephone ringing, busy tone, and dialing.

Do you know how your telephone operates? Or how a local telephone call is completed? Or what services are offered by your local telephone office? This chapter tells you about the telephone—how it works, how calls are handled, and what services are available—and introduces you to the telecommunications network.

Telephone Components

Although telephones have differed over time in shapes and sizes, as shown in Figure 3-1, all telephones function in the same way and contain the same basic components: a transmitter and a receiver, a switchhook mechanism, a ringer or other type of alerting device, and a rotary or pushbutton dial. Figure 3-2 shows the arrangement of the telephone components. A circuit board, called a network assembly, is mounted inside the telephone and contains places to connect the transmitter to the receiver and to connect the ringer, dial, and outside lines.

■ The Transmitter and the Receiver

The transmitter and the receiver usually are housed in a handset constructed of molded plastic. The transmitter converts voice vibrations into electrical

FIGURE 3-1   Telephones

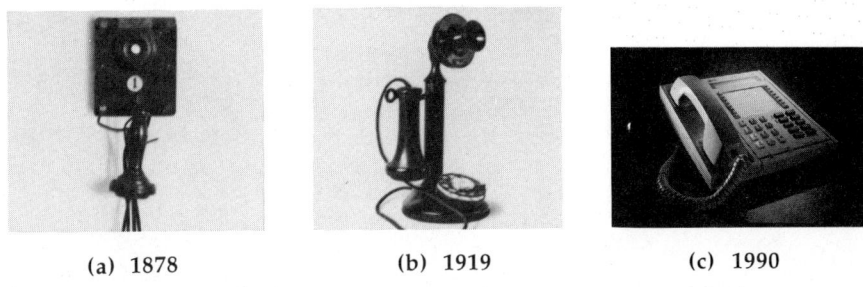

(a) 1878   (b) 1919   (c) 1990

(a) and (b) Courtesy of AT&T Archives. © Provided by Hello Direct, Inc., Catalog of Business Telephone Accessories, 140 Great Oaks Blvd., San Jose, CA 95119.

impulses. These impulses are then transmitted over telephone wires, radio waves, or satellite. The telephone receiver converts the incoming electrical impulses to sounds.

When you look at the telephone mouthpiece, all you see is a protective cover with holes in it. Behind the holes, however, is a miniature transmitter that has two basic components: the diaphragm and the carbon chamber shown in Figure 3-3(a). The diaphragm is a circular piece of very thin aluminum with an outer edge that is fixed firmly to a circular frame in the mouthpiece. The diaphragm's outer edge remains secure while the rest of the surface is free to vibrate. On the underside of the diaphragm, there is a small gold-plated brass dome that rests in a chamber containing small carbon granules. When the handset is lifted from the cradle, the granules in the chamber become part of the electrical circuit and the current passes through them.

When you speak into the mouthpiece, sound waves or vibrations pass through the holes and strike the diaphragm, which causes it to vibrate in

FIGURE 3-2   Telephone Components

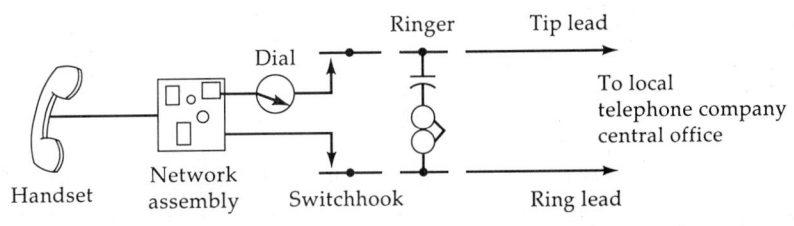

FIGURE 3-3 The Telephone Handset

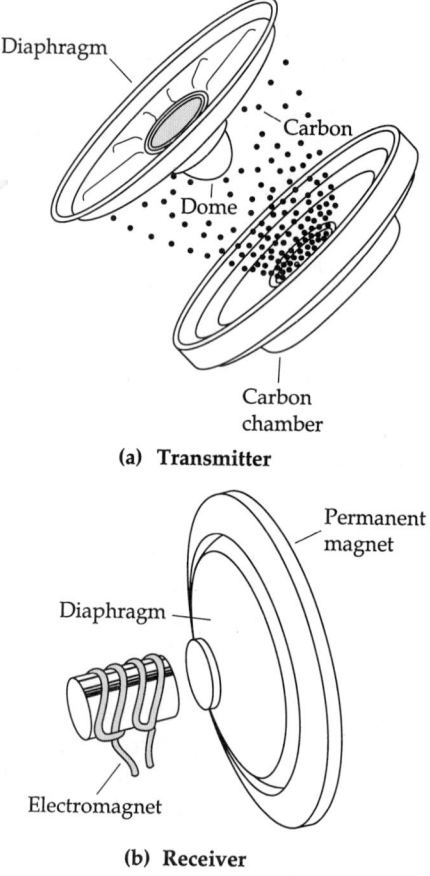

(a) Transmitter

(b) Receiver

the same pattern of vibrations as the words you are speaking. This, in turn, causes the small dome on the underside of the diaphragm to vibrate in the carbon chamber that is part of the electrical circuit. Each vibration causes the dome to compress the carbon granules. When the carbon granules are closer together due to compression, more current flows through the circuit. As the pressure decreases, the granules have greater space between them and the amount of current flowing through the circuit is reduced. It is at this critical point that speech is converted from sound waves or vibrations into electrical signals (impulses). The resulting signals are carried by two wires, called the tip and ring leads, to the distant telephone, where a receiver at the listening telephone converts them back into audible sounds so the signals can be heard as words.

Once the transmitter converts your words into electrical signals, it becomes the job of the receiver to convert them back into audible sounds so they can be heard as words. As shown in Figure 3-3(b), the receiver consists of three basic components: a diaphragm, an electromagnet, and a disc-shaped permanent magnet. The diaphragm is different from the transmitter's diaphragm because it performs as a speaker. Although it also is fixed to a circular frame, its frame is made of permanently magnetized iron. Under the diaphragm is an electromagnet in the form of a cylinder made of soft metal with a thin wire wound around it forming a coil. Surrounding the magnetic iron diaphragm frame on the underside of the diaphragm is a disc-shaped permanent magnet. This permanent magnet provides a constant pull on the diaphragm's outer ring (called the armature). When the electrical current from one telephone's transmitter flows into the coil of another telephone's receiver, the coil forms an electromagnetic field that aids or opposes the permanent magnet. The magnetic forces in the receiver are alternately increased or decreased depending on the direction in which the alternating current is flowing. The variation in magnetic pull results in the flexible armature moving in and out. The diaphragm also moves in and out at the same rate and thus pulls and pushes the air, setting the air into vibration at the same rate. This air vibration is the "voice" you hear in your telephone receiver.

■ The Switchhook

The **switchhook**, a "plunger" beneath the telephone handset, is an electrical make-and-break connection that turns the telephone on and off. It signals the "central office switch" (explained in the next section) and incoming callers that the telephone is either idle or in use.

■ The Rotary Dial or Pushbutton Keypad

The **rotary dial** or **pushbutton keypad** is a way of sending out coded information over the telephone. This information tells the switch what number is being dialed. The dial system, which came into general use in the 1920s, eliminates the need for an operator when making local calls. As explained in the next section, the types of dial telephone commonly used today are the rotary dial phone, shown in Fig. 3-4(a) and the pushbutton phone, which uses dial pulsing or dual tone multi-frequency (DTMF) electronic signaling, shown in Fig. 3-4(b).

■ The Ringer

A ringer, operated by electric current, alerts a person that someone is calling on the telephone. The ringer is mounted inside the base of the telephone and is connected to the **tip and ring leads**.

FIGURE 3-4 **The Dial System**

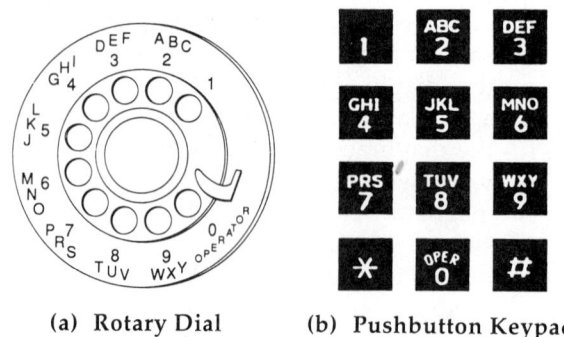

(a) Rotary Dial   (b) Pushbutton Keypad

Courtesy of Hello Direct, Inc., Catalog of Business Telephone Accessories, 140 Great Oaks Blvd., San Jose, CA 95119.

Basic Telephone Operations

■ The Central Office

The first telephones were linked point-to-point, as shown in Figure 3-5(a). As the number of telephone subscribers increased, the number of lines also increased, as shown in Figure 3-5(b). A simple formula for figuring how many connections a telephone system would need is $X(X - 1)/2$ with X representing the number of telephones in the system. For example, for ten telephones to be connected point-to-point, you would need forty-five telephone lines [$10(10 - 1)/2$]. How many connections would 10,000 telephones or 180 million telephones require? If there were only a few telephones in the world, connecting them point-to-point would be quite simple.

The situation in Figure 3-5(b) can be improved considerably by introducing switching at a central location, as shown in Figure 3-5(c). A **switch** connects lines to form a transmission path between two subscribers. All calls are routed through a switch housed at what is called a **central office**, which reduces the number of transmission paths considerably. The primary purpose of a central office switch is to provide a physical path for the call.

Switching. Telephones are joined to switching equipment in central offices throughout the country. Two wires, referred to as the tip and ring leads, connect each telephone to a central office switch, as illustrated in Figure 3-6. These wires are used to send signals and provide a transmission path to a central office. This path—a communications link between your telephone and the serving central office—is also referred to as a *local loop* (also called a *line*).

FIGURE 3-5   Connecting Telephones

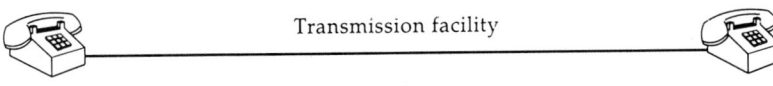

(a) Early Telephones Connected Point-to-Point: One Line

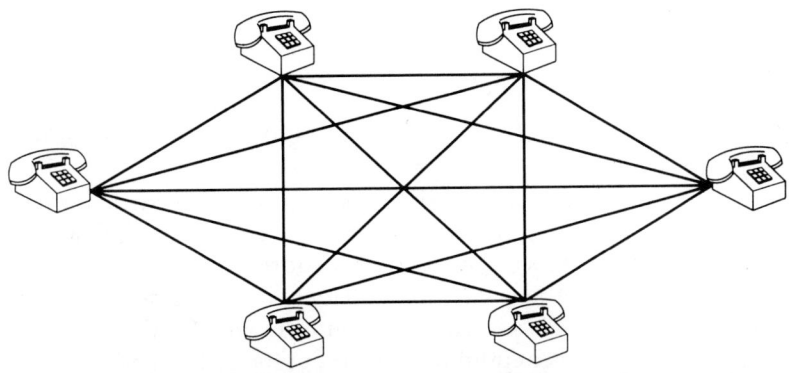

(b) Numerous Telephones Connected Point-to-Point: Too Many Lines

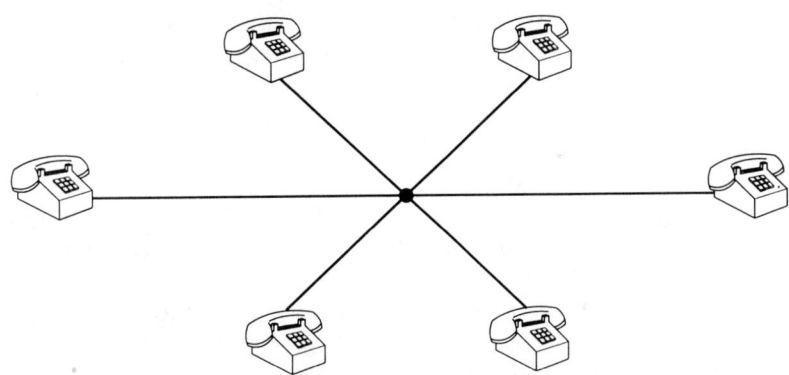

(c) Numerous Telephones Connected Via a Central Switching Location: Fewer Lines

When you lift your telephone receiver, a switch inside your telephone closes; a condition known as going **off-hook** occurs. Current then flows from the local switch (the central office) to your telephone, which in turn alerts the local switch to a request for service. When you replace your telephone receiver, a condition known as going **on-hook** occurs. The current ceases to flow, and the local switch registers a disconnect. This signal triggers a series of events that return the sections of the network to idle status, ready to participate in other calls.

FIGURE 3-6 **Local Loop Between Central Office and Telephone**

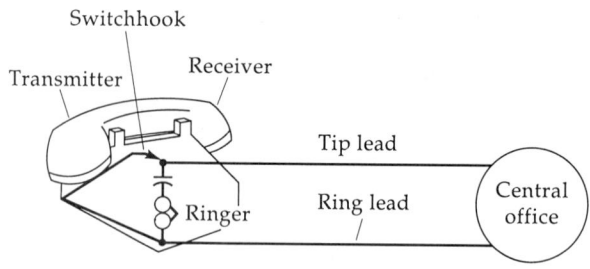

Dial Tone. When your central office switch receives a request for service, it connects equipment to the caller's line that applies a dial tone, indicating that the caller may send address information by dialing or keying the called number. The type of telephone instrument, dial or pushbutton, to be used is an essential piece of information for the local switch if it is to connect the proper equipment to accept the codes that make up the called number.

Rotary Dial. With a rotary dial, each digit of the number being called is transmitted by interrupting the off-hook current as the dial returns to its rest position. The rotary dial opens and closes the connection between the telephone and the local telephone office according to the number of digits dialed. This signaling method is called **dial pulsing**.

Pushbutton Keypad. A pushbutton keypad phone can also use dial pulsing. As each button is depressed, the corresponding number of clicks is heard. Other pushbutton keypad phones, called Touch-Tone* phones, use **dual tone multi-frequency** (DTMF) signaling, which replaces dial pulses with electrically produced tones for network signaling. When each button is depressed, two tones are generated simultaneously causing a signal of combined frequencies in tones ranging from 697 to 1477 Hz. For example, the digit "2" is made up of frequencies 697 Hz and 1336 Hz. The signal, which is audible to the caller, is transmitted to the caller's central office switch. Special receivers in the switch convert the signals into a form that can be used by its switching system.

You can determine whether a phone is dial pulsing or Touch-Tone by pressing 7-4-2-4-7-7-7 4-4-7-4-2. If you hear "Mary Had a Little Lamb," your telephone is Touch-Tone. If you hear clicks, you will not be able to access computerized phone services without adding a tone dialer to the phone. Another way of determining the type of pushbutton phone is to examine

---

*Registered service mark of AT&T.

Basic Telephone Operations

the printing on the bottom of the phone. An FCC certification number should be followed by certain letters: TE-R indicates that the phone is a rotary dial or a pushbutton keypad with dial pulsing. TE-T is a phone with DTMF tone signaling. TE-E is a phone that has both dial pulsing and DTMF allowing the user to select the mode desired.

■ Local Telephone Calls

A central office switch connects its own subscribers with each other. When a call involves only one switching system, it is called an **intraoffice call**. The central office switch also has trunks to other local central office switches, as shown in Figure 3-7: A central office switch can be connected directly to another central office switch, or it can be connected through a tandem office switch. The term "tandem" refers to any switching system that connects trunks to trunks. A call between two switches is called an **interoffice call**.

Figure 3-8 illustrates how a local call is made. Suppose your telephone number is 235-1300 and you wish to call 235-7744—a local call. The first three

FIGURE 3-7 Direct and Alternative Routes for a Local Call

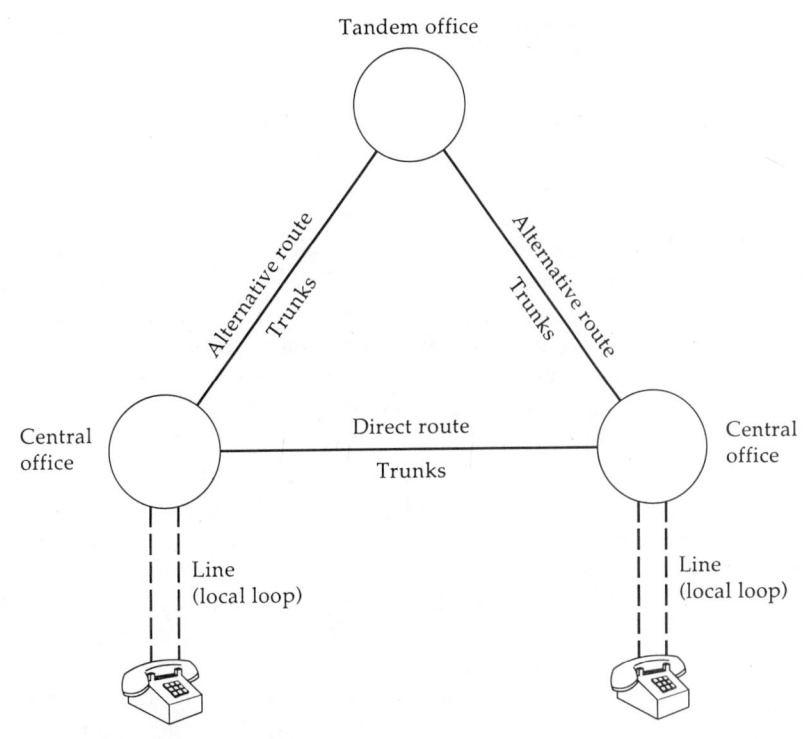

FIGURE 3-8 Making a Local Call

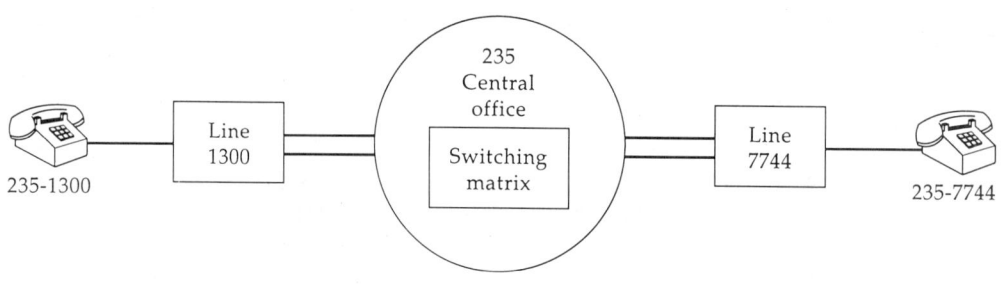

digits, called the central office prefix or exchange, identify the central office switch of the number you are calling. In this case your telephone and your friend's use both the same central office switch: 235. The last four digits, called the line number, identifies the line circuit within that central office switch. Line 1300 is physically connected by the tip and ring leads to this central office switch, as is Line 7744. These leads send signals to provide a transmission path to the central office switch. Thus your phone conversation is connected to your friend's phone through loops or lines through the central office switch.

Now suppose that you are calling your uncle in a neighboring town. His number is 659-3310. Your telephone is served by central office switch 235. Your uncle's telephone is served by central office switch 659. Since many calls are placed between the two switches, a number of trunks provide a direct route between them, as shown in Figure 3-7. In addition, a tandem office switch provides an alternative route for calls between the two central office switches. Figure 3-7 shows an example of a local tandem office switch. Through the tandem office switch, local switching systems (central office switches) are connected to each other.

When the central office switch translates the first three digits of the number you dial, in this case 659, it determines that your call is to another central office. Your call is not an intraoffice call; instead, it is an interoffice call and must be connected to a trunk going to another central office switch. Routing information stored in the central office switch equipment tells which outgoing trunks are idle. If an idle trunk is found that directly connects your central office switch with your uncle's central office switch, then that trunk will be used for your call.

If all the direct trunks are busy, then the central office equipment will investigate whether any outgoing trunks are available using the tandem switching office, as also shown in Figure 3-7. If an idle trunk is available, your call will be routed through the tandem office switch. If all trunks to the tandem office switch are busy, your call will not be completed. You will then hear a reorder tone, often called a fast busy tone, since it has 120 interruptions per minute (ipm) rather than the 60 ipm of the busy tone.

■ The Numbering Plan—Domestic and International

Numbering Plan Area. The public telephone network uses a numbering plan that identifies each telephone by a unique address. Most of North America is divided into geographic calling areas, called **Numbering Plan Areas**. Each calling area, which contains a number of central office switches located throughout its area, is assigned a three-digit identification code. These three digits are called the *area code* or *NPA (Numbering Plan Area) code*, as shown in Figure 3-9. No two telephones within each geographic calling area have the same seven-digit telephone number (central office switch number and line number).

To make a long-distance call, the caller must usually dial either a zero or a one followed by ten digits to make a connection. The zero or one goes to a toll office switch. The zero alerts the toll operator to assist the caller in making the long-distance call, while the one accesses a long-distance carrier.

The three digits following the zero or one represent the area code. This code identifies the area or group of central office switches to be selected. The next three digits identify the particular central office switch, and the last four digits specify the line number within that switch. See Figure 3-10.

When a call is made within the same area code to a central office switch other than its own central office switch, the number dialed omits the area code but usually begins with the digit one followed by the seven-digit phone number. This number is referred to as a "one plus seven-digit number." If the area code is included when making a call within the same area code, a recorded announcement advises the caller to dial again or dial for operator assistance. See Figure 3-11 in which line 436 dials line 483, both in the 407 area.

Special Numbers. A few area codes, called **special area codes** (SACs) have been set aside for special purposes, such as 800 toll-free service numbers, 900 Dial-IT (sports updates, investment information, lottery information, etc.), and Western Union TWX service (510 or 710 or 910).

The International Numbering Plan. The **International Numbering Plan** is a plan developed by the Consultative Committee on International Telephone and Telegraph (CCITT), which assigns an international prefix, a combination of digits, to each country to allow it to access the international network. The international prefix assigned to North America is 011. (The CCITT, a forum for member countries of the United Nations, sets communications standards to facilitate communication among countries.)

Once you have dialed your international prefix to gain access to the international network, you dial the called party's international number. This number consists of the called party's country code, city code, and local

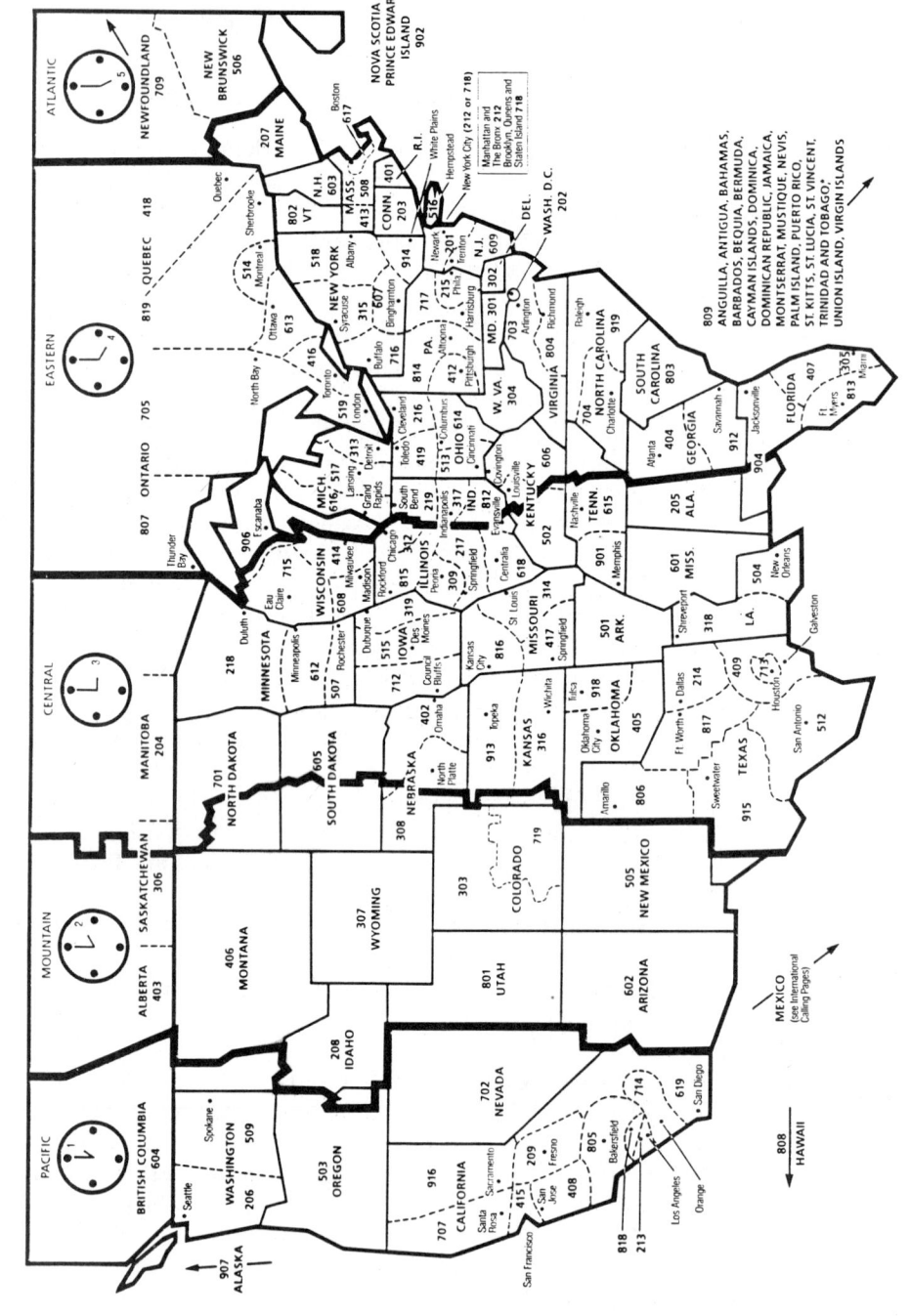

FIGURE 3-9 Numbering Plan Area Code

Copyright, NYNEX Information Resources Company, 1989. Printed by permission of NYNEX Information Resources Company.

FIGURE 3-10 A Long-Distance Connection

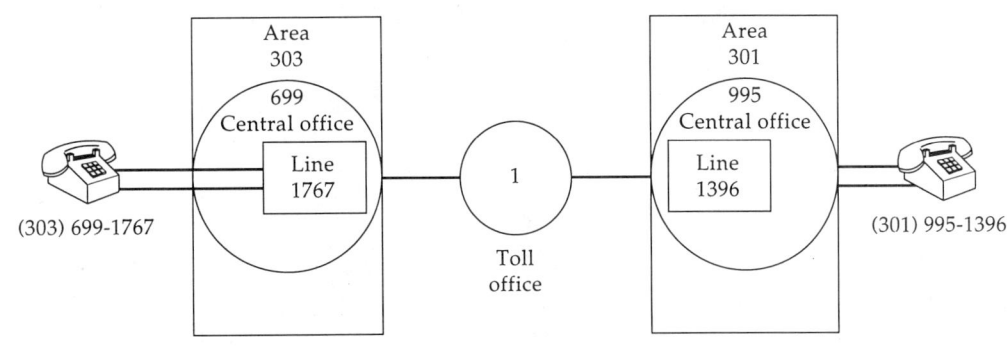

number. Country codes typically consist of a two- or three-digit number that identifies the world zone of a country, followed by a country code of one to three digits, as shown in Figure 3-12. North America and the Soviet Union have each been assigned one digit to represent both the world zone number and the country code. North America is assigned 1, and the Soviet Union is assigned 7. Other countries have been assigned two- or three-digit numbers.

For example, to dial Sydney, Australia, from the United States, you would dial 011 to access the international network, then the country code 61 (world zone 6 and country code 1), 2 for the city code, and then the local

FIGURE 3-11 Placing a Call Within the Same Area Code Using "One-Plus" Dialing

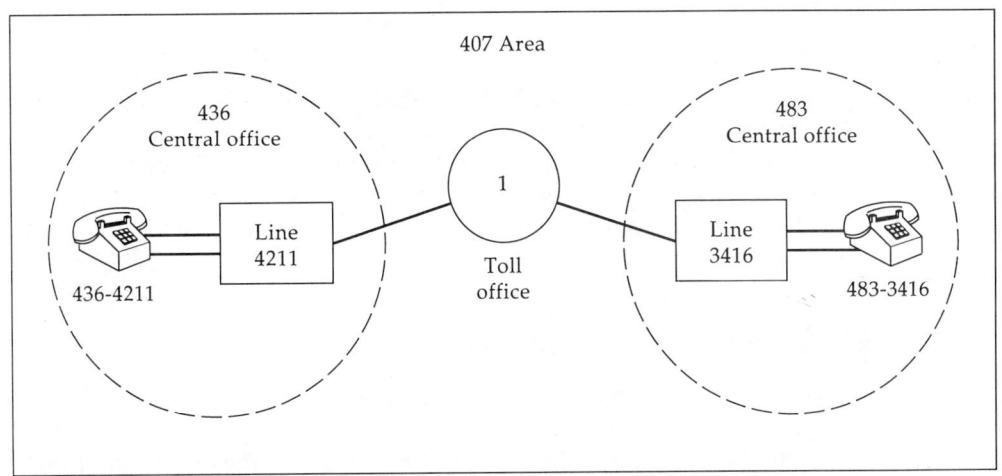

FIGURE 3-12   **International Numbering Plan: Examples**

Argentina   54   *The country code (world zone and country code) is 54.*
Buenos Aires   1   *The city code for Buenos Aires is 1.*

Other examples:

Australia	61	Hong Kong 852
Melbourne	3	Hong Kong 5
Sydney	2	Kowloon 3
Bolivia	591	Iceland 354
La Paz	2	Akureyri 6
Santa Cruz	33	Hafnarfjordhur 1
Chile	56	Norway 47
Santiago	2	Bergen 5
Valparaiso	31	Oslo 2
Egypt	20	Yugoslavia 38
Cairo	2	Belgrade 11

number of the person in Australia being called. If telephone equipment is not available for dialing direct, you would dial long distance and give the operator the codes. If someone in Australia calls a person in Florida, the same number format is used. The person in Australia dials 0111 to access its international network followed by the United States' country code of 1, the Florida area code of either 407 or 305, and the seven-digit central office number.

Exchange Services

Services provided through the central office switch are called "exchange services." Access to these services is obtained by the local loop, the communications channel that connects the subscriber's telephone to his or her central office switch. Services available to subscribers range from basic local calling with a standard rotary-dial telephone to custom or class calling services.

■ Basic Exchange Services

The local central office switch provides any customer located within its geographic area with basic exchange services such as local calling. A local call is a call to any person within the same local calling area of the calling subscriber's central office switch. A local calling area, or exchange area, is a designated geographic area and may be served by several central office switches.

Exchange Services

In addition to local calling, basic exchange services also include operator assistance on local calls, telephone repair service, emergency service, and usually directory assistance. Some telephone companies now charge for local directory assistance.

Local Calling Plan. Bell telephone companies offer customers various local calling plans. Although plans differ from state to state, two typical plans are flat-rate service and measured-rate service. The trend in the Bell System is toward measured-rate service because it generates more revenue.

- **Flat-rate service** is a fixed monthly charge that permits the subscriber to make an unlimited number of outgoing local calls.
- **Measured-rate service** is a fixed monthly charge for a limited number of local outgoing calls plus an additional charge for each call in excess of this number.

911 Emergency Service. The telephone company provides a universal central office number, 911, for emergency service bureaus engaged in assisting local government in protecting the safety and property of the general public. The cost of implementing and maintaining this **911 emergency service** is usually paid by county and state governments. They obtain equipment from either the telephone company or a vendor of their choice.

The 911 number can access directly a variety of emergency agencies such as the police, fire, or emergency medical service. The 911 service was established by the Bell System in 1968 in response to a recommendation by the Presidential Commission on Law Enforcement and Justice that a single (police emergency) number be established wherever practical.

The two types of services are Basic 911 (B911) and Enhanced 911 (E911). Basic 911 service includes the following features:

- **Forced disconnect** of the calling line to prevent tying up a line with unnecessary calls.
- **Called party hold** to retain control of the connection regardless of the calling party's action.
- **Emergency ringback** to the calling station.

The major difficulty in using the basic service is that in many places the boundaries of emergency agencies do not coincide with the boundaries of the local areas served by a telephone company. In some places, one local area may have several different combinations of emergency jurisdictions. In such cases, emergency calls must be routed to the correct emergency agency on the basis of the location of the calling party. The enhanced 911 service provides the routing logic required to perform this task. This service also includes features that display the calling party's telephone number and address at the public safety answering station, such as at a police station.

For example, once a call reaches the public safety answering point (PSAP), such as the police, the caller can tell his or her location and describe the problem. But should a caller forget or be unable to give this information, the caller's telephone number appears on a display screen at the PSAP as soon as the call is answered. If the caller hangs up and more information is needed, contact can be reestablished right away. An automatic location identifier enables the caller's address to appear on the display screen within seconds after the 911 call is answered. Even if verbal contact cannot be reestablished, emergency assistance can still be dispatched. This feature is especially important when a caller is unable to communicate effectively for any reason—age, a language barrier, panic, injury, or shock. It can also save critical minutes that might otherwise be lost when a caller tries to describe an unfamiliar location or gives the wrong address.

■ Custom Calling Services

In addition to basic exchange services, central office switches in most areas have the capability of offering **custom calling services**. These services take advantage of the stored-program control of electronically operated switches, as explained more fully in the next section of this chapter. No special equipment or installation is needed on the subscriber's premises. Custom calling services include Call Waiting, Call Forwarding, Three-Way Calling, and Speed Calling.

Call Waiting. Call Waiting allows you to be engaged in a call and still be reached by another caller. A short beep informs you that another call is waiting to be accepted. If you ignore the first beep, you will hear a second beep in ten seconds. The party calling you hears only the normal ringing. You can place the first call on hold and answer the second call by quickly pressing and releasing the switchhook (flashing). To return to the first call, press and release the switchhook again. You can switch back and forth between the two calls as often as you wish. If you hear a beep and want to end the first call, hang up. Your telephone will immediately ring with the second call.

You can also put Call Waiting on hold so that you can talk without interruption. To cancel Call Waiting before you dial a call, you dial a special two-digit code. Your new conversation will not be interrupted by Call Waiting. To cancel Call Waiting while you are on a call requires that you also subscribe to the Three-Way Calling service. All you must do is press the switchhook once to put your call on hold and get a dial tone. On hearing the dial tone, you dial a special two-digit code. You are automatically reconnected to your original call, which will not be interrupted by Call Waiting. Call Waiting automatically returns for your next call when you hang up the telephone.

Call Forwarding. Call Forwarding lets you transfer your calls to any telephone that you can direct-dial without operator assistance by dialing a special code sequence. For example, from a rotary dial telephone you dial a two-digit code and wait approximately 5 seconds for a dial tone. Then you dial the number that will be accepting your calls. You will hear two short tones, then normal ringing. Call Forwarding is in effect when the party answers. At that time you can tell them that they will be receiving your calls.

While Call Forwarding is activated, all incoming calls to your telephone line are automatically transferred to the designated telephone. To cancel Call Forwarding from rotary dial telephones, dial another two-digit code and wait about 5 seconds for two beeps and a dial tone. If you forward your calls outside of your local calling area, you will be charged for any calls forwarded from your number to the distant number. For example, if you forward your calls to a number in another state, the person calling you is charged for a call only from his or her telephone to your number. You are charged the long-distance rate from your number to the forwarded number in the other state.

Three-Way Calling. Three-Way Calling lets you add a third party to your existing conversation without operator assistance. First, you press and release the switchhook to place your call on hold. You will hear three beeps, then a dial tone. Next you dial the third party's number. You can talk before including the original caller. To begin the three-way call, press and release the switchhook. All three parties will be on the line.

Speed Calling. Speed Calling lets you call frequently called numbers by dialing only one or two digits. For example, instead of dialing a ten-digit number, you dial a one- or two-digit number. The central office switch then translates the two digits into a ten-digit number. The switch allows you to select storage for either eight or thirty telephone numbers. The eight-number storage capacity uses a one-digit code; the thirty-number storage capacity uses a two-digit code.

■ Class Calling Services

Some central office switches also have the capability of offering to subscribers additional service options, referred to as **class calling services**. These calling services are usually available only if both the called and calling telephone numbers are located within specific local exchanges that have access to electronic switches using advanced technologies. Some of these services are also available on customer premise equipment, such as PBXs and Centrex systems (discussed in Chapter 5). The class calling options include Special Ring, Call Block, Selected Call Forwarding, Number Identification, Return Call, Repeat Call, and Call Trace.

Special Ring. Special Ring, also called Priority Ring, allows you to assign a distinct ring to each of several callers, usually no more than six. Whenever one of these callers phones you, a distinctive ring alerts you that it is one of your chosen callers. If you subscribe to Call Waiting, a Custom Calling service that lets you take two calls at a time on your line at once, Special Ring will signal you with a Special Tone.

Call Block. Call Block allows you to predetermine that certain people may not call you by blocking their telephone numbers from calling your telephone number. A blocked caller will reach a recording that tells of your unavailability.

Selected Call Forwarding. Selected Call Forwarding is the same as Call Forwarding except that you determine which calls you want forwarded by entering up to six callers' numbers.

Number Identification. Number Identification allows the number calling you to be displayed on your telephone screen to view before answering the telephone. This option also serves as a trace on all incoming calls. This feature may not be available from some telephone companies, since it also reveals nonpublished telephone numbers.

Return Call. Return Call allows you to call back the last number that called you, whether or not you answered the ring. Return Call is particularly helpful when you are unable to reach a telephone before it stops ringing.

Repeat Call. Repeat Call redials the last number you dialed, even if it was busy. For example, when you receive a busy signal, you dial a one- or two-digit code, and Repeat Call keeps dialing the number you are trying to reach for as long as 30 minutes and alerts you with a special ring when it gets through.

Call Trace. Call Trace lets you initiate a trace of the number of the last call you received. Your telephone company receives the number traced; you must contact your local business telephone office for additional instructions.

■ Business Exchange Services—Centrex Services

The central office also offers business exchange services called Centrex services. Centrex services emulate the services offered by private branch exchange (PBX) and automatic call distributor (ACD) equipment located on the customers' premises. With PBX and ACD services, customer lines first connect to switching equipment on their own premises. This switching equipment then connects to a central office switch, as shown in Figure 3-13(a).

When these same services are provided by Centrex, the customer's lines are connected directly to the central office switch, as shown in Figure 3-13(b). This setup reduces the amount of equipment required on the customer's premises. Chapter 5 discusses Centrex services and PBX systems more fully.

Exchange Services

FIGURE 3-13   Other Central Office Services

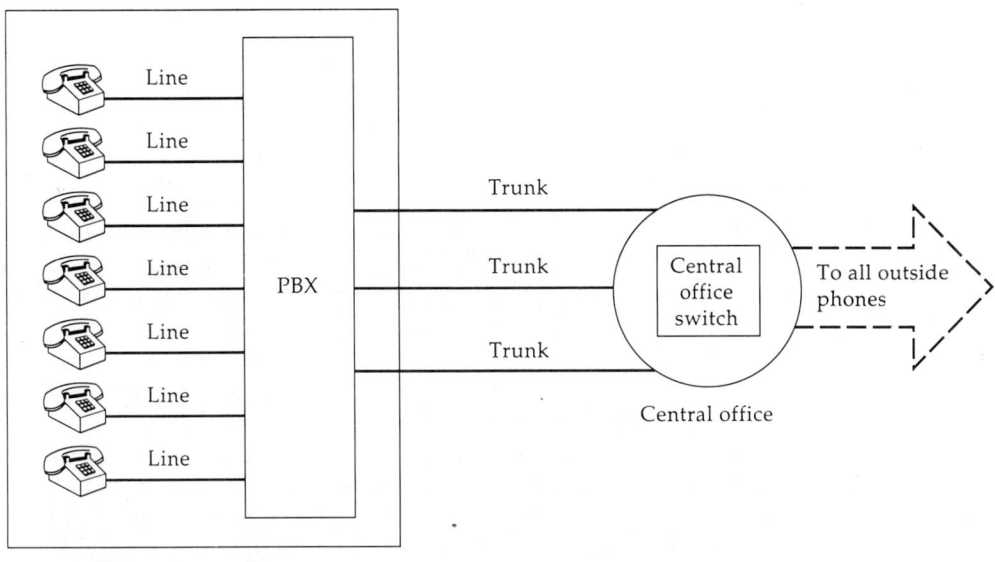

(a) PBX Concept

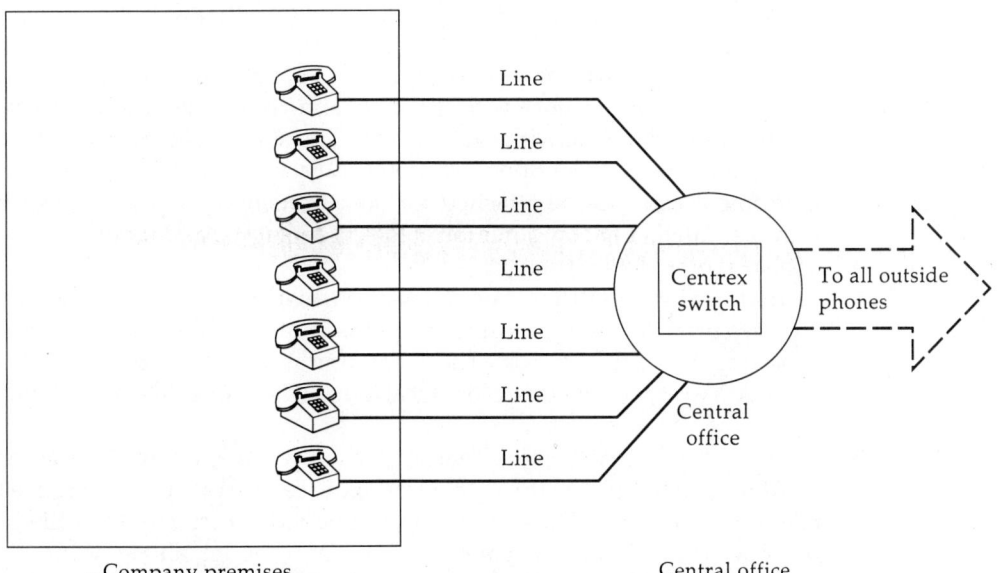

(b) Centrex Concept

The Telecommunications Network

The purpose of the first telephone system was to connect electrically two telephones to allow a conversation to take place between the two users. Today's telephone system still carries out the same purpose, even though technologies have changed how the task is accomplished.

■ Telecommunications Network Defined

Before defining a telecommunications network, two concepts should be defined. What is meant by a network? A **network** is a system of interconnected elements represented by nodes (switches) and by links that interconnect the nodes. A network provides services to many widely dispersed telephone customers.

What is meant by traffic? **Traffic** is the flow of information through the network. Traffic may be generated by a telephone conversation or be the result of data, video, and audio services.

A **telecommunication network** may be defined as a system of interconnected facilities designed to carry the traffic that results from a variety of telecommunications services. These services are discussed in Chapter 4 and include toll (long-distance) services, WATS, and private line services.

■ Physical Facilities of the Telecommunications Network

The physical facilities of the network can be divided into three categories: station equipment, transmission facilities, and switching systems.

Station Equipment. Station equipment is usually located on the customer's premises. Its purpose is to originate and receive signals and to enable customers to interface with the network. The station equipment most commonly used is the telephone instrument, discussed earlier in this chapter. Equipment can also be attached for data transmission, such as electronic printers, intelligent computer terminals, video units, and facsimile units.

Transmission Facilities: Local Loops (Lines) and Trunks. Transmission facilities provide the communication paths to carry information between two subscribers in the network. The communication paths are referred to as circuits. Two types of circuits are local loops (also called lines) and trunks.

Local Loops. As you just learned, when you dial a number, the signals go from your telephone through wires to the central office switch of the local telephone company. These wires, as mentioned earlier, are also called lines or local loops. Thus both your telephone and the telephone of the person you are calling are connected by lines or local loops to a central office. As you talk, signals are being transmitted in both directions simultaneously. If your line and that of the party you are calling use *the same central office switch*, the call connects directly over local loops, as shown in Figure 3-7.

Trunks.   Trunks are the transmission circuits (links) that carry telephone calls between switching offices. Trunks connect central office switches, as shown in Figure 3-7. They can also form a network of trunks to connect phone calls between remote locations.

Switching Systems

Function.   The basic function of a switching system is connecting communication paths. The two essential parts of a switching system are the switching network and the control mechanism. The *switching network* contains individual switching devices used to connect the communications path. The *control mechanism* directs the operation of the switching devices.

The switch detects the service needed. It recognizes the code numbers of the calling telephone and the called telephone. It sets up the circuit connection for a transmission path that is to send the information from the calling telephone to the receiving telephone.

Other functions include the following:

- Receiving and sending network control signals between itself and customer terminals and other switching systems.
- Administering and maintaining the system, including:
    Managing the network so that traffic can be rerouted to avoid congestion,
    Measuring traffic loads of the system's various components,
    Recording call-related information for billing for services,
    Maintaining the running of the system.
- Providing enhancements, such as custom and class calling services (discussed in the previous section) and Centrex services (discussed in Chapter 5).

Types of Switches.   The three basic types of switches are manual, electromechanical, and electronic. AT&T's first switching systems were manually operated switchboards consisting of sockets connected to a line and a set of wires or cords with plugs at both ends. A connection was made by plugging the ends of a cord into two jacks associated with the correct lines.

Manual Switches.   The first operators were young boys, as shown in Figure 3-14, but their language and behavior soon proved them unsuitable. In 1878, Emma M. Nutt became the first female employee to operate a switchboard in Boston. Thus began a long tradition of employing female operators. Figure 3-15 illustrates a typical switchboard operation in 1883. Operators were seated on wooden chairs separated by panels known as annunciator drops. These annunciator drops gave visual indications of

FIGURE 3-14   Early Central Office

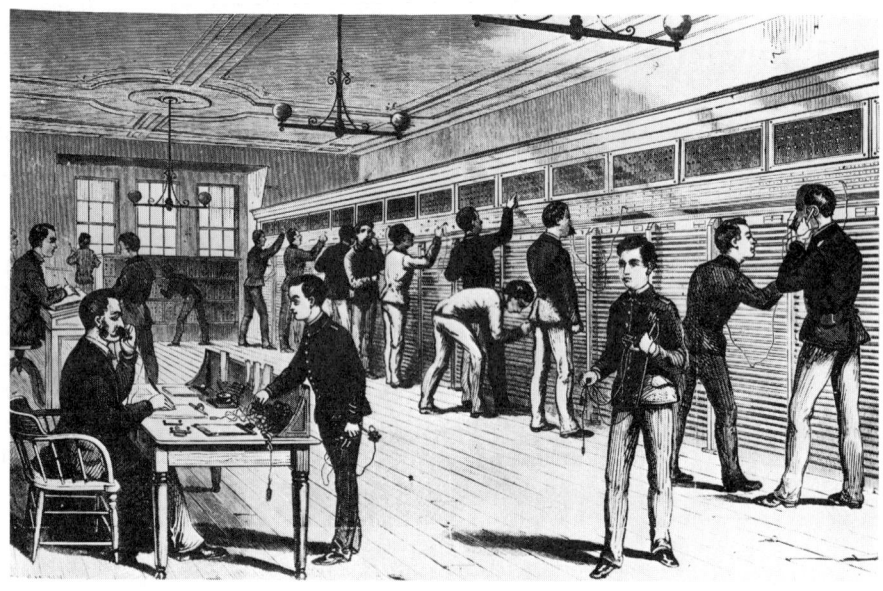

Courtesy of AT&T Archives.

telephone lines requesting service. The telephone company closed its last "cord board," which was in Bath, Maine, in 1982.

Electromechanical Switches.   To help manual operators and later to replace them, electromechanical switches were introduced. These switches emulated an operator's tasks. Communicating information to the customer without voice was provided. For example, dial tone replaced "Number please," audible tones replaced "I'm ringing that number," and busy signals replaced "That number is busy." A means for selecting a path and for setting up the path by closing switches replaced inserting a plug into a jack.

The two main types of electromechanical switching systems are the step-by-step (SXS) switching system, known worldwide as the Strowger switch, after its inventor A. B. Strowger, and the common control switching system (crossbar switch). The Bell System installed the first Strowger switch in 1919 and introduced the crossbar switch in 1938. These switches are currently being replaced by electronic switches.

The electromechanical switch operates by first scanning a switchboard panel for lights indicating that someone wants to make a call, then recording the location and identity of the caller, locating the line being called, and completing the connection if the line is not busy. If the line being called is

FIGURE 3-15 Manual Telephone Switchboards

Courtesy of AT&T Archives.

busy, the calling party receives a busy signal. When the switchboard panel lamps indicate that both parties have disconnected, the switch releases the connections.

The switch recognizes the number assigned to each caller and calling party. The dial on the phone electrically sends the number being called to the central office switch. As the dial is operated, the electric circuit between the caller and the central office switch is opened and closed a number of times, depending on the digit or letter dialed.

Electronic Switches. The first **electronic switch** (ESS), made possible by the invention of the transistor in 1947, was introduced in 1960. These ESS switches are computer controlled. They are often referred to as stored-program-controlled (SPC) machines to distinguish them from electromechanical switches. Figure 3-16 shows the basic components of an electronic switch—the 5ESS switch.

The heart of the 5ESS is the communication module, which connects the switching modules to each other and to the administration module. The communication module serves as a central switchboard for voice, data, and

FIGURE 3-16 **The Basic Components of the 5ESS Switch**

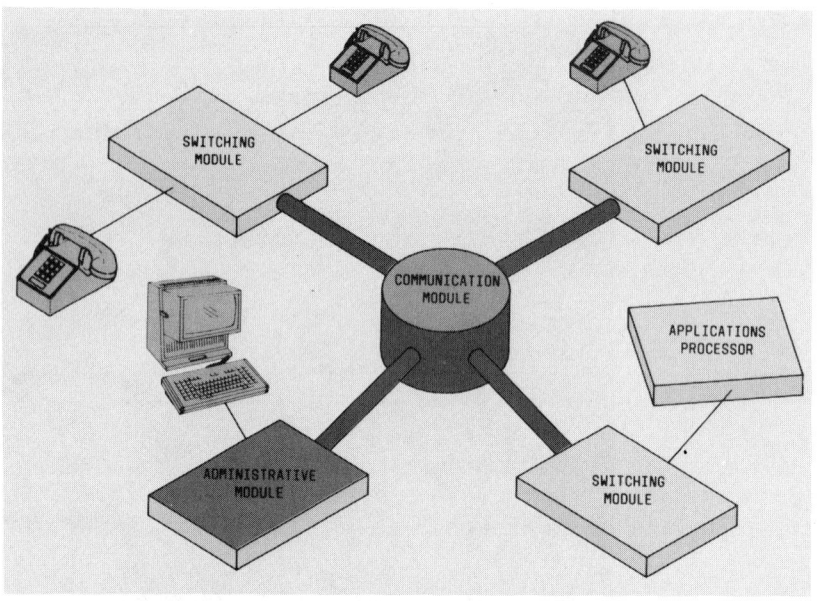

message switching. For example, it performs the routing of control messages between processors and the transfer of calls between switching modules. Its major components are a time-multiplexed digital switch that establishes the communication paths between the switching modules and the administration module, and a message switch that transmits control and administrative messages.

Each switching module has its own dedicated, duplicated processor with line and trunk interface units. The switching modules automatically handle most of the steps necessary to process calls while they consult with the administrative module only for routing information. Additional switching modules can be added to provide the ESS switch with more capacity.

The administrative module performs those tasks that are best handled centrally, such as call routing, resource allocation, and centralized maintenance functions. For example, the administrative module runs diagnostics, isolates troubles, and corrects troubles so that the effects on the switch's performance are minimal. Other tasks include data storage and backup capabilities. The applications processor is a separate minicomputer that connects to the 5ESS switch and provides additional interactive feature capabilities. For example, an applications processor can be connected to a given 5ESS switch to support one or more business customers.

The switch uses two types of memory: program store and call store. **Program store** is a semipermanent memory in which executable instructions

(EI) are stored. EI provides the switch with call processing procedures. Included are the logical steps for making telephone connections and providing services, such as custom and class calling services, and instructions about how and when to perform in various situations. Self-diagnostic programs that constantly evaluate the functioning of the switch are also supplied.

Call store is memory used for short-term storage of information. The "electronic scratchpad," as it is called, temporarily stores such information as the status of calls in process and available routes for connecting calls. Information in this memory is continually being changed as calls are processed. The switch uses this information to determine which lines are initiating calls and selects the best transmission paths for connection.

Electronic switches (ESSs) use either *space-division networks* or *time-division networks*. The type of network chosen depends on the characteristics of the line and trunk transmission environment in which the system will be used. Space-division networks are compatible with analog transmission facilities, while time-division networks are compatible with digital ones.

In space division networks, calls are separated from each other in space; in other words, each call travels over a different route. In time-division switching, calls travel over the same path but are separated from each other in time. Each telephone is connected to a common path by a switch.

Compared with earlier switches, electronic switches offer the following advantages:

- More calls can be handled.
- Calls can be processed faster.
- The switch requires less space because of its compact size.
- New routines and features can be easily introduced by changing stored program instructions.

The most recent electronic switch is the 5ESS, which is a digital time-division electronic switching system designed to serve central offices with 1000–100,000 lines. Its administrative module includes duplicate and active standby units to prevent service interruption or data loss when faults occur.

Summary

The telecommunications network consists of station equipment, transmission facilities, and switching equipment. Station equipment, such as a telephone, connects to a local central office switch by lines and then to other central offices and/or tandem offices by trunks. Although the basic function of the switch is to connect lines and trunks, sophisticated switches, such as the 5ESS, can provide customers with custom and class calling services.

Key Terms

Basic exchange services
Central office
Class calling services:
    Call Block
    Call Trace
    Number Identification
    Repeat Call
    Return Call
    Selected Call
      Forwarding
    Special Ring
      (Priority Ring)
Custom calling services:
    Call Forwarding
    Call Waiting
    Speed Calling
    Three-Way Calling

Dial pulsing
Dual tone multi-frequency
Electronic switch:
    Call store
    Program store
Flat-rate service
International Numbering Plan
Interoffice call
Intraoffice call
Measured-rate service
Network

911 emergency service:
    Called party hold
    Emergency ringback
    Forced disconnect
Numbering Plan Area
Off-hook
On-hook
Special area code
Switch
Switchhook
Telecommunications network
Tip and ring leads
Traffic

Self-Quiz

Indicate whether the statement is true or false.

1. All telephones contain a transmitter and a receiver, a switchhook mechanism, an alerting device, and a rotary or pushbutton dial. T/F
2. When you lift your telephone receiver, a condition known as on-hook occurs. T/F
3. The local calling plan favored by the Bell System is a flat-rate service. T/F
4. Transmission circuits that connect central office switches are called trunks. T/F
5. Electronic switches are referred to as stored-program-controlled machines to distinguish them from electromechanical switches. T/F
6. Electronic switching systems use either space-division or time-division networks. T/F

Complete each of the following statements.

1. The telephone instrument component that signals the central office that your telephone is either idle or in use is the _____ .
2. The path between your telephone and the serving central office is called a _____ .
3. Any switching system that connects trunks to trunks is called a _____ .
4. The first three digits of your telephone number identify _____ .
5. If all trunks to the tandem office switch are busy, you would hear a(n) _____ .
6. The flow of information through a network is called _____ .

Match Column A with Column B.
Which feature in Column A can you use to solve the problem in Column B?

Column A
(a) Call Block
(b) Call Waiting
(c) Number Identification
(d) Return Call
(e) Speed Calling
(f) Three-Way Calling

Column B
____ 1. You do not want to receive any calls from a particular telemarketing company.
____ 2. You would like to know who is calling you before answering the telephone.
____ 3. When you cannot answer your telephone before it stops ringing, you would like to be able to call the person back.
____ 4. You would like to discuss a project on the telephone with two people at the same time.
____ 5. You would like to cut the time spent dialing frequently called numbers.
____ 6. You would like others to be able to reach you even when you may be talking to someone else.

■ *Review Questions*

1. Explain what happens to your voice when you speak on the telephone.
2. Describe what each component of the telephone instrument does.
3. How many lines would you need to link 31 telephones point-to-point?
4. Your telephone number is 661-7710, and your friend's number is 661-3311. Describe how the central office uses these numbers when you call your friend?
5. What happens when the central office switch receives your request to call your friend in a nearby town?
6. How does the Numbering Plan Area help in assigning unique addresses?
7. What information do you need to make a call from New York City to Paris, France?
8. (a) What is the difference between a local calling plan using flat-rate service and one using measured-rate service?
   (b) Which plan is more advantageous for a business? Why?
9. Which feature of the 911 emergency service do you consider most important to a business?
10. Suggest one or two business situations in which each of the following would be helpful: Call Forwarding, Call Waiting, Speed-Calling, Three-Way Calling.
11. Suggest one or two business situations in which each of the class calling services would be helpful?

12. (a) Who provides custom calling services? Do you need special equipment? Why?
    (b) Who provides class calling services? Do you need special equipment? Why?
13. (a) What are the functions of a switching system?
    (b) How does a switching system process your call?

▪ *Activities/Projects*

1. Describe how a call is made, such as a call connecting to the central office and/or tandem offices, in each of the following situations. Include a diagram for each one.
   (a) A call placed from your home telephone to your next-door neighbor.
   (b) A call placed from your home telephone to a friend's telephone in the next town.
2. (a) What calling services does your local telephone company offer to its subscribers?
   (b) What calling services has your school or company selected for its use?
3. Visit your local police and/or fire departments to find out what kind of 911 emergency services they are using and the features offered by these services. What kind of equipment are they using? Does the equipment connect to the central office switch? What geographical area do the services cover? What is the cost of the services? How helpful have the services been? Do the services have any limitations?
4. Arrange to visit one of your local telephone company's central offices. Before the visit, prepare a list of questions that you would like answered.

▪ *Case:* Selecting Exchange Services

The president of CST Oil and Gas Consulting is a geologist who employs one full-time staff assistant, another geologist. He also hires other geologists, engineers, and oil workers as needed for such jobs as land work (leasing and title opinion) and oil production within the local area. Time in the office is spent computing and analyzing data and keeping in contact by telephone with business associates, particularly investors, and with oil production workers. The president is experiencing telephone problems, some of which are listed below.

- Although the consultant uses an answering machine both at the office and at home, he often attends meetings at other local companies, making it difficult for investors and geologists to reach him immediately.
- While talking on the telephone with one person, the consultant believes that he may be missing other incoming calls.
- Some clients would be annoyed to be placed on hold while the consultant answers another incoming call.
- Time is often wasted trying to get a line to a busy number.
- Telephone conferences with two people can be helpful when trying to solve immediate problems.

(a) How can the consultant improve his productivity and communications with others? What are your recommendations?
(b) Suppose that you recommend custom calling services and/or class calling services. Which services would you recommend to this company? Why? What would be the monthly and annual costs? The consultant's local telephone company charges the following fees for custom calling services and class calling services:

Custom Calling Services		**Class Calling Services**	
Call Forwarding	$2.57 per month	Call Block	$5.00 per month
Call Waiting	$2.58 per month	Call Forwarding*	$0.25 per activation
Speed Calling	$2.10 per month	Call Trace	$3.00 per activation
Three-Way Calling	$3.15 per month	Priority Ring	$1.25 per month
		Repeat Call	$1.25 per month
		Return Call	$2.00 per month
		Select Call Forwarding	$0.25 per activation

*Class Call Forward is offered on a pay-as-you-use basis; otherwise it is the same as Custom Call Forwarding.

Additional Readings

Hugh J. Beuscher, Kenneth J. Kush, and James R. Thomas, "Electronic Twins Protect 5ESS Switch Operations," *AT&T Bell Laboratories Record*, May 1985, pp. 22–26.

Bruce E. Briley, *Introduction to Telephone Switching* (Reading, Mass.: Addison-Wesley Publishing Company, 1983).

E. Bryan Carne, *Modern Telecommunications* (New York: Plenum Press, 1984).

M. T. Hills, *Telecommunication Switching Principles* (Cambridge, Mass.: MIT Press, 1979).

Tom Smith, *Anatomy of Telecommunications* (Geneva, ILL.: abc TeleTraining, 1987).

David Talley, *Basic Electronic Switching for Telephone Systems* (New York: Hayden, 1975).

David Talley, *Basic Telephone Switching Systems*, 2nd edition (New York: Hayden, 1979).

CHAPTER 4

The Public Telephone System

The Bell System in 1982
  The American Telegraph and Telephone Company
  Independent Telephone Companies

The Bell System After Divestiture
  The New AT&T
  The Twenty-Two Bell Operating Companies
  Regional Bell Operating Companies
  Independent Telephone Companies
  Long-Distance Competitors

The Public Switched Telephone Network
  PSTN Defined
  Hierarchy of Switching
  Dynamic Nonhierarchical Routing

Local Access and Transport Areas or Market Service Areas
  IntraLATA and InterLATA Calls
  Regulatory Agencies

Long-Distance Carriers
  Equal Access
  How an OCC Operates
  Resellers
  Bypassing the PSTN

Long-Distance Services
  AT&T Communications
  MCI Communications
  Wide-Area/Bulk-Rate Services

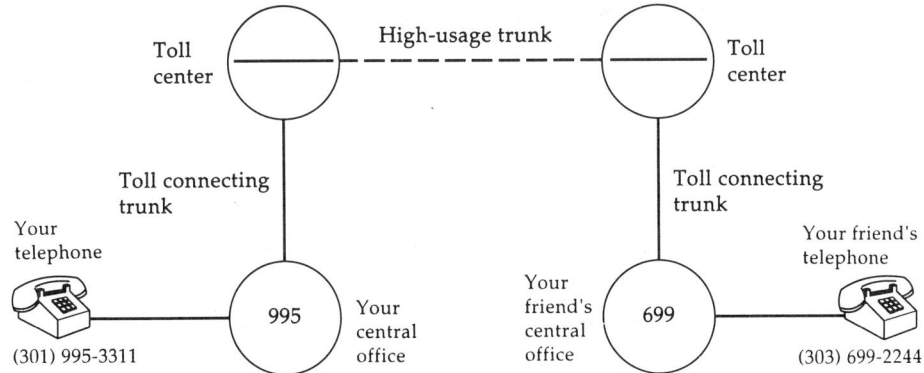

Private Lines
  Tie Lines
  Foreign Exchange
  Remote Call Forwarding
  T-1 Lines

Selecting a Long-Distance Carrier
  Cost of Using a Carrier for Long-Distance Calling
  Other Factors to Consider
  Application

CHAPTER OBJECTIVES

After studying this chapter, you should be able to

1. Describe how the Bell System changed after divestiture.
2. Explain the difference between IntraLATA and InterLATA.
3. Give an example of how a long-distance call is completed by using AT&T's switching hierarchy.
4. Give an example of how a long-distance call is completed by using other common carriers.
5. Discuss how a company can bypass the PSTN.
6. Describe the operation of the different types of private lines.

The American Telephone and Telegraph Company (AT&T) was incorporated in 1885 as a subsidiary of the American Bell Telephone Company. It was commonly referred to as the Long-Distance Company until 1899, when it became the parent company of the then evolving Bell System.

By 1982, the Bell System had grown to a huge, regulated monopoly. The dissolution of the company in 1983, as a result of antitrust action, was observed in the *1983 AT&T Annual Report* as follows:

> At midnight on December 31, 1983, the Bell System passed into history, bringing to a close a unique and memorable chapter in the chronicle of American business enterprise.
>
> Long bound together by a common commitment to make telephone service available to everyone in the country at an affordable price, AT&T and its associated companies—that is, the Bell System—gave the United States the biggest and best communications system in the world.
>
> Let it be noted, then, that Bell System people did what was asked of them. They provided excellent telephone service at low cost. And in doing so, they honored what in 1927 a former AT&T president described as the company's "unusual obligation to the public to see to it that the service shall at all times be adequate, dependable and satisfactory to the user."
>
> The record of the Bell System was one of promises kept, and we are proud of that record. The future of the Bell System's separate parts is promising. But we can only regret that an unyielding combination of technological, regulatory, legal, and political pressures brought to an end what very well may have been the most successful large scale business organization in history.
>
> It has been said that the character of a business, in greater or lesser measure, is a composite of the character of all the people who work in it— *or ever did*. In that sense, then, the *spirit* of the Bell System will live on in the new AT&T and in the now-divested Bell companies.[1]

This chapter presents the reader with an overview of the transformation of AT&T from a regulated monopoly to a number of fully competitive businesses with the options now available to long-distance users.

The Bell System in 1982

The divestiture agreement of 1982 broke up the largest company in the world, with assets of $155 billion and one million employees.

■ The American Telephone and Telegraph Company

Figure 4-1 shows the structure of the Bell System as it was before divestiture. AT&T's organization operated as a partnership which consisted of the

FIGURE 4-1 **The Bell System at the End of 1982—A Single Integrated Organization**

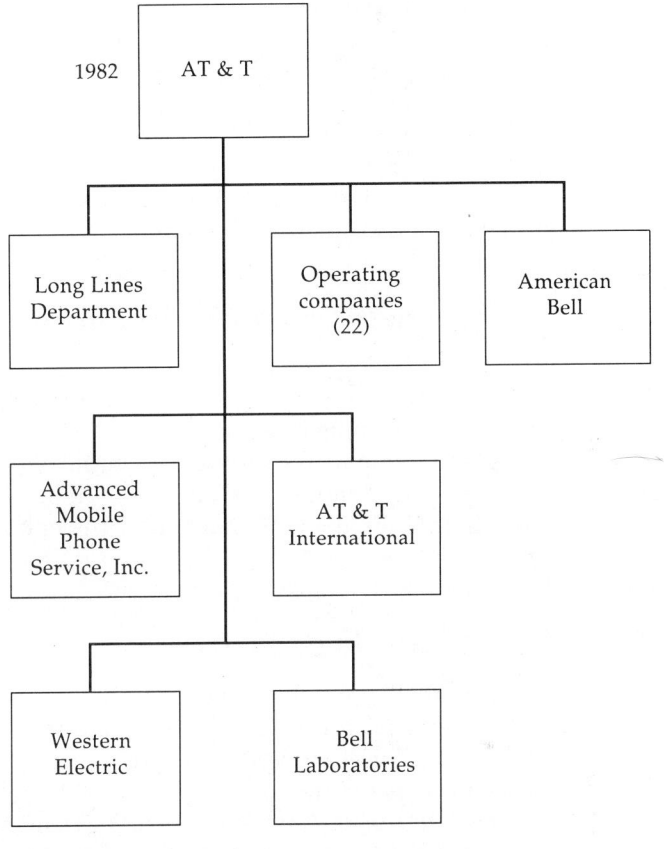

Copyright, 1982, AT&T, reprinted by permission.

twenty-two Bell operating companies, AT&T Long Lines, Western Electric, Bell Laboratories, American Bell, and AT&T International. The product of this partnership was service.

The twenty-two **Bell operating companies** (BOCs) such as New York Telephone, Southwestern Bell, and New England Telephone built, operated, and maintained the local and intrastate networks and provided service for customers within the communities they serviced.

AT&T Long Lines built, operated, and maintained most of the interstate network of long-distance lines and thus provided interstate and international communications services for people throughout the United States.

Western Electric, Bell Laboratories, American Bell, and Advanced Mobile Phone Services, Inc. were involved with AT&T's equipment. Western Electric was the manufacturing and supply unit of the Bell System. The Bell System's

BOCs and Long Lines purchased 80% of their equipment from Western Electric, which accounted for 90% of Western Electric's revenues. The prestigious Bell Laboratories was AT&T's research and development organization. American Bell was created on January 1, 1983, as a result of the Federal Communications Commission's Computer Inquiry II. Its function was to design and market computer premises equipment manufactured primarily by Western Electric. Advanced Mobile Phone Services, Inc., formed seven cellular radio subsidiaries.

International Lines was formed to market the Bell System's products worldwide and to apply Bell System technology and products to the needs of international business customers.

■ Independent Telephone Companies

In 1982 the Bell System served over 80% of the 180 million telephones in the United States, which covered 30% of the nation's geographical area. The remaining 36 million telephones were served by about 1450 independent telephone companies that were not affiliated with the Bell System. The independent companies worked with each other and interfaced with the Bell System through the U.S. Independent Telephone Association.

The Bell System After Divestiture

On January 8, 1982, the Justice Department and AT&T reached a settlement of the antitrust suit that called for the dissolution of AT&T Bell Telephone System. Federal court approval of the detailed restructuring plan with modifications was granted on August 24, 1982; January 1, 1984, was set as the target date for its completion. The agreement came to be known as the **Modified Final Judgment** (MFJ)—a modification of the Final Judgment in the 1956 Consent Decree.

On January 1, 1984, the telephone industry in the United States as it was known for over half a century no longer existed. The U.S. Department of Justice ended a ten-year antitrust suit by making an agreement with AT&T to break up the largest company in the world. The breakup of AT&T, also referred to as the "the divestiture of AT&T," resulted in the following new companies: AT&T, the twenty-two Bell operating companies, and the seven regional Bell operating companies.

■ The New AT&T

AT&T continues to own research, development, and manufacturing facilities; to provide long-distance telecommunications services; and to market a broad range of telecommunications and information equipment, products, and systems in the United States and abroad. The MFJ required that AT&T divest itself of the twenty-two BOCs but allowed AT&T to keep its subsidiaries by renaming or restructuring them.

To better focus on customer needs and to give individual business units more operating responsibility and more decision-making authority, in 1989, the new AT&T reorganized into 19 business units supported by AT&T's divisions, such as sales, manufacturing, human resources, legal, and development. Currently, five group executives provide support for the business units and divisions. These executives support domestic communications services, communications products, network systems, computer systems, and international efforts. Following are AT&T's markets and a brief description of the units that serve them.[2]

Business Markets. *Business Communications Services* markets long distance services for business customers. *Business Communications Systems* offers premises products and customer service to business customers with more than 80 phone lines. *General Business Systems* offers premises products, systems, and customer service to businesses with under 80 telephone lines. *AT&T Paradyne* offers data communications equipment, such as multiplexers and modems, to both large and small customers. AT&T Data Systems Group is composed of three business units: *Networked Computing Systems* develops and markets systems that provide business solutions through distributed computer systems; *UNIX Software Operation* is responsible for the development, marketing, and licensing of UNIX System V software; and *Synchronous Terminal Products* offers data terminal systems including those that interact with customer mainframe computers. *AT&T American Transtech* offers information and other support services for companies providing financial services. *AT&T Credit Corporation* offers creative financing for AT&T and other companies' products.

Consumer Markets. *Consumer Communications Services* markets AT&T's domestic long distance services to residential users. *Consumer Products* designs, develops, sells, and leases communications products for the home and very small business.

Federal Government. *Federal Systems* markets a complete array of AT&T products and services to the U.S. government.

Telecommunications Industry. AT&T Network Systems consists of five business units: *Switching Systems* manufactures and markets telecommunications switches; *Transmission Systems* manufactures markets transmission equipment; *Media Products* manufactures and markets fiber-optic and copper cable and specialty fibers; *Operations Systems* makes and markets software and hardware that support telecommunication systems and networks;

and *Cellular Systems* manufactures and markets radio and switching systems that support mobile phone networks.

Electronics Industry. *AT&T Microelectronics* designs, manufactures, and sells advanced electronic components and power systems for AT&T and other high-technology firms worldwide.

International Markets. *The International Communications Services* unit, known in many countries as AT&T Communications, provides international long distance services that link U.S. customers to consumers and businesses abroad.

Research and development continues to be the responsibility of *AT&T Bell Laboratories*, the world's foremost research and development establishment.

■ The Twenty-Two Bell Operating Companies

The twenty-two local Bell operating companies (BOCs) have remained primarily unchanged. The MFJ, as approved by federal judge Harold H. Greene, prescribed the following business for the twenty-two divested Bell operating companies:

- Offer local exchange service within specified geographical operating areas
- Provide equal access to their exchanges to all long-distance carriers
- Continue control over Yellow Pages directory publications
- Sell customer premises equipment but not manufacture it
- Handle cellular mobile communications services
- Offer voice storage retrieval, voice messaging, expanded audiotex, and electronic mail services (Judge Greene, March 1988)

■ Regional Bell Operating Companies

The twenty-two BOCs were grouped into seven **regional Bell operating companies** (RBOCs), also called regional Bell holding companies or holding companies. These companies are entirely independent of AT&T and each other. The map in Figure 4-2 shows the RBOCs and their operating companies.

The RBOCs are holding companies whose main business is local telephone service. However, these companies may participate in unregulated businesses that are not related to the telephone industry. Since the RBOCs no longer receive technical support from AT&T's Bell Labs, Western Electric, and other AT&T subsidiaries, each of the seven RBOCs currently funds one-seventh of the cost of a new service organization known as Bell Communications Research, Inc. or BELLCORE. This support organization provides many of the services formerly provided by AT&T, including new production evaluation, assignment of new area codes, and special projects requested by the BOCs.

FIGURE 4-2 The RBOCs and Their Operating Companies

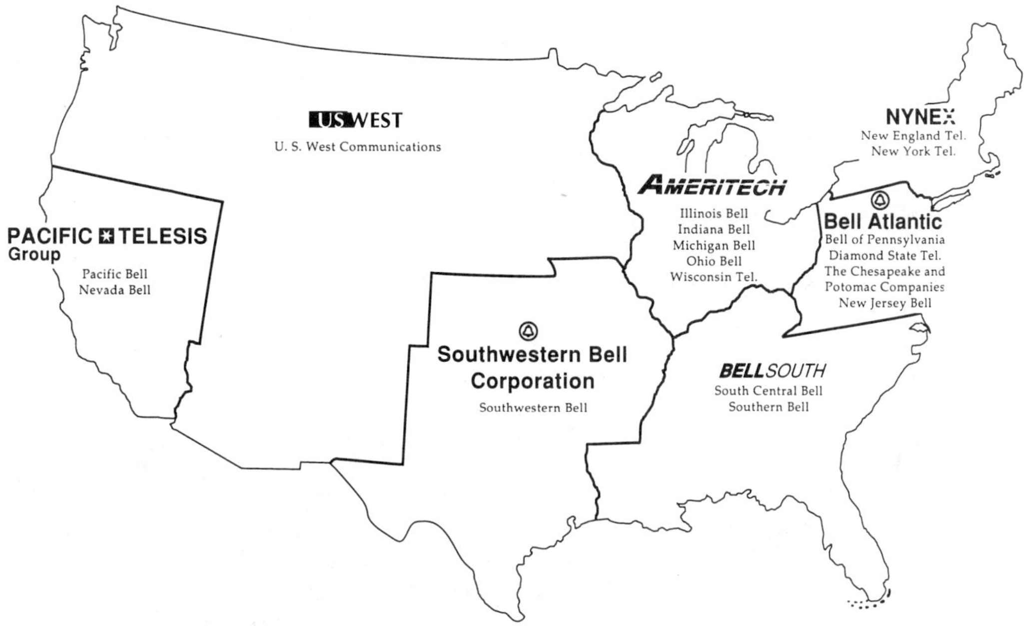

US WEST
U. S. West Communications

NYNEX
New England Tel.
New York Tel.

AMERITECH
Illinois Bell
Indiana Bell
Michigan Bell
Ohio Bell
Wisconsin Tel.

PACIFIC TELESIS Group
Pacific Bell
Nevada Bell

Bell Atlantic
Bell of Pennsylvania
Diamond State Tel.
The Chesapeake and Potomac Companies
New Jersey Bell

Southwestern Bell Corporation
Southwestern Bell

BELLSOUTH
South Central Bell
Southern Bell

Courtesy of Bellcore.

- ## Independent Telephone Companies

   Independent telephone companies continue to handle local calling within their assigned territories. Although many continue to merge or are purchased by other companies, as of the end of 1988, the United States Telephone Association reported that the independent companies numbered 1371 with 130 million access lines to their own central office switches. Their company switches access AT&T and other common carriers when their subscribers request long-distance calling. Examples of independent companies are GTE, United Telecommunications, Inc., and Contel Service Corporation. United Telecommunications, for example, operates as the local telephone company in 17 states serving 3000 communities in rural and suburban areas.

- ## Long-Distance Competitors

   Although AT&T Communications is the major supplier of long-distance services, other long-distance competitors, referred to as the **other common carriers** (OCCs), provide interstate service in competition with AT&T. An

OCC is a common carrier other than AT&T that is licensed by the Federal Communications Commission (FCC) to provide long-distance services.

Currently among the largest OCCs are MCI Communications, US Sprint, ITT/US Transmission, ALC/Allnet, and Western Union. OCCs own and operate their own microwave and/or satellite networks. These networks connect into the local BOC and independent exchanges, making it possible for OCC subscribers to use the same telephones as they do for AT&T calls.

The Public Switched Telephone Network

■ PSTN Defined

The *public switched telephone network (PSTN)* is the largest traffic network in terms of both equipment utilization and traffic volume. The PSTN consists of two interdependent parts: the local network (sometimes called the exchange area network) and the long-distance network.

As you recall from Chapter 3, a switching system in a telecommunications network interconnects telephones or other telecommunications terminals of many customers on demand and economically. The local central office switch interconnects local subscribers and has trunks to other local central office switches. Some central office switches add tandem office switches that function solely as switching points between local central office switches. In addition, each central office switch has trunks to at least one toll office switch—another switching center. This toll office is the gateway to the long-distance network. In order for the PSTN to extend centralized switching systems to a large number of long-distance users, AT&T has developed a hierarchy of switching offices.

■ Hierarchy of Switching

AT&T set up a network that is a well-defined **hierarchy of switching centers** with specific rules established for its operation. The hierarchy consists of five classes, as shown in Figure 4-3.

AT&T divided the United States into ten regions and Canada into two regions. Each region is served by a *regional center*, with all regional centers connected by "final" trunks. Regions are subdivided into sections served by *sectional centers*. These centers are in turn subdivided into primary areas served by *primary centers*. Within each primary center are *toll centers*. The hierarchy proceeds downward from classes 1, 2, 3, and 4 and finally to class 5 offices. Note that the class 1 regional centers are connected by a final trunk.

In Chapter 3 you learned how a telephone instrument connects to a central office by a local loop or line. The term "central office" is commonly used to mean "central office switch." Similarly, the term "regional center" refers to a "regional center switch." Central offices are also referred to as

FIGURE 4-3 The AT&T Switching Hierarchy

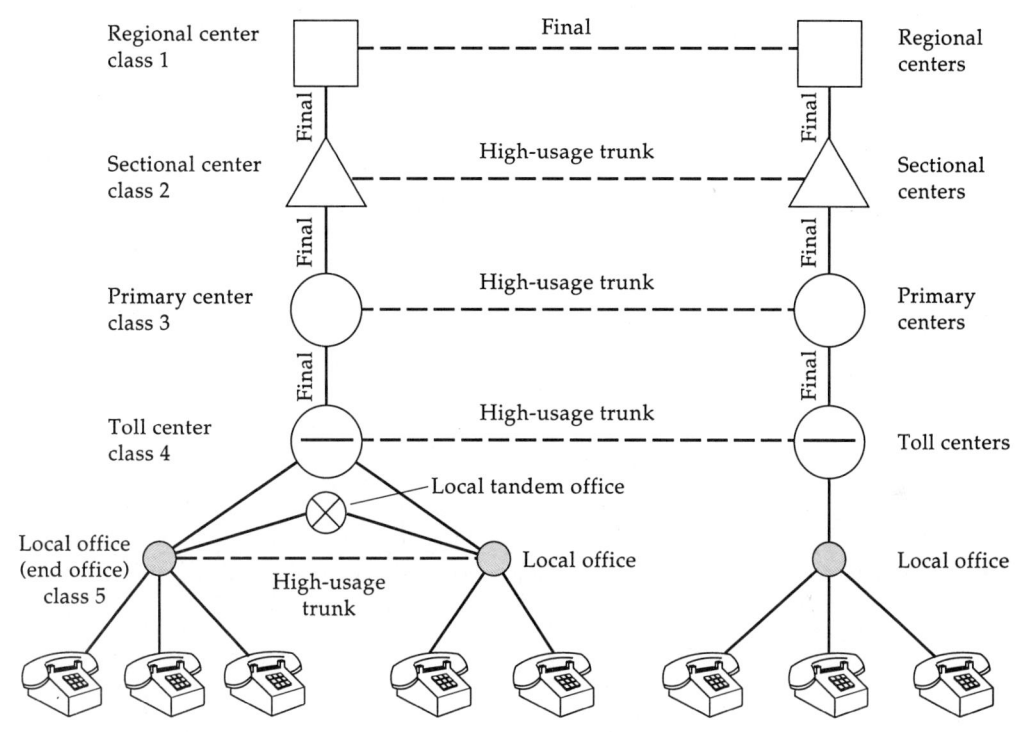

local offices or **end offices** since all subscriber calls originate or terminate at these offices. End offices are class 5 offices, the lowest level of the hierarchy.

The *toll network* is defined as class 4 and the higher switching offices (toll centers, primary centers, sectional centers, and regional centers) plus the trunks that interconnect each. Trunks that interconnect to the desired level 5 central office are classified as either high-usage or final trunks. *High-usage trunks* can be established between any two switches if the trunks are available. Offices that connect trunks in the toll network (class 4 to class 1) of the public switched telephone network are called *toll offices*. However, offices (class 5 offices) that connect trunks within a metropolitan area are called *local tandem offices*, as shown in Figure 4-4.

A calling customer's call first goes to the local office (class 5 office). A class 5 (end office) can connect the calling customer to the receiving person's class 5 office directly with a high-usage trunk, as shown in Figure 4-4. If the call is a toll call, the class 5 office can "home on class 4." An office is said to home on the higher-level office in the hierarchy to which its final route connects. The class 5 office homes on class 4 toll office (toll center) and

FIGURE 4-4 Possible Routes for Completing a Call Using AT&T Switching Hierarchy

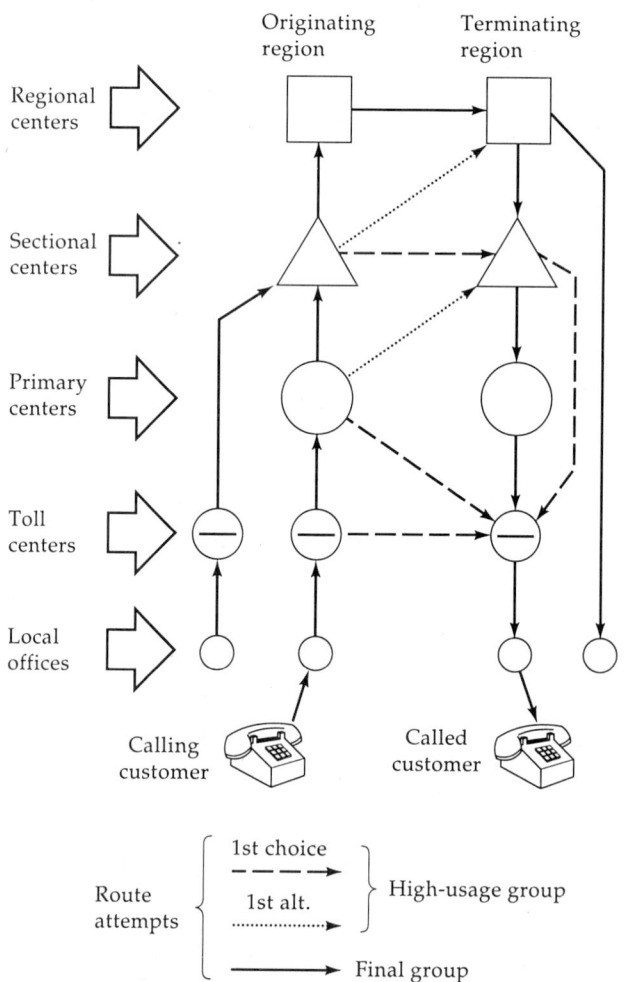

Copyright, 1984, AT&T Bell Laboratories, reprinted by permission.

requests that office to complete the call to the receiving party's class 5 office. If a high-usage trunk is available, it is used to connect a final trunk to the call. If no high-usage trunks are available at this level, then the class 4 toll office requests a class 3 toll office to complete the call. The procedure is repeated through class 1. If all trunks are busy, the call is blocked, and the caller receives a reorder tone.

The basic rule for routing a toll call is to use as few trunks as possible. The maximum number of trunks that may be used in a connection is nine,

Since the breakup of AT&T and implementation of long-distance traffic handled by carriers other than BOCs, and OCCs have been building their own networks and hierarchies. Their hierarchies are similar to AT&T's but range from one to no more than three classes.

■ Dynamic Nonhierarchical Routing

Call completion using AT&T's hierarchy of switching is considered to be via a direct route. If trunks are busy, the call may not be completed. AT&T has introduced the *dynamic nonhierarchical routing (DNHR) system* to provide indirect routing when needed. Calls on the direct hierarchy that receive a fast busy, meaning that all circuits are busy on the direct route, are now routed to DNHR switches to complete the call. When a call is identified as being a DNHR call, dynamic routing rules controlled by a computer are used to complete the call using DNHR switches. Figure 4-5 shows a DNHR network configuration.

Local Access and Transport Areas or Market Service Areas

Before divestiture the BOCs and independent telephone companies handled all calls within the state, including all in-state long-distance calls. The MFJ required that new geographical areas be defined to distinguish the local calling market from the long-distance one. These local geographical areas are called *local access and transport areas (LATAs)*, also referred to as *market service areas (MSAs)*. LATA boundaries generally coincide with standard metropolitan statistical areas (SMSAs). In 1989, there were 198 LATAs within the United States.

■ IntraLATA and InterLATA Calls

A LATA is a geographic area within which a BOC and/or one or more independent telephone companies are responsible for handling local customers' calls as well as any toll calls that originate and terminate within this area. These calls are referred to as **intraLATA calls**.

All calls between LATAs, within a state or across state lines, must be handled by AT&T or one of the other OCCs. These calls are called **interLATA calls**. They may be intrastate (between LATAs within a state) or interstate (between states).

For example, Pacific Bell, a BOC, offers both local and long-distance services within ten of California's eleven LATAs. However, Pacific Bell cannot provide long-distance service from one LATA to any of its other LATAs, even when it serves both LATAs, but it does handle toll calls between distant parts of the same LATA. The geographical areas of the LATAs in California

FIGURE 4-5 Dynamic Nonhierarchical Routing (DNHR) Network Structure

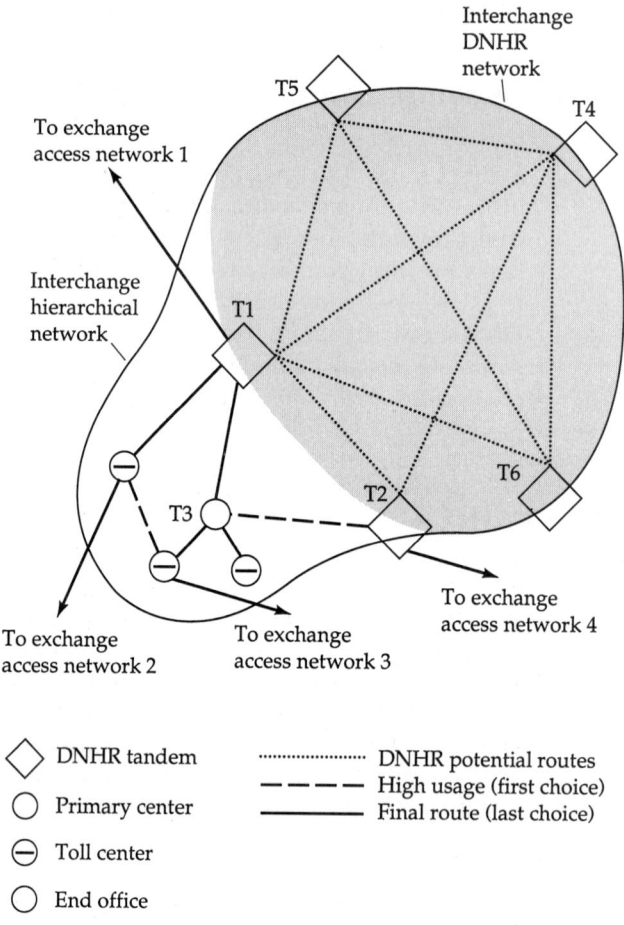

Copyright, 1984, AT&T Bell Laboratories, reprinted by permission.

are illustrated in Figure 4-6. Note that Pacific Bell does not handle all intraLATA calls in California; private companies such as General Telephone also offer intraLATA services in assigned geographical areas. The State Public Utility Commission of California is considering a proposal, The California Plan for Rate Stability, that would open intraLATAs to competition, allowing companies to compete with each other for subscribers. Pacific Bell supports this plan, since it would base telephone rate of return not on cost but on operating efficiency.

FIGURE 4-6 **Local Access and Transport Areas in California**

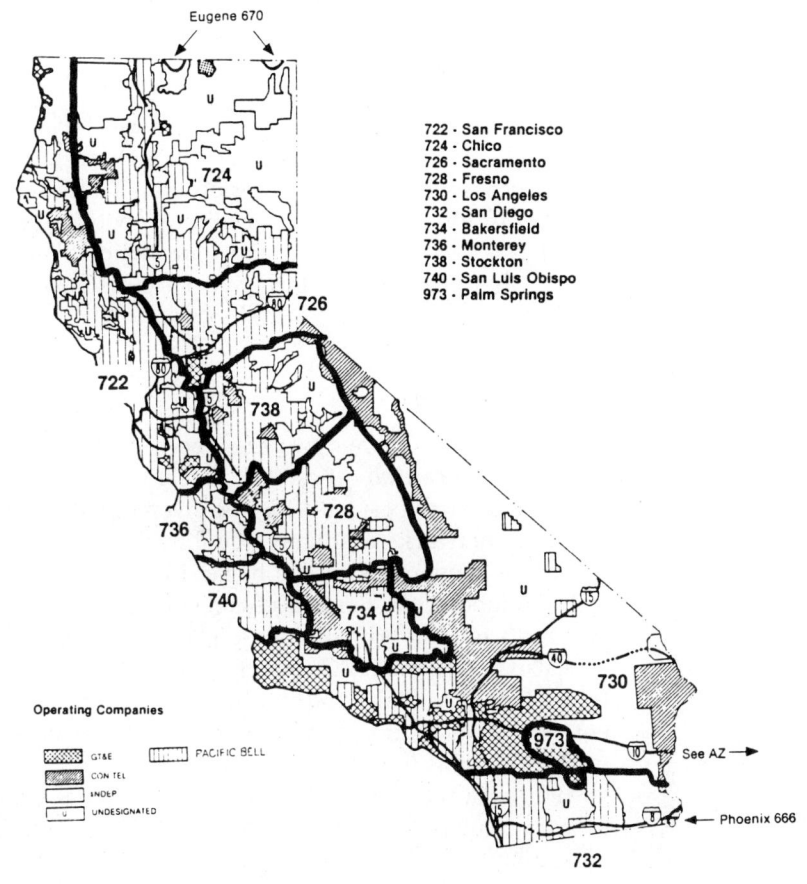

Courtesy of CCMI/McGraw-Hill.

Since the BOCs handle the intraLATA calls, which may be local or toll calls but are never interstate calls, the BOCs are referred to as **intraexchange carriers**. Since AT&T and the OCCs handle calls between LATAs, they are called **interexchange carriers**.

■ Regulatory Agencies

State public utility commissions still maintain jurisdiction over all calls within their state, including calls between LATAs in their state. Interstate-interLATA calls are subject to regulation by the FCC. Independent telephone companies are not directly affected by the creation of LATAs and are not required to establish such areas within their territories.

Long-Distance Carriers

Until the early 1970s, long-distance services including those made through local exchanges of independent telephone companies, could be transmitted only over AT&T's long distance network. Today AT&T is no longer the sole supplier of long-distance services. Calls between LATAs within states and between LATAs with other states are handled by both AT&T and OCCs. OCCs offer managers alternative long-distance services from which to choose.

■ Equal Access

Access to interexchange carriers—both AT&T's and OCCs'—is at the subscriber's local central office. The divestiture agreement required that other common carriers besides AT&T be given **equal access** to the local telephone company networks of quality equal to that enjoyed by AT&T. The MFJ ordered the conversion, which began in mid-1984, to be basically completed by September 1986. Equal access resulted in the nation's phone subscribers having to select a primary long-distance carrier, such as AT&T or MCI. The MFJ also makes the OCCs easier to use. To access an OCC prior to MFJ, you typically had to dial extra numbers to link into the OCC network and then enter an identification number. Now users may be able to dial long-distance numbers just as they do for AT&T.

For example, if your local central office has arranged one-plus-dialing for a particular OCC, then to access that OCC, you dial 1 plus the area code and calling number. If your central office does not have one-plus-dialing, then you must dial extra numbers to access the OCC and then enter an identification number. AT&T is currently converting its central office switches to include one-plus-dialing for OCCs.

Equal access has made OCC services directly accessible to 80% of the population. However, OCCs must now pay local telephone companies increased fees for their new and improved local links. The result is that the typical savings the OCCs provided in predivestiture days have shriveled dramatically. For example, in 1985, MCI rates ranged from 12 to 35% lower than those of AT&T, but by 1988, MCI rates for additional minutes were only a fraction of a penny less than those of AT&T.

■ How an OCC Operates

As discussed in the previous section, when you place a long-distance call using AT&T as a carrier, your call reaches your central office (class 5) and then goes over a **toll-connecting** trunk to class 4 toll office. If a high-usage

FIGURE 4-7 **Using an OCC for Long-Distance Calling**

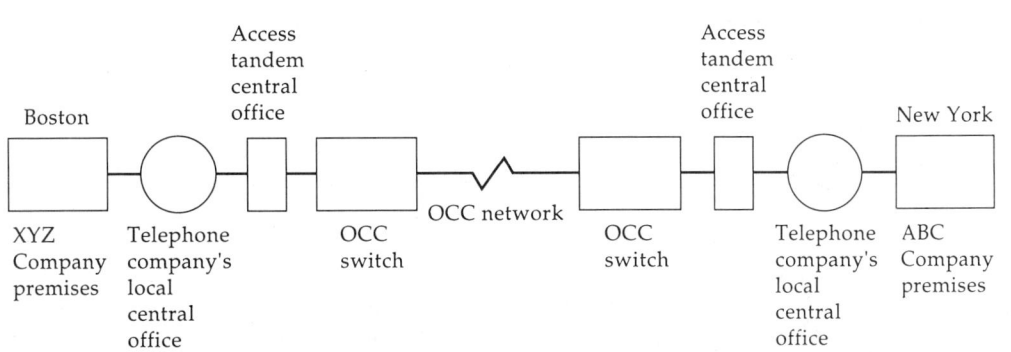

trunk is available, your call can then connect to a final trunk and to the calling party's class 4 toll office. From this toll office your call connects to the calling party's central office (class 5), and the call connection is completed.

Suppose that you decide to place a long-distance call from Boston to New York using a carrier other than AT&T—an OCC. OCCs have their own circuits between Boston and New York City. They may be the OCC's own microwave system or a leased circuit from AT&T or another common carrier.

Figure 4-7 illustrates the placement of a call using one of the OCCs. In Boston your phone call first connects by loop (line) to your central office and then by trunk to an access tandem central office and its microwave system or leased circuit. The access tandem central office serves as the gateway between the BOC's central office and the OCC. Your call is completed by connecting to the access tandem central office in New York City and then to the local central office of the party being called, which completes the call. Note that your call uses a BOC to access the OCC and to complete the call.

The type of connection that a long-distance carrier chooses determines the quality of service the carrier provides to its subscribers. An interexchange carrier connected to a local switch by a four-wire line can provide better service than an interexchange carrier connected by a two-wire line. The interexchange carrier decides which type of access to choose.

■ Resellers

Resellers lease long-distance services at quantity discounts from AT&T and OCCs and then resell them to customers on a shared basis. Resellers differ from OCCs in that they *lease services*, while OCCs *lease or build their own networks*. For example, two services often obtained by resellers are WATS and foreign exchange, both of which will be discussed in the next sections.

Continued existence of resale common carriers depends on the continued availability of volume discounts for leasing long-distance services. A limitation of resellers is that customers must be able to originate calls from the reseller's local area. When away from the local area, the customer must make long-distance calls at regular long-distance rates to access the reseller's equipment location to use its services. This procedure is more costly than simply dialing the long-distance number directly.

■ Bypassing the PSTN

Bypass occurs when a company buys or leases lines to complete its transmission without going through a BOC exchange—a central office. Bypass tends to be used by telephone subscribers who decide that they can supply their own telephone service more cheaply than by using the local central office. Large corporations and government agencies that spend more than $1 million in telephone costs and/or have high-volume telephone usage are frequent bypassing users. Bypassing is made possible by using such transmission media as communications satellite, microwave radio, fiber optic cable, cellular radio, and coaxial cable. For example, Aetna Life and Casualty bypasses the PSTN when it uses fiber optics to transmit voice, video, and data from one building to another. Westinghouse Electric links facilities around the world through its own digital microwave system.

Figure 4-8 illustrates two types of bypass: private (complete) bypass and carrier bypass. A *private (complete) bypass* occurs when a company installs its own transmission system, such as a fiber-optic or microwave system, to interconnect directly to its warehouse or sales offices. A *carrier bypass* occurs when a carrier sets up its own transmission facilities directly between itself and the customer, usually a large-volume telephone user. A company can

FIGURE 4-8   Types of Bypass

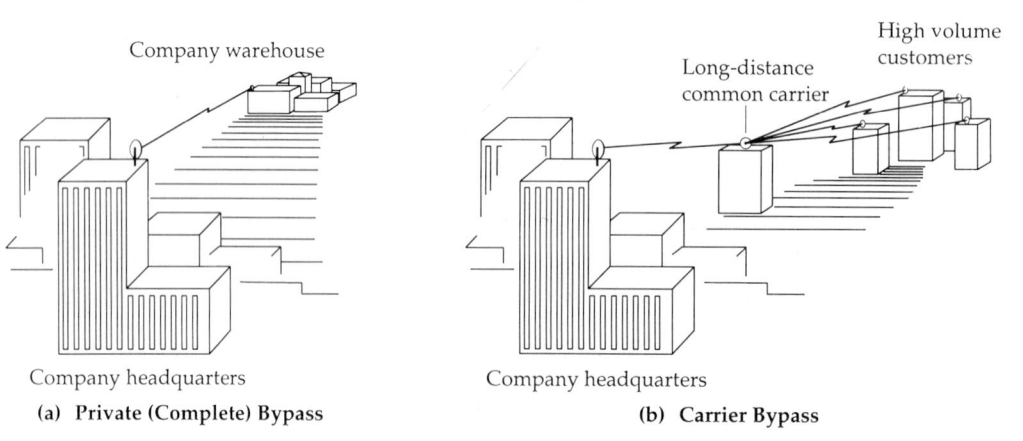

(a) Private (Complete) Bypass   (b) Carrier Bypass

Courtesy of *Telephone Engineer & Management*. Edgell Communications, Chicago, Illinois and Digital Microwave Corporation.

install microwave or satellite transmission antennas on roofs of its offices and plants to connect directly to a long-distance carrier, such as AT&T or OCC. In this way the company avoids paying the charges for using the BOC's facilities.

Long-Distance Services

■ AT&T Communications

Although AT&T cannot provide local service, AT&T is still the dominant carrier in the long-distance market. AT&T's long-distance service can be accessed through a local central office switch.

Types of Long-Distance Services. AT&T Communications offers long-distance services that include:

- Station-to-station calls
- Calling Card calls
- Collect calls
- Operator-assisted station-to-station calls
- Person-to-person calls

The cost of a call depends on distance, call duration, time of day, day of the week, and class of service (such as station-to-station, person-to-person, or Calling Card). A user accesses AT&T's long-distance service through the central office switch. Service is available between all points in the United States and between the United States and 250 countries or territories.

Dialup Services. The typical way to place a long-distance call is to dial a 1 and the local number or a 1 plus an area code followed by the local number. This service is called **dialup service** or *direct distance dialing (DDD)* service. AT&T's dialup services compete with discount services provided by owners of alternative networks and by resellers of AT&T WATS services. Dialup services are used primarily by consumers, small businesses, branch offices, and larger business for spillover traffic from bulk calling service lines.

International Services. AT&T provides international long-distance services between the United States and over 250 countries or territories. Of these countries, 146 can be directly dialed by about 65% of the U.S. population.

Low-Volume Bulk Calling Services. AT&T offers three direct-dialing plans for business customers making out-of-state long-distance dialup calls: PRO WATS I, PRO WATS II, and PRO WATS III (formerly called PRO America). No special access lines are required, so customers can make and receive calls as usual.

For a flat monthly charge of $12, AT&T's PRO WATS I offers users a 10% discount on station-to-station long-distance interstate calls and a 5% discount on credit card calls. Since the breakeven point is $120 ($120 × 0.10 = $12), callers with more than $120 in monthly interstate AT&T long-distance calls save by using this service.

AT&T's PRO WATS II and PRO WATS III are also direct-dial calling services. PRO WATS II is designed primarily for customers with monthly telephone charges ranging from $500 to $2000, and PRO WATS III is for customers with monthly charges of $2000 or more. Also included are discounts on interstate calls: 23–28% for PRO WATS II and 33–38% for PRO WATS III. Calling card discounts for PRO WATS II's interstate calls are 10%; and for PRO WATS III's interstate calls, 15%.

Additional costs for these three services include a one-time installation charge and a fixed monthly charge. In 1989 the installation charge was $10, PRO WATS II cost $80 a month, and PRO WATS III cost $300 a month. PRO WATS II and PRO WATS III are possible alternatives to Wide-Area Telecommunications Services (WATS), which will be explained later in this chapter.

■ MCI Communications

MCI Communications is the largest of the OCCs and the leading competitor of AT&T. MCI is available as a primary carrier in approximately 65% of the United States. In 1972 the company, the first OCC to be licensed by the FCC, began its long-distance telephone service between St. Louis and Chicago. MCI's long-distance services include both voice and data transmission. A brief description of the dialup services offered by MCI is as follows.

Dial-1 is a one-way, dial-in/dial-out, multipoint service that permits users to make and receive calls on local telephone facilities. For long-distance calling, subscribers access the MCI network by dialing 1 plus the area code and number, using any rotary or pushbutton (tone) telephone. Subscribers can make both interstate and international calls similar to AT&T's calling areas. Rates are charged on a per-minute basis.

Both AT&T and OCCs also offer 10XXX service that allows a user to access any carrier desired. For example, suppose your primary carrier is AT&T and you want to make a long-distance call using MCI facilities. You dial 1-00222 to access MCI plus one, the area code, and the local number of the person you are trying to reach.

Figure 4-9 compares the services offered by AT&T, MCI, and three other common carriers: Allnet, US Sprint, and Western Union.

■ Wide-Area/Bulk-Rate Services

Wide-Area Telecommunications Service (WATS) is a long-distance plan that offers bulk rate for calls that are directly dialed station-to-station using the toll-telephone network. The two types of WATS are outward WATS and inward WATS, as shown in Figure 4-10.

FIGURE 4-9 Examples of Services Offered by AT&T and OCCs, 1989

Carrier/Toll Services	WATS and Equivalent Services
AT&T Communications: Dial-It 900 Service, Interstate LDMTS	MEGACOM 800 Service, PRO WATS, Readyline
MCI Communications: Dial-1 Service, MCI Calling Card, 10XXX Service	PRISM Services (WATS), MCI 800 Services
Allnet Communications: Allnet Interstate MTS	Allnet WATS
US Sprint, Phone Card: Direct Dial US Sprint, Ultra 800 Services	Sprint WATS, US Sprint Direct
Western Union: Western Union Long-Distance Services	WATS, INWATS

FIGURE 4-10 Outward and Inward WATS

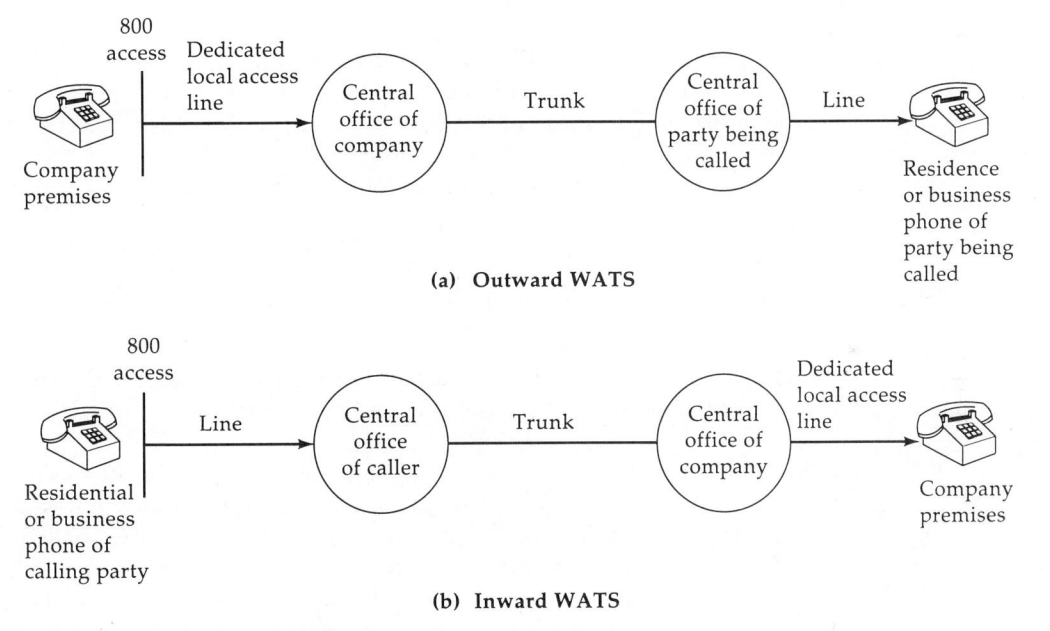

(a) Outward WATS

(b) Inward WATS

Outward WATS. With AT&T's **outward WATS** you can call other locations and receive discounts that increase as your calling volume increases. Outward WATS services are voice-grade facilities that can be used for voice and data transmission between points in the contiguous United States and between the U.S. mainland and Alaska, Hawaii, Canada, Puerto Rico, and the U.S. Virgin Islands. Initially, only AT&T provided WATS services. By 1986, OCCs such as MCI were offering outward WATS.

Inward WATS. AT&T's **inward WATS**, called *800 Service*, operates similarly except that it allows outsiders to call your business without charge. You pay for the calls—at a discount that increases as call volume increases.

Local Access Line. Inward and outward WATS usually require that a customer have a dedicated access line. A **dedicated access line** is a circuit assigned to a customer for exclusive use between the customer's telephone equipment and the central office.

Cost. The cost for a WATS line includes the charge for each dedicated local access line (one-time installation charge and a fixed monthly charge) and the usage charge for the services. The usage charge is based on the number of hours per month, time of day, day of the week, and service areas called. Day rates are higher than evening rates, night and weekend rates being the lowest. The cost per usage hour decreases as interstate usage increases during the day and evening periods.

Geographical Coverage Plan. The 48 contiguous states are divided into 58 service areas. The geographical coverage of WATS from any of these service areas is determined by the band of service to which the customer subscribes.

Customers subscribe to one of the following five bands:

- Band 1 provides interstate coverage to nearby states.
- Bands, 2, 3, and 4 provide intermediate coverage.
- Band 5 includes the 48 contiguous states, Hawaii, Puerto Rico, the Virgin Islands, and Alaska.

For the band of service selected, a rate is assigned to the first 25 hours of use, the next 75 hours of use, and then over 100 hours of use.

Other 800 Services. *AT&T 800 Service Canada* is available between Canada and the United States. *AT&T International 800 Service* accommodates those customers in the contiguous United States who wish to receive calls from specific overseas countries and eliminate overseas charges to the callers. This service is provided through a service component called a *County Access Capability* (CAC). The overseas network control arrangement permits customers to subscribe to AT&T's International 800 Service from specific countries.

AT&T's *MEGACOM and MEGACOM 800* services are designed for business customers whose long-distance bills exceed $12,000 a month—about 1000 hours of usage per month per location. Costs for these services are based on mileage and duration of each call, plus a fixed monthly charge. The MEGACOM service allows customers to call any exchange in the United States, Puerto Rico, and the U.S. Virgin Islands. Customers with MEGA-COM 800 can create their own toll-free calling area, such as California area codes only, whereas customers with AT&T 800 Service who choose a particular band are obliged to accept calls from the entire area the band covers.

AT&T recently added the *800 Readyline*, an inward calling service, to its WATS services. The 800 Readyline, designed for companies with less than 15 hours of 800 traffic per month, is aimed at small businesses, although larger AT&T 800 service customers may find the service helpful for promotional and seasonal applications.

The 800 Readyline permits customers to use their existing phones lines instead of using dedicated local access lines. It features two-way calling, that is, customers may place their outgoing calls over the same lines that are used to receive 800 calls. This service requires no modification to existing equipment. It can be used with any calling feature provided by the local central office. For example, customers with call forwarding can transfer their calls to another number during business hours.

Evaluation of Services. Both AT&T WATS and 800 Services offer national coverage and extend to Canada and 18 foreign countries. These services are also attractive to large-volume long-distance telephone users as an attractive alternative to traditional long-distance dialup services. No minimum usage requirement or minimum monthly usage charges apply.

The major drawback to AT&T WATS/800 services is that the banding arrangement does not permit distance-sensitive pricing. For example, if you have Band 2 service and place a call outside of this band, you will be billed the appropriate long-distance rate.

Private Lines

A private line (also called a dedicated or leased line) is a dedicated transmission channel for the customer's exclusive use between two locations. Private lines generally provide transmission in two directions. These lines are used for voice and data when traffic patterns justify the cost. For example, a leased line can be less expensive than dialup services when a significant amount of traffic is destined for one location.

Private lines have certain drawbacks.

- Private lines may be expensive to install.
- The speed of installing a private line, from the time the order is placed to actual installation, may take longer than anticipated. Such a situation can make it difficult to make plans for its services. A private microwave system can be set up overnight.
- The increasing cost of the local-loop portion of the line is causing fixed monthly rates for private lines to increase.
- The private line may not be fully utilized, making long-distance dialup services more cost effective.

Types of private lines available from AT&T and OCCs are tie line, foreign exchange, remote-call forwarding, and T-1 lines.

■ Tie Lines

A **tie line** (also called a tie trunk) is a private leased or dedicated telephone circuit provided by a common carrier that links two remote offices together without using the public switched telephone network. Each line supports only one call at a time. Users can pack the line with traffic and still pay only a fixed monthly charge. As shown in Figure 4-11, a tie line connects two switching devices, such as two private business exchanges, one at each location. To access the tie line from either location, a user dials a specific number to connect to the tie line. Once the connection is made, the user can dial any extension at the remote location. A tie line makes it possible for locations separated by distance to operate as though they were in the same building. In 1988 the cost of a tie line from a Boston office to a Chicago office was $2000 to install and approximately $900 a month.

■ Foreign Exchange

Another type of private line is **foreign exchange** service (FX). FX enables a subscriber to be served by a distant or "foreign" central office rather than by its own local central office, as shown in Figure 4-12. With a FX private line the user's dedicated line ends in a local exchange that is outside, or foreign to, the company's local service area—usually in another city. For example, a subscriber leases a line from the local telephone company. One end terminates in the subscriber's own telephone equipment. The other end terminates in a central office of a distant city. A user in the subscriber's office who accesses the FX line receives a dial tone from the distant city. To place a call, the subscriber dials a seven-digit number to reach any telephone in that city. A subscriber's calls to customers in the distant exchange area are treated as local calls instead of toll calls.

Costs of FX include an installation charge and a fixed monthly charge for telephone service in the distant city, connection to both central offices, and the mileage between the two locations—from the subscriber's telephone

FIGURE 4-11 Tie Line

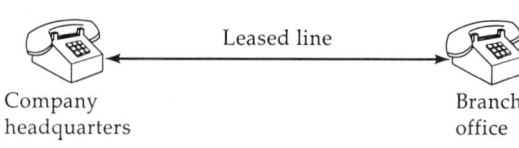

FIGURE 4-12   Foreign Exchange Service

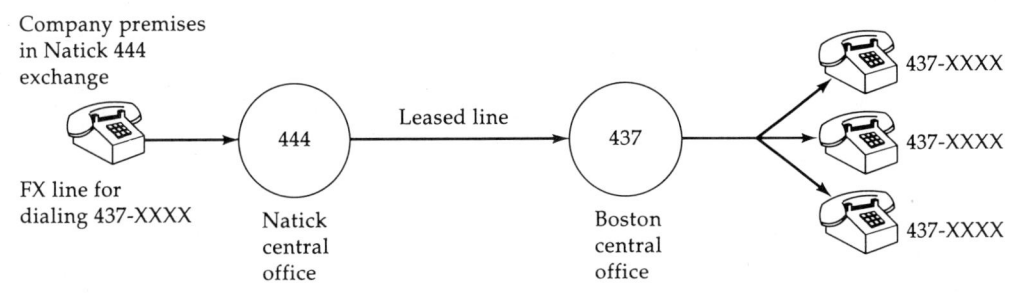

FIGURE 4-13   Foreign Exchange Costs for a Company Located in Natick with a Boston Telephone Number*

One-time installation charge	$351.00
Monthly charges:	
Boston telephone service (measured)	$ 20.00
Mileage charge (from Natick to Boston, 16 miles)	
First 9 miles: $6.79 per mile	
Over 9 miles: $1.97 per mile	$ 72.93
Central office connect charge (Boston)	$ 5.09
Central office connect charge (Natick)	$ 5.09
Total monthly charges	$103.11

*The figures represent 1988 rates and are intended only as an illustration of the cost of foreign exchange services.

to the distant central office. An example of FX costs for a company located in Natick, Massachusetts, calling locally in Boston is illustrated in Figure 4-13. For subscribers who make sufficient calls to a particular distant exchange area the fixed monthly charge for FX service can be less than the sum of the toll charges they would otherwise pay.

■ Remote Call Forwarding

Remote call forwarding (RCF) is a one-way line that allows a company with customers located in another city to call the company as a local call. Suppose your company is in Natick, Massachusetts, but your customers are located in Boston. With RCF your customers' calls can be handled by the central office in Boston as local calls. Customers call your Boston number; their calls are forwarded automatically to your Natick number over long-distance lines,

FIGURE 4-14 Remote Call Forwarding

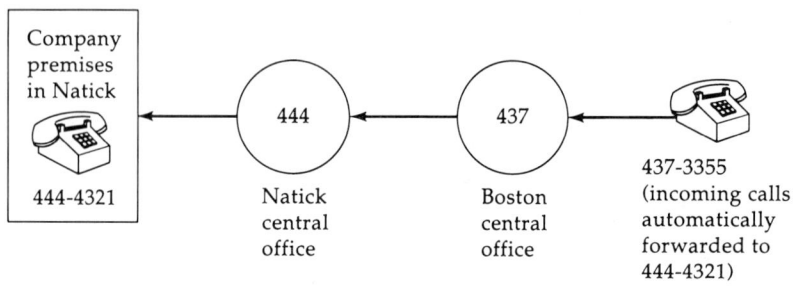

as shown in Figure 4-14. Your RCF phone number is listed as a local Boston number in either the Boston White Pages, the Boston Yellow Pages, or both. It is like having a branch office without really being there.

The cost for RCF service includes a fixed monthly charge plus the cost of each call from the Boston central office to Natick at direct-dial rates. In this case you would pay a $16.97 monthly rate plus long-distance charges for each call from any of your Boston customers using RCF. If your business expects more than ten calls a day, you should consider 800 Service instead.

■ T-1 Lines

Traditional private lines, such as the ones just discussed, handle one circuit at a time. **T-1 lines**, which are digital lines, can handle 24 voice channels between two points, such as central offices, customer premises, or a combination of both, on two pairs of copper wires. The cost is about 16 times that of a single-circuit private line. Full duplex transmission requires two twisted pairs (one for each direction). The 24 voice channels are digitized and then combined (multiplexed) onto a single 1.544 Mbps data stream where they are transmitted over two pairs of wires. At the receiving end, they are returned to their original state.

Selecting a Long-Distance Carrier

OCCs are in fierce competition with AT&T and each other. Information about carriers can be obtained from the carriers, through tariff updating services (for carriers who are regulated), and through product information services. The following factors should be considered in selecting a carrier.

■ Cost of Using a Carrier for Long-Distance Calling

Cost items to be considered when comparing carriers are the following.

Minimum Charge. Carriers may have a minimum charge, sometimes called a service surcharge or a minimum billing charge. Other carriers have no such charge.

Installation Charge. A carrier may charge for installing or converting to its service.

Access Charge. In addition to the cost of the call, which is usually based on distance, some OCCs may charge an access charge. The charge may be a flat fee per call or a flat fee for each minute of use.

Billing Increments. Most carriers, including AT&T, use a billing increment of 1 minute. However, some OCCs bill usage in fractions of a minute, such as every 6 seconds, for certain services. For example, ITT bills every 6 seconds for its ITT Business Class service with a 30-second minimum.

Volume Discounts. To encourage use of services, AT&T and some OCCs give volume discounts on certain services, such as WATS. For example, ITT gives a volume discount on its Business Class service of 5% on usage ranging from $100 to $1999 and 10% over $2000.

Time of Day Discounts. Rates may be lower or discounts given for calls placed during the evening or during night/weekend rate periods.

Authorization Codes. An OCC generally provides the subscriber with one authorization usage code. A charge may be included for additional codes.

Cost of Long-Distance Services. Costs of the various long-distance services, such as station-to-station, Calling Card, collect, and operator-assisted, vary among the carriers, some carriers offering discounts calling plans such as AT&T's PRO WATS I, II, and III. The cost of the different types of private lines also varies among carriers.

■ Other Factors to Consider

Other factors to consider are the following.

Customer (User) Profile. The number of calls per week, time of calls, and length of calls must be considered in choosing a long-distance carrier. See Figure 5-30.

Areas Served. A carrier may service only certain geographical areas. For example, the carrier may allow calling only from a certain area of the United States or calling to and from the United States and one or two countries outside the United States.

Customer Service. Customer service, such as 24-hour telephone assistance and convenient service locations, should be available to subscribers.

Information about the quality of services can be obtained by talking with other users of the carrier being considered.

Dialing. Some central offices offer one-plus-dialing for specified OCCs. If the central office does not offer one-plus-dialing for the OCC that you are considering, information should be obtained about the availability and cost of an automatic dialer for the OCC's access and authorization codes.

Individual Accounting. Some carriers provide two-digit accounting codes to be used when placing a call. The code identifies the user or the department to be charged for the call.

■ Application

After evaluating the costs and services of a dozen carriers the state of Florida selected Microtel, Inc., a Florida-based fiber-optic long-distance company to provide intrastate digital private lines and WATS services for its SUNCOM telecommunications network. Florida will save about $7.2 million over a three-year period compared to the rates it has been paying to AT&T.[3] Figure 4-15 shows how Microtel, one of the OCCs, handles a WATS call.

Summary

"Nineteen eighty-three was a year in which we took apart the world's largest business enterprise and reshaped it into separate and independent organizations. When the year was done, there was a new, more compact AT&T. There were seven new regional holding companies, into which were grouped the twenty-two local Bell operating companies. And there was a new service organization to provide centralized technical support to the regional companies."[4] The BOCs now handle calls within specified geo-

FIGURE 4-15 Using an OCC (Microtel) for WATS Calling

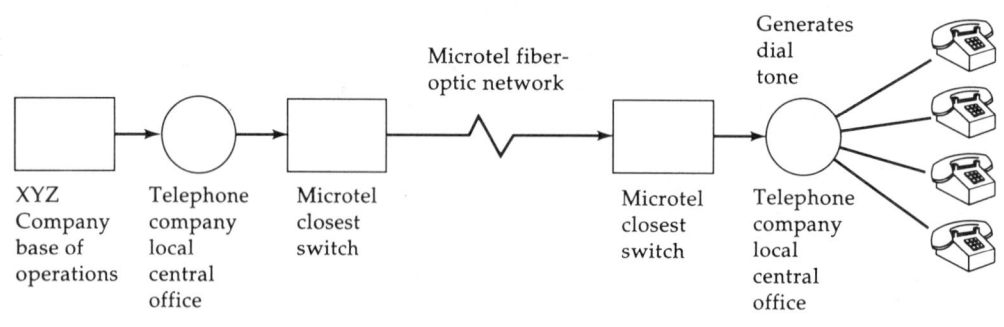

graphic areas, called LATAs, while long-distance carriers handle calls between LATAs, that is, within and between states. Other common carriers compete with AT&T to provide long-distance services.

Customers access interexchange carriers via their local central office, as required by the Modified Final Judgement, the divestiture agreement. AT&T's well-defined hierarchy of switching centers extends its centralized switching centers to all long-distance users, OCCs combining these with their own switching centers. Some long-distance users bypass the central office by using transmission media such as communication satellite and microwave.

Key Terms

Bell operating companies (BOCs)
Bypass
Dedicated access line
Dialup service
End office
Equal access
Foreign exchange
Hierarchy of switching centers
Interexchange carrier
InterLATA call
Intraexchange carrier
IntraLATA call
Inward WATS
Modified Final Judgment
Other common carriers (OCCs)
Outward WATS
Regional Bell operating companies (RBOCs)
Remote call forwarding
T-1 lines
Tie line

Self-Quiz

Indicate whether the statement is true or false.

1. The divestiture agreement of 1982 broke up the largest company in the world, both in assets and in number of employees. T/F
2. The divestiture of the AT&T Bell Telephone System resulted in the twenty-two Bell operating companies being grouped into seven regional Bell operating companies and being somewhat dependent on AT&T. T/F
3. The toll network consists of class 4 and higher switching offices. T/F
4. Calls between LATAs within a state or across state lines are handled by AT&T or one of the OCCs. T/F
5. A class 5 office can also be called a toll office or a tandem toll office. T/F
6. An example of a private bypass is a transmission system installed by a company to interconnect its sales office directly to the local BOC exchange. T/F

Complete each of the following statements.

1. Long-distance competitors of AT&T are called _____ .
2. The maximum number of trunks that may be used in a long-distance calling connection, using AT&T's switching hierarchy, is _____ .

3. The geographic area within which a BOC is responsible for handling local subscribers' calls as well as any toll calls that originate and terminate within this area is called a _____ .
4. The divestiture agreement required other common carriers to have equal access to _____ .
5. Companies that lease long-distance services at quantity discounts from AT&T and then resell them to customers on a shared based are called _____ .
6. Suppose you place a long-distance call using AT&T as your carrier. If all of the trunks to the calling party are blocked from your class 3 toll office, your call would then overflow to _____ .

Match Column A with Column B.

Column A
(a) Dialup service
(b) Foreign exchange
(c) Inward WATS
(d) Outward WATS
(e) Remote call forwarding
(f) Tie line

Column B
____ 1. AT&T's direct distance dialing.
____ 2. Allows outsiders to call your business without charge.
____ 3. Allows a company to call other locations at lower prices.
____ 4. A leased line that connects two switching devices, one at each office.
____ 5. A leased line that enables a subscriber to be served by a foreign central office.
____ 6. A leased line that allows a company with customers located in another city to call the company as a local call.

■ *Review Questions*

1. How has the Modified Final Judgement changed AT&T?
2. How has the breakup of AT&T helped the OCCs?
3. What is the difference between an intraLATA call and an interLATA call? Give examples.
4. (a) What is the meaning of "hierarchy of switching offices"?
   (b) How would a call to a friend in another city be switched through the hierarchy?
5. What is the difference between an end office and a toll office?
6. How do intraexchange carriers and interexchange carriers differ from each other?
7. (a) Explain what happens when you place a call in Chicago to a friend in New York City using AT&T as a carrier. (Draw a diagram showing the Central Office, etc.)
   (b) Explain what happens when you place a call in Chicago to a friend in

New York City using OCC. (Draw a diagram showing the Central Office, etc.)
8. (a) What is the difference between resellers and OCCs?
   (b) Why would a company want to consider using a reseller?
9. How can a telephone subscriber bypass the local central office? (Draw a diagram.)
10. (a) How does AT&T WATS differ from foreign exchange?
    (b) How does foreign exchange differ from remote call forwarding?
11. What is the difference between dialup services and a private line?
12. What factors should you consider when selecting a long distance carrier?

■ Activities/Projects

1. What type of private or leased lines would you recommend for each of the following situations?
   (a) A sales office in Monroe, Louisiana, and its corporate headquarters in Stillwater, Oklahoma, use AT&T's direct distance dialing for calling between the locations. Calling between the offices averages about six or seven hours each weekday and three or four hours on Saturday.
   (b) The sales territory of a telemarketing department of a manufacturing company in Pullman, Washington, is the northwest United States.
   (c) A company in Boulder, Colorado, clocks six or seven hours of calling a day to various clients in Denver, Colorado, a distance of 50 miles.
   (d) Most of the customers of an equipment repair company are located in New York City, about 20 miles from the company. If the customers have to pay a toll charge to call the company, they will not use the company's services.
   (e) A retail company located in Seattle, Washington, would like its customers throughout the country to be able to telephone orders without charge.
2. Are you using the long-distance carrier that provides you with the lowest rates? Obtain a copy of the long-distance charges that have appeared on your telephone statement (or a friend's) for the past 6 months. Also obtain the current rates of two long-distance carriers. (A call to 1-800-555-1212 information will give you the carriers' toll-free numbers.) Calculate what the charges would have been if either of these carriers had been used. Have you selected the carrier with the lowest rates for your calls? Are there any other factors you would consider in the selection of a long-distance carrier?

■ Case: Should This Company Use WATS for Long-Distance Calling?

The cost of your company's long-distance telephone calls exceed $1800 each month. An analysis of past telephone statements resulted in the following long-distance calling pattern for a typical week.

Report of Your Company's Long-Distance Telephone Calling for a Typical Week (Monday through Friday)

Calling Distance Mileage	Number of Calls per Week	Average Length of Each Call
Day Calling:		
10–292	200	3.5 minutes
293–430	100	3.5 minutes
431–925	50	3 minutes
926–1910	20	3 minutes
1911–3000	20	3 minutes
3001–4250	20	3 minutes
Evening Calling:		
10–292	32	4 minutes

You have decided to investigate the cost of using AT&T and MCI WATS for the company's long-distance calling. Information about each service is given below. How much would it cost per month to use each service? Should you select one of these services? If so, which one? What are your recommendations?

(a) AT&T's PRO WATS II Virtual Banded Calling Plan, Per hour billed in 6-second increments after an initial 30 seconds. (July 1, 1989 prices.)

Mileage	Day (per hour)	Evening (per hour)
0–292	$11.52	$ 8.82
293–430	$12.24	$ 9.36
431–925	$13.20	$10.02
926–1910	$13.62	$11.10
1911–3000	$14.34	$12.96
3001–4250	$16.74	$14.52

Note: No local access lines are required; detailed billing is provided. Customers are charged a monthly account fee of $80. Service covers all outbound lines. Installation charge is $10.

(b) MCI's PRISM PLUS Plan, Billed in 6-second increments. (July 1, 1989 prices.)

Mileage	Day (per minute)	Evening (per minute)
0–292	$0.2052	$0.1443
293–430	$0.2227	$0.1560
431–925	$0.2342	$0.1677
926–1910	$0.2416	$0.1736
1911–3000	$0.2582	$0.1853
3001–4250	$0.3014	$0.2165

Note: A volume discount based on total monthly domestic usage of MCI PRISM PLUS is given: 10% discount for usage totaling up to $125; 12.5% discount for bills totaling between $125 and $1000; and 20%, over $1000.

Notes

1. C. L. Brown, "Report of the Chairman," *1983 AT&T Annual Report* (New York: American Telephone and Telegraph Company, 1984), p. 3.
2. *Fact Book* (New York: AT&T, 1989), pp. 1–13.
3. "Microtel Awarded Florida Contract," *The Miami Herald*, December 7, 1987.
4. "1983: An Epilogue," *1983 AT&T Annual Report* (New York: American Telephone and Telegraph Company, 1984), p. 4.

Additional Readings

Gerald R. Ash and Vernon S. Mummert, "AT&T Carves New Routes in Its Nationwide Network," *AT&T Bell Laboratories Record*, August 1984, pp. 18–22.

Byron Belitsos and Jay Misra, *Business Telematics* (Homewood, Illinois: Dow Jones–Irwin, 1986), Chapter 9.

H. M. Boettinger, *The Telephone Book: Bell, Watson, Vail and American Life, 1876–1983* (New York: Stearn Publishers, Ltd., 1983).

John Brooks, *Telephone: The First Hundred Years* (New York: Harper & Row, Publishers, 1976).

Donald F. Burnside, "Last-Mile Communications Alternatives," *TPT*, April 1988, pp. 57–60.

Steve Coll, *The Breakup of AT&T* (New York: Collier, MacMillan, 1986).

Edwin Diamond, Norman Sandler, and Milton Mueller, *Telecommunications in Crisis: The First Amendment, Technology, and Deregulation* (Washington, D.C.: CATO Institute, 1983).

Samuel A. Simon, *After Divestiture: What the AT&T Settlement Means for Business and Residential Telephone Service* (White Plains, N.Y.: Knowledge Industry Publications, 1985).

CHAPTER 5

Business Telephone Systems

The Interconnect Industry
  The Carterfone Decision
  Computer Inquiry II

Key Telephone Systems
  Evolution of Key System Technology
  1A2 Key Telephone System—An Electromechanical System
  Electronic Key Telephone System
  Hybrid Key Telephone System
  KTS Functions/Features
  KTS Costs
  The Key System Market

Private Branch Exchanges
  Evolution of PBX Technology
  PBX Components and Operation
  PBX Features
  PBX Architecture—Centralized or Distributed
  The PBX Market

Centrex Services
  Evolution of Centrex Services Technology
  Centrex Services Operation
  Centrex Services Features
  Centrex Services Rates
  Centrex Services Market

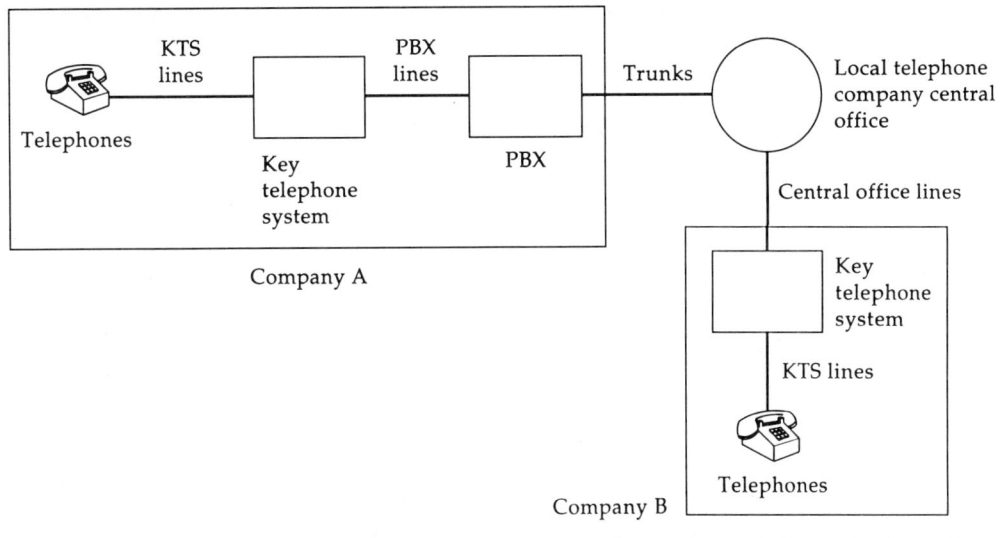

Comparison of PBX Systems and Centrex Services
Selecting a Business Telephone System
    Phase 1: Analyze the Current Telephone System
    Phase 2: Specify the Requirements of the New Telephone System
    Phase 3: Select the New Telephone System

CHAPTER OBJECTIVES
After completing this chapter, you should be able to

1. Distinguish between the different business telephone systems.
2. Define the three types of key telephone systems.
3. Explain typical features of business telephone systems.
4. Describe the operation of a business telephone system.
5. Weigh the pros and cons of each business telephone system.
6. Develop plans for selecting a business telephone system.

How would you solve each of these common business telephone problems?

    a. Your department members are often away from their desks. Their telephone keeps ringing, or callers are left fuming on hold.

b. You want to have your incoming calls answered even when you are on the telephone or away from your desk.
c. You are tired of trying to get through to a busy telephone extension.
d. You want to know the long-distance telephone charges incurred weekly by each member of your department.
e. You want to add a third party to an existing call.

Business telephone system features that offer solutions to these problems are as follows: (a) *Call Pickup* allows you to redirect people's calls to your phone by dialing a simple code; (b) *Call Forward* redirects your incoming calls to another phone; (c) *Automatic Callback* allows you to be called back when a busy extension becomes free; (d) *Station Message Detail Recording* provides records of telephone activity; (e) *Add-On Conference* allows you to add a third party to your conversation. These features are discussed in this chapter.

Today, business organizations have many options for selecting, installing, and managing their own telephone services. Many employees must now learn more than they ever wanted to know about telephone operations. Others welcome the knowledge for use in better controlling and improving their business communications and operations.

This chapter discusses the interconnect industry and the basic business telephone systems: key telephone systems (KTSs), private branch exchanges (PBXs), and Centrex services. An understanding of these systems, including their technical evolution, how they operate, and features that they offer, helps end users to make intelligent, informed decisions when evaluating and selecting the type of telephone system that best meets their needs.

The Interconnect Industry

The U.S. telephone system market was once the chief domain of AT&T's Bell system. Today, the market is shared by over thirty other manufacturers and many distributors, interconnect companies, local Bell telephone companies, and the seven regional Bell operating companies (RBOCs).

■ The Carterfone Decision

Before 1968, subscribers could not legally attach non-Bell equipment to Bell lines. Bell system tariffs stated that the telephone company had the right to deny service to any subscriber found to have attached foreign equipment (non-Bell equipment) to its public switched network. (Tariffs refer to regulations concerned with the cost and the conditions of telephone service that are approved by the state and federal regulators.) This regulation was based on the belief that such attachment might damage the delicate mechanisms of the entire network.

The Carter Electronics Corporation, a Texas manufacturer of mobile radio devices, challenged this regulation. The company sued the public telephone companies in order to be allowed to connect its radio devices to the public switched telephone network (PSTN). In 1968 the Federal Communications Commission (FCC) ruled in favor of Carter Electronics. Customers were now allowed to purchase their own switching services, including telephone instruments, key telephone systems, and private branch exchanges, and were permitted unrestricted interconnection of all devices to the network.

This landmark decision, known as the **Carterfone Decision**, marked the birth of the **interconnect industry**. The new industry of nontelephone company manufacturers and distributors arose to supply customers, by sale, rental, or leasing, with equipment that connects to existing Bell and independent networks. Manufacturers of this equipment were no longer limited to supplying equipment to independent telephone companies and the Bell operating companies. They could now supply the entire business community.

■ Computer Inquiry II

In 1980 the Federal Communications Commission in its Computer Inquiry II ruled that customers premises equipment, such as private branch exchanges and telephones, could be offered on a deregulated basis through a separate AT&T subsidiary. In June 1982, in response to Computer Inquiry II, AT&T organized American Bell, now known as AT&T Information Systems, to provide customer premises equipment to telecommunications customers.

Key Telephone Systems

A computer software development company in Portland, Maine, began business with one single-line telephone. Business is now booming, and the company requires additional staff and more telephones. Telephone demands are being met by adding three more telephones and another outside line. What kind of telephone system should the company's owner select? After evaluating the different telephone systems the owner selected a 1A key telephone system with telephone set buttons for holding calls and accessing an intercom line (for employees to talk with each other) and two outside lines.

When a company requires more than one or two single-line telephones to talk to the outside world, the company usually considers purchasing a **key telephone system** (KTS). As shown in Figure 5-1, a KTS consists of a key service unit (center), a power supply (left), and a number of telephone instruments (right). Expansion cartridges (center front) can expand a system from two outside lines and eight extensions to six outside lines and sixteen extensions. Each telephone has access to more than one PSTN central office telephone line or other lines and the capability of performing other desired functions. A PSTN central office is a common carrier location where customer lines terminate in a switching capability. The switch connects the customer's local line to another local line or to the long-distance network.

Figure 5-2 shows the basic relationship between the PSTN central office, single-line telephones, and a key telephone system. In addition to allowing users to share a few lines, a KTS offers such functions as answering or originating a call on a selected telephone line, putting a call on hold, and using an intercom line to talk with another employee at the same location.

FIGURE 5-1 A Key Telephone System (KTS): The Businesscom 616

Courtesy of TIE/communications, Inc.

FIGURE 5-2 Connecting a Key Telephone System and Single Telephone to the Central Office

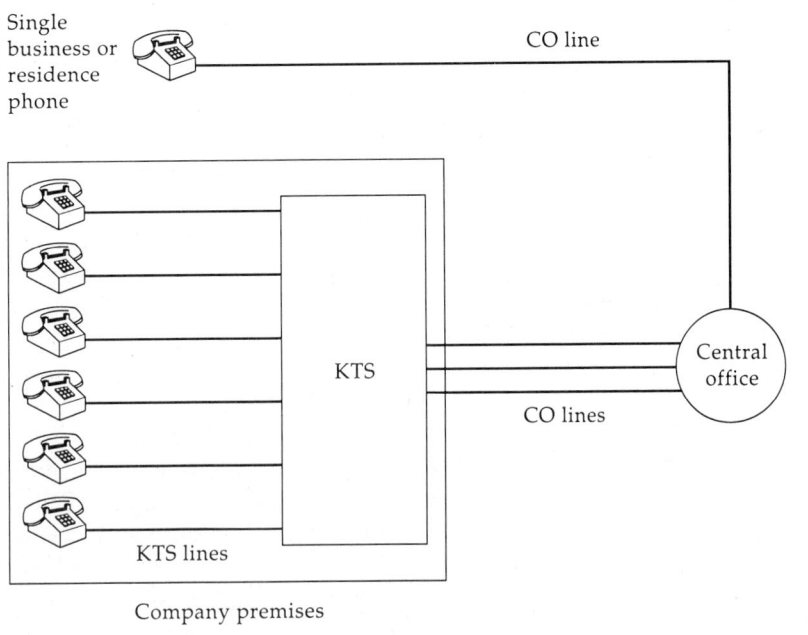

■ Evolution of Key System Technology

The term "key" is a carry over from the early days of telegraphy and telephony, when a key was used to close a specific circuit or break electrical contact mechanically. During the first two decades of the 1900s, whenever a business needed more telephone service, a line and a telephone were added. As offices became swamped with single-line telephones, a better solution for increasing telephone service had to be found.

In the mid-1920s, AT&T responded with the first KTSs, called wiring plans. They consisted of a collection of wires, switches, and lamps to help customers communicate with each other. Each customer's plan was unique, making installation and maintenance for technicians extremely difficult. These wiring plans eventually developed into the 1A key telephone system, an electromechanical system introduced by AT&T in 1938. For the first time, all system components and wiring were specifically defined, making installation and maintenance easier. In 1963, AT&T introduced the 1A2 KTS, which was smaller than the 1A KTS and much easier to install. Today, the three basic types of key telephone systems are the 1A2 KTS, the electronic key telephone system, and the hybrid key telephone system.

■ 1A2 Key Telephone System—An Electromechanical System

The **1A2 KTS** is still considered the standard key system in the electromechanical industry. To many this key station, shown in Figure 5-3, is known only as "the one with six built-in buttons." Five of the six buttons are assigned for the intercom, central office, PBX, or other outside lines, and the sixth, a red button, is assigned for hold. A light under each button tells the status of the line: ringing, busy, on hold, or idle. Not only does the key system provide end-users with access to two or more outgoing lines, but it is easy to operate. The end-user just pushes a button to access an outgoing line. Line availability is quickly determined by noting which buttons are not illuminated. Some users prefer the simplicity of this key telephone system to more complicated electronic telephone systems with their numerous features. The durability of these systems is evidenced by the fact that they have lasted for so many years. The popularity of these key systems with very small business users is expected to continue.

The 1A2 KTS, an electromechanical system, features solid-state components, printed circuit boards, and miniature relays. Its system components, shown in Figure 5-4, are the key service unit (KSU), the power supply, and the telephone station (terminal) equipment—the multiline telephones that connect to the KSU via multiwire cables. The KSU, an equipment cabinet that can be wall- or desk-mounted or floor-standing, contains the circuitry

FIGURE 5-3 The Classic 1A2 Key Telephone System

Courtesy of AT&T Archives.

Key Telephone Systems

FIGURE 5-4 The Components of a 1A2 KTS

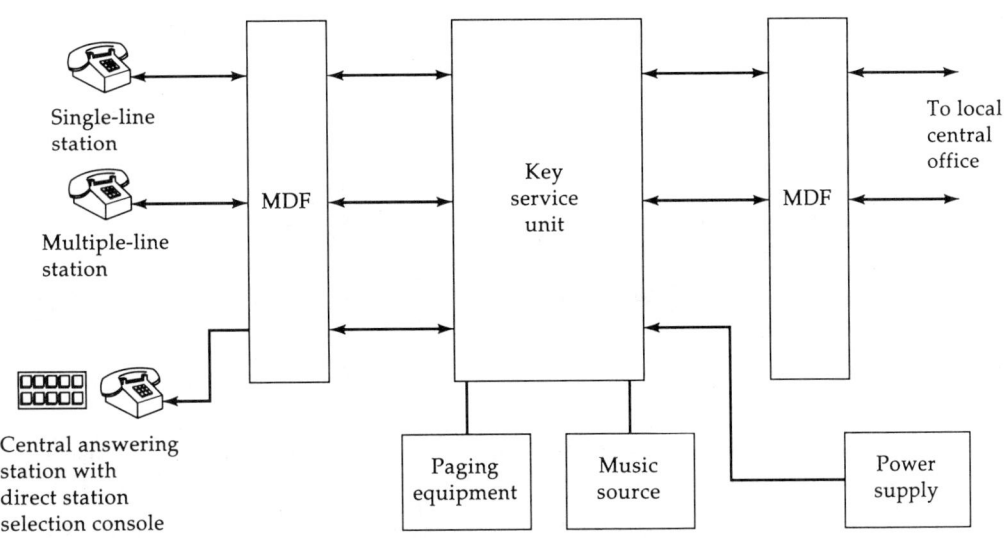

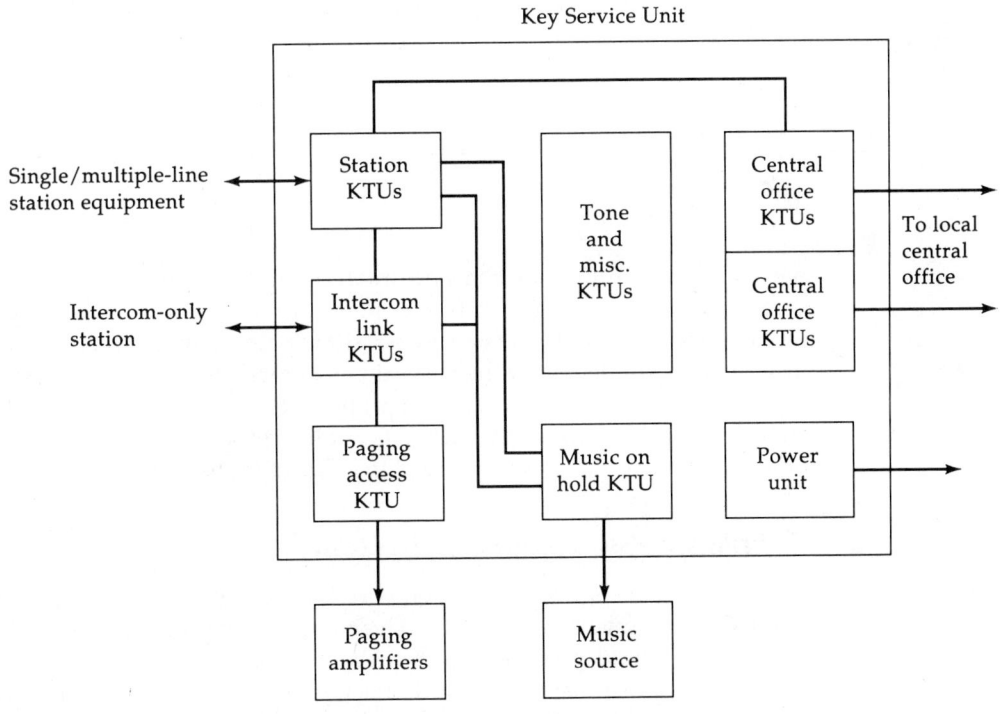

Redrawn courtesy of Datapro Research Corporation.

FIGURE 5-5 Key System Configuration

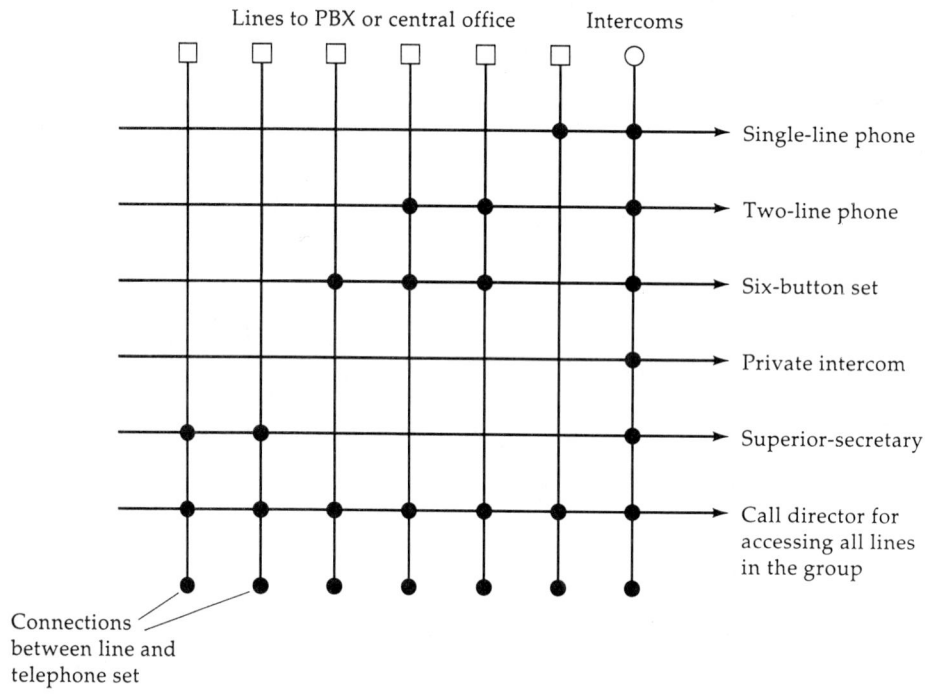

that provides the distribution and integration paths to make the system work. A cable requiring twenty-five pairs of wire connects each key telephone station to the KSU. Figure 5-5 shows how key stations connect to outside lines. In the matrix the vertical lines represent telephone lines to the central office (or a PBX), and the horizontal lines represent user stations. Each dot that appears at an intersection of a vertical and a horizontal line indicates that the station is equipped to connect to that line.

■ Electronic Key Telephone System

After a study of its telephone needs, an interior design company decided that it should replace its 1A2 KTS. The company selected an electronic key system that would provide such features as call pickup, call forwarding, paging, and speed dialing. An added benefit was that the same key system could be used when the company's telephone needs expanded to require more sophisticated telephone systems such as PBX or Centrex systems.

In the 1970s, **electronic key telephone systems** (EKSs) using microprocessors and integrated circuit chips became available. (A microprocessor is an electronic circuit, usually on a single microchip, that performs arithmetic, logic and control operations, customarily with the assistance of small internal memory, also on the chip.) EKSs offer features unavailable to electromechanical systems. Installation charges for EKSs are less than those for 1A2s because installing electronic systems requires less time and uses fewer materials. Features are easy to implement through computer programs stored in the system's memory. A major drawback, however, is that electronic key sets are often designed to interface with particular control equipment and may not be compatible with other systems.

Components and Operation of EKSs. Electronic key telephone systems replace electromechanical control with microprocessor control and reduce the number of cable pairs per station from twenty-five to three or four. For example, when a microprocessor detects an incoming ring, it signals a station. The station user responds by depressing a button to pick up the incoming call. The telephone set then sends a data message to the controller, which connects the incoming line to the station. The user can hold calls by depressing the hold button, which applies a flashing lamp signal to the line button.

Capacity. The capacity of a key system is indicated by the maximum number of lines to the PSTN central office and the key telephone stations that can be implemented. A 6 × 18 key system offers a maximum of six central office lines and a maximum of eighteen key telephone stations. The ratio of stations to central office lines is usually three to one. Most key systems also include one or more intercom lines for station-to-station conversations within the system.

Hybrid Key Telephone System

Recently, manufacturers introduced a **hybrid key telephone system (HKTS)**. The hybrid system is intended to combine the best features of the key system, such as low cost and easy-to-use features, with the cost-maintenance and advanced system features commonly associated with private branch exchanges (PBXs). PBXs are discussed in the next section.

Key systems are more limited than PBXs in the number of trunk lines that they can handle. Since each telephone can access every incoming line, there must be a button for each line. Anyone can pick up a ringing line and, in effect, act as a receptionist. As more stations are added to a key system, one key set can be turned into a console, with a receptionist announcing calls to other key set users through the intercom. For large systems this arrangement becomes impractical.

In 1979, AT&T marketed the first hybrid system, the Horizon Communications System. A Horizon telephone station is shown in Figure 5-6.

FIGURE 5-6   A Horizon Key Telephone Station

Courtesy of AT&T Archives.

Although this system is no longer being manufactured, it is one of the most widely used systems and is still being actively traded on the used equipment market. The Horizon system was the first system to provide users with the ability to perform their own administrative telephone changes, such as changing feature configurations, restricting stations from dialing outside the local area, reassigning existing telephones without wiring changes, and changing extension numbers as desired.

Examples of state-of-the-art hybrid systems include TIE/Communications' Data Star Hybrid (1986) and AT&T's Merlin Plus (1987) and Merlin II (1987) shown in Figure 5-7.

For example, an insurance company uses a hybrid key telephone system to connect directly to its central office. The system supports six central office lines and twelve stations with expansion of sixteen stations (6×16). When the company requires a larger system, it plans to continue using the key systems to connect to either a PBX or a Centrex system.

In addition to the present twelve telephone stations the system components include the key service unit (KSU) and the power supply. The KSU contains all the circuitry required to support central office lines, station sets, and intercom paths as well as provide for an external system alarm, common audible ringing, and station ringing. All switching and features are controlled by a stored system program. Each key telephone set contains a microprocessor and communicates with the main microprocessor in the KSU by two sets of twisted-pair wires. Cables also connect the KSU to the central office, to the power supply, and to each key station.

The FCC determines whether a system is classified as a key or a hybrid telephone system. Classification is based on the way the system accesses the

FIGURE 5-7 Examples of Current Hybrid Key Telephone Systems

(a) The Merlin Plus System

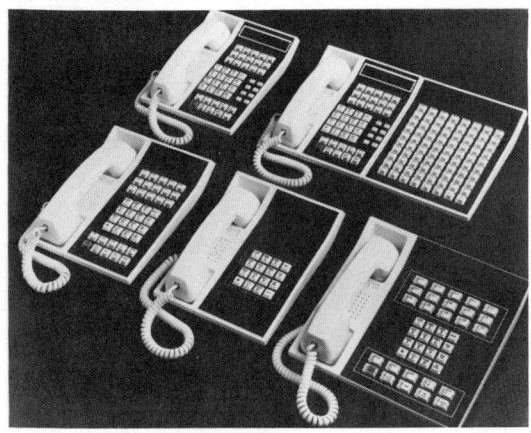

(b) Data Star Hybrid Family

(a) Courtesy of AT&T Archives. (b) Courtesy of TIE/Communications, Inc.

central office from a single-line telephone. For example, if a single-line telephone can access only one line, the system is classified as a key system. If a single-line telephone has access to a pooled group of lines, the system is classified as a hybrid. Some systems are dual-registered because their software options allow them to be configured for either pooled-line access or one-line only from a single-line telephone.

■ KTS Functions/Features

Key telephone systems are designed for small and medium-size companies with fewer than 100 telephone lines, although a few systems exceed this limitation. Systems range from a few telephone stations and central office lines to those with 128 stations and 36 lines. The majority of systems have twenty-four or fewer stations and eight or fewer central office lines.

Key systems can be stand-alone telephone systems or be used behind (as an adjunct to) PBX or Centrex systems. PBX and Centrex systems are discussed in the next sections. Standard features of KTSs include the following:

- *Call pickup*: The telephone has the ability to answer a line from more than one telephone.
- *Call hold*: The telephone has the ability to place a line on hold while being used for another call.
- *Supervisory signals*: The telephone contains lamps that indicate when a line is ringing, off hook, or on hold.

- *Common ring*: Only one alerting device rings to indicate incoming calls.

Other available features include paging, intercom, music on hold, and access to centralized dictation machines.

Electronic and hybrid key systems also offer enhanced features such as the capability to program features and restrictions on multibutton keysets.

- *Programmable buttons*: Programmable buttons (soft keys) on telephone keysets can be assigned added telephone lines and other features. For example, buttons may be used to provide one-button access to intercom numbers or to selected features, such as speed dialing numbers.
- *Changing calling restrictions*: Users can configure an entire system by restricting access to long-distance lines on some telephones and by expanding unlimited long-distance access on others.

In addition, hybrid key systems add PBX-like features, such as automatically routing calls over the least-cost facilities.

■ KTS Costs

KTS equipment costs less than PBX and Centrex systems (described in the next sections). In addition, the telephone company often charges less for KTS telephone lines than for PBX telephone lines.

■ The Key System Market

The key system market includes many vendors, all offering similar products. As a result, the selection of a key system is often based on price.

Most key telephone system manufacturers do not sell their products directly to end-users but market them through distributors, independent telephone companies, interconnect vendors, retailers, or Bell operating companies. Two large telephone system interconnect companies, Contel Executone and Tel Plus, order telephone systems from equipment manufacturers to be produced according to their specifications. They then sell them to customers under their own label. According to a 1987 study by Northern Business Information,[*] the ten leading key system manufacturers in 1987 were (ranked in order) AT&T, TIE/communications, Toshiba, Isoetec, NEC America, Vodavi (marketed by Premiere and Tel-Plus), Iwatsu, Inter-Tel, Matsushita (marketed by Panasonic and Contel Executive), and Trillium.

---

[*]Northern Business Information of New York City is an independently owned and operated research company. The company produces and publishes reports on the telecommunications equipment market, the telecommunications services market, and company strategies and the *Telecom* Bulletin, a monthly that lists research reports and services.

Private Branch Exchanges

A bank with forty branches serving twenty cities and towns has been experiencing the following telephone problems: Bank customers have been complaining about being placed on hold indefinitely. Employees are not using the least expensive route when placing their calls. Compared to last year, telephone charges have increased 150%, indicating that telephone abuse may be occurring. Unauthorized calls are also being made after normal working hours. Bank employees spend time dialing frequently placed interbranch calls. After an evaluation of the situation the bank installed a new telephone system, a private branch exchange, on its premises. The private branch exchange included features that addressed each of the bank's telephone problems and increased the overall efficiency of its telephone operations.

Most business calls are internal calls—employees talking with employees within the organization. Employees also access the public telephone network for outside calls, but not everyone does so at the same time. The average employee uses the telephone for less than five minutes during each hour.

Private Branch Exchange (PBX) systems were developed to handle in-house calls and to reduce the number of outside lines by having users sharing lines. A PBX is another type of business telephone system that provides private telephone service to an organization (internal calling) and also allows calls to be transmitted to and from both the public switched telephone network and private networks outside the organization. As the PBX systems became less dependent on the plug-and-cord concept, they were referred to as Private Automatic Branch Exchanges (PABXs). When computerized PBXs were introduced, they were called Computerized Branch Exchanges or CBXs. Since computerized systems make up nearly all the systems built today, the distinction between CBX and PABX has become less important, and the generalized term PABX or PBX is now common in referring to any private switching system. The term PBX is used in this book.

A PBX is actually a switch, a specialized minicomputer performing telephone switching within an organization's private network. It is located on a company's premises where all lines terminate. As discussed in Chapter 3, the primary purpose of a switch is to create and maintain a path for signals to travel between the calling party and the called party. The switch handles all internal calls, both calls originating and calls terminating within the organization.

The PBX switch also routes telephone calls that go outside the company, as shown in Figure 5-8. The telephone lines that connect a PBX switch with the telephone company's central office are called trunks. For example, an organization with 200 telephone extensions connects through a PBX that may have about sixteen trunks. When a call comes into the PBX, the PBX determines the extension of the called party, makes the correct connection, and rings the extension.

FIGURE 5-8 The PBX and the Central Office

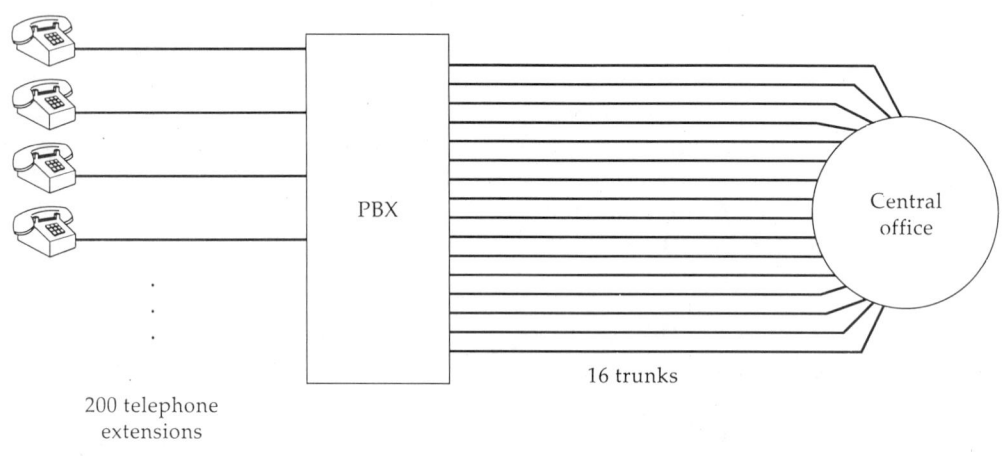

Evolution of PBX Technology

First-Generation PBXs. A model of the first commercial telephone switchboards, which was installed at New Haven, Connecticut, in 1878 is shown in Figure 5-9. These early PBXs were manual switching systems with operators, called PBX attendants, using cords and plugs to complete the calls. An operator manually performed the switching function by plugging the end of a cable into an access point for each destination on the central switchboard. The connection was maintained until the operator unplugged the cable.

Second-Generation PBXs. The second generation of PBXs performed the switching function mechanically rather than manually. Technology was based on how the telephone company's central offices operated. Switch systems evolved from using space-division switching to time-division switching. Computer-controlled programmable switches were introduced.

Third-Generation PBXs. In the mid-1970s, digital rather than analog switching techniques became more attractive for central office and PBX switches. These digital PBXs, often referred to as "third-generation," include the bulk of current PBX offerings. They are characterized by digital switching, control, and transmission and create a completely digital system with digital telephones converting voice conversation from analog to digital at the source. These systems are capable of integrating voice and data, full call processing, least-cost routing, and traffic measurement.

Digital PBXs require *conversion of analog signals to digital ones* before passing through the switch. The *control function* of the PBX switches also are

FIGURE 5-9 First-Generation PBX

Courtesy of AT&T Archives.

digital, evolving from the operator manually controlling the cords and plugs, to mechanical control, and then to computer control using stored programs.

The *transmission of signals* between user phones and the switches also changed from analog to digital. A codec is placed in each user's phone so that signals can be transmitted throughout the entire system in digital form. A *codec* (abbreviated from COder-DECoder) is a device that transforms signals from analog to digital at one end and from digital to analog at the other end.

Fourth-Generation PBXs. These PBXs, now being introduced, perform all the third-generation functions as well as integrate local area networks (to be discussed in Chapter 7) with PBX technologies. Figure 5-10 shows a diagram of a leading PBX, AT&T's System 75. The System 75 uses digital switching to integrate the processing of voice and data.

■ PBX Components and Operation

The four components of a PBX are systems control, switching matrix, trunks, and peripheral equipment. The basic operation of electronic PBXs is similar to that of the manual switchboards of the past. Operations once performed by the switchboard attendant are now performed electronically.

Systems Control. The *control processor* is a complete computer system with a full complement of memory, peripheral equipment for input/output and bulk storage, and systems software. The types of hardware and software used in control processors vary, but all perform the same basic functions: controlling, managing, and monitoring PBX operations.

FIGURE 5-10   An Example of a Present-Day PBX System

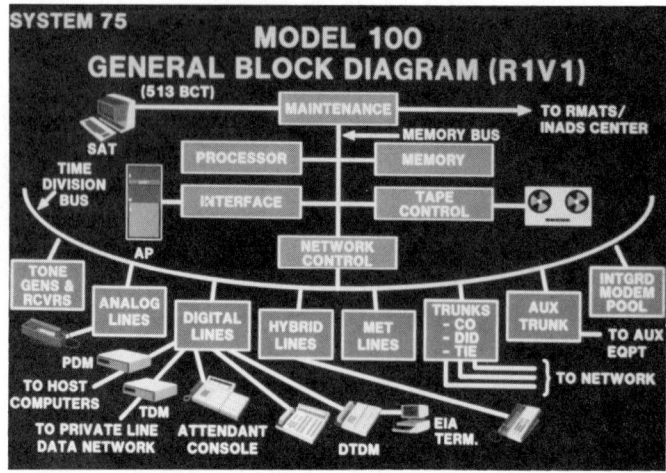

Courtesy of AT&T Archives.

The control processor provides the logic, memory, and switching circuitry for a system plus the port circuit packs that provide links to voice and data terminals and trunks. It also contains equipment that supplies power, power backup, ringing signal voltage, and software-type recording and playback capabilities. All of these elements along with the connecting paths are known collectively as the communications switch or just the *switch*. The switch is the heart of the system; it processes all the signals involved in completing voice and data calls.

Switching Matrix.   The basic function of the **switching matrix** is to switch telephone calls. The matrix creates and maintains a path for signals to travel between the calling party and the called party. The two types of switching used are space-division switching and time-division switching. *Space-division switching* requires a physically separate pathway for each call, as shown in Figure 5-11. *Time-division switching* shares a single high-speed pathway for all calls.

Trunks.   As discussed in the first part of this section on PBXs, trunks connect the PBX switch with the central office switch for outside calls. Trunks can be incoming, outgoing, or a combination of both. Many PBXs have special trunks to provide access to cheaper long-distance service, such as trunks for WATS lines, foreign exchange, and 800 numbers. A *foreign*

Private Branch Exchanges

FIGURE 5-11 **Space-Division Switching Matrix**

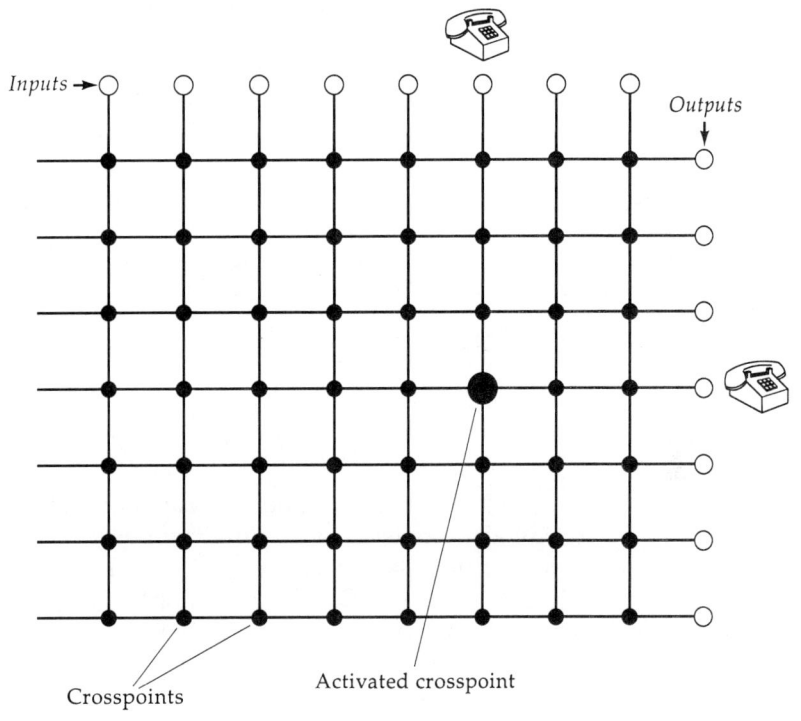

exchange trunk connects a PBX directly to a central office other than its local central office.

Trunks, called **tie trunks**, directly connect two PBX systems. Organizations that operate multiple PBXs can link all of their PBXs with tie trunks. **Direct inward dialing** (DID) trunks route incoming calls directly to the desired stations, bypassing the system's attendant. Figure 5-12 shows the relationships between a central office, a company's PBX system, a key system, and single-line telephones.

Most digital PBX systems are nonblocking. A **nonblocking PBX** means that the switch can handle simultaneous conversations among all users by having enough pathways to carry all the traffic. A **blocking PBX** limits the number of calls that can be made simultaneously. To determine the capacity of a blocking PBX, the question you should ask is, "How many of the lines can be engaged in calls at any point in time?" You should also know the difference between the number of calls and the number of active stations. When the call is internal, two company stations are active; when the call is to an outside party, only one company station is active.

FIGURE 5-12 **Relationship Between a Company's Switching Systems and a Central Office**

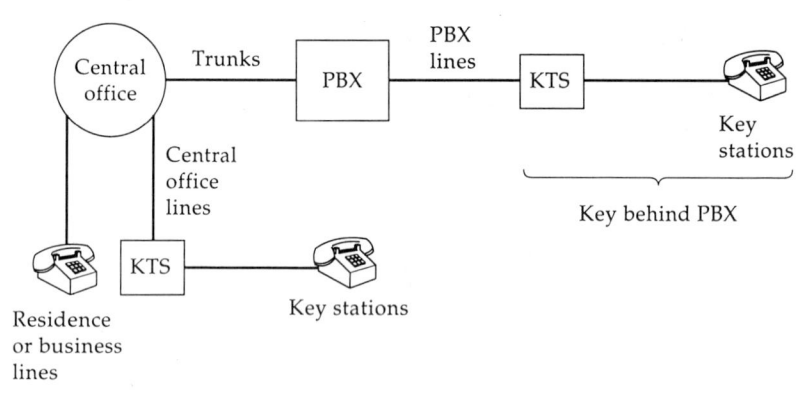

Voice PBXs are seldom nonblocking because rarely does a PBX installation use all of its telephones simultaneously. As a digital PBX increases its support of data calls between terminals and computers, the demand for more lines increases. Data conversations usually tie up switching pathways for much longer periods of time than voice communications, leaving fewer lines to be shared by occasional voice users.

Peripheral Equipment. Peripheral equipment includes all the devices that can be connected to the *system switch* to provide access to PBX services and features. Types of peripheral equipment are station terminals, data interface equipment, attendant consoles, and devices to enhance the capabilities of the system. Devices to enhance the system include speaker paging equipment, headsets, speakerphone, and message waiting.

Station Terminals. **Station terminals** may be (a) voice telephones or (b) data terminals (either stand-alone or integrated with the voice equipment).

The interface between the user and the system is the telephone set or voice terminal, such as the single-line telephone and the electronic key set. *Nonvoice terminals*, such as microcomputers and teletypewriters, can interface if compatible with the switch. The *single-line telephone* can access most of the system's features, ranging from the basic touch-tone telephone to telephones with speakerphone and speed dialing features.

Although most PBX systems support standard single-line telephones, the trend is toward *electronic key sets*. These key sets include multiline appearance, information displays, features that operate easily, and buttons that are programmable. They cost substantially more than single-line telephones and require their own control equipment. Most key sets are **proprietary key**

Private Branch Exchanges 143

sets, that is, they conform to individual vendor specifications for signaling, transmission, and control. Proprietary key telephones from one vendor may not work with another vendor's PBX.

Many key telephone systems, both electromechanical and electronic, can be used with a PBX, a setup referred to as a **key behind PBX**. But key and PBX compatibility depends on the particular systems being considered.

Data terminals are user/system interactive that combine visual display and portable keyboard with a variety of voice and data services alone or together. The terminal shown in Figure 5-13 has full voice and data communications. It combines the display and keyboard of a data terminal with the functions of a telephone instrument, referred to as an integrated voice/data terminal (IVDT). Some PBX systems offer a proprietary IVDT, while others support IVDTs manufactured by other vendors.

A data terminal that allows the PBX systems manager to manage the PBX is the **system access terminal** (SAT). The SAT attaches directly to the PBX control processor rather than to the system's switch. It allows the manager to administer the system's features and services by just pressing the appropriate button to make a change to its software and/or hardware, rearrange equipment (such as removing and adding voice terminals), and make wiring changes. The manager maintains the system by monitoring its performance, conducting tests to detect errors in the system, and then correcting them. With the SAT the PBX manager generates reports that determine the system's status and efficiency. Data from the Station Message Detail Recording feature, to be discussed in the section on PBX features, also assists

FIGURE 5-13   Integrated Voice/Data Terminal

Courtesy of AT&T Archives.

FIGURE 5-14   **Sample PBX Report**

```
                          SELECTION REPORT
                           COMPANY NAME

                   DURATION(  10:00 - 18:00:00)
   DATE   TIME   DURATION  EXT  ACC  DIALED DIGITS       TYP ACCOUNT CODE    COST $
   ----   ----   --------  ---  ---  -------------       --- ------------    ------
   03/23  10:42AM  10:00  5300   64                      WST                   1.79
   03/23  11:01AM  12:00  3011    4  663-2828            FX  41363             5.01
   03/23  11:15AM  10:00  1122    9  1-315-681-0846      IST 335678            0.93
   03/23  11:29AM  11:00  2400    9  9872011222333413129312459
                                                         OCC 95643             3.74
   03/23  11:35AM  22:00  1011    9  1-213-324-5012      OST 12345             9.76
   03/23  00:05AM  10:00  4622    9  1-419-643-7474      OST 54321             1.49
   03/23  06:05PM  11:00  4500    9  1-818-643-7474      OST 34671             3.02
   03/23  01:16PM  30:00  4355    9  1-206-999-5478      OST 54321            13.20
   03/23  01:16PM  30:00  2388    9  1-206-888-4587      OST 88644            13.20
   03/23  02:35PM  15:00  1122    9  987101127856561819888 3200
                                                         OST                   4.60
   03/23  02:53PM  12:00  4155    6  1-206-324-5151      WST                   2.86
   03/23  03:02PM  35:00  2388    8                      ---                   6.30
   03/23  03:22PM  25:00  2400    9  987201126345761315365 7219
                                                         OCC                   1.72

       TOTALS            3:53:00                                              67.62

       TOTAL CALLS 13
                                      TOTAL TIME
                                      SPENT ON              TOTAL COST FOR
                                      13 CALLS              13 CALLS
```

Copyright, AT&T, reprinted by permission.

in keeping track of the PBX's usage and costs. Figure 5-14 shows a sample report.

Data Interface Equipment.   PBX systems can support data terminal equipment by using an *EIA RS-232-C interface*. (For more information about EIA RS-232-C, refer to Chapter 6, particularly Figure 6-7.) The RS-232-C interface consists of a data line circuit packet that can connect up to a certain number of compatible terminal equipment. One arrangement for connecting a PC to a company's PBX system is shown in Figure 5-15.

Attendant Consoles.   Today's PBX systems may require using one or more **attendant consoles**, as shown in Figure 5-10 though some systems can operate without any. With the attendant console the operator can monitor and supervise the general operation of the system.

■ **PBX Features**

PBXs that operate by automatic switching and can store computer programs perform many functions that previously required operator intervention. Anything that goes beyond the basic function of making or receiving a telephone call is considered to be a "feature." PBX manufacturers and dealers offer "feature packages" designed to meet the needs of the different

FIGURE 5-15 **PBX Interfacing with Terminal Equipment**

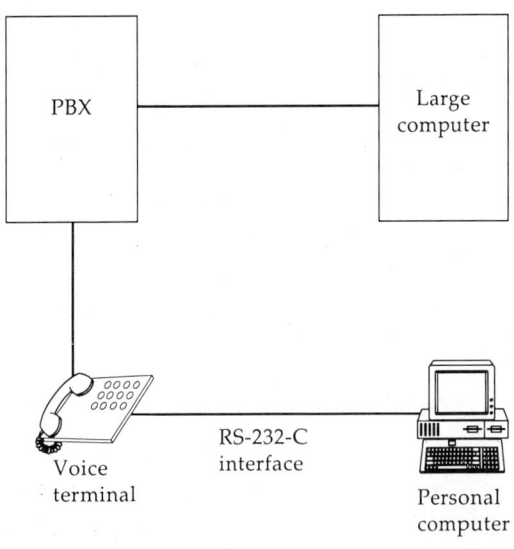

types of organizations. "University packages," "restaurant packages," and "banking packages" are available to name a few. Feature packages are usually computer software programs to load into the PBX system. Features can also be purchased separately, such as automatic call distribution (ACD) for handling a large number of calls.

Standard features come with the system, although what is standard varies among vendors. *Optional features* require additional equipment and/or software. *Custom features*, those designed for a particular system, must be programmed by using the system access terminal. PBX features can be grouped according to user—station, attendant console, system, and application.

PBX Station Features. PBX features available to someone at a telephone or console are called *station* or *user features*. For example, station users can now set up their own conference calls and redial automatically. Common station features are described in Figure 5-16. Features are assigned to a particular telephone station according to its **class of service**. Class of service defines whether or not a station user has access to certain features, such as speed dialing or automatic callback. For example, the "call restriction feature" that is assigned to a very low class of service may permit only internal calls. A *night class of service* automatically restricts service after normal working hours, which prevents calls being made on the system beyond working hours by unauthorized parties.

FIGURE 5-16 **Common Station Features of PBX Systems**

Add-On Conference: Allows a station user to hold any outgoing, internal, or incoming call; dial another person; and add the original call to the connection for a three-way conversation.

Automatic Callback: When the number you dial is busy, the call is automatically completed as soon as both lines are free.

Call Forwarding: Allows a station user to automatically transfer calls to an alternate station within or outside the system. Can be set to forward all of your incoming calls, only those occurring when the line is busy, or only incoming calls after programmed number of rings.

Call Park: Allows a user to place a call on hold and then pick it up at any telephone station.

Call Pickup: Allows a person without leaving his or her station (desk) to answer a call ringing at another station by dialing a simple code.

Call Waiting: A busy telephone line can receive an audible signal indicating that an additional call is waiting. The second call can then be answered while the first call is placed on hold.

Camp-On: Allows an attendant console operator or station user to queue an incoming call to a busy station. When the station becomes idle, the call is automatically completed.

Consultation Hold: Allows a telephone user to hold an established call, dial another telephone for a private conversation, and return to the original calling party.

Direct Outward Dialing: Allows a station user to place an outgoing call just by picking up the telephone and dialing the desired number. No attendant is necessary.

Distinctive Ringing: Unique ringing patterns tell you the type of call you are receiving. One ring indicates an inside call. Two rings indicate a call from outside the system.

Executive Override: Allows a station to interrupt a busy line or preempt a long-distance trunk if the station's class of service is higher than the class of the user.

Hands-Free Answer: Allows user to answer an internal call and talk without lifting the handset.

Last Number Dialed (LND): Allows the last outside number dialed to be redialed automatically when the user activates the LND feature.

Private Line: Allows a given number of lines in the system to be programmed as private outside lines. No other station can use them, and no line status appears on any other station.

Speed Calling (Speed Dialing): Frequently called numbers can be reached by dialing one- or two-digit codes or by simply pushing a button of an electronic feature telephone.

Station Hunting: Allows an incoming call directed to a busy telephone line to automatically ring an alternative telephone line for completion.

PBX Attendant Console Features. The attendant console was discussed in the section on peripheral equipment. The attendant console operator answers, extends, and/or transfers calls to users within the organization as well as controls some of the system's functions. Many of the same features found on station equipment are also included on attendant consoles, such as call-waiting, executive override, camp-on, intercom, and paging.

The attendant console also includes features designed to make the console operator's tasks easier and more efficient, such as indicators to show when outside or inside trunks are busy, "automatic recall to the attendant," and "station number and class of service displayed on the console." The attendant console also controls some of the functions of the system, such as limiting a station terminal only to making internal calls.

PBX System Features. System features deal with the entire PBX system for the purpose of making it operate efficiently. Examples of *system features* are the following.

Station Message Detail Recording (SMDR). This feature offers a printout of all call traffic. Evaluation of the printout allows management to determine such items as originating station of all calls; time, date, and duration of each call; the type of call (for example, long-distance, WATS, foreign exchange, or tie line); the number dialed; and the cost of the call. With this information, costs can be allocated, calling patterns analyzed, and unnecessary calls identified.

Call Restriction. The **call restriction** feature allows management to control telephone costs by restricting stations from dialing outside their local area on central office lines. Managers can program stations individually or collectively. A station can be restricted from dialing outside the local area on central office lines or dialing only certain extensions in the local area, or not at all. If desired, specific central office lines, such as WATS lines, may be programmed to override the station's toll restriction and allow long-distance dialing. The system also may be programmed to recognize a PBX trunk access code, allowing proper toll restriction operation in systems installed behind PBXs, such as key sets.

Music on Hold. This feature provides music or other audible indication to a party on hold waiting in a queue. (A queue is an ordered sequence of calls waiting to be processed.) The music lets the waiting caller know that the connection is still in effect.

Night Answer. When the operator goes off duty, this feature allows the attendant console operator to direct all calls to a night console or to other answering stations.

Automatic Routing of Calls (ARS). This feature, also called Least-Cost Routing (LCR), reduces long-distance charges by analyzing the dialed numbers and automatically selecting from a given group of carriers and services the lowest outgoing route available, as shown in Figure 5-17. Route selection takes into account time of day and distance rates. This feature, which is software controlled, must be updated as tariffs and prices change.

Remote Location Access. This feature permits callers from the public switched telephone network to access the system and then use its features and services. For example, a salesperson can use the organization's facilities to call potential customers all over the country from the convenience of his or her home.

Automatic Call Distribution (ACD). Nothing is more frustrating to a caller than to be placed on hold indefinitely or to be transferred needlessly by an overburdened phone system. **Automatic call distribution** (ACD) provides the means for efficiently handling a large number of calls to a specific department, such as sales or customer service. ACD, a computerized switching system, automatically distributes incoming calls in sequence to the next available "operator," referred to as an "agent."

ACDs are of two types: stand-alone ACD systems and PBX-integrated ACDs. *Stand-alone ACDs* are dedicated to the incoming call-handling function and are preferred for more complex ACD applications. These systems usually include advanced features, generate more comprehensive reports, and are more costly. *PBX-integrated ACDs* consist of special software added to the basic operating software of a PBX. These systems are more suitable for smaller, simpler applications. Most PBX vendors offer the ACD feature as an option.

An ACD system constantly monitors each line or trunk for indications of an incoming call. When a call is detected, the system directs it to a group of agents, called a *split*, for handling. The system then searches for the available agent who has been waiting the longest and assigns that agent the

FIGURE 5-17 **Example of ARS Routing Pattern from Providence to New York City**

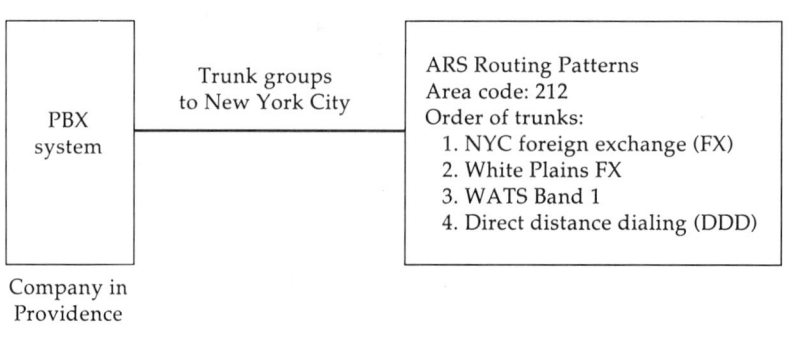

call. When all agents are busy, the call enters the queue; if it remains for a preset time without being answered, it is connected to one or two announcements. Such announcements assure callers that they have reached the correct number and that their calls are not being ignored. The queue is served sequentially, providing first-in, first-out call answering.

When an agent becomes available, the ACD provides the agent with a trunk-group identification and then connects the call to the agent's position for servicing. During the time the agent and customer are connected, the system monitors both the agent position and the trunk to detect any changes in status. When the agent releases the call, the system removes the connection through the switch, classifies the line as inactive, and makes that agent available for subsequent calls. A diagram of a typical ACD set up for a travel agency is shown in Figure 5-18.

An ACD system also collects and stores operational data, compiles and reports operating status and statistics, and prepares summary reports for computer screen display or printing. ACD can generate reports automatically on a user-defined schedule or on demand. For example, the "Agent

FIGURE 5-18 Typical ACD Arrangement

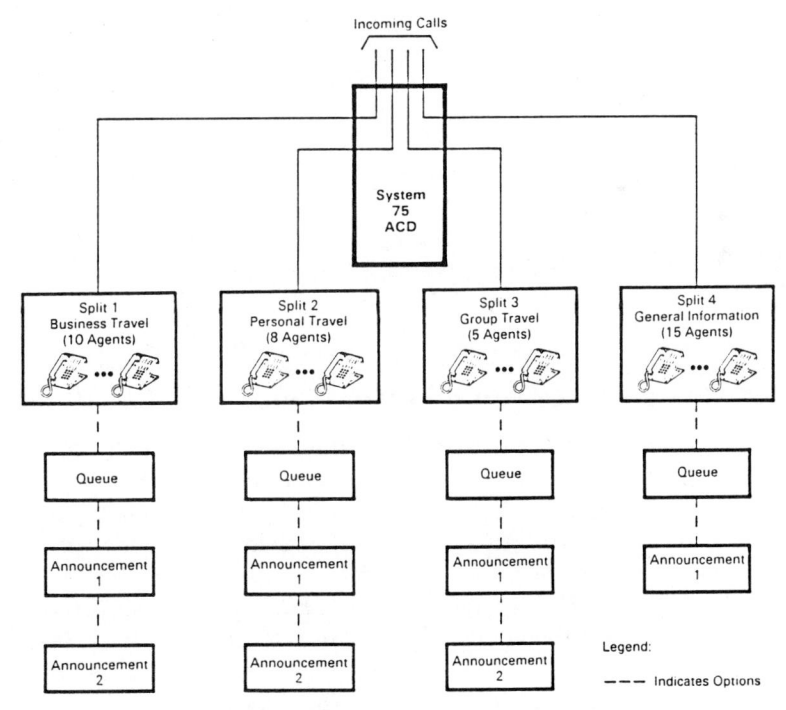

Copyright, 1987, AT&T, reprinted by permission.

Performance Report" can be displayed on the supervisor's computer screen and updated as changes occur. This report tabulates the calls handled, transferred, and originated by each agent plus the percentage of time spent in talking, wrapping up, or awaiting a call.

Applications suited for an ACD system require a heavy volume of incoming calls, usually handled by a particular group of employees. Most callers are interested in accessing a service rather than a particular individual. For example, travel agents, customer service departments, mail-order stores, and airline reservationists use ACD to answer incoming calls and handle customer requests and/or orders.

PBX Application Features. Application features, such as voice processing, energy/property management, message center service, and directory, can enhance PBX systems. These add-ons can be supported by a separate minicomputer or integrated into the system by adding special software to the PBX's operating software. (Similar enhancements are also available for key systems and Centrex services.)

Voice processing offers such features as telephone answering, voice mail, caller routing, and voice bulletin boards. (In Chapter 9, these features are discussed more fully.)

Energy/property management provides building management services, such as controlling employees entering and exiting, monitoring and controlling energy usage, and sounding alarms for smoke, fire, and other hazardous conditions.

Message center service (MCS) is staffed by agents who answer calls and take messages for system users. Users then call the MCS to retrieve their messages.

Directory is a feature that allows terminal users to key in a name and retrieve an extension number from the system's directory. The directory contains an alphanumeric listing of all user names and extension numbers.

■ PBX Architecture—Centralized or Distributed

PBX systems differ in their architectural structure of the location and the interconnection options among the control processor, the switch, and the access interface. If these elements are located in one place, the system is referred to as *centralized* and consisting of a central node (because there is only one control computer authority).

In contrast, a *distributed system*, as shown in Figure 5-19, consists of several nodes, each of which is capable of independent operation. Each node has its own control processor, switch, and set of access interfaces with its own group of stations. The nodes are linked together so that they appear to be a single, larger system. If a link fails, users on that system still receive PBX service, but they do not have direct access to users on other nodes.

FIGURE 5-19 Distributed PBX Systems

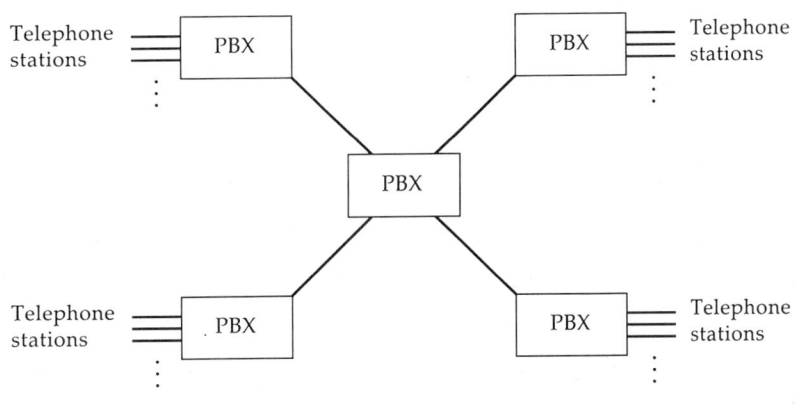

■ The PBX Market

PBX systems are integrating a variety of diverse office systems, such as voice processing and energy/property management, making them even more attractive to business. Competition is fierce among PBX vendors as well as between PBX and the local telephone companies that sell enhanced Centrex services. Northern Business Information reports that the three major PBX vendors in 1988 were AT&T, NTI, and IBM/Rolm, followed by Mitel, NEC America, Fujitsu, GTE, and Siemens.

A whole new "after market" has emerged for PBXs that have completed their first tour of duty, AT&T being the major reseller. Estimations are that this market will be more than $1 billion by 1995.[1]

Centrex Services

A small midwestern university decided to upgrade its key telephone system and selected Centrex services rather than a PBX system. Not only did Centrex provide PBX-like features, but it required no major investment in equipment, since the switch is located at the telephone company's central office and not at the university.

Centrex (CENTRal EXchange) **service** is a central office–based business telephone system. Switching equipment is usually located at one of the telephone company's central offices, although it can be located on the customer's premises. The central office controls the switching functions for the customer's telephone system, the customer's telephone lines connecting directly to the central office, as shown in Figure 5-20. The system offers PBX-type features plus additional features that give the telephone stations the

FIGURE 5-20 Centrex Connections

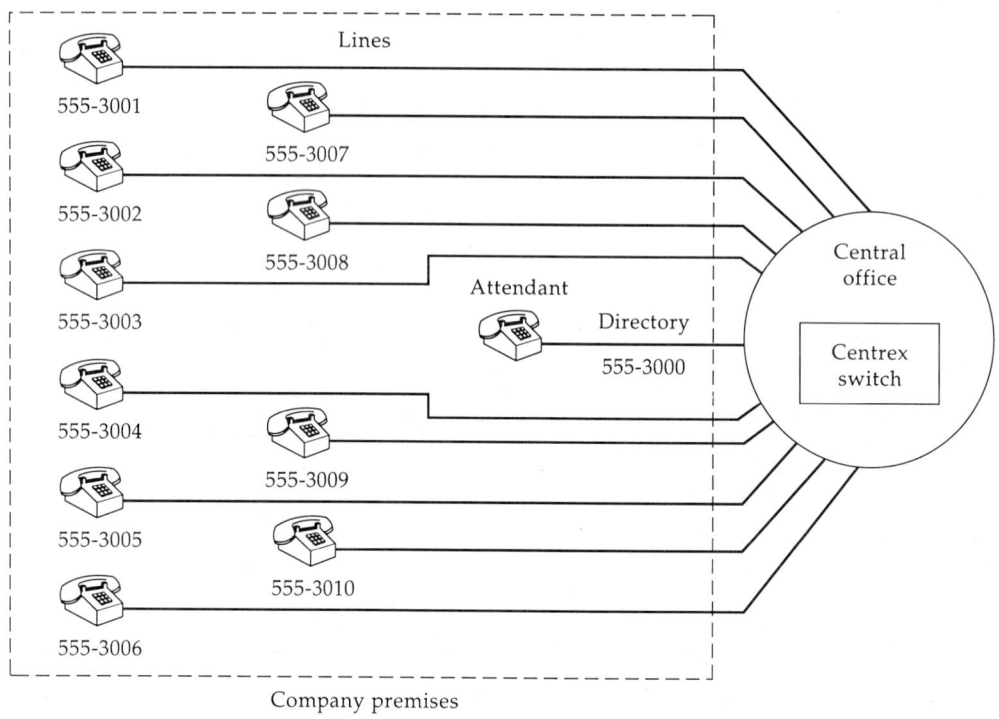

characteristics of both an individual line and a PBX line. For example, a telephone attendant on the company's premises can provide directory information to both company employees and outside callers. To reach the company attendant in Figure 5-20, an employee dials the extension 3000.

Centrex eliminates the need for a customer to lease or buy switching equipment. Such a consideration is especially important for customers that cannot afford a system or feature capabilities that they may not use initially but may need at a later time.

A customer also does not need to worry about outgrowing Centrex's capacity and system and feature capabilities. Centrex offers a customer the potential of virtually an unlimited number of stations and is continually updating system and feature capabilities without cost to the customer.

The telephone company's central office maintains and administers Centrex for its customers. For example, a central office staff inspects and maintains the equipment 24 hours a day and provides uninterrupted backup power with engine-powered generators. Customers may lose their building power, such as lighting and air conditioning, but Centrex telephone lines will still be operating.

■ Evolution of Centrex Services Technology

The Bell System introduced Centrex in the 1960s as the prime switching service for medium- and large-size users. Through the 1960s and the early 1970s, Centrex achieved a major portion of this market. In the late 1970s, Centrex began lagging behind in technology advancement, while PBX systems began using computer-based technology. The final abandonment of Centrex was expected to occur with the Bell divestiture in 1984; instead, Centrex has become a proven money maker for the regional Bell operating companies (RBOCs), appealing to all types and sizes of users. The RBOCs are striving to retain a majority of the companies that already use Centrex as well as to attract new customers.

■ Centrex Services Operation

Central offices use chiefly AT&T's analog 1AESS switch or digital 5ESS switch and Northern Telecom's DMS 100 switching system. These analog and digital switches provide computer-controlled, time-division switching. The majority of large metropolitan-area businesses are presently being served by AT&T's 1AESS analog switch. This equipment provides customers with such capabilities as voice mail, electronic mail, message center, modem pooling, and direct interface with digital carrier systems.

A Centrex system requires that each customer have on its premises station equipment, such as electronic or hybrid key systems. On-premise attendants are required only if calls are to be screened. For efficient operation, equipment should be compatible with the Centrex system. See Figure 5-21.

Centrex allows callers to dial extensions directly from outside the company (direct inward dialing) and employees to dial outside numbers directly from the extensions (**direct outward dialing**). DID is equivalent to an individual line service while DOD differs from an individual line service only by requiring the dialing of an outgoing access code, usually "9." Calls between stations in a Centrex system require dialing 4 or 5 digits of the seven digits required for local calls. More than one company can be served from the same central office. For example, the 536 exchange in the 617 area could have the following three Centrex customers: Company A uses 536-2100; Company B, 536-3200; and Company C, 536-6000. Within these three number groups, several hundred telephone numbers associated with each Centrex customer are listed. For example, Company A lists 536-2100, 536-2101, 536-2102, 536-2103, and so on.

FIGURE 5-21   Connecting a Key System to a Centrex System

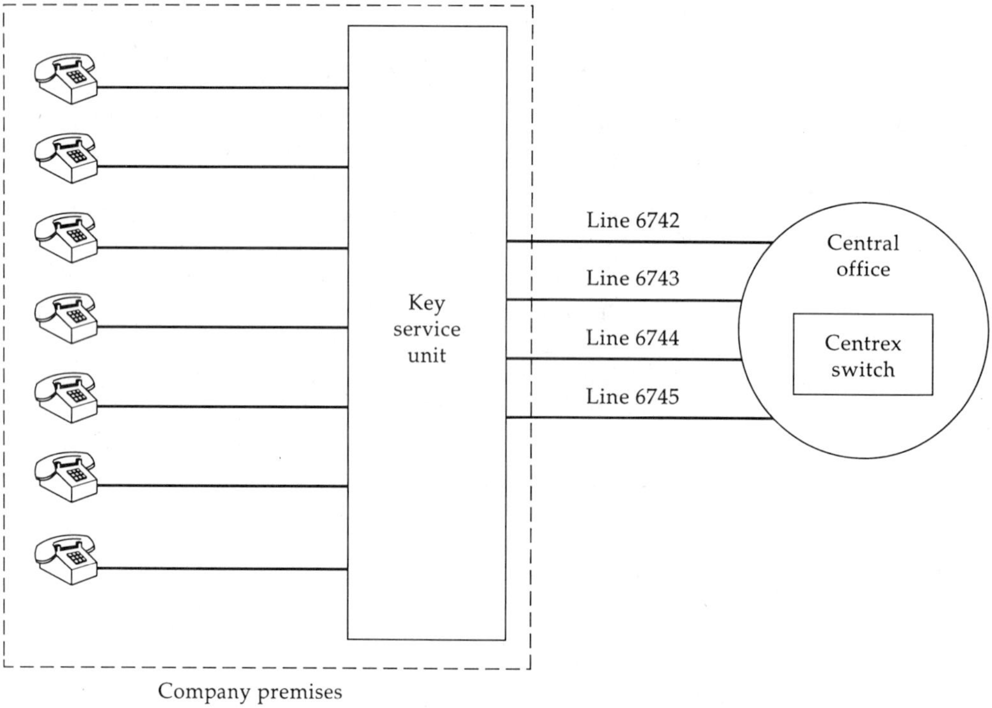

```
Line 6742
Line 6743
Line 6744
Line 6745
```

Key service unit

Central office

Centrex switch

Company premises

■ Centrex Services Features

As was previously mentioned, Centrex offers features similar to those of a PBX including the ones described in Figure 5-16. Centrex uses a building block approach to features: The customer customizes the system by choosing the features desired. At any time the customer can add features to or delete features from the entire system or individual telephones.

Centrex allows customers to reduce service costs by doing their own station moves and feature changes from a computer system on their own premises. They can also use their own microcomputer to download this information to a telephone company's computer system that then sends it during off-peak hours to the central office switch. For example, by using an on-site computer system a station move can be administered in 15–20 minutes.

Hardware/software upgrades to the central office's switch provide Centrex enhancements, such as integrated voice/data, voice mail, electronic mail, and modem pooling. The RBOC's newest Centrex services offer customers services that include both expanded voice and data capabilities, facility management, and cost management. Some RBOCs offer central office local networks that connect a company's computer to its switch. Most RBOCs offer real-time station message detail recording (SMDR) that provide customers with records of calling activity.

■ Centrex Services Rates

Each RBOC has its own rate structure and payment options. Centrex rates are based on the following:

- End-user line size
- The customer's distance from the central office
- The length of the service contract
- Optional Centrex services selected

Centrex customers are often locked into a three-, five-, or seven-year contract. In states where Centrex is regulated, the telephone company may offer rate stability plans that set Centrex charges for a period of years. Although the offer guarantees that rates will not be raised by the RBOC, they can still be increased by the state commission. A RBOC can also file a tariff for an individual case to allow the RBOC to design rates for a specific system arrangement, which gives the RBOC a competitive edge over PBX vendors. In states where Centrex is deregulated or detariffed, Centrex users are offered reduced rates to compete with PBX vendors.

■ Centrex Services Market

Centrex services are offered by the seven RBOC's Bell operating companies under various names, such as Centraflex, Centron, Intellipath, Premiere, Nova Centrex, Business Pak, and Essx. Centrex service cannot be owned by the customer, although some customers would like such control. Centrex is not available in all areas of the United States. Where it is available, feature capabilities depend on the type of switching equipment located at each central office and its associated software. However, the most technologically advanced central office switches provide Centrex features that are fully competitive with the latest PBX equipment.

Comparison of PBX Systems and Centrex Services

As was mentioned at the beginning of this chapter, the Carterfone Decision makes it possible for end users to choose terminal equipment as well as service and equipment suppliers of their choice. One of the biggest decisions an organization makes is choosing between Centrex service or a PBX for handling its communications requirements. Should the organization own or lease a telephone switch located on its premises, or should the organization lease the use of a switch located on a telephone company's premises? Large organizations with a wide range of communications requirements often develop a plan that takes advantage of both PBXs and Centrex.

Before making a decision, a company should compare PBX systems and Centrex services. Although each alternative has advantages and disadvantages, the decision should be based on the organization's individual requirements. Figure 5-22 presents a comparison of the pros and cons of PBX systems and Centrex services.

FIGURE 5-22 **Summary: A Comparison of PBX Systems and Centrex Services**

PBX	Centrex Service
A capital investment for equipment is required, unless leased.	No capital investment for equipment is required.
PBX switch is owned by the customer.	Centrex service cannot be owned by the customer.
PBX switch can become obsolete.	Telephone company is continually updating the switch.
Switch is housed on customer premises.	Switch is housed at the local central office.
Customer must provide floor space, environmental conditions, and insurance to protect against loss.	Central office is responsible for providing floor space, environmental conditions, and insurance to protect against loss.
Electrical failure shuts down the switch except for trunk lines.	Uninterrupted electrical backup power is supplied by reserve electrical power.
Customer is responsible for administration and maintenance of switch.	Central office is responsible for administration and maintenance of switch.
Features fully competitive with Centrex services.	Features fully competitive with PBX system.
Some systems have traffic blocking.	Nonblocking traffic is virtually provided.
PBX usually requires an attendant to process calls.	Centrex service does not require an attendant unless calls must be screened.
PBX customer is responsible for obtaining software updates.	Central office automatically updates system software.
An additional capital investment may be required for upgrades.	No capital investment is required for upgrades.
Many vendors offer PBX systems at a wide range of prices.	Centrex service offered only by regional Bell operating companies.
Mileage charges apply only to trunks.	Mileage charges apply to every telephone line.

Selecting a Business Telephone System

Is the company planning to purchase or lease a business telephone system from scratch? Or is the company planning to replace or upgrade its present system?

For example, if the company's present key system has the basic capacity, it may be cheaper to upgrade then to replace the system. On the other hand, if the company decides to change its key system, the company may select one of the following alternatives:

- Replace its key system with a larger key system.
- Trade its key system for a PBX or Centrex service.
- Keep its key system to use behind (adjunct to) a PBX or Centrex service.

Before the company can make any decision, such as whether to purchase a new business telephone system or upgrade the old one, the company must determine its user needs as well as project its needs five years hence. The system must have growth capacity. After the details of the proposed telephone system are specified, vendors' offerings can be evaluated. Then the company selects the vendor that is to provide the system.

The selection of a business telephone system requires a planned approach. The suggested plan consists of three phases: (1) analyze the current telephone system, (2) specify the new telephone system, and (3) select the new telephone system.

■ Phase 1: Analyze the Current Telephone System

Obtain the following information:

- A description of the present telephone system, how it operates, who uses it, and how they use it. Figure 5-23 suggests questions that should be asked of users.

FIGURE 5-23 Suggested Questions for Determining an Employee's Use of the Telephone

1. How often do you use your telephone on a typical day?
2. Is telephone contact with people outside your office an essential part of your job?
3. Is telephone contact with people within your office an essential part of your job?
4. How many times per week do you make long-distance telephone calls?
5. How many calls do you usually receive each day from outside the company?
6. How many calls do you usually receive each from within the company?
7. When receiving calls, do callers complain about getting a busy signal?
8. When placing a call, does it take a long time to receive a dial tone?
9. How would you rate your telephone service?

- A description of the telephone system features that are desired and that will improve telephone efficiency.
- A projection of the company's anticipated voice communications needs for the next five years based on projected company growth.
- A projection of the company's current and future data communication needs. For example, is the business telephone system to accommodate data communications?

Sources of data about the present telephone system and its usage include individual users, department managers, switchboard attendants, and the telephone company.

- Collect data from individual users by administering questionnaires about current internal and external telephone use, type of equipment, features being used, and features desired.
- Conduct interviews with department managers to review questionnaire results and obtain suggestions for improving the present telephone system.
- Conduct interviews with switchboard attendants to determine operating patterns, functions performed, and suggestions for improving the present telephone system. Operators can be observed or asked to keep a record of their activities.
- Obtain information from the local telephone company about how often and when trunks are used.

■ Phase 2: Specify the Requirements of the New Telephone System

On the basis of the information collected in Phase 1, prepare the specifications for the new telephone system.

- Describe the present telephone system configuration and operation.
- Identify the operating features that are of value to users' operation and improved efficiency for conducting business.
- Develop a proposed telephone system configuration and operation. What type of business telephone system do you need? Key? PBX? Centrex? Describe the type and quantity of central trunks, extension lines, station equipment, and possible attendant position equipment that will be needed.

■ Phase 3: Select the New Telephone System

Prepare the RFP. Prepare a formal Request for Proposal (RFP) to be submitted to vendors. The proposal specifies the new telephone system and the information that vendors must present. Also specify the physical location and features of the present system and the major features required of the new system. Request that the vendors submit an installation schedule and cost information (basic cost information, optional features costs, installation costs, and maintenance charges). Ask for copies of instructional manuals for users of the system. Evaluate the adequacy of this material for use in initial and ongoing training of system users.

Select Vendors and Suppliers. Select both potential vendors and suppliers at this time to ensure and coordinate quality service. What is the vendor's nearest location? Financial stability? Reputation for maintenance service? Ask suppliers the same questions. Talk with users of the proposed system to determine how the system, the vendor, and the suppliers have carried out their responsibilities.

Evaluate the RFP. As proposals are received from vendors, evaluate each one according to prices, support, and options offered. A rating scale based on the requirements of the RFP may be devised. Include the following questions in the evaluation:

- *System expandability*: To what extent can the system be expanded beyond the company's initial requirements? Does the system have sufficient capacity to meet the company's future expansion needs?
- *System operation*: Is the system easy to operate? Does it offer operating flexibility, such as programmable buttons?
- *System features*: Although vendors' products may have similar or identical features, they are likely to perform differently. What does each feature do? Is it easy to use?
- *Customer service and support*: Is the vendor reputable? Does the vendor have a strong record for customer support?
- *Present business telephone system*: Can the company's present telephones be used with the new system? If so, when upgrading to the new system, telephone replacement costs will be decreased.

Negotiate Contracts. After you have selected the vendor, negotiate the contract. Do not sign standard contracts. Instead design the contract to meet the company's requirements of installation, testing, warranty, and service needs. Ask your company's legal department or your lawyer to review the contract.

Prepare for the System Changeover. Prepare a time schedule for changing from the old to the new system. Appoint an employee to direct the changeover.

Training and Follow-up. Develop a plan for training employees and evaluating their use and knowledge of the new telephone system. The plan should include periodic follow-up evaluation with more training as needed.

Failure to develop and implement such a plan results in unsatisfactory use of the system. Employees often view change within an organization with cautiousness. Management must help employees to realize the benefits that the change in the communications systems will provide.

Summary

The birth of the interconnect industry was marked by the landmark Carterfone Decision. With so many new telecommunications products and services now coming to the market, users discover that they are ill-prepared to make intelligent, informed decisions about which products and services to select. Shopping for a business telephone system, whether it is a key system, a PBX, or Centrex services, involves analyzing present telephone needs, determining the features and functions the company currently needs, projecting needs for the next three to five years, and evaluating vendors' products. Each type of system offers a variety of enhancements that contribute to performing telephone operations efficiently.

■ *Key Terms*

Attendant console
Automatic call distribution
Blocking PBX
Call restriction
Carterfone Decision
Centrex service
Class of service
Direct inward dialing
Direct outward dialing
Electronic key telephone system
Hybrid key telephone system
1A2 KTS
Interconnect industry
Key behind PBX
Key telephone system
Nonblocking PBX
Private Branch Exchange
Proprietary key sets
Station terminals
Switching matrix
System access terminal
Tie trunk

■ *Self-Quiz*

Indicate whether the statement is true or false.

1. The standard key system in the electromechanical industry is the 1A2KTS.   T/F
2. A nonblocking PBX means that the switch can handle simultaneous conversations among users.   T/F
3. Whether or not a station user has access to certain features is determined by the user's class of service.   T/F
4. The standard features of a PBX are those that require additional equipment and/or software.   T/F
5. Switching equipment of Centrex services is typically located on the users' premises.   T/F

6. Centrex limits its customers to a specific number of stations based on the size of the switch. T/F

Complete each of the following statements.

1. The landmark decision that marked the birth of the interconnect industry was the _____ .
2. A 9 × 27 key system has the capacity of _____ .
3. The telephone lines that connect a PBX switch to the telephone company's central office are called _____ .
4. A PBX can be connected directly to a central office other than its own local central office by a(an) _____ .
5. Trunks that connect two PBX systems are called _____ .
6. PBX systems can support data terminal equipment by using a(an) _____ .

Match Column A with Column B
Which feature in Column A would you select to solve each problem in Column B?

Column A
(a) Automatic callback
(b) Call forwarding
(c) Call park
(d) Call waiting
(e) Consultation hold
(f) Direct inward dialing
(g) Private lines
(h) Speed dialing
(i) Station hunting

Column B
___ 1. You must dial lengthy codes to access major customers.
___ 2. You have calls to make but do not want to miss an important call.
___ 3. The number you dial is busy.
___ 4. Your main client has been grumbling about how difficult it is to reach you.
___ 5. You need to provide the caller with information stored in files in another office.
___ 6. Customers calling the order department often get a busy signal, while others must wait seemingly forever.
___ 7. You will be working in another office but do not want to miss any of your calls.
___ 8. While talking with one person, you need to dial some others for information and then return to the first person.
___ 9. An important project requires that you have an exclusive line.

Review Questions

1. (a) How has the Carterfone Decision affected the telephone industry?
   (b) What is the interconnect industry?
2. What are the characteristics of each type of key telephone system?
3. Explain the meaning of "12 × 36 KTS."

4. What are the major differences between a key telephone system, a PBX, and a Centrex service?
5. Under what circumstances might a key telephone system be combined with a PBX?
6. Why might a customer prefer Centrex service to PBX or vice versa?
7. What key, PBX, or Centrex feature(s) would you select to solve each of the following problems?
   (a) You call the company's five branch offices located in nearby cities two or three times a day.
   (b) You attend many meetings, but you do not want to miss important calls.
   (c) You frequently need the participation of two or three people in a single telephone conversation.
   (d) You need to know who is making long-distance calls in your company, the length of each call, and its cost.
   (e) You are constantly redialing to get through to businesses with busy numbers.
8. What information can help you in selecting a business telephone vendor?
9. What questions do you need answered when you are evaluating a vendor's business telephone system?
10. (a) How does automatic call distribution (ACD) operate?
    (b) Under what circumstances should a company consider using ACD?

■ *Activities/Projects*

1. Visit an office that uses a key, PBX, or Centrex system. Obtain information about how the system operates, its capacity (number of stations and lines), the features it offers, why the company selected the system, and its weaknesses and strengths. Discuss your findings.
2. With a small group, discuss the following: Should a company own or lease a telephone switch located on its premises, or should a company lease the use of a switch located on a telephone company's premises?
3. Study the current telephone system at a school or office of your choice. What features would you suggest for this system? Why? For suggestions, refer to Figure 5-23 and the section on "Phase 1: Analyze the current telephone system."
4. Prepare a formal Request for Proposal for a business telephone system to be used in an organization of your choice.

■ *Case:* Should a Company Replace Its Key System?

A Georgia public relations company is considering replacing its present key telephone system with another one. A study of existing telephone conditions reveals the following problems: No control exists over who places long-distance calls; the secretaries have difficulty locating the person being called; after-hour telephone service is limited to an answering service; a secretary has no way of being reminded to attend to a customer on hold; conference capability needs improvement; holding parties may disconnect; the intercom interrupts users when they are using the telephone; distribution of incoming calls is often delayed; users cannot communicate when using the telephone, which adds to cost of long-distance calls as well as results in missing important calls; and no way exists of obtaining information about outgoing calls such as calling costs.

The present electronic key system consists of a key service unit, a power supply, thirty electronic key stations, eight outside lines, and one station intercom. The proposed electronic key system consists of a key service unit, a power supply, thirty electronic key stations, eight outside lines, three station intercoms, one call processor, one all-call page, and one speakerphone. The proposed system offers features that would address the company's telephone problems, such as those listed in Figure 5-23.

Cost of the present telephone system: After leasing the system for several years the company purchased the system from Southern Bell for $1000 in 1985. The monthly utility line charges are $880.00, including federal and state taxes per month.

Cost of the proposed telephone system: The monthly utility line charges would be $880.00, including federal and state taxes per month. The total cost of the system is $21,258.42. Cash terms are 25% down payment of $5314.60 with agreement, 50% of $10,629.21 due on installation, and the balance of $5314.60 due 30 days from installation. Lease terms for a seven-year lease with purchase option of $1 are $518.28 per month for 84 months with first and last two months in advance ($1554.84).

Should the company continue using its present system? Or should the company replace the present system with the proposed one? What is your recommendation? Why?

Notes

1. Ben Harrison, "PBX Growth Patterns Take New Directions," *TPT*, May 1988, pp. 62–68.

Additional Readings

"All About Key/Non-PABX Telephone Systems," *Datapro Reports on Telecommunications*, June 1988, pp. TC08-001-101–TC08-001-160.

"All About PABX Systems," *Datapro Reports on Telecommunications*, April 1988, pp. TC07-001K-101–TC07-001K-123.

Elizabeth Mazur, Mary Perhay, Monica Sentoff, and John Spencer," New Voice and Data Features for Centrex," *The Record*, May 1985, pp. 4–9.

James H. Morgan, "The Telecom RFP: Three Pages or 50?" *Telecommunication Products + Technology*, August 1987, pp. 64–67.

Kent Nutt, "The Next Generation in ACD Products," *Telecommunications*, May 1987, pp. 124–128.

Jeffrey Rosenwald, "PBXs Enhance Day-to-Day Business Transactions," *Administrative Management*, March 1988, pp. 33–37.

Lorraine Stemmler, "Big PBXs, Small Differences," *Network World*, February 15, 1988, pp. 1, 37, 40, 46.

CHAPTER 6

Data Communication Networks and Hardware

Terminals
  Types of Terminals
  Selecting a Terminal
Buffers
Modems
  Modem Defined
  Modem Configuration
  Types of Modems
  Modem Features
  Selecting a Modem
Point-to-Point and Multipoint Networks
  Point-to-Point Network
  Multipoint Network
  Multiplexing Networks
Front-End Processors
Packet-Switching Networks
  Packet-Switching Routes
  Types of Packet-Switching Networks
  X.25 Standard
  Advantages of Packet-Switching Networks
  Selecting a Packet-Switching Network

CHAPTER OBJECTIVES

After studying this chapter, you should be able to

1. Describe the different kinds of terminals.

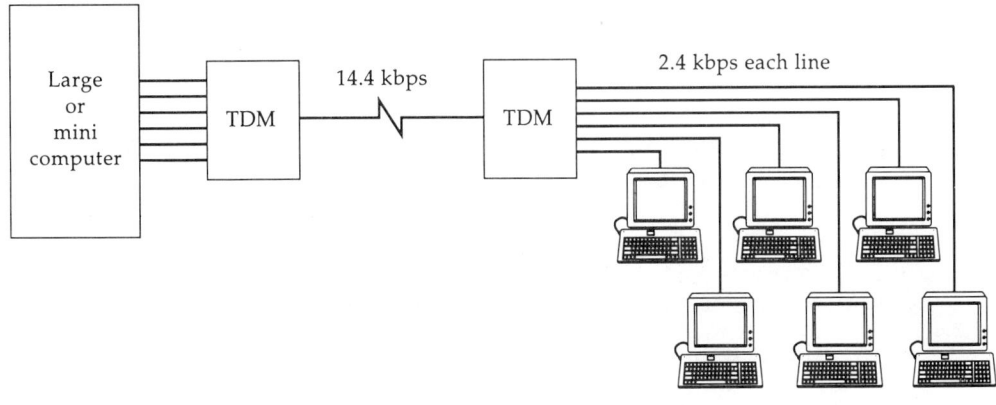

2. Define and specify the functions of the following hardware: modems, multiplexed modems, stand-alone multiplexers, and front-end processors.
3. Distinguish between analog and digital bridges.
4. Select a modem with the appropriate features and compatibility.
5. Suggest hardware for point-to-point, multipoint, and multiplexed networks.
6. Distinguish between circuit- and packet-switching networks.

A manufacturing company that uses a computer, telephone, and a modem to send data to its sales office recently exchanged its low-speed modem for a high-speed one. The low-speed modem runs at 300 bps, while the high-speed modem runs at 2400 bps. Data that previously took three hours to transmit at a cost of $66.68 is now transmitted in 25 minutes at a cost of $8.33.

By reconfiguring its network a bank cut its monthly communications costs by 65%. Originally, the bank used a separate telephone line and two modems to connect each of its four terminals to its mainframe computer in another city. By installing two modem multiplexers, one connecting to the mainframe computer and the other to the four terminals, the bank eliminated three telephone lines and six modems. Another company set up the network shown in the above diagram that allows six devices to communicate with a large computer by sharing one high-speed digital line and using two time-division multiplexers but no modems.

This chapter describes the basic network configurations and accompanying hardware used for communicating data over the public and private telephone networks. The information will assist you in understanding the chapters that follow. The opening diagram shows a network configuration of a host computer communicating with terminals. To increase the efficiency of a host computer, some of its tasks can be performed by other equipment, such as modems and front-end processors, as explained in the sections that follow. The *mainframe or host computer* is the control computer or one of a collection of computers in a data communications system. Its purpose is to provide the primary data processing functions, such as computation, database access, special programs, or programming language. Other major components of the network are the following:

- **Data terminal equipment** (DTE), which includes any digital device, such as terminals, printers, or computers that transmit data.
- **Data communications equipment** (DCE), which includes any device, such as a modem, attached to the transmission or communications line that manipulates the transmitted signal or data.
- *The medium,* such as dial or leased telephone lines or metallic cable, over which the signal is sent.

Terminals

The purpose of a network is to electronically transmit encoded voice, text, data, and images from one physical locale to another. Encoding transforms input data or signals into signals that can be transmitted. The data terminal equipment's function is to extract the encoded electronic information from the network, perform any necessary code conversion and/or data manipulation, and present the information in an appropriate format to the receiver. Terminals are the nodes, also called the end points, within the communications network. They transmit and/or receive data.

To communicate with a host computer, the terminal must match the task and the characteristics of the existing network. A poor choice of terminal can reduce the efficiency of the network by slowing the transmission and increasing costs.

■ Types of Terminals

Terminals are classified according to the amount of built-in capability. The three types of terminals are dumb terminals, smart terminals, and intelligent terminals, as shown in Figure 6-1.

Dumb Terminals. At the low end of both price and performance is the **dumb terminal.** It is a low-speed terminal that transmits only in asynchronous mode (in which characters travel individually down the line as they are keyed in by the operator). Dumb terminals are limited to operating online

FIGURE 6-1 Types of Terminals

(a) Dumb Terminals

(b) Smart Terminal

(c) Intelligent Terminal

(a) and (b) Courtesy of Qume Corporation. (c) Courtesy of DAVOX Corporation.

and a character at a time. Although these terminals can receive and/or transmit signals, serving as input and/or output devices, they have no local processing capability. Since these terminals do not have the capability to be addressable, they cannot be polled by the host computer. **Polling** occurs when the host computer asks a terminal whether it is ready to receive or send data.

Dumb terminals often lack error-checking capability for making certain that data arrives without any transmission errors. A transmission error on a report or letter may be easily recognizable from its meaning, but in other situations an error can be critical, such as a misplaced zero on a bank statement.

How are dumb terminals used? These terminals are often associated with minicomputer environments that also operate asynchronously. They are typically located near a minicomputer, eliminating the need for telephone links and thus avoiding transmission errors associated with telephone line disturbances. When these terminals are hard-wired directly to the host computer, they do not require intelligence for line sharing capabilities or polling.

Smart Terminals. **Smart terminals** are synchronous devices that transmit at high speed entire blocks of data rather than individual characters. Although these terminals cannot be programmed by the user, they do contain built-in firmware that allows them to perform specific functions, such as editing and storing data. (Firmware is software prepared in the factory and permanently stored within the computer's read-only memory. Firmware can be changed only if the hardware itself is changed.) Since these terminals employ microcomprocessors, they can be polled, can store data, and can acknowledge whether data was received and whether there were errors. They can automatically retransmit in case a message is not received intact. However, these terminals still rely on the host computer's processing power for manipulating data.

Intelligent Terminals. In addition to having the characteristics of smart terminals, **intelligent terminals** accept programs written by the user and process data with little assistance from the host computer. The more intelligent the terminal, the more functions it can perform without using the host computer's resources; some can even operate as stand-alone computers. Since the host computer no longer has to handle data from these terminals, it can work on other tasks that make more efficient use of its power.

Like smart terminals, intelligent terminals can reduce transmission errors through error-checking and can automatically retransmit in case a message is not received intact on the other end. Some intelligent terminals operate asynchronously. These devices operate as stand-alone devices, such as the popular personal computer (microcomputer). Since these devices are not connected to a host computer, they cannot be polled, cannot acknowledge the data received are without errors, and contain no memory. To trans-

FIGURE 6-2 Guidelines for Selecting a Terminal

- What keyboard features, such as detachable keyboards, separate numeric keypads for data entry, and special function keys, are important in your application(s)?
- What terminal functions, such as terminal emulation, line-oriented editing, and text editing, do you need?
- How will your terminals communicate to the host computer?
- What forms of data presentation are suitable for your application(s)?

mit data over telephone lines, they must use communication software and an interface to accommodate a modem. If necessary, these terminals can accept programs that allow them to be addressable and polled.

■ Selecting a Terminal

Before selecting a terminal, obtain the answers to the following questions:

- For what application(s) will you use the terminal? Define the application(s).
- What format of data (asynchronous or synchronous) will the host computer handle?
- How much intelligence does the terminal need to process the information?

Figure 6-2 identifies guidelines for selecting a terminal:

Buffers

A host computer can transmit data faster than the data can be processed by a terminal or a printer. Instead of decreasing the host's speed to match that of the terminal's, a storage area, called a **buffer**, is added to both the host and the terminal to compensate for the differences in transmitting rates, as shown in Figure 6-3. As each character is keyed into a terminal, it is moved to the terminal's buffer. After a certain amount of data are entered, the terminal's buffer transfers the stored data to the host's buffer. When the host's buffer receives sufficient data, it releases the data to the computer for processing. Buffers make it possible for the terminal to transmit data efficiently and the host to process data with fewer interruptions.

Modems

As was discussed in Chapter 2, analog transmission lines are designed to carry analog or voice signals, while digital lines carry digital signals, such as those produced by a computer or a terminal. Before data computers and

FIGURE 6-3   Buffer Configuration

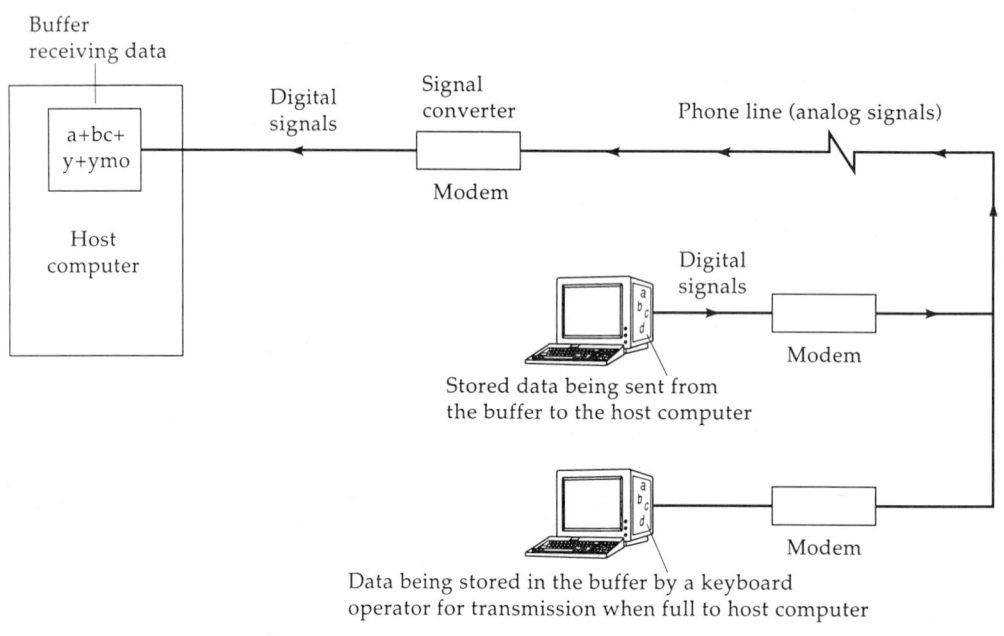

terminals can exchange information over analog public or private telephone lines, a modem has to be placed between the computer or terminal and the telephone line to convert digital signals into the proper form for transmission. Figure 6-4 shows computers sending information to each other over analog lines.

■ Modem Defined

A **modem** (MODulator/DEModulator) is defined as an electronic device that converts computer or terminal electrical digital signals to analog signals so that data can be transmitted over an analog transmission line (also called a circuit). Digital signals are modulated to make sounds similar to those heard on a Touch-Tone® telephone. At the receiving end of the transmission line a modem reconverts the analog signals to digital ones so that the data can be used by the receiving computer or terminal. Figure 6-4 shows a modem accepting digital signals from the sending device and converting them into analog signals that are sent over the public switched telephone network. At the receiving end, a corresponding modem reconverts the analog signals into digital ones.

FIGURE 6-4 Basic Data Communications Configuration

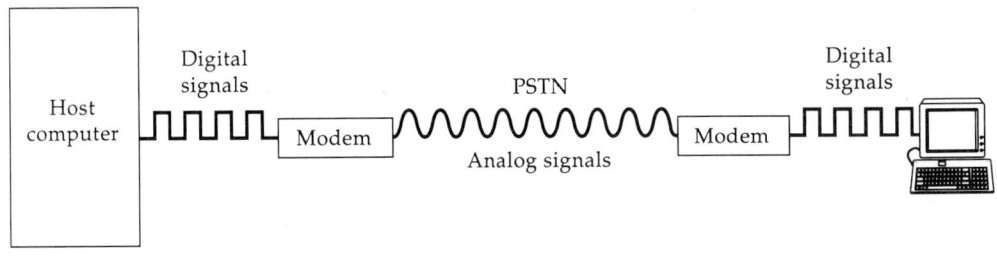

Originally, all communication lines were analog, but in recent years, telephone companies have built digital lines for carrying data. When the transmission line is digital, a digital device, called a **data service unit** (DSU/CSU), serves as the interface between the computer and the digital network, as shown in Figure 6-5. The DSU converts the digital signals from the data terminal equipment to the form required for operation with the digital network, while the CSU is the circuitry for interfacing to the digital lines.

DSUs are not classified as modems because they do not convert digital signals to analog ones for transmission. Since the DSU/CSU is a simpler electronic device than a modem, it can cost less to connect to a digital line than to an analog line. Voice can also be transmitted over digital lines, as discussed in Chapter 2, by using a codec/decoder (codec), a device that encodes voice for digital transmission. Figure 6-5 shows how computers or terminals and telephones connect to digital lines.

FIGURE 6-5 Connecting Computers and Telephones to Digital Lines

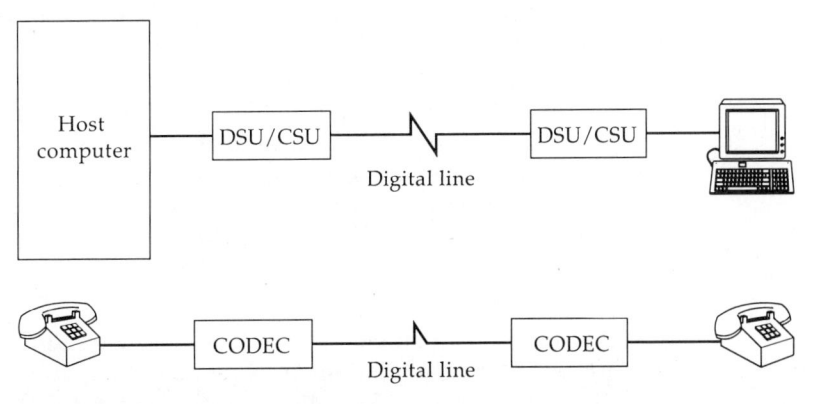

Modem Configuration

Basic Components. Although different types of modems are available, all units share basic components: a power supply, a transmitter, and a receiver. The power supply uses 120 to 220 V alternating current and transforms it into direct current voltage for operating the modem's internal circuitry. The transmitter changes the digital data into analog form, while the receiver reconverts the data to the original digital form. All modems use some type of computer software to execute communication commands. Modem vendors either provide their own software or use software of other vendors.

Dumb and Smart Modems.

Dumb Modems. The first modems were *stand-alone dumb modems*. These modems performed only the function of sending and receiving data.

Smart Modems. In recent years, modems with more capabilities, referred to as smart or intelligent modems, have emerged. *Smart modems* contain microprocessors and operate under the control of program software. In addition to sending and receiving data these modems perform such functions as answering calls automatically, checking passwords, storing names and telephone numbers, and performing diagnostics on existing conditions within the modem, the attached terminal, and the communications network.

Smart modems can be stand-alone modems, plug-in modems, or rack mount modems. A *stand-alone modem*, also called an external modem, is a separate unit placed on the desktop. Figure 6-6(a) shows a typical stand-alone modem with a front-panel display. These modems require an RS-232 port to connect a cable from the modem to the computer. A stand-alone modem is particularly convenient to use when installing or developing new components of a communications systems.

A plug-in or internal modem is an optional device installed on a circuit board and mounted into an empty slot in a microcomputer's central processing unit, as shown in Figure 6-6(b). These modems save desk space, do not require their own power supplies, and are usually less expensive than stand-alone units. But placing a modem inside a microcomputer has drawbacks: The microcomputer's performance is sacrificed. The load of the microcomputer is increased. Space is used that may be needed for another option board within the microcomputer.

A **rack mount modem** can hold a number of modem cards, as shown in Figure 6-6(c). Modem racks are tailored for central computers and even for local area networks.

Equipment Interface. Data communications equipment such as modems and data terminal equipment must have compatible interfaces for connection. An electrical connection between the modem and the data terminal

Modems

FIGURE 6-6 Smart Modems

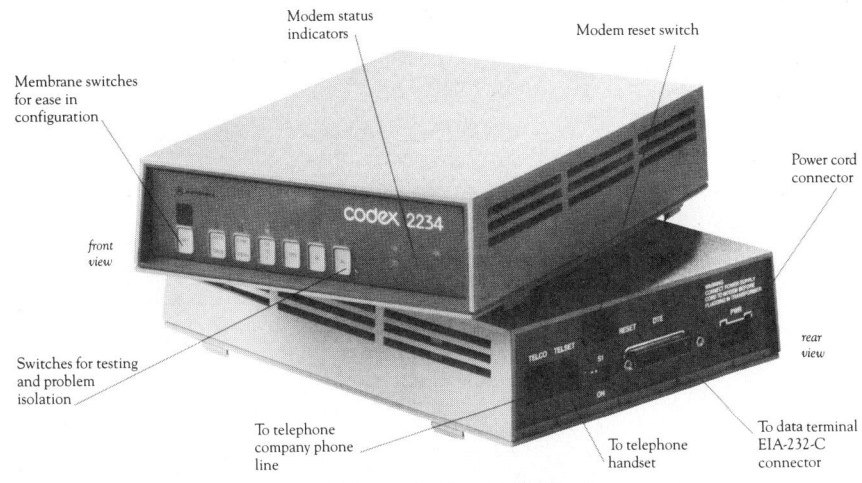

(a) Stand-Alone Modem

(b) Plug-In Modem (Internal View)

(c) Rack-Mount Modem

(a) and (c) Courtesy of Codex Corporation. (b) Courtesy of Concord Data Systems, Inc.

equipment is called an **interface**. When you select computer-modem interfaces, you need to be knowledgeable about the capabilities of interface connections and which ones are essential for various system configurations. To ensure compatibility between different brands of equipment, the Electronic Industry Association (EIA) in cooperation with computer and modem manufacturers and Bell Laboratories developed a standard for the interface—the RS-232. The RS-232 standard defines the electrical characteristics of the signals in the cables that connect a terminal to communications equipment.

Each pin of a 25-pin connector or plug is assigned a particular circuit-controlling function, as shown in Figure 6-7. Most electrical interfaces in the United States conform with this standard. For example, the EIA RS-232-C or the EIA-232-D standard assures plug-for-plug compatibility between modems and all data communications devices whose manufacturers subscribe to this interface standard. The Consultative Committee on International

FIGURE 6-7   EIA-232-D Interface Connector Pin Assignments (Revision of RS-232-C)

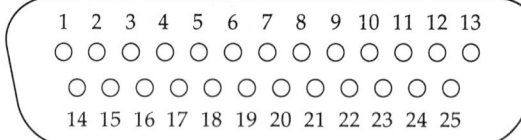

Pin	Function
1	Shield
2	Transmitted data
3	Received data
4	Request to send
5	Clear to send
6	DCE ready
7	Signal ground
8	Received line for signal detector
9	Reserved for testing
10	Reserved for testing
11	Unassigned
12	Secondary received line signal detector/data signal
13	Secondary clear to send
14	Secondary transmitted data
15	Transmitter signal element timing (DCE source)
16	Secondary received data
17	Receiver signal element timing (DCE)
18	Local loopback
19	Secondary request to send
20	DTE ready
21	Remote loopback/signal quality detector
22	Ring indicator
23	Data signal rate select (DTE/DCE source)
24	Transmit signal element timing (DTE source)
25	Test mode

(Note: DCE = Data Communication Equipment; DTE = Data Terminal Equipment)

© Electronic Industries Association. Reprinted with permission.

Telegraph and Telephone (CCITT) has developed an interface identical to RS-232-C called V.24/V.28 that allows data communications equipment to be plug-compatible worldwide. In January 1987 the EIA issued EA-232-D, a revision of the popular RS-232-C. Note that the EIA has dropped the prefix "RS" for EIA-232-D. In March 1987 the EIA introduced the RS-530. The RS-530 achieves data rates 20 kbps higher than the EIA-232-D.

■ Types of Modems

As summarized in Figure 6-8, modems can be classified in a number of ways, such as by operation mode, transmission type (asynchronous or synchronous), transmission medium, line-servicing group, and transmission line connection.

Operation Mode. Modems operate in one of three transmission modes: simplex, half-duplex, or full-duplex. As discussed in Chapter 2, the *simplex mode* allows unidirectional data transmission, that is, data can be either transmitted or received by the modem. The *half-duplex mode* allows data transmission in either direction, but not simultaneously. *Full-duplex mode* allows simultaneous transmission in both directions by using two transmission paths, one for each direction.

A modem typically operates in either half- or full-duplex mode. But in half-duplex mode, transmission is delayed while the modem switches from receiving to transmitting or vice versa. With full-duplex transmission the communication links are open in both directions at the same time, which eliminates modem switching.

Transmission Type. To achieve an orderly data flow across a communication facility, a time relationship, called *synchronization*, must exist among the bits that make up the messages. As discussed in Chapter 2, the two forms of synchronization are asynchronous and synchronous. In *asynchronous transmission*, each character is sent one character at a time, usually as it

FIGURE 6-8   Types of Modems

Operation modes: Simplex, half-duplex, or full-duplex modes.
Transmission types: Synchronous or asynchronous.
Transmission media: Twisted-wire, coaxial cable, fiber-optic cable, microwave, or satellite.
Line-servicing groups: Narrowband, voiceband, wideband, or limited-distance modems.
Transmission line connections: Direct-connect or acoustic modems.

is being keyed. Each character contains its own start and stop bits in order to synchronize operations between the transmitter and the receiver. In *synchronous transmission*, data characters and bits are transmitted in a continuous stream at a fixed rate with the transmitter and receiver synchronized. As a result, data characters are transmitted without individual start and stop bits with the transmitter and receiver synchronized by a clock signal, which provides greater efficiency. Because synchronous transmission is faster and more efficient, modems that can handle higher speeds are synchronous.

Transmission Medium. Modems operate on voice-grade dialup telephone or private (leased) voice-grade telephone lines as well as other media. Modems may be classified according to whether the intended transmission medium is a dialup line or a leased line. The three types of physical lines used to carry data are metallic, dialup, and leased.

A *metallic (copper) line* is a direct-connect line that can be described as a permanent cable connection between two devices, dedicated to the user who purchased or leased it, and generally located within the user's facility. Although the metallic line provides high-speed capability, no alternate circuits are available if the line develops problems.

Dialup lines access the public telephone switched network, allowing you to route data to any destination with access to a telephone. Because of their narrow bandwidth, dialup lines are the slowest of the three physical mediums. Another problem of dialup lines is noise, which can create data errors. However, modems with automatic error detection and error correction capabilities are available. If you do not need to transmit large volumes of data at high speeds across the country, dialup lines can be cost-effective.

For long-distance communications, *leased lines* (private lines or dedicated lines) can be obtained from a common carrier, such as your local telephone company. Like the metallic line, the leased line is a permanent connection. Leased lines are economical if your use justifies the flat monthly rate. They are usually four-wire, full-duplex lines. Leased lines can be installed between separate facilities within a city or between different cities.

Line-Servicing Groups. Modems can be classified by four line-servicing groups: narrowband, voiceband, wideband, and limited-distance or short-haul modems.

Narrowband modems use asynchronous transmission over four-wire lines at a speed of 300 bits per second (bps). These modems are used with slow-speed terminals, such as teletype terminals. (Bits per second is the unit for measuring the speed of data transmission—the rate at which bits are sent over a data link. Baud rate, often confused with bit rate, is the number of single transitions per period of time on the telephone line. The baud rate and bit rate are typically the same at 300 bps (300-bps rate equals 300 baud).

The baud rate cannot exceed 2400 baud or approximately the bandwidth of the telephone line. Transmission above 2400 bps is accomplished by coding or increasing the number of bits per baud. For example, transmission of 4800 bps at 2400 baud is encoding two bits per baud, while transmission of 9600 bps at 2400 baud is encoding four bits per baud.)

Voiceband modems, also called long-haul modems, are usually classified as follows: low-speed modems (up to 1200 bps), medium-speed modems (up to 4800 bps), and high-speed modems (9600 bps and above). However, some vendors classify low-speed modems up to 600 bps, medium-speed modems from 1200 to 3600 bps, and high-speed modems 4800 and above. Typical speeds are 300, 1200, 2400, 4800, 9600, 14,400, 16,800, and 19,200 bps. Asynchronous modems typically operate at a transmission speed of 1200 bps, 2400 bps being the upper limit, and may be assigned to handle both asynchronous and synchronous transmissions. A comparison of the costs of sending 360,000 bytes of data at different rates is shown in Figure 6-9.

Wideband modems, sometimes called broadband modems, are similar to voiceband modems except that they operate in a different part of the frequency spectrum and use more bandwidth to transmit more information or transmit it faster. They make use of the fact that the wider the bandwidth, the faster the possible transmission speed. A wideband group facility is usually a single channel that takes up the same bandwidth as twelve voice-grade circuits. The modems serving these lines handle speeds from 19.2 kbps to 64 kbps. To justify the expense of operating this network, a large amount of data must be transmitted.

Limited-distance modems are short-haul modems that are used for transmissions ranging from one to about 20 miles. These modems, requiring metallic (copper) lines, are generally used to transmit data within company facilities at speeds usually ranging from 2400 to 19.2 kbps, some units supporting higher rates to a maximum of 1.5 Mbps. Limited-distance modems are less expensive than either voiceband or wideband modems because, by operating within a company's facilities, they eliminate the telephone

FIGURE 6-9   **Comparative Costs of Sending 360,000 Bytes of Data by PSTN**

Rate of Speed (bps)	Transfer Time	Cost of Call ($20/hour)
1200 bps	50 min	$16.67
2400 bps	25 min	8.33
9600 bps	6 min, 5 sec	2.08
19,200 bps	3 min, 7 sec	1.04

company's monthly line charges. They can be used in asynchronous or synchronous transmissions.

For example, the headquarters of a clothing manufacturer just opened a sales office located 8 miles away. The question is which type of modem to use to link the facilities. Heavy data traffic is expected between the company's host computer and the sales office's terminals. With heavy data traffic the company should select a synchronous modem and install a dedicated line. Because of the short distance, a short-haul modem, which provides a higher speed than other types of modems, can be used. The modem should be able to operate at either half- or full-duplex mode.

Transmission Line Connection. A modem is connected physically to a transmission line either by directly connecting wires or by telephone coupling—a mechanical connection that requires no direct or permanent connection to the communications facility.

Direct-Connect Modems. Today most modems, known as **direct-connect modems**, are physically wired to the telephone line by using a common modular plug and a jack, as shown in Figure 6-10. Connections are either two-wire or four-wire, the two-wire connection being dial lines and the four-wire being leased or private lines. The four-wire connection uses two communication circuits to provide full-duplex operation. A two-wire set up can provide full duplex by cutting the transmission capacity in half.

One of the advantages of a direct-connect modem is that extraneous sounds cannot enter the system as they can with the acoustic modem discussed below. Also, by hard-wiring, you gain the capability of high transmission speed and less chance of an accidental disconnect. But permanent wire connections limit the modem's portability and require installing a jack if no modular jack is available.

FIGURE 6-10 A Direct-Connect Modem

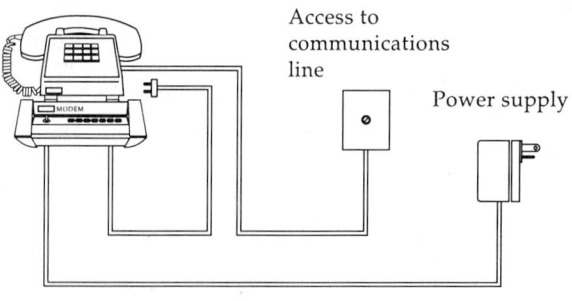

FIGURE 6-11 An Acoustic Modem

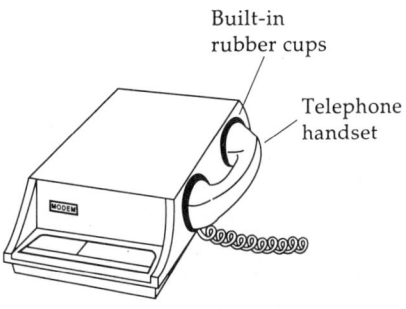

Acoustic Modems.   Despite the simplicity and reliability of connecting directly to the network, places exist where modular plugs and jacks are not available and not likely to be available, such as telephone booths, key telephone set installations, and overseas locations where registered U.S. modems have not been approved or equipped with proper line connectors or are difficult to use. In such situations, **acoustic modems**, also called *acoustic couplers*, can be used. Instead of being hard-wired directly to a dial telephone line, an acoustic modem has built-in rubber cups that fit a standard telephone handset, as shown in Figure 6-11. After you dial the telephone number of the receiving device and hear a special tone from its modem, you then place the telephone headset on the coupler to form the transmission connection. The connection is acoustic, rather than electrical.

Acoustic modems are easy to use but are prone to error because of external noise or vibration, and they can be easily disconnected by accidentally removing the handset from the modem. These modems are asynchronous and limited to a maximum speed of 1200 bps. They are small, lightweight, portable, and usable with any standard telephone. Acoustic modems are usually compatible with low-speed Bell modems and cost less than direct-wire connection modems.

For example, a journalist traveling in Africa can connect a laptop computer and an acoustic modem to any available telephone to transmit news events to a New York City publication.

Transmission Line Features

Analog Leased Line Conditioning.   You can make sure that transmitted data arrive working the way they left by conditioning the transmission line. **Line conditioning** refers to improvements made in the signaling characteristics of transmission lines that make it possible to transmit high volumes of data at high speeds with low error rates. Most leased lines are adequate to support data at 4800 bps and possibly 9600 bps but these lines become unacceptable at higher speeds. To ensure a clean line at the higher speeds, one without impairments such as attentuation and delay distortions, line conditioning becomes necessary. Dialup lines cannot be conditioned because you use a different line each time you transmit; thus, you would have no idea which line to condition. Common carriers (telephone companies) are responsible for adding conditioning equipment to leased lines for a monthly charge. For example, equalizers compensate for problems dealing with frequency response while amplifiers adjust the transmitting signals to their correct level.

Available to both leased lines and dialup lines are modems of 2400 bps and higher that contain built-in equalizers that adjust incoming signals for inconsistencies in the transmission medium. These equalizers are especially helpful to dialup lines where no other methods of line conditioning are available.

Data Compression. **Data compression** techniques allow data to be sent at high speeds with lower-speed modems. For example, a user can transmit data at 2400 bps while using a 1200 bps modem. Data are transmitted in reduced form and reconstructed at the receiving end of the transmission line. The bit patterns of individual characters can be compressed, for example, by using only four bits instead of eight to send numerical data. Frequently recurring words like "and," "the," and "it" are transformed into single characters. The start, stop, and parity bits are stripped from the data stream. The result is an effective transmission rate that is actually 20–200% higher than the basic transmission rate. Data that would otherwise have to be transmitted over a high-speed line can be compressed and transmitted at a lower speed. Another advantage is that eavesdropping does not work with compressed data.

Types of Data Compression. The two types of data compression are basic and advanced. *Basic data compression* increases throughput by as much as a factor of two. **Throughput** is the number of bits, characters, or blocks of data that can pass through a data communications system when the system is working at saturation. The results of basic compression is that a modem that can send data at a maximum speed of 2400 bps can now achieve throughput speeds of 4800 bps. Since the practical speed limit of a dialup line is 9600 bps, users can now use a 9600 bps modem to send an average text or spreadsheet file at 19,200 bps over dialup lines.

Advanced data compression, which is more expensive and complex, increases throughput by a factor of three. For example, advanced data compression enables a modem with a maximum speed of 2400 bps to transmit data at a speed of 7200 bps. Thus a modem with data compression provides the user with higher transmission rates without the need to purchase a more costly modem to attain them.

Standards. Modem manufacturers are beginning to include data compression features to increase throughput. Manufacturers that are not using their own data compression proprietary standards usually select the de facto standards of Hayes Microcomputers, Inc., or Microcom, Inc.

Modem Compatibility. The exchange of control signals between modems at each end of a transmission line, referred to as "handshaking," is necessary when establishing a connection. Standards govern the signals that are required for setting up and terminating calls and for transmitting information. For a handshake to occur, modems must be compatible with each other—an important requirement if modems are to operate efficiently on a network. If a company purchases all modems from the same vendor, compatibility is generally ensured. However, a company typically mixes modems from different vendors for the following reasons:

- Since data communications networks are often developed in stages, equipment is procured as needed. As a result, organizational changes in vendor companies may prevent continued use of the same vendor.
- In some organizations, more than one person may purchase modems for the same network, each person selecting different modem vendors.
- The vendor selected to replace aged or malfunction modems may not be the original vendor.

Bell Standards. Modems that are compatible with national and international standards are likely to be compatible with each other. In the United States, AT&T has established standards for modem configurations. All modems intended for use in the Bell system must be compatible with these standards as well as meet the regulations imposed and enforced by the Federal Communications Commission. Examples of Bell standards are as follows:

- Bell 103: 300 bps, full-duplex, asynchronous, dialup
- Bell 212: 1200 bps, full-duplex, asynchronous/synchronous
- Bell 212A: Bell 212/103

The numbers identify a basic circuit configuration, and the letter following the number identifies the number model and features. Modems from different manufacturers are compatible with each other as long as they follow the same Bell standards.

CCITT Standards. The CCITT recommendations for modem configurations are designed to comply with international standards for data transmis-

FIGURE 6-12 Modem Standards

Speed	Bell Standard	CCITT Standard
300 bps	103	V.21
1200 bps	212A	V.22
2400 bps	224	V.22bis
9600 bps		V.32

sion. CCITT's most popular recommendations for modem configurations are V.22 and V.22bis (second iteration of the standard) for medium-speed dialup units and V.32 for 4800 bps and 9600 bps dialup units. The philosophy of CCITT V.XX modem specifications is that newer, faster modems are to be backward-compatible with their earlier counterparts. For example, a 2400 bps V.22bis (2400 bps full-duplex, asynchronous/synchronous) modem will be compatible with its 1200 bps V.22 modem. Figure 6-12 identifies the modem standards for Bell Standard and CCITT by speed.

CCITT modems have little or no vendor-to-vendor compatibility, since CCITT requirements contain many options that can be widely interpreted by vendors. CCITT V.XX recommendations are directed toward European telephone facility specifications. Since signaling conventions and equipment differ from continent to continent, modems designed primarily for use on European facilities may have compatibility problems when used on North American networks.

Hayes Compatibility. Another type of compatibility common to modems used with microcomputers is the Hayes command structure, a de facto industry standard. Hayes compatibility is concerned with modem commands, modem responses (OK, ring, connect, etc.), and the ability to provide settings that are compatible with various communications programs. For example, modems that are compatible with the Hayes Smartmodem 1200 obey twenty-two modem commands and sixteen register settings stipulated for that device. These modems should also comply with Bell 103 at 0–300 bps, Bell 212A at 1200 bps, and possibly CCITT V.22 standards.

■ Modem Features

Manufacturers of modems provide features that increase operating flexibility, such as simplifying operations for inexperienced users. Yet one manufacturer's features can be another manufacturer's options. You should request the vendor to specify which features are factory installed and which ones may be added later.

Security Equipment. If data encryption equipment is used, eavesdroppers or telephone line tappers can be prevented from obtaining sensitive data. This equipment scrambles data before it reaches the modem and the telephone line.

Password Security Equipment. "Password locks" can prevent unauthorized persons from gaining access to computer ports via dialup or leased telephone lines. One type of lock, which either is placed between an asynchronous modem and a computer or is part of the modem, requests a password sequence before connecting the caller to the computer. On receipt of the correct password sequence an advanced version of this lock hangs up, consults its memory, and calls back the authorized user system. This procedure results in increased security and reverses the charges for the longer portion of the call. These locks also include other safeguards to prevent passwords and phone numbers from being altered or discovered.

Field-Selectable Switch. Some modems contain a *field-selectable switch* that allows the modem to operate at any of the standard speeds up to its maximum capacity. For example, with this feature a Bell 212, which ordinarily operates at 1200 bps, can operate at 300 bps to communicate directly with a Bell 103 modem, which operates only at 300 bps.

Strapping options allow the user to set operating configurations for the modem. For example, the user can switch from half- to full-duplex operations or from two- to four-wire transmission or can convert a point-to-point modem into a multipoint one.

Figure 6-13 describes other available features.

■ Selecting a Modem

To select a modem, you need to know the volume of data to be transmitted and the speed and distance at which it is to travel. Questions to answer are the following:

- What volume of data will you be transmitting? Volume is the number of characters per transaction and the number of transactions per day. Traffic volume determines the transmission speed and whether dialup or leased lines should be used.
- How fast do you want to transmit?
- How far will you be transmitting? Distance determines whether you need short-haul modems for a metallic line or long-haul modems for your telephone line.

Figure 6-14 suggests additional questions to consider when selecting a modem, while Figure 6-15 lists questions for selecting a vendor.

FIGURE 6-13 Features Available on Modems

Adaptive Rate System (ARS): Allows a modem to continuously sense varying line conditions and adjust according to the highest possible speed.

Alternate Voice/Data Capability: Allows a user to alternate voice transmission with data transmission on the same line.

Asynchronous-to-Synchronous Converter: Permits asynchronous data terminal equipment to operate with a synchronous modem.

Autoanswer: Automatically answers and hangs up the telephone for each call by manipulating the telephone disconnect functions; the handset remains off the hook.

Autodial: Allows automatic dialing from the computer keyboard or from a program stored in the modem or computer.

Autoredial: Redials a busy line or tries to reestablish an unintentionally broken connection.

Built-In Diagnostics: Test the modem's circuits to ensure that they are operating satisfactorily before being set up to send and receive signals.

Built-In Speaker: Allows a user to hear the modem dialing and connecting to a telephone line. Also provides on-screen prompts telling whether the call to the other computer is being completed successfully.

Call Timer: Keeps track of the connect time of each call and displays it on a status screen or elsewhere. This feature serves as a reminder of accruing telephone charges.

Dial Backup: Allows a user to switch from a leased line to a dial line or lines in the event the private line should fail.

Fallback Speed: Allows a synchronous modem to reduce its speed to accommodate line conditions and the speed limits of other communication devices.

Help Aid: Gives a user step-by-step on-screen instructions to get a computer online.

Modem Substitution Switch: Allows a user to reroute data through a "hot" spare modem, one that is already powered up, in the event the original modem fails.

Multiple Speed Selection: Allows a user to continue transmitting, even while the quality of the telephone line is degrading, by falling back to a lower transmission speed, thus reducing the error rate.

Multiport Capability: Allows several communications lines to be handled by a single modem (similar to a basic multiplexer).

Number Storage: Stores at least one called number so that a user can request redialing the last number with one command. Some autodial modems have memories sufficient to store directories and a number of commands.

Strapping Options: Allow a user to set operating configurations for the modem. For example, the user can switch from half- to full-duplex operations or from two- to four-wire transmission or can convert a point-to-point modem into a multipoint one.

Timeout Functions: Serve as safeguards against forgotten connections accruing large telephone line charges. For example, some modems have a timer that hangs up the connection when no data transmission activity occurs for a specified period of time.

Voice Over Data: Allows a user concurrent voice and data operation usually with short-haul modems designed to be used with voice/data PBXs.

FIGURE 6-14 Guidelines for Selecting a Modem

- Is the modem compatible with Bell and CCITT standards?
- Does it offer the Hayes commands?
- What standard does it use for data terminal interface?
- Will the modem interface be compatible with your terminals?
- Will the new modem be able to communicate with any existing ones?
- Will the modem be used for dialup, leased, or metallic line operation?
- Will the modem be used in a point-to-point or multipoint configuration?
- What kind of diagnostic capabilities do you need?
- What kind of error rate can you accept?
- What is the modem's mean time between failures?
- What features should the modem have?
- What is involved if you want to add modem options?
- Does the modem have network control capability to keep your network running despite network problems?

FIGURE 6-15 Guidelines for Selecting a Vendor

- Select a reliable vendor.
- Request a demonstration of the modem that you are considering.
- Ask for references from businesses similar to yours.
- How long has the vendor been doing business?
- How many modems has the vendor sold?
- Is the vendor financially stable?
- Is the vendor knowledgeable about the current state of electronics, communications, and manufacturing techniques?
- What kind of applications does the company offer?
- What kind of maintenance service(s) does the vendor provide?
- Does the vendor provide reasonable repair turnaround charges?
- Does the warranty protection last for a reasonable time?

Point-To-Point and Multipoint Networks

■ Point-To-Point Network

The previous section discussed connecting two computers by a single telephone line using two modems. This configuration, two computers (nodes) connected by a single communication link, is called a **point-to-point network**. Dialup telephone lines are ordinarily point-to-point lines because one and only one terminal usually has the exclusive use of the channel.

Suppose you own a furniture business. You have set up a point-to-point network for transmitting data between a smart (synchronous) terminal in the order entry department and a host computer located in another part of the same building. Data transmission is over a leased line using a pair of

FIGURE 6-16 Point-To-Point Network

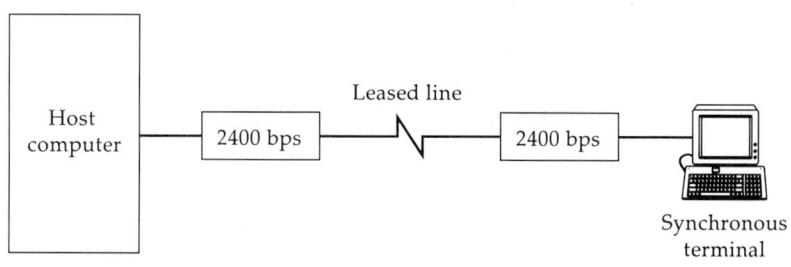

2400 bps half- or full-duplex synchronous modems. You selected a smart terminal because order entries require the operator to manipulate the cursor, perform some editing, and check for accuracy before sending the information to the host computer. To be compatible with the terminal, you selected synchronous modems. You decided on a leased line because a dialup line is more expensive for frequent transmissions. Figure 6-16 shows the point-to-point network that you designed.

But you soon discover that you need more terminals to perform the order entry tasks. You then link three more terminals to the host computer. Now you have four terminals, each linked in a point-to-point configuration to the mainframe or host computer by its own leased line and modem, as shown in Figure 6-17. Each telephone line connects through a modem to one of the host computer's port. A **port** is a point of access into a computer, the

FIGURE 6-17 Point-To-Point Network for Four Terminals

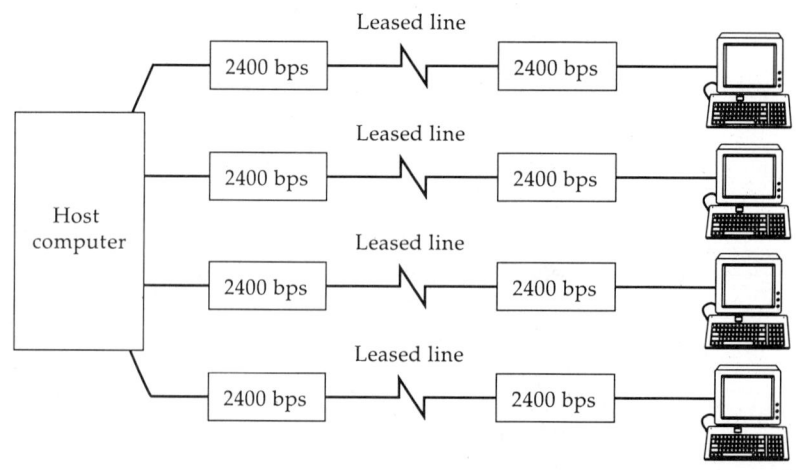

FIGURE 6-18   **A Company Using a Point-To-Point Network to Access Information Sources**

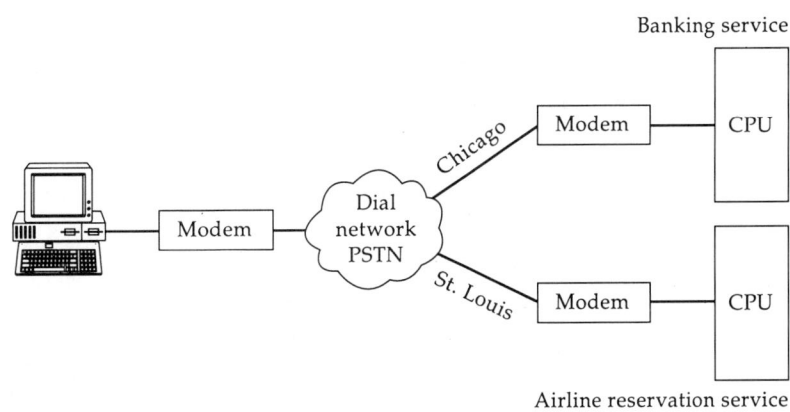

number of computer ports determining the number of simultaneous users the computer can accommodate.

Figure 6-18 shows how another company uses a point-to-point network for its applications. Here, an office with one personal computer and one modem uses the dial network to access airline and banking services, each at different times.

■ Multipoint Network

The new point-to-point configuration that you just set up for your furniture business, shown in Figure 6-17, has increased your equipment costs and your telephone charges. Since the four terminals are transmitting to the same place, you decide to have them share the same telephone line. What you are doing is changing the network configuration from point-to-point to multipoint. A **multipoint network** consists of two or more terminals (also referred to as nodes or drops) sharing the same communications link, which is normally a private or leased line.

You set up your network so that the four terminals and their modems share one leased telephone line and one of the host's modems, as shown in Figure 6-19. By using this network design you have eliminated the three leased lines between the terminals and the host computer, three of the host's modems, and three of the host's ports.

But now only one terminal can transmit at a time. Since terminals cannot transmit simultaneously, the host computer polls each one, in a predetermined order, asking whether it has data to transmit. Polling requires that terminals be smart or intelligent terminals so that they can provide sufficient

FIGURE 6-19 "Polling" Multipoint Network

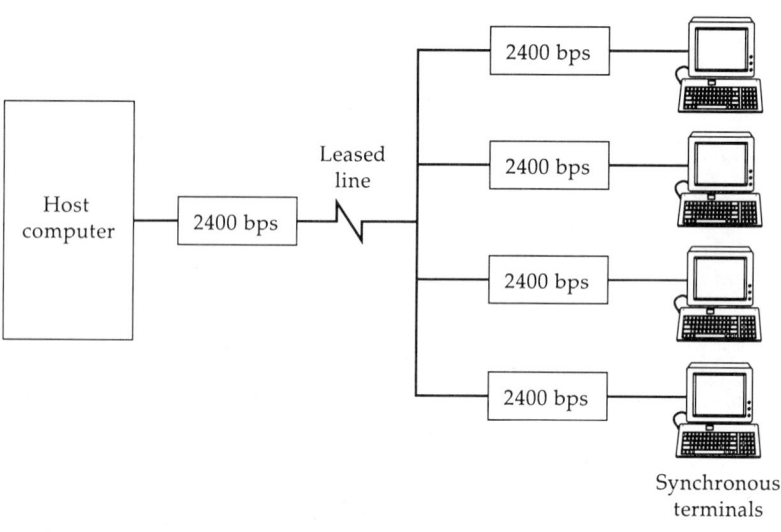

intelligence to be addressable, have buffers for storage, and be synchronous. Where many terminals share the same line, as in this multipoint or "polled" network, you use a leased line and modems that operate synchronously to permit higher transmission speeds and that include error-protection capabilities to reduce error rates.

A drawback to polling is that communication between a terminal and the host computer can be slowed because each terminal must wait its turn to transmit. However, polling time can be reduced by using high-speed modems.

Another application of a company using a polling multipoint network is described in Figure 6-20. In this case, a national chain store's host computer automatically polls the minicomputers at each of its three stores in Atlanta, Chicago, and New York. Each store transmits the day's transactions to the host computer each night when telephone rates are cheaper. The company uses Codex's modem 2230 full-duplex at speeds up to 2400 bps in asynchronous/synchronous mode.

Analog Bridge. The polling multipoint network just described has all the terminals (drops) located in the same building. But a multipoint network can also be set up for offices that are located elsewhere—within the same city or in other cities. In this type of configuration the local telephone company's central office in the area in which the terminal is located sets up a multipoint connection by providing an **analog bridge** that connects the terminal to the company's leased line.

FIGURE 6-20   A Company Using a Multipoint Network to Night-Poll Remote Offices

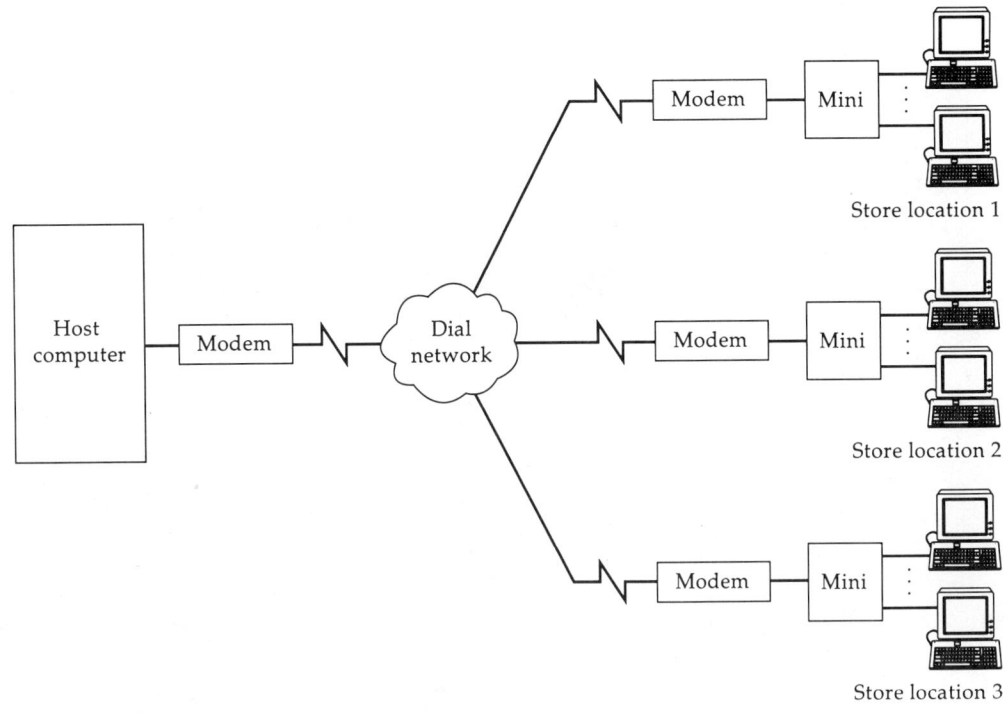

Redrawn courtesy of Codex Corporation.

Suppose four of your company's branches are located in an area that is 2000 miles from the host computer. If you use a point-to-point network to connect each terminal, you require a total of 8000 miles of leased lines and eight modems. You can cut these costs by using a multipoint network and analog bridges. Each branch's terminal connects to its local central office, which sets up a multipoint connection to the host computer, as shown in Figure 6-21. Each central office (represented by circles in Figure 6-21) provides an analog bridge that connects the terminal to the company's leased line. The telephone company's central offices are actually providing a series of point-to-point segments and analog bridges to link the terminals to the multipoint network. With this multipoint configuration you not only have cut costs, but have increased the efficiency of data traffic between the terminals and the host computer.

Digital-Sharing Device. Another way to increase your network's capacity and cut costs is by using a digital-sharing device that can treat up to a maximum of six point-to-point lines as if they were a single multipoint line.

FIGURE 6-21   **Multipoint Network Using Analog Bridges**

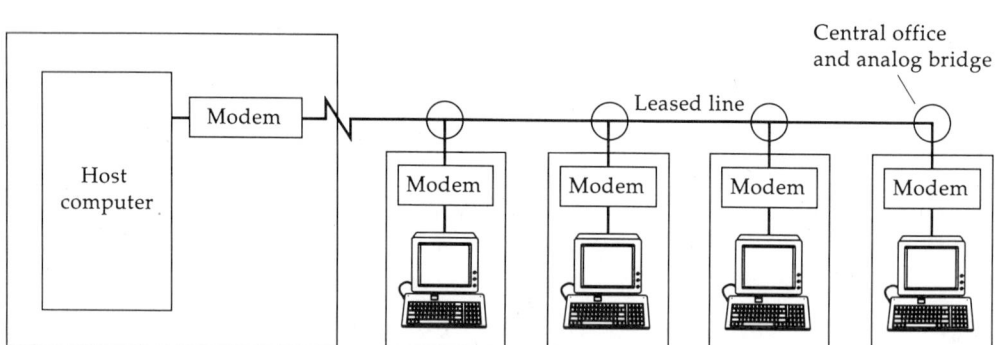

By linking up to six terminals within fifty feet to a *digital-sharing device*, the number of modems is reduced from six to one. For example, you can use the digital sharing device to improve the network configuration shown in Figure 6-19. By connecting this device to the terminals in the order entry department, only one modem is needed, instead of four, to connect to the transmission line, as shown in Figure 6-22(a).

A digital-sharing device can also be used to expand the port capacity of a host computer, as shown in Figure 6-22(b). When the device is placed next to the host computer, it reduces the number of ports required for point-to-point connection. Modems, terminals, and/or other DCE and DTE can share a single connection with one of the host's ports. A drawback is that the digital-sharing device allows only one DCE or DTE to communicate with the host computer or remote modem at a time.

■ Mutliplexing Networks

You now decide to split the circuit so that you can send more than one transmission at the same time. What you are doing is called *data multiplexing*; you are placing two or more separate transmissions on a single transmission circuit. This task is accomplished by multiplexed modems or stand-alone modems that combine two or more slow-speed lines into a single-high speed line.

Multiplexed Modems.   Suppose the work of your four data entry operators in your furniture company has increased sufficiently to require that they transmit simultaneously. Since the polling network in Figure 6-19 no longer meets your requirements, you could install a costly point-to-point leased

FIGURE 6-22   Multipoint Network Using a Digital-Sharing Device

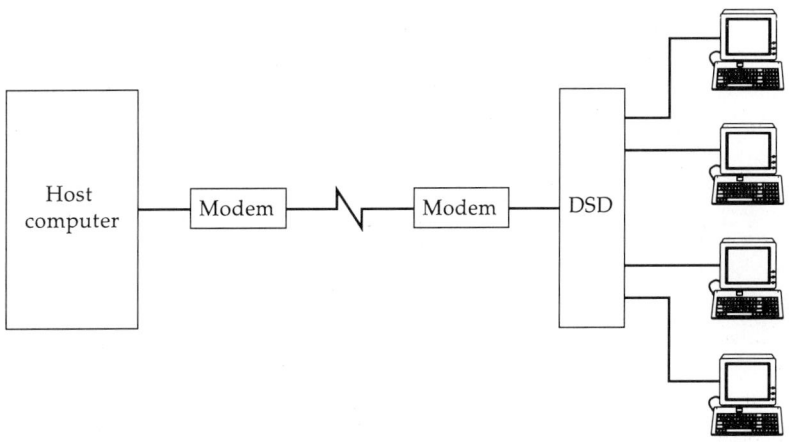

(a) Reducing the Number of Modems

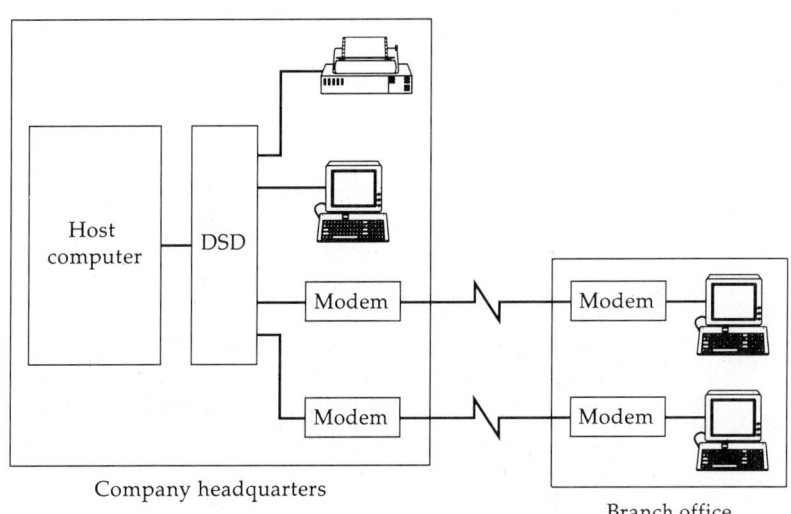

(b) Expanding the Host Cmputer's Port Capacity

line for each terminal operator. Instead, you decide to use multiplexed modems, which split the transmission channel into four or six subchannels.

Each **multiplexed modem** has an internal four- or six-channel multiplexer. A four-channel modem allows data to be transmitted simultaneously over a leased line by combining four subchannels into one leased line for

FIGURE 6-23 **Using Multiplexed Modems**

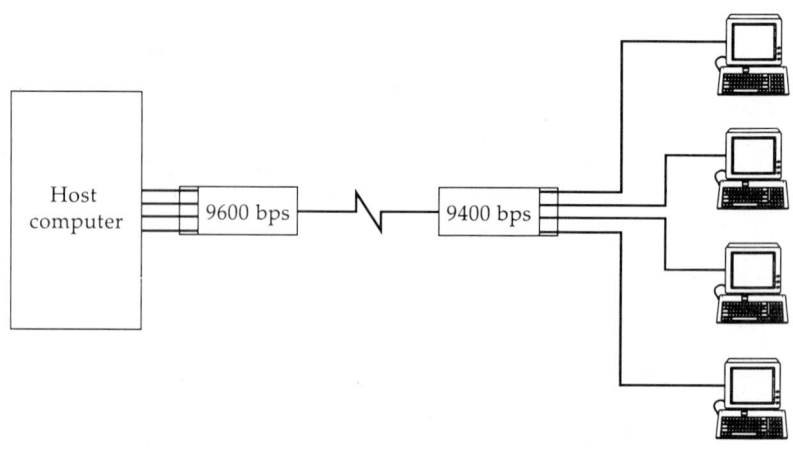

synchronous transmission, as shown in Figure 6-23. The sum of the speed of the individual channels cannot exceed the total line speed. For example, a 9600 bps modem would allow four 2400 bps channels to be connected. In addition to the two multiplexed modems the host computer requires four computer ports. Compared to Figure 6-19, you have replaced the four 2400 bps modems with two 9600 bps multiplexed modems.

A few weeks after setting up the multiplexed modems, you decide to move one of the terminal operators along with a terminal to a sales office three miles away. Since the terminal operator at the sales office still needs to access the host computer, all you have to do is purchase two 2400 bps modems. One modem connects the operator's terminal to the local telephone line, while the other modem links the line to the operator's vacated 2400 bps channel in your office. The data now runs from the sales office over the telephone line to your office, to the 9600 bps modems, and to the host, as shown in Figure 6-24. Your new costs include two 2400 bps modems and a local telephone line.

The configuration that links the terminal in the sales offices to the 2400 bps modems is called a *tail circuit*. The link between the 2400 bps modem and the 9600 bps multiplexed modem is a digital one.

Stand-Alone Multiplexers. Up to this point, all the network configurations have been designed for synchronous terminals and modems operating at the same speed. Suppose that your requirements again change. You are now considering using more than four terminals to transmit simultaneously, possibly mixing synchronous with asynchronous terminals, and transmitting some data at higher speeds and other data at lower speeds. For one

FIGURE 6-24 Using Multiplexed Modems with One Terminal at a Remote Site

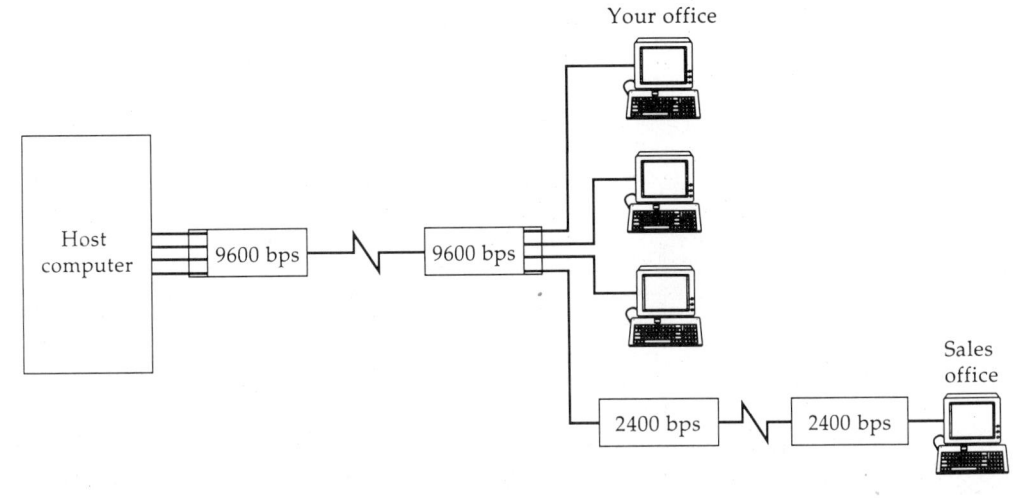

or more of these reasons you should consider installing stand-alone multiplexers.

A multiplexer, often called a "mux," combines the transmission of several slow-speed terminal transmissions into one higher-speed voice-grade line connecting to the host computer. A second multiplexer demultiplexes the signal back into lower-speed transmission and routes each terminal's input into one of the host computer's ports. Now instead of using four separate telephone lines for the four terminals, only one line is used. Typical multiplexers operate in maximum multiples of eight, sixteen, or thirty-two simultaneous transmissions over a single transmission circuit.

Multiplexing Techniques. The two basic multiplexing techniques, discussed in Chapter 2, are frequency-division multiplexing (FDM) and time-division multiplexing (TDM). Two advanced versions of TDM are T-1 multiplexing and statistical multiplexing (statmuxing).

Frequency-Division Multiplexing (FDM). **Frequency-division multiplexing** divides the voice circuit into multiple low-speed channels that are separated by guardbands to prevent crosstalk. Each terminal is assigned its own channel, as shown in Figure 6-25. Because the circuit is divided into a limited number of data channels, FDM can support only a small number of devices.

The maximum speed of an FDM circuit is 1200 bps. The sum of the terminal transmission speeds cannot exceed the speed of the high-speed link. FDM does not require modems because the multiplexers are analog

FIGURE 6-25 **Frequency-Division Multiplexing**

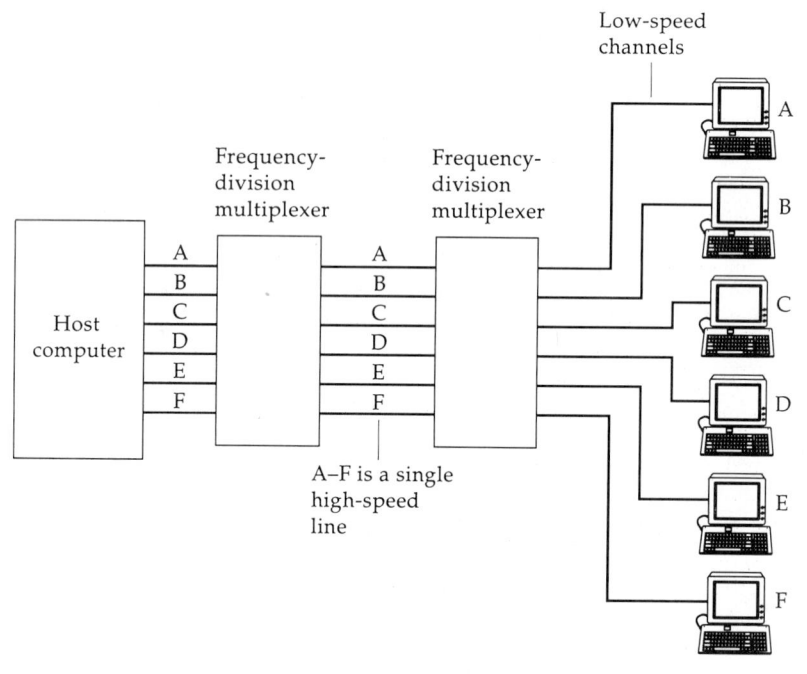

devices. FDM is used to connect multiple slow-speed data terminals over voice channels. Generally, FDM is used for low-speed asynchronous full-duplex, leased line transmission. FDM allows dumb terminals to share a voice circuit although the terminals are still not addressable preventing them from being polled.

Time-Division Multiplexing (TDM). **Time-division multiplexing** (TDM), another multiplexing technique, operates digitally and thus requires modems on a point-to-point analog line, as shown in Figure 6-26. In TDM a common transmission path is shared by a number of terminals on a cyclical basis, each terminal being assigned a time slot. In other words, each terminal uses the total bandwidth of the high-speed line exclusively for a short time slot. The multiplexer collects data in a predetermined order from each synchronous terminal or asynchronous terminal, a process called interleaving. It next transmits the data continually over leased lines at equal to or less than the sum of the separate terminal transmission speeds. The order in which terminals transmit never changes. When a terminal has no data to send, its time slot goes unused. The high-speed link between the multiplexers transmits data at the modem's top speed, such as 9600 bps, because the entire bandwidth is used rather than subchannels. When a high-speed dig-

FIGURE 6-26 Time-Division Multiplexing

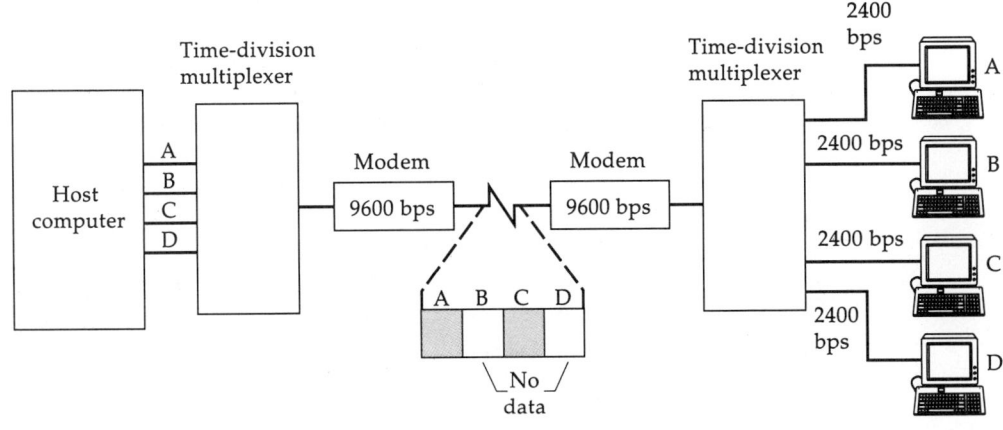

ital transmission circuit is used with time-division multiplexers, no modems are required, as shown in the opening diagram to this chapter. The time-division multiplexer in this case allows up to six devices to share one high-speed digital line, as long as the sum of the data rates does not exceed 14.4 kbps.

T-1 Multiplexing. The T-1 facility discussed in Chapter 4 uses T-1 multiplexers. These multiplexers are time-division multiplexers that accept information from multiple data, voice, or video channels and combine it for transmission over a single T-1 communication facility. Figure 6-27 shows twenty-four 64 kbps voice channels and a time-division multiplexer at each end of the digital line to concentrate the circuit at one end and to separate

FIGURE 6-27 T-1 Multiplexing

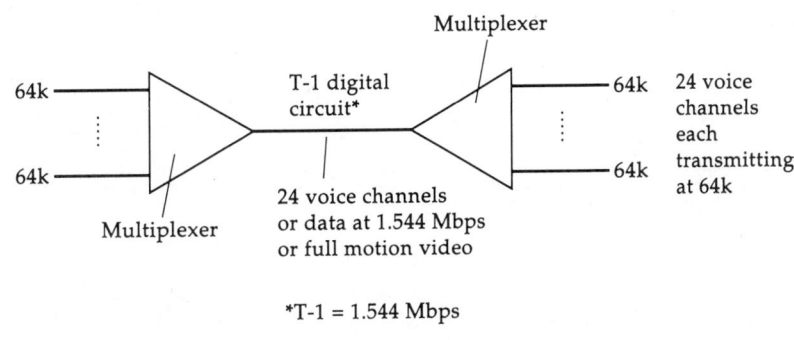

the voice channels at the other. Note that the 24 voice channels times 64 kbps equals 1.536 Mbps. By adding 8 kbps for control and synchronization, the total bps is 1.544 Mbps, the speed of the T-1 circuit.

Statistical Multiplexing. **Statistical multiplexing** eliminates multiple parallel lines by merging the digital links at one end into one high-speed transmission line, then sorting them out at their destination. Statistical multiplexers, also called statmuxes or intelligent time-division multiplexers, make use of the idle times in a TDM circuit. They allocate bandwidth to "active" terminals only. When a terminal has no data to send, it receives no allocated time on the line. Figure 6-28(a) shows a company's original network; Figure 6-28(b) shows the same company's network using statistical multiplexing. The statmux collects data from the terminal and then sends the data to the receiving end with the address of the receiving terminal. On the average, asynchronous terminals tend to transmit 10% of the time, while synchronous terminals transmit 30% of the time. A statmux is shown in Figure 6-29.

Multiplexing still saves money on telephone bills and equipment costs, as shown in Figure 6-28. Statmuxes improve circuit utilization by minimizing idle time between transmission. These multiplexers are more costly than FDMs and TDMs and must be monitored to prevent overloads.

FIGURE 6-28   Statistical Multiplexing

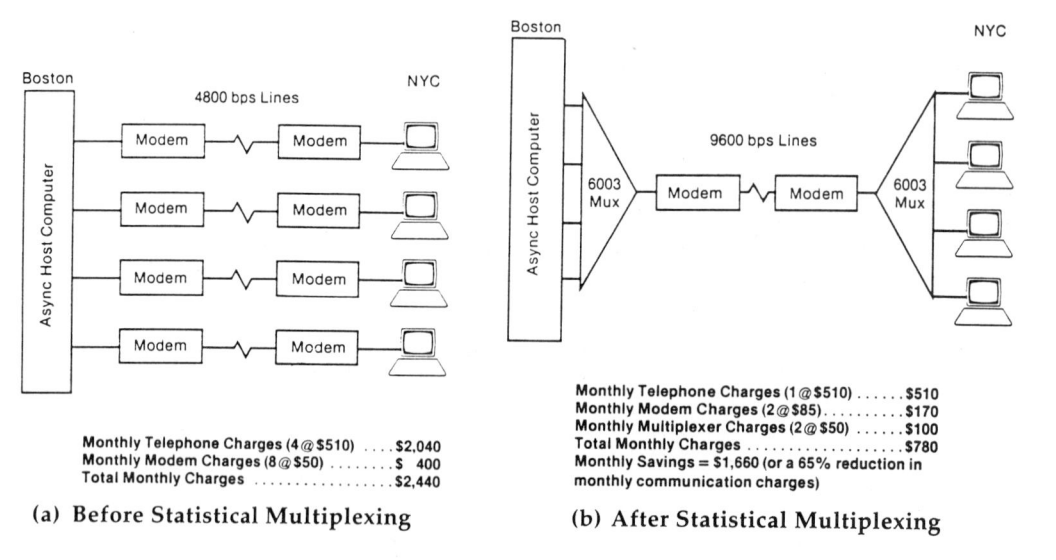

Courtesy of Codex Corporation.

FIGURE 6-29   A Statistical Multiplexer

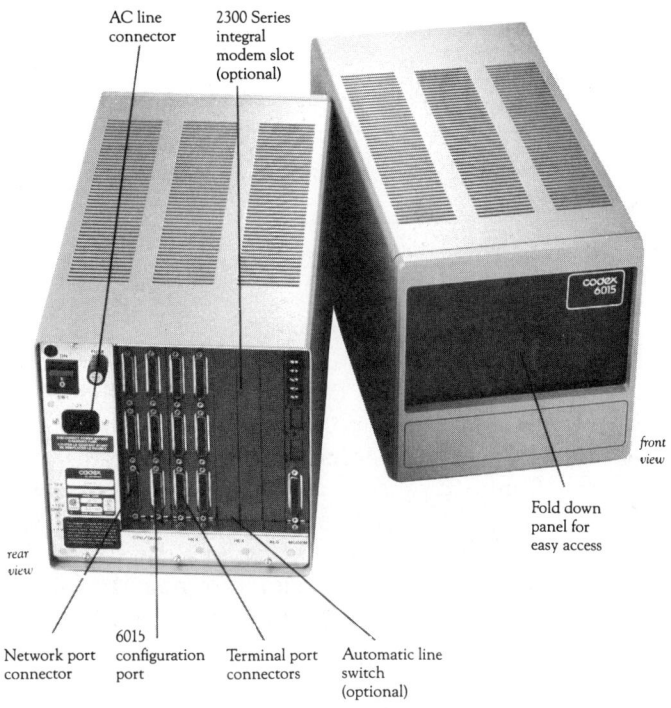

Courtesy of Codex Corporation.

Front-End Processors

A **front-end processor** (FEP), also known as a transmission control unit or a communications controller, is a mainframe computer, a minicomputer, or a microcomputer that has been programmed to perform communication tasks for a host computer. It is installed between the front of the host computer and its modem(s), as shown in Figure 6-30. A widely used front-end processor is the IBM 3705.

By relieving the host computer of routine tasks, the FEP enables the host computer to increase its speed and capacity. For example, an FEP that receives data a bit at a time can, after receiving the whole message, pass the information at very high speeds to the computer. Figure 6-31 lists the major functions performed by FEPs equipped with the appropriate software.

The number of ports on a front-end processor determines the number of terminals that can connect to it. The digital-sharing device previously

FIGURE 6-30 **Front-End Processor**

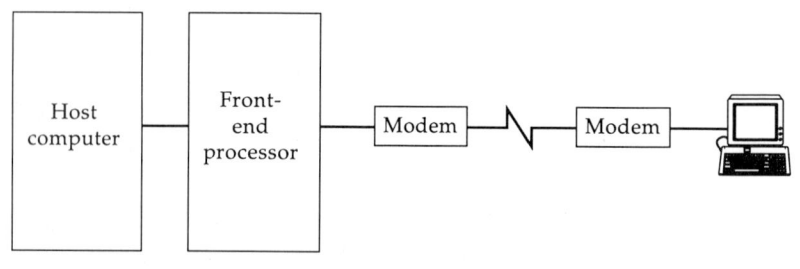

discussed can extend the FEP's port capacity by treating point-to-point communication lines as though they were a single multipoint line. The device is placed between the FEP and DCE and DTE. In this way an FEP port is expanded to handle more than one modem, terminal, and/or other device, either remote or local. This device can be used to avoid installing a second front-end processor when all of the ports of the first front-end processor are occupied. A drawback is that it allows only one terminal to transmit at a time. The use of port devices may be a temporary solution until a new network can be configured or new hardware purchased. Figure 6-32 compares connecting the ports of a front-end processor to terminals with and without a digital-sharing device. With a digital-sharing device, up to six terminals or modems in any combination can share one of the front-end processor's ports.

FIGURE 6-31 **Functions of Front-End Processors**

Poll terminals by asking each one whether it is ready to send or receive data.
Record messages by logging inbound and outbound messages.
Convert incoming data codes and formats to those of the host computer.
Record statistics by maintaining records of network performance and traffic.
Detect and correct transmission errors initiated at the terminals before they are received by the host computer.
Automatically route messages to a backup terminal when a terminal or circuit is not working.
Queue by placing incoming messages in transmission order for processing by the host computer.
Respond to simple inquiries directly without contacting the host computer.
Assemble and disassemble data input at varying line speeds and in synchronous or asynchronous formats to ensure that the host computer receives only complete messages.
Keep system parts operating when the host, terminal, or transmission line fails.

FIGURE 6-32 Using a Digital-Sharing Device with a Front-End Processor

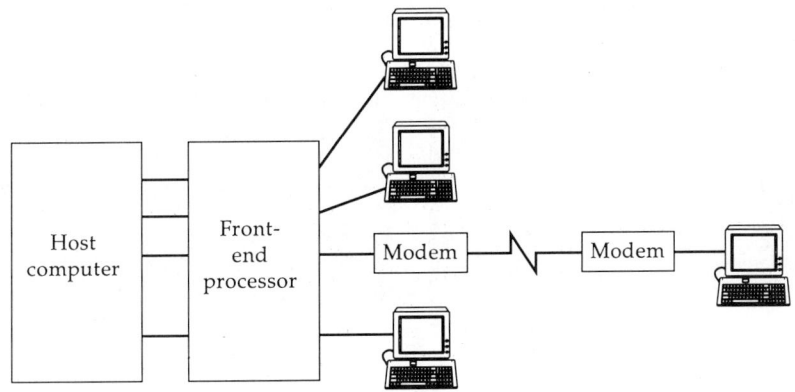

(a) Without a Digital-Sharing Device

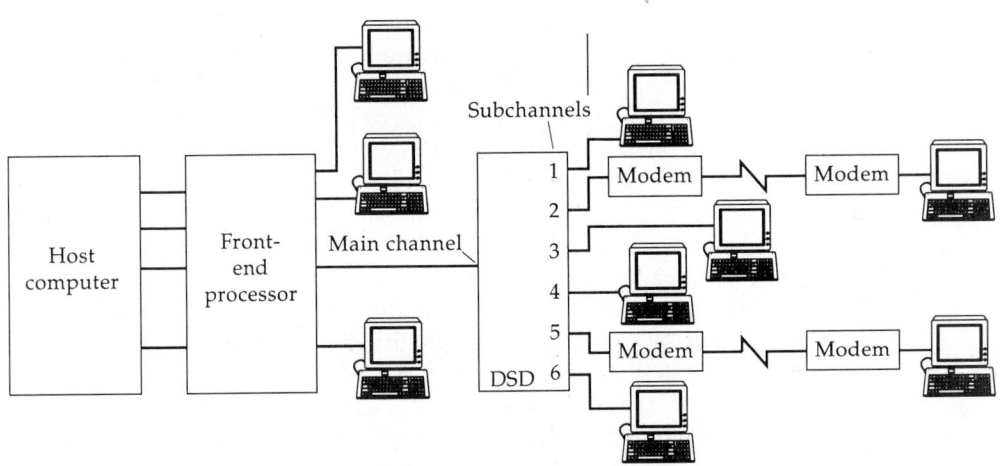

(b) With a Digital-Sharing Device

Packet-Switching Networks

The two major methods for transmitting messages are circuit switching and packet switching, as shown in Figures 6-33(a) and 6-33(b). The public switched telephone network is a *circuit-switching network* in which a communications path is established between the sender and the receiver and is held for the duration of the transmission. During the connection the circuit is dedicated to the sender and the receiver, allowing them to interact without

FIGURE 6-33   The Two Major Switching Methods

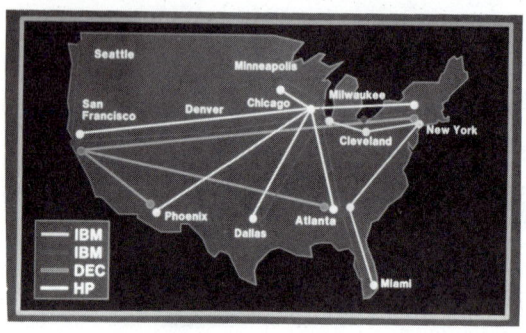

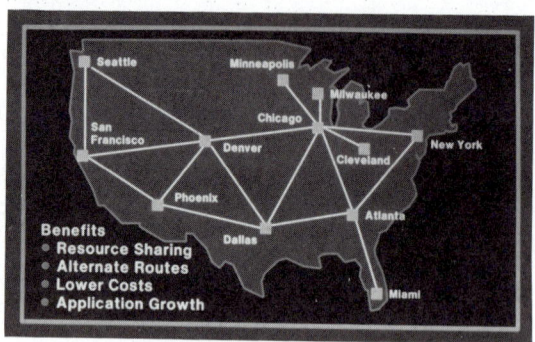

(a) Circuit-Switched Network   (b) Packet-Switched Network

Courtesy of Hughes Network Systems.

any delay or for providing continuous transmission of data. The circuit established for transmission is completely independent of the message being sent, whether voice or data. Since the circuit cannot be shared between its other users, inefficiencies and underutilization of the transmission medium result. Figure 6-33(a) shows examples of dedicated circuits.

A **packet-switching network** (PSN) is a form of time-division multiplexing based on user demand. A digitized message is broken into small discrete units called *packets*. Large messages may be divided into many packets. Individual packet size varies depending on the equipment used to generate and receive packets and the nodes (switches) that transport them. Each packet, which is constructed by the computer, is addressed as though it were a piece of mail and sent individually through many locations across the network to its final destination, where it is converted back into unpacketed form. A packet is generally of a specified length, containing bits for synchronization, control information, a message number, the numbers of current and last packets, destination and source addresses, acknowledgment, error checking, and data. Figure 6-34 shows the structure of a typical packet. Note that the CRC (cycle redundancy check) field allows detection of transmission errors within the packet.

Components of a PSN are shown in Figure 6-35. Messages are packetized by a packet assembler/disassembler (PAD), a converter device that is similar to a modem. The assembled packets are transmitted over public or private networks and then reassembled at the receiving end by another PAD. Each PSN consists of nodes— **packet-switching** computers or packet switches that relay each packet over the network to its final destination. These nodes route hundreds of packets of data each second around the network. Remote terminals are connected directly into the network by PADs. Other components of a PSN include the network operation center (NOC) that monitors the network and provides diagnostic programs as

FIGURE 6-34 Packet

Preamble	Destination address	Source address	Type	Data field	CRC*
8	6	6	2	46–1500	4

Bytes

*CRC (Cyclic Redundancy Check) field allows detection of transmission errors within the packet.

Courtesy of Hughes Network Systems.

needed; the network access system (NAS), a security device that performs such tasks as authenticating user passwords; and gateways that link the network to other networks.

For example, suppose that you want to send a message from your Chicago office to an office in New York City. With a computer, a telephone, and a modem you dial the telephone of the packet-switched network provider.

FIGURE 6-35 Components of a Packet-Switching Network

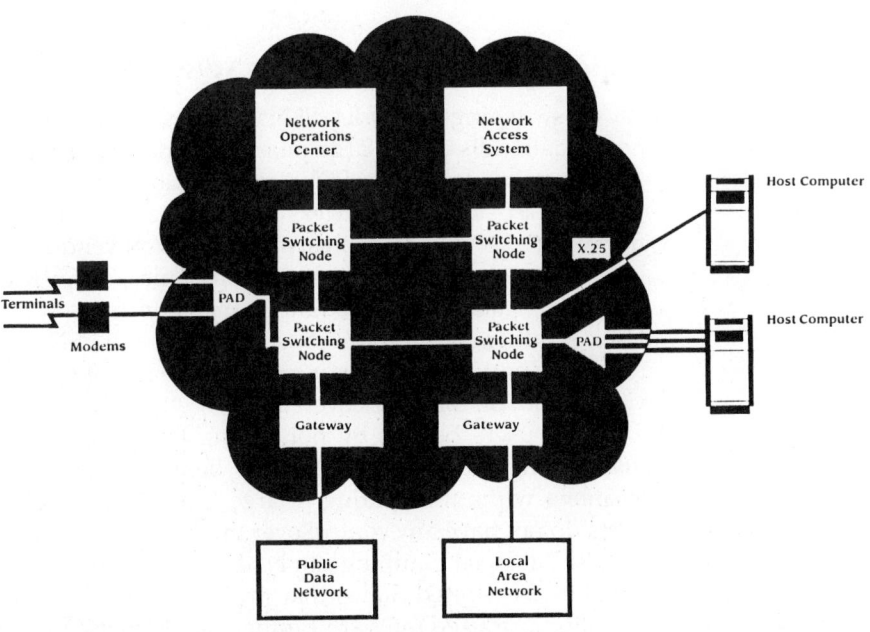

Courtesy of Bolt Beranek and Newman, Inc.

Your dialup telephone line connects you to the entry node of the packet-switching network. Once your message is received by the entry node, it is broken into packets. Network nodes then switch each packet over the packet-switching network to an exit node in New York City, each taking its own individual path and arriving in New York City possibly out of sequence. As shown in Figure 6-33(b), one packet may go from Chicago to New York City, another from Chicago to Atlanta and then to New York City, and so on, or all packets may go from Chicago to New York City. Each packet has appended control information that identifies that part of the message it represents. At the exit node the packets are assembled into proper form and order and sent by dialup line to the receiving office in New York City. The final delivery of information is rapid so that to a user it appears as a dedicated end-to-end channel.

■ Packet-Switching Routes

Packet-switching networks are designed to include at least two alternative high-speed paths from one node to any other. Packet-switching networks are either permanent or switch virtual circuits. A *permanent virtual circuit*, similar to a dedicated voice circuit, establishes the same route through the network for all users. A *switch virtual circuit* selects the best path for each packet transmission. In the example shown in Figure 6-36, each packet has the same entry node but takes a different route to reach the same destination.

■ Types of Packet-Switching Networks

Packet-switching networks (PSNs) are designed for users with a large number of data calls and a large quantity of data that must be transmitted between various locations. PSNs can be public, private, or hybrid networks. *Public packet-switching networks* are supplied to the public by **value-added network** (VAN) vendors or carriers. The VAN vendor leases telephone facilities, often from local telephone companies, to provide packet-switching nodes in major cities throughout the country as well as to connect with PSNs of other countries. VAN users access the PSN by an 800 number or a toll call. The VAN charges users on the basis of connection time and data volume, not on distance covered.

VAN users benefit by not having to be responsible for operating or maintaining the network. Another benefit is that they can link multiple locations without requiring a large initial system expenditure. However, users do not have any control over the network, its services, or its changing fees, so financial planning can be difficult. Examples of providers of public PSNs in the United States that provide data service to a large number of small users at fixed rates are Tymnet and Telenet. Other public PSNs include Datapac (Canada), Transpac (France), PSS (England), and Europnet (connects major European cities).

FIGURE 6-36   Packet-Switching Routes

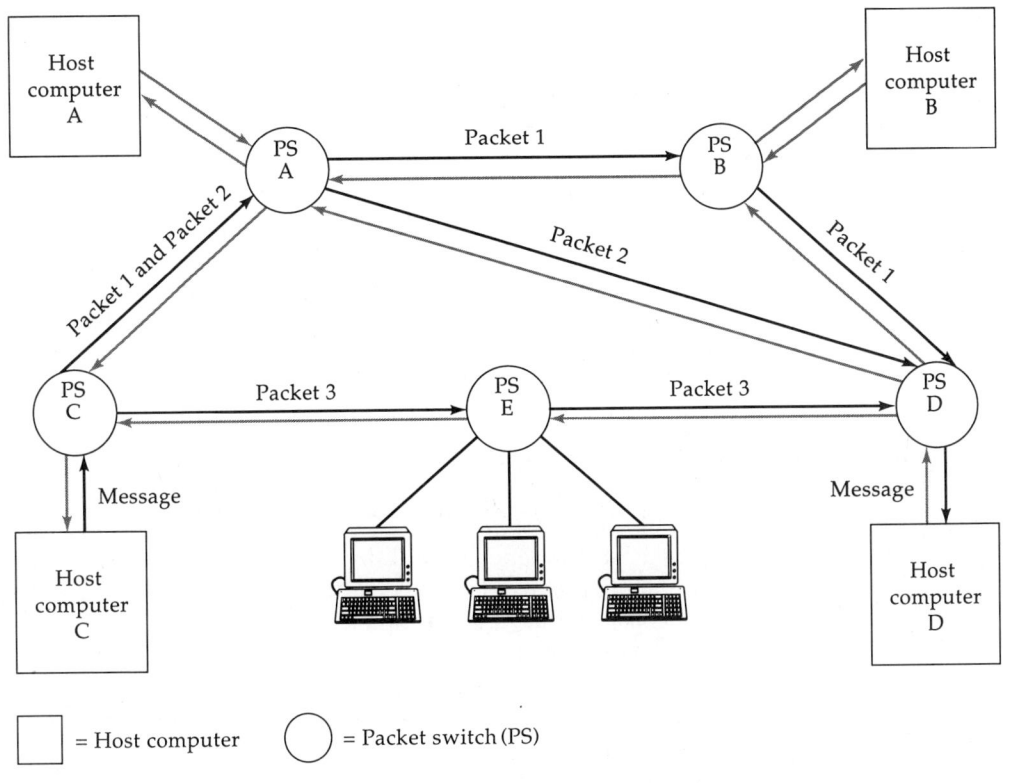

A *private packet-switching network* is one that is tailored to the needs of a particular organization. The transmission facilities for interconnecting the switching nodes, users, and computer systems are leased from common carriers. The network is used only by those who know of its existence and how to access it and who are authorized to use it. For example, the U.S. government currently owns and operates numerous private data networks for remote terminal access to central computers and databases, electronic mail, bulk documents, and file transfers among mainframe computers and personal computers. Hewlett-Packard sets up private packet networks tailored to customer needs.

Private PSNs require expenditures for packet-switching equipment and for recurring operations and maintenance. Compared to public PSNs, they provide better network security, predictable costs over the life of the network, and control over how and when to add or modify the network's technology.

A *hybrid packet-switching network* is a combination of public and private ones. This type of network allows an organization to set up its own network but use public PSNs to connect with remote locations where its low traffic volume does not justify a private PSN.

- **X.25 Standard**

    For different kinds of terminal equipment to access a public PSN, the CCITT developed the X.25 standard to permit connectivity. The X.25, also called the Interface between Data Terminals Operating in the Packet Mode on Public Network, specifies the rules for user access to a PSN, for setting up a data call from one computer to another, for exchanging data, and for terminating the call. With this standard, any user's computer can connect to both domestic and international networks using the same standard. For example, the X.25 tells how to convert the digital signals from various types of data equipment into a form that can be processed by a PAD to connect to a data network, such as Telenet.

- **Advantages of Packet-Switching Networks**

    Packet-switching networks offer the following advantages:

    - The message cost is independent of distance and time. Large volumes of data are transmitted at fixed costs regardless of the distance between end points. The charge is based on the quantity of packets transmitted, not on the time or distance involved.
    - Dissimilar data terminal equipment can use the network. To provide a common interface for connection between different packet vendors, a series of standards, such as the X.25, was developed.
    - Connectivity is available internationally.
    - Packet-switched networks offer total data security.
    - Packet-switched networks allow facilities to be shared efficiently by users.
    - Built-in transmission safeguards maintain data integrity. Packet switches retransmit lost or corrupt data.
    - Transmission delays are reduced because messages are broken into smaller segments—packets.
    - A private network may be cost-effective for a large organization with dispersed locations and a high volume of traffic, particularly if the off-peak hours of the network services can be resold.
    - The user has control over the private network. For example, a company with a private network has control over such areas as planning; quality, reliability, and availability of facilities; security; cost; and geographic coverage that might not be available from the public network.

- **Selecting a Packet-Switching Network**

    Since packet-switching networks vary in size and capabilities, a company should base the selection of a network on its traffic load, public access or

FIGURE 6-37 Guidelines for Selecting a Packet-Switching Network

- How many ports does the PSN support?
- What types of interfacing devices does the PSN use?
- What line speeds does the PSN support?
- What are the maximum number of nodes supported per network?
- What are the packet sizes supported?
- What is the packet throughput in packets per second per node?
- What is the number of simultaneous calls per second that can be accommodated?
- What network management information does the PSN provide?

private access or both, and the type of channel interfaces. The selection of a vendor is based on the amount of network control the user requires as well as the experience and services the vendor offers. A company should examine the performance of the packet-switching network, such as the items listed in Figure 6-37.

Packet-switching networks offer a cost-effective alternative for transmitting data and possibly voice. Telephone companies, independent carriers, and private companies are establishing PSNs to replace leased lines for data communications.

Summary

The purpose of a network is to electronically transmit encoded voice, text, data, and images from one physical location to another. To transmit data over a network requires data terminals equipment, data communication equipment, and a medium. The terminal, whether it is a dumb, a smart, or an intelligent terminal, must match the task and the characteristics of the existing network. So that data can be transmitted over an analog public or private telephone network, a modem must be used to convert digital signals to analog ones. At the receiving end, the modem reconverts them to their original form. When the circuit is digital, a digital service unit is required.

A multipoint configuration or the use of other equipment can be more economical than a point-to-point configuration in which each terminal transmits over its own dial or leased lines to the host computer. For example, multiplexed modems and stand-alone multiplexers using frequency-division multiplexing, time-division multiplexing, or statistical multiplexing can provide more economical ways of transmitting data. Host computers can be relieved of routine tasks by programming front-end processors to perform them. Digital-sharing devices can extend the port capacity of front-end processors, computers, and modems. Packet-switching networks offer users an alternative to circuit-switching networks including leased lines and dialup lines for transmitting data.

Key Terms

Analog bridge
Buffer
Data communications equipment
Data compression
Data service unit
Data terminal equipment
Digital-sharing device
Front-end processor
Interface
Line conditioning
Line-servicing groups:
Limited-distance modem
Narrowband modem
Voiceband modem
Wideband modem
Modem:
  Acoustic
  Direct-connect
Multiplexed modem
Multipoint network
Stand-alone multiplexers:
  Frequency-division multiplexer
  Time-division multiplexer
  Statistical multiplexer
Packet-switching network
Point-to-point network
Polling
Port
Rack mount modem
Terminal:
  Dumb terminal
  Intelligent terminal
  Smart terminal
Throughput
Value-added network

Self-Quiz

Indicate whether the statement is true or false.

1. A modem converts digital signals to analog ones for transmitting data over a voice line.   T/F
2. High-speed modems are asynchronous, while low-speed modems are synchronous.   T/F
3. All modems intended for use in the Bell system should be compatible with the Bell standards.   T/F
4. The narrower the bandwidth, the faster the possible transmission speed.   T/F
5. Modems that allow higher data speeds at lower transmission costs use line conditioning.   T/F
6. Multiplexed modems require that the sum of the individual channels does not exceed the total line speed.   T/F

Complete each of the following statements.

1. The basic components of a data communications network are _____ .
2. An example of an intelligent asynchronous device is a(an) _____ .
3. Modems that handle speeds from 19.2 kbps to 64 kbps are called _____ .
4. A modem that has built in rubber cups that fit a standard telephone handset is called a(an) _____ .
5. A network that requires terminals to take turns transmitting is called a(an) _____ .
6. To transmit data from two synchronous and two asynchronous terminals simultaneously to a host computer requires _____ .

Match Column A with Column B.

Column A
(a) Analog bridge
(b) Buffer
(c) Digital port-sharing device
(d) Dumb terminal
(e) Front-end processor
(f) Smart terminal

Column B
____ 1. Cannot be polled by the host computer.
____ 2. Links geographically dispersed terminals in a multipoint network.
____ 3. A synchronous terminal that transmit blocks of data.
____ 4. A computer that performs communication tasks for a host computer.
____ 5. Compensates for the different data rates between a transmitting device and a receiving device.
____ 6. Links terminals within the same buildings to reduce the number of modems needed.

Redesign the following network.

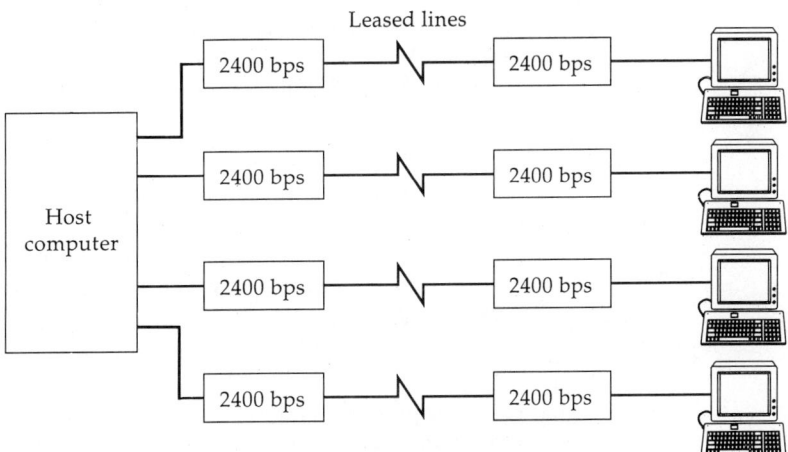

1. Change the network to a polling multiline network.
2. Change the network to one using 9600 bps multiplexed modems.
3. Change the network in (2) to allow one terminal to perform as a tail circuit.
4. Change the network in (1) to one using time-division multiplexing.

Review Questions

1. (a) Describe the characteristics of the three types of terminals.
   (b) Describe an office situation in which each type of terminal would be the best choice.

2. How is a buffer helpful to the sender and the receiver?
3. (a) Describe the four-line servicing groups.
   (b) Describe an office situation in which each type would be particularly suitable.
4. (a) How are modems with data compressors helping business activities?
   (b) How is throughput affected by using a 2400 bps modem with basic data compressor techniques?
   (c) How is throughput affected by using a 2400 bps modem with advanced data compressor techniques?
5. (a) What criteria do you consider to be most important when selecting a modem? Why?
   (b) What features would you want a modem to have? Why?
6. (a) What is (are) the difference(s) between a point-to-point and a multipoint network?
   (b) How can a network using analog bridges be both a multipoint and a point-to-point network?
7. How can a digital-sharing device be of help when setting up a network?
8. When could you use a multiplexed modem and not a stand-alone multiplexer?
9. (a) How does frequency-division multiplexing differ from time-division-multiplexing?
   (b) Is a time-division multiplexing or a statistical multiplexing better for transmitting data? Why?
10. How can a front-end processor be of help in operating a network?
11. (a) What is the difference between circuit-switching and packet-switching networks?
    (b) Describe how a document is sent over a packet-switching network?
    (c) Distinguish between public and private packet-switching networks. Give examples.
12. Referring to Figure 6-36, select the possible routes for the following messages.
    (a) Host computer A sends a message to host computer B.
    (b) Host computer D sends a message to host computer C.

▪ *Activities/Projects*

1. Visit a computer facility of an organization of your choice to examine how a modem operates. Obtain the following information:
   (a) Classify the modem according to operation modes, transmission type, transmission medium, line-servicing group, and transmission line connection.
   (b) Construct a diagram of how the modem connects to the telephone and the computer.
   (c) Describe the procedure for sending data including the commands entered into the computer.

2. In each of the following situations a company must set up a data communications network that is economical and provides the appropriate transmission media, modems or multiplexers, terminals, and data speeds. Construct a diagram of the network that you would recommend. Also include a description of each of the network components.
   (a) A lumber store has opened a branch store in the next town, a distance of three miles. Data traffic is expected to be heavy between the main store's host computer and the branch store's terminal.
   (b) Three companies need to access a host computer in Philadelphia via the dial network to simply key in numbers. An Allentown, Pennsylvania, company needs to access the Philadelphia store six to nine hours a week, while the other two companies, one in Hartford, Connecticut, and the other in Providence, Rhode Island, each require only three "connect" hours a week.
   (c) Four research laboratories in New Hampshire and Maine with similar data communications tasks often must access the company's host computer in Chicago. The frequent transmissions required between the labs' terminals and Chicago's host computer make dial lines uneconomical. However, four leased point-to-point connecting each lab with the host computer total 4000 miles of leased lines and require four host computer ports.
   (d) A company with headquarters in Boston has branch offices in Denver, Portland (Oregon), Salt Lake City, and Seattle. To connect each branch office's synchronous terminal with Boston's host computer could require eight modems and four point-to-point lines totaling 8,900 miles of leased lines.
3. A company with headquarters in Denver and branches in Philadelphia, Pennsylvania, Washington, D.C., West Palm Beach, Florida, Atlanta, Georgia, and Las Vegas, Nevada, exchange documents with each other daily.
   (a) Using these locations, construct a diagram illustrating a circuit-switching network.
   (b) Using these locations, construct a diagram illustrating a packet-switching network.
   (c) Discuss how a document is sent by each method.
   (d) Which network configuration would you prefer? Explain why.

■ *Case:* **Comparing Costs of Network Operations**

A Baltimore office of an accounting firm is using a synchronous terminal with a 4800 bps modem to communicate point-to-point with a host computer in Hartford, Connecticut. The monthly telephone charge for the leased line is $620 per month. The monthly modem charge for each of the two 4800 bps modems is $50.

Peter Jenkins, the company administration manager, would like to add three more terminals to the Baltimore office. He is considering enlarging the point-to-point network, with each terminal having its own line and modems, because he believes it would be an easy way to expand the network. You have been asked to recommend a network that includes the four terminals. You obtained the following cost information to help in preparing your analysis. Prices used are estimates. Modem and multiplexer prices represent typical equipment. Their costs are based on a three-year lease. The monthly charges for hardware are as follows:

	Monthly Charge 3-Year Lease	Purchase Price
2400 bps modem	$36	$540
4800 bps modem	54	1450
9600 bps modem	62	1695
19,200 bps modem	248	7315
Statistical multiplexer, 4-channel	55	1500

(a) Construct diagrams of the company's present network and the expanded ones that are being considered.
(b) Calculate the cost of the equipment for each of the present and proposed networks.
(c) What are your recommendations? Why?

■ *Additional Readings*

Noel J. Boulanger, "Safe at Any Speed," *Digital Review*, May 2, 1988, pp. 59–71.
"Buyers Guide: Modems," *PC Week*, June 25, 1988, pp. C/17–C/29.
C. Kenneth Miller, "Standards Battles Rage On," *TPT*, November 1987, pp. 48–52.
Dave Powell, "Are Standardized Modems an Illusion," *Telecommunication Products + Technology*, June 1987, pp. 21–32.

CHAPTER 7

Networks: Local- and Wide-Area Networks

Local-Area Networks and Wide-Area Networks
  Local-Area Network Defined
  Wide-Area Network Defined
  Why LANs and WANs?

LAN Technology
  LAN Hardware Components
  LAN Software Components
  LAN Topologies
  LAN Access Methods
  LAN Transmission Media
  LAN Transmission Methods

LAN Standards
  The OSI Model
  IEEE 800 Standard for LAN
  De Facto Standards

Commercial LANs—The Hardware Configuration

LANs to LANs to WANs
  LAN Hierarchy
  Span Technology

Alternatives to LANs
  Floppy-Disk Exchange
  Data Switches
  SubLANs
  Data PBX
  Multiuser Systems
  Central Office Local-Area Network

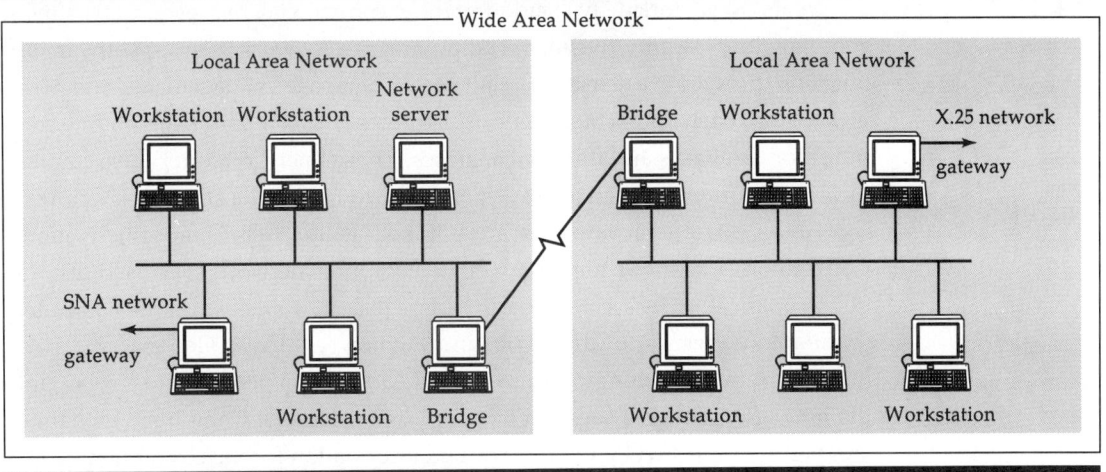

Selecting and Managing a LAN
Do You Need a LAN?
Selecting a LAN
Managing a LAN

Integrated Services Digital Network
ISDN Technology and Operation
Comparison of ISDNs and LANs
Benefits of ISDN

CHAPTER OBJECTIVES

After studying this chapter, you should be able to

1. Distinguish between local- and wide-area networks.
2. Explain the technology of LANs.
3. Identify the LANs protocols and standards including the OSI model.
4. Describe how LANs are connected to LANs and LANs to WANs.
5. Select alternatives to LANs.
6. Identify criteria for selecting a LAN.
7. Describe the duties of a LAN manager.
8. Discuss ISDN.

Martin Marietta Astronautics of Denver links twelve IBM microcomputer compatibles and fifty-eight Macintoshes into a network. Engineers use the network to share files, develop computer-assisted-design drawings, and exchange research proposals.[1]

In its New York City headquarters a commercial real estate investment company links twenty-five microcomputers on a network to share software application programs such as spreadsheets, database management, and word processing. Each microcomputer can also access the company's mainframe computer for databases and financial analyses. These microcomputers also communicate with others located in branch offices throughout the state of New York.

About 300 microcomputers were linked at the 1988 Democratic National Convention, making it the largest microcomputer network ever used at a national political party's convention. Nine separate subnetworks of computers (local-area networks) in three sites in downtown Atlanta, Georgia, and party headquarters in Washington were linked. The Atlanta police could also tap into the network through a series of communication servers. Computers exchanged messages, monitored bus traffic, tracked information for the convention's chairperson, delivered data to the press, kept track of important guests, and monitored convention operations.

During the 1980s, microcomputers and minicomputers became firmly established in offices and factories. Microcomputer users soon wanted to share computer files, programs, and storage as well as peripheral devices. The need to exchange data within and among departments as well as with others at remote sites resulted in developing networks for computers to talk to each other. A *network* is a communications system that allows attached devices, such as computers, to communicate.

The opening scenarios describe networks of computers communicating with each other in close proximity as well as at a distance. The purpose of this chapter is to present basic information about these networks and how companies manage and utilize them. Knowledge of the technology of the operation of these networks is necessary for selecting and managing them.

Local-Area Networks and Wide-Area Networks

■ Local-Area Network Defined

A **local-area network**, referred to as a LAN, is generally defined as a privately owned network that offers reliable high-speed communication channels for connecting information processing equipment, such as micro-

FIGURE 7-1 Characteristics of a Local Area Network

- It interconnects two or more communicating devices.
- It is usually limited to a geographical area that includes a section of a building, an entire building, or a cluster of buildings.
- It is owned, administered, and used by a single organization. (It is not subject to Federal Communications Commission regulations.)
- It supports operations at moderate to high data rates with a consistently low error rate. (The range is from 500 kbps for low-speed LANs to over one billion bps for fiber-optic LANs.)
- It supports full connectivity among its workstations, every workstation being able to communicate with each other.
- It may consist of many types of equipment and applications integrated into a discrete physical entity. Devices are connected by a continuous structural medium such as a single cable.
- It can transmit data, voice, and video signals.

computers, in a limited geographic area. The network is controlled by computer software that allows linked microcomputers to exchange information and share software and peripherals.

A LAN can transmit data, voice, and video signals, although at this time most LANs transmit only data. Data is assembled into packets for transmission on a packet-switching network and restored to its original form at the receiving end, as was discussed in Chapter 6.

What makes a LAN a LAN? The characteristics of a local area network are identified in Figure 7-1.

■ Wide-Area Network Defined

By contrast, a **wide-area network**, referred to as a WAN, connects computers that are geographically separated across a city, across a country, or in different countries. Transmission is by dialup, leased lines, other common carriers, microwave, and satellite systems. Bridge devices connect two LANs of the same topology while gateway devices connect two dissimilar LANs. (See the chapter opening diagram.)

A type of WAN called a metropolitan-area network (MAN) is a data network that links together LANs at different sites within a city. Links are usually digital circuits leased from the telephone company. For example, the nine LANs used at the 1988 Democratic National Convention were linked in a MAN. A WAN links MANs together so that companies in one city can access the data resources in another city or country.

Why LANs and WANs?

About 80% of all company documents travel a short distance—typically within an office or building or between a group of buildings. LANs provide immediate, inexpensive delivery of these documents. The remaining 20% of the documents travel outside of this area. They are delivered by communicating at a distance with other LANs using wide-area networks.

Figure 7-2 lists some of the reasons why organizations network microcomputers.

According to International Data Corporation, a market research company in Framingham, Massachusetts, the market value of LAN shipments in 1987 was $824 million. By 1992 the value is projected to be $2.7 billion, over 3.6 million LANs having been installed. Among the leading companies in the LAN market are 3Com Corporation, Novell, IBM Corporation, Digital Equipment Corporation, Wang Laboratories, Apple Computer, and AT&T's Information Systems.

FIGURE 7-2   Reasons for Networking Microcomputers

Reason	Comment
To share expensive peripherals, such as high-priced letter-quality printers, optical character readers, modems, and devices that emulate host computers	For example, a laser printer, an expensive peripheral, outputs documents faster than information can be generated by a single microcomputer. By linking microcomputers together to allow printer sharing, the printer gets more use, and its cost becomes a shared expense.
To share software application programs, such as word processing, spreadsheets, and databases	Employees may use one or a group of application programs, produced either commercially or written specifically to perform certain tasks. Computer networking allows employees to access and share the same programs. For example, a microcomputer network allows a user to download a word processing program, prepare a document, and then store it. Other users can make changes to the document because they have access to the same version of the word processing program.
To share data files	By networking computers, employees can exchange files or documents that others have prepared.
To share common databases	For example, employees typically need access to the company's database of customers that lists important information about each one. By using a computer network they can share a computer database and make better use of the company's investment in preparing and maintaining the databases.

FIGURE 7-2 Continued

Reason	Comment
To interconnect to mainframe computers and/or minicomputers	By networking, employees can access mainframe and minicomputer data files and databases.
To send and receive electronic mail	For example, microcomputer users scattered throughout an office building or working different shifts can talk with each other electronically by exchanging short text messages at minimal cost.
To share the workload among several microcomputers or workstations at the same time	Load sharing increases the organization's return on its microcomputer investment.
To be able to expand the LAN	By adding one or more microcomputers, companies can avoid having to add more expensive equipment such as a minicomputer or a host computer.
To back up files of all microcomputer users on the network	Users often forget to back up their individual files. Since files of LAN users are stored on the network's hard disk, only one person needs to be responsible for remembering to back up the disks periodically.
To provide a high data transfer rate	Many networks can reach data transfer speeds of up to 10 Mbps, and some reach over 150 Mbps.
To communicate with other LANs located nearby or at a distance	Communicating with LANs and WANs provides users with access to more information resources.

LAN Technology

Before a company can decide whether or not to install or expand a LAN and what is needed for satisfactory operation, basic knowledge of LAN technology is necessary. This section examines the LAN configuration and control schemes that are prevalent today.

■ LAN Hardware Components

The major LAN hardware components include microcomputers with network interface cards, network servers, and the cables that connect them with each other, as illustrated in Figure 7-3. The network interface card that is installed in the microcomputer is attached to the LAN cable and allows the microcomputer to communicate with the network. The server directs the network operation.

FIGURE 7-3   A LAN with Workstations, a Network Interface Card, Cable, and a Network Server

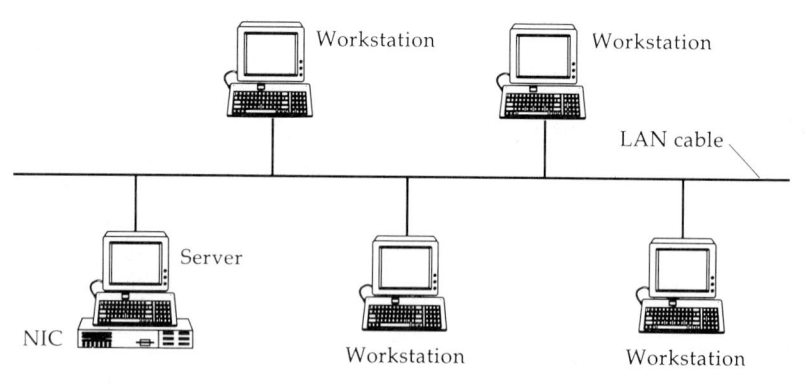

Redrawn courtesy of Novell, Inc., Provo, Utah.

Workstations.   A microcomputer with an installed network interface card is defined as a **workstation**. Workstations, the taskmasters of the network, run the application programs, process the data by retrieving needed programs and files from a network server, and then return them when finished.

Network Interface Card.   The **network interface card** (NIC) is a circuit board that plugs into an expansion slot of a microcomputer to make the physical connection between the workstation and the network cable, as shown in Figure 7-3. This component determines how a workstation will access the network. The NIC controls the data transmission rate, the network (cable) access method, the size of message units (packets), and message-addressing information.

Servers.   An important component of the LAN is the *network server*, also called a *file server*. (The term refers to both hardware and software.) The hardware server, linked by cable to the workstations, is a special-purpose computer whose main function is to serve the needs of the workstation users. The server's hard disk contains the network operating system and the workstations' data, files, and application programs. Peripherals such as printers and modems can be attached to the server for workstations to share.

Dedicated, Specialized, and Nondedicated Network Servers.   A **dedicated server** is a computer designed exclusively to serve the network. Not only may a LAN have one or more network servers, but it may also have one or

FIGURE 7-4   A Network Server Menu

```
┌ Main Menu ─────────────────────────────────────────────┐
│   Directories and Files                                │
│   Printer Connections                                  │
│   Shared Resources                                     │
│   Log Out                                              │
│   3+Mail                                               │
│   Network Menu                                         │
│   Word Processing Programs                             │
│   2nd Quarter Reviews                                  │
│   Personnel Data                                       │
│   Marketing                    ┌ DOS Utilties ════════╗│
│   Sales Forecasting            │  DISKCOPY            ║│
│   DOS Utilties                 │  CHKDSK              ║│
│   Applications                 │  FORMAT              ║│
└────────────────────────────────┴──────────────────────╝┘
```

Courtesy of 3Com Corporation.

more **specialized servers**. These servers handle specific network services. Examples of specialized servers are database servers, print servers, and communication servers. A **nondedicated server** is a microcomputer that functions as both a server and a workstation. When the microcomputer is not being used as a server, it operates as a workstation. This type of server generally does not have the performance capabilities of a dedicated server, especially if numerous workstations are attached to it.

Operating a LAN. When a workstation user wants to use application programs, such as a word processing program, or retrieve a file from the network server, the user types the name of the application program or the file at the DOS prompt and presses the return key or refers to a menu like that shown in Figure 7-4. A request for the program or file is then sent to the workstation's network interface card, over the network cable, and finally to the server. The server responds by retrieving a copy of the requested item from its hard disk and sending it over the network cable to the requesting workstation.

The workstation user can store files (or documents) either on the workstation's local storage device, if it has one, or on the server's hard disk. Some workstations contain floppy disk drives or hard disks, while others are *diskless workstations*—without floppy disk drives or hard disks. Diskless workstations are less expensive; they rely on the contents of the network server's hard disk to access programs and store data files. They also prevent users from physically copying information from the network.

■ **LAN Software Components**

LAN software components include the network operating system, the workstation operating system, and application programs.

Network Operating System Software. The LAN server runs two operating systems: a host operating system and a network operating system. (An operating system is a collection of programs that allows a computer system to supervise its own operation.) The *host operating system* enables the server to perform its own operations, including loading the network operating system software onto its system. The LAN's network operating system (NOS), which is a group of software programs residing on the server's hard disk, manages the network by performing functions such as the following:

- Provides services to the workstation user. For example, if the user wants a list of the LAN's available resources, the user asks the NOS.
- Supports application programs, such as word processing, spreadsheet, and database, so that they will run on the network.
- Controls the operation of services, such as sharing files and peripherals, for all workstations on the network.

Figure 7-5 identifies leading NOSs and the corresponding workstation operating system and host operating system that must be used with each one.

Workstation Operating Systems. Each LAN workstation uses its own operating system to perform its tasks, including accessing the server(s) for files, data, application programs, and other services. The server can download the operating system to the workstation, or the workstation may have its own system. The operating system most commonly used by LAN workstations is Microsoft's Disk Operating System (DOS), as Figure 7-5 shows.

Network Application Program Software. Application programs, such as word processing, spreadsheets, and databases, are stored on the server's

FIGURE 7-5 Network Operating Systems

Network Operating System	Workstation Operating System	Host Operating System	Network Vendor
NetWare	DOS, MAC, OS/2	NetWare	Novell
MS-NET	DOS	DOS	Microsoft
3+Share	DOS	DOS	3Com
PC-Network Program	DOS	DOS	IBM
PC-NFS	DOS	DOS or Other	Sun
VINES	DOS	UNIX 5	Banyan
3+Open	OS/2	OS/2	3Com
Lan Server	OS/2	OS/2	IBM
Star Group	DOS	UNIX 5.3	AT&T

disk. Since a LAN creates a multiuser environment, application programs must be specifically written for the network.

■ LAN Topologies

LAN topology defines the physical and logical ways in which network nodes are linked together. A *node* is an intelligent device, such as a workstation, a server, or an interconnecting equipment facility, that is attached to a network. A *link* is the communication path between two nodes. The two basic types of connections used for building LAN topologies are point-to-point and multipoint. As discussed in the previous chapter, a *point-to-point connection* connects two nodes by a single communication link, while a *multipoint* or *multidrop connection* consists of several nodes sharing the same communications link, but only one node transmitting at a time.

The three common network topologies, shown in Figure 7-6, are star, bus, and ring. A *star topology* connects all nodes (stations) to a central node, which routes data to the appropriate place. A *bus topology* connects all nodes to one cable running the length of the network. A *ring topology* connects all nodes in a closed loop. Note that both the star and the ring are point-to-point connections, while the bus is a multipoint connection.

Physical Topology. The **physical topology** determines the way cables run and the way the nodes are physically connected to each other. The selection of a particular physical topology depends on the situation. For example, when all the nodes, such as workstations, are in one room, the bus configuration can easily connect them. When the nodes are scattered throughout offices that are wired to a central telephone system, the star configuration enables each node to be connected by a wire to a wiring closet, which is a termination point for customer premises wiring.

FIGURE 7-6 **Common Topologies Used in LANs**

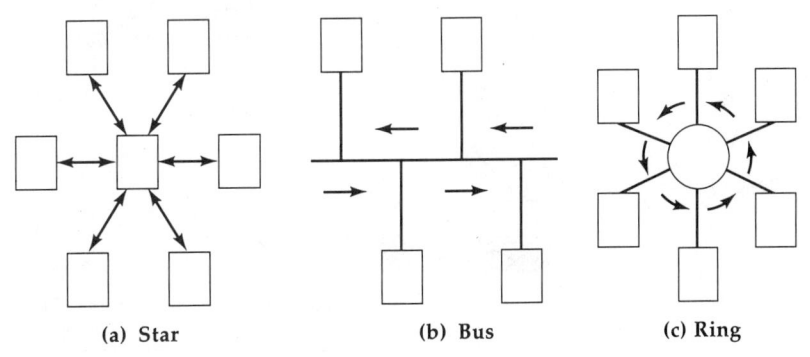

(a) Star   (b) Bus   (c) Ring

Logical Topology. The **logical topology** describes how signals flow between nodes and how they interact. The choice is either a peer-to-peer network or a hierarchical network, as shown in Figure 7-7. A **peer-to-peer network** allows every node to have equal access to the network. Each node can send and receive data at any time without having to seek permission from a central node. Conversely, a **hierarchical network** does not allow each

FIGURE 7-7   Logical Topology

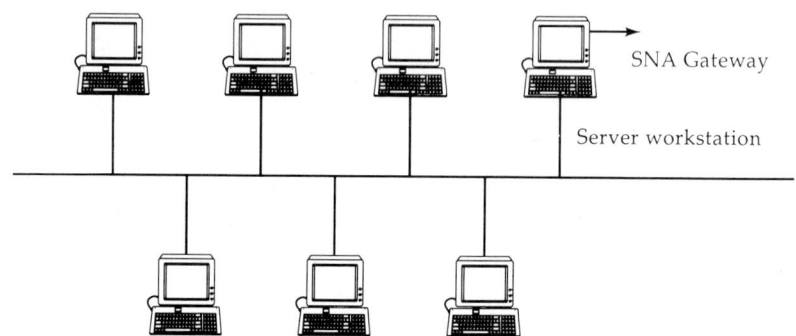

(a)   Peer-to-Peer Network of Workstations (Bus Configuration)

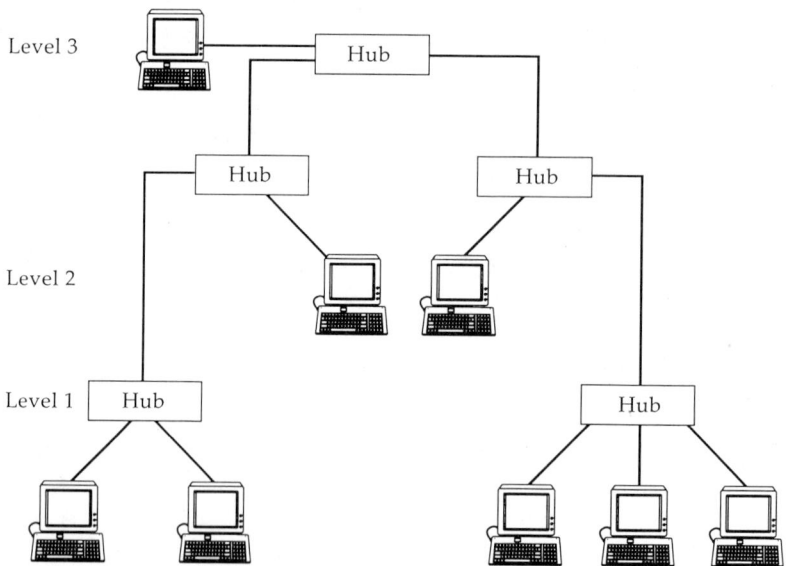

(b)   Hierarchical Network of Workstations (Star Configuration)

node equal access to the network. Instead, designated nodes control access to the network, all data transfer taking place through the control nodes.

Star Topology. The **star topology**, the oldest and simplest of the LAN arrangements, links each outlying workstation, or node, to a central workstation, which is the network server, as shown in Figure 7-8. Examples are StarLAN by AT&T and others and Arcnet by Datapoint, Standard Microsystems, and Pure Data. The star network uses no shared cable; each node (workstation) has its own dedicated cable. If a problem in the central switch occurs, then each station also develops trouble. Total loss of communication can occur when the central switch ceases to operate, but a malfunctioning workstation or its cable will affect only that workstation.

Ring Topology. In **ring topology**, shown in Figure 7-9, workstations, or nodes, are connected only to their adjacent neighbors on the ring and to no other node. Signals are sent unidirectionally from a source node around the ring from node to node until they reach their destination. The topology can be designed so that the failure of one node will not disrupt the operation of the remaining ones. To add a new node, the ring must be broken. An example is IBM's Token-Ring.

Bus Topology. The "linear" **bus topology** consists of a linear length of cable, called a bus or trunk, that is shared by all the workstations, or nodes,

FIGURE 7-8 Workstations in the Star Topology

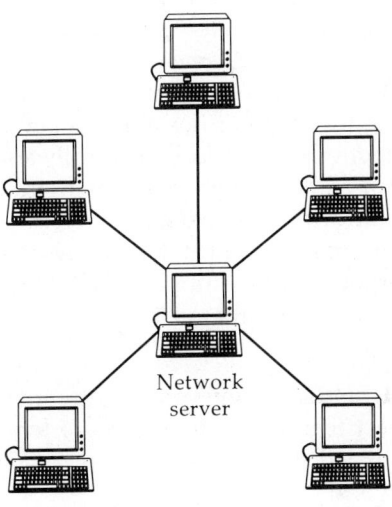

FIGURE 7-9 **Workstations in the Ring Topology**

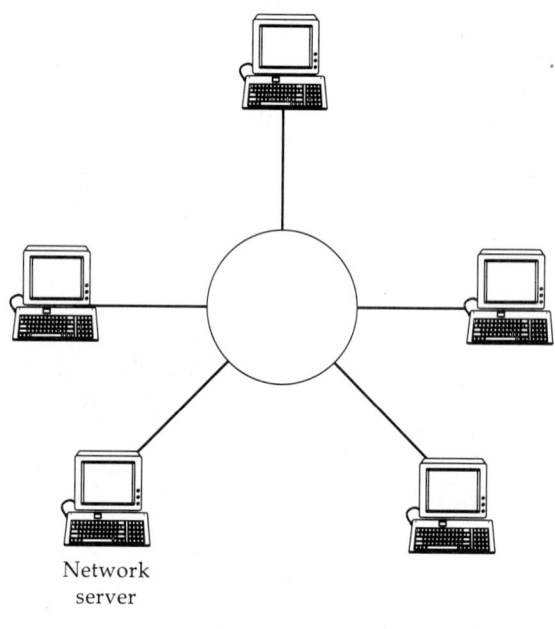

Network server

on the network, shown in Figure 7-10. All nodes receive transmitted data and discard the data not addressed to them. In such a configuration there must be management of who is broadcasting, to whom, and for how long. Some bus networks are managed by a central node, or hub, but the prevailing method is to establish a set of transmitting procedures obeyed by all nodes. Bus networks are easily and relatively cheaply installed. New nodes can be added or deleted without causing downtime for the network. The network's diagnostic features can locate cable faults, although if the cable fails at any point, the entire network stops functioning. An example is Ethernet, which is supported by Xerox, Digital Equipment Corporation, 3Com, Novell, and others.

Hybrids. Many vendors offer hybrid architectures to take advantage of the best features of two or more topologies. Examples are token-buses, star-shaped rings, star-buses, and daisy-chains. Figure 7-11 shows two types of hybrids.

Figure 7-12 identifies factors to consider when selecting a LAN topology.

FIGURE 7-10 **Workstations in the Bus Topology**

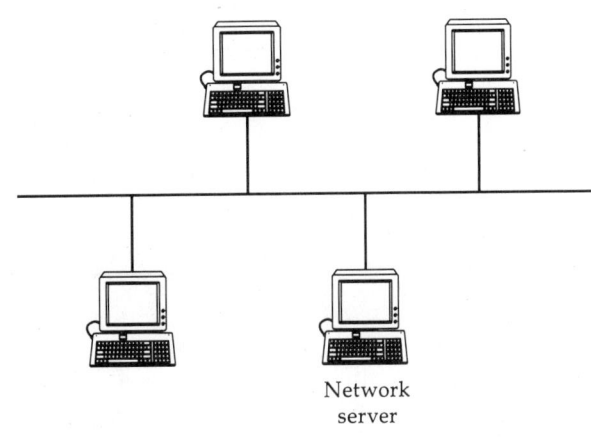

Network server

■ LAN Access Methods

Because LANs with media-sharing topologies use a single cable to carry signals to every node, two messages cannot be on one cable in the same place at the same time, or conflicts or collisions will occur. To determine which node gets the network, LANs use one of two types of network access methods: noncontention-oriented (polling) methods or contention-oriented methods.

Noncontention-Oriented Methods. **Noncontention-oriented methods**, referred to as polling methods, determine the order in which nodes can take turns accessing the network so that message-sending nodes do not collide with each other and thus do not require retransmission. The two most commonly used noncontention methods are roll-call polling and token passing.

Roll-Call Polling. A common polling technique is **roll-call polling**, also called *centralized polling*. This method uses a master or control node to query each node in turn, asking, "Node 1, do you wish to speak?," "Node 2, do you wish to speak?," and so on. If the node wishes to speak (or "transmit"), it sends its message. If not, the master node polls the next node in sequence. The master node decides which node is to access the network at any one time. Although polling avoids collisions, the network carries no information during the time spent polling nodes that have no messages to transmit.

FIGURE 7-11   Hybrid Architectures

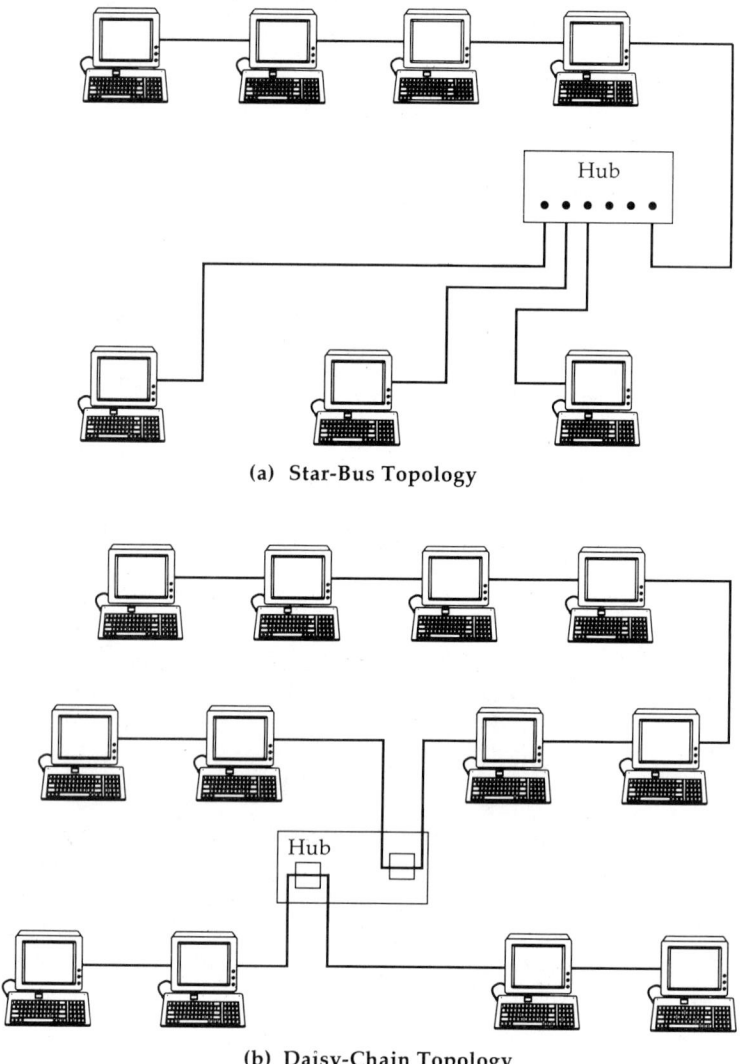

(a) Star-Bus Topology

(b) Daisy-Chain Topology

Token Passing.   Although token passing can take place on a bus, it is primarily used with ring topologies. In **token passing**, users can transmit messages on the network only after they have gained control of an electronic token, which is passed from node to node throughout the network. If the token is clear, that is, no message is attached, the node that is processing the token may attach a message and transmit it to the next node. That node

FIGURE 7-12 Factors to Consider in Selecting a LAN Topology

- The users' objectives
- The network's ability to continue to recover after the failure of one or more of its workstations
- The network's physical constraints, such as its data rates, maximum operating distance, maximum number of stations, and channel error rate
- The cost of the system, including installation and operational costs

---

will retransmit the message to the next one and so on down the line. The token does not clear until the addressed node receives the message and processes it. The network has a built-in intelligence that gives each node a chance to pass the token along or communicate in sequence. Occasionally, tokens get damaged, lost, or duplicated. An advantage of token passing is that it is deterministic, that is, a particular node knows exactly how long it must wait to gain access to the line. This advantage is not available in contention-oriented methods.

Contention-Oriented Methods. **Contention-oriented methods** anticipate conflicts or collisions and use them to allocate the common channel. These methods are used by bus topologies, a popular one being Carrier Sense Multiple Access with Collision Detection (CSMA/CD). Variations of this contention technique include Carrier Sense Multiple Access (CSMA) and Carrier Sense Multiple Access with Collision Avoidance (CSMA/CA). The differences among these methods are minimal.

CSMA/CD. The **CSMA/CD** method allows any node that is about to transmit to first sense that the channel is free, a procedure referred to as "listen before talking." If the network is idle, the node can transmit; if another node begins to transmit simultaneously, the transmissions collide; the result is a garbled message. On detecting a collision, each node involved backs off and abandons its transmission, waits a brief interval, and then tries to retransmit.

The major drawback of this access method is that it is stochastic, not deterministic. In other words, this method does not guarantee that a node's message will arrive within a certain period of time. In most applications this is not a serious problem, only a matter of an electronic message arriving within a few seconds instead of a few milliseconds.

Comparison of CSMA/CD with Token Passing. CSMA/CD works well with networks that have bursts of intermittent traffic. The token-passing method is more desirable when it is necessary to control the amount of time a node must wait for access.

FIGURE 7-13   LAN Transmission Media

	Twisted-Pair Wire	Baseband Coaxial Cable	Broadband Coaxial Cable	Fiber-Optic Cable
Partial Bandwidth	1.5 Mbps–10 Mbps	10 Mbps	400 MHz	>150 Mbps
Media Expense (U.S. $/km)	$300	$1500–$5000	$1500–$5000	$300–$6000
Installation Expense	Low	Medium	High	Low
Cable Weight (kg/km)	50	75–750	150–1500	30–170
RFI/EMI* Susceptibility	High	Medium	Low	None
Freedom from Crosstalk, Echoing, and Ringing	Low	Medium	High	Very high
Spark Hazard	High	High	High	None
Data-Transfer Reliability	Low	High	High	Very high
Transmission Security	Low	Low	Low	High

Source: Copyright 1988, 3Com Corporation. Reprinted with permission from *CONNECT, The Journal of Computer Networking*, Summer 1988. All rights reserved.
*Radio frequency interference (RFI) and electromagnetic interference (EMI) refer to the intrusion of unwanted signals into a cable.

■ LAN Transmission Media

LAN transmission media, the physical links over which the data travels, can be any of three guided media: twisted-pair wire, standard (thick) or thin coaxial cable, and fiber-optic cable. Figure 7-13 summarizes their characteristics. The type of medium selected determines the speed at which the network can operate, the cost of installation, the ease of maintenance, immunity from radio and electromagnetic interference, and even the type of network that can be installed. For example, fiber-optic cable can carry signals at up to 100 Mbps while the rate of twisted-pair wire ranges from 1 to 10 Mbps. As you recall, the greater the bandwidth, the more information that can be sent through a system a given time. Unless the cable is already in place in the office, the cost of the cable and installation can be more than 50% of the cost of the entire LAN installation.

Twisted-Pair Wire.   Twisted-pair wire, otherwise known as common telephone wire, is unshielded twisted copper wire, the least expensive medium available for LAN installations and the easiest medium to install. Since it is the same type of cable as is used for telephone systems, existing telephone cable may be used for some LANs, which eliminates the expense of rewiring the office. Twisted-pair wire is preferable for low-cost, short-distance LANs such as small networks that link microcomputers.

The susceptibility of twisted-pair wire to electrical interference can be overcome by using shielded twisted-pair wire. This medium is like the typical telephone twisted-pair wire but is insulated against electrical interferences and noise, is more precisely made, and can support higher data transmission rates and a longer cable length for a single LAN. A drawback is that shielded twisted-pair wire is one of the most expensive media. The Travelers Corporation has installed about 2.5-million feet of shielded twisted-pair wiring to create about fifty-five IBM token rings that link about 10,000 workstations at corporate headquarters in Hartford, Connecticut.

Coaxial Cable. Coaxial cable, currently the primary medium for LANs, can link more than 1000 devices in a single LAN network. Networks can be built with thin or thick (standard) coaxial cable. Both types of cable are shielded wire, which insulates them against electrical interferences or noise, making them especially suitable for noisy offices. Thin coaxial cable is normally used inside open areas or in small networks, while thick coaxial cable is used as a backbone in traditional wired systems or in areas of high electrical noise.

Fiber-Optic Cable. Compared to twisted-pair and coaxial cable, fiber-optic cable is much thinner and can carry more channels. Its size makes it possible to fit into extremely small spaces, while its high security makes it ideal for outside installation between buildings. Its bandwidth supports data speeds far in excess of the needs of most LANs.

The cost of fiber-optic cable, once a disadvantage in comparison to other media, is now comparable to standard (thick) coaxial cable. Although fiber-optic cable is essentially maintenance-free, installation still requires special tools and skills. Improvements in this technology will result in fiber optics becoming a preferred medium for users.

The U.S. Military Academy in West Point, New York, has one of the largest fiber-optic networks of its type in a university setting. The $4.2 million installation includes more than 4500 ports. Delta Airlines uses a fiber system that links Delta's three operating facilities at Hartsfield International Airport, Atlanta, Georgia. St. Joseph's Health Center in Orange, California, recently installed a fiber-optic network because of its cost-effectiveness as a transmission medium.

Fiber-Optic Data Distribution Interface. An important development in the LAN industry is the proposal by the American National Standards Institute (ANSI) X379.5 Committee of the first fiber-optic network standard, called the Fiber-Optic Data Distribution Interface (FDDI). In an FDDI network, workstations are physically connected by fiber-optic cable in a ring topology. Data is transmitted sequentially around the ring at 100 Mbps or more, ten times the speed of Ethernet. A network can support as many as 500 stations and cover up to 200 kilometers in total network length without using additional signaling equipment, such as repeaters.

An FDDI configuration consists of a primary ring and a secondary ring. This topology allows the network to continue operating in the event that one of the stations on the ring fails or if one of the cable segments is disabled. FDDI-2 supports synchronous traffic and includes circuit-switching capability so that voice and video can be integrated on the same network. FDDI-2 also allows PBXs to be connected to the network to support combined voice and data traffic.

■ LAN Transmission Methods

Baseband, rather than broadband, is the transmission method most often used for office LANs because of its lower cost and ease of operation.

Baseband Network. As you recall from Chapter 2, *bandwidth* is the measure of the range of frequencies a communication network can transmit. A **baseband network** devotes its entire bandwidth to a single channel in order to carry one signal at a time. Since baseband signals on a LANs are always digital, the sending device places each signal onto the cable without modification of any kind. Each node (workstation) on a baseband network usually shares the cable through a form of time-division multiplexing.

Broadband Network. A **broadband** network divides its bandwidth into subchannels so that multiple applications including voice, data, and video can be sent simultaneously. By using frequency-division multiplexing to divide the bandwidth, each channel transmits signals at a different frequency to support its own application.

Since broadband networks use analog signals, digital data must first be converted to analog before transmission, as by the modems in Figure 7-14.

FIGURE 7-14   Broadband Connection

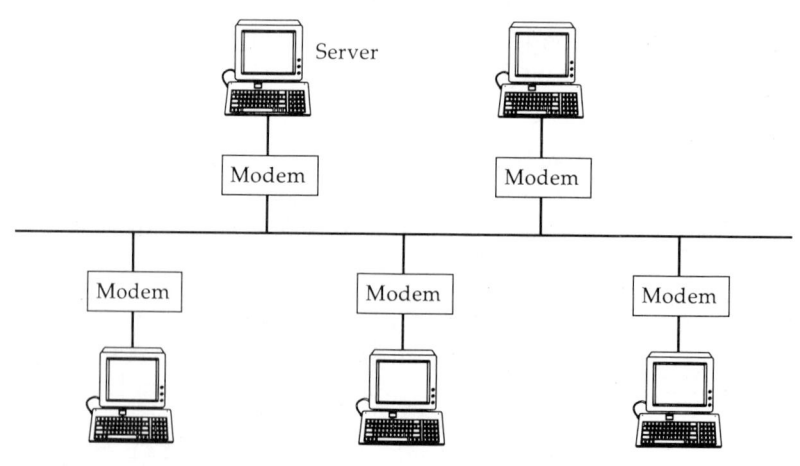

Courtesy of Novell, Inc., Provo, Utah.

A broadband network can span up to 55 miles, while a baseband network can transmit only a couple of miles before the signal weakens beyond recognition. Coaxial cable and fiber-optic cable are better suited for broadband transmission than is twisted-pair wire. Although broadband systems are more complex, they provide higher data rates over greater distances than do baseband systems.

For example, a utility company wanted its 8000 employees located in San Ramon, Hayward, and San Diego, California, and Japan to communicate with each other using both computer and voice communications. The company selected a broadband LAN to accommodate both types of communications. The network was subdivided into department LANs, each LAN having no more than 100 nodes (workstations) and one to three servers.

LAN Standards

Since the early days of computers, a continuing problem has been one vendor's computer being able to accept data created by another vendor's computer. At one time the only solution was to retype the data—a task that is both time-consuming and fraught with errors. The attraction of LANs is that they allow communications between equipment of different vendors. Users can purchase equipment that solves their individual local processing needs and still be able to share resources and communicate with others.

Two terms that are commonly used when discussing LANs are connectivity and interoperability. **Connectivity** is the ability to tie devices together physically, such as linking microcomputers and interconnecting heterogeneous hardware systems and components to pass data. **Interoperability** goes beyond connectivity; it allows users from diverse environments to correctly interpret and respond to the data received. For example, interoperability means that you can transfer a document from a Digital system to an IBM system, revise or edit it, and then return the document to the original system for additional editing or revision.

To ensure equipment connectivity and interoperability, there need to be common standards used by the same or different vendors. Communications standards are formally adopted and widely accepted rules that describe an agreed-on way in which computers should communicate, such as the transmission media between communicating computers, the type of interface between a computer system and a transmission medium, and the format of the transmitted message.

Standards are defined at both national and international levels. A national standard is developed by a national standards organization and adopted by vendors and suppliers in that country, while an international standard is developed by international organizations and adopted by vendors and suppliers worldwide. An example of an international organization is the Geneva International Standards Organization (ISO), which includes national standards organizations worldwide. Manufacturers that adopt the same standards for the design and building of their hardware and software can assure users that their systems will communicate with each other. For more information on how ISO develops standards, refer to the article by Richard Desjardins.[2]

■ The OSI Model

In 1981 the ISO set forth the *open systems interconnection (OSI) reference model*. The purpose of the **OSI model** is to allow computers worldwide to exchange data with each other, independent of manufacturer or implementation of technology. The OSI model is considered to be the industry's primary blueprint for network products for the next decade with the majority of the world's computer vendors implementing and supporting these protocols. The *Corporation for Open Systems (COS) International*, a nonprofit research and development consortium, selects products and services operating under the OSI and places its seal on them.

The OSI model divides the total data communications task into seven separate functions or "layers." These functions include the preparation of messages and data and their actual transmission onto the network. The model is hierarchical, so each layer provides certain services to the layer above it as well as using the services of the layer below it. The layers in one system communicate with the corresponding (peer) layers in the other.

Description of Each OSI Model Layer. Each layer has its own *protocol*, sets of rules for how information is exchanged over a computer network, with standards for each protocol set by the ISO. Figure 7-15 presents the seven layers of the OSI model and each of their functions. Within each layer are protocols that define message formats and rules for message exchange between communicating systems. The first four layers, referred to as the *transport protocol*, define protocols that enable a workstation or a network system to pass data to another system. These layers deal with the mechanical and electrical specifics of connecting to the transmission medium, the error-free transmission of data, and transmission of data to correct destinations.

Once the data arrives at its destination, the protocols at the top three layers come into play. These protocols interpret the received data and make it available to applications for the end-user. Without these layers, transmitted data would be meaningless to user applications and therefore unusable.

For example, in an electronic mail application the lower-layer standards ensure that a memo written on vendor A's system is transmitted accurately to vendor B's system. The higher-layer standards ensure that the received message is understood by the mail application on vendor B's system and made available to the addressed person or persons on vendor B's system.

Figure 7-16 shows how a LAN communicates with another LAN using the OSI model. Data flows down from the application layer to the physical layer, picking up additional overhead, which defines the communication

FIGURE 7-15   The Open Systems Interconnection Reference Model

- *Layer 1: Physical Standard.* Establishes the physical medium between the computer and the network. It specifies the physical and electrical characteristics of cables and connectors and other hardware responsible for encoding and physically transferring data between workstations on a network. For example, it specifies the type, length, and thickness of cable; the number and location of prongs on a plug; and the voltage requirements.
- *Layer 2: Data Link Protocols.* Packages the data for transmission and unpackages them for receipt. It ensures that both sender and reviewer agree on synchronization, error detection, recovery procedures, and initiation and operation procedures. For example, it detects and corrects bit transmission errors, assembles outgoing messages into blocks called frames, disassembles incoming frames, and acknowledges that a message has been successfully transferred.
- *Layer 3: Network (or Packet) Protocols.* Sets up a path through the network and defines the procedures by which connections between systems are established, maintained, and terminated. Decisions about the network address, routing, and switching are made at this layer. Recovery from some transmission errors is also provided. For example, it translates logical addresses into physical addresses and picks the LAN network route if more than one is available on the LAN. It defines the procedures for connecting different packet-switching networks.
- *Layer 4: End-to-End Transport Protocols.* After a route through the network has been set up by the network-level protocols, this layer organizes messages into the correct form for the selected transmission service and also performs some network management tasks.
- *Layer 5: Session Protocols.* Establishes the connection for transferring data between the sender and the receiver—just like the telephone dial tone when you get ready to make a telephone call. Other protocols specify the way in which connections are to be terminated or released and the structuring of the communications dialog, such as whose turn is it to speak, for how long, and half- or full-duplex communications. Still others address buffering and queuing of messages and interrupting, reusing, and resynchronizing sessions.
- *Layer 6: Presentation Protocols.* Performs data translation, data encoding/decoding, formatting, and syntax. Messages are formatted and translated to enable the receiving system to understand and use them. These functions adapt the information-handling characteristics of one application process to those of another process. This layer also handles data encryption/decryption and disguising one device as another. For example, disguising devices may be making a workstation appear as a 3270 terminal by interposing hardware (emulation card) or software.
- *Layer 7: Application Protocols.* Receives messages from sending programs in one computer and hands them over to receiving programs in the second computer. It provides the interface between the communications environment and the application using it. It is where formatted data is finally delivered to the user. This layer does not carry out applications, such as word processing; instead, it supplies functions, such as file transfer or electronic mail, that allow the workstation users to communicate with other systems on the network. It is responsible for getting the appropriate screens, menus, and headers to the user workstations.

FIGURE 7-16 **Communicating LANs**

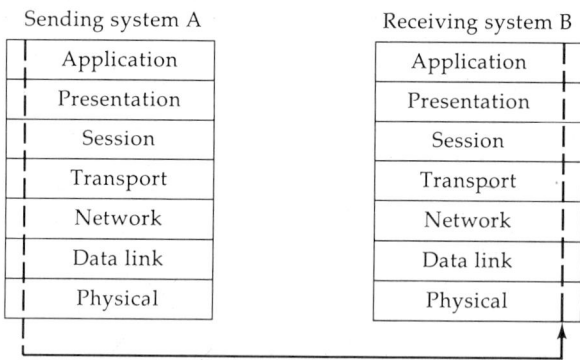

language and format. The receiving computer, which is connected to a different LAN, receives the information on the cable at the physical layer and picks off overhead information to retrieve the actual data.

Benefits of the OSI Model. The OSI model offers computer vendors and users three major benefits:

- *Data exchange between users is easier.* Users can buy equipment from one vendor and expect it to work with equipment from another OSI-supporting vendor.
- *Users can choose the best system for the application regardless of vendor.* Users are not limited to selecting a system based on whether it will communicate with existing systems. Standards protect users' hardware and software investments.
- *The establishment of the OSI model allows manufacturers to concentrate on developing and enhancing user applications.* No longer do they have to spend their resources on how to interconnect with each other's equipment.

■ IEEE 800 Standard for LAN

LAN standards are being produced by Project 802 of the Institute of Electrical and Electronics Engineers (IEEE), a professional society based in the United States. The **IEEE 800 standards**, which have also been adopted by ISO, deal with the first and second layers—the physical and link layers—of the ISO model. They specify the physical medium and how data are sent. Figure 7-17 provides a summary of major standards.

For example, vendors that apply the 802.3 standard to their equipment, such as Digital Equipment Corporation (DEC), Hewlett-Packard, and 3Com

FIGURE 7-17 Summary of Major Standards

Level 7	CCITT X.400: Message-handling system (electronic mail)
Level 6	
Level 5	CCITT X.225
Level 4	DECnet
	TCP/IP: Transmission Control Protocol/Internet Protocol
	XNS: Xerox Network System
Level 3	CCITT X.25 defines the public data network according to interface, link control, and packet exchange procedures
Level 2	IEEE 802.7 is the feasibility of the broadband research group.
	IEEE 802.6 defines Metropolitan Area Network (MAN).
	IEEE 802.5 defines the token-passing ring implementation.
	IEEE 802.4 defines the token-passing bus implementation.
	IEEE 802.3 defines the CSMA baseband bus implementation, which is identical to Xerox's and Digital Equipment Corporation's Ethernet LAN. Also defines two other cabling systems known as StarLAN and Cheapernet, also called Ethernet.
	IEEE 802.2 defines the data link control layer that is independent of the other standards.
	IEEE 802.1 defines the overall work of the committee in an outline form, including a discussion of the internet working protocol.
Level 1	CCITT X.20 and X.21 defines public data network interface operations. X.20 covers asynchronous, character-oriented equipment for public data networks. X.21 is the equivalent for synchronous equipment.
	CCITT V.35 describes an electrical protocol for serial communication. It is designed specifically to interface with high-speed modems, supporting transmission speeds up to 64 kbps and cable lengths up to 200 feet.
	EIA RS-232 defines the interface between data terminal equipment and data communication equipment.

IEEE = Institute of Electrical and Electronics Engineers; CCITT = Consultative Committee on International Telegraph and Telephone; EIA = Electronic Industries Association.

Corporation, can participate in multivendor LANs to exchange information. But since the IEEE 802.3 is a data link layer standard, it ensures only that data is transferred reliably and accurately between systems in a multivendor LAN. The standard is not concerned with interpreting messages received by destination nodes. Interpretation is the responsibility of higher-level standards. Thus the IEEE 800 standards allow connectivity, but it does not provide interoperability.

■ De Facto Standards

Since the process of defining and approving national and international standards is a lengthy one, **de facto standards** are used where official standards have not been fully defined or widely implemented. Prior to development of the OSI model and while it was still in early stages of definition, several research agencies and major computer manufacturers defined their own communications standards, with models similar to OSI, to support the networking of their own systems. Figure 7-18 compares OSI with other models.

The *Manufacturing Automation Protocol (MAP)* and *Technical and Office Protocol (TOP)* apply the OSI model to meet specific application problems. MAP permits full plant automation for communications between heterogeneous computers and programmed devices, while TOP integrates business systems, engineering design and analysis, and publishing systems. TOP networks can transfer and accept data from the MAP networks, thus linking the engineering and office environments to the factory.

A de facto standard that is similar to the OSI reference model at each of its seven layers and can interface with it is *Transmission Control Protocol/ Internet Protocol (TCP/IP)*. TCP/IP, developed by the Department of Defense's Advanced Research Projects Agency Arpanet computer network, enables many different types of computers to communicate in a mixed vendor envi-

FIGURE 7-18 Comparison of OSI with TCP/IP, IBM's SNA, and DEC's DNA

Layer (ISO Model)	TCP/IP	SNA	DECnet
7 Application	End-user	End-user	Application layer
6 Presentation	Telnet File Transfer Processor (FTP)	Network addressable units	
5 Session	(None)	Data flow control	(None)
4 Transport	Host-to-host	Transmission control	Network services
3 Network	Transmission control Protocol	Path control	
			Transport
2 Data link	Internet Protocol	Data link control	Data link control
1 Physical	Physical	Physical	Physical

Reprinted with permission from *Electronic Design*, (Vol. 36, No. 12) May 26, 1988. Copyright 1988, VNU Business Publications, Inc.

ronment. Xerox's *Xerox Network Systems (XNS)* architecture model also conforms to the OSI model.

IBM's *System Network Architecture (SNA)*, another de facto standard, is a structured set of layered protocols governing how IBM products can interact with each other. IBM plans to use SNA within its environment and OSI protocols for outside access.

The *Digital Network Architecture (DNA)* is DEC's standard, with its communication software and hardware products, referred to as DECnet. DECnet enables DEC's computing systems to communicate with other systems. DEC plans to phase in OSI by first allowing DECnet and OSI to coexist in DEC machines by communicating either protocol and then later to eliminate DECnet, without any of the migration being noticeable to users.

Commercial LANS— The Hardware Configuration

The basic LAN technology and the LAN standards, discussed in the previous sections, are packaged by companies into various hardware configurations such as Ethernet and Token-Ring. Hardware configurations deal with the first and second levels of the OSI model.

The oldest and most widely installed LAN technology was developed by Xerox's Palo Alto Research Center in California in early 1970s. But it was not until 1980 that Xerox Corporation, DEC, and Intel Corporation developed an Ethernet specification. Today, nearly every major computer vendor supports the Ethernet hardware configuration, with DEC providing the largest number of Ethernet products. Ethernet introduced a new trend in data processing by allowing devices of different manufacturers to communicate directly with one another.

The leading hardware configurations currently offered by vendors are Ethernet, Token-Ring, and Starlan, which are compared in Figure 7-19. Companies that offer them are listed in Figure 7-20. These hardware configurations are used as transport protocol by upper-level protocols, such as Ethernet using TCP/IP, DEC's DECnet, or Xerox's XNS.

LANs to LANs to WANs

■ **LAN Hierarchy**

LANs can mirror a company's organizational structure. Small companies may have a single LAN, while larger companies have a hierarchy of LANs, ranging from work group or department to organizationwide LANs. Figure 7-21 shows a company's LAN hierarchy from work group to departmental

FIGURE 7-19 Comparison of LAN Features

	3Com Novell Ethernet	IBM Token-Ring	AT&T StarLAN	AT&T StarLAN 10	Datapoint Arcnet
Cabling Topology	Bus	Ring	Star; daisy-chain	Star	Bus; star; or combination; daisy-chain
*Transmission Speed**	10 Mbps	4, 16 Mbps	1, 10 Mbps	10 Mbps	25 Mbps
Transmission Media	Coaxial (baseband/broadband); fiber-optic; twisted-pair	IBM cabling system; twisted-pair (baseband); fiber-optic	Twisted-pair (baseband); fiber-optic	Twisted-pair (baseband); fiber-optic	Coaxial; fiber-optic; twisted-pair
Transmission Method	Baseband	Baseband	Baseband	Baseband	Baseband
Access Method	CSMA/CD	Token passing	CSMA/CD	CSMA/CD	Token passing
Max. No. of Devices†	100	72–260	20–1000+	20–1000+	255
Max. Cable Length of Single Segment	1000–3000 ft	330 ft	400 ft daisy 1600 ft star	100 meters TWP 2 km fiber	22,000 ft
Industry Standard	802.3	802.5	802.3	802.3	De facto

*Identifies the maximum rate in bits per second (bps) at which information travels over the cable medium. For example, Ethernet runs at 10 Mbps.
†Indicates the maximum number of devices that can be attached per cable segment.

FIGURE 7-20 **Vendors Supporting IEEE Standards**

StarLAN	AT&T, 3Com, Banyan, Novell, Intel.
Ethernet	AT&T, Digital Equipment Corporation, Hewlett-Packard, Novell, Sun, 3Com, Xerox, and others.
Token Ring	IBM, Excelan, Micom-Inerlan, 3Com, Ungermann-Bass, Novell, Teltone, Proteon.

level. This company's Northeast Regional Sales Group includes Toronto, Hartford, and Westboro office staffs, each an example of a work group. At the next level of the hierarchy, the work groups connect to each other and to the Regional Sales Department.

Work Group. The basic LAN networking unit within an organization is the work group, which typically contains from two to twelve workstations.

FIGURE 7-21 **An Example of a Company's LAN Hierarchy from Work Group to Departmental Level**

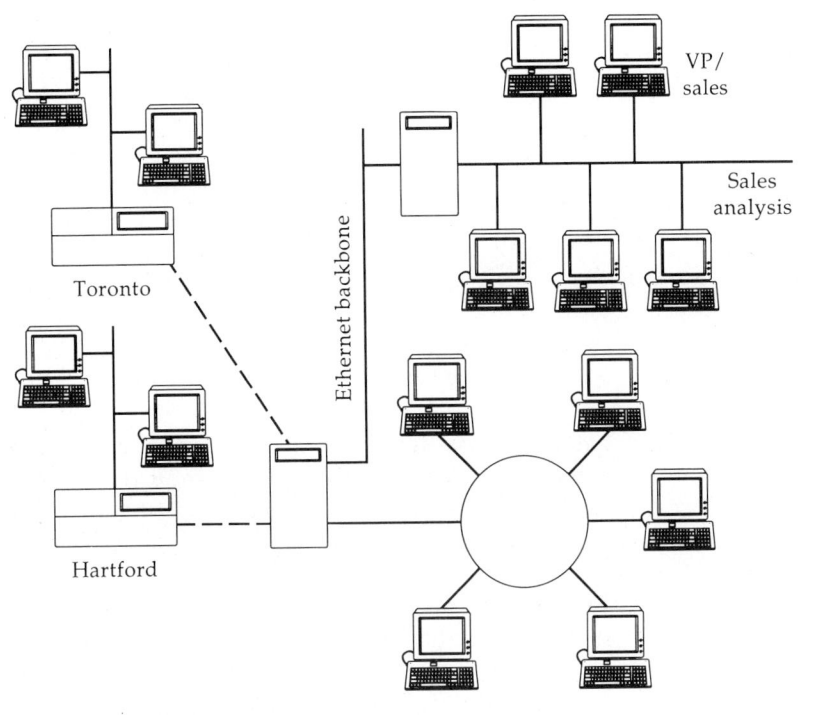

Redrawn courtesy of Banyan Systems, Inc.

Users perform both individual and shared computer tasks such as moving files electronically between workstations and sharing peripheral devices.

Departmental Level. The next level of networking, the departmental LAN, links work group LANs with each other and may include connections to minicomputers and mainframe computers.

Organizational Level. The third level of networking, the organizational level, links together all of the organization's LANs as well as its minicomputers and mainframes.

■ Span Technology

Once a work group links its microcomputers, it soon wants to expand the size of its LAN or connect to other LANs or WANs. Such connections are made possible by spanners—specifically repeaters, bridges, routers, and

FIGURE 7-22 **Internetworking at the Different OSI Layers**

OSI Layer	Spanner
7 Application	⎫
6 Presentation	⎬ gateway
5 Session	⎭
4 Transport	
3 Network	router
2 Data link	bridge
1 Physical	repeater

gateways. The definition of spanners differs among vendors. For example, some vendors include routers in their definition of bridges. Figure 7-22 shows the OSI layer(s) at which each span operates. In 1987 the span business totaled $58 million; it is projected to be $544 million by 1991.[3]

Repeaters. **Repeaters** are hardware devices that operate at the first layer of the OSI model. They extend the length of a cable by repeating all electrical signals from one segment to the next.

For example, Ethernet's standard specifies that a single segment of cable cannot exceed 1640 feet (500 meters). By interconnecting two segments with one repeater you can extend the cable length of your Ethernet network to reach a maximum distance of 3280 feet (1640 × 2), as shown in Figure 7-23. But repeaters cannot repeat forever. Ethernet is limited to five segments of 1640 feet (500 meters) each—a total of 8200 feet (2500 meters). Repeaters can also be used when workstations are too far apart for reliable transmission.

Bridges. A **bridge** is a device that connects two LANs of the same topology, such as token ring to token ring or Ethernet to Ethernet, as shown in Figure 7-24. Since bridges operate below the operating system level, they can connect two LANs of the same topology but different network operating systems. Because bridges operate at the data link layer, layer 2 of the OSI model, they are protocol-independent and transparent. *Protocol independent* means that they operate below level 3, the network operating level of OSI. *Transparent* means that users are unaware of being bridged to another LAN.

Workstations on bridged LANs can communicate as if they were on a single network. For example, files from one LAN can be accessed by another LAN. Electronic messages can be sent between LANs; application software can be shared. A user on one LAN may access a document from another LAN, make corrections, and send it back.

FIGURE 7-23   Repeaters

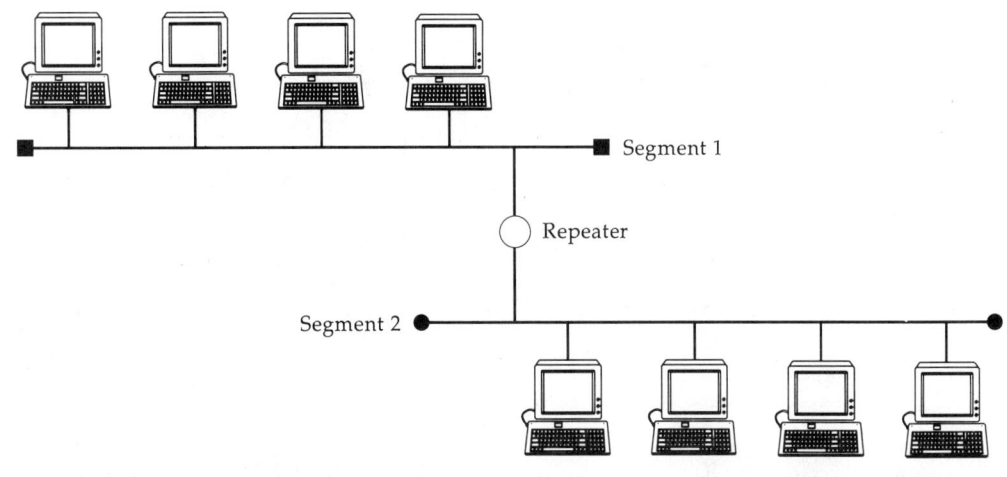

FIGURE 7-24   Two LANs Connected by a Bridge

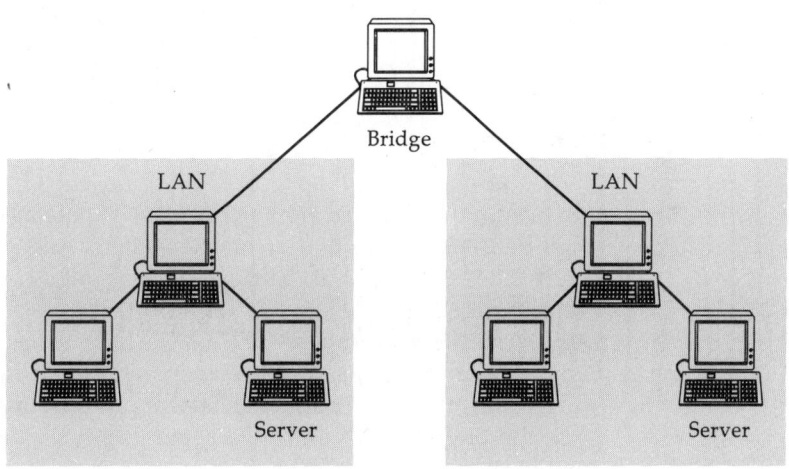

Bridges are used for the following purposes:

- *To extend the capacity of a LAN.* A LAN that has reached its maximum capacity, such as maximum number of nodes or obsolete hardware, can be expanded by bridging it to another LAN and to create a larger network. The new LAN allows more nodes to be added and/or provides updated hardware, as shown in Figure 7-25.

FIGURE 7-25   Extending a LAN's Capacity

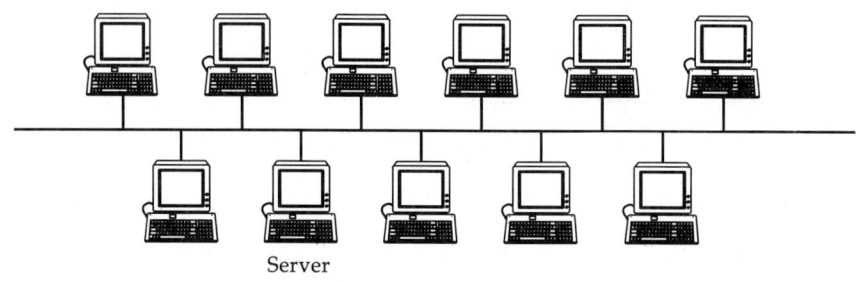

(a) The Original LAN Before Division

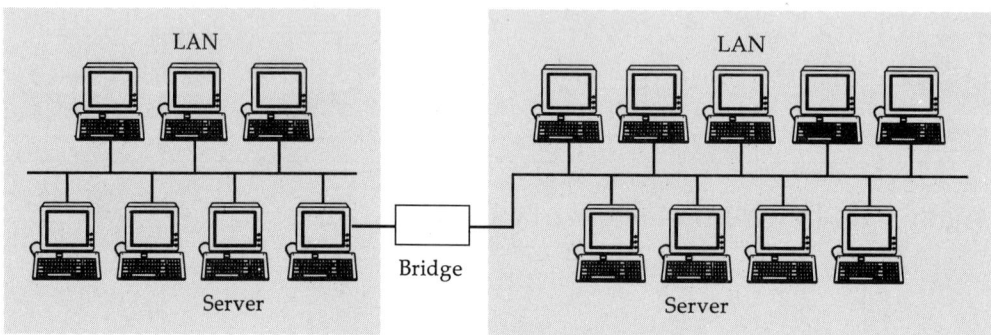

(b) Two LANS After Division

- *To increase a LAN's processing speed*. A LAN that has too many workstations, can be divided into two or more smaller LANs. Each workstation communicates as before but, being part of a smaller LAN, can communicate at a faster rate.
- *To extend the distance of a LAN*. A LAN that has reached its maximum distance can be divided into two separate LANs and joined by a bridge. A LAN that originally spanned 4000 feet can now expand 8000 feet by dividing the original LAN into two separate LANs joined by a bridge in the network server.
- *To connect LANs that use different media*. A bridge can connect a coaxial-cable Ethernet and a twisted-pair Ethernet without having to rewire them.
- *To serve as the access point for multiple LANs to access a high-speed backbone network*, as shown in Figure 7-26. The only nodes on the backbone are bridges to other networks. The backbone is usually a network capable of long distances.

For example, Moses H. Cone Memorial Hospital, the largest general hospital in the Greensboro, North Carolina, area has saved 20% of the cost

FIGURE 7-26 **LAN Connecting to a Backbone Network**

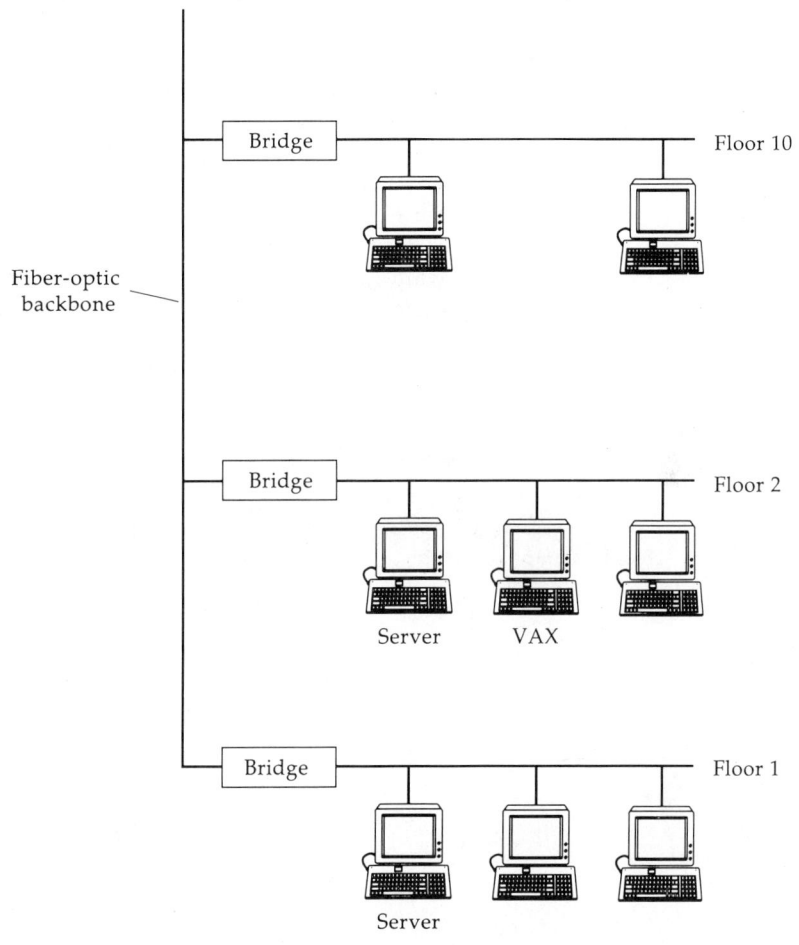

of a traditional mainframe system by going the LAN route. Each department designs its own LAN system suited to its environment while sharing a LAN backbone to connect to departments and exchange patient information.

Bridges are either local or remote. *Local bridges* link LANs within the same building or building complex, such as connecting work groups into internetworks. *Remote* bridges connect remote LANs into wide-area networks. For example, a network in your office can be connected into a city-wide, countrywide, or worldwide network even if they use different types of network hardware. In this way you can tie your company's LANs into a WAN. Remote bridges operate over dialup lines, microwave, or satellite systems.

Routers. A **router** connects LANs at the network layer, layer 3, of the OSI model. Routers are protocol-sensitive and therefore can connect only two LANs using the same network operating systems but can support LANs using different types of hardware.

Like bridges, routers pass packets between networks. But they operate more slowly and are more complex than bridges. A router accepts packets from one LAN that are addressed to another LAN. It inspects the layer 3 address and decides which LAN must receive the packet. If more than one LAN network is involved, the router takes the shortest direct route, as shown in Figure 7-27. Campuses are interconnected through remote routers with campuses running TCP/IP protocols. With routers there is more than one possible route between any two networks. Routers also interconnect departmental-level networks within each campus, allowing departments to independently administer their own networks.

FIGURE 7-27 Routers

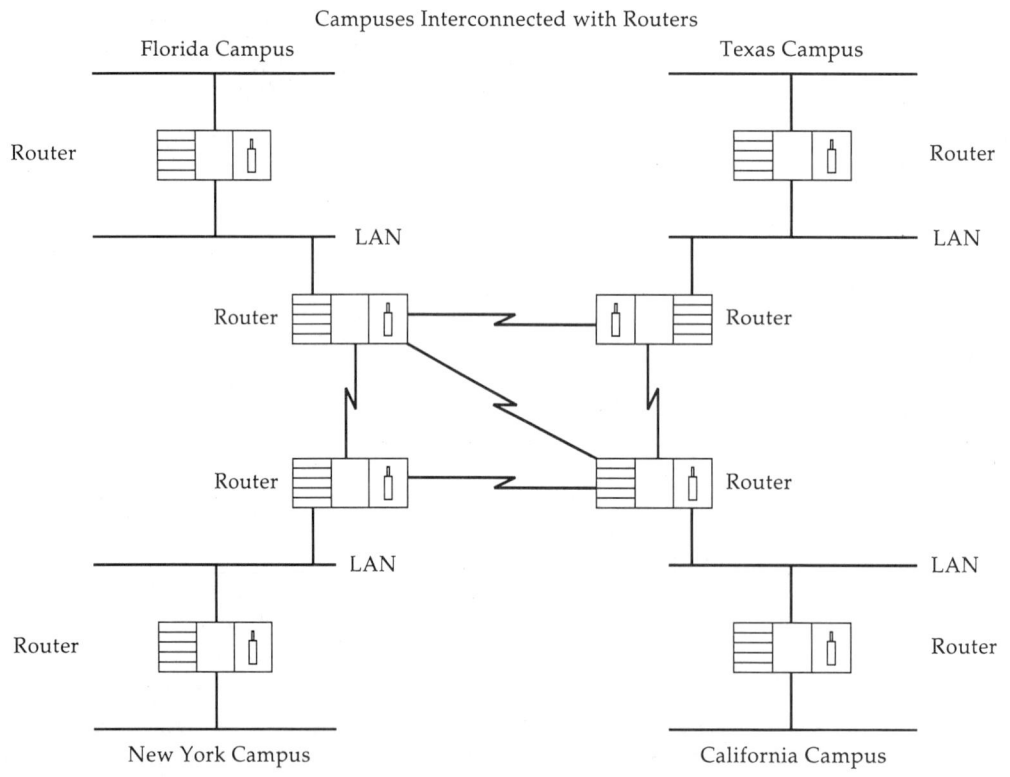

Redrawn courtesy of 3Com Corporation.

LANs to LANs to WANs   **245**

Gateways. A **gateway** is a device designed to interface two dissimilar networks. It translates the protocols of one network to the protocols of another network like a language interpreter translating from one language to another.

In Figure 7-28 a gateway connects two incompatible networks, such as an Ethernet LAN running DECnet with a Token-Ring LAN running TCP/IP,

FIGURE 7-28   Gateway Connecting Ethernet LAN to Token-Ring Running TCP/IP

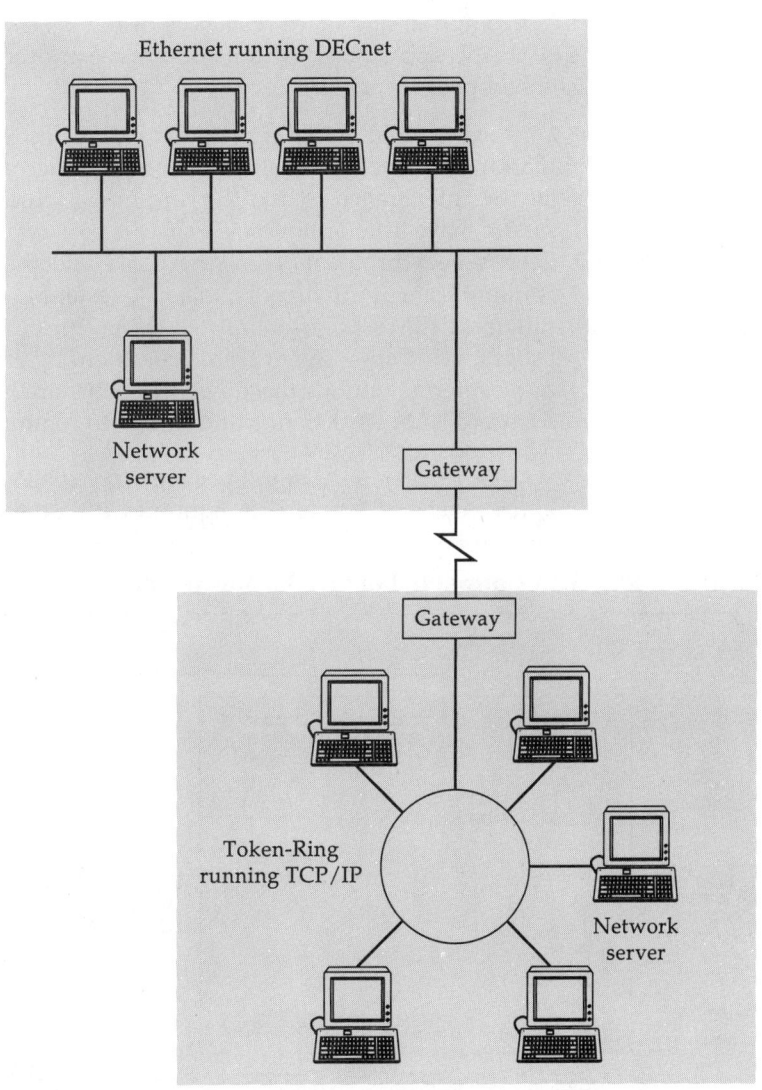

and allows them to communicate. It changes the framing or packaging of a message to a format that another network with different protocols can understand. For example, a gateway can convert the protocols of a DEC network into ones recognizable by an IBM network and vice versa. It allows bidirectional flow of information between the two vendors' networks so that any node in either network can access any node in the other network.

LAN to Mainframe Computer or Minicomputer. LAN users often need to access information stored in mainframes or minicomputers. A LAN and an IBM mainframe can be connected by using IBM's SNA gateway allowing the LAN computers to share resources of the SNA network, shown in Figure 7-29. LANs access a mainframe or a minicomputer by using terminal emulation or peer-to-peer protocols:

- Terminal emulation allows LAN workstations to appear as terminals to a mainframe. The terminal emulation approach assumes that the host has all the intelligence, while the terminals, which are actually microcomputers, have little or none.
- Peer-to-peer protocols allow the LAN and the mainframe computer to communicate as intelligent equals. An example of peer-to-peer communications is IBM's Logical Unit 6.2 (LU6.2) protocol, a computer software program that allows peer communication. By offering the same programming interface on all machines, it allows any two intelligent machines, such as a LAN workstation and a host, to communicate as equals or peers.

Minicomputer to Mainframe Computer. DEC minicomputers and IBM mainframe computers are often found within the same company. For exam-

FIGURE 7-29   LAN Connected to an IBM Mainframe

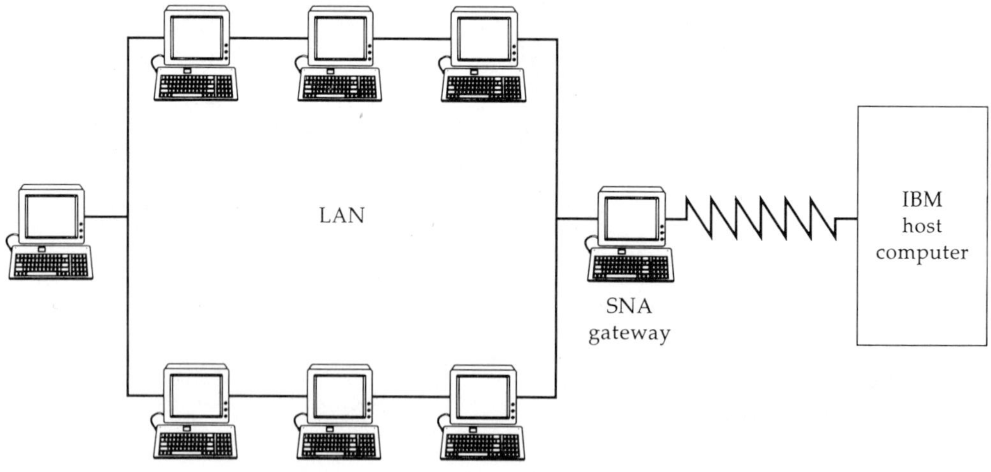

FIGURE 7-30   DEC Minicomputer Connected to IBM Mainframe

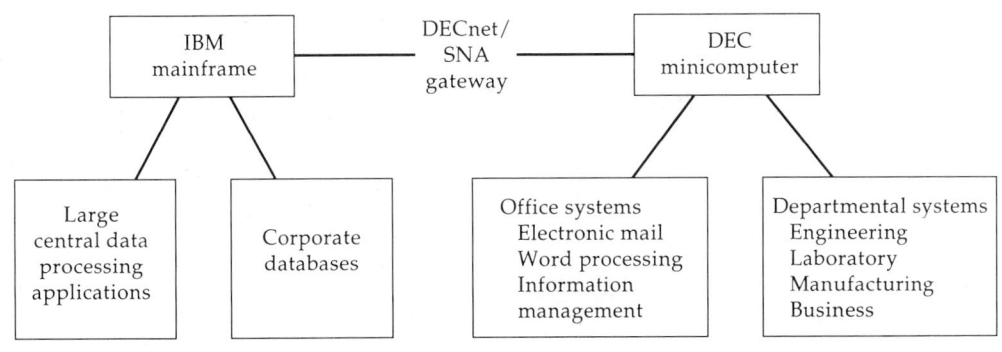

ple, a company typically uses DEC's VAX equipment (minicomputers) to perform department applications and IBM mainframes to house large databases or run central administrative functions, such as accounting and payroll. Although these systems have dissimilar networks, they can communicate and share resources with each other by using a DECnet/SNA gateway, as shown in Figure 7-30.

X.25 LAN Gateways.   CCITT X.25 gateways allows a LAN to connect to public packet-switching networks that use the CCITT X.25 protocol, such as Telenet and Tymnet. X.25 gateways can be microcomputers with X.25 adapters cards and software, or they can be dedicated devices with X.25 hardware and software. The X.25 standard specifies the rules for user access to a packet-switching network, for setting up a data call from one computer to another, for exchanging data, and for terminating the cable. Figure 7-31 shows an X.25 gateway connecting an Ethernet LAN to an X.25 network.

Alternatives to LANs

A LAN is not the only way to move information among microcomputers. Alternative technologies, if they meet users' needs, may offer easier, faster, and less expensive ways of accomplishing the same goals. Alternatives to LANs are identified in Figure 7-32 and described below.

■ Floppy-Disk Exchange

The cheapest and the most cost-effective way for microcomputers to share information is to exchange floppy disks. This alternative is suitable when users need to exchange only a limited number of files or send a few documents to a printer connected to someone else's microcomputer.

FIGURE 7-31 X.25 Gateway Connecting LANs to a Public-Packet Switching Network

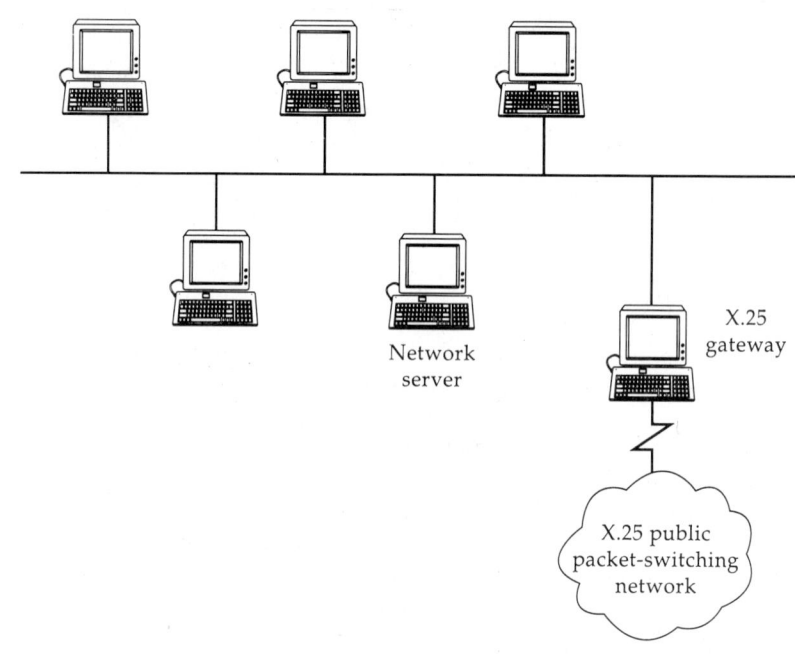

FIGURE 7-32 Alternatives to LANs at a Glance

Data switch:	Uses a switch to connect microcomputers for sharing peripherals.
SubLAN:	Uses the RS-232 serial ports to connect microcomputers for sharing peripherals and files.
Data PBN:	Uses a "smart switch" (using circuit switching) to perform many of the same functions as a LAN.
Multiuser system:	Is a mainframe that interfaces with dumb terminals.
CO LAN:	Connects a company's computer along with its telephone to the local telephone company's switching equipment using twisted-pair wire to perform the same functions as a LAN.

- ## Data Switches

For offices that require only peripheral sharing, such as sharing a printer or a modem, a manual or an automatic data switch (also called a peripheral sharing device) might be a cheaper choice than a LAN. A **data switch** is a device that makes a temporary connection between different devices such as telephones, microcomputers, terminals, or printers.

FIGURE 7-33 **The Manual Data Switch Connecting Four Microcomputers to One Printer**

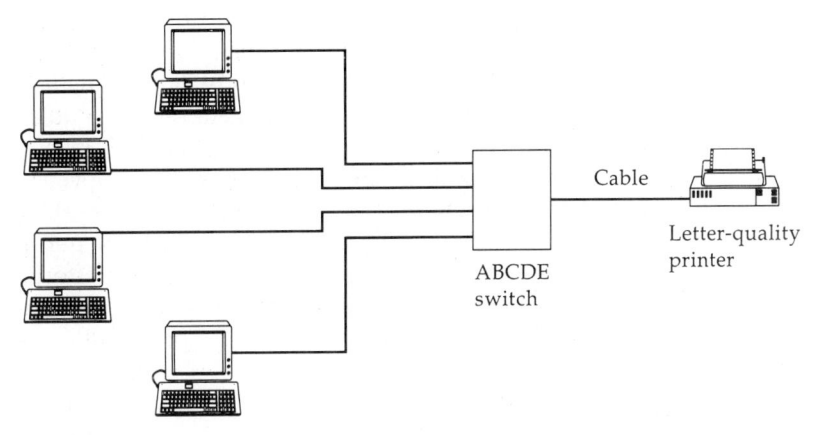

Manual Data Switch. A *manual data switch*, shown in Figure 7-33, is connected by cable to two to four microcomputers, allowing them to share one peripheral for their output. When microcomputer A, for example, wants to use the printer, the data switch must be on the "A" setting. If not, someone must manually rotate the data switch to this setting.

A variation of this peripheral device is the **crossover data switch**, which allows two computers to share two peripherals, such as a printer and a modem or two different types of printers, shown in Figure 7-34.

Automatic Data Switch. A switch can be automatically directed from a user's desk with a microcomputer and appropriate computer software. The switch can connect as many as twenty microcomputers to a peripheral, each one being connected directly to the switch.

FIGURE 7-34 **The Crossover Data Switch (a Manual Data Switch) Connecting Two Microcomputers to Two Different Types of Printers**

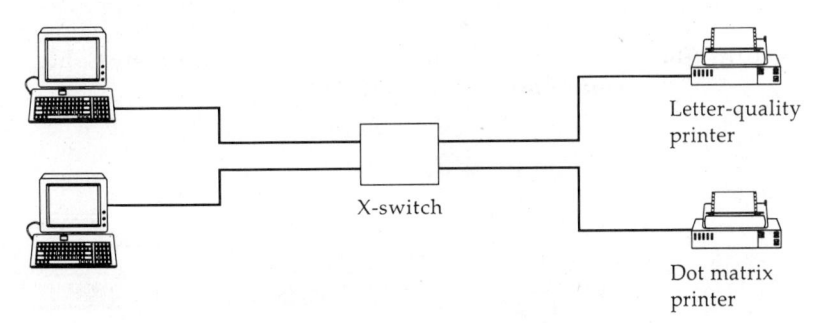

When the automatic switch receives a document from one of the microcomputers to be output, it stores the document in its temporary buffer. As soon as the peripheral is available, the document is output automatically. This queuing frees the microcomputer for other uses while the buffered document or documents wait their turn to be printed. These switches are either an external stand-alone box or a board installed inside the peripheral. The board functions as an intelligent buffer, spooler, and data switch while appearing as a dedicated printer to each microcomputer. For example, the owner of a small business with six staff employees who frequently operate microcomputers wanted each employee to be able to access the company printer from his or her desk. However, the owner did not want to invest in any unnecessary equipment and could not afford a printer for each employee. The owner's solution was to select an automatic peripheral-sharing device—an automatic data switch for printer sharing.

■ SubLANs

SubLANs, also called low-cost LANs or zero-slot LANs, connect microcomputers by using their standard RS-232 serial ports instead of LAN network interface cards. These LANs offer a small business or a department within a large organization a permanent networking solution or an introduction to more expensive networks.

Technology. A simple arrangement is joining the serial communication ports of two microcomputers by cable in a point-to-point configuration, as shown in Figure 7-35. Files, for example, can be transferred between the microcomputers by running a communications software program with files transfer capability.

Another arrangement is connecting microcomputers in a star configuration with one microcomputer designated as the hub machine and the others as satellites, as shown in Figure 7-36. The hub machine is a microcomputer with a hard disk and a serial port for each device. Port boards containing either two or six ports per board are available. For example, to connect eighteen microcomputers, you would install three six-port serial boards in the hub machine.

FIGURE 7-35 Two Microcomputers Communicating by Cable and Using Communications Software

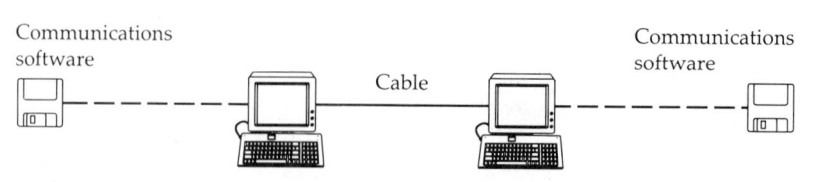

FIGURE 7-36 **Microcomputers Sharing Each Other's Files, Printers, and Disks**

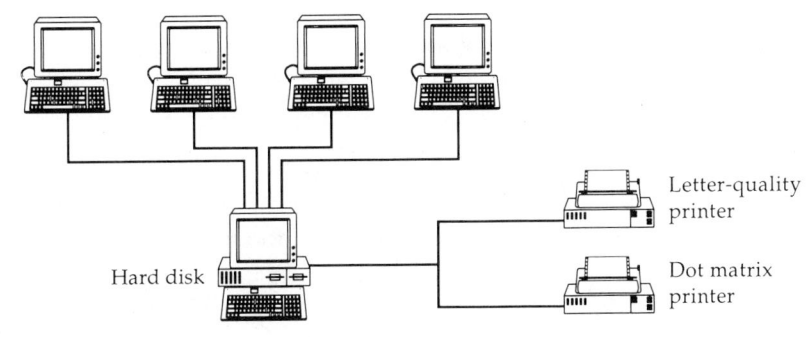

Functions. SubLANs offer many of the functions of the higher-priced LANs but generally are about one-fourth to one-fifth of their cost. Functions of subLANs typically include the ability to communicate with other subLAN users and share peripherals and files. Safeguards, such as file locking, record locking, and password access, are available to prevent unauthorized access to confidential information. (File locking is a feature of the operating system that limits access to a data file to one user at a time. Record locking is a feature of the operating system that allows individual records to be locked to prevent accidental erasure, particularly when records are accessed simultaneously by two or more users.) Remote access allows a user at a distant location to become a satellite on the network through a modem connection, shown in Figure 7-37. Some subLANs contain a special node on

FIGURE 7-37 **Local PCs and a Remote PC with a Modem Sharing Files, Printers, and Disks**

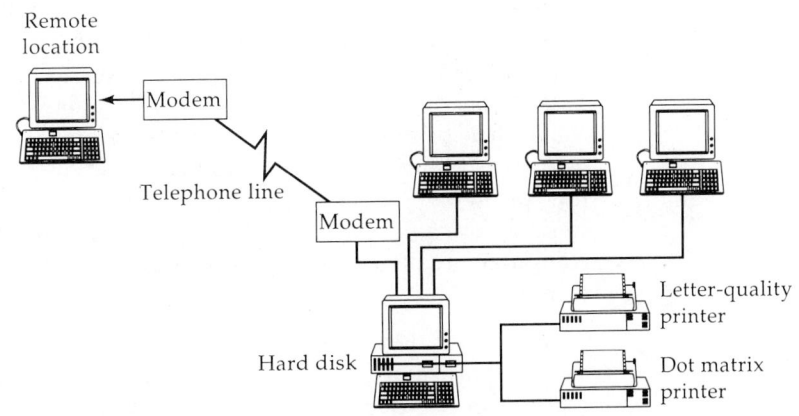

the network to allow users to interface to a dissimilar network or system, such as an IBM mainframe.

Compared to higher-priced LANs, subLANs have certain drawbacks:

- The transmission rate of subLANs is low. Although the transmission speed can reach 100 Mbps, the average is 19.2 kbps.
- The transmission distance between microcomputers is limited. SubLANs can run reliably to a maximum of 500 feet, which is usually sufficient for networking a workgroup. By adding a higher-speed port, an RS-422 port, the transmission distance can be increased to 2000 feet. Users who are located at a distance from the hub machine can use modems to dial into the network.
- The number of users that can be attached to the network is limited.

■ Data PBX

An even smarter switch is a **data PBX**, shown in Figure 7-38. Data PBXs, also called digital PBXs, handle data traffic and also perform LAN functions, such as connecting microcomputers so that they can communicate with each other—and at a much cheaper price. The architecture is similar to integrated voice/data PBXs with both consisting of a central control device, a switching matrix, and a set of interface cards for connection through the transmission medium to the workstation. Data PBXs compete with the more costly voice/data PBX as well as with multiplexers and LANs. Data PBXs offer the following capabilities:

- *Port Selection*. A data PBX allows a user to access more than one mainframe computer or minicomputer without having a dedicated cable running between each user's terminal and host computer.
- *Port Sharing*. Adding a port for every user becomes too costly. Instead, a data PBX allows users to share ports, which maximizes their use. When a user requests a port, the user is routed to the first available port, or if all ports are being used, the user is put in a queue. Port sharing makes use of the circuit switch concept, which allows users to be connected only as needed.
- *Resource Sharing*. As with LANs, data PBXs allow users to share peripherals, such as printers and/or modems. A printer at each workstation would be expensive and inefficient, since each user usually does not need a full-time printer.
- *Fallback Switching*. A data PBX allows fallback switching. If a mainframe computer breaks down, the data PBX can quickly switch to a backup computer.

The main difference between a data PBX and a LAN is that a data PBX uses *circuit switching* while a LAN uses *packet switching*. Since packet switching does not use dedicated circuits, LAN cable is shared among its users when transmitting small packets of data. With data PBXs, transmissions

FIGURE 7-38   Data PBX

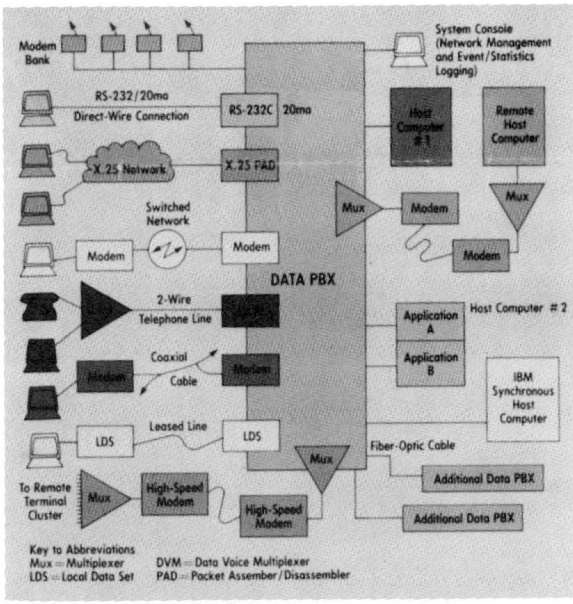

Reprinted from *Digital Review*, June 15, 1987. Copyright © 1987 Ziff Communications Company.

follow the wire of a dedicated connection to their destination. Other differences include the following:

- A LAN typically connects intelligent devices, such as microcomputers, with an increasing number of LANs supporting devices that connect to minicomputers and mainframe computers. Although a data PBX can connect microcomputers, it usually connects dumb terminals to systems such as mainframe computers and minicomputers.
- A data PBX is limited by a specific number of circuits. If a data PBX has five lines connecting to a mainframe, then it can support only five terminal connections at one time; other users are placed in a queue. A LAN is limited by its bandwidth. Theoretically, a LAN cable has no limit on the number of users it can support, but the more users there are, the slower the transmissions are.
- A data PBX costs between $100 and $200 per port, while a LAN can cost between $500 and $1000 per connection (1988 prices).
- Since a data PBX uses a star topology with all communication going through its central processing unit, security on a PBX can be controlled more easily than on a LAN.
- Data PBXs can use twisted-pair wire already present in offices for telephone systems. The use of this medium gives data PBXs an advantage over those LANs requiring use of coaxial cable or shielded twisted wire.

FIGURE 7-39 CPU Placement: LAN versus Multiuser System

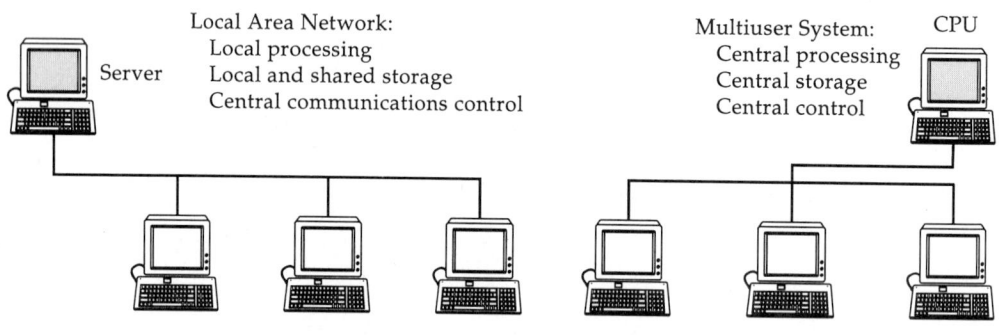

- Data PBXs, like voice PBXs, provide telephone management information through their station message detail recording (SMDR) ports. As discussed in Chapter 15, while voice PBXs, through their SMDR feature, provide telephone management information, data PBXs provide similar information about data use.
- Data PBXs transmit data at a slower rate than LANs—19,200 bps versus over 10 Mbps. Even though data PBXs use a dedicated path and LANs use a shared one, the difference in speed is still a major factor.

To take advantage of both systems, gateways can be added to connect both LANs and data PBXs.

■ Multiuser Systems

A **multiuser system** is a mainframe computer or minicomputer that interfaces with attached dumb terminals or sometimes with intelligent terminals and microcomputers. The mainframe computer consists of a control processing unit (CPU) with central storage and input and output processing. All processing is performed by the CPU. One of the major differences between a multiuser system and a LAN is the placement of logic, memory, and the level of resource sharing, as shown in Figure 7-39. Although a multiuser system requires a large investment for its CPU, terminals cost less than microcomputers.

A department's LAN may connect to other LANs within an organization and yet still connect to the organization's mainframe computer. As was discussed earlier in the chapter, gateways permit LANs and mainframes to access each other. Some multiuser systems prefer to use microcomputers rather than dumb terminals. Such a multiuser system then begins to look like a LAN, as shown in Figure 7-40(a). Systems are also appearing that include both microcomputers and multiuser systems on the same network, as shown in Figure 7-40(b).

FIGURE 7-40 Merging LANs and Multiuser Systems

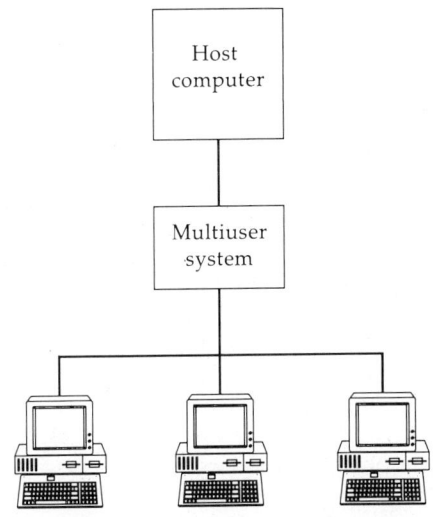

(a) A Multiuser System Connecting Microcomputers to Host Computer

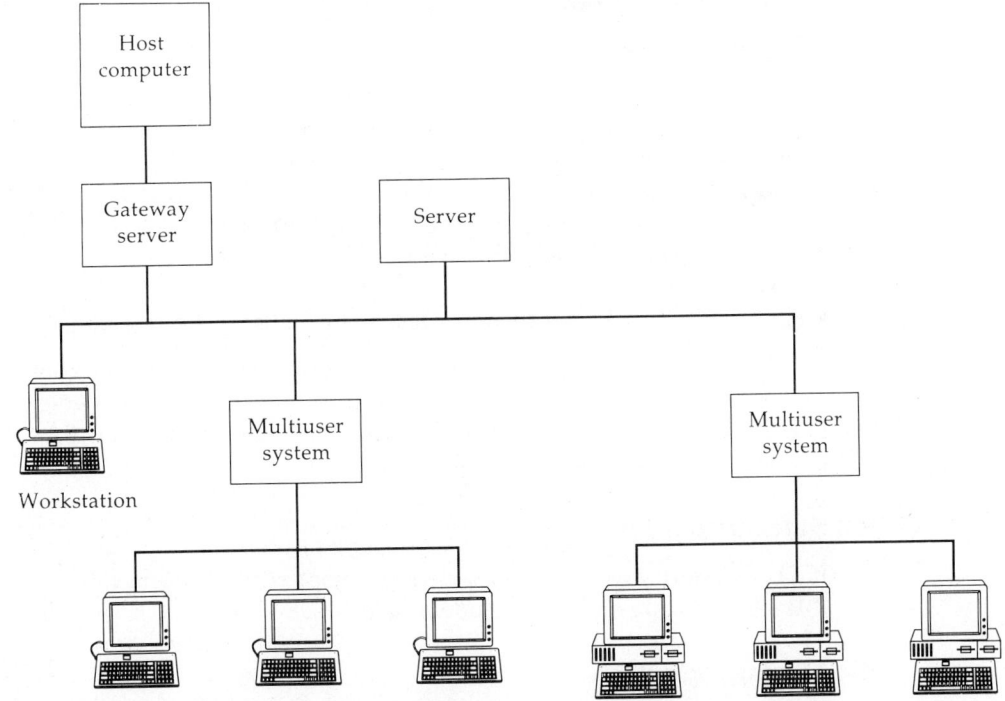

(b) Multiuser Systems Connected to LAN and to Host Computer

- **Central Office Local-Area Network**

  The Bell operating companies can support an organization's LANs, such as Ethernet and Token-Ring, through Centrex services. A *central office LAN*, also called **CO LAN**, operates by the local telephone company's central office connecting a customer's computers to its switching equipment by twisted-pair wire.

  This alternative has certain benefits. First, users make no capital investment beyond the purchase of a small data/voice multiplexer (DVM). The DVM is connected to the customer's telephones and computers. It allows both computers and telephones to be used simultaneously over twisted-pair wire. At the central office, another DVM splits the mixed data and voice transmission; voice signals are routed to their destination via normal channels. Data signals are sent to a central office–based data-switching unit. This unit transmits the data signals to their destination—a computer that is located on or off the customer's premises. The second benefit is that users do not maintain the CO LAN. The CO LAN is maintained by the local telephone company or a service vendor.

Selecting and Managing a LAN

- **Do You Need a LAN?**

  To determine whether you need a LAN or an alternative LAN, consider the following questions:

  - What are your present networking requirements? Find out to what extent employees share peripherals, share computer files, and work on the same computer data simultaneously.
  - What must you do to satisfy your current requirements?
  - What do you anticipate that your requirements will be five years from now?
  - How can you satisfy both your present and future requirements?

  For example, if employees share only peripherals, then a data switch or a subLAN may be the answer. If you do not want to invest in LAN equipment or maintain it or are not sure what your future requirements will be, then perhaps you should consider a CO LAN.

- **Selecting a LAN**

  If a LAN alternative is to be selected, develop criteria for selecting it. Figure 7-41 suggests questions to include in selecting a LAN.

- **Managing a LAN**

  The management of a LAN is concerned with overseeing and maintaining the network. Typical duties of a LAN manager are listed in Figure 7-42.

FIGURE 7-41 Suggested Questions to Ask in Selecting a LAN

- Should you standardize on one type of a LAN?
- Can products of different manufacturers be selected?
- Is connectivity possible with all devices, even those from the same manufacturer?
- Will the LAN be interoperable with other LANs?
- Does the LAN perform the users' functions without requiring replacing or adding costly interface equipment?
- Will the LAN reduce office costs?
- Will the LAN increase the flexibility of your office's operations?
- Is the LAN transparent to the user?
- Is the LAN's transmission speed appropriate for the user's applications?
- Does the LAN provide users with sufficient circuit capacity and device support to meet present and future needs?
- What is the maximum cable distance allowed between workstations and their access points?
- Are there many access points to the transmission cable available throughout the site?
- Are gateways available for communicating with LANs at remote sites?
- Does the LAN support nonproprietary standards, such as IEEE?
- Will the LAN enable incompatible machines to talk to each other?
- Can the LAN communicate with microcomputers, terminals, minicomputers, and mainframes?
- Can the LAN communicate with equipment from different vendors without requiring changes to either vendor's system? In other words, is multivendor communication possible?
- What is the cost of the LAN per node?

Integrated Services Digital Network

By 1995, just about every telephone and/or computer user will be affected by ISDN. **ISDN**, an acronym for *integrated services digital network*, is not a network in the physical sense; instead, it is a standard means of providing a single, global digital communications network with common interfaces and access techniques. Users can access simultaneously on demand voice, data, facsimile, image, and video communications through a single standard interface, as shown in Figure 1-2(b). The ISDN concept is the result of work done by the Consultative Committee on International Telephone and Telegraph (CCITT).

Existing communication networks are designed for a specific service, such as telephone, data, or facsimile transmission. Customers use different terminals and access methods, while sharing transmission and switching equipment. With ISDN, users can conveniently access all services because they receive all communication services at one entry point. ISDN is designed to reduce communications costs and simplify using and managing multiple communication services, such as voice, data, and facsimile.

FIGURE 7-42   Typical Duties of a LAN Manager

- *Install and configure the LAN initially and when changes are made.* The continual growth of a network makes installation and configuration an ongoing task.
- *Manage the server's hard disk.* Set up and maintain a directory structure that enables users to easily locate the desired directories and files. Establish policies for creating new directories, deleting unneeded files, and using a specified amount of disk space.
- *Diagnose network problems and initiate repair.*
- *Set up and implement procedures for users to report problems, configure changes, and additions.*
- *Back up the network.* Back up each server's hard disk to protect users' files in case the disk crashes. Next transfer files that are not being used to a tape and then delete them from the hard disk. Files can be retrieved from the tape if users need them.
- *Maintain an operations log.* For each file the LAN should provide a record of dates and times of log-on and log-off with the user's name. If a file is misused, the manager can refer to the log to identify who had access to it.
- *Monitor network usage and activity daily.* Find out how files are being used and who uses them. This information helps to distribute files evenly among the servers so that one server is not more active than the others. A record of file users helps to find out who is using files carelessly.
- *Monitor network traffic daily.* Analyze network traffic to identify problems and determine whether the LAN should be expanded.
- *Establish a security system to govern access to the server and its files and programs.* Implement security features and procedures. Set up user passwords to log onto the system, giving rights to directories and files. Mark files shareable, nonshareable, read-only, or manipulate.
- *Itemize and charge users for network time.* This information also allows a user's work to be charged to specific customers.
- *Provide orientation and training to LAN users.*
- *Test software to determine whether it operates satisfactorily on the LAN.*
- *Make certain sufficient copies or licenses of application software packages are available for users.* Many vendors still have a one-user license policy, although some are offering server-based prices that allow any number of users to run an application program.
- *Plan for network growth.*

■ ISDN Technology and Operation

ISDN evolved from the digital T-1 system, which allows twenty-four conversations to be multiplexed. In the T-1 application, analog to digital conversion occurs in equipment that is located in each switching office, with repeaters used at regular intervals along the cable, microwave, or satellite route. By installing T-1 systems, companies can avoid the cost of installing a separate line for each individual trunk, which is especially costly when digital communication is required. Thus T-1 maximizes transmission while minimizing the cabling requirement. As the high-speed transmission of data also became possible, a demand for combined voice/data transmission developed—and thus ISDN evolved.

Recent developments in digital technology allow the use of subscriber lines' twisted-pair wire that is already in place in businesses and homes. A subscriber can access ISDN via a standard modular telephone jack, where voice and/or data traffic is multiplexed into a digital bit stream and sent to its destination. A PBX or a telephone company or both provide the switching function.

The Basic Interface or 2B + D. The basic ISDN communication line from the terminal to the local network consists of three separate channels. Two of them, referred to as B channels, are used for voice, packet-switched, or circuit-switched data. Each one operates at 64 kbps, making it capable of transmitting fifty times faster than most microcomputer modems, which transmit digital data over an analog network.

The third channel, the D channel, is always open and provides the user with a link to the network. This channel, which operates at 16 kbps, allows a user to be in constant contact with the network while using one or both B channels for separate purposes. The D channel provides the signaling to set up user calls as well as allows packet-switched data to be transmitted while the B channels are carrying voice, data, or other information. This ISDN access is referred to as the *basic interface or 2B + D*.

Primary Rate Interface. A second type of access standardized by CCITT is the *primary rate interface*. This access has a transmission rate of 1.544 Mbps and can provide twenty-three separate B channels and one D channel for signaling. Using this *23B + D configuration*, the primary rate interface can connect digital PBX systems directly to ISDNs.

Reference Point Interfaces. ISDN terminals permit users to access an ISDN at work, at home, or wherever ISDN is available. However, existing equipment, such as a telephone, microcomputer, or facsimile machine can be made ISDN-compatible by using a conversion device referred to as a terminal adapter (TA). The *reference point interfaces*, referred to as R, S, T, and U, define the network demarcation points at which different devices interconnect with the integrated network. For example, the R interface connects non-ISDN equipment to ISDN services; the other three interface reference points maintain the separation between the signaling and bearer channels, such as the S interface connecting network terminating equipment and an ISDN terminal or terminal adapter.

ISDN uses the OSI model, beginning transmission at the end-user location at the application level and proceeding through the layers to the physical layer on which the communication is transported. From there it travels through the network, which may involve several switching stations for long-distance transmission to the targeted end-user, where the transmission then begins its way up through the various levels to the application level.

■ Comparison of ISDNs and LANs

ISDN is often listed as a competitor of LANs. Both provide high-speed information exchange among local users. Most PC LANs are resource-sharing environments and not communication environments. Even at 64 kbps, ISDN is slower than many LANs and is probably not suitable for certain applications, such as computer-aided design (CAD), which demands constant resource access by many remote users. Although ISDN was not intended to replace LANs applications, some form of LAN ISDN may be desirable, such as using ISDN as a gateway.

■ Benefits of ISDN

ISDN enables users to access a digital network that can be reconfigured for maximum efficiency. Managers of telephone services and computers are provided with tools far superior to anything now available and at lower costs compared to nonintegrated networks.

ISDN offers a range of services, such as desk-to-desk videoconferencing; high-speed, high-resolution color facsimile; and services created to meet a user's unique needs. Technical benefits of ISDN include easy multiplexing for sharing facilities, using digital technology for communications, integrating transmission and switching, regenerating signals for long-distance transmission, monitoring performance for maintenance, and easy encryption for privacy and security.

Existing ISDN services offer a company a chance to conduct its own ISDN trials, giving it an opportunity to save money on applications while providing experience with ISDN. To prepare for such a trial, a company should set up a plan similar to the following:

- Find out about the ISDN plans of their local carrier and the interexchange carriers serving their area.
- Identify suppliers of ISDN equipment and the applications that they offer.
- Determine how ISDN services will affect the applications and replacement for other ways of communicating.
- Compare the costs of ISDN with the benefits achieved.

In addition to revolutionizing how companies do business, ISDN will play a critical role in the development of future information technologies.

Summary

Today, companies have information stored in many places—the corporate headquarters' mainframe computer(s), the divisions' minicomputers, and the departments' LANs. Local- and wide-area networks connect these computers to allow them to share their resources. Network spans, particularly bridges and gateways, create connectivity and interoperability between similar and diverse network elements. Companies considering LANs should also investigate LAN alternatives such as data PBXs and CO LANs. All of these networks can increase office productivity and reduce the cost of communicating. Meanwhile integrated services digital network (ISDN), a network architecture that represents a fundamental change in the way voice and data traffic will be managed in the future, is being introduced. ISDN provides a standardized way to interface equipment and services to enable voice and data signals to be integrated over all-digital transmission and switching facilities, which can be controlled by the end-users.

■ *Key Terms*

Alternative LANs:
  CO LAN
  Crossover data
    switch
  Data switch
  Data PBX
  Multiuser system
  SubLAN
Connectivity
De facto standards
IEEE 800 standards
ISDN
Interoperability
Local area network
Logical topology:
  Hierarchical network
  Peer-to-peer network

Network access methods:
  Contention-oriented
    method
  CSMA/CD
  Noncontention-
    oriented method
  Roll-call polling
  Token passing
Network interface card
OSI model
Physical topology
Servers:
  Dedicated server
  Nondedicated server
  Specialized server

Spanners:
  Bridge
  Gateway
  Repeater
  Router
Topologies:
  Bus
  Ring
  Star
Transmission methods:
  Baseband
  Broadband
Wide-area network
Workstation

■ *Self-Quiz*

Indicate whether the statement is true or false.

1. Dumb terminals connected to a mainframe in a star configuration are an example of a LAN.   T/F
2. The bus topology is an example of a multipoint connection.   T/F
3. A network access method that is designed so that no collisions occur among nodes that wish to transmit is token passing.   T/F
4. A server that handles only communication tasks is classified as a specialized server.   T/F
5. The basic functions of a LAN network is determined by the network operating system.   T/F

6. The spanner that connects a mainframe with a LAN is a bridge.   T/F
7. Integrated services digital network is a standardized way to interface equipment and services to enable voice and data signals to be integrated over all-digital transmission and switching facilities.   T/F

Complete each of the following statements.

1. The transmission method that devotes its entire bandwidth to a single channel in order to carry one signal at a time is called _____ .
2. The LAN transmission medium with the largest bandwidth is _____ .
3. The LAN transmission medium that is most susceptible to noise from outside sources is _____ .
4. The logical topology that allows every node to have equal access to the network is called _____ .
5. A microcomputer becomes a workstation when _____ .
6. The ability of all system elements to exchange information between equipment from same or different vendors is called _____ .

Match Column A with Column B.

Column A
(a) CO LAN
(b) Crossover data switch
(c) Data PBX
(d) LAN
(e) Manual data switch
(f) Multiuser system
(g) SubLAN

Column B
___ 1. Allows two computers to share one printer.
___ 2. Networks microcomputers by using RS-232 ports.
___ 3. Allows two computers to share two printers.
___ 4. Networks terminals through a mainframe.
___ 5. Microcomputers connect to switching matrix through interface cards.
___ 6. Uses DVMs to connect customers' equipment to its own switching equipment.
___ 7. Connects microcomputers and printers to a network server.

Specify the level of the OSI model that deals with each of the following functions:

___ 1. Specifies cable requirements.
___ 2. Deals with the method for accessing the network.
___ 3. Organizes messages into correct form for the selected transmission.
___ 4. Ensures that no data is lost or duplicated.
___ 5. Determines whose turn it is to talk.
___ 6. Determine which character code to use.
___ 7. Contains functions for getting users on the computer and associated with the right application.

Review Questions

1. What makes a LAN a LAN?
2. (a) How can a LAN increase the productivity of a department?
   (b) How can a LAN be used by schools and/or colleges and universities?
3. (a) What are the functions of LAN server software?
   (b) How do the networking operating system, workstation operating system, and network application program software relate to each other?
4. Compare the three common network topologies.
5. How do the operations of token passing and CSMA/CD differ?
6. Compare the baseband and broadband transmission methods.
7. What do each of the layers of the OSI model do when a message is being exchanged?
8. (a) How can you link two LANs, each running Ethernet, located within your office building?
   (b) How can you link two LANs, each running StarLAN, located in different countries?
   (c) How can you connect a LAN to a company's mainframe?
   (d) How can you link two LANs when one uses Ethernet hardware while the other uses token ring but both use DECnet?
9. What are the differences between each of the following:
   (a) A data switch and a subLAN.
   (b) A multiuser system and a data PBX.
   (c) A LAN and a central office LAN.
10. What criteria would you use for selecting a LAN?
11. What do you consider to be three most important duties of a LAN manager? Why?
12. What are some of the technical benefits of ISDN?

Activities/Projects

1. Examine Figure 7-41. Suggest at least two other questions that the LAN manager should add to this list of suggestions for selecting a LAN.
2. Prepare a diagram showing the configuration of the LANs described in one of the scenarios included at the beginning of this chapter.
3. Visit an organization of your choice that links computers, such as microcomputers, terminals, minicomputers, and/or mainframes. Obtain answers to the following questions.
   (a) Is the computer network a LAN or an alternative to a LAN?
   (b) Describe the computer network according to its topology, transmission medium, transmission method, and network access method
   (c) Draw a diagram of the network configuration.
   (d) Describe the computer hardware and software being used.
   (e) What tasks does the computer network perform?

(f) Does the network communicate with other computer networks? If so, describe how these networks communicate. Include a diagram of the configuration.

4. For each of the following situations, prepare a diagram of a LAN configuration. Label each item on the diagram.
   (a) You would like to extend the original cable of your department's Ethernet LAN to twice its size.
   (b) The LAN in your department contains the maximum number of workstations that can be attached to it and seems to operate slowly because of its heavy use.
   (c) You would like to link the sales department's LAN with the marketing department's LAN. Both offices are located on the same floor of the office building. Both departments' LANs run token ring.
   (d) You would like to link the accounting department's LAN with another department, which is located in the same building but on another floor. Your department runs an OSI-based Ethernet LAN, while the other department runs an OSI-based token ring LAN. You are located on the second floor, while the other department is located on the sixth floor.
   (e) You would like to link the department's LAN to the company's mainframe.
   (f) You would like your department's LAN to communicate with the LAN at the branch office, which is located two miles from you. Both your LAN and the branch office LAN run Ethernet and OSI networking system.
   (g) You would like to connect your department's LAN to the organization's mainframe.

5. After investigating the current developments of ISDN, discuss the role of ISDN in telecommunications and how it will affect you both at work and at home.

■ *Case:* **Increasing Productivity with LANs**

A real-estate company employs seven support employees and thirty salespeople at its main facilities and handles both commercial and noncommercial real estate. Each employee has his or her own microcomputer containing a hard disk and a communications port and a serial port. You have been asked for recommendations on how to improve operations. Include with your recommendations a diagram for each situation.

(a) The two secretaries in the president's office would like to use a laser printer to output work from their microcomputer. Each secretary generates two or three hours of printing a day. The high cost of a laser printer does not permit one to be assigned to each secretary.

(b) The four secretaries that report to the office manager each have a microcomputer. The printer is attached to secretary Mary's microcomputer. When the other secretaries want to print documents, each one must arrange with Mary for the use of her microcomputer. Occasionally, the secretaries share disk files by making a copy of the disk file or letting the other person borrow it for a short time. One of the secretaries works at home two days a week, using the same kind of microcomputer as in the office.

(c) The salespeople are spread out in four offices, all within the same location (ten in Office A, four in Office B, eight in Office C, and eight in Office D). To obtain information about properties and other real estate matters, the salespeople must obtain hard copy information or borrow floppy disks from Tom, the sales secretary, or from each other. This process is time-consuming and often does not provide up-to-date information. A printer connected to Tom's microcomputer is available for their use when he is not using it. Some salespeople are currently using different word processing programs. Many would like to start using spreadsheet software for their work.

(d) A branch office located a distance of ten miles from the main office has four salespeople and one secretary, each person having his or her own microcomputer. They also need information from the salespeople at the main office as well as to share information with them. At present, the information is delivered by anyone who is available.

(e) The salespeople also have available to them a microcomputer that is linked to the county real estate board's mainframe. Although the salespeople can use this machine to access valuable information about properties, they usually do not want to interrupt their present activities to go to a machine that is in another office and may be in use.

■ Notes

1. Jon Swartz, "Users Share Enthusiasm for 3+Mac," *MacWeek,* November 17, 1987.
2. Richard Desjardins, "Enterprise Networking Event: Its Significance Will Prove OSI Can Really Work," *Communications Week,* June 6, 1988, p. 18.
3. George F. Colony, *The Network Strategy Report* (Cambridge, Mass.: Forrester Research, Inc., December 1987), p. 2.

■ Additional Readings

Advanced NetWare Theory of Operations, Version 2.1 (Provo, Utah: Novell, Inc., 1987).
Rowland Archer, *The Practical Guide to Local Area Networks* (New York: McGraw-Hill Book Company, 1986).
The AT&T Starlan Network vs. IBM Token Ring Network (Middletown, N.J.: AT&T Information Systems, 1986).
Bill Buffam, "Telecommuting on the ISDN Highway," *Network World,* September 25, 1989, pp. 65–70.
Judith Davis, "PC LANs Revisited," *Patricia Seybold's Office Computing Report,* April 1988, pp. 1–20.
James S. Fritz, Charles F. Kaldenbach, and Louis M. Progar, *Local Area Networks: Selection Guidelines* (Englewood Cliffs, N.J.: Prentice-Hall, Inc., 1985).
James Harry Green, *Local Area Networks: A User's Guide for Business Professionals* (Glenview, Ill.: Scott, Foresman & Company, 1985).

Introduction to Local Area Networks (Maynard, Mass.: Digital Equipment Corporation, 1982).

Richard G. Lefkon, *Selecting A Local Area Network* (New York: American Management Association, 1986).

"Local Area Networks Annual Report: Multiusers vs. LANs," *Administrative Management*, September 1987, pp. 24–30.

John R. Logan, "Surviving the Technology Accelerator," *Communications/Information Systems Planning Service* (Boston, Mass.: The Yankee Group, 1988).

Martin Pyykkonerv, "Plan for Your LAN," *Datamation*, October 15, 1987, pp. 109–110.

Networks and Communications Buyer's Guide: 1988 July–September (Maynard, Mass.: Digital Equipment Corporation, 1988).

Patricia Schnaidt, "Installation Tips," *LAN Magazine*, October 1987, pp. 20–22.

Jon William Toigo, "Chart Your Best Course to a Low-Cost LAN," *PC Resources*, October 1989, pp. 83–90.

Periodicals

Connect: The Journal of Computer Networking is published quarterly by 3Com Corporation, 3165 Kifer Road, Santa Clara, CA 95052.

The Government Guide to LANS is published quarterly by Government Technology Services, Inc., 14130-B Sullyfield Circle, Chantilly, VA 22021.

LAN: The Local Area Network Magazine is published monthly by Telecom Library, 12 W. 21st Street, New York, NY 10010.

LAN Times is published bimonthly by Novell, Inc., 748 North 1340 West, Orem, UT 84037.

CHAPTER 8

Microwave and Satellite Communications

Microwave Radio
  Microwave Radio Defined
  Microwave Radio Evolution
  Microwave Radio Technology and Operation
  Comparison of Fiber-Optic Cable, Leased Lines, and Microwave Radio
  Planning a Microwave Radio System

Satellite Communications
  Satellite Communications Defined
  Satellite Communications Evolution
  Satellite Technology and Operation
  Comparison of Satellite Communications with Fiber-Optic Networks

Selecting a VSAT System
  Planning a VSAT System
  Selecting a VSAT System

Teleports
  Teleport Defined
  Types of Teleports
  Teleport Operation
  Profile of a Teleport
  Teleport Issues and Trends

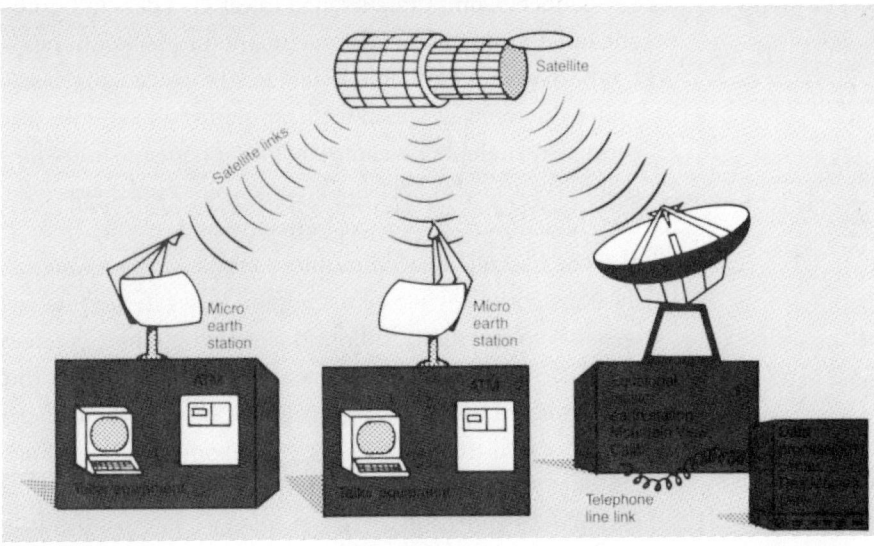

Courtesy of Financial Information Trust, Des Moines, Iowa.

CHAPTER OBJECTIVES

After studying this chapter, you should be able to

1. Describe the technology and operation of a terrestrial microwave system.
2. Discuss the planning of a terrestrial microwave system.
3. Describe the technology and operation of a satellite communications system.
4. Discuss teleports and their importance to business.
5. Compare microwave radio and satellite systems with fiber-optic cable and leased lines.

At Financial Information Trust, Des Moines, Iowa, individual microwave earth stations on the users' premises beam signals from automatic teller machines and teller stations to a satellite in space. From there the data is sent to Equatorial's master earth station in Mountain View, California, and back to the data processor in Des Moines via telephone lines. After the transaction is processed, the output data travels the same path in reverse back to the member savings institutions. The entire process averages five seconds, including the second and a half for processing.

Tandem Computers needed to set up a data link connecting mainframes in one building with a mainframe in another building that was located across the California freeway. Cable could not be considered because digging a tunnel under the freeway was not practical. Telephone links also were not an option because the telephone company did not operate a 10 Mbps data link, the speed required by Tandem. The company's only choice was a 23 GHz microwave system, which proved to be cost-effective and reliable.

The Catholic Telecommunications Network of America leases office space in the New York/New Jersey teleport and uses its satellite facilities five hours each weekday to downlink audio and video programs to receiving dishes at the Chancery/Diocesan Pastoral Centers and Catholic hospitals throughout the country. Programs are then either downlinked to regional deaneries or taped for distribution within the dioceses for 15-million cable households to access. Program offerings include ecumenical, educational, and Spanish-language productions for children and adults. The satellite facilities are also used to conduct teleconferences and send "satellite" mail.

As discussed in Chapter 2, companies can choose guided media, such as twisted-pair wire, coaxial cable, and fiber-optic cable, and/or unguided media, such as terrestrial microwave radio and satellite communications, for their communications system. By being knowledgeable about the available technologies, a company can better select and implement the most appropriate media for its operations. This chapter presents the technology, operations, and applications of microwave and satellite communications systems and compares these systems with fiber-optic cable systems. Teleports, an important distribution vehicle for information, are also discussed.

Microwave Radio

Once the exclusive use of military applications, long-haul common carriers, and utility companies, terrestrial microwave radio is now an essential part of transcontinental communications. Every telephone call, data message, and television program that is transmitted across the country uses a microwave system some of the time. This communication system has become an alternative to the wireline telephone networks.

Microwave radio, also referred to as terrestrial microwave radio, is suited for voice, data, and video and can connect PBXs and LANs. For example, when a blaze destroyed a central office switch of the Illinois Bell Telephone Company, thousands of users' networks were rendered useless. The loss of voice and data lines prevented businesses from carrying out their business activities, such as contacting their customers. One company in-

FIGURE 8-1 **Microwave Radio Applications**

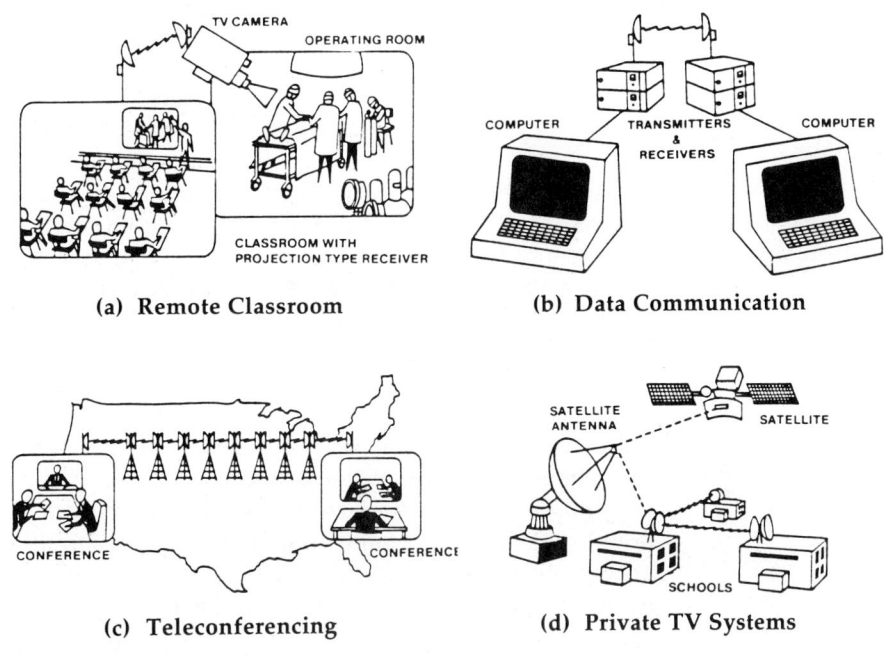

(a) Remote Classroom

(b) Data Communication

(c) Teleconferencing

(d) Private TV Systems

Courtesy of International Microwave Corporation.

stalled a line-of-sight microwave link with an AT&T switching office about two miles from the company's headquarters. The company then used AT&T networks to complete outgoing long-distance calls. Other examples are illustrated in Figure 8-1.

■ Microwave Radio Defined

Microwave is a term that tends to be used loosely to refer to radio (electromagnetic) waves in the frequency range from about 1 GHz (1 gigahertz, or 1 billion hertz) and upward. **Microwave communication** includes radio signals used by terrestrial microwave systems and by earth stations via satellite, although the term is often used to refer only to terrestrial microwave radio systems.

Microwave radio systems can be defined in terms of the frequencies at which they operate, such as between 1 and 23 GHz. Others prefer to describe these systems as being a radio operating between two points via a focused beam of high-frequency radio signals. As discussed in Chapter 2, terrestrial microwave radio is a point-to-point medium with microwave antennas usually located at substantial heights above the ground and spaced 20–30 miles apart (see Figure 2-35).

The Federal Communications Commission (FCC) has divided the microwave region, with frequencies between 1 GHz and 100 GHz, into frequency bands, each band covering a defined range of frequencies, to be shared by different types of users, such as private, commercial, government, and military. Within the entire range of microwave frequencies, only the frequencies between 1 GHz and 23 GHz are designated for conventional communications by private users and by common carriers who derive revenue by reselling communications services to end-users. Frequencies above 23 GHz are designated for military radar applications and some commercial applications. Another band that will be available to private users and common carriers for future systems will be the 31 GHz frequency band.

Short-haul microwave systems use frequencies of 18 GHz and 23 GHz and can travel a distance from several hundred feet to about 15 miles and possibly more. In contrast, *long-haul microwave systems* use frequencies between 1 GHz and 12 GHz and can travel a distance of 30 miles. In major metropolitan areas, congestion in low-frequency bands, such as 12 GHz and below, makes it difficult to secure a path and license for new long-haul systems. However, short-haul microwave systems using 18 GHz and 23 GHz frequencies are currently available to private users and common carriers. In some areas, only the 23 GHz frequency is available, especially in major metropolitan areas such as New York City, where nearly every frequency has been taken except 23 GHz. Throughout the country the 23 GHz frequency offers more spectrum than is available in all the other frequencies combined. Capabilities range from short-distance, low-speed data links to systems that can transmit over 15 miles at speeds of 45 Mbps, the equivalent of 672 64-kbps voice-grade circuits.

According to Dataquest, Inc., of San Jose, California, the market for short-haul microwave systems operating at 18 GHz and 23 GHz reached $59.4 million in 1987 and $75.4 million in 1988 and is projected to be $180.0 million in 1993. Among the leading vendors are Digital Microwave Corporation, Harris Farinon, Hughes Communications, AT&T, Motorola, Inc., Racon, Inc., Rockwell International Corporation, and International Microwave Corporation.

■ Microwave Radio Evolution

Microwave is an outgrowth of the thousands of radio experiments performed in the 1920s. Before the radio boom, radio pioneers had discovered that shortwave (high-frequency) radio waves, those with frequencies between 2 MHz and 30 MHz, were ideal for long-distance communications.

■ Microwave Radio Technology and Operation

Microwave Path. Microwave signals are usually thought as constituting a "beam" of energy. To accommodate wavelengths, the path to be traveled by the microwaves requires a **line-of-sight** connection; that is, an open-air

FIGURE 8-2 Line-of-Sight Between Two Locations

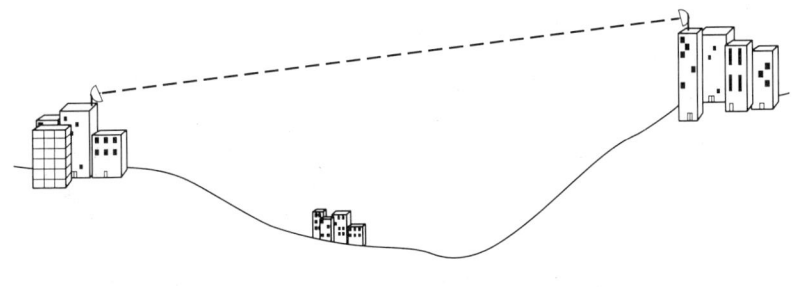

transmission path, between the sending and receiving locations. Such an open-air transmission path is one that is free of obstructions, such as buildings, trees, and other objects, as shown in Figure 8-2. Although a line-of-sight is often thought of as a straight line from a transmitter to a receiver, it is neither a straight line nor a straight path. The microwave is subject to reflection, refraction, and the curvature of the earth. To determine whether a line-of-sight exists between two sites, a visual determination for shorter distances is usually sufficient. Where longer paths are involved, a field study might be required.

The space above and below the line-of-sight, called **Fresnel zones**, must be kept free of obstruction along its entire length for optimal system performance. Fresnel zones are circular orbits that surround the line-of-sight path between the two antennas. The Fresnel zone clearance is maximum at the midpoint of the path, as shown in Figure 8-3. For example, the midpoint Fresnel zone clearance at 23 GHz ranges from 14.5 feet for a ten-mile path to 5.0 feet for a one-mile path.

Signal Loss. The movement of microwaves away from their source is described by the term *propagation*. A wave propagates through the atmosphere from the transmitter to the receiver. Propagation characteristics of microwaves are a function of frequency, transmitter power, and antenna design. However, using the earth's atmosphere as the transmission medium can cause certain signal loss problems not experienced by other media. Types of signal loss include the following.

Free Space Attenuation. The microwave signal expands as it travels away from the source, so the receiving station "sees" only a portion of the radiated energy. This "loss in energy" is called *free space loss* or *free space attenuation*. Although free space loss accounts for a significant signal loss between the transmitter and the receiver, this loss is accounted for when a microwave system is being designed.

FIGURE 8-3 Fresnel Zone Clearance

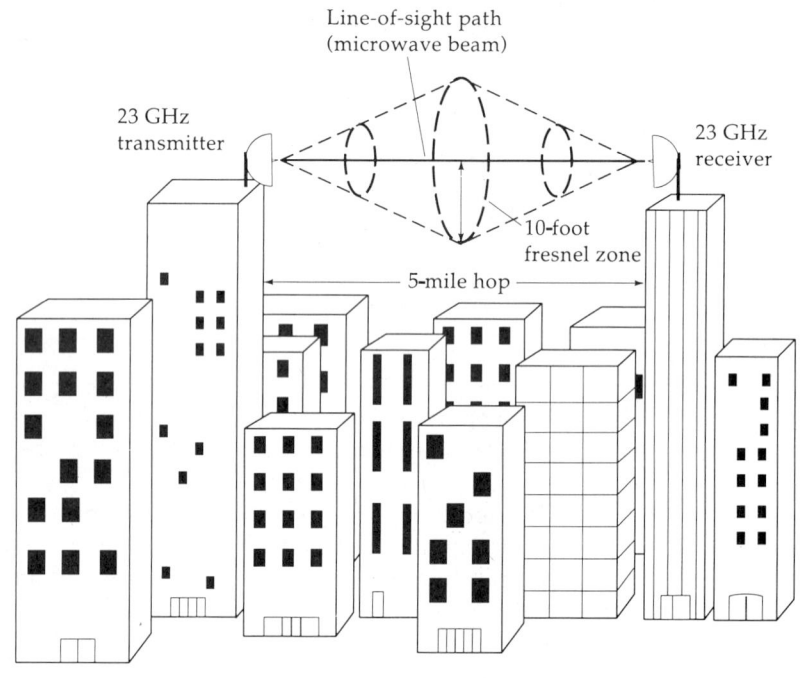

Absorption. Absorption is signal loss between a transmitter and a receiver that is caused by water vapor in the air. Absorption increases with rain intensity and frequency and requires that path lengths at frequencies of 11 GHz and higher be shorter. Rain intensity, not annual rainfall, affects the microwave signal.

Fading. Fading is the variation in signal intensity that is caused by multipath propagation and atmospheric refraction changes. As conditions deteriorate, the signal becomes weaker; when they improve, the signal becomes stronger. For example, heavy ground fog can cause atmospheric refraction to noticeably reduce a signal's strength.

Transmission. Microwave radio transmission involves combining a message signal with a carrier signal by modulation. The modulated carrier that contains the message signal is then transmitted through the atmosphere via electromagnetic radiation to the receiver, where it is demodulated and the message signal extracted. By using carrier signals of different frequencies, different radio transmissions in the same geographical area will not interfere with one another.

FIGURE 8-4 **A Microwave Terminal**

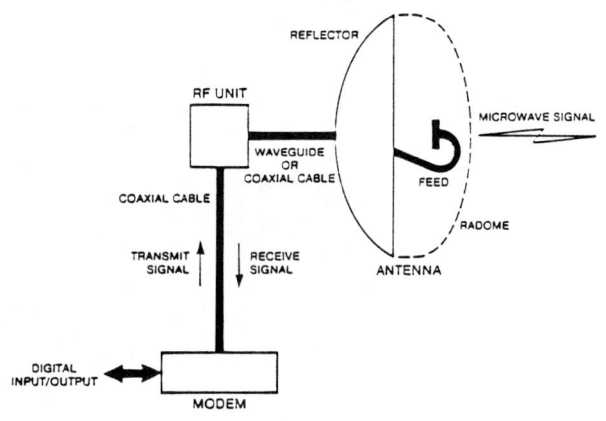

Courtesy of Digital Microwave Corporation.

A microwave radio system, classified as either digital or analog, includes a microwave radio terminal linked by microwave, called a microwave *hop*, to another microwave terminal. The basic components of a digital radio terminal are a digital modem, a radio frequency (RF) unit, and a parabolic dish antenna, as shown in Figure 8-4. Each terminal transmits and receives information to and from the opposite terminal. The systems operate in full-duplex mode by using a single antenna at each end for both transmitting and receiving.

The modem and the radio frequency (RF) unit, which houses the transmitter and the receiver, modulate the digital signals. The sending antenna radiates the signals to the receiving antenna, where they are directed to its RF unit and modem, amplified, and converted to their original form. Each microwave radio link uses two radio frequency channels, as shown in Figure 8-5. One frequency is used to transmit and receive in one direction, and the other in the opposite direction.

FIGURE 8-5 **Microwave Radio Link**

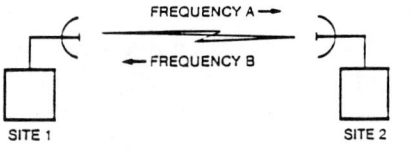

Courtesy of Digital Microwave Corporation.

FIGURE 8-6   Microwave Antenna

Courtesy of Racon Incorporated.

Antenna.   The function of the antenna is to radiate transmit signals and capture receive signals. *Antennas* used for short-haul microwave systems are typically the parabolic reflector type, often called *dish antennas,* such as the one in Figure 8-6. A waveguide feed, with its opening at the focal point of the parabola, directs the outgoing transmit signals to the parabolic reflector, whereby the signal is radiated in a beam from the antenna. Since this beam separates as the distance from the sending antenna to its destination increases, the receiving antenna captures only a small portion of the original signal. The portion captured by the parabolic reflector of the receiving antenna is focused at the opening of the waveguide and directed to the RF unit. Waveguides are rigid hollow pipes—square, oval, or circular in cross section. Coaxial cable is also used to transport microwave signals but with less efficiency than waveguides for a given distance.

Antennas are typically mounted outdoors on a rooftop or antenna tower, but they also can be located indoors behind a clear, nonlead glass window. Outdoor antennas usually have a protective cover over the front of the dish, called a *radome,* to protect the feed and the reflector surface.

Repeater.   High-frequency microwave systems (in the range of 18 GHz and 23 GHz) are typically used for transmissions up to 10–15 miles. As discussed earlier in the chapter, the path between the two terminals must be clear of obstacles—the so-called line-of-sight requirement. When the point-to-point distance between two radio terminals needs to be extended or redirected around line-of-sight obstructions such as hills and tall buildings, a device called a *repeater* can be used. The repeater is placed between

FIGURE 8-7 Microwave Repeaters

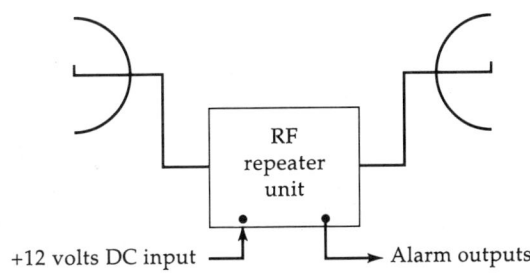

the two radio terminals and is used to redirect and/or boost the signal, as shown in Figure 8-7. Alarm outputs identify any signal problems between the receiver and the transmitter.

Repeaters are either active and passive. *Active repeaters* extend the path length beyond normal operating distances. The active repeater, which is essentially two back-to-back radio terminals, receives the signal, then regenerates and retransmits a clean new digital signal. Thus an active repeater establishes two discrete microwave paths. *Passive repeaters* are used only to redirect the signals.

Multiplexers. A microwave system may be augmented by using T-1 multiplexers designed to accept twenty-four channels of data/voice signals and to combine these channels into a 1.544 Mbps data stream. The microwave system at the University of Southern California at Los Angeles uses two T-1s so that the system can handle forty-eight outgoing long-distance calls simultaneously. A backup battery system prevents service interruptions during power failures. Figure 8-8 shows a network configuration that includes multiplexers.

Cost of Systems. Prices range from $15,000 for a basic low-capacity system to more than $50,000 for a system that provides high-capacity channels.

Microwave System Licensing. The FCC requires that a license be obtained to operate a microwave system. A license application must include documentation verifying that no interference with previously installed links will occur, specifying the exact location of the antennas and the models of the radio system to be used, and stating that the system complies with American National Standards Institute (ANSI) standards for microwave radiation levels. A licensed frequency coordination company assigns frequencies to each radio site so that its transmissions do not interfere with those of others.

FIGURE 8-8 A Microwave Radio System with Multiplexers

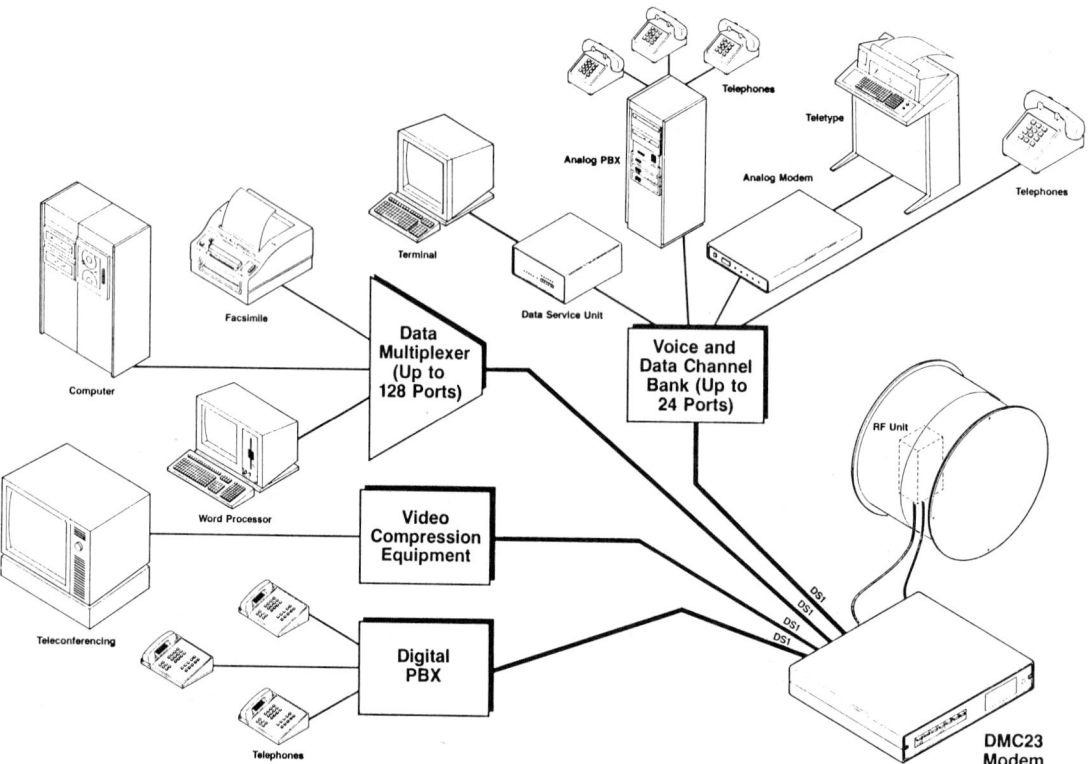

Courtesy of Digital Microwave Corporation.

Microwave Radio Applications. Microwave radio systems can transmit both analog and digital signals. The most common application of analog systems is teleconferencing (see Chapter 13). With digital systems, data can be transmitted from microcomputer to microcomputer or from microcomputer to mainframe computer. Another application is serving as a bridge between parts of a network, each in different locations. Microwave systems also transmit digitized voice, known as T-1 carrier signaling, and are capable of providing twenty-eight or more voice and data lines over a single path.

Network Northeastern of Boston's Northeastern University uses a microwave-based instructional television fixed service that operates on four microwave channels. Each channel simultaneously broadcasts one of Network Northeastern's programs. All programs are broadcast live from specially equipped classrooms at the university's Boston campus. A microwave transmitter broadcasts to an omnidirectional antenna on top of the Prudential Tower, which then transmits to a receiver dish at each company location.

Also included is a telephone talk-back service operating over ordinary telephone lines. For a company to participate, it must have line-of-sight to the Prudential Tower so that it can receive all four channels without the use of repeaters. If the company meets this requirement, Network Northeastern provides and installs the antenna dish, down converter, power supply, and external cabling for the participating company. The company installs its own internal cabling from the entrance of its building to its classrooms and television monitors. Figure 8-9 illustrates Network Northeastern Broadcast System.

A division of Kaiser Permanente Medical Care Program in northern California has installed a microwave system that links its twenty-seven hospitals and health care facilities in the area. Its system is the nation's largest private microwave system in the health industry. Kaiser Permanente selected the system to reduce communication costs, to maintain network control, and to ensure network reliability in case of a natural disaster, such as an earthquake. The system consists of repeaters, thirty-two microwave radio paths, and one fiber-optic cable link to transmit voice, data, and video to twenty-seven sites. Fiber-optic cable was not selected for the entire installation because of the possibility of its being severed during a natural disaster. Although the microwave tower may take a jolt during an earthquake, causing the path to be lost momentarily, the path generally returns after the first jolt.

FIGURE 8-9 **The Network Northeastern Broadcast System**

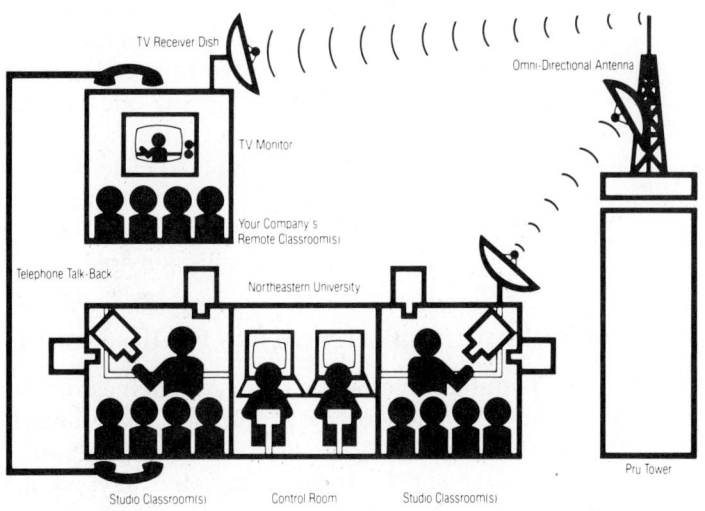

Courtesy of Northeastern University.

Microwave systems are linking a company's LANs from one building to another. These systems allow a LAN to be extended several miles at a 10 Mbps data rate. For example, universities and state and local state governments with locations scattered throughout an area use microwave systems to connect their LANs, especially when roads, shopping centers, and neighborhoods restrict the available right-of-way.

■ Comparison of Fiber-Optic Cable, Leased Lines, and Microwave Radio

Installing a microwave radio system requires a large capital outlay for equipment, possibly a leased line backup system, rooftop space rental, equipment rentals, licensing, and maintenance fees. Yet a microwave system may have a payback period as short as nine months and may result in savings of many thousands of dollars over the system's life.

To decide whether to select a fiber-optic cable, leased lines, or a microwave radio system, the costs of the systems should be compared for a specific period of time. Costs can be simply totaled and compared, or a cash-flow analysis that includes the company's current cost of capital can be calculated.

Other factors also need to be considered such as site locations, speed of transmission, and lead time needed for installation. For example, if a company (or college or university) has several buildings close together on its own property, it should select fiber-optic cable. But if the buildings to be linked are separated by a highway or property owned by another party, microwave radio should be selected. When a highway separates two sites, the user must obtain the rights-of-way to run the cable under the road. Rights-of-way can be purchased from the local telephone company, a utility company, or a railroad. If no conduit exists under the highway, the user must pay a construction firm to burrow one—a time-consuming and expensive procedure. Furthermore, any transmission facility laid in the ground can be accidentally dug up and damaged. The Bell operating companies run "Dig Safe" campaigns designed to inform those planning to dig to check with them first. Factors to consider when comparing these transmission methods for short-haul distance transmission are listed in Figure 8-10.

■ Planning a Microwave Radio System

Planning a microwave radio system includes tasks such as equipment specification, site and route selection, path analysis, and FCC licensing. The PERT chart in Figure 8-11 illustrates the basic steps and approximate time requirements for implementation of a typical microwave system. PERT (Program Evaluation and Review Technique) is a technique that breaks down a planned project into identifiable tasks that must be done in a certain order or at a certain time. It takes into account the fact that parts of a project have a "network" relationship.

FIGURE 8-10 Factors to Consider in Comparing Microwave Radio, Fiber Optics, and Leased Lines for Short-Haul Distance Transmission

- How quickly can the system be installed?
  Microwave systems can be installed within one or two months, including licensing, while the other choices may take as many as several months.
- How long is the installation expected to remain in service?
  A fiber-optic system will probably last longer than a microwave system.
- Does the system allow for company growth?
  Both fiber-optic cable and leased lines have more reserve bandwidth available than does microwave, allowing for growth over a long time period.
- Can the rights-of-way be obtained?
  Obtaining rights-of-way may be a problem for fiber-optic systems but not for microwave systems.
- Does the geographical area experience heavy-intensity rainfalls?
  Heavy rainfall causes attenuation between the microwave transmitter and the receiver.
- Can the system handle the required data link speed?
  High data link speeds might not be available from the telephone company.
- How much bandwidth does the system offer?
  Fiber optics offers more bandwidth than the current microwave systems.
- Is there an unobstructed path between the transmitting antenna and the receiving antenna?
  Microwave systems require a clear line-of-sight with towers required at one or both ends to obtain the required path. The length of cable between the indoor unit and the antenna is limited to either 500 or 1000 feet.
- How secure are the transmissions?
  Microwave transmission sent over specific frequencies is easier to tap into than cable buried in the ground.
- How costly is the system?
  Fiber-optic systems cost less than microwave systems. Leasing high-speed data lines is more expensive than the other two choices.

To establish a point-to-point microwave communications link, first select the two antenna sites and determine whether a clear transmission path can be established between them. For short distances you can visit one of the proposed antenna locations and see whether the path to the opposite location is clear of obstructions. For longer distances you might need to use binoculars. If locating the opposite site is still difficult, a compass might be needed to locate the site coordinates.

Even with line-of-sight clearance, objects might still be near the transmission path. These objects can obstruct the microwave beam and cause a loss in signal strength at the receiver or cause signal interference or attenuation of the received signal. To determine the amount of clearance required for obstacles, the Fresnel zones are calculated.

Next an extensive path analysis is performed to determine how the system will perform. A balance sheet, such as the one in Figure 8-12, shows

FIGURE 8-11   Microwave Project PERT Chart

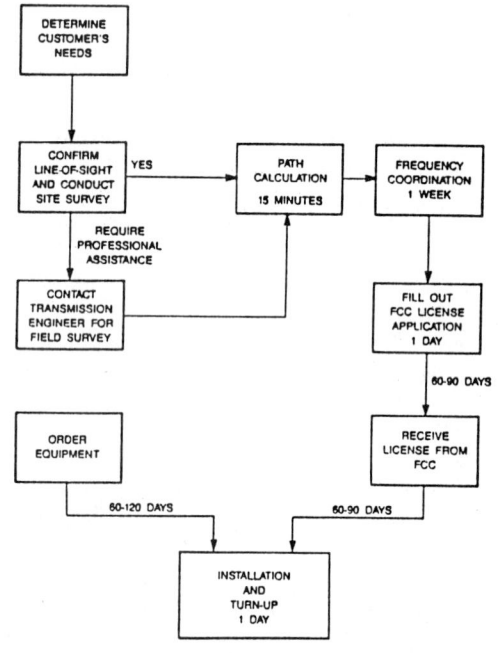

Courtesy of Digital Microwave Corporation.

the gains and losses of the radio signals as they travel from the transmitter to the receiver. After the proposed site has been studied and the equipment selected, system licensing must be obtained from the FCC.

If you are considering installing a microwave system, you should contact a microwave system vendor. The vendor will perform these planning tasks for you and assist you in obtaining an FCC license.

Satellite Communications

Over forty years ago, British author-scientist Arthur C. Clarke proposed the first theory of satellite communications and accurately predicted that space stations would be placed 22,300 miles above the equator. Today, satellite transmission is important not only as a transmission medium but also as a networking method, competing with such methods as packet switching and multiplexing.

Satellite communications include voice, data, and video applications in either a receive-only or an interactive mode. Typical applications are making

FIGURE 8-12 Microwave Path Balance Sheet

(1) Path Name: _____

                                 Site A: Site B:

(2) Site Name: _____ _____

(3) Path Length: _____
   or
   Coordinates: Latitude: _____ _____
                      Longitude: _____ _____

(4) Antenna Azimuths: _____ _____

GAINS:

(5) Transmitter Output Power: _____ dBm

(6) Antenna Gains: _____ dB _____ dB

(7) Total Gains (Sum of items 6, 7A & 7B): _____ dB

LOSSES:

(8) Free Space Losses: _____ dB

(9) Atmospheric Losses: _____ dB

(10) Jumper Losses: _____ dB _____ dB

(11) Pad Losses: _____ dB _____ dB

(12) Misc./Safety Factor Losses: _____ dB _____ dB

(13) Total Losses (Sum of items 8, 9, 10A, 10B, 11A, 11B, 12A & 12B): _____ dB

(14) Unfaded Receive Signal Level (@ 10^{-4} BER) (Item 7 less item 13): _____ dBm

(15) Receiver Sensitivity (@ 10^{-4} BER): _____ dBm

(16) Fade Margin (@ 10^{-4} BER) (Item 14 less item 15): _____ dB

Courtesy of Digital Microwave Corporation.

reservations, point-of-sale, inquiry and response, bulk file transfer, electronic mail, remote printing, high-speed digital facsimile, broadcast news wire, and stock quotation services. For example, more than a dozen newspapers, such as the *Wall Street Journal*, *USA Today*, the *International Herald Tribune*, and *Pravda*, transmit pages daily via satellite. The Paris-based *Herald Tribune* transmits simultaneously via satellite to four countries on two continents. *Time* magazine transmits weekly its entire magazine from New York to Hong Kong and Singapore via satellite. *USA Today*, after being completely edited and composed in Arlington, Virginia, is transmitted by satellite five days a week to thirty-three printing plants in the United States and to three in Europe and Asia. Each plant is equipped with an earth station 5 meters (approximately 16 feet) in diameter and three facsimile recorders. Signals are sent in one eighth of a second to Contel's ASC-1 satellite, which then beams them to earth to be received simultaneously in another eighth of a second by all the printing plants. A typical black-and-white page is transmitted in three to four minutes. Figure 8-13 diagrams the operation.

284   Chapter 8 • Microwave and Satellite Communications

FIGURE 8-13   Producing *USA Today* by Satellite

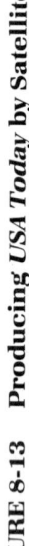

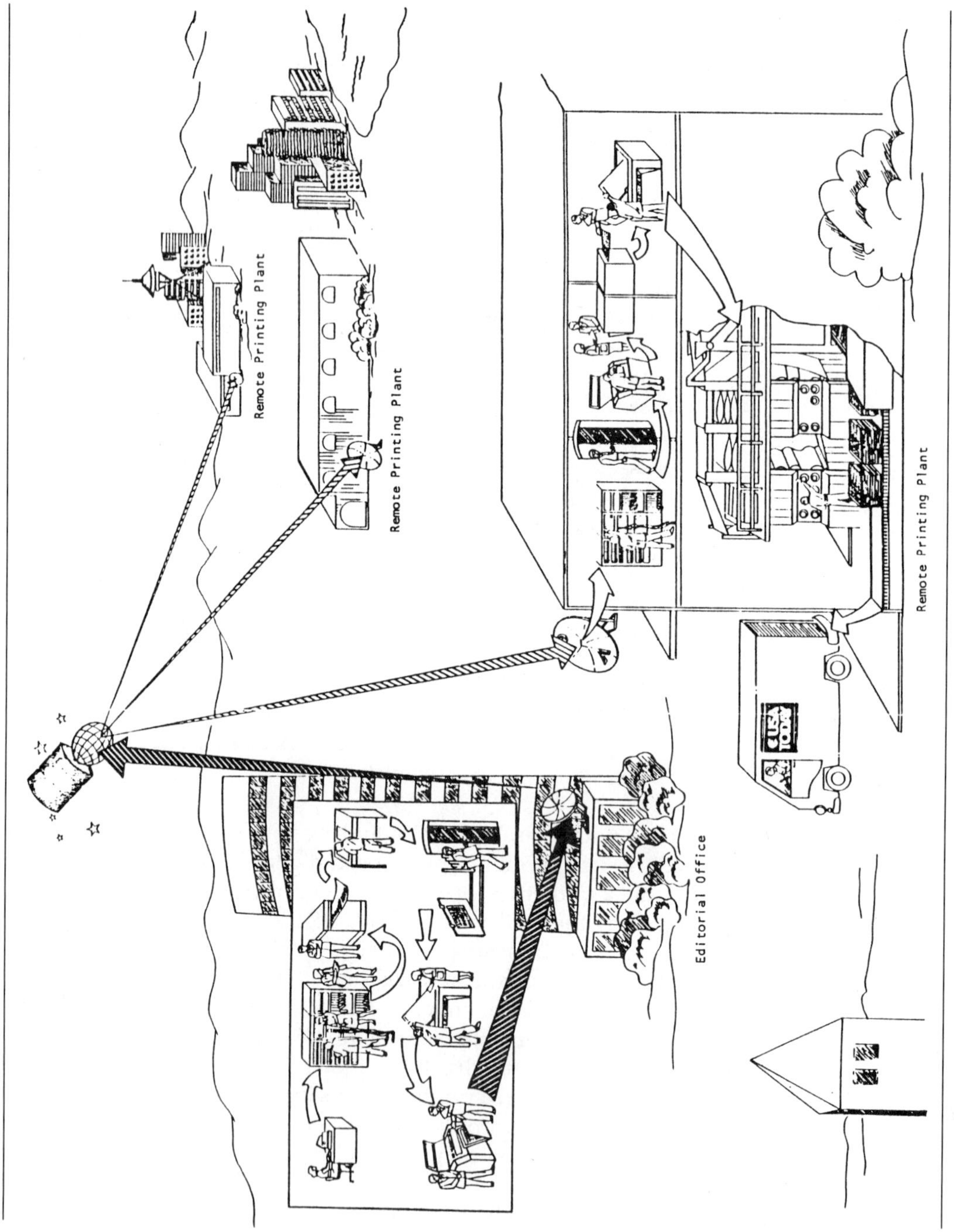

Courtesy of Gannett Co., Inc.

FIGURE 8-14   A Satellite System

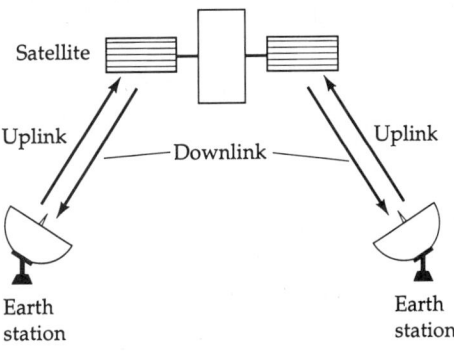

■ Satellite Communications Defined

The term *satellite* can be defined as "a man-made object designed to orbit the earth." **Satellite communications** is "the use of orbiting satellites to relay transmissions from one earth station to another or to several other earth stations" by means of microwave. An **earth station** is "a ground terminal that uses antennas and associated electronic equipment to transmit, receive, and process communications via satellite."[1] A satellite system as shown in Figure 8-14 is used not only for voice and data applications but also for facsimile transmissions, electronic mail, teleconferencing, and paging systems.

■ Satellite Communications Evolution

Since the 1960s, satellite technology has advanced dramatically from an experimental state to an established one. In 1962, AT&T launched the first communications satellite, Telstar, which had only twelve voice circuits. By contrast, INTELSAT VI, scheduled for launching in the fall of 1989, will carry 24,000 voice circuits plus three television channels with a maximum potential of 120,000 voice circuits.

In 1983, small earth stations, commonly called very small aperture terminals (VSATs), were introduced. These small earth stations have revolutionized satellite applications by bringing satellite communications directly to the end-user's location and becoming a cost-effective alternative to terrestrial communication methods. VSATs are explained later in this section. In the 1960s, earth stations with 30-meter antennas sold for $10 million; those being placed into service in 1988 cost under $10,000.

FIGURE 8-15 A Satellite Network

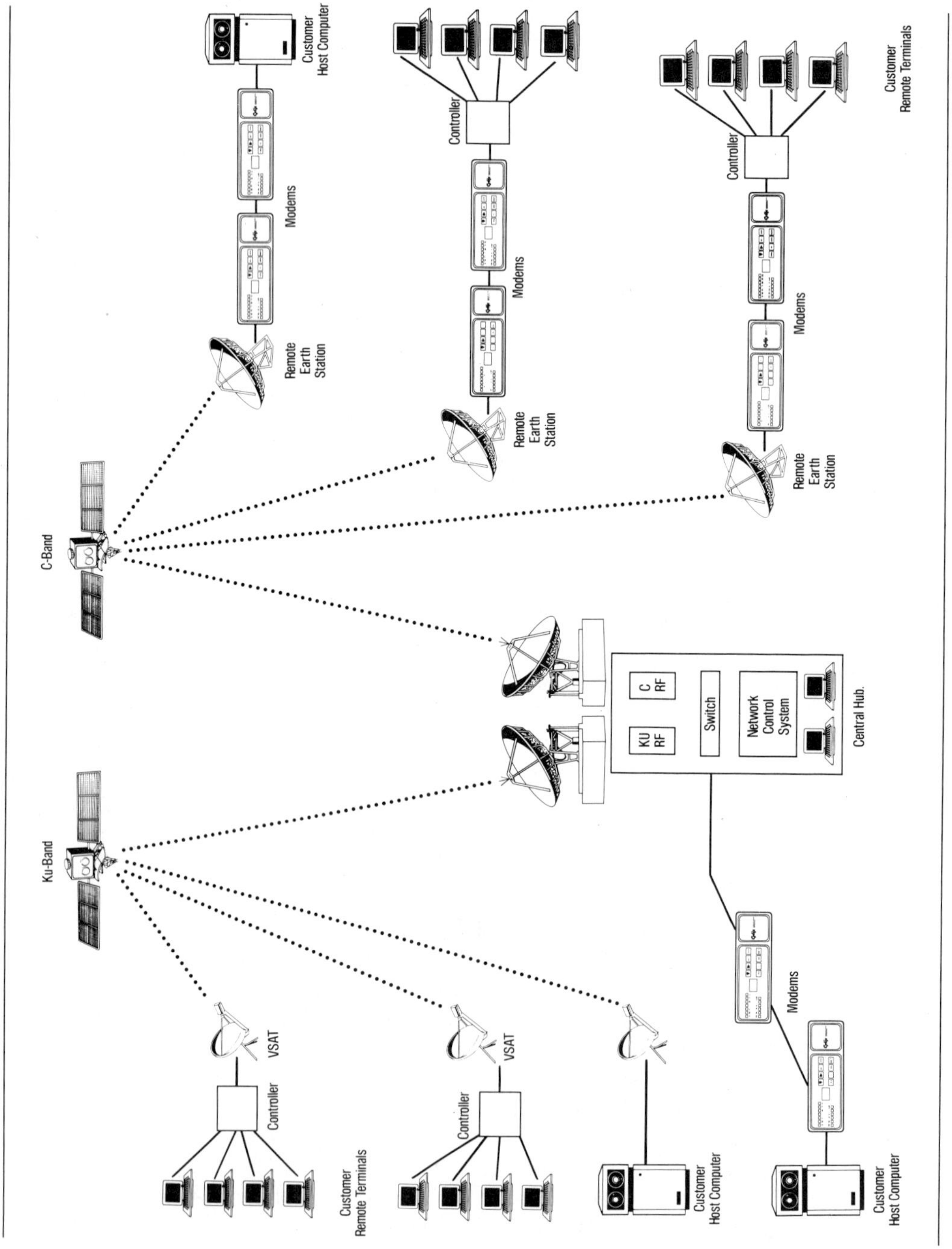

Courtesy of Cylix Communications Corporation.

■ Satellite Technology and Operation

As shown in Figure 8-14, an earth station beams **uplink** signals in the form of radio waves to a satellite in outer space. Once the satellite receives the weak signals, it amplifies the signals' power and then retransmits or **downlinks** the signals to one or more earth stations. The earth stations detect the weak signals received from space and extract them. The uplink beam uses one set of frequencies while the downlink beam uses another set of frequencies so that they do not interfere with each other. Uplinks are more carefully regulated by the FCC and are more expensive than downlinks.

Sending and receiving stations can be located any place in view of a satellite. An uplink beam can receive its input by direct cable links from telephone lines, computers, and broadcast studios, as shown in Figure 8-15. For example, television stations typically send signals by cable to an uplink, which in turn sends them to a satellite for transmission to one or more earth receiving stations.

A narrow beam from the satellite illuminates a portion of the earth's surface, referred to as a **footprint**. As shown in Figure 8-16, the footprint defines the precise area of the earth in which the signal can be received. A satellite's footprint may range from several hundred miles to several thousand miles in width, depending on the application. For example, a satellite used for television broadcasts has wide footprints, while a satellite used for point-to-point messages has narrow footprints.

Footprint maps, like the one shown in Figure 8-17, which are provided with every communication satellite, specify the *effective isotropic radiated*

FIGURE 8-16 Typical Ku-Band Satellite Footprint—Continental United States

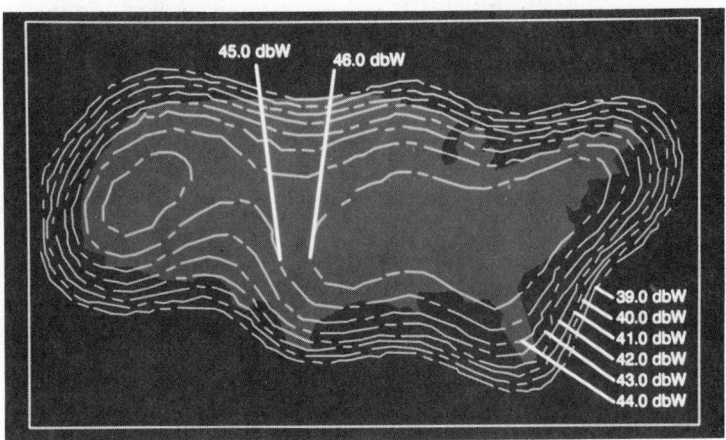

Courtesy of Cylix Communications Corporation.

FIGURE 8-17 Footprint Map

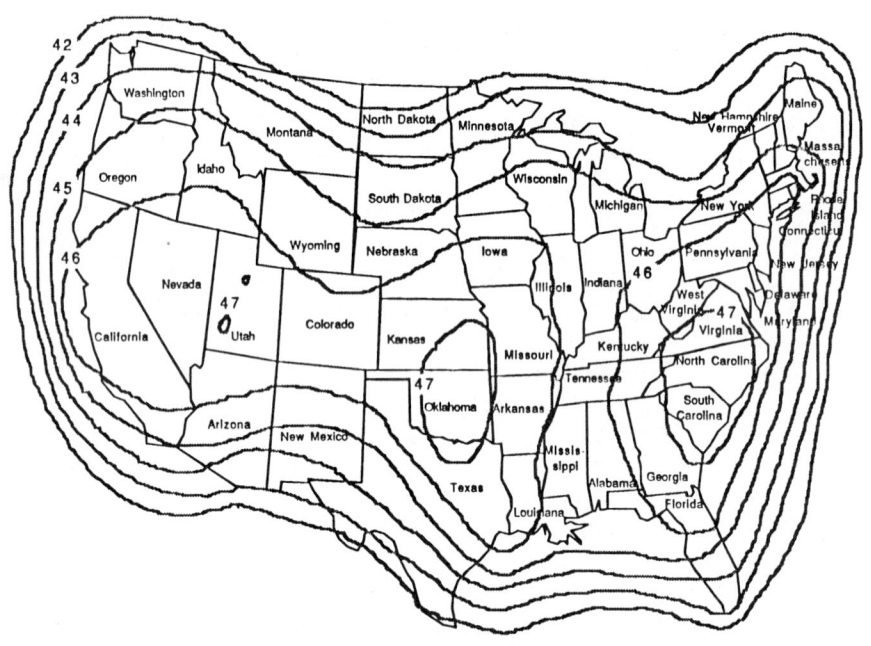

Courtesy of Cylix Communications Corporation.

power (EIRP). The EIRP is a measure, expressed in decibels, of the power levels reaching the earth. As a signal travels from the downlink antenna to earth, it spreads out in a conelike beam and becomes weaker. This weakening of power is called the *free space path loss*. As you would expect, the free space path loss increases as the distance between the communication satellite and the earth station increases. The power received at an earth station must be adjusted for free space path loss.

The Satellite. A satellite's primary function is to relay signals from earth station to earth station. Communications satellites encircle the earth in a ring 22,300 miles above the equator, usually separated from each other by 3 degrees, as shown in Figure 8-18. Since this orbit is confined to one circular path, the number of satellites that can be active at one time for coverage of specific portions of the earth is limited.

Satellites are geostationary; that is, they appear to remain in one position relative to a particular point on earth by rotating at the same speed as the earth. One of the satellite's maintenance functions is to maintain its position in orbit. A satellite's *altitude control apparatus* keeps the antennas precisely

FIGURE 8-18 **Communication Satellites**

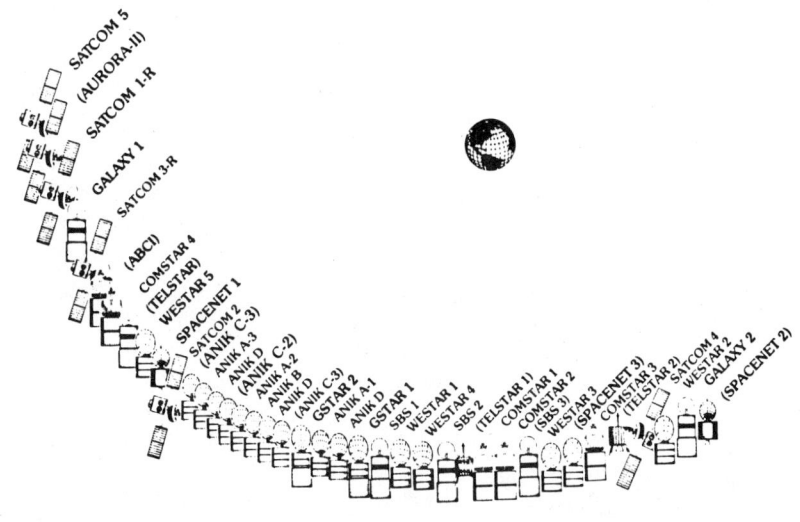

Courtesy of Scientific-Atlanta, Inc.

aligned toward the earth. A satellite's *stationkeeping system* corrects the system's orbit to ensure that it maintains its assigned position. Other maintenance functions include generating and storing electrical power for the satellite's own use and monitoring the performance of its components.

Satellites must be extremely light and reliable. Current satellites range in weight from several hundred to a few thousand pounds, their weights being limited by the power of the launch vehicle. Once a satellite is in orbit, it must function without any possibility of repair for its entire working life. Because of weight and fuel-carrying limitations, the U.S. National Aeronautics and Space Administration (NASA) space shuttle, which launches satellites, cannot reach the altitudes necessary to retrieve satellites in geosynchronous orbit. The expected life of a communication satellite now in orbit or planned for the near future ranges from seven to ten years. During its life, the satellite must operate with more than 99% reliability.

A satellite's power is generated by solar cells when the satellite is illuminated by the sun and by batteries during darkness. A communications satellite consists of an antenna, one or more transponders, and a control circuit. Earth stations send signals to the satellite's antenna, which then sends them to one of the satellite's transponders.

The **transponder**, a microwave repeater on board the satellite, receives, amplifies, and reconverts the uplink signals and then retransmits them to the antenna, which sends them to their destination earth station(s) within the particular satellite's footprint. Satellites carry multiple transponders, each with a bandwidth of 30–70 MHz. For example, AT&T's Telstar 3 contains thirty transponders, twenty-four working and six spare, each with a bandwidth of 36 MHz. The number of transponders and the power available to each one determine the communications capacity of the satellite. Since newer satellites carry more powerful transponders, they can carry more signals than older satellites.

A communications satellite carries one or more antennas. Each antenna has more than one transceiver and usually more than one reflector for radiating signals and gathering them from earth stations.

The Signal Element

Modulation. Signals can be transmitted over satellite channels in either analog or digital form. In general, all broadcast television and most voice telephone transmissions use analog signals, while all dedicated data transmissions and an increasing number of voice telephone transmissions use digital signals.

Bandwidth. A satellite's wide bandwidth enables it to carry more signals than any other medium currently being used commercially. The bandwidth of a given signal is a function of its frequency and of its strength. For example, a satellite transponder typically offers 36 MHz bandwidth at frequencies from 4 GHz to 6 GHz. A satellite that carries twelve or twenty-four transponders would then have a total bandwidth of 432 MHz or 864 MHz, respectively (36 × 12 or 36 × 24).

Frequency Bands. As was explained in Chapter 2, separate frequencies are used for the two directions of transmission—the uplink and the downlink. The spectrum of frequencies is expressed in frequency pairs, such as 6/4 GHz band pair. Of the two frequencies in each pair, the higher figure represents the uplink, while the lower represents the downlink.

Commercial communication satellites today operate at C-band, Ku-band, or a hybrid of C-band and Ku-band frequencies. Future satellites will use higher-frequency bands, such as Ka-band. Figure 8-19 lists the uplink and downlink frequencies of the three bands. Both the C-band and the Ku-band have usable bandwidths of 500 MHz, while the Ka-band has a bandwidth of 3500 MHz. Whether to choose the C-band or Ku-band satellite networks depends on the user's applications. For example, if a small earth station is to be used within a city congested with C-band frequencies, then Ku-band frequencies would be selected.

C-Band. The first commercial satellites built for INTELSAT, an international satellite organization, operated in the **C-band** frequencies, the uplink frequencies ranging from 5.925 GHz to 6.425 GHz and the downlink fre-

FIGURE 8-19 **Communications Satellite Frequency Bands**

Frequency Bands (GHz)	Uplink (GHz)	Downlink (GHz)	Bandwidth (GHz)
C 6/4	5.925–6.425	3.700–4.200	500
Ku 14/12	14.0–14.5	11.7–12.2	500
Ka 29/19	27.5–31.0	17.7–21.2	3500

quencies ranging from 3.7 GHz to 4.2 GHz. The C-band is shared with terrestrial microwave radio systems that requires close coordination of spacing and antenna positioning to prevent interference. Interference between satellites and between satellites and microwave is prevented by using high directional antennas. The C-band is still used particularly for satellite applications dealing with television distribution and international voice and data communications.

A particular benefit of C-band is that climatic effects from heavy rainfall are minimal. A drawback of C-band is that large antennas are needed for transmit/receive operations to avoid interference to and from adjacent satellites. Another drawback is that sharing frequencies with terrestrial services requires frequent coordination. Terrestrial interference in C-band limits its use in major metropolitan areas.

Ku-Band. Introduced in the United States in the early 1980s by Satellite Business Systems, **Ku-band** is experiencing rapid growth in use and is becoming the preferred frequency band. Examples of Ku-band satellites in orbit as of April 1988 are Satellite Business Systems' SBS, GTE's Spacenet, Hughes' ASC, GTE's GStar, and RCA's Satcom.

The Ku-band uplink in the United States is 14–14.5 GHz, while the downlink is 11.7–12.1 GHz, its primary applications being commercial satellite communications. The primary benefit of Ku-band frequencies is that they are used exclusively by satellite; they are not shared with other terrestrial systems. Users can set up earth stations virtually wherever they desire, including metropolitan areas where frequency congestion prevents placing C-band earth stations. Other benefits are as follows:

- Compared with C-band, the Ku-band has a narrower footprint, making it possible for earth station antennas to be smaller and cheaper.
- The narrower beam of the Ku-band satellite allows the spacing between satellites to be 2 degrees, which allows more satellites to be in space.

The primary drawback of Ku-band (and Ka-band) is susceptibility to rain attenuation, which results in lower reliability. The problem may be reduced by selecting earth stations that are located where heavy rain is less likely to occur or by designing circuits to tolerate the effects of the rain. Ka-band frequencies are even more susceptible to attenuation. Although

Ka-band frequencies offer more bandwidth, more technology developments are needed before Ka-band frequencies are available for general use.

Domestic and International Satellites. Domestic satellites are owned and operated by COMSAT, AT&T, Satellite Business Services, Western Union, GE American Satellite, and GTE. International nonmilitary satellites are the responsibility of the International Telecommunications Satellite Organization (INTELSAT) and Pan American Satellite.

INTELSAT. Created in 1964, **INTELSAT** is an international satellite organization operating under a treaty with 112 countries. The organization owns and operates commercial communication satellite systems that are used by countries worldwide for international communications and by more than 25 countries for domestic communications. The United States through its signatory, Communications Satellite Corporation (**COMSAT**), holds the largest share in INTELSAT at 25.6%, followed by the United Kingdom with 13.9% and France with 4.5% as of April 1988. (A signatory is a member government or its designated telecommunications entity that has committed itself to meet annually to consider issues related to the financial, technical, and operation aspects of INTELSAT. COMSAT, a government-regulated private organization, is the U.S. member of INTELSAT.)

INTELSAT satellites carry two-thirds of the world's international telephone services and virtually all international television transmissions. When you telephone overseas, send a telex, data, or facsimile from one country to another, or view a television broadcast of an international event, the transmission is most likely being handled by INTELSAT. For example, INTELSAT's international television services offer regular telecasts of international events, such as the Winter and Summer Olympics, World Cup Soccer, U.S. presidential elections, the Academy Awards, and Wimbledon.

The world's first commercial communication satellite, Early Bird (INTELSAT I), launched in 1965, transmitted twenty simultaneous telephone conversations between the United States and Europe. Early Bird, like all subsequent commercial satellites, was placed in geostationary orbit 22,300 miles above the equator. INTELSAT VI has a capacity of 120,000 simultaneous two-way telephone circuits and at least three television channels utilizing both K-band and C-band (6/4 GHz and 14/11 GHz, respectively). In 1988, INTELSAT had fifteen satellites in geosynchronous orbit with more than 680 earth stations linking together more than 165 countries.

Figure 8-20 shows a diagram of INTELSAT VI.

Pan American Satellite. Pan American Satellite Corporation, established in 1984, launched its PAS 1 Satellite to become INTELSAT's first competitor. The PAS 1 satellite beam covers the Caribbean, Central and South America, the continental United States, and western Europe. Transmission costs are substantially less than those of INTELSAT.

FIGURE 8-20   INTELSAT VI

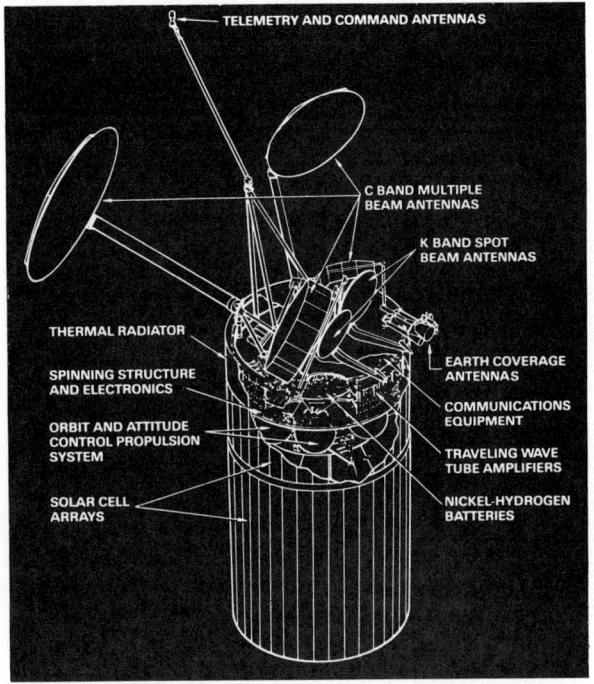

Reproduced courtesy of INTELSAT.

Earth Stations.   Earth stations can be receive-only or two-way stations. Large antennas, also called dishes, made of perforated metal, wire mesh, fiberglass, or solid metal for receiving satellite broadcasts are familiar sights at hotels and television stations, in back yards, and in rural areas. Antennas range in size from 30 meters (about 100 feet) in diameter to very small ones. The antenna size is directly related to the intensity of the satellite signal. By doubling the signal power the antenna can be decreased in size, and a 10-foot dish, for example, can be replaced with a 7-foot one.

Receive-Only Earth Station.   The antenna's function at a receive-only earth station is to detect signals from a communications satellite and funnel the signals into a device called a *feedhorn* or *feed*, as shown in Figure 8-21. The feedhorn directs the signals into a small, boxlike low-noise amplifier (LNA) or low-noise converter (LNC), which amplifies the signals' power many thousands of times. These signals are then sent via coaxial cable to an indoor receiver/modulator, which downconverts and demodulates the signals into a form that can be understood, for example, by any television set. The receiver may be located several hundred feet from the antenna.

FIGURE 8-21 **Transmission from Satellite to Earth Station**

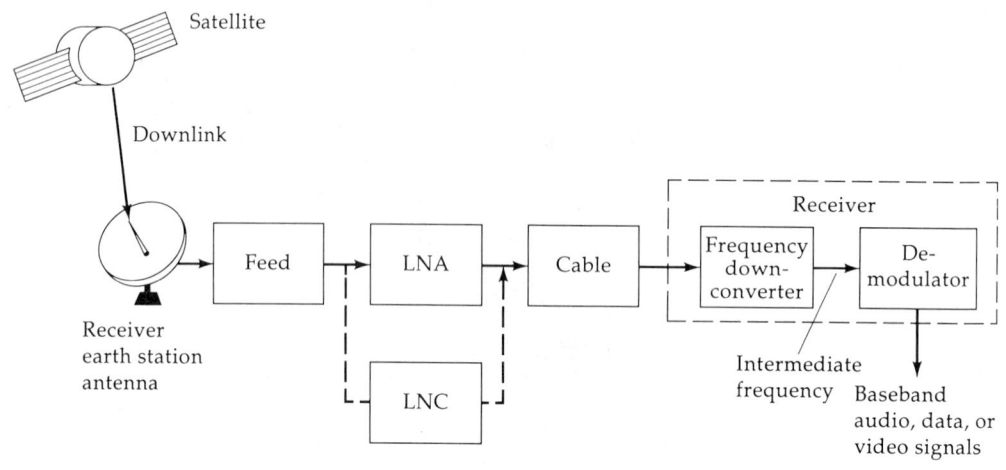

The antenna must be of adequate size and quality to capture signals from a distant satellite. It also must be accurately aimed toward the satellite to avoid detecting messages and noise from unwanted terrestrial and satellite sources. Other requirements include being durable, aesthetically pleasing, and able to maintain its accuracy for years.

Transmit Earth Station. The basic transmit earth station contains the basic receiving equipment plus an exciter, a high-power amplifier (HPA), a transmit reject filter, and interconnecting cable, as shown in Figure 8-22. The earth station antenna is equipped with a feed capable of radiating a 6 GHz uplink signal. At the transmit earth station the exciter accepts the baseband audio, data, or video signals, modulates them, and then upconverts the signals. The HPA amplifies this signal to the required power output level for the uplink RF signal toward the satellite.

VSAT Technology. A very small aperture terminal (**VSAT**) is a small earth station with an antenna (dish) only 2–6 feet in diameter. Dishes as small as 19 inches in diameter, about the size of a normal house fan, and flat dishes are expected to be available shortly. The VSAT's small size also makes it less likely to be banned by city zoning laws than the large conventional satellite dish.

According to Link Resources, a marketing research firm, the VSAT market increased from $99 million in 1985 to $416 million in 1988, with $765 million projected for 1990. In 1984, VSAT earth stations cost $30,000–$50,000. By 1986 the same terminals could be purchased for $6,000–$15,000; and by 1988 the cost was $2,000 for a receive-only VSAT. The cost of a VSAT

FIGURE 8-22   Transmission from Earth Station to Satellite

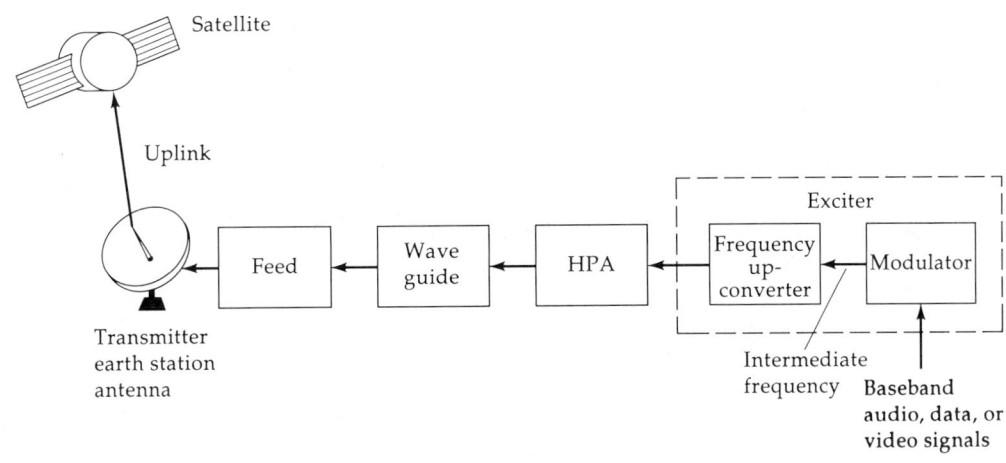

network depends on the particular business applications. The higher the data rate the VSAT can transmit, the more costly the terminal.

VSAT Operation and Technology.   In a VSAT network a master earth station acts as the hub of a star network with a number of small earth stations forming the points of the star. The master station transmits a high-power signal to the satellite, compensating for the receiving limitations of the VSAT. To make up for the weak signals sent by the VSAT, the hub requires a large antenna, at least 5 meters (16.4 feet) in diameter, to perform its functions. A larger dish may be necessary if the area is experiencing heavy rain or if the hub is to uplink both video and data.

Transmission.   VSAT networks transmit signals by multiplexing methods. Multiplexing, as discussed in Chapters 2 and 6, is using a common channel to make two or more subchannels. The common channel can be split by frequency into narrower bands, each constituting a distinct subchannel (frequency-division multiplexing), or its full channel bandwidth can be accessed by multiple users taking turns (time-division multiplexing). When these techniques are used in satellite transmission, they are referred to as *multiple access techniques*, in particular, **frequency-division multiple access** (FDMA) and **time-division multiple access** (TDMA). The majority of VSAT networks rely on TDMA accessing methods for sending and receiving data signals.

Owning or Sharing Hubs.   Users can purchase, operate, and maintain their own *private VSAT network*. This alternative is usually considered only by large companies, since a master hub can cost over $1 million. Most VSAT users use a *public VSAT network* in which they share a master hub that serves as the center of the network. Carriers such as AT&T offer shared hubs to users who cannot afford or prefer not to purchase their own master hubs. Users can lease or purchase a whole or a percentage of a transponder, depending on their requirements. In this way an organization can easily increase its VSAT transmission capacity as its communication demands change. The cost of VSAT service in a shared hub environment is usually between $300 and $500 per month, the installation charge per site averaging $2000–$5000. The cost of equipment for each VSAT site is about $10,000. A network can be installed and fully operational in three to six months.

VSAT Configurations. VSAT configurations use either C-band or Ku-band frequencies. C-band is less costly than terrestrial networks for low-end data rates, while Ku-band is less expensive for high-end data rates.

VSATs can be set up to operate as either a receive-only or a receive/transmit configuration with VSATs installed at geographically dispersed sites. Four possible VSAT network configurations are as follows. Figure 8-23(a) shows a point-to-multipoint configuration. A company's host computer broadcasts messages to the VSAT sites through the hub, also called the master earth station (MES). This type of network is used by organizations to broadcast messages to branches as well as by corporate video networks.

Figure 8-23(b) diagrams a two-way VSAT network. Here the VSAT remote sites exchange data with the host computer through the master earth station. Several company networks with their host computers and VSATs share the master hub. The point-to-point network shown in Figure 8-23(c) allows VSAT sites to communicate with each other through the master hub but does require a double satellite hop. This configuration is suitable for file transfers and batch-processing applications and certain interactive data applications. In Figure 8-23(d) the hub is located at the host computer's site. This configuration requires several VSATs at various locations to justify the cost of the network.

Benefits and Drawbacks. VSAT networks have become particularly attractive to businesses for routing data to hundreds of geographically dispersed sites and for applications that require quick response times from a central database. Among the increasing number of VSAT users are K mart, Farmers Insurance, Days Inn of America, Red Roof Inns, Avis Rent-A-Car, Mobil Corporation, Toyota Motor Sales, Inc., Chrysler Motor Corporation, pharmaceutical distributor McKesson Corporation, brokerage house Edward D. Jones & Company, and federal agencies such as the U.S. Departments of Agriculture and Interior.

Benefits of VSATs include the following:

FIGURE 8-23 Possible VSAT Network Configurations

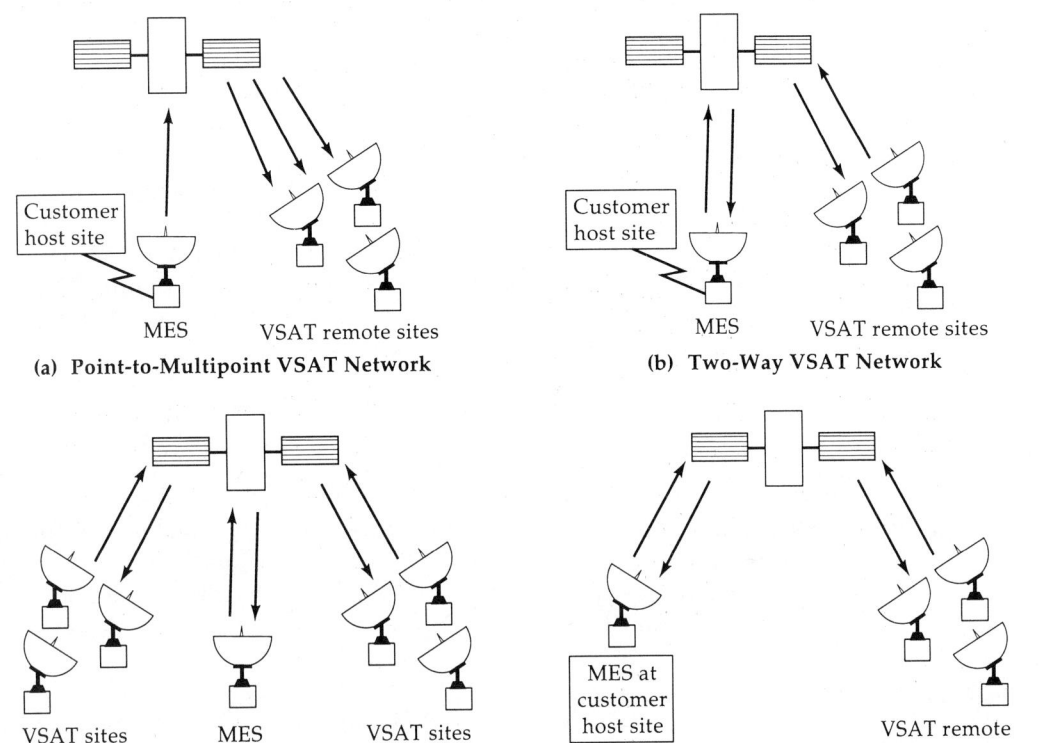

Redrawn by permission from *Teleconference Magazine*, Volume 6, Number 2, "VSATS: Very Small Aperture Terminals," by Joseph Freitag, Jr.

- The cost of transmitting by satellite is independent of the distance between the sending and the receiving stations.
- Since all satellite signals are broadcast, the cost of a satellite transmission does not change regardless of the number of stations receiving the transmission. For example, Burlington Coat Factory, a New Jersey–based retailer, links more than 100 stores by VSATs. The stores connect to a central hub for transferring inventory data, purchase orders, electronic mail, and credit card authorizations. The company estimates that its VSAT network saves about $350,000 annually compared to the cost of a terrestrial network.[2]
- Since the satellite is insensitive to the location of the dishes and users need to communicate only intermittently, the satellite channel can be shared by many users, which results in network savings.

- VSATs operate quickly. Burlington Coat Factory's VSAT network has reduced the time required to process credit card transactions from 40 seconds to 7 seconds.
- VSATs are reliable. VSAT bit-error rates are one in 10 million, while telephone line error rates are one in 100,000.
- VSATs are flexible. Users can expand their networks as data traffic grows. The addition or moving of VSATs does not disturb the rest of the network. VSATs are compatible with most data protocols and data terminals.
- The small VSAT dish allows it to be quickly mounted on rooftops or next to office buildings.
- Compared to terrestrial transmission methods, VSAT networks are more efficient, since they do not rely on expensive terrestrial circuits. By placing a VSAT terminal at each end user's site the telephone company's central office, the "last mile loop," can be bypassed.

Among the drawbacks of VSATs are the following:

- Since satellite signals are broadcast, they lack security unless they are encrypted. If an earth station is within sight of the satellite and is tuned to the proper frequency, it can intercept any signal the satellite transmits.
- Propagation delay can be a problem for one-way and two-way transmissions. Propagation delay, caused by delays in the transmission medium, refers to the time lost between the transmission of a signal and the time it is received.
- Weather or other atmosphere conditions can be a problem. For example, signals operating at Ku-band or Ka-band frequencies are affected by rain absorption.

VSAT Application. A first-of-its kind VSAT reservations system has helped to boost Days Inns, the lodging chain, to become one of the top hotel chains in the industry. The VSAT system sends reservation data from point to point in eight seconds—about ten times faster than the WATS service that Days Inns previously used. With VSAT the company knows exactly what its communications costs will be for the next five years, which allows it to better plan its network future.

The VSAT system allows the hotel chain to update software at each site by downloading bulk files and to broadcast video employee-training programs. Days Inns is considering generating additional revenue by renting its facilities for videoconferencing. Other applications being considered are in-room entertainment, electronic mail, and voice applications.

Days Inns examined several alternative technologies before deciding that a VSAT network would be the most cost-effective. Leased lines would have been more expensive and less flexible, a packet-switched network would have left the chain at the mercy of tariff changes, and the dialup system that was in place was costly and very slow. The only drawback to the

VSAT system has been the initial capital outlay of $10,000 for hardware and installation per site. As of 1988, the chain had 750 sites linked to the network.

Six-foot roof-mounted dishes are installed at each site. The Ku-band signal is hubbed through GTE Spacenet Corporation facilities in New York and beamed through GTE's GSTAR II satellite. Since the system is interactive, the IBM 3090 host computer at corporate headquarters can inventory all rooms, and a reservations agent can book rooms for a Days Inns hotel from any other hotel in the chain. The system currently provides only video and data communications over the 9.6 kbps satellite circuit.

Satellite Communications Standards and Licensing. Satellite communications are regulated by the FCC in the United States and by the International Radio Consultative Committee (CCIR), a branch of the International Telecommunication Union (ITU). Satellite carriers set their own standards for designing systems but must comply with FCC standards for radio frequency spectrum and satellite positioning. Since most users obtain satellite services from a satellite carrier, they are not concerned with the performance of the satellite and earth station equipment, although they are concerned with the circuit performance established by the carrier. The Consultative Committee on International Telephone and Telegraph offers circuit performance recommendations, but compliance is voluntary in the United States.

In a 1986 decision the FCC waived an earlier requirement that called for the licensing of each VSAT earth station. The FCC now requires an application describing the system operation and the applicant for each master earth station over 5 meters in diameter and a second application for the type of VSATs to be used in the network. The company pays a $5000 fee for the entire network rather than a licensing fee for each earth station.

■ Comparison of Satellite Communications with Fiber-Optic Networks

Although long-distance traffic currently accounts for almost 40% of satellite use, long-distance carriers are increasingly shifting to fiber-optic networks. Fiber optics, which uses beams of light to transmit information, transmits telephone traffic more efficiently than does satellite communications. Signals transmitted by fiber-optic cable do not have to travel to an orbiting satellite and are not subject to the propagation delays experienced by satellite transmissions. However, deciding which transmission technology to select still depends on the particular applications. Although most fiber-optic networks tend to be designed for point-to-point transmission, they can complement satellite technology, resulting in integrated networks, as shown at the beginning of the chapter. Industry analysts believe that the future of satellite communications lies in applications made possible by VSATs.[3] Factors to consider in deciding between fiber optics and satellite are listed in Figure 8-24.

FIGURE 8-24 A Comparison of Satellite and Fiber-Optic Systems

Feature	Satellite Systems	Fiber-Optic Systems
Right-of-way	Not a major cost factor.	A major cost factor.
Bandwidth	Bandwidth of 500 MHz may be increased to 3 or 4 GHz.	Optical-fiber cable may provide about a 500 MHz bandwidth. Number of cables can be increased at no added trenching cost.
Flexibility	Easy to reconfigure.	Difficult to reconfigure.
Security	Signals must be encrypted for security.	Must be encrypted to protect the message in case of tapping.
Delay	About 0.50-second roundtrip delay.	Much less delay than satellite for reasonable distances.
Future expansion	Much easier to expand. Only needs a terminal added to include a new user.	Every new path is done independently, so expansion is costly and perhaps not feasible.
Immunity to interference	Transmission subject to interference from adjacent system and jamming.	Not susceptible to external noise and electromagnetic interference.
Reliability	A mature and reliable technology.	An evolving technology, especially for undersea installation.
Availability	Affected by adverse weather conditions.	Very high unless physically disabled.
Cost	Depends on link capacity.	Depends on location, distance, and link capacity.

Eugene Cacciamani and M. Hassein Sharifi, "Designing Efficient Satellite and Fiber-Optic Networks," *Telecommunication Products + Technology*, April 1987, p. 48. Courtesy of Networking Management (formerly TPI), PennWell Publishing Co., Westford, Massachusetts.

Selecting a VSAT System

■ Planning a VSAT System

Selecting a VSAT system requires careful planning. Answers to the following questions will assist in determining your VSAT system requirements.

- What applications will the company run on the VSAT system?
- Where are the earth stations to be located?
- Where is the hub station to be located?
- Will one-way or two-way earth stations be appropriate for the applications?

- How much voice, data, and/or video traffic do you expect now and during the life of the network?

■ Selecting a VSAT System

After you have determined your VSAT system requirements, you are ready to select a system. The following questions will serve as a guide in the selection process.

- Which vendors provide all of the VSAT services? Which vendors provide only certain VSAT services? For example, who provides transponder space? Who provides network management and control? Who handles network installation? This information is particularly important for users who prefer one-step shopping for communications equipment, services, and support. Some companies offer a single point of contact for the various services; only a few actually own the transponder space, manufacture VSATs, and operate service organizations. For example, when K mart Corporation set up its VSAT system, GTE Spacenet served as the single point of contact and transponder space supplier. GTE Spacenet contacted NEC America, Inc. to supply the small earth stations; Mosler, Inc., of Hamilton, Ohio, to assist in network installation; and Telenet Communications Corporation to provide network management and control. Another company contacted AT&T to set up its VSAT system. AT&T provided all services but contacted Harris Corporation to provide the VSATs.
- Does the vendor provide a shared hub station, a private hub station, or both? How many hubs does the vendor have? Where is each one located? How far is the vendor's shared hub station from your VSATs? You might have to run one or more leased lines from your offices to the hub. For example, one vendor has only one shared hub, which is located in California; another vendor has its shared hub in New York City.
- Do you own your building? VSAT users who do not own their buildings must seek landlord approval to install a VSAT on the roof or attach one to the side of the building. Local zoning restrictions may also present problems to users. Will the point-of-contact vendor assist you in handling landlord and zoning issues?
- Who should you select to maintain and provide field support services? Although a vendor's own support group may be more familiar with the vendor's product, a third-party support service might offer more diversified knowledge of VSAT maintenance.
- What data protocols does the VSAT services vendor support? Examples of protocols you might want to have supported are IBM's, SNA, SDLC, BCS, X.25, asynchronous, and bisynchronous.
- Does the system use Ku-band or C-band?

You should also seek information about VSAT systems from vendors' customers and VSAT users within your industry. Careful planning and selection will enable you to choose the system that is right for your company.

Teleports

The news that the United States and the Soviet Union had signed a landmark treaty to reduce the size of their nuclear arsenals was transmitted from the United States to European audiences by the European Broadcast Union via New York's Teleport. Before 1987, television networks sent and received television signals overseas by using satellite antennas in West Virginia and Maine.

■ Teleport Defined

Although earth stations had been operating in the United States for several years, it was not until 1982 that the New York–New Jersey Port Authority and Merrill Lynch coined the term "The Teleport" to describe a shared satellite communications facility diagrammed in Figure 8-25. What is a teleport? A **teleport**, as defined by the World Teleport Association (WTA), is "an access facility to a satellite or other long-haul telecommunications medium incorporating a distribution network serving the greater regional community and associated with, including, or within a comprehensive related real estate or other economic development."

The World Teleport Association (WTA), founded in 1984, addresses the growing need for cooperation on a global level in transnational telecommunications and has been active in developing teleports that combine satellite and terrestrial communications with real estate developers who create teleport office parks. WTA publishes a quarterly newsletter and a worldwide

FIGURE 8-25 The Teleport Concept

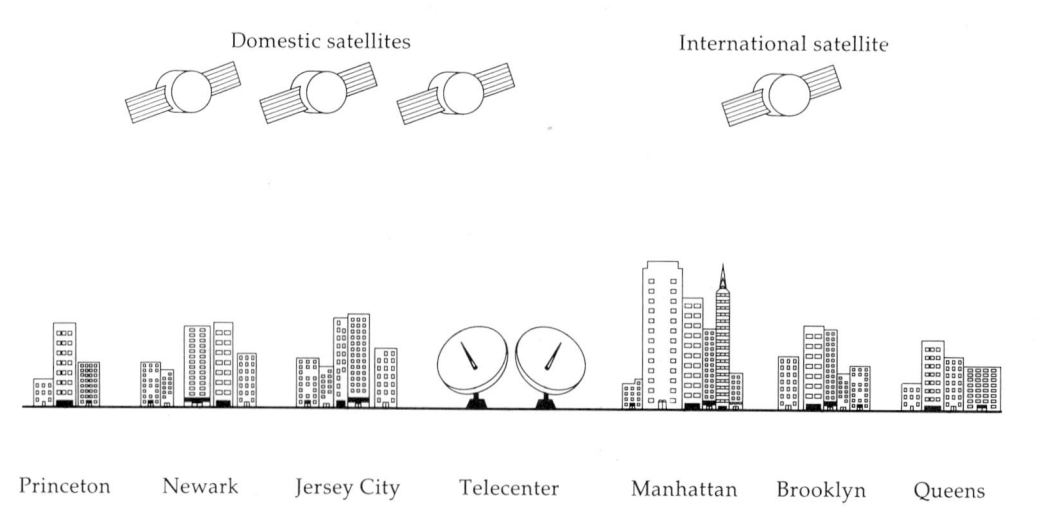

Redrawn courtesy of Teleport Communications.

directory of teleport operators and organizations, provides technical and marketing information, conducts seminars, and provides consulting services and industry education. Regular members are organizations that operate, are constructing, or are planning a teleport. Associate members are organizations that provide related facilities or services or represent membership organizations that complement the association's activities and demonstrate an interest in the teleport concept.

In other words, a teleport is a communication distribution center that allows its customers to share access to receiving and transmitting voice, data, and video information via satellite, fiber optics, and microwave without directly incurring the large expense of their construction. It is an information infrastructure whose purpose is to promote both regional economic development and world trade. An easy way to understand the teleport concept is to compare it to a shipping port or an airport—both of which dispatch traffic to other locations. At one time, shipping ports were essential to any city that wanted to be a major business center, while today airports are located in nearly every important city worldwide. Teleports will soon become the ports that identify international centers of business activity. They will replace transporting passengers and cargo with transmitting information.

The number of teleports currently operational, planned, or under construction is thirty in the United States and about fifty worldwide. Among the leading teleports are the New York/New Jersey Teleport, the Bay Area Teleport (San Francisco), United Video (Chicago), the Dallas/Fort Worth Teleport, the Houston Teleport, and the Washington International Teleport. By 1995, 200 teleports are expected to be operating in the United States, according to Frost and Sullivan, a consulting firm in New York City.

■ Types of Teleports

A teleport can be classified by type of customer or whether it is facility-based or real-estate based.

Type of Customer. Teleports classify their customers as either common carriers or end-users. The majority of teleport market to end-users, some market to carriers, and others, such as the New York/New Jersey Teleport and the Bay Area Teleport, market to both. In less populated metropolitan areas the difference between having carrier customers or not determines whether the teleport will have early financial success, particularly in the absence of video traffic.

Facility or Real-Estate Based. The majority of the nation's teleports are facility-based teleports, while the majority of international teleports are real-estate-based. A **facility-based teleport** is one in which users of the teleport are not physically located at the teleport site. These teleports derive their sole revenues from teleport operations and tend to be mainly analog facilities with long-term contracts to provide video service to cable television or broadcast television industries.

The newer and larger teleports in the United States are **real-estate-based teleports** and are located in teleport office parks, also referred to as business parks. These teleports offer shared telecommunications services to tenants located at the teleport office park as well as to others and also attract business and economic development to the area.

▪ Teleport Operation

While all teleports serve as a port for information, no two are identical. Each is designed to suit the economic activity of the area it serves. Given the appropriate conditions, teleports may thrive in any region, and the region may thrive from the presence of the teleport.[4]

Teleports provide subscribers with satellite communications, microwave, and fiber-optic distribution networks and VSAT network support. Their transmit-and-receive facilities interconnect with long-haul domestic satellite and terrestrial networks as well as provide international services. Teleports are installed, maintained, and managed by teleport companies.

Regulatory Constraints. Foreign teleports are operated through government control, while teleports in the United States must compete with each other. U.S. teleports are subject to federal and state laws governing common carriers and other telecommunications services, radiation emissions standards, and other zoning constraints. However, they are not subject to full FCC regulations, since they do not have the power to control the market; instead, they operate as nondominant common carriers.

Customers. Television and radio broadcasters, cable television providers, and system operators are heavy users of teleports. Other major teleport customers are currently in the communications, financial, and data processing industries.

Services Offered. Among the uses of teleports are the following:

- Radio and television companies use teleports to create, distribute, and deliver programming. In fact, television is a major business at such teleports as the Dallas/Fort Worth Teleport, the Houston International Teleport, and Teleport Denver (Colorado).[5]
- Teleports offer cost efficiencies and special services for exchanging electronic data—for example, between corporate headquarters and regional offices, between suppliers and vendors, and among governments and their agencies.
- Data transmissions are becoming a major business for many teleports. For example, London's Mercury Telecommunications' Thameside Teleport now provides 60% of the traffic in digital Intelsat Business Services be-

tween the United States and the United Kingdom. The Bay Area Teleport provides digital services to support such companies as Intel Corporation and Hewlett-Packard and to tie together state and local government offices.
- Major long-distance telephone companies, such as AT&T, RCA, Argo Communications, and US Sprint, use teleports.
- Teleports offer VSAT services. By leasing VSAT hub capacities a company eliminates the high capital costs of building its own master hub.
- Videoconferencing is another service offered by teleports. (See Chapter 13.) London's Mercury Communications and US Sprint (using the New York/New Jersey Teleport) recently linked 150 representatives of the United Kingdom's largest companies for a 45-minute videoconference. The Dallas/Fort Worth Teleport (DFWT) links the offices of Texas Instruments, retailer J. C. Penney, and other corporate customers for business television meetings. The DFWT even helps one of its customers to conduct livestock auctions via satellite; bidders participate by using their own earth stations and telephone-linked personal computers.
- LAN support or complete LAN installation and maintenance is also offered to teleport customers.

■ Profile of a Teleport

On March 11, 1987, the New York/New Jersey Teleport helped to make sound-recording history by conducting the world's first transcontinental recording. As if they were in the same room, but in reality 3000 miles apart, musicians Stevie Wonder in California and Nile Rodgers in New York recorded a song together by using The Teleport's fiber-optic cables, satellites, and digital recorders. Nile Rodgers's guitar accompaniment was encoded as bits of computer data and beamed like a television signal to a remote recording studio. In his Los Angeles office, Stevie Wonder added his voice track simultaneously to the song, and the music was sent back to New York instantly with the quality of a compact disc.

> "This is wild," said Quincy Jones from a studio in Los Angeles. "Are you sure you guys are in New York."
> "Are you sure you're in Los Angeles?" answered Nile Rodgers from Master Sound Astoria at Kaufman Astoria Studios in Queens, New York.
> "Amazing," said Stevie Wonder.[6]

The New York/New Jersey Teleport is headquartered in a multimillion-dollar office complex on a 350-acre office park on New York City's Staten Island. Figure 8-26 shows an aerial view of The Teleport. The Port Authority undertook the real estate development of the teleport by leasing the land for The Teleport from the City of New York. (The Port Authority, which borders on two states, is a powerful economic force. This unique entity possesses powers normally reserved by local governments. For example, its responsibilities include the development and management of ports, transportation,

FIGURE 8-26 New York/New Jersey Teleport

Courtesy of The Port Authority of New York and New Jersey.

and related facilities within a 50-mile radius of the Statue of Liberty in New York Harbor. Its income is generated from the operation of transportation facilities, such as bridges, tunnels, rail systems, seaports, and the New York World Trade Center. In addition, it has the ability to issue bonds to the public. The Port Authority's involvement with The Teleport has simplified zoning and other approvals for its tenants. Its review procedure replaces public hearings, zoning, and other regulatory approvals.) Teleport Communications–New York (TCNY), a joint venture of Merrill Lynch Telecommunications Inc. and Western Union Communications System Inc., is building, operating, and marketing The Teleport. TCNY began operating the fiber-optic network and satellite communications in 1985 and its office park in 1987.

The Teleport's office park with its intelligent buildings provides state-of-the-art shared tenant services, including a 150-mile regional fiber-optic network, a satellite communications center, and tenant communications services. (An intelligent building is a building that through a single source provides its occupants/tenants with automated technologies to perform such office functions as controlling temperature, pressure, and humidity to both maximize the comfort of the building's occupants and minimize the energy used; providing efficient lighting; providing fire and security protection; integrating data and word processing operations; and providing a telecommunications system.) The Teleport currently operates an 11-acre, 16-antenna earth station facility. Its fiber-optic cable provides an alternative to the local telephone company by providing long-distance carriers with last-mile links. It also links the switching centers of long-distance companies with each other and links long-distance operating centers with their customers. By connecting long-distance carriers serving the New York area with each other, TCNY is performing its role as a telecommunications port and thus becoming the hub for long-distance telecommunications transport. The Teleport offers voice, data, and video services to businesses located at the site as well as to over eighty major office buildings in the region. Among the present tenants are Recruit USA (Japan's leading publisher), the Catholic Telecommunications Network of America, and Dun & Bradstreet. TCNY has also become a major provider of satellite transmission and receiving facilities for the region's broadcasters, such as ABC, CBS, and NBC, by transmitting news and sports to affiliates across the country.

Hockey, basketball, and baseball games played in locations across the country continue to be transmitted back to New York. When the *NBC Nightly News* and *The Today Show* went to China, it was TCNY that downlinked nearly 100 hours of broadcast material and transmitted the material over its fiber-optic network to NBC studios in Rockefeller Center.

■ Teleport Issues and Trends

Some of the trends and issues concerning teleports are as follows:

- Future teleports will become less dependent on satellite transmission. Instead, they will interface with existing fiber carriers and local telephone companies to provide transmission services to their customers.
- Teleport operations will experience more government influence. For example, regulations that affect local telephone service and customer rates may also affect teleports. The economic importance of teleports is being recognized by favorable tax strategies and other incentives that promote investing in the growth of teleports.
- Teleports will provide one-stop communications services including last-mile access, trunking, equipment, repair, and billing.
- Teleports will become ISDN gateways for customers. Integrated services digital network (ISDN) is the integration of voice, data, image, and text over one interoperable digital network.
- Teleports will improve or strengthen the economic development of their areas. "We've seen significant evidence that The Teleport is fulfilling an economic development role in helping to bring and retain jobs in the New York–New Jersey region," says Douglas Beardsley, vice-president and general manager of Merrill Lynch and Fidelity Communications (a subsidiary of Fidelity Investments). "And we've come to believe that teleports can be a major benefit to cities everywhere."[7]

The growth of teleports worldwide can be impeded in the following ways:

- A country's reluctance to liberalize the regulation of telecommunications can hinder teleport construction. The worldwide trend is toward deregulation of telecommunications.

- Technological incompatibility of teleport operations is a major problem. As a result, pressure for worldwide standards is increasing.
- Teleports must attract capital to set up their facilities. The margin between the cost of the services and what the market will bear must be at a high enough rate to allow teleport operators to make a profit.

Summary

Although any electromagnetic wave with a frequency between 1 GHz and 100 GHz can be defined as a microwave, the frequencies commonly used for microwave radio systems range from 1 GHz to 23 GHz. Available microwave radio frequencies for business users and common carriers are 18 GHz and 23 GHz, which are used for short hauls. Satellite communications is based on the use of geosynchronous satellites with applications using microwave frequencies in the C-band and Ku-band. Microwave radio systems are designed for point-to-point applications, while satellite systems are particularly suited for point-to-multipoint applications. The introduction of VSAT networks is making satellite use possible at affordable costs. INTELSAT is responsible for international nonmilitary satellite communications. Microwave radio and satellite communications offer companies alternatives to fiber-optic cable and leased lines.

As the world increases its dependence on the flow of information, it will also become more dependent on teleports. They will be the transporters of information and will thus identify the major business centers worldwide.

Key Terms

COMSAT
Fresnel zones
INTELSAT
Line-of-sight
Microwave
  communication
Microwave radio systems

Satellite communications:
  C-band, Ka-band,
    Ku-band
  Earth station
  Footprint
  Frequency-division
    multiple access

Time-division
  multiple access
Transponder
Uplink/downlink
VSAT
Teleport:
  Facility-based
  Real-estate-based

Self-Quiz

Indicate whether the statement is true or false.

1. The line-of-sight between a transmitter and a receiver is a straight line. T/F
2. A VSAT network includes a master hub and a number of small earth stations in a star configuration. T/F
3. The Federal Communications Commission requires microwave systems to be licensed for operation. T/F

4. INTELSAT owns and operates its own worldwide commercial communication satellite systems.   T/F
5. COMSAT is a special type of satellite.   T/F
6. The majority of the nation's teleports are real-estate-based ones.   T/F

Complete each of the following statements.

1. Short-haul private microwave systems use frequencies of _____ .
2. To link college buildings that are located close to each other, you should select a _____ network.
3. To link a company's buildings that are separated by property owned by another party, you should select a _____ network.
4. The portion of the earth's surface illuminated by a narrow beam from a satellite is called a(an) _____ .
5. The transmission format commonly used in satellite communications for sending and receiving analog and digital signals is _____ .
6. A facility that offers end-users and common carriers a range of telecommunications services including satellite communications, microwave, and fiber-optic distribution networks is called a _____ .

Match Column A with Column B

Column A
(a) Absorption
(b) Altitude control apparatus
(c) Fading
(d) Fresnel zones
(e) Hop
(f) Transponder

Column B
____ 1. Keeps the satellite antenna precisely aligned toward the earth.
____ 2. A microwave repeater onboard a satellite.
____ 3. The microwave link between two terminals.
____ 4. Loss between a transmitter and a receiver caused by rain intensity and frequency.
____ 5. A variation in signal intensity caused by multipath propagation and atmospheric refraction changes.
____ 6. Area surrounding a microwave's line-of-sight path that must be free of obstruction.

Review Questions

1. Describe the components of a microwave system.
2. How can a microwave system overcome the line-of-sight requirement?
3. (a) Describe two situations in which microwave radio systems would be a better choice than satellite systems.
   (b) Describe two situations in which satellite systems would be a better choice than microwave communications?

4. When would you select a microwave system rather than a fiber-optic system for short-haul transmission?
5. Describe how messages are sent by satellite communications.
6. (a) What is the difference between C-band and K-band?
   (b) Which one would you recommend to a company for its satellite communications? Why?
7. How can VSAT networks benefit a company?
8. What impact does INTELSAT have on satellite communications?
9. Would you prefer to use satellite communications or fiber optics for long-distance communications? Why?
10. How is a teleport similar to an airport or a shipping port?

■ *Activities/Projects*

1. Prepare to discuss the following topic: Although the 1984 divestiture agreement removed the long-distance market from the local telephone companies, they continue to control local service facilities, sometimes preventing would-be competitors, such as TCNY, from using them. In 1987, TCNY petitioned the FCC to enforce its right to interconnect directly its 150-mile fiber-optic network serving the New York metropolitan area and northern New Jersey to New York Telephone's network through its central offices. TCNY needs this arrangement to compete successfully with New York Telephone in order to provide dedicated local links to the business community and long-distance carriers. Should TCNY and the New York Telephone Company have the same interconnection privileges? Should the New York Telephone Company be restructured to promote competition? Should a Divestiture II take place to remove the local telephone company's monopoly?
2. Visit an organization that has a microwave or a satellite system. Describe how the system operates and the system's purposes.
3. You have been asked to give a presentation about using satellite communications for production and sales training of a company's field personnel and for transferring its data. What would be the configuration of the system? What equipment would the company need? Include a diagram of the network configuration with your presentation.
4. Set up a checklist for planning and selecting either a microwave or a satellite communications system for an organization of your choice.

■ *Notes*

1. Graham Langley, *Telephony's Dictionary*, 2nd edition (Chicago, Ill.: Telephone Publishing Corporation, 1986), pp. 108, 270.
2. Fred Kelly, "The VSAT Network Finally Comes of Age," *TPT/Networking Management*, November 1988, p. 31.

3. Herb Brody, "Big Hopes for Small Dishes," *High Technology Business*, November 1987, p. 43.
4. Robert Annunziata, "What Is a Teleport?" *Telecommunication Products + Technology*, February 1987.
5. *WTA Update*, Spring 1988, p. 1.
6. *Teleport Communications 1987 Expanding Frontiers.*
7. *WTA Update*, Autumn 1988, p. 6.

Additional Readings

Frank Baylin and Brent Gale, *Satellite Today: The Guide to Satellite Television*, 2nd edition (Columbus, Ohio: Universal Electronics, Inc., 1986).

Arthur Epley, "Why You Should Use Microwave to Link Data," *TPT/Networking Management*, October 1988, pp. 51–54.

Robert E. Friess, "Microwave Brings in the Last Mile," *Telephone Engineer and Management*, May 1, 1987.

E. W. Fthenakis, *Manual of Satellite Communications* (New York: McGraw-Hill, 1984).

Bruce Jennings, "Short-Haul Microwave—A Versatile System," *Telecommunications*, June 1988, pp. 47–48.

Andrew Lipman, Robert Sugarman, and Alan Cushman, editors, *Teleports and the Intelligent City* (Princeton, N.J.: Dow Jones, 1986).

Mark Long, *The Ku-Band Satellite Handbook* (Indianapolis, Ind.: Howard W. Sams & Company, 1986).

G. Maral and M. Bousquet, *Satellite Communications Systems* (New York: John Wiley & Sons, 1986).

J. M. Noodhoven van Goor and G. Lefcoe, editors, *Teleports and the Information Age* (New York: Elsevier Science Publishers, 1987).

Tom Shimabukuro, "Securing Satellite Signals," *Telecommunications Products + Technology*, June 1988, pp. 21–26.

Bob Wallace, "The Long and Short of Short-Haul," *Network World*, June 13, 1988, pp. 1, 39–46.

Periodicals

Satellite News, a weekly newsletter of the latest developments in the satellite industry, is published by Phillips Publishing, Inc., 7811 Montrose Road, Potomac, MD 20854.

Teleport Report is a newsletter published monthly by the Teleport Communications Group, Teleport 1, One Teleport Drive, Staten Island, NY 10311-1011.

Via Satellite is published monthly by Phillips Publishing, Inc., 7811 Montrose Road, Potomac, MD 20854. It features articles, company profiles, and market analyses of the latest trends, opportunities, and challenges in the satellite industry.

PART III

Telecommunications Applications

CHAPTER 9

Electronic Mail

Electronic Mail Defined

Evolution of Electronic Mail

Telex
   Origin
   How Telex Operates
   Domestic Telex
   International Telex
   Benefits and Drawbacks

Computer-Based Message Systems
   CBMS Defined
   How Electronic Mail Operates
   Types of CBMSs
   Benefits and Drawbacks of CBMSs

Electronic Mail Standards
   The X.400 Standard
   The X.500 Standard

Electronic Data Interchange
   EDI Defined
   How EDI Operates
   EDI Standards
   Benefits and Drawbacks of EDI

Selecting an E-Mail System

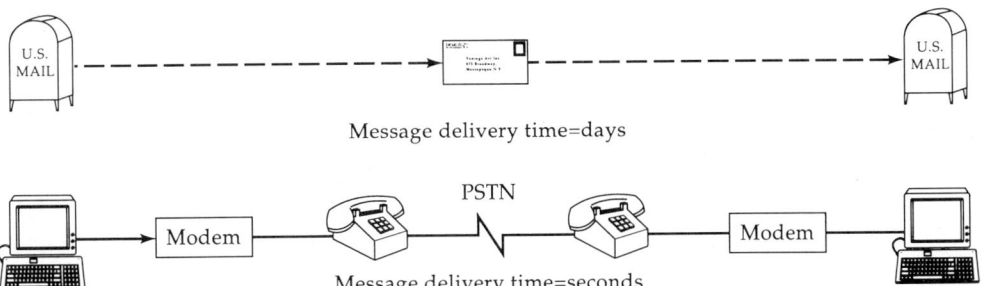

CHAPTER OBJECTIVES

After studying this chapter, you should be able to

1. Define electronic mail.
2. Describe telex.
3. Explain how a computer-based message system operates.
4. Distinguish between in-house and public service electronic mail systems.
5. Discuss electronic data interchange.
6. Select an electronic mail system.

With a few strokes of his computer a New England sales representative for a large, Ohio-based, manufacturing company uses electronic mail to check every morning with his home office for messages and sales leads. Every evening he keys order information into his computer to be sent to the home office. By using electronic mail his orders are not only accurate but also processed immediately. And he saves over $100 on monthly telephone calls to the home office.

Hiroshi Karamashi and Susan Franklin are partners: He paints fabric in Tokyo, and she markets it in New York. They both subscribe to BUSINESSnet, an electronic mail service. On Thursday afternoon, February 14, Susan receives a large order. She immediately sends the information to Hiroshi's electronic mailbox for him to read and answer when his workday begins. The first item that Hiroshi will see when he turns on his computer is

No.	Delivered	From	Subject	Lines
1	FEB 14	S. FRANKLIN	MORE GOOD NEWS!	23

Hills Department Stores, a chain operating in the mideastern United States, can now have an order into their supplier's order-processing system on Monday that reflects store-by-store sales through the previous Saturday night. The company has electronic partnerships with its key suppliers, which allows it to transmit by computer specially formatted purchase orders to each supplier. Once the suppliers receive the information on their computers, they process it immediately—no more having to reenter the information manually into their order-processing system. This procedure, electronic data interchange, results in reduced order processing time, fewer errors, and better in-stocks.

Electronic (E-mail) has become an integral part of business communications. Walter E. Ulrich, consulting partner of Coopers and Lybrand, who tracks the E-mail industry, predicts that the number of mail messages will increase from 3 billion in 1988 to 10 billion in 1991. About half of the current 6-million E-mail users send messages only on internal company systems and are unable to communicate electronically with other systems.[1] Consulting company Link Resources estimates that the electronic mail industry will be a $1.5 billion industry by 1995.

This chapter presents an overview of electronic mail, its evolution, its applications, and its standards. The types of electronic mail discussed in this chapter are telex, computer-based message systems, and electronic data interchange. Voice mail and facsimile are discussed in Chapters 10 and 11, respectively.

Electronic Mail Defined

The Electronic Mail Association (EMA), a trade association of the electronic mail industry, defines **electronic mail** as "the generic name for the noninteractive communication of text, data, images, or voice messages between a sender and designated recipient(s) by systems utilizing telecommunication links." (Founded in 1983, the Electronic Mail Association, 1919 Pennsylvania Avenue, NW, Suite 300, Washington, DC 20006, publishes a quarterly newsletter and a membership directory and serves as a clearinghouse for information about the electronic messaging industry. Members include system operators, equipment manufacturers, corporate users, and industry consultants.) While the term "electronic mail" refers to all types of noninteractive communication, such as computer-based message systems, voice mail, and facsimile, it can also be more narrowly defined to refer to only computer messaging, as discussed in this chapter. This definition of electronic mail includes the transmission of items such as messages, stories, texts, and briefs from one computer or terminal to another. In this form its most common use is as an in-house system that links a company's employees. Public access networks that connect subscribers to other systems also are becoming increasingly popular.

Evolution of Electronic Mail

Electronic mail systems originated with the invention of the telegraph by Samuel Morse in 1840. Telex was introduced in the 1930s, followed by TWX (typewriter exchange service) in the 1950s. International telex followed in the 1950s, and facsimile, computer-based messages systems, and electronic data interchange came in the 1970s with more advanced systems in the 1980s.

As more and more people received electronic mailboxes, that is, computerized storage for receiving and storing electronic messages, more people started communicating electronically. Some companies that were using in-house electronic mail started offering their computers to outside companies for a fee. For example, companies such as MCI Communications, United States Sprint-Telenet, Western Union, IT&T, AT&T, and General Electric began selling electronic mail software and allowing their electronic mail services to be accessed by their customers' computers. All that customers needed were computers with communications capability, such as communications software, a telephone, and a modem for transferring data from computer to computer over telephone lines, as shown at the beginning of this chapter.

Telex

For many years the transmission of data overseas was limited to telex services. Telex is a point-to-point low-speed electronic mail service that is available virtually throughout the world. It allows users to communicate with each other through interconnected terminals in which the receiving terminal prints out the message on paper or on a screen (see Figure 9-1). Although telex is being replaced by higher-speed services in North America, it is still one of the primary means of electronic communication throughout the rest of the world, particularly in Third World countries. Companies can take advantage of an already established public network for setting up a telex transmission system. Equipment can be rented, and messages can be transmitted via common carrier lines. Also for some companies, other forms of electronic communication are not available or their systems are not compatible with other companies' systems. For example, Boeing Company

FIGURE 9-1 Telex Terminals

(a) Early Model

(b) Current Model

Courtesy of Western Union Corporation.

transmits 15,000 telexes daily to suppliers and subcontractors, but the company would send most of these messages by some other form of electronic mail if recipients had the capability to receive and send and their equipment was compatible with Boeing's. In 1988, telex subscribers numbered 1.5 million worldwide.

■ Origin

Telex is the oldest keyboard-oriented message system available to users. **Telex I**, the original version, owned and operated in the United States by Western Union, had its beginning in Germany in the 1930s. **Telex II**, previously called the *teletypewriter exchange service* or **TWX**, was formerly owned and operated by AT&T. In the 1960s it was acquired by Western Union, which then connected Telex I and Telex II subscribers through a system of computer "store-and-forward" switching systems. Store-and-forward is a method of transmitting data that does not require an immediate reply. The data is held in storage until it is convenient for it to be sent to its destination. In 1980 the addition of "real-time" transmission (transmission in which there is no significant delay) allowed customers the option of choosing either system.

■ How Telex Operates

A message is first keyed in at the sending terminal and sent over telephone lines to another terminal, where it is printed. A transmission path is established and held through the call period while information between the parties is exchanged in printed form. Specialized typewriter-based devices, typeprinters and teletypewriters, are used for both input and output, as shown in Figure 9-1. Telex I uses the Baudot code, the standard code for start-stop teletypewriter operation, for transmission, while Telex II uses ASCII code. (ASCII code, the American Standard Code for Information Interchange, is one of the major transmission codes used for information interchange among data processing systems, data communication systems, and associated equipment.) Transmission speed for Telex I is 50 characters per second (66 words per minute) and for Telex II is 110 characters per second (120 words per minute). Both services, however, are slower than the 1200 to 9600 bps transmission speeds of other international services.

To increase the usefulness of telex, a message switched network service is now used in conjunction with telex. This service, *Infomaster*, permits a store-and-forward capability that has several benefits:

- It allows a subscriber to transmit a message to another subscriber's destination even when the destination terminal is busy. This capability eliminates the need to redial until a successful connection can be established.
- It allows more powerful data terminals to be used for sending and receiving messages.
- It enables different types of terminals to communicate with each other.
- It permits either single-address or multi-address messages to be sent. A maximum of 250 multi-address messages can be sent per broadcast, which allows information to be expedited easily from one sender to many receivers.

■ Domestic Telex

Domestic telex offers its subscribers an answer-back feature, which informs the sender that the message has been received even if the terminal is unattended. Other options are available to telex subscribers through Western Union's central computer, including automated conversion of telex messages into telegram or mailgram messages for delivery to nonsubscribers.

Western Union's domestic telex business has been adversely affected by the proliferation of facsimile equipment and more advanced electronic mail systems. One of the ways in which Western Union has responded to industry changes is by introducing EasyLink and offering an economy telex service that uses ordinary telephone lines rather than special access facilities to connect to the telex network. EasyLink, an advanced electronic mail service that is discussed in the next section of this chapter, can communicate with telex terminals for both domestic and international transmission. Its subscribers also can access an electronic mail directory that contains both telex and EasyLink subscribers.

For a moderate volume of electronic mail services, the monthly cost of telex is low. A subscriber's monthly bill typically includes

- A charge for access to the communications network

- A measured usage charge for the amount of time spent on the network
- A rental charge for terminal equipment; the charge depends on the terminal model and features selected and the type of interface: Telex I to Telex I, Telex I to Telex II, Telex II to Telex I, and so forth

■ International Telex

In most foreign countries, telex is the primary form of electronic mail. In the United States, domestic services connecting with foreign networks for international service transmit in the telex mode. International telex communications to and from the United States are handled by international record carriers (IRCs). The term "international record carrier" refers to organizations dealing only with the transmission of the printed or written word. Since these organizations now engage in telephone business, the organizations are now being called "international service carriers." Included are MCI International, Western Union Corporation, and TRT/FTC Communications. MCI International acquired Western Union International (not affiliated with Western Union Telegraph Company) in 1983 and RCA Global Communications in 1988. Western Union Corporation acquired ITT World Communications in 1987 and changed its name to WU World Communications, Inc. Pacific Telecom, Inc. acquired TRT Telecommunications Corporation in 1989. FTC Communications was acquired in 1986 by National Gateway Telecom, a subsidiary of Pacific Telecom. Pacific Telecom is currently combining the operations of FTC Communications and TRT Telecommunications Corporation.

■ Benefits and Drawbacks

As an electronic mail service, telex offers these benefits:

- The cost is low.
- It offers both domestic and international service.
- The services are used throughout the world.
- It offers immediate or store-and-forward delivery service.

Telex service has the following drawbacks:

- The service is slower than other types of electronic mail services.
- Copy output quality is poor on older terminal models, making their use not suitable for business distribution requiring high-quality output.
- The service is designed for exchanging brief messages, not for transmitting lengthy documents and reports. Since the transmission rate is slow and the usage charges are high, the cost of transmitting lengthy documents will be high.

Although telex is not the best choice for long text transmissions, it is successfully used by international businesses for delivery of short messages.

Computer-Based Message Systems

As costs of traditional mail delivery systems continue to increase, companies are becoming more interested in alternatives, such as electronic mail. The type of electronic mail that is becoming most familiar to the average information employee is a computer-based message system (CBMS), commonly referred to as electronic mail or E-mail.

The first computer messaging systems were introduced in the early 1970s by such users as the scientists working on Arpanet. (In 1968 the Advanced Research Projects Agency (ARPA) of the U.S. Department of Defense began a project to implement a nationwide computer network. This network allows a large number of dissimilar computers to communicate with each other.) They communicated with one another by leaving messages on each other's terminals. These early systems were the forerunners of integrated information systems used within companies and commercial long-distance network services.

■ CBMS Defined

A **computer-based message system** (CBMS) is a form of electronic mail that allows computers and/or terminals to communicate with each other for the purpose of sending and receiving text and data messages—short messages, memos, and other documents. A CBMS uses text processing and file managing for creating, editing, storing, sending, retrieving, and rerouting messages. A host, such as a mainframe computer or a LAN server, enables these functions to be handled easily. CBMS users access the host to perform these functions. Figure 9-2 describes the basic services of CBMSs.

A CBMS is used for everything from office chitchat, recording telephone messages, and scheduling meetings to exchanging documents and files and generating hard copy. Users can create and edit online information. Messages can be obtained from computer memory, spreadsheet, and graphics;

FIGURE 9-2 Basic Services of Computer-Based Message Systems

Create a message:	The sender keys a message into a computer.
Edit a message:	The sender revises message before transmission using text-editing or word processing functions.
Send a message:	The sender transits a message to one address or broadcasts to many addresses simultaneously.
Scan a message:	The receiver checks messages for identity of sender, subject, and date/time.
Read a message:	The receiver views a message with options to print, store, or delete.
Store a message:	The user files a message for short term or archives.
Retrieve a message:	The user recalls a message for reuse.

database information can be accessed; and messages can be electronically filed. From virtually any terminal, users can access messages and store, dispose, file, print, and reroute messages at will, mail output being in the form of a computer screen or hard copy. The receiver need not be present to receive messages.

How Electronic Mail Operates

The Basic Components. The components generally required to operate a CBMS at both the sending and the receiving workstations are shown in Figure 9-3. They can be described as follows.

- A CBMS can consist of a computer, communications software, a modem, and a telephone. A mainframe computer, minicomputer, or microcomputer with a hard disk directs the operations of the CBMS. Since output can be a computer screen or hard copy, a printer for message output is optional. Messages can be printed at a central laser printing site and/or delivered by U.S. mail or a courier service.

FIGURE 9-3 **CBMS System Configurations**

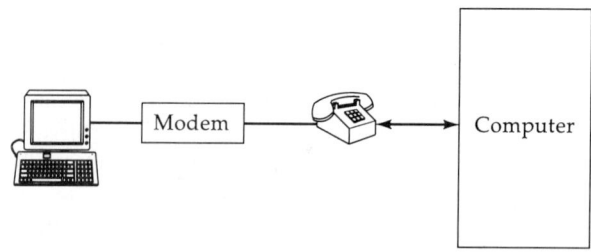

(a) Dialup Access Configuration

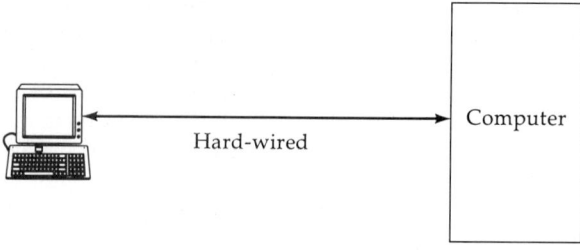

(b) Direct Connect Configuration

- A CBMS can be a direct connect configuration consisting of a computer terminal hard-wired to a mainframe computer, a minicomputer, a microcomputer, or a LAN.

For example, with communications software and a modem connecting a computer and a telephone, access to the recipient's E-mail network can be made and the message retrieved. With similar software and equipment a user who is away from the office can access his or her company's internal E-mail system as well as other systems. The scenario at the beginning of this chapter describes a user of electronic mail. AT&T Mail, an E-mail service of AT&T, goes one step further: It allows its subscribers who are away from their computers to telephone its service by touch-tone telephone and request their messages to be read to them by voice synthesis. Voice synthesis is discussed in Chapter 10.

The *data transmission speed* at which an E-mail message is sent is measured in bits per second (bps) for both text and, where applicable, nontext or binary files. Typical transmission speeds are 300, 1200, and 2400 bps, some being as high as 9600 bps.

How to Use CBMS. CBMSs can be operated with menus or commands. Figure 9-4 shows the menu from the E-mail component of Data General's Comprehensive Electronic Office (CEO) system. The user selects the desired mail activity from the menu by keying the appropriate number.

A CBMS that uses a combination menu and a command system is the Dialcom Message Service offered by Dialcom, Inc. A brief explanation of how to use such a system follows.

FIGURE 9-4 **Data General's CEO E-Mail Menu**

```
Msgs: New: 0            Jul 10,85  7:35 AM Document:
                                   MAIL

       --) 1. Inbox           (Process received mail)
           2. Short message   (Compose and send messages)
           3. Mail a document (Send an existing document)
           4. Mailing lists   (List, create, or change mailing lists)
           5. Get mailing list (Get a copy of a mailing list)
           6. Change inbox    (Survey another user's inbox, if authorized)
           7. Mail a file     (Send a non-CEO file)

       Enter choice: 1




            To return to the previous menu, press the CANCEL/EXIT key.

            For assistance here (or on any other menu or question), press the HELP key.
```

Courtesy of Data General Corporation.

The Dialcom Message Service allows you to create, send, and receive office messages—electronically. Each user of the system has an electronic mailbox to receive messages from other users. To see what is in your mailbox, you identify yourself by typing "scan" or "s." You are immediately provided with a visual summary of your messages: who sent each message, the date and time delivered, and the subject. You specify the message you want to read first by typing "read" or "r" and the unique message number.

To create a message, simply type "send" or "s," and the system will automatically prompt you to specify the name or ID of the recipient, the subject of the message, and the text. When you are finished, you enter ".send" on a line by itself. You then receive a display verifying that the message was sent and an interpersonal message (IPM) number assigned by the computer to uniquely identify your message. If you want the message placed at the top of the recipient's stack of unread mail, you type "ex" (express priority) after the recipient's name. When the message is sent, the recipient's terminal beeps if he or she is online. If you want the computer to automatically send you an acknowledgment when the recipient has read your message, you type, ".r" on a line by itself but before you type the send command. Figure 9-5 shows how easy it is to scan your mailbox and read your computer mail.

CBMS Features. Features that are available on many CBMSs are described below.

Text processing or *word processing* features included on CBMSs range from a few to many. Most systems include an online *help* feature that gives instructions and information on how to use the system's features. An *online user directory* feature provides a list of subscriber/user names and E-mail addresses that a user can access when using the CBMS.

A *send message* feature puts a message in the recipient's electronic mail box. A *deferred message sending* feature allows the user to select a particular time for sending a message rather than sending it immediately. A *delivery confirmation of message* feature lets you know whether the message that you sent has been received and, if so, the time and date of its delivery. A *forward message* feature allows a message to be read by one or more other readers.

Protocols, such as X.PC and X.Modem or proprietary protocols, are error-checking rules that govern the transfer of data in a communications system.

Interfaces provide access to other public E-mail services, in-house E-mail systems (such as IBM's PROFS and DISOSS, Data General's CEO, and DEC's All-In-One), and telex.

Network access offers a user the ability to transmit a message to a network mailbox supplied by the network vendor or by a third party, to leave that message stored, and to have it forwarded later to the appropriate receiving party.

FIGURE 9-5 **How to Scan Your Mailbox and Read Your Mail on Dialcom Message Service**

RECEIVE MESSAGES*	
To read your messages, enter name and password. Your password will not appear on the screen	Please sign on >**id ABC123** Password: **L345**
You ask to access mail	Dialcom Computer Services On At 13:21 04/30/88 EST Last on At 16:03 04/29/88 EST Mail Call (0 Read 2 Unread, Total 2) >**Mail**
You are now ready to use the mail service	Send Read or Scan:**Scan**

You get a summary of each message	1 From: R.JANKA (NNC023) Delivered:
	           Fri 30-Apr-88 10:21 EST
	           Sys 146 (29)
	Subject: Budget Overruns
	Mail Id: IPM-146-860106-748395710
	
	2 From: M.HUGHES (NCC228)
	           Fri 30-Apr-88 11:05 EST
	           Sys 146 (6)
	Subject: Down to the Wire
	Mail Id: IPM-146-880124-302948399

You ask to see Number 2	Read or Scan:**r 2**

After reading, you delete the message	To: B.EDWARDS (NCC304)
	Cc: S.KELLER (NNC075)
	From: M.HUGHES (NCC228)
	           Fri 30-Apr-88 11:05 EST
	           Sys 146 (6)
	Subject: Down to the Wire
	Mail Id: IPM-146-880124-302948399
	
	Bill,
	
	Are we going to make that 3:00 deadline we promised Houston?
	
	Marcia
	
	Disposition:**d**

*The commands in bold print are entered by the user.

The *X.400 standard*, as described later in the next section, is an international standard for exchanging electronic text and data messages. It allows messages from dissimilar E-mail systems to be easily exchanged.

Batch mail processing/transmission allows the system to "bundle" mail messages and send them to other mail systems at a selected processing time. Some systems bundle mail several times a day; others process mail only overnight.

An *accounting log* feature tells a user or system manager who is using the mail system at any given time, who has used it previously, and how many messages have been sent and received by each user.

Binary file transfer feature lets users directly transmit any type of binary data or file, such as spreadsheets, database files, address lists, and desktop publishing files. EasyLink allows users to send and receive binary files directly, with no conversion to ASCII text before transmission.

An **upload text** feature allows users to upload text and binary files to the CBMS. With this feature, users save online charges by preparing messages offline and then uploading them for transmission. When working offline, users can use their own word processing programs. This feature allows users to store or download received messages into their own computer files.

Save/file/copy/delete features put the message in a permanent filing area or in the wastebasket. A print feature tells the computer to print a hard copy of the message. Other hard copy features include output to the U.S. Postal Service or a courier service. Options may include paper delivery within four hours, overnight, or within a day or two. *International paper delivery* is another option. For example, a sender who is using MCI Mail, an E-mail service, can transmit a business letter from his or her computer by modem to the recipient's city. MCI Mail prints out the letter, places it in an addressed envelope, and mails the letter in the recipient's city for next-day delivery. The sender need only type one letter and a list of people who should receive it. At $2 for three pages, the MCI Mail price is considerably less than that of Federal Express and avoids the need to print, address, and stuff envelopes.

For example, suppose you want to send an overnight letter to each of your ten branch managers. If you use Federal Express, you must type each letter and the envelope address and then stuff each letter into an envelope or pay someone to do the task. Federal Express charges $15 per letter for overnight delivery or a total of $150 for ten letters. If you use MCI Mail, the total cost is only $90 ($9 × 10)—and you do not have to prepare each letter for mailing.

Output to *facsimile machines* is another feature. For example, subscribers of EasyLink, another E-mail service, can designate a facsimile machine for the receipt of messages or send messages directly to any facsimile machine by using a facsimile telephone number. Because of lack of standardization of formats, it is not yet possible to reverse the direction, that is, to fax to an E-mail system.

Access to *voice mail* through the CBMS mailbox is another feature, to be discussed in Chapter 10.

Electronic data interchange (EDI) enables business transaction documents, such as purchase orders and invoices, to be transmitted in a standard format to another computer. EDI is discussed later in this chapter.

■ Types of CBMSs

CBMSs are of two types: in-house CBMS systems and public electronic mail service (subscription) systems. An *in-house CBMS* is one that a company operates on its premises for its own benefit. A **public electronic mail service** allows subscribers to share the use of a third party's off-site computer to communicate with other subscribers of the service and other E-mail systems without investing in the installation of a similar type of computer.

In-House CBMSs. Many organizations have their own internal electronic mail systems. Such a system, for example, allows employees in different departments to converse with one another easily and without having to leave their desks. These systems can be grouped as follows: (1) stand-alone E-mail software that runs on mainframes, minicomputers, and microcomputers; (2) LAN E-mail software designed to run on a local area network; and (3) integrated office systems that include E-mail as a key component.

Stand-Alone E-mail Software. E-mail software packages run on mainframes, minicomputers, and microcomputers using modems. New equipment can be purchased, or existing computer equipment can be upgraded to handle E-mail software.

LANs Software. E-mail systems are considered a necessary tool for LANs. LANs users can exchange not only messages but also binary files (spreadsheets) with other work groups and with mainframe E-mail systems. LAN network operating systems may include E-mail as part of its system or as an option. Independent suppliers also offer E-mail programs (software packages) that can run on a variety of LANs. Examples are CC:Mail from PCC/Systems and Network Courier from Consumer Software. These and other packages are listed in Figure 9-6.

Comprehensive Office Systems. Another type of in-house system is a *comprehensive office system* that supports a wide range of office and personal functions. The most popular systems are listed in Figure 9-7. These systems require a substantial investment in computer equipment and software. To make using the system worthwhile, a company must have a sufficient number of users.

For example, Data General's CEO connects terminals to a minicomputer or a mainframe computer. This system includes word processing; electronic

FIGURE 9-6 **E-Mail Software Packages for LANs**

E-Mail Software	Vendor
3+ Mail	3Com Corporation
Instant Mail Manager	Western Union Corporation
The Network Courier	Consumer Software
Mail-Net	NetSoft
CC:Mail	PCC/Systems

FIGURE 9-7 **In-House Comprehensive Office Systems with E-Mail**

E-Mail System	Vendor
All-In-One	Digital Equipment Corporation
Professional Office System (PROFS)	IBM Corporation
Comprehensive Electronic Office (CEO)	Data General
Wang Office	Wang Laboratories

mail; electronic filing; administrative support (for example, electronic calendar, telephone message pad, phone directories, and scheduling); integrated use of database, spreadsheet, graphics, mailing, and filing, and word processing; and access to other systems, such as public E-mail services, Wang word processing users, and telex.

Public Electronic Mail Services. An alternative to an in-house system is a public electronic mail service offered by a third party. Subscribers communicate to the public E-mail services by computer via circuit-switched (PSTN) or packet-switched carriers. Some of the public E-mail service vendors have their own communications networks; others lease them.

Services are accessible by modem from anywhere in the country. Companies typically use these services to communicate with their company's branch offices and/or customer and clients. Figure 9-8 lists the eight largest public E-mail services in the nation.

How Public E-Mail Services Operate. To use any public E-mail service, you need a computer—any dumb or intelligent terminal, word processor, or microcomputer will do—and communications software. If your computer is not hard-wired to a mainframe, you also need a modem and a telephone. You then use the equipment and the software to access the public service provider in one of the following ways:

- You can telephone the service provider directly.

FIGURE 9-8 U.S. Public E-Mail (Subscription) Services Providing Electronic Mail, 1987–1988

Vendor	Service	Active Mailboxes, June 1988	Messages per Month
Western Union	EasyLink	175,000	7.5 Million
US Sprint	Telemail	165,000	4.8 Million
Dialcom	Dialcom Services (US)	140,000	3.8 Million
CompuServe	InfoPlex & CIS	450,000	3.3 Million
MCI Communications	MCI Mail	100,000	1.8 Million
GE Info Services	Quik-Comm (& GEnie)	150,000	1.6 Million
AT&T	AT&T Mail	40,000	1.7 Million
McDonnell Douglas	OnTyme	50,000	1.1 Million
Others		215,000	1.3 Million
Public E-mail Total:		1,485,000	26.9 Million
Annual Growth Rates, 1987–1988:		18%	29%

Courtesy of International Resource Development, Inc., New Canaan, Connecticut, a management consulting research firm and publisher of *Electronic Mail & Micro System*, a twice-monthly newsletter.

- You can telephone a local number to access a value-added network, such as Tymnet, Telenet, Uninet, and the service provider's own value-added network, that will connect you with the service provider.
- You can call an 800-number to access a value-added network. The charge for using the 800-number varies. A typical rate is 25 cents per minute.

Most public E-mail service providers allow a user the option of working either online or offline. This option allows a user to control his or her connect time to the host (public E-mail service's) computer. Users work offline by downloading data from a mainframe computer and storing it on a microcomputer's hard or floppy disk. Or they can create E-mail messages on a hard or floppy disk and then upload them to the E-mail system. When users upload messages to the host computer, they direct the host to transmit the messages to their destinations. Messages can be output to mailboxes of other subscribers to the service and/or to hard copy output, such as to printers, telex, the U.S. Postal Service, or a courier service.

For example, you may first prepare messages offline using your own word processing package. When the preparation of the messages is completed, you connect to your service provider, such as Dialcom, by making a local or long-distance telephone call to Telenet, a value-added network. Once Telenet connects you to Dialcom, you can upload your messages and give instructions for their destination. You could also prepare messages while connected to Dialcom, but you would be paying connect time while doing so.

For a rental fee, your service provider will provide you with an electronic mailbox for storing and receiving messages. To send mail to any electronic mailbox, however, you must know its computerized address. A service provider may offer all of the CBMS features described in the section on CBMS features or only some of them.

Cost of Using Services. The cost of using these services varies from one company to another. Since services can be priced in many different ways, prospective users should perform a cost analysis that applies to their organization's usage requirements. Figure 9-9 compares the costs of selected services. Typical costs are

- One-time sign-up fee
- Fixed monthly charge, regardless of usage
- Access charges based on the amount of service used; for example, charges based on units of information exchanged (such as characters or per message), or according to the number of minutes connected, or for both units of information and online time
- Charge for sending messages and recipient's use of the service in retrieving it
- Charge based on the method of delivery chosen, such as E-mail, U.S. Postal Service, or express courier

In-House E-Mail Combined with Public E-Mail Service. An organization can combine its in-house system with one of the public E-mail services for external E-mail service. For example, an organization can use Digital's All-In-One or IBM's PROFS for in-house E-mail applications and one of the public E-mail services for external E-mail. Figure 9-10 shows how a user of All-In-One connects to GE Information Services Quik-Comm, a public E-mail service. Through Quik-Comm, All-In-One users can send and receive to other Quik-Comm users as well as access users of telex and other comprehensive office users, such as IBM's PROFS.

Another example is Chrysler Corporation's E-mail network that connects its offices to district managers and over 6500 of its dealerships. Chrysler runs IBM's PROFS on its in-house mainframe. District managers and dealers use their personal computers to interface to PROFS through GE's Quik-Comm. Messages generated on PROFS that are addressed to either a district manager or a dealer are sent to Quik-Comm, which converts them into a format that can be accessed by the manager or dealer's personal computer. The PCs run a customized version of GE's PC Mailbox, a software package that allows its users to write, edit, receive, send, print, file, and retrieve E-mail messages.

FIGURE 9-9 1989 Charges and Features of Public E-Mail Services: AT&T Mail, MCI Mail, and EasyLink

	AT&T Mail (AT&T)	MCI Mail (MCI)	EasyLink (Western Union Corp.)
Charges			
Service fee	$30 (annual)	$25 (annual)	$2.50/mo. per mailbox
Monthly minimum charge	n/a	n/a	$25 minimum usage
WATS charges per month	n/a	$0.15	n/a
Estimated Costs			
50 words (300 characters)	$0.40	$0.45	$0.35*
250 words (1500 characters)	$0.80	$0.75	$0.60
1000 words (6000 characters)	$0.80	$1.00	$0.90
Connect-time charge	no charge	no charge	$0.35–$0.50/minute using AT&T 800 depending on bps rate
Online charge to create and edit messages	$0.20 (400 characters) $0.45 (401–7000 characters) $0.45 (over 7000 characters)		
Paper mail			
Postal service delivery, 1 page (domestic)	$2.00 (7000 characters)	$2.00 (3 pp)	$1.50; $0.50 each additional page
Currier service delivery			
Overnight letter	$7.50 (7500 characters)	$9.00 (6 pp); $1.00/each additional 3 pages	$3.95 ½ page; $0.50 each additional ½ page
Same-day delivery	$27.50 (7500 characters)	not available	Telegram: $4.25 + $0.10 per/word
Facsimile	$0.55 (1500 characters) $0.40 (1500 additional characters)	$0.50 1st 28 lines; $0.30 next 28 lines	$0.55 ½ page; $0.35 each additional page
Network access	AT&T Mail Network	Tymnet; MCI 800 Service	Tymnet
Data speed (bps)	1200; 2400	300; 1200; 2400	300; 1200; 2400
Connections to other Electronic Mail Services			
Public	Envoy 100	CompuServe; Missive; Dialcom	EasyLink in the UK; Missive in France
Private	DEC All-In-One; IBM PROFS	MCI, DEC All-In-One; IBM PROFS; Wang Office	IBM PROFS
X.400 compatibility	yes	yes	no

*Rates are for a baud speed of 1200 bps.

FIGURE 9-10 **Connecting an In-House System to a Public E-Mail Service**

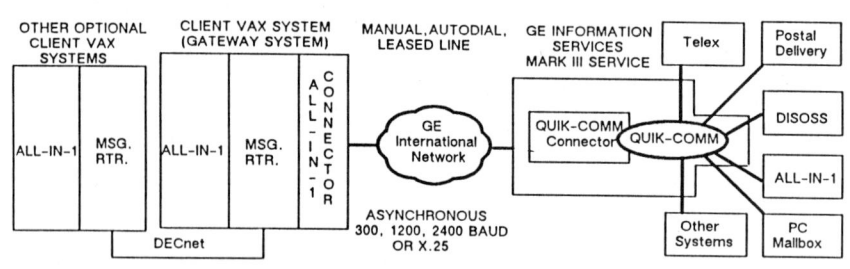

Courtesy of GE Information Services.

- **Benefits and Drawbacks of CBMSs**

  Among the benefits of CBMS are the following:

  - Telephone tag is reduced by eliminating the time spent trying and retrying to reach someone by telephone to convey a message.
  - The time spent in lengthy telephone conversations is reduced.
  - Fast delivery of information is provided so that users can use information proactively rather than reactively in a competitive business environment.
  - Paper handling and accompanying costs are reduced by decreasing the volume of print messages.
  - The receiver is provided with a permanent record.
  - Gateways are provided to other public and private E-mail systems.
  - The problem of the sender and the receiver each being in different time zones is resolved. For example, users can communicate across time zones in which it might not be convenient to contact recipients by telephone, as described in the second scenario at the beginning of this chapter.
  - Immediate confirmation that the message was received can be provided.

    CBMS has the following drawbacks:

  - Users often forget to check their E-mail. Some systems provide reminders, such as a blinking light on the receiver's telephone to signal new mail.
  - Some users dislike keyboarding or do not know how to keyboard.
  - Some users have difficulty learning and using the E-mail system.
  - Message security can be a problem unless a password system is used.

Electronic Mail Standards

- ### The X.400 Standard

  After an organization selects an E-mail service, it might be unable to communicate with organizations using other E-mail services. For example, each service uses different commands to execute the same functions. The command "to exit" from an E-mail service varies from "bye" or "exit" to "off" or "quit." The problem is to decide which service's commands to use when the sending and the receiving services are different.

Two vendors, CompuServe and MCI Mail, have agreed to use the commands of the originating service. But such a solution is not always possible or feasible. Instead, a standard must be established that specifies rules that a system must follow to allow it to exchange messages with other systems. The Consultative Committee on International Telephone and Telegraph (CCITT) is developing an E-mail standard concerned with message routing and handling—the **X.400**. This standard is part of CCITT's model for communicating between dissimilar computer-based systems. It is designed for manufacturers to use in developing products that will allow dissimilar computer-based messaging systems to communicate. Dialcom, Inc., and Telenet Communications Corporation are the first companies to offer domestic, commercial X.400-based messaging services. The creation of the X.400 international messaging standard has made the concept of a global messaging network a reality.

For example, the American Bar Association in Chicago relies on public E-mail services, specifically those provided by Telenet Communications Corporation and Dialcom, to pass vital legal information between members nationwide. Without the X.400 standard the various members' private systems would be unable to communicate.

Operation. What is commonly referred to as the X.400 standard is actually a collection of ten CCITT recommendations, ranging from X.400 to X.430, as listed in Figure 9-11. The X.400 standard defines the basic structure of an E-mail message—its architecture, protocols, and formats—so that virtually all E-mail users can exchange messages, even if they do not use the same type of E-mail system. Message content can include digital voice, graphics, facsimile, image, text, and binary data communications.

FIGURE 9-11 **X.400 Series of Recommendations**

X.400	Message Handling Systems: System Model-Service Elements
X.401	Message Handling Systems: Basic Service Elements and Optional User Facilities
X.408	Message Handling Systems: Encoded Information Type Conversion Rules
X.409	Message Handling Systems: Presentation Transfer Syntax and Notation
X.410	Message Handling Systems: Remote Operations and Reliable Transfer Server
X.411	Message Handling Systems: Message Transfer Layer
X.413	Message Handling Systems: Message Store
X.419	Message Handling Systems: MHS Application Protocols
X.420	Message Handling Systems: Interpersonal Messaging User Agent Layer
X.430	Message Handling Systems: Access Protocol for Telex Terminals

The X.400 distinguishes between message preparation and receipt and message transfer. Message preparation and receipt are supported by functional units called **user agents** (UAs). Message transfer is supported by **message transfer agents** (MTAs). Users prepare messages with the assistance of UAs, such as text editors and word processors. Once the user has prepared the message with the aid of an UA, the MTA is responsible for delivering it. MTAs provide store-and-forward delivery services between UAs in the same way that post offices provide delivery of paper mail. When the message is ready to be sent, the originating UA transfers an "envelope" containing the delivery address and the message contents to the MTA for delivery. MTAs carry messages in "envelopes" from originating UAs to the receiving UAs without opening them or interfering with their contents.

X.400 consists of three basic protocols. P1 handles the message relay. P2 governs the format of the message. P3 simplifies the microcomputer interface by translating the microcomputer software's messaging commands to a format compatible with the electronic mail format.

Benefits. The X.400 standard enables messages to be exchanged among different makes and kinds of computers and communication devices without altering the layout of the original message. The acceptance of X.400 facilitates E-mail communication within the United States and with other countries. It provides a guideline for linking existing computer mailbox systems to each other and to telex, videotex, facsimile machines, microcomputers, and internal E-mail systems, as shown in Figure 9-12.

For example, an E-mail user in the United States can send a message to a user at a mainframe terminal in Japan as shown in Figure 9-12. The user in Japan can receive the message by using the mainframe E-mail application. The only requirements are a data link connecting the LAN and the mainframe and an X.400 gateway on both systems. Without an X.400 gateway, a separate gateway for each device on the network is needed to connect the systems.

■ The X.500 Standard

E-mail users want an easy way of locating recipients' E-mail addresses, regardless of whether they are on the same system. For example, current users of MCI Mail and CompuServe can send electronic messages to each other. But before they do so, either they must know the recipient's exact E-mail address and the routing to reach the network or they must telephone the recipient to obtain his or her E-mail address. Neither MCI Mail nor CompuServe subscribers can search the directories of each other's systems. Without an E-mail address, a message cannot be sent.

Directory Capabilities. The CCITT is developing recommendations, the X.500 standard, for a universal directory system. The standard recommends

Electronic Mail Standards

FIGURE 9-12   **Connecting E-mail Systems with X.400 Gateways**

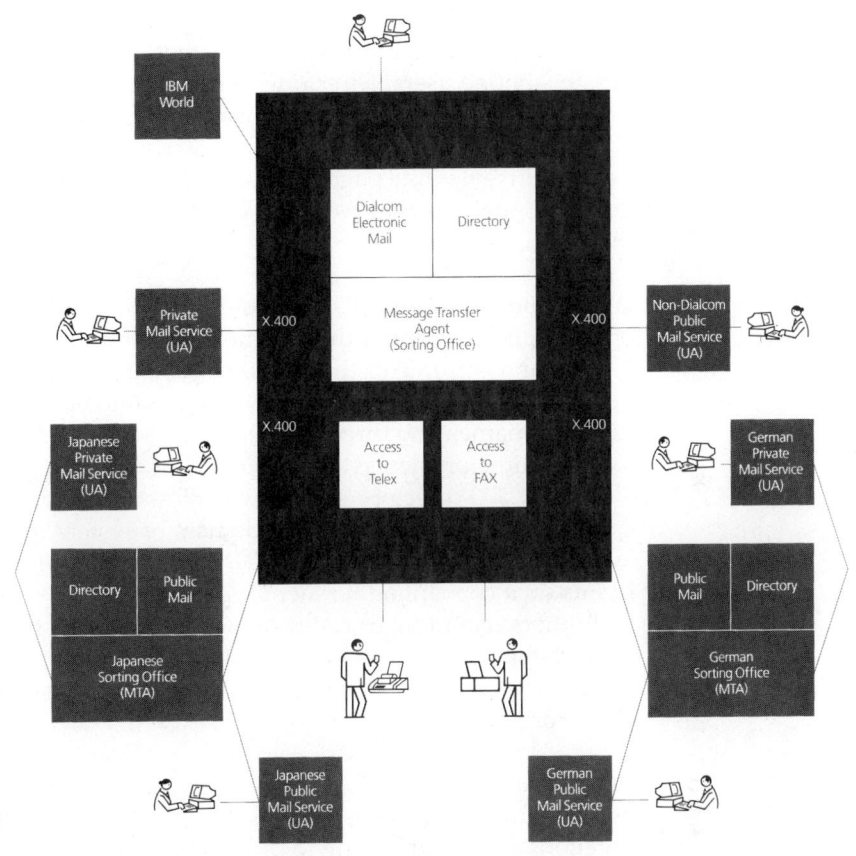

Courtesy of Dialcom, Inc.

how electronic directories of users should be developed. The X.500 standard will allow X.400 users to look up the network addresses of other X.400 users anywhere in the world. The directories will have search and retrieve capabilities for obtaining network addresses, user names, and other information as well as include database update capabilities.

For example, a sender is usually charged for sending messages regardless of whether the message reaches its intended recipient. The present X.400 standards permit a user to check whether a specific connection can be made to the destination E-mail address by sending a probe. All a probe does is give the user a yes-no confirmation of whether the recipient exists without actually sending the message. With the X.500 capability of full directory search, a sender can locate an E-mail address when only part of the E-mail address is known, such as knowing only the recipient's name and company but not the precise E-mail system used.

Users. Electronic directories are designed for any person or device that can be reached by a communications network, including residential and business telephone users. Directories will be available for E-mail users as well as users of electronic data interchange (described in the next section) and facsimile machines. An electronic directory could replace the telephone companies' current white pages and yellow pages. Access to the directory would include E-mail users as well as telephone users with digital telephones with displays.

Operation. As with X.400 recommendations, the X.500 standard is another application under the OSI model and must be compatible with it. The X.500 standards mirror those of the X.400 messaging standards. The X.500 includes directory-service agents performing the function of an MTA for directory names and directory-user agents performing the function of a UA for local directory access and control.

The X.500 directory service will allow E-mail users to have an address consisting of the country, public domain or system, private domain (such as a comapny E-mail system), and user identifier. Currently, each E-mail system has its own convention for identifying user names; some use actual names, and others use number codes or a combination of letters and numbers. E-mail systems that use the X.500 will adopt a common method of identifying users or else install software to translate their own user names to the X.500 formats.

Privacy and Security Issues. The massive distributed databases that are possible under X.500 raise questions about privacy and security. Many corporations will be unwilling to provide their employees' telephone numbers and other data for electronic access. Private individuals will prefer not to give personal data beyond name, telephone number, and postal address. Government regulations also control employee and private individual's privacy. Such regulations differ widely throughout the world. Any organization that is developing an electronic directory will need to consider privacy issues.

The X.500 standard addresses the issue of security by offering two types of address authentication. A simple level of authentication requires an identifier and a password, similar to the access requirement of most public E-mail systems. For addresses requiring more security, a digital signature in the form of an encrypted description is required. Without prior knowledge of the encryption key, access to devices on a private network would be impossible for unauthorized users.

New Market. The X.500 standard could create a new market for electronic directory services. Public and private organizations could offer their electronic directories for others to access for a fee. For example, some law firms might decide to make their internal E-mail addresses and related information available to selected clients through X.500 for a fee. Local telephone companies might market white-page telephone listings. Companies that currently issue facsimile directories for a fee, as discussed in Chapter 11, can now market their services globally and electronically with the X.500 standard.

Electronic Data Interchange

Another rapidly growing electronic mail application is electronic forms, referred to as **electronic data interchange** (EDI). In simplest terms, EDI is computer-to-computer transmission of business transaction documents, such as purchase orders and invoices, between two companies. Companies that use EDI for exchanging documents are often referred to as "partners" or "trading partners." The research firm Input of Mountain View, California, projects that the EDI market will expand to $88 million by 1992. Link Resources Corporation in New York estimates that the number of companies using EDI will increase from 3,780 in 1987 to 10,530 in 1991. The third scenario described at the beginning of this chapter describes a company using EDI.

Traditionally, organizations have used the telephone and/or the U.S. Postal Service for exchanging business documents such as purchase orders and shipping invoices. In recent years the explosive growth of paper exchanges has been forcing companies to seek alternatives in processing their massive amounts of data. Although computers assist in preparing these paper documents, a more expedient method is needed to reduce document transmitting time. Many organizations are choosing EDI for handling their transactions. EDI reduces transmitting time as well as inventory investments and paper processing costs. Organizations no longer need to rely on paper, telephones, telex, and the mail to exchange information, since EDI now performs these tasks.

For example, a chemical company reported that EDI reduced its paper-processing costs from $16 to $2 per order. Another company reported a decrease in costs from $75 to $5 per order.[2] As of 1988, EDI has been adopted by over twenty-five industries such as the grocery, automotive, drug, and chemical industries.

■ EDI Defined

The McDonnell Douglas Corporation, one of the originators of the EDI concept, defines EDI as "the computer-to-computer exchange of intercompany and intracompany business documents in a public standard format." An EDI application consists of the following three components:

- Computer-to-computer exchange of data

- Intercompany/intracompany business documents
- Data in a public standard format

In other words, EDI transfers machine-readable, electronically coded documents from one organization's computer to a trading partner's computer. Standard message formats have been adopted by individual industries to allow computers to exchange common business documents such as purchase orders and invoices.

The machine-readable characteristic of EDI differentiates it from E-mail (CBMS) and other textual transmissions: E-mail is the person-to-person exchange of unformatted messages in a textual format. The form of these messages cannot generally be read or understood by a computer application. Figure 9-13(a) illustrates the business cycle without EDI; Figure 9-13(b) illustrates the business cycle using EDI.

■ How EDI Operates

Through EDI, an organization sends a purchase order from its computer via telephone lines or other communications facilities to the computer of another organization. First, the data contained in the business document is translated into an EDI format—an electronically coded, public standard format. Messages in this format are then transmitted to the receiving partner, who on receipt translates them into their original format.

For a sender and a receiver to communicate electronically requires that both use the same standard EDI format. Translating documents from a sender's internal format to an accepted EDI format is achieved with the help of software, referred to as **translator software**. Similar software is used by the receiving partner to translate the coded document back into its original form.

Media. Formatted data representing a business document can be set up as follows: It may be recorded on a paper or magnetic tape or a disk and transported to the receiving company by U.S. mail or courier service, or it may be transported via public or private telecommunications media.

Method of Transfer. The sender and the receiver or a third party must set the location of the mailbox, the protocol, and the transmission parameters. The criteria for selecting the method of transfer includes these elements: distance of transport, required delivery time frame, volume of transactions, number of destinations, frequency of transport, compatibility of media, costs, security, and reliability. A computer-to-computer transfer of documents takes place in one of the following four ways.

- A formatted magnetic tape or diskette delivered by courier service, such as the U.S. Postal Service
- Point-to-point telephone connection between organizations

FIGURE 9-13 **Electronic Data Interchange**

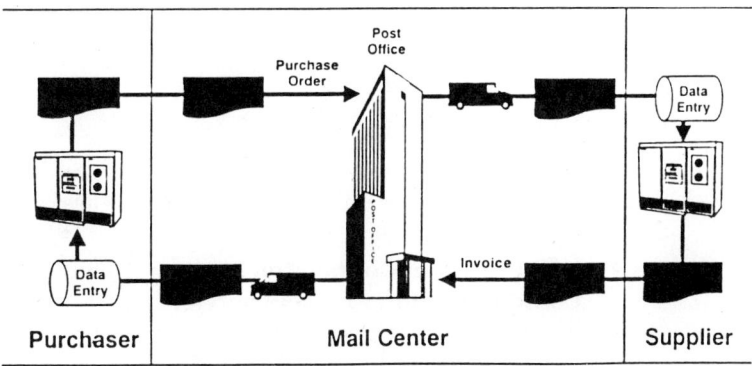

(a) Without EDI

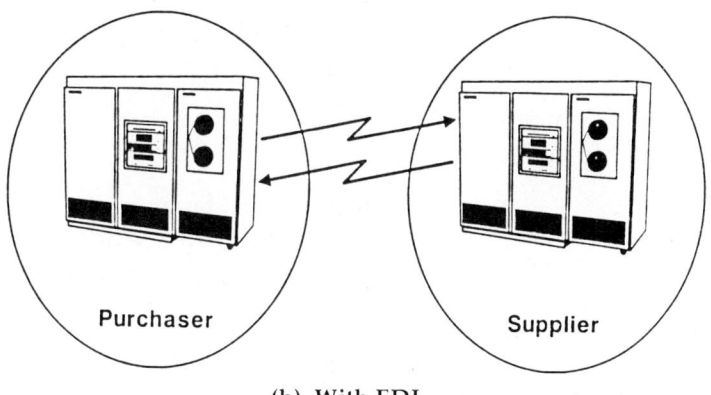

(b) With EDI

Courtesy of McDonnell Douglas Corporation.

- Value-added network
- Third-party communications service

As shown in Figure 9-14, the first method uses a *courier service*. This method is impractical when cost of transport, security of connection, and speed of delivery are important considerations.

The second method, *point-to-point connection between partners*, is diagrammed in Figure 9-15. This method is commonly used by organizations that deal with a limited number of businesses or when the transaction volume is high between two organizations. Both organizations must accommodate the same communication protocols and ANSI X.12 format, a standard explained in the next section. The method is expensive and should be justified by the volume of data, the speed of delivery, and the cost of connection.

FIGURE 9-14 **U.S. Mail or Courier Service Delivering Magnetic Tape or Diskette**

Used with permission of ASC X.12 Secretariat, Data Interchange Standards Association.

FIGURE 9-15 **Point-to-Point Connection between Partners, Both Using the Same Communication Protocol and ANSI X.12 Format**

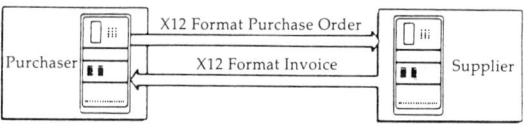

Used with permission of ASC X.12 Secretariat, Data Interchange Standards Association.

In the third method, diagrammed in Figure 9-16, a *value-added network* provides mailbox service for both partners using the ANSI X.12 formats. Selection of this method is determined by easy adaptation of each partner's own line speed, protocol, multiple destinations, and times of day when they would be transmitting.

The fourth method, the *third-party communications service*, is preferred by a company that does business with a number of other companies or that is involved in cross-industry activity in which communications standards vary widely. A diagram of this method is shown in Figure 9-17.

This method allows organizations to transmit to an EDI service provider rather than transmit directly to each other. The **EDI service provider** serves as a clearinghouse and offers a variety of other services that make EDI more accessible and cost-effective. With this method the partners, such as the purchaser and the supplier, do not have to be concerned about translating standard formats or negotiating line speeds, protocols, multiple destinations, and the time of day to transmit. The third-party service provider performs these tasks.

The third-party service provider also provides its users with an electronic mailbox. Mailbox service allows documents to be sent or received at times convenient to each user's operations.

Examples of third-party services are McDonnell Douglas EDI*Net and GE Information Services EDI*EXPRESS System. These services provide

FIGURE 9-16 Value-Added Network Providing Mailbox Service for Both Partners Using the ANSI X.12 Format

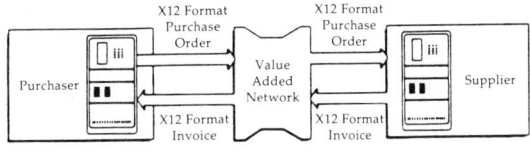

Used with permission of ASC X.12 Secretariat, Data Interchange Standards Association.

FIGURE 9-17 Third-Party Communications Service Providing Mailbox and ANSI X.12 Standard Translation Services

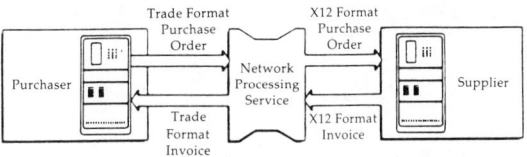

Used with permission of ASC X.12 Secretariat, Data Interchange Standards Association.

"partners" with electronic mailboxes, interconnection, and translation software. For example, your company's microcomputer can operate as a stand-alone workstation or as a front-end to an in-house mainframe. EDI*PC, a software package, translates the documents entered directly into the microcomputer or transferred from the mainframe to the microcomputer and then transmits them to EDI*EXPRESS, where they pass through various EDI*Express processing steps, such as document and format translation and compliance checking. Your trading partners use their EDI*PC systems to retrieve the documents that EDI*EXPRESS has delivered. Your company can also use EDI*PC to retrieve documents sent to you and placed in your EDI*EXPRESS mailbox. Figure 9-18 shows a configuration of GE Information Services EDI*EXPRESS Systems.

Also, in the third scenario at the beginning of this chapter, Hills Department Stores are using third-party communications services—GE Information Services EDI*EXPRESS and IBM Information Network and Quick Response Services. With these services, Hills Department Stores can easily implement EDI with their many suppliers. They do not have to waste time developing data formats and transmission protocols with each EDI partner.

FIGURE 9-18 GE Information Services EDI*EXPRESS System

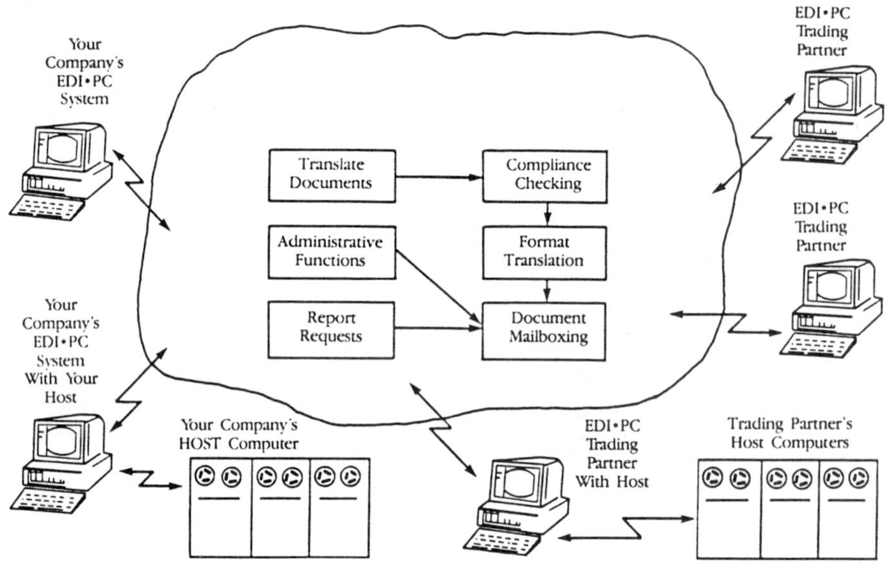

Courtesy of GE Information Services.

■ EDI Standards

An organization that conducts transactions with many organizations faces the task of supporting many incompatible private electronic document formats. EDI standards allow an industry to develop a common document format for data interchange. These standards facilitate the electronic interchange of data in a standard format among the same or different computers and communication systems.

The ANSI X.12 Standard. National EDI standards for the electronic interchange of business transactions between and within industries are being developed by ANSI X.12, a committee appointed by the American National Standards Institute (ANSI). The X.12 committee is developing generic standards for individual documents relating to order placement and processing, shipment and receiving information, invoicing, payment, and cash application data.

The universal adoption of EDI standards makes it possible for organizations to use a single standard format for interchanging data. Virtually all major third-party communications services as well as most translation software providers support **X.12** standards. With additional coding, the ANSI

X.12 standards can be modified, if necessary, to meet the requirements of specific industries. A number of industries have defined their own forms of EDI within the ANSI X.12 standard, while other industries have developed their own standards. Examples of industry implementations of ANSI X.12 include the chemical industry (CIDX), the electrical industry (EDX), the electronic industry (EIDX), automotive industry (AIAG), the health care industry, the metals industry, and the office products and furnishings industry. Other industry-developed standards are the grocery industry (UCS), the warehouse/distribution industry (WINS), and the transportation industry. For example, SuperValu Stores uses the grocery industry's standard (UCS) for formatting its purchase orders.

A brief overview of the standard helps in understanding its components. The ANSI X.12 data interchange standards consist of

- The *transaction set standards*, which define the procedural format and data content requirements for specified business transactions, such as purchase orders and shipping invoices.
- The *data entry dictionary*, which defines the precise content for data elements used in building transaction sets. For example, "CA" is defined as the unit of measure for "case."
- The *segment directory*, which provides the definitions and formats for the codes used in building transaction sets.
- The *transmission control standards*, which define the formats for the information required to interchange data.

In EDI the term *transaction set* refers to a single business document that is transmitted electronically between one company's computer and another company's computer. For example, in the railroad industry a transaction set was developed for bills of lading and freight bills. The data included in a transaction set convey the same information as a conventional printed document. Each transaction set contains three areas:

- The *header area*, which contains preliminary information related to the entire document, such as the company's name and address
- The *transaction set line item area*, which describes the actual business transaction, such as quantities, description, and price
- The *transaction set summary area*, which includes control information and figure totals

The entire contents of the document are transmitted electronically by being divided into these three basic areas, each of which is coded for transmission.

The conventional invoice shown in Figure 9-19 illustrates the three basic areas of a transaction set. To facilitate an electronic transmission, the information in the document is converted to EDI format by using the appropriate EDI symbols compiled in the ANSI X.12 Data Directory.

FIGURE 9-19 The Three Basic Areas of a Transaction Set

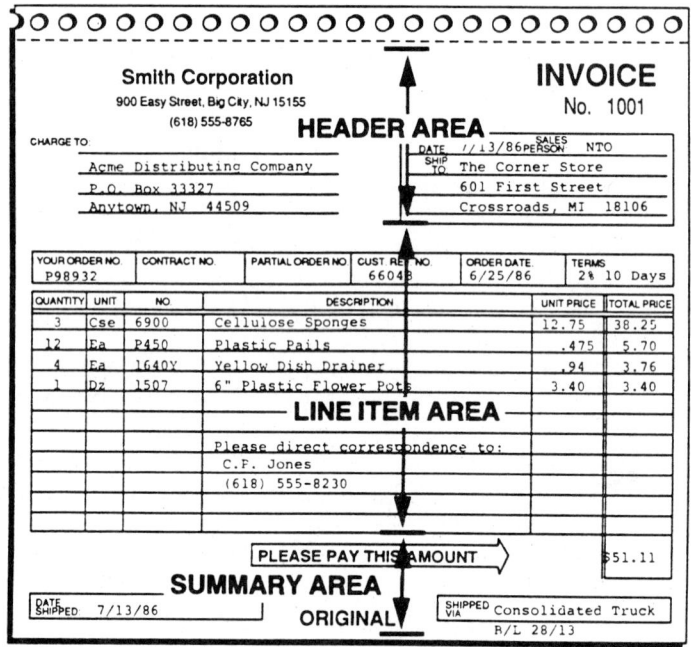

Used with permission of ASC X.12 Secretariat, Data Interchange Standards Association.

EDI and the X.400 Standard. As discussed earlier in this chapter, X.400 allows users to exchange E-mail among dissimilar equipment using private or public networks. The integration of X.400 with EDI will simplify the transmissions of EDI documents between the various private, public, and international networks. Many organizations currently rely on third-party service providers for EDI. If two organizations use different third-party providers for EDI services, the two organizations cannot easily exchange documents. When X.400 is integrated with EDI, a common connection between the different third-party services allows the two organizations to exchange documents. Similarly, a user of DEC's All-In-One E-mail system could send EDI documents to a third-party EDI service used by one of its customers.

■ Benefits and Drawbacks of EDI

Among the benefits of EDI are the following:

- It improves inventory and materials management by reducing the size of the company's inventories.

- It reduces purchasing, sales, and production cycles. For example, one company reports that it takes a minimum of seven days for a purchase order to be processed from the time the order is mailed until the order is confirmed. EDI reduces the time to two days.
- It reduces errors that are caused when data has to be keyed in more than once.
- It decreases clerical and administrative expenses. EDI reduces the labor needed to prepare business documents. It eliminates time previously wasted on minor inquiries about contents of these business documents. Express mail expenses are also eliminated.
- It improves the speed and accuracy of customer service. For example, EDI provides faster turnaround than is available from other services such as mail or courier services.
- It provides format-to-format translation. An organization can still use its own private formats and trade with partners who use either public or private formats. Software handles each organization's document translations from private to public format and back again to the originating organization's format.
- It establishes closer partnerships with customers by improving order and delivery schedules.

The biggest drawbacks to using EDI are the costs of setting communication links and developing software to perform the necessary transactions.

Third-party service providers are solving the problem of setting communication links by supplying mailboxes to which organizations can send their documents. Low-cost, off-the-shelf EDI software that adheres to the ANSI X.12 standard is now available, allowing manufacturers and suppliers the option of establishing their own links.

Selecting an E-Mail System

Before selecting any type of E-mail system, a company must determine whether it needs the system. A suggested plan for selecting an E-mail system, such as a CBMS, consists of three phases:

1. Analyze the present internal and external methods of communication.
2. Specify the requirements of the CBMS.
3. Select the CBMS.

Phase 1: Analyze the company's present methods of communicating, both internally and externally. Your analysis helps to determine whether you should install a CBMS. Suggested questions for gathering data are

- Who receives information?
- How is it sent?
- Who sends information? How is it read?

FIGURE 9-20 Planning Checklist

Planning is essential to ensure that an electronic message-handling system meets company needs. A checklist of questions such as the following should be circulated throughout the organization to determine requirements.

- What is the potential number of users?
- What method of communication is currently used?
- What is the average message length?
- How time-sensitive are the messages?
- Do all users require terminals or microcomputers?
- What is the projected volume of messages?
- What type of traffic is anticipated: domestic or international?
- Is the existing terminal population adequate for a CBMS?
- What is the makeup of the user population: computer novices or experts?

Reprinted with permission from the February 1987 issue of *Infosystems* magazine. Copyright 1987, Hitchcock Publishing Company. All rights reserved.

- Are messages being sent or received from other time zones?
- Who would use a CBMS?
- How many employees would use a CBMS?
- How many employees have access to computers?

Phase 2: Specify the requirements of the CBMS. If your analysis results in a decision to install a CBMS, then conduct an analysis to obtain information to help specify your CBMS requirements. Figure 9-20 offers suggestions.

Phase 3: Select a CBMS. Most potential customers consider cost the major factor. In selecting an E-mail system, other considerations can be as important, or possibly even more important. Figure 9-21 suggests questions for evaluating each system (there are usually two or three) being considered. Also talk to customers of the vendors you are considering. Your options include adding an E-mail system to your existing computer facility, installing a comprehensive information system, and obtaining the services of a public electronic mail service.

Summary

Among the types of electronic mail are telex, computer-based message systems, electronic data interchange, voice processing, and facsimile. Although domestic telex is being replaced by more sophisticated E-mail systems, international telex is still one of the primary means of electronic communications in many countries other than those in North America and between countries.

The type of E-mail that is becoming most familiar to information employees is computer-based message systems (CBMS), particularly in-house

FIGURE 9-21 Suggested Checklist for Selecting a Computer-Based Message System

Basics
- Is it easy to install?
- Is it easy to administer?
- Is it easy to use?
- Does it include help screens for using the system?
- Is it command- or menu-driven or both?
- Does it provide prompts for heading items, such as "To," "From," "Subject," "Blind carbon copy," and "Reply to?"
- Is it a multiuser system?
- Can it perform batch-processing transmissions?
- Does it have an online user directory?
- Does it offer text-editing features?
- Is it accessible while the user is working on other applications?
- Does it automatically notify the user of incoming mail audibly or visually, such as with an on-screen message?
- Can a user invoke the mail program while in another application, read and send messages, and then return to the original application?
- Does it include a calendar for daily appointments and allow scheduling of meetings?
- Does it provide for paper mail including overnight or same-day delivery?
- Does it provide a facsimile connection?

File Transfer
- Can text files be sent and received?
- Can binary files (spreadsheets and databases that have been created offline) be sent and received?
- Can text, graphics, and voice annotations be included in the same document?

Security
- Does it provide security for private messages equivalent to physical mail's sealed, opaque envelopes?

Voice Mail
- Can it integrate CBMS mailboxes with voice mail?

Gateways
- Does it provide a gateway to mainframe mail systems?
- Does it provide a gateway to public E-mail systems?
- Does it access telex?
- Does it provide standards that comply with CCITT X.400 messaging standards?
- Does it provide proprietary gateways to systems such as IBM's PROFS and DEC's VAXMAIL?
- Does it comply with the X.500 standard?

systems. Employees use them for such activities as office chitchat, recording telephone messages, scheduling meetings, exchanging document and files, and generating hard copy. A CBMS may be directed by a mainframe or a LAN server or be part of a comprehensive office system. Public E-mail services allow users to share a third-party's off-site computer for more E-mail options. By using CCITT's X.400 standard, any individual or organization can exchange information; and by using CCITT's X.500 standard for electronic directories they can obtain electronic telephone numbers. The selection of an E-mail system is based on an analysis of the company's present internal and external methods of communicating. Although most potential customers consider cost the major factor when selecting a CBMS, other factors can be as important, or possibly even more so.

Electronic data interchange allows computer-to-computer transmission of business transaction documents, such as purchase orders and shipping invoices, between two companies. Standards for these documents are being developed by the ANSI X.12 committee and other industry groups.

■ *Key Terms*

Computer-based message system
EDI service provider
Electronic data interchange
Electronic mail
Public electronic mail service
Telex I and II
Translator software
TWX
Upload text
X.12
X.400:
  Message transfer agents
  User agents
X.500

■ *Self-Quiz*

Indicate whether the statement is true or false.

1. The preferred method of computer-to-computer transfer of business documents is by VANs.   T/F
2. EDI requires more employees to process business documents.   T/F
3. Translator software converts the data in a business document into a standard format suitable for computer transmission.   T/F
4. An advantage of a third-party EDI service is that it provides each of its users with an electronic mailbox.   T/F
5. Telex is a primary form of electronic mail in many foreign countries.   T/F
6. Telex is replacing facsimile machines.   T/F

Complete the following statements.

1. The hardware and software components that a user must have to operate a CBMS are _____ .
2. Error-checking rules that govern the transfer of data in CBMSs are called _____ .
3. An example of a public E-mail service provider and the service offered is _____ .
4. An example of an in-house comprehensive office system is _____ .

5. Two organizations using different third-party providers for EDI services can exchange documents easily if EDI is integrated with _____ .
6. A CBMS feature that allows a user to prepare messages before signing onto the E-mail CBMS system is _____ .

Match Column A with B.

Column A
(a) X.12
(b) X.500
(c) X.400
(d) CBMS
(e) EDI
(f) UA

Column B
___ 1. CCITT's standard for communicating with dissimilar computer systems.
___ 2. CCITT's standard for an electronic directory.
___ 3. ANSI's generic standard for exchanging business transaction documents.
___ 4. Computer-to-computer transfer of standard format business transactions documents.
___ 5. Computer-to-computer transfer of unformatted text and data.
___ 6. Deals with message preparation and message receipt.

Review Questions

1. (a) How does telex operate?
   (b) How has Infomaster affected its operation?
   (c) How has telex been affected by the new office technologies?
2. Each of the following companies would like a CBMS. Specify the type of CBMS (mainframe, LAN, comprehensive office system, public E-mail service) you would suggest for each situation and explain why.
   (a) A company with ten to twelve employees currently has no computers but would like the employees to be able to communicate with each other.
   (b) A department with microcomputers networked for exchanging files and sharing peripherals would like to add a CBMS.
   (c) A company with eighty employees with access to a mainframe for business applications would like to add a CBMS.
   (d) A company of 100 employees would like a CBMS that combines E-mail with other functions such as scheduling, integrated word processing, spreadsheet, and database.
   (e) A company of forty employees would like a CBMS that enables it to communicate with other CBMSs and telex.
3. Suggest two or three ways to reduce the cost of using a public E-mail service.
4. What is (are) the difference(s) between CBMS and EDI?
5. How does EDI operate?
6. Explain how the following standards can benefit a company when it is dealing with other companies: ANSI X.12, CCITT X.400, CCITT X.500.
7. How can EDI be used at a university? Suggest applications.

8. Which method of transfer would you recommend for transmitting documents by EDI? Why?
9. What information would you need to determine whether your college or company should install a CBMS?
10. Examine Figure 9-21 the checklist for selecting a CBMS. Add two or three suggestions to this list.
11. When selecting a CBMS system, what three capabilities do you consider to be the most important for the system to possess? Why?

■ *Activities/Projects*

1. You must decide whether using the telephone, the U.S. Postal Service or a computer-based message system, such as a public electronic mail service, would be preferable for delivery of messages between New York City and San Francisco.
   (a) Calculate the cost of transmitting a 200-word verbal message from New York City to San Francisco by telephone. With AT&T as your long-distance carrier, the day telephone rate is $0.25 for the first minute and $0.25 for each additional minute. The evening rate is $0.16 for the first minutes and $0.17 for each additional minute or fraction thereof. The average person speaks at a rate that can vary between 120 and 180 words per minute.
   (b) Calculate the cost of transmitting a 200-word message from New York City to San Francisco by using MCI Mail, a public E-mail service. Refer to Figure 9-9 for rate information. The baud rate of the modem used for delivery of computer-based messages is 1200. Assume six characters per word.
   (c) Would you recommend transmitting by telephone, U.S. Postal Service, or by a public E-mail service? Why?
2. Visit an organization of your choice to find out whether any business transactions, such as purchasing, sales, and shipping, are conducted with EDI.
   (a) If so, describe how EDI operates.
   (b) If not, describe the procedure the organization uses to purchase supplies. How many copies of a purchase order are prepared? Who receives a copy? Could EDI be used by this organization? Is the organization considering its use?
3. Compare two CBMSs. Compose a message for transmission by computer from your hometown to a city of your choice. Calculate the cost of sending the message by two of the public electronic mail services. Base your calculation on the systems and rates listed in Figure 9-9. Compare the costs of the two systems.
4. Employees accustomed to traditional methods of messaging may not want to change to CBMS. How would you, as a manager or a supervisor, approach this situation?

Case: Which Public E-Mail Service Provider Should It Be?

As information-processing manager of a company located in Portland, Oregon, you have been asked to select a public E-mail service. The following information is available to you.

The average length of a message to be transmitted is fifty words, and the average document is four pages long. Messages will usually be time-sensitive. Each user will be transmitting an average of ten messages a day and four or five documents a week. Some users require hard-copy output: facsimile and same-day service. Some also require access to other CBMSs such as DEC's All-In-One and IBM's PROFS. Many of the company's customers are located in New York City, Philadelphia, and Chicago. Users are not knowledgeable about computers.

(a) What criteria would you use in selecting an E-mail service?
(b) Of the public E-mail services listed in Figure 9-9, which one would you select? Why?

Notes

1. Frances Seghers, Jeffrey Rothfeder, and Robert D. Hof, "Electronic Mail: Neither Rain, Nor Sleet, Nor Software . . . ," *Business Week*, February 20, 1989, p. 36.
2. "Paperless Buying Nets Multiple Benefits," *Electronic Buyers News*, April 6, 1987.

Additional Readings

Michael Braum, "Signed, Sealed and . . . Delivered," *Network World*, June 27, 1988, pp. 53, 56, 57, 60.

Michael Braum, "Return Receipt Requested," *Network World*, July 4, 1988, pp. 35, 46, 47.

Dennis Eskow, "Lawyers Warn: Don't Break Up Your E-Mail," *PC Weekly*, September 11, 1989, pp. 81, 85.

Willie Schatz, "EDI: Putting the Muscle in Commerce and Industry," *Datamation*, March 15, 1988, pp. 56–64.

Mary Sumner, "The Organizational Impacts of Electronic Mail," *Office Systems Research Journal*, Spring 1987, pp. 1–19.

Libby Trudell with Janet Bruman and Dennis Oliver, *Options for Electronic Mail* (White Plains, N.Y.: Knowledge Industry Publications, Inc., 1984).

Benjamin Wright, *EDI and American Law: A Practical Guide* (Alexandria, Va.: TDCC: The Electronic Data Interchange Association, 1989).

Periodicals

Electronic Mail and Micro Systems is a twice-monthly newsletter covering technology, user, product, and legislative trends in graphics, record, and microcomputer communications. It is published by International Resource Development, Inc., 21 Locust Avenue, #1C, New Canaan, CT 06840, (203) 966-2525.

CHAPTER 10

Voice Processing

Voice Processing Defined

Voice Processing Evolution

How to Use Voice Processing
   Operating a Voice Processing System
   Voice Processing System Features

Voice Processing Technology
   Digitized Speech
   Text-to-Speech Conversion
   Voice-to-Text Conversion

Types of Voice Processing Systems
   Stand-Alone Voice Processing Systems
   Integrated Voice Processing Systems
   Automated Office Systems
   Service Bureaus

Voice Processing Functions and Applications
   Telephone Answering
   Caller Routing
   Interactive Messaging
   Information Providing
   Transaction Processing

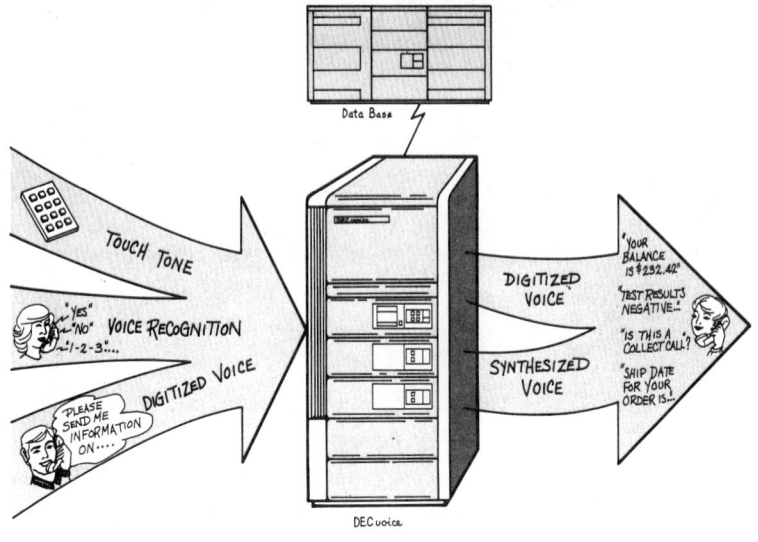

Courtesy of Digital Equipment Corporation.

Benefits and Drawbacks of Voice Processing
  Benefits of Voice Processing
  Drawbacks of Voice Processing
Selecting a Voice Processing System

CHAPTER OBJECTIVES

After studying this chapter, you should be able to

1. Define voice processing.
2. Describe how to use voice processing.
3. Describe the technology of voice processing.
4. Distinguish between digitized voice, voice synthesis, and voice recognition.
5. Describe voice processing functions with examples of applications.
6. Select a voice processing system.

At 5 P.M. a manager in San Francisco discovers that she needs important information from the New York sales office for a presentation the next morning. She telephones the New York office and places her request via voice message. When

353

she arrives in her office the next day, the information is waiting for her in her voice mailbox.

When calling American Airlines, you might reach a voice bulletin board—an "audiotex." A voice answers, "Thank you for calling American Airlines Automated Information System. For flight arrival and departure information, press 1. For fare and schedule information, press 2. For assistance any time, press asterisk and zero." If the caller presses the 1 on a touch-tone telephone and then keys in the flight number, the voice reports the flight's status. An operator assists anyone calling from rotary-dial telephones.

College students register for classes from their home telephone. They gain access to their school's computerized registration system by calling a special telephone number and then using the telephone's keypad to enter their student or social security number for identification. Courses are chosen, added, or dropped simply by entering the right code. The voice processing system leads the students through the call with easy-to-understand instructions. The system automatically verifies each entry against the school's computer files to make certain students register only for course sections that are open and for which they qualify. If a course is full or another problem arises, a touch of a key can bring a live operator on for assistance.

Using only his voice, Dr. Arthur L. Chambers, III dictates reports directly into Kurzweil VoiceEM (for Emergency Medicine) system, edits them on the computer screen, and orders an instant printout. The procedure, done entirely by voice, takes minutes and solves problems of illegible handwriting as well as delays in transcribing reports dictated to tape. Dr. Chambers is Director of Emergency Medical Services, Nash General Hospital, Rocky Mount, North Carolina.

In each of these situations the telephone is combined with a computer to handle some form of voice processing—sending, receiving, recording, and/or redirecting messages.

Message handling is a challenge to business, since telephone calls often fail to reach the intended party on the first try. The calling party might receive a busy signal, be put on hold, or have the call go unanswered. The called party might be away from his or her desk, be located in a different time zone with different working hours, or already be talking with someone else on the telephone. Repeated phone calls become necessary. So-called "telephone tag" has added an estimated $4 billion annually to the cost of doing business.[1] Telephone answering machines, message answering services, and receptionists have not solved the problem. The solution is proving to be voice processing, another form of electronic mail. This chapter describes voice processing, its operation and technology, and its usefulness to business.

Voice Processing Defined

Voice processing is the technology of computers speaking, storing human voice and understanding, and reacting to human speech.[2] It is a computerized delivery system that provides telephone callers with automatic access to information bases, services, and operation. But instead of a computer keyboard, requests are made by using a touch-tone telephone as a terminal to interact with the computer. Information can be requested and communicated from almost any telephone in the world. (Not all pushbutton telephones are touch-tone phones; some are pulse dialing telephones. Pushbutton adapters are available that convert these telephones and rotary-dial telephones into touch-tone telephones. An adaptor can be temporarily attached to an existing telephone by replacing the plastic mouthpiece. Also available is a battery-operated pocket-size unit that can be attached to an existing telephone for permanent use.)

Voice processing is the umbrella term for the various voice functions, such as telephone answering, caller routing (automated attendant), interactive messaging (voice mail), information providing (audiotex), and transaction processing. It also includes the various technologies—voice recognition and voice synthesis. Each of these functions and technologies is discussed in the sections that follow.

Chapter 9 discussed computer-based message systems. Before examining voice processing in depth, we should note the similarities and differences between the two systems. These systems complement each other. Both automate the delivery of messages over a private or public switched telephone network.

- *Voice processing systems* are appropriate for brief, one-way messages, while *computer-based message systems* lend themselves to long documents that can be edited and reproduced.
- *Voice processing systems* allow messages to be sent and retrieved from any telephone that has access to the network, whereas *computer-based message systems* require a computer terminal for input and output.
- In a *voice processing system*, messages are immediately authenticated by the caller's voice. A *computer-based message system* does not provide the same positive identification of the sender.

Voice Processing Evolution

First-generation voice messaging systems, introduced in 1976, were room-sized and required external cooling, special wiring, and other features of a computer environment. Subscribers could use these systems only for sending messages to each other.

In 1980, Voice Message Exchange (VMX), formerly ECS Telecommunications, introduced a second-generation system, a stand-alone digitized voice mail system. The company installed the first unit at 3M company headquarters in St. Paul, Minnesota. VMX is recognized as the inventor of digital voice messaging and is credited with setting the pace for the voice messaging industry. These early systems were limited to voice store-and-forward messaging—telephone answering and message notification. Compared to first-generation systems, they were somewhat smaller, required special electric treatment, and were expandable but at a high cost.

Second-generation systems have been replaced with systems that use 32-bit microprocessor chips and can be the size of a small copier, fitting nicely into an office environment. These third-generation systems offer numerous capabilities at lower prices. Since Rolm Corporation's introduction of the first completely integrated voice messaging system in 1982, many systems now integrate with PBX and Centrex systems.

Other recent voice processing advancements include computers that speak written text and other computers that convert speech into text. Progress is being made in developing speaker-independent voice response systems in which a computer is able to understand and respond to the speech of any person.

Today, both large and small businesses use voice processing systems. According to Probe Research, a market research firm based in Morristown, New Jersey, sales revenues of voice processing services and equipment generated more than $450 million in 1987 and are expected to grow to $2.5 billion by 1992—a 50% annual sales growth.

How to Use Voice Processing

Most companies install voice processing systems primarily to improve their internal communications. When a company installs a system, it soon discovers that the system changes the way the company conducts its business. For example, no longer do employees play telephone tag. Messages are now clearer and can be delivered and/or received at any time from any time zone, and fewer secretaries are needed to take and deliver messages. A recipient may respond directly to the caller by keying in the caller's extension (as long as the caller is on the system). Or the recipient can forward messages to a third person or a group by just pressing a button. For employees to use the system effectively, however, they must understand how it operates and what it can do.

■ Operating a Voice Processing System

The company assigns to each of its system users (also called subscribers) a voice mailbox. A "voice mailbox" refers to the section of computer memory that is allotted to each system subscriber. Voice messages in digitized form are delivered to and stored in these mailboxes. When messages are to be played, they are retrieved and reconverted to the originator's voice. Messages can be saved, deleted, or routed to other users

How to Use Voice Processing

Accessing the System. Assume that your company has a voice processing system and a person from another company decides to telephone you. This person, referred to as a nonsubscriber, dials your company's phone number and hears a voice say:

"Enter the extension of the person you are calling or press zero for the information center."

Instead of reaching a live operator, the caller has reached a special function called an automated attendant. Your caller responds by keying your extension number on his or her phone keypad.

Your extension is busy. After four rings, a "voice" gives the caller choice of the following prompts:

"The extension you are trying to reach is busy. Make another choice:
Key in 1 to leave a message for this party.
Or key in another extension.
Or key in 2 to go to a live operator."

In response to these choices, your caller decides to leave a message and so keys in the number 1.

Recording Messages. The caller is directed to your mailbox and hears your greeting:

"This is _____. I cannot come to the phone just now. Please leave a message when you hear the tone. When you complete your message, please press the number sign. I shall return your call as soon as possible. Thank you."

Your caller then dictates his or her message and presses the number sign when finished. Messages may be limited to a specified period of minutes. If so, the caller is given a brief warning to signal that the end of the recording is approaching. The "voice" also may ask when the message is to be delivered. The caller keys in a number to indicate immediate delivery or keys in the time of day and date for later delivery. Once the caller presses the send key, the voice mail system informs *you*, the called party, that a message is waiting.

Receiving Messages. Once you are informed that a message is waiting for you, you decide you want to hear your messages. To access your own mailbox, you key your personal mailbox number and a special password from any touch-tone phone. Password protection prevents others from obtaining access to your personal mailbox. The system's voice offers you a menu of choices:

"Key in 1 to review messages.
Or key in 2 to send a message.
Or key in 3 to check receipt of a message.
Or key in 4 to change personal options."

FIGURE 10-1 Pocket Reference Guide

TO BEGIN:
- DIAL _____
- ENTER YOUR MAILBOX NO. _____
- PRESS [*]
- ENTER YOUR PASSCODE
- TO MAKE A MESSAGE, ALWAYS ENTER THE SYSTEM THROUGH YOUR MAILBOX FOR CONVENIENT ANSWERING
- ALWAYS PRESS [WXY 9] TO EXIT THE SYSTEM

User Commands

```
                    1    ABC 2   DEF 3  — DISCARD
ANSWER —
GIVE   —          GHI 4  JKL 5   MNO 6  — MAKE
                                        — KEEP
PLAY   —          PRS 7  TUV 8   WXY 9  — EXIT (SEND)
REVIEW —                                — USER OPTIONS
BACKWARD —         *    OPER 0    #    — FORWARD
```

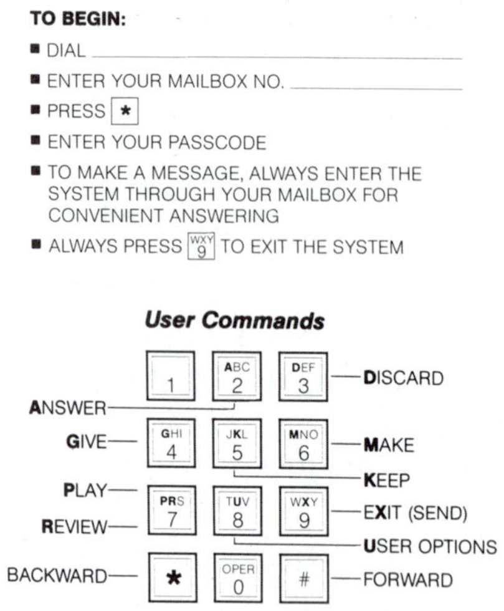

Courtesy of Centigram Corporation.

You select the first choice. When you key in the number 1, the system automatically checks for any messages that are waiting for you. If you have messages, you can listen to each message or key in a scan code to move quickly through the message.

A dial overlay or pocket reference guide (Figure 10-1) that lists the various system command codes is helpful when using a system. System users can construct their own overlays or pocket guides if the vendor does not provide one.

Redirecting Messages. Suppose that you decide to redirect one of the messages you received to another system user. You then key in the code that tells the system you want to resend a message. Next you key in the extension of the system user who is to receive the message and press the send key. Figure 10-2 shows a flowchart of various ways you can move around a voice processing system.

■ Voice Processing System Features

Features of a voice processing system are accessed through a touch-tone keypad. Features that are available on many voice processing systems are described below.

FIGURE 10-2 Flowchart of a Voice Processing System: Voice Memo™

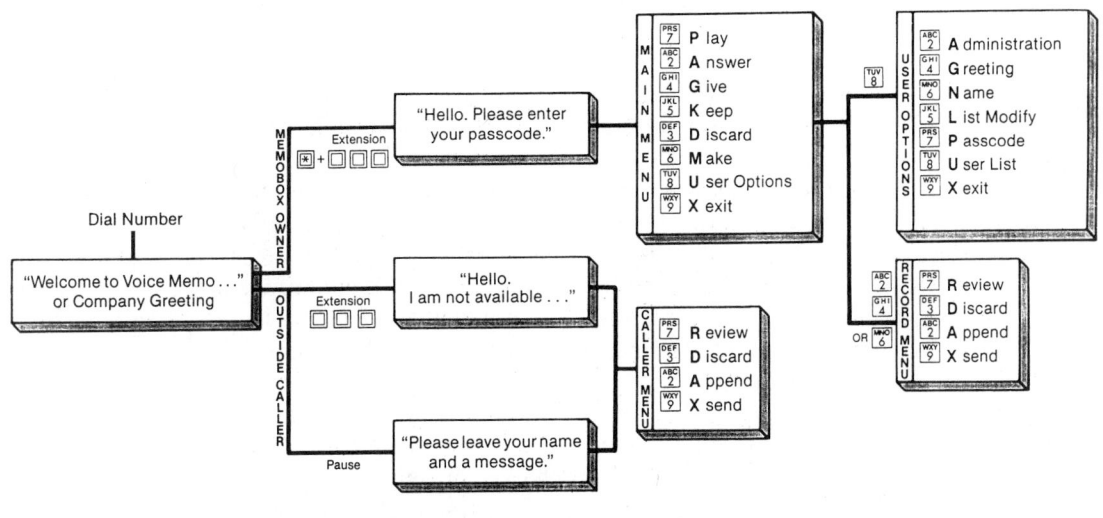

Courtesy of Centigram Corporation. ™Trademark of Centigram Corporation.

The *password feature* protects a user's mailbox from unauthorized access. For example, to restrict access to sensitive information, a caller dials a specified authorization code, or password, before listening to the contents of the mailbox.

Experienced users, both subscribers and nonsubscribers, can skip standard voice prompts with *prompt override*.

The *scan feature* allows a subscriber to review messages waiting in his or her mailbox before listening to each message in its entirety.

After listening to each message, the subscriber uses the *save feature* to either save or erase the message.

The *visitor or guest key feature*, also called a guest mailbox, allows a mailbox owner to give a code to others for accessing his or her box.

When a nonsubscriber is assigned access to a guest mailbox on the system, the nonsubscriber uses the *reply feature* to respond to a received message from another subscriber or a nonsubscriber.

With the *redirect feature* a subscriber can reroute a received message to another subscriber's mailbox or to a distribution list of mailboxes.

The *annotate feature* allows a subscriber to add comments to a received message before rerouting it to others.

After the subscriber or nonsubscriber creates a message, the *edit feature* allows its creator to add to, delete, or revise it.

A subscriber may create lists of mailbox users and broadcast messages to these lists. The **broadcast feature** allows a subscriber to automatically send the same voice message to multiple mailboxes with one command. This feature is suitable for sending announcements and general information to various groups of personnel.

The *delivery verification feature* notifies the sender when a voice message has been delivered.

The *message notification feature* informs the called party of a waiting message by special telephone ringback, a visual indicator lamp on the phone, and/or visual messages on terminal screens. A system without this function requires the subscriber to call the system and inquire for his or her messages.

Paging service links a voice processing system to a paging system. A caller can request that the called party be paged by pressing a key.

With *message delivery options* the subscriber can choose among such options as to hear messages immediately, hear the length of the message and the sender's name, hear messages only on request, or hear new messages only.

The *voice networking* feature links voice processing systems at remote locations as well as two or more systems at a single location. Networking allows subscribers with mailboxes on one system to exchange voice messages with subscribers on other systems of the same manufacturer. For example, a subscriber to a company's system in Dallas can send messages to subscribers of the company's other systems in New York, Washington, and San Francisco by making one local call. Figure 10-3 illustrates how one company is networked.

With this feature an urgent message can be transmitted between systems immediately, multiple messages can be transmitted per network call and using least-cost routing, or nonurgent messages can be held for overnight delivery when transmission rates are cheaper, as shown in Figure 10-4. Lack of technical standards for the voice processing industry prevents the networking of systems from different vendors.

The *call statistics* feature generates information about the system's use for whatever period of time is desired, such as last month, this month, this week, today, or even this hour. Information may include the percentage of used disk, the number of calls per port, the number of calls directed to extensions, the number of calls directed to the live operator, the number of messages stored, the number of messages purged, and use of the various functions.

Voice Processing Technology

Voice processing technology can be classified according to voice generation techniques and voice-to-text conversion (voice recognition). Voice generation techniques include digitized speed (digital recording) and text-to-speech conversion (speech synthesis).

FIGURE 10-3 Voice Networking at a Company with Several Locations: AspenNet®SM

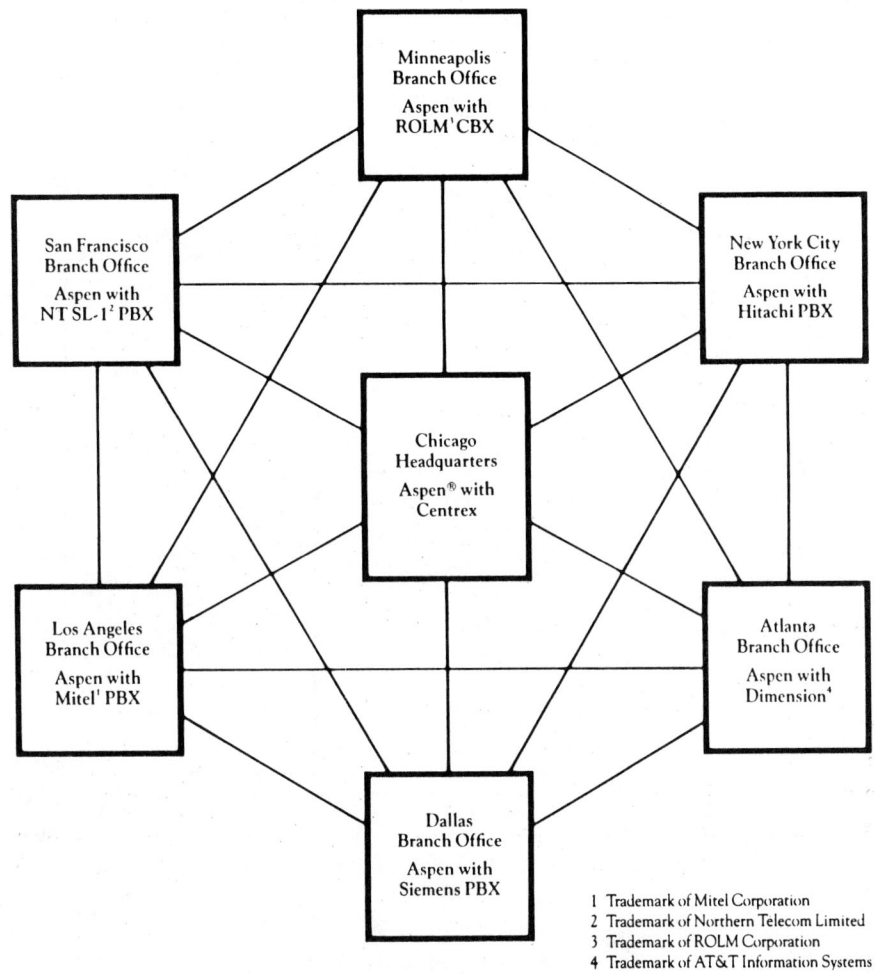

Courtesy of Octel Communications Corporation. ®SM Trademark and service mark of Octel Communications Corporation.

■ Digitized Speech

In **digitized speech**, a computer converts human speech into digital signals for storage on a computer disk and then, when commanded, reconverts the signals to human speech for someone to hear. The first scenario at the beginning of the chapter describes digitized speech.

FIGURE 10-4 Networking Routes for Voice Messages Using Low-Cost Alternatives: AspenNet®SM

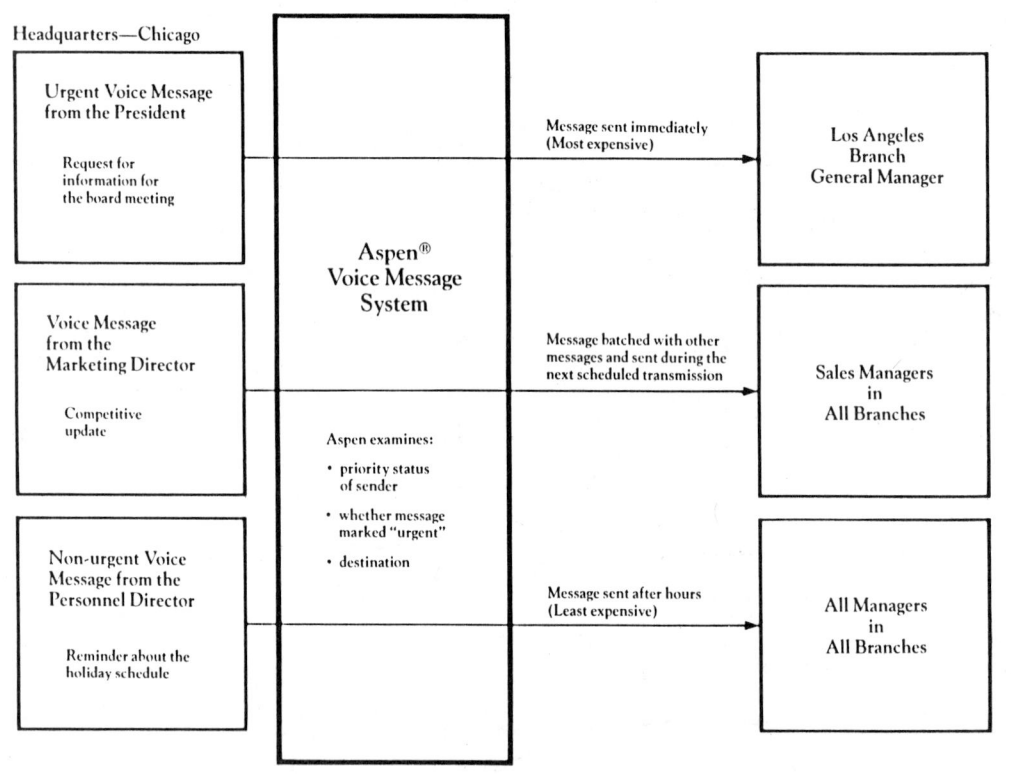

Courtesy of Octel Communications Corporation. ®SMTrademark and service mark of Octel Communications Corporation.

System Components. The components of a voice processing system for digitized speech include its computer, specialized computer software that controls the system's operation, a codec device that converts analog voice signals into digital form and then reconverts them, and disk storage that stores the digitized voice messages. The input/output units for the system are two-way telephone and/or tie lines that connect the voice processing system directly to the public switched telephone network, a key telephone system, or a PBX or Centrex system, as diagrammed in Figure 10-5. Examples of units that house voice processing equipment are shown in Figure 10-6. Voice processing systems range from a 4-port system for up to 75 users to a 72-port system for up to 7500 users. The four systems shown in Figure 10-6 can be integrated with most PBXs and Centrex and networked with each other to offer company-wide voice messaging among remote locations.

Voice Processing Technology 363

FIGURE 10-5 Network Configuration of a Voice Processing System: Aspen®

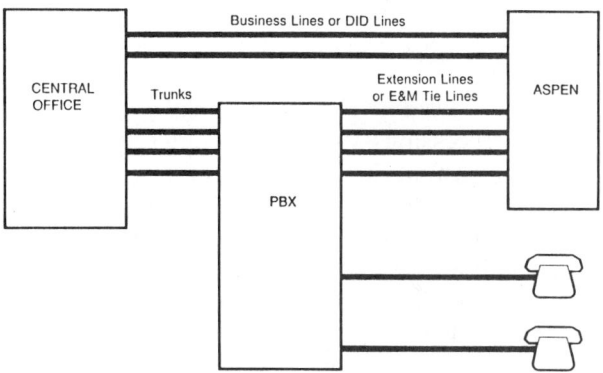

Courtesy of Octel Communications Corporation. ®Registered trademark of Octel Communications Corporation.

FIGURE 10-6 Voice Processing Equipment

Courtesy of Octel Communications Corporation.

System Capability. The capability of a voice processing system to support voice traffic depends on the following factors:

- The number of available ports
- The amount of computer storage space available for voice message storage

Selecting the Correct Number of Ports. The number of ports on a voice processing system determines the number of users who can access the system at the same time and, on many systems, the number of incoming and outgoing telephone lines attached to the system. If 800 people try to call a 24-port voice message system at exactly the same time, 776 of them will get a busy signal. However, it is very unlikely that 800 people will try to call a system at the same time.

To determine the number of ports needed to support a given number of subscribers based on the probability that a specific number of users will attempt to call at the same time, you should calculate the following variables.

1. Calculate the weighted average number of minutes per day that subscribers and/or outside callers use the system.
2. Determine the percentage of those minutes that occur during a peak (busy) period.
3. Calculate the maximum acceptable probability that a caller to the voice processing system will encounter a busy signal during this peak period.

Calculation of the weighted average number of minutes per day of use involves several factors. First, the minutes of port time used per day includes the number of minutes the subscriber is in voice mail as well as the number of minutes an outside caller uses to leave messages for a subscriber. That is, a voice mail message is counted twice, once for the sender and once for the recipient. Second, the number of minutes of usage per day includes direct and indirect usage. Direct usage includes time the subscriber is depositing or reviewing messages and overhead time, that is, administrative functions and listening to prompts. Indirect usage includes telephone answering, message taking, and message notification outcalling. Third, although it is difficult to predict exactly how a particular person will use a voice processing system, knowledge of the person's present communication patterns helps to determine usage. However, instead of studying an individual's communications pattern in detail, the user population is divided into groups of individuals who have similar communications patterns, such as shown in Figure 10-7. An analysis of typical groups of users also gives a better approximation of actual usage than calculating an average based on the total organization. In Figure 10-7, the single weighted average of 6 minutes per user is what is used in determining the number of ports. Although no actual subscriber may use the system for 6 minutes per day, the calculation provides an average usage profile.

FIGURE 10-7 **Hypothetical Calculation of Weighted Average Minutes of Usage per Subscriber**

Category of Subscriber	Number of Persons	Average Daily Minutes per Person			Total Minutes per category
		Direct	Indirect	Total	
Executive	5	5	2	7	35
Manager	20	6	4	10	200
General professional	80	4	2	6	480
Service technician	30	5	0	5	150
Order entry clerk	20	2	8	10	200
Other clerks	30	2	1	3	90
Secretary	15	3	1	4	60
Total weighted average	200	4	2	6	1215

Note: Weighted average is total minutes divided by total users—e.g., 1215/200 = 6. Weighted averages of four minutes direct and two minutes indirect are similarly calculated.
Courtesy of Octel Communications Corporation.

The percentage of total daily minutes that occur during a peak (busy) period is another variable that must be determined. If most of the system's usage occurs during a particular hour of the day, then a large number of ports will be needed to ensure that not too many callers receive a busy signal. Conversely, if usage is spread evenly over the day, fewer ports will be needed.

The standard measure used in traffic analysis is *busy hour peak*, which is expressed in terms of the percentage of calls occurring during the busiest hour of the day. Busy hour peak is simply the percentage of total traffic that occurs during the busiest hour of the day. A busy hour peak of 15% means that 15% of the day's total traffic occurs during a one-hour period and the remaining 85% occurs during the remaining twenty-three hours of the day. For example, a busy hour peak of 10% for a PBX is considered very "flat" or even usage while a busy hour peak of 17% for a PBX is considered very heavy usage. Busy hour peak percentages tend to be lower in situations where many users are calling across time zones. Voice message systems used for general purposes tend to have lower-peaked patterns than PBXs for the following reasons:

- Subscribers from other time zones call during nonbusiness hours.
- The call completion rate is close to 100% with voice messaging.
- Subscribers often access the system to review messages during off-peak hours.

- The maximum acceptable probability is that a caller to the system will encounter a busy signal during the busy hour.
- Transactions are typically one-third to one-fourth as long as "real-time" telephone conversations.

The maximum acceptable probability that a caller to the voice processing system will encounter a busy signal during the busy hour peak is referred to as *grade of service*. Grade of service is measured as the percent probability that a given call during the busy hour peak will be blocked and will encounter a busy signal. For voice processing systems, the standard grades of service are P.02 (2% probability of a busy signal), P.03 (3% probability), and P.05 (5% probability). In off-peak hours, the grade of service may be the same or even higher.

Figure 10-8 shows the total number of ports that Octel Communications Corporation suggests for simultaneous access to one of its voice processing systems. Calculations are based on the total number of users, whether they use the system lightly or heavily, and how heavy the load is during the busy hour peak. For example, suppose a company's usage is described as 6 minutes per user and 14% usage during the busy hour peak. If the company has 600 potential users, then according to Figure 10-8, 16 ports should be ordered.

Note that 12 ports will support only 472 users at P.02 while 16 ports support 702 users. The 600 users on 16 ports will enjoy a grade of service better than P.02 and the system can allow for future growth. The company

FIGURE 10-8 Number of Subscribers that Aspen® Ports Can Support at a P.02 Grade of Service

Usage Category	Weighted Average Usage per User per Day (minutes)	Busy Hour Peak (% of calls)	Number of Users Supportable at P.02 (number of ports)					
			4	8	12	16	20	24
Heavy Usage Very peaked usage	8	18%	45	151	275	409	549	692
Medium Usage Medium-peaked usage	6	14%	78	259	472	702	941	1187
Light Usage Not-peaked usage	4	10%	164	544	992	1474	1977	2494

Courtesy of Octel Communications Corporation. ®Registered trademark of Octel Communications Corporation.

could also decide to order 12 ports and experience a grade of service slightly poorer than P.01 during the busy hour peak.

Determining the Correct Amount of Computer Storage Space. In addition to determining the number of ports for the voice processing system, the amount of computer storage space, specifically disk storage, for messages must also be determined. For example, if 500 users of a system require a relatively large number of ports because they are heavy users of the voice processing system, then they will probably require a large amount of disk storage.

The amount of message retention on a voice processing system affects the system's storage needs along with message volume and peak loads. Longer average retention of messages results in higher storage needs. Factors that tend to increase retention are

- Subscribers infrequently accessing their mailboxes to review messages
- A large number of messages being archived
- Loading messages after a weekend or after hours for the receiver
- Placing a large number of messages for future delivery in the system
- Including a large number of limited-use subscribers who pick up their messages infrequently

To determine storage requirements, you should estimate the average storage requirements at any "snapshot" point in time. For each category of users, estimate the average number of messages that are stored and the average length of each message. Stored messages include both messages that are waiting to be reviewed and those that have been skipped or saved in the archives. The storage requirements for each category of users is determined by multiplying the number of messages by the average length of message by the number of people in the category. The sum of the requirements of all categories gives the total message storage requirement, as shown in Figure 10-9. To this figure is added, the storage requirement for personal greetings, which is the normal "snapshot" storage requirement for the application.

You also need to determine how much the peak storage requirement will differ from the average "snapshot" requirement. In many applications, differences will be small because the rate at which messages are deposited and retrieved are similar for each hour of the day. In some situations, however, many messages will be deposited at one time and not retrieved until a few hours later. Such a pattern might occur because of heavy communication across time zones. When the peak requirement is greater than the "snapshot" requirement, a peak estimate should be calculated and added to the average "snapshot" figure. In Figure 10-9, an adjustment is made for peak requirements as well as for group sends, which is the same message sent to multiple destinations but only stored once on a disk. For example, Figure

FIGURE 10-9 Hypothetical Calculation of Weighted Average Storage per Person

Subscriber Category	Number of Subscribers in Category	Average Number of Messages Stored	Average Length of Message (seconds)	Total Storage Required for Group (minutes)	Average Storage per User (minutes)
Executive	5	6	45	23	4.5
Manager	20	6	30	60	3.0
General Professional	80	5	30	200	2.5
Service Technician	30	7	20	70	2.3
Order Entry Clerk	20	5	30	50	2.5
Other Clerks	30	3	30	45	1.5
Secretary	15	2	30	15	1.0
Total	200			463	2.3

Personal Greeting Requirement:
  Number of Users*
    100*   ×   Average Greeting 10 Seconds   16   0.1

Plus Peak Load Adjustment
  463 minutes × 15%**   69   0.3

Less Adjustment for Group Sends***
  532 minutes × −10%   −53   −0.2

Total Adjusted Storage Requirements   495   2.5

*Not all subscribers have a Class of Service that allows a personal greeting.
**Estimated need as a safety factor.
***The same message sent to multiple destinations is only stored once on the disk. This is a weighted average estimate for this group, based on use of group lists and sending to more than one individual mailbox. It is calculated after adjusting for peak load.
Courtesy of Octel Communications Corporation.

10-10 shows that one disk drive with 38 hours of storage will support 570 subscribers requiring heavy storage, 760 subscribers requiring medium storage, and 1560 requiring light storage.

The calculated weighted average for storage requirements per user is used to determine the amount of computer storage needed. Figure 10-9 shows that storage requirement per user is 2.5 minutes for 200 users. Figure 10-10 shows the number of disk drives required for storage based on the weighted average per user and the number of prospective users on the system. If the weighted average storage requirements per user were 2.5 minutes and the number of subscribers were 200, then you would need 1 disk drive. If the number of subscribers were 900, then you would need three storage drives. When you cannot make a detailed analysis of all users or user groups, then use the per-user average for similar groups that you have analyzed.

FIGURE 10-10   **Number of Subscribers Supportable by Different Numbers of Disk Drives**

Number of Drives	1	3	4	6	8	10	12	14	16
Hours of Storage	38	57	95	114	152	190	228	266	304

Weighted Average Storage Requirements per User (minutes)	Subscribers Supported (per drive and hour quantities above)								
Heavy storage: 4.0	570	855	1140	1710	2280	2850	3420	3990	4560
Medium storage: 3.0	760	1140	1520	2280	3040	3800	4560	5320	6080
Light storage: 1.5	1520	2280	3040	4560	6080	7500	7500	7500	7500

Courtesy of Octel Communications Corporation.

With any voice messaging system, a trade-off exists between level of service and cost. A system with too little disk space tends to have a negative impact on users, for example, when they are told the system cannot accept more messages. The system administrator can monitor disk usage, and if capacity is scarce, can encourage users to free up more space. The initial system should contain adequate storage capacity so that disks do not fill up immediately. If initial storage calculations are close to the maximum number of subscribers supportable by a particular number of disks, then consider adding additional disk capacity. Another solution would be to restrict the use of personal greetings and possibly reduce class of service allowance until storage usage can be monitored.

■ Text-to-Speech Conversion

In text-to-speech systems the computer reads text and creates synthesized speech from the text. **Speech synthesis** allows a caller with a touch-tone phone to access an electronic mail message or a word processing document directly from the computer without using a computer terminal or the assistance of a telephone operator. The computer then recites the message or document over the telephone to the caller. Speech synthesis is also used as the output method for such applications as telephone directories, weather reports, and inventory and other database applications.

Text-to-speech conversion is accomplished by the computer converting textual information stored in machine-readable code (ASCII) into a computer-generated voice that synthesizes human speech. The task of synthesizing speech begins with establishing the phonemes of a language and digitizing these sounds for computer storage. **Phonemes** (typically vowels, consonants, and diphthongs) are among the basic units of sound that make up words. The computer is then programmed to construct phonemes based on letter combinations. Text that is to be computer-generated is then analyzed phonetically by separating each word into a series of individual phonemes and then generating the phonemes in the proper sequence to speak words and sentences. Phoneme-based speech is usually not natural-sounding. However, this technology makes it possible for ASCII text to be output as voice just as easily as it can be sent to a printer or modem.

Digital's DECtalk. *DECtalk,* a product of Digital Equipment Corporation (DEC), is an example of a text-to-speech system. The product, shown in Figure 10-11, is a small, modem-sized unit that is connected to a computer via an RS-232-C terminal port. The synthetic speech produced by DECtalk can be output to a speaker or a telephone, as diagrammed in Figure 10-12.

DECtalk converts standard ASCII text from a computer into human speech. DECtalk speaks with a wide range of voices, speech rates, and intonation patterns. Voice types can be adult male, adult female, or child. Speech rates can range from 120 to 300 words per minute, and the speaking mode can be either full sentence, word-at-a-time, or letter-at-a-time. DEC-

FIGURE 10-11 DECtalk Equipment

Courtesy of Digital Equipment Corporation.

FIGURE 10-12 The DECtalk System

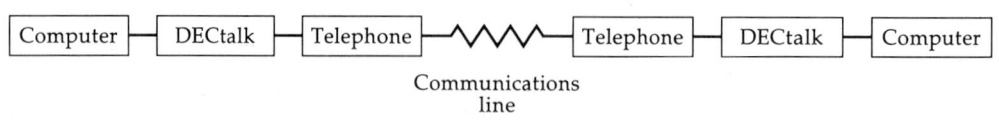

Redrawn courtesy of Digital Equipment Corporation.

talk's built-in vocabulary includes familiar and frequently used words, numbers, and abbreviations. A user can also build an auxiliary dictionary for trade terms, acronyms, and other special words. In addition to dictionaries, DECtalk contains a library of letter-to-sound rules to increase its pronunciation capabilities. With these rules, DECtalk can generate educated guess pronunciations for unfamiliar words or letter combinations not found in its dictionaries.

DECtalk, through its DECtalk VAX/All-in-One office automated system software, provides a solution for applications that need telephone access and/or voice output of information stored on a computer system. For example, users who do not have immediate access to their computer terminal or workstation can use a touch-tone telephone from any location at any time to access and "listen to" their electronic mail and electronic calendars or to "proofread" word processing documents. DECtalk provides keyboard-shy executives with an easy way to scan their electronic mail by reading critical items and leaving the remaining ones for printing or processing by assistants.

From a phone, a caller can do the following:

- Listen to all new messages or select specific mail for reading.
- Delete mail messages.
- Retrieve and listen to documents stored on All-in-One.
- Stop, pause, resume, and repeat the reading of mail.
- Adjust the speaking rate at which mail is read.

DECtalk Mail Access includes a telephone interface with voice prompts and a help facility to allow the user to access messages easily.

■ Voice-to-Text Conversion

In voice-to-text systems, also called voice recognition systems, the computer listens to the human voice and transforms it into text. **Voice recognition** is the ability of the computer to transform the wavelengths of the human voice into computer text. Voice input activates a recognition program in the computer that translates voice into a code to which the computer can respond. Current voice systems are speaker-dependent: The system recognizes only the voice that has trained it.

A voice recognition system allows text either to be viewed on a computer or to be printed without someone having to transcribe and edit the material. Since the services of a transcriptionist are bypassed, productivity and efficiency are increased. Kurzweil Applied Intelligence has developed and applied *Kurzweil Voice works (KVW)*, a voice recognition system with a working vocabulary of between 5,000 and 10,000 spoken words or phrases. Vocabulary can be expanded by creating trigger words or phrases for calling up standardized or repetitive text. This approach works like computer keyboard macros; one or two words instantly bring an entire paragraph or page of text to the screen.

The primary application of KVW is to automate the creation of written text, the fundamental activity in the office. Once users train KVW to understand their speech patterns, they can use the telephone to dictate text and immediately see the words appear on the screen as they are spoken.

KVW overcomes voice recognition problems of limited accuracy, insufficient vocabulary size, and excessive sensitivity to background sound. Other problems of speech recognition systems are dealing with continuous versus discrete speech and handling the normal variations in speech that occur from one person to another.

VoiceEM. A successful application of voice recognition is described at the beginning of the chapter and shown in Figure 10-13. VoiceEM was developed by Dr. Arthur L. Chambers, III, director of Emergency Services at Nash General Hospital, Rocky Mount, North Carolina. The Kurzweil VoiceEM system has a 1000-word vocabulary that meets emergency room needs.

Future Market. Despite the increasing demands for written documents, the supply of secretarial staff and skilled legal and medical transcriptionists continues to shrink. With diminished support, the work force has had to become progressively more self-sufficient. Speech recognition can help to offset the general lack of typing and computer skills. A major applica-

FIGURE 10-13 **Emergency Room Doctor Dictates to Computer**

Courtesy of Kurzweil Applied Intelligence.

tion of voice recognition will be automatic dictation and transcription or "voicewriting."

Digitized Speech Compared to Synthesized Speech. Users tend to prefer digitized rather than synthesized voice. Although digitized voice requires more disk storage than synthesized voice, it more closely resembles the intonation of the human voice. However, office applications are combining digitized voice with voice synthesis. For example, when you call your bank for your current balance, a digitized voice greets you, but a synthesized voice tells you your balance.

Combining the Three Technologies: Digitized Speech, Speech Synthesis, Voice Recognition. DEC's DECvoice Response System incorporates these three technologies, as illustrated at the beginning of the chapter. DECvoice transforms the ordinary telephone into an efficient information delivery system by enabling callers to communicate interactively with a database to enter and retrieve information. Many applications require more than one voice processing technology to ensure effective interaction with a database. A cash management application, for example, might require voice recognition as a supplement to touch-tone input to enable non-touch-tone telephone users to input account numbers. Up-to-date account information—account balances, credit card balance, interest rates, credit line, last loan payment, and so on—would be provided by synthesized speech. Similarly, a field service dispatching application might use synthesized speech for relaying information from the database to callers, digitized voice to allow callers to leave comments, and voice recognition to permit the use of non-touch-tone telephones to access the database.

Types of Voice Processing Systems

An organization that is considering the installation of a digitized voice processing system can select one of the following options: a stand-alone system, an integrated PBX or Centrex system, an automated office system, or a service bureau.

■ Stand-Alone Voice Processing Systems

A **stand-alone voice processing system** (also called freestanding) as shown in Figure 10-14 performs the basic voice processing functions: telephone answering, message store-and-forward, and call routing. Some systems use a dedicated microcomputer for programming its operation. Other systems require at least an IBM PC XT or an equivalent with a 20-megabyte hard

FIGURE 10-14 **Stand-Alone Voice Processing Equipment**

Courtesy of Brooktrout Technology, Inc.

disk, a voice data board inserted into one of its expansion slots, and voice processing software.

A stand-alone system connects to a telephone system through a single-line extension; many stand-alone systems can also interface with PBX and Centrex systems. When interfaced to a PBX, the system can perform transaction processing and information retrieval, to be explained in the next section on voice processing applications. Stand-alone systems are intended for businesses with five to ten telephones and also are suitable for individuals and small employee groups, such as a department within a larger company.

■ Integrated Voice Processing Systems

Voice processing systems can be integrated with PBX or Centrex systems by using a special communications link between the two systems whereby each can give certain commands to the other. For example, the voice processing system can tell the PBX to turn the message waiting light on for a particular phone. Or the PBX can tell the voice processing system that "the call being forwarded on Line 4 is coming from extension 789 because it was busy." An **integrated voice processing system** offers users advanced features such as the following:

- A *message notification feature* alerts the subscriber that a message is waiting.
- A *message delivery feature* allows a subscriber's calls to be forwarded automatically to his or her voice mailbox, to an operator, or to another extension

FIGURE 10-15 Voice Processing Configuration: DVX Network®

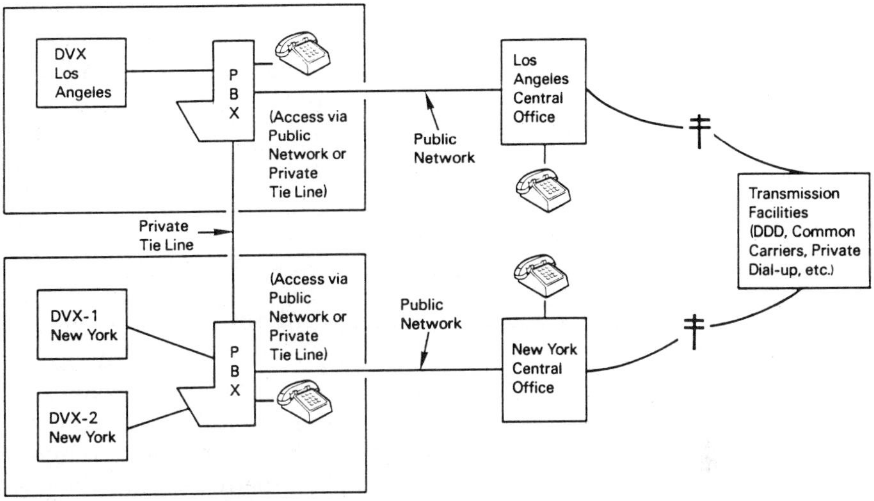

Courtesy of Wang Laboratories, Inc. ®Trademark of Wang Laboratories, Inc.

after a certain number of rings or when the subscriber does not wish to be disturbed by a ringing phone. With unintegrated systems the user must have two telephone numbers, a PBX or Centrex number and a voice mailbox number; callers must dial a second number to reach a voice mailbox number if the caller does not answer the telephone.

- The *transfer to operator feature* allows a caller inside the voice mail system to transfer out of that system and go to a human attendant.

Some PBX vendors offer voice processing as an option. Integration on a PBX system usually requires an addition of a minicomputer that is dedicated to voice processing applications and a control channel for the exchange of information, such as called party's identify, between the minicomputer and the PBX. Whether an organization has the option of implementing voice processing with Centrex depends on the capabilities of the local telephone company's central office. Figure 10-15 shows how Wang's voice processing system connects internal and external calls to the company's PBX.

■ **Automated Office Systems**

Voice processing systems are also integrated with automated (comprehensive) office systems, such as Wang Laboratories' Wang Integrated Office Solution (WIOS), Digital Equipment Corporation's All-in-One, IBM's Professional Office System (PROFS), and Data General's Comprehensive

Electronic Office (CEO). **Automated office systems** typically offer the following features:

- *Automated attendant* allows all incoming calls to be answered automatically and gives the caller the choice of entering the desired extension number, talking to an operator, or leaving a voice message.
- *Voice messaging* allows a WIOS user to retrieve, create, reply to, or forward voice messages by following the display prompts and pressing the appropriate key on the system. Telephone conversations can also be recorded by using this feature.

- **Service Bureaus**

Service bureaus offer companies the use of voice applications without the expense of purchasing their own systems. Service bureaus place storage space on their computers at the disposal of subscribers. Users access the bureau's own computer through a local or 800 number. This approach allows a company to explore voice messaging before purchasing a system and at the same time provides the company, especially one with widespread locations, with a quick way to establish a messaging network.

For example, GTE Telemessager, a service bureau, has voice mail computers in twelve of the nation's cities. Companies rent mailboxes on Telemessager's computers. Examples of other companies that offer service bureau equipment are VMX, Commter, WISC, Async Voice Message Service, and Wang Information Service Corporation SVX Service Bureau.

Subscribers pay a one-time setup fee, a monthly rental charge for each mailbox, and connect time charges. Although fees vary by service bureau, number of mailboxes on the system, and extent of service, the cost of basic monthly service per mailbox ranges from $20 to $30 plus phone charges.

Voice Processing Functions and Applications

A voice processing system can provide one or more of the following functions: telephone answering, caller routing, interactive messaging, information providing, and transactions processing. A voice processing application often includes two or more of these functions. Each of these functions is described below with examples of applications.

- **Telephone Answering**

Telephone answering allows subscribers and nonsubscribers to leave messages for subscribers as they would on an ordinary telephone answering machine. The system "plays" a recorded greeting to a caller and proceeds to take the caller's message. Once the system receives a message, it can phone the called party at any remote telephone location with news that a message is waiting.

Both voice processing systems and telephone answering machines accept and store messages from any telephone for later playback by the intended recipient. The similarity of these message-handling systems ends there. A simple telephone answering device provides analog message recordings on magnetic tape of 30 to 60 minutes duration and generally serves a single user. Voice processing systems record messages in computer memory rather than on magnetic tape; thus they can provide hundreds of hours of storage time for thousands of users.

■ Caller Routing

Caller routing, also known as "automated attendant," manages the system by answering calls and allowing callers to route themselves to the desired extension by keying the appropriate button on a touch-tone telephone. Callers hear a recorded message that presents them with a menu of options, as shown in Figure 10-16. Some system software allows callers to key the employee's name, rather than the extension, to automatically route their calls.

A caller should be offered a menu of no more than six choices at one time, three choices being the ideal number. Otherwise, the caller might not

FIGURE 10-16 Routing Calls: Aspen® Customized Call Routing Menu

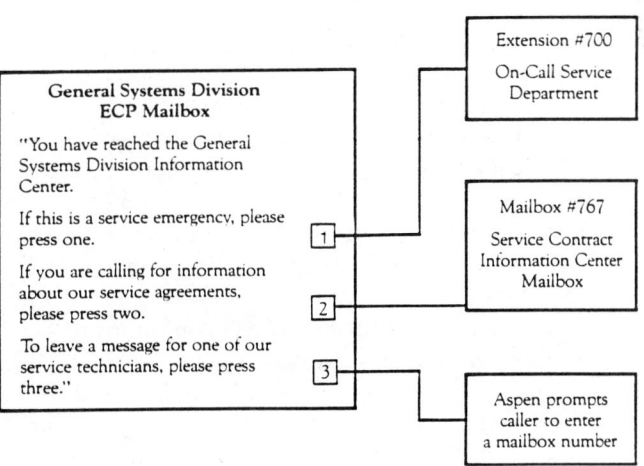

Redrawn courtesy of Octel Communications Corporation. ®Registered trademark of Octel Communications Corporation.

be able to remember the various options to make satisfactory decisions. A caller tends to remember the first and last choices but not the ones in between.

■ Interactive Messaging

Interactive messaging, also called "voice mail" or **voice store-and-forward**, provides for "nonsimultaneous" conversations that allow a subscriber to send messages to one or more subscribers or groups of subscribers as well as to reply to these and other voice messages.

For example, an executive could inform a half dozen managers that a meeting has been canceled without having to place individual calls. The voice processing system will dial a list of telephone numbers and deliver a spoken message to each one.

■ Information Providing

Information providing, also called "audiotex," is a voice bulletin board that gives a caller access to prerecorded information in a listen-only mode. A caller is directed to a section of a computer's prerecorded files—a voice mailbox that contains a prerecorded message containing the information that the caller seeks.

The caller reaches the mailbox by using a telephone keypad to key numbers in response to prerecorded telephone prompts. The caller is then told that he or she is to make a choice; then the choices are explained. On completion the audiotex asks the caller for a decision. However, the caller can interrupt at any time and make a choice. Messages can be recorded live as in voice mail or constructed from a vocabulary of natural-voice, prerecorded words and/or phrases.

Public bulletin boards allow nonsubscribers to call in and hear a variety of prerecorded announcements. *Subscriber bulletin* boards are password-protected. Only subscribers can hear these announcements. Any number of callers can access the same bulletin board simultaneously.

The first major audiotex application based on digitized voice, Dow-Phone, was introduced by Dow Jones and Company in 1984. For a yearly fee plus charges for connect time, Dow Jones provides subscribers with a voice bulletin board of the latest finance news and stock information. This service is provided through direct communication with Voicemail International.

Another audiotex user is the airline industry. Airline companies offer arrival and departure information and flight schedules by telephone. The opening of this chapter describes American Airline's use of audiotex.

Physicians can dial Medical Economics, an audiotex service that publishes updates to the *Physician's Desk Reference*. For example, physicians can seek information on drug interactions by just keying in the code number for the drug in question and listening to the update.

■ Transaction Processing

Transaction processing, also referred to as "voice response," provides a telephone interface with an external computer for access to its database or other information, such as order entry. The voice processing system asks the caller a series of prerecorded questions using digitized speech. The caller responds by keying numbers on his or her keypad. The system then provides the requested information by converting textual machine-readable code in the database into synthesized human speech.

For example, transaction processing can allow bank customers to use any phone to access an 800 number to their bank and then key in their passwords and account numbers to find out about their accounts. A synthesized voice responds, giving information about their bank balances, credit card payments, and whether certain checks have been cashed. To transfer deposits between bank accounts, a digitized and/or synthesized voice leads the caller through the steps to complete the transaction. The customer responds by pressing appropriate buttons on the telephone keypad.

Benefits and Drawbacks of Voice Processing

■ Benefits of Voice Processing

Voice processing provides the following benefits.

Elimination of Telephone Tag. The most frequently mentioned benefit of voice processing, particularly voice mail, is the elimination of the time waster—telephone tag. Since voice mail is a one-way form of messaging, it does not require the recipient to be present to receive a message. Once the caller delivers a voice message, the caller can forget about it. The caller knows that the recipient will receive the message.

With voice mail, any caller who must contact people in different time zones can do so easily, as described in the first scenario at the beginning of this chapter. The caller leaves the message in the recipient's voice mailbox when convenient. The recipient retrieves the message in his or her time frame. Communication is faster, more efficient, and convenient for both the caller and the recipient. Since less time is spent volleying with the telephone, productivity increases.

Easy Access. Voice response can be accessed by anyone with a pushbutton telephone. Rotary telephones and pulse-dial pushbutton telephones can be used by attaching a *tone generator*—a device that produces the same tones as

FIGURE 10-17 Tone Generators

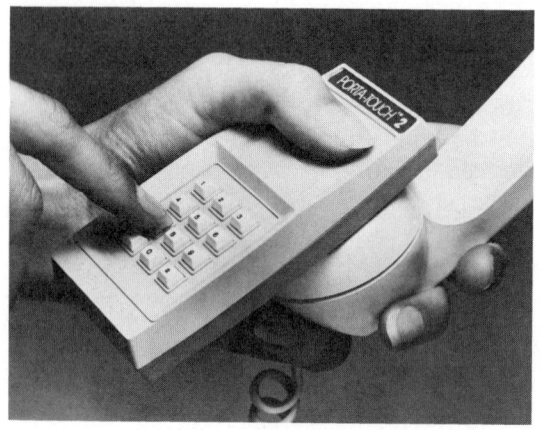

(a) Permanent Adaptor Added to an Existing Telephone

(b) Battery-Operated Portable Adaptor

Courtesy of Periphonics Corporation, 4000 Veterans Highway, Bohemia, NY 11716.

a touch-tone telephone—to input commands. Figure 10-17 shows two types of tone generators.

Relative Ease of Use. Voice processing can be used by individuals who are not keyboard-oriented, such as managers and other executives.

Capability to Combine with Other Electronic Systems. Voice processing can be used in combination with other electronic systems, such as electronic mail systems.

No Unanswered Calls. With a voice processing system, no call is left on hold when an extension is busy or does not answer. The system is available 24 hours a day, seven days a week.

Privacy. Because each person is assigned his or her own voice mailbox, confidential information can be left for the recipient.

Shorter Call. The length of an average telephone conversation is between four and five minutes, whereas the length of a voice processing call is about one minute or less.

Convenient One-Way Communication. System users, whether in the office or elsewhere, can retrieve stored messages from any location and send messages to other voice processing subscribers—just by using any touch-tone telephone.

PBX and Centrex Connections. Voice processing functions can be integrated with private branch exchange (PBX) and Centrex systems.

Reduced Costs. The cost of computer hardware has decreased, as has the cost of information storage. With compression techniques, large amounts of digitized voice can be stored using less memory than was possible in earlier voice systems. Systems that originally cost hundreds of thousands of dollars could be purchased for less than $100,000 by 1989. Low-end voice products have also emerged; some systems are available for less than $1000.

Reduced Number of Interoffice Memos. Broadcasting permits two or more recipients to hear exactly the same message delivered in the caller's voice.

■ Drawbacks of Voice Processing

Although voice processing systems can enhance a company's productivity, an incoming caller should be able to return to a human operator at any time. In some working areas, such as sales and customers complaints, a human operator might be preferred for all incoming calls. Other drawbacks of voice processing systems are the following.

No Common Terminology. The manufacturers of various voice processing systems are not consistent in the use of terms. For example, the term "call processing" might mean "telephone answering" to some manufacturers, while to others the term encompasses all of the voice processing functions.

No Technical Standards for Voice Processing Systems. Companies with large voice processing systems and vendors of these systems support adopting the Audio Message Interchange Standard (AMIS) for voice processing systems. AMIS would establish a uniform means of transmitting control information and messages between heterogeneous systems, its adoption making it possible to network voice processing systems from different vendors.

High Costs for Voice Processing Systems. Although voice processing system costs are decreasing, they are still considered to be more costly than other forms of electronic messaging.

User Resistance. Some people cannot talk easily to a machine and will simply hang up on reaching a voice processing system.

No Written Records. Voice mail provides no written record of the messages unless someone takes time to transcribe them or a voice recognition/response system is used, such as VoiceEM.

Selecting a Voice Processing System

Before selecting a voice processing system, a company must determine whether a voice processing system is needed.

The suggested plan consists of three phases: (1) analyzing the present internal and external methods of communicating, (2) specifying the requirements of the voice processing system, and (3) selecting the voice processing system.

Phase 1: Analyze the company's present methods of communicating, both internally and externally. Obtain the following information:

- What is the company's volume of calls? Check telephone statements.
- What is the pattern of external correspondence? Information can be obtained from department employees and the company's mail department.
- What is the pattern of internal correspondence? Information can be obtained from department employees and the company's mail department.
- What are the company's calling activities? Information can be obtained from the company's telephone operators.

Phase 2: Specify the requirements of the voice processing system. If your analysis results in a decision to install a voice processing system, then conduct a traffic analysis to determine the requirements of the system. Obtain the following information:

- What is the desired message-handling capacity?
- What is the minimum number of tie trunks that will be needed?
- How many more trunk lines, extensions, etc. will be needed?
- How many users expect to use the system?
- What is the range of message length?
- Will the existing PBX need to be modified? If so, what are the needed modifications that will be needed?

To be certain that the system will have sufficient capacity to operate satisfactorily at all times, periodically conduct a traffic analysis to determine whether the system needs updating.

Phase 3: Select the voice processing system. Use the checklist in Figure 10-18 to evaluate each system (usually two or three) being considered. Also talk to other customers of the vendor(s) you are considering. Your options include renting or purchasing voice processing equipment or obtaining the services of a service bureau. Often a company will experiment with voice mail by first renting mailboxes from a service bureau. This experience helps the company to determine its voice processing system requirements and to decide whether it should buy or rent equipment.

FIGURE 10-18 **Voice Processing System Checklist**

Use this checklist to evaluate each voice processing system being considered.
Company: _____ Product: _____

System Architecture
- Can the system expand by adding ports and disk storage?
    Single node maximum number of ports:
    Single node maximum number of hours:
- Does the system have networking capabilities? If yes, what is the network system capacity?   Number of ports: Number of hours:
- How many mailbox addresses are available for users?
- Can the manufacturer's smallest system grow into its largest?
- Can the system support batch networking?
- Can the system interface with Centrex, key systems, and most PBXs?
- Does the system integrate with any PBXs? Which ones?
- Does the system have redundant message and user directories?
- Is a random-access storage device available for backup and system updates?
- Does the system have special tone detection circuits?
- Can additional processors and memory be added when more ports are added?
- Does the system need a special environment (air conditioning, flooring)?
- Is battery backup available?

System Management Features
- Are messages date and time stamped?
- Are there menu-driven commands? How many?
- Does the system provide usage reports such as:
    Traffic statistics   Message traffic by type of message   Billing reports
    System disk use   Users reports
- Can the system be maintained in-house?
- Does the system have remote diagnostics?
- Can group distribution lists be created? How many?

User Capabilities
- Can outside callers do the following:
    Listen to their own message before sending it?
    Erase and rerecord their message?
    Add to their message after they have reviewed it?
    Mark a message urgent?
    Return to the operator?
    Leave a message in more than one mailbox without returning to the operator?
- Can users send the same message to several destinations?
- Can users hear destinations confirmed?
- Are different delivery options available, including priority and future delivery?
- Can special listen-only mailboxes be provided?
- Are help prompts available at all decision points?
- Can each user record his name?
- Can system greetings be selected instead of personal greetings?
- Are there user directories?
- Can each user change his or her password?
- Does the system support message waiting notification?
- Is training provided?

Courtesy of TELECONNECT Magazine, New York, NY. September 1987, p. 139.

Summary

Installing a voice processing system soon changes the way a company performs its tasks. Voice processing is the generic term that includes the following functions: telephone answering, caller routing, interactive messaging, information providing, and transaction processing. Advances in the technologies now make it possible for a computer to speak written text, to convert speech into text, and to answer and respond to any person conversing with it.

The selection of a voice processing system should first include an analysis of the present internal and external methods of communicating. If a system is to be installed, the system's requirements are determined by a traffic analysis, followed by periodic analyses to maintain satisfactory operation. The selection of a voice processing system is based on the system architecture, system management features, and user capabilities.

■ Key Terms

Broadcast feature
Digitized speech
Phonemes
Speech synthesis
Voice processing
Voice processing functions:
   Caller routing (automated attendant)

Information providing (audiotex)
Interactive messaging (voice mail)
Telephone answering
Transaction processing (voice response)
Voice processing systems:
   Automated office system

Integrated voice processing system
Service bureaus
Stand-alone voice processing system
Voice recognition
Voice store-and-forward

■ Self-Quiz

Indicate whether the statement is true or false.

1. Voice processing can be sent and retrieved from any telephone that has access to the network. T/F
2. The first completely integrated voice messaging system was introduced by Rolm Corporation in 1982. T/F
3. Messages are stored on a computer disk by converting them to analog signals. T/F
4. The computer can deliver a voice message that is constructed from words and/or phrases that have been prerecorded and stored. T/F
5. For voice processing systems, the standard grades of service are P.02, P.03, and P.05. T/F
6. The number of ports on a voice processing system determines the number of users who can access the system at the same time. T/F

Complete each of the following statements.

1. Basic units of sounds that make up words are called _____ .
2. An example of a text-to-speech system is _____ .
3. The ability of the computer to transform the wavelengths of the human voice into computer text is called _____ .
4. The type of voice processing system intended for small business with five to ten telephones is the _____ .
5. The voice processing feature that allows a subscriber to automatically send the same voice message to multiple mailboxes with one command is the _____ .
6. The voice processing feature that allows a subscriber to add comments to a message before rerouting it to others is the _____ .

Match Column A with Column B.

Column A
(a) Audiotex
(b) Automated attendant
(c) Telephone answering
(d) Voice mail
(e) Voice processing
(f) Voice response

Column B
____ 1. Records the caller's message in computer memory.
____ 2. Answers calls and allows callers to route themselves to the desired extension.
____ 3. Dials a list of calls and delivers a spoken message to each one.
____ 4. Gives a caller access to prerecorded information in a "listen-only" mode.
____ 5. Includes all of the voice system's functions.
____ 6. Asks the caller a series of prerecorded questions using digitized speech and provides requested information by converting textual machine-readable code in the database into synthesized human speech.

■ *Review Questions*

1. How does a voice processing system differ from a telephone answering machine? From a computer-based message system?
2. Describe how a subscriber receives voice messages on a voice processing system.
3. Which voice processing feature would you use for each of the following situations:
   (a) You have just received a voice message. Before you send it to your superior, you would like to add a comment.
   (b) You would like to send the same voice memo to all of the members of three departments.
   (c) You would like to know the number of incoming calls for yesterday.

(d) You would like to make some changes to the message you just recorded.
4. What are the basic components of a voice processing system for digitized speech?
5. How many ports should a company order to support a voice processing system that has a weighted average of 6.0 minutes per user, 14% busy hour peak, and 900 potential users at P.02 grade of service? Refer to Figure 10-8.
6. (a) How much storage space should a company order to support a voice processing system that has a weighted average storage requirement of 4.0 minutes per user and 900 potential users at P.02 grade of service? Refer to Figure 10-10.
   (b) Could you manage with less than the recommended storage space? Explain.
7. How do digitized speech, speech synthesis, and voice recognition systems differ?
8. How does a stand-alone voice processing system differ from an integrated one?
9. What types of costs does a company subscriber to a voice processing service bureau pay?
10. What functions can a voice processing system perform? Give an example of each.
11. How can audiotex help a company? Give an example.
12. (a) What are the advantages of a voice processing system?
    (b) What are the disadvantages of a voice processing system?
13. What factors should you consider when selecting a voice processing system?

■ Activities/Projects

1. Discuss the following issues.
   (a) How will voice processing affect the way business conducts its operations?
   (b) Should voice processing standards be established that allow messages to be transmitted between heterogeneous systems?
   (c) How will voice synthesis and voice recognition affect office tasks?
2. Arrange to access two or three voice processing systems in order to become familiar with how such a system operates. To identify organizations with these systems, consider large organizations that deal with the public, such as banks, chain hotels, and airlines. They can be accessed through 800 numbers. Also check with your local telephone company for suggestions.
3. Evaluate a voice processing system. Refer to Figure 10-18 in this chapter for suggestions. Prepare a report of your findings.

■ Case: A Paper Nightmare

Over 500 field salespeople are on the road taking orders from wholesalers and retailers. The hundreds of orders that these salespeople generate each day result in a massive paper-handling and order entry operation. Twenty-two home-office employees are required to open mail and process the day's orders.

Order entry error rates are running close to 5%, and the manual operation costs run an average of $2.75 per order. The average order takes three days from the time the salesperson is in the store followed by his or her mailing the order to the company until the order is loaded for processing on the company's computer. Confirmation of an order is mailed soon afterward.

How could a voice processing system help this company? Suggest how the company could use one or more of the voice processing functions to solve its nightmare.

Notes

1. Harry Whittelsey, "Talking Mailboxes," *Management World*, February/March, 1987, p. 34.
2. *The Book on Voice Processing* (Bohemia, N.Y.: Periphonics Corporation, 1982).

Additional Readings

Tobin L. Alexander, "Voice Processing," *Data Base Monthly*, September 1987, pp. 44–46.

Tom Bidgett and Kathy Spurgeon, "Voice Processing Applications: Laying the Foundation for the Technology of Tomorrow," *Digital News*, December 1988, pp. 39T–46T.

Sam Dickey, "Getting the Message with Voice Mail," *Today's Office*, July 1987, pp. 47–51.

S. F. Ehrlich, E. A. Akiba, and L. K. Munson, *The Organizational Impact of Voice State and Forward Technology* (Lowell, Mass.: Wang Laboratories, Inc., 1983).

Paul F. Finnigan and James G. Meade, "Audiotex: The Telephone as Data-Access Equipment," *Data Communications*, November 1986.

James L. Flanagan, "Synthesis and Recognition of Speech: Teaching Computers to Listen," *Bell Laboratories Record*, May/June 1981, pp. 146–151.

James E. Greene and Joe and Marks S. Elliott, "Can We Talk," *Communication Age*, January 1986.

John Hunter, "By Word of Mouth," *Network World*, September 25, 1989, pp. 55–62, 86.

Paul Kneisel, "Talking Data," *Inbound/Outbound Magazine*, October 1989, pp. 24–28.

Megin J. Paznik, "Voice Mail: Pitfalls and Promises," *Administrative Management*, March 1987, pp. 16–25.

Daniel I. Stusser, "Technology Now Offers More Than Just Voice Mail," *TPT*, July 1987, pp. 18–28.

Voice Processing Demonstrations

For demonstrations of how one or more voice processing systems operate, telephone the following numbers. These demonstrations enable you to interact with a voice recognition, a digitized voice, or a voice synthesis system.

Digital Equipment Corporation (DECvoice): (508) 493-8255
Natural Microsystems Corporation: (800) 692-8766 or (508) 651-2186 (in MA)
OKI Semiconductor: (800) 832-6654 Extension 462
Texas Instruments: (512) 250-4114

CHAPTER 11

Facsimile

Facsimile Defined

Facsimile Evolution

Facsimile Technology
  Fax System Components
  Sending and Receiving
  Printing
  Transmission Facility

Facsimile Equipment Standards
  Classification of Fax Machines
  Machine Protocol and Transmission

Facsimile Equipment
  Types of Equipment
  Placement of Equipment
  Equipment Features
  Special Fax Equipment

Public Facsimile Services
  Users of Public Fax Services
  Companies Offering Public Fax Services
  Services Available to Fax Owners

Facsimile Applications

Benefits and Drawbacks of Facsimile
  Benefits of Facsimile
  Drawbacks of Facsimile

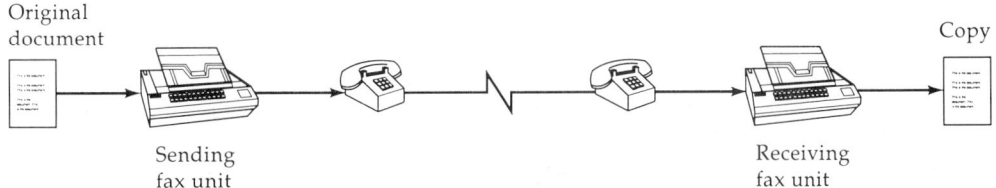

Selecting a Fax System
    Phase 1: Evaluate Your Current Delivery System
    Phase 2: Select a Fax System

CHAPTER OBJECTIVES

After studying this chapter, you should be able to

1. Define facsimile.
2. Describe how a facsimile system operates.
3. Specify facsimile equipment standards.
4. Select appropriate facsimile features and/or equipment.
5. Describe public/private facsimile services.
6. Select a facsimile system.

Shannon, Gracey, Ratliff and Miller, the largest law firm in Fort Worth, Texas, doesn't worry about whether important papers will get to their destination in time. The company uses facsimile machines to send their documents—at a transmission speed of 16 seconds per page. To send a large number of documents quickly by any other means would result in prohibitive mailing costs. When desired, these facsimile machines can be easily programmed to transmit without an operator in attendance. Liquid Air of Walnut Creek, California, one of the nation's four largest manufacturers and distributors of industrial and commercial gases, relies heavily on facsimile transmission to send messages between its Walnut Creek headquarters and its twelve regional administrative offices as well as to receive fast responses from customers. Sending a four-page letter by regular mail at 25 cents is cheaper, but it takes a week for the letter to travel from Walnut Creek to New York City and another week for a response. With facsimile transmission, messages are received within seconds.[1]

These companies are using a form of electronic mail called "fax," short for facsimile. The term "fax" can be used as a noun ("I sent the document on my fax."), as an adjective ("My fax number is in the directory."), or as a verb ("Fax me that document immediately."). This chapter discusses technology, equipment, and applications necessary for selecting and managing a facsimile system.

Facsimile Defined

Facsimile (fax) transmission is the sending and/or receiving of an exact replica—a facsimile—of the original document from one location to another by using communication lines, as shown in Figure 11-1. Just about any type of document—copies of typewritten and handwritten documents, graphs, charts, business forms, weather maps, fingerprints, signatures, and photographs—can be sent to any location in the world that has a telephone line and a fax hookup. Although a fax unit can resemble an office copier, as shown in Figure 11-2, it differs in being able to send and receive copies over telephone lines. In fact, fax is sometimes referred to as telecopying—photocopying at a distance.

Facsimile Evolution

The first fax system, the transmission of a crude image over a short distance, was patented by Scottish clockmaster Alexander Bain in 1842. Yet fax remained a relatively underutilized technology until Xerox launched its "long-distance xerography" in 1962 and the Carterfone court decision in 1969 permitted fax documents to be sent over regular telephone lines. Still, busi-

FIGURE 11-1 The Facsimile System

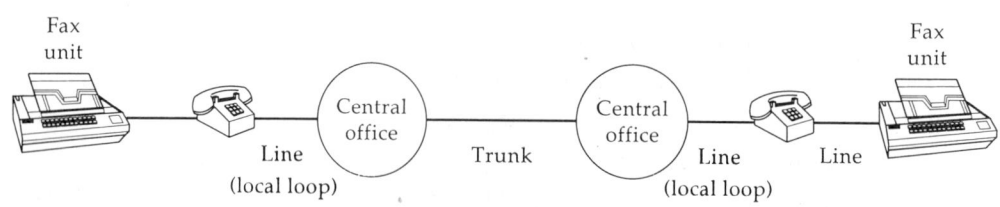

nesses were slow to use fax systems because of costly equipment and long-distance transmission costs, slow transmission speed, poor copy quality, and noncompatible equipment.

About a decade ago, the Japanese discovered that fax would overcome the incompatibility of their complex Kanji alphabet. Since all international standards for communicating text are based on the Roman alphabet, the Japanese were required to translate their native Kanji to the Roman alphabet for telex transmission and then back to Kanji for use at the receiving end. This procedure not only was time-consuming but also resulted in meanings being lost when translated. By revitalizing fax the Japanese not only eliminated time consumption and translations but became the major manufacturer and user of fax.

Since 1980, advances in fax technology and decreasing equipment transmission costs have overcome previous fax problems and stimulated fax use by business. The U.S. fax market is led by Japanese office automation companies that manufacture and market these systems. Fax units are sold primarily by fax manufacturers directly and by office product dealers. The leading fax distributors in the United States are Canon USA, Fujitsu Imaging Systems of America, Harris/3M, Murata Business Systems, NEC America, Panafax Corporation, Pitney-Bowes Facsimile Systems, Ricoh Corporation, Sharp Electronics Corporation, and Xerox Corporation.

CAP International, Inc., a marketing and research company in electronics imaging based in Norwell, Massachusetts, reports that as of January 1989, approximately 2 million fax units were installed in the United States. CAP forecasts compounded annual growth rates of 43.2% from 1986 to 1992,

FIGURE 11-2 A Facsimile Machine

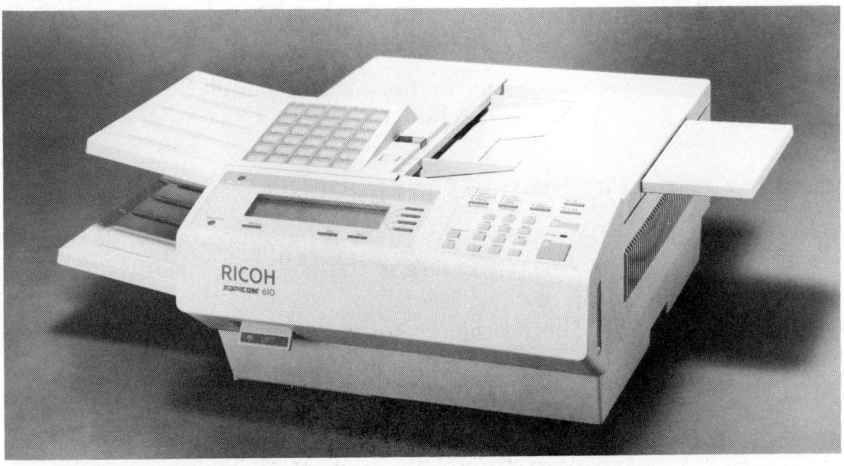

Courtesy of Ricoh Corporation.

created a $2 billion market by 1989. By the year 2000, nearly every business in the United States will have a facsimile machine.[2]

The largest growth area for fax is small business. Of the 3 million small businesses with twenty or fewer employees, only 3% are currently using fax. Fax systems are now more affordable and can easily be cost-justified. As more and more businesses use fax machines, they will expect others, such as their suppliers and customers, also to have these devices. In fact, the question "What is your fax number?" is being asked as often as "What is your telephone number?" Fax numbers are now an essential part of business card and letterhead information.

A second large growth area for fax is large businesses. Although most large businesses already own at least one fax unit, many of them need additional units to move documents instantaneously within the organization, particularly when the company has multiple locations.

Facsimile Technology

Facsimile is a system that converts hard copy images into signals suitable for transmission over communication lines. Connected to telephone company lines, as shown in Figure 11-3, a fax machine first scans the original document and then converts the scanned image into analog or digital signals for transmission by the public switched telephone network, fiber optics, microwave radio, or satellite communications. The receiving fax machine reconverts the signals into a duplicate—a "fax"—of the original image. As shown in the diagram in Figure 11-3, the transceiver connects to the electrical power, a telephone instrument, and the telephone line by an FCC certified jack. It is also possible to provide a temporary, indirect connection to the telephone line by using an acoustic coupler. The connection is made by placing the handset directly onto the acoustic coupler. Before transmitting, the acoustic coupler requires the sender to establish verbal contact with the receiver via the telephone. The connection is then made by placing the telephone handset directly in the ports of the coupler unit. Figure 11-3 also describes how to use a fax machine to send and receive documents.

■ Fax System Components

A facsimile system consists of four components: a fax transmitter (document scanner), a modem, a transmission facility, and a fax receiver (recorder or printer).

The *transmitter* (document scanner) scans the original document and converts the images into electronic signals for transmission.

The *modem* at the transmitting site changes the electronic signals into audible signals that are acceptable to the transmission facility and tests the line to determine the speed of the data.

The *transmission facility*, such as the public switched telephone network, connects the sending and receiving stations and transmits the data to the

FIGURE 11-3 **Fax Machine Operation**

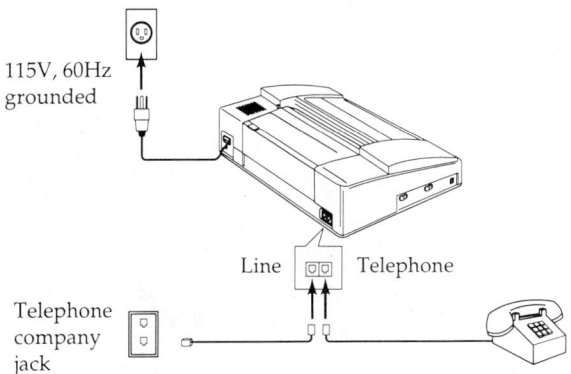

1. Prepare your fax machine for sending and receiving documents.
   Connect your fax machine to a telephone line—the network over which the fax machine communicates to another fax machine.
   Connect your fax machine to a telephone instrument.
   Plug your fax unit into an electrical outlet to obtain power.
   Check that the fax machine contains paper—usually roll paper—to print any document it receives.

2. Send your document.
   Insert your original document into the document feeder of the fax machine.
   Dial the telephone number of the fax machine that is to receive the copy.
   Once the connection is made, press the "transmit" key on your fax machine and a replica of your document will be transmitted.

3. Receive a document.
   To receive a document, turn on your fax machine (or keep your machine on throughout business hours). You do not have to be present to receive a document.

receiving unit. The modem at the receiving end reconverts the audible tones to their former state.

The *receiver* (recorder or printer) accepts and reproduces the data, usually on paper.

Originally, the facsimile transmitter and receiver were separate units. As shown in Figure 11-4, they are now combined into one unit, a **transceiver**, to provide two-way transmission and may have a built-in telephone.

■ **Sending and Receiving**

The transmitter scans the original document and dissects it into minute picture elements called pixels. **Pixels** are tiny dots that form letters, numbers, symbols, and pictures, as shown in Figure 11-5. The number of pixels

FIGURE 11-4 Facsimile Transceiver

Courtesy of Canon U.S.A., Inc.

used for each character determines the resolution or sharpness of the image; the higher the number of pixels, the higher the resolution.

The transmitter focuses reflected light from the original document onto a photoelectrical cell. The contrasting dark and light areas that are picked up by the reflected light are converted into analog or digital signals, depending on the method used.

The *analog processing method* is associated with fax units that transmit at speeds ranging from two to six minutes, while the *digital processing method* refers to fax units that transmit at speeds under one minute.

FIGURE 11-5 Pixels

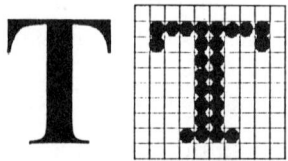

- The **analog processing method** scans every part of an original, such as the characters, the spaces between characters, the spaces between lines, and the margins.
- The **digital processing method** analyzes a document in terms of its actual picture elements and converts them into binary codes of 1's (black) and 0's (white). Since digital signals are more compact than analog ones, digital signals result in faster transmission.

Whether the fax unit uses an analog or a digital processing method, either type of signals must be conditioned or converted by a *modem*. A modem, usually built into the fax transmitting terminal, converts these signals into analog signals that can be sent over an analog communications line. A modem at the receiving end reestablishes the original signals, which activates a *graphic recording device or a printer*. Fax units can transmit both alphanumeric and graphic characters—in other words, any information that can be recorded on paper.

■ Printing

Various methods are used for reproducing or printing documents encoded into fax signals. The most common fax printing methods are also the ones most often used in ordinary office copying.

- The methods that are used for analog transmission are electrolyte and electrosensitive (coated paper techniques) and electrostatic and dielectric (plain paper techniques).
- The methods that are used for digital transmission are thermal printing for low-resolution fax and ink jet or laser printing for high-resolution fax.
- The method that is used for transmitting photographs is the photographic technique.

■ Transmission Facility

Most fax transmissions use the voice channel of the public switched telephone network (PSTN) which requires signals to be in analog form. As discussed in Chapter 2, problems such as signal delay, distortion, and attenuation impair transmission. For example, changes in daily temperature can cause static, while heavy traffic on telephone lines can produce signal interference or crosstalk. Such impairments can result in spurious black and white spots, blank areas, and smearing on the reproduced copy. Transmission alternatives available for fax transmission include the following:

- *Dialup or WATS voice lines that travel through the PSTN.* To overcome noise, some fax systems offer error-clearing capabilities. These systems slow the transmission as necessary and retransmit the document when errors occur.

- *Dedicated (leased, private) telephone lines.* A dedicated line directly connects a fax machine at one location to a fax machine at another location and thus eliminates problems associated with two central office switches and accompanying impairments. A drawback of this alternative is that fax communication is limited to only one remote fax machine. Communication with other fax units is still over the PSTN.
- *Packet-switched data networks.* These networks arrange digital signals in packets that permit easy error checking and efficient routing. Packet-switched networks are more reliable and less costly than direct distance dialing or dedicated telephone lines.
- *Value-added common carriers.* Common carriers with established telephone networks offer fax users special rates to transmit over their lines. They offer options such as full compatibility with all types of fax units, fax features including store-and-forward, and the capability of interfacing with telex networks.

Facsimile Equipment Standards

A fax user must be capable of communicating with other fax users, whether or not they are using the same type of equipment. Fax standards assure users that fax units will be compatible with each other for sending and receiving documents and help prospective purchasers to select units that best meet their needs.

■ Classification of Fax Machines

To establish technological compatibility between units, fax manufacturers are complying with standards recommended by Study Group XIV of the Consultative Committee in International Telephone and Telegraph (CCITT). (The CCITT, a forum for member countries of the United Nations, sets communications standards to facilitate interbrand compatibility for all types of communications equipment. The committee meets every four years to officially sanction the work of its study groups. Study Group XIV was chartered to investigate fax equipment and its operation over various transmission facilities.) The CCITT categorizes fax machines into four groups, based on the transmission speed of an 8½" by 11" sheet of paper. Figure 11-6 describes each group. The higher-speed fax machines save on telephone company charges.

Groups 1, 2, and 3 fax machines use dialup (analog) telephone lines for transmission. Modems change electrical signals so that they are suited for transmission. For example, when Group 3 machines communicate, their digital signals are changed to analog ones for transmission and then reconverted to digital ones at the receiving end. Group 3 machines, the prevailing technology, transmit at a faster rate than Group 1 and Group 2 machines, some Group 3 machines being able to interface with other automated equip-

Facsimile Equipment Standards

FIGURE 11-6 **CCITT Classification of Facsimile Equipment**

Class of Fax Machine	Signal	Transmission Speed of an A4 Page[1] (8½" × 11")	Network(s)	Year Approved by CCITT
Group 1	Analog	4–6 minutes	PSTN[2]	1972
Group 2	Analog	2–3 minutes	PSTN	1976
Group 3	Digital	Less than 1 minute	PSTN	1980
Group 4	Digital	Less than 10 seconds	ISDN, CSDN, PSDN[3]	1988

[1]A4 refers to the standard size of paper (210 × 297 millimeters or 8.27 × 11.69 inches) established by the International Organization of Standards.
[2]Public switched telephone network.
[3]Integrated services digital network, circuit-switched data network, and packet-switched data network are digital networks. Specifications for use of Group 4 fax on the PSTN have not yet been completed.

ment, such as intelligent copiers and microcomputers. Some Group 3 machines have the capability, called **downward capability**, of communicating with Group 1 and/or Group 2 machines, transmitting at the rate of the slower machine.

Group 4 machines require a digital data network rather than an analog network. These units provide faster transmission speeds, error-free transmission, and plain paper printing and copying. They also can interface with other automated equipment. However, Group 4 machines are more expensive than Group 3 machines and are only now becoming commercially available. Figure 11-7 describes the three classes of Group 4 fax machines.

■ Machine Protocol and Transmission

CCITT standards for Group 3 fax units specify machine protocol and transmission including the size of the paper the equipment handles, the way the document is read by the scanner, the code that is used, the methods and speed at which the information is sent, and the protocol by which two units establish contact.

FIGURE 11-7 **Classification of Group 4 Facsimile Equipment**

Class 1 fax machines transmit and receive fax documents only.
Class 2 fax machines transmit fax documents only and receive fax, telex, and mixed-mode (text and images generated from computers and other office systems) documents.
Class 3 fax machines generate, transmit, and receive fax, telex, and mixed-mode documents.

Paper Size. The Group 3 standard requires fax units to handle at least the standard paper size of ISO B4, which is 210 × 297 millimeters (approximately 8½ × 11 inches). An optional paper length is ISO B4, which is 364 millimeters or approximately 14 inches. Or a fax unit may have an "unlimited length of paper" option, which is intended for fax units that do not precut paper to any given length. Paper sizes in the United States and Canada are expressed in inches; in other countries, such as in Germany and Sweden, they are expressed in millimeters, based on the standard sizes established by the International Standards Organization. For example, reference ISO A4 refers to standard 210 × 297 millimeters or 8.27 × 11.69 (approximately 8.5 × 11) inches. To convert from inches to millimeters, multiply by 25.4.

Resolution. Image **resolution** is determined by (1) the size of the smallest character that can be legibly scanned and printed and (2) the sharpness or quality of the fax output. It is expressed in number of horizontal and vertical lines per inch (1pi). Horizontal resolution refers to the number of times a scanner or printing element stops along the width of a page. Vertical resolution refers to the number of times the scanner or printing element stops or marks down the length of a page.

The CCITT Group 3 standard for horizontal resolution requires that the scanner read the entire width of the document up to 8.46 inches (215 mm). The scanner must read 1728 points along the 8.46-inch line, which is equal to approximately 204 lines per inch. The CCITT Group 3 standard for vertical resolution requires that the scanner read these 1728 points 98 times per inch going down the page. As an option, equipment may also read 196 lines per inch to produce a higher-quality image when needed. Lower resolution suffices for text-only documents. A high line-per-inch resolution, which shows more detail, is critical for graphics and other types of image documentation. But resolution is related to transmission time: A decrease in line resolution will decrease the time and cost of transmitting a document. Figure 11-8 lists the standards for image resolution for Groups 3 and 4.

FIGURE 11-8 Standards for Image Resolution for Groups 3 and 4

	Resolution (Horizontal by Vertical Lines per Inch)		
Group 3 Required	200 × 200	200 × 100	
Group 4 Required	Class 1	Class 2	Class 3
	200 × 200	200 × 300	200 × 300
Optional	200 × 300	200 × 200	200 × 200
	200 × 400	200 × 240	200 × 240
		200 × 400	200 × 400

Courtesy of CAP International, Inc., Norwell, MA.

Data Compression Code. The information read by the fax scanner is put into code before it is transmitted. The **data compression code standard** for Group 3 is the **Modified Huffmann code** (MH), a binary, one-dimensional horizontal scheme. As an option, the manufacturer may use a two-dimension code called the **Modified Read code** (MR), which transmits at a faster rate than MH. Some manufacturers also use proprietary codes that transmit at even faster rates. To obtain the faster rates, both the transmitting fax and the receiving fax must employ the same data compression codes. Group 4 uses an advanced version of MR for data compression—a more efficient data compression code than Group 3.

Signaling Rate. As was discussed in Chapter 2, information is transmitted as signals at a certain speed with a modem regulating the operation. The CCITT signaling rate standard for Group 3 is 4800 bits per second (bps) with the ability to slow down to 2400 bps for fax units that can transmit only at this speed. As an option, manufacturers may incorporate 7200 and 9600 bps speeds. Although fax units with lower-speed modems are cheaper, they increase transmission time and thus increase telephone costs. The CCITT standard for Group 4 is 56,000 bps (56 kbps) over data lines.

Protocol. The CCITT has defined the following five phases for the fax process—from establishing contact between the sending and the receiving fax units, to their transmitting documents, and ending with their disconnect. Most fax machines complete these phases automatically.

- Phase A: Call setup (the sending fax and the receiving fax establish contact).
- Phase B: Electronic handshaking (once the fax units have established contact, they must exchange information—electronic signals—to be certain that they are compatible and synchronized. The exchange of preliminary information is known as the **handshake protocol**).
- Phase C: Fax message transmission.
- Phase D: Confirmation (postmessage procedure).
- Phase E: Call release (disconnect).

The protocol for phases A, B, D, and E is commonly referred to as the "T.30 protocol." Phase C is called the "message transmission phase."

Facsimile Equipment

■ Types of Equipment

Fax systems can be classified as stand-alone units, multifunction units, or integrated units.

Stand-Alone Fax Units. Stand-alone fax units do not have multiple functions. They perform only the fax function.

Multifunction Fax Units. Until recently, all fax units were stand-alone devices, but now **multifunction fax units** (hybrid devices) are available. These units combine the fax function with other office technologies, as described in the following examples.

Fax Copier. A fax with a copy function allows the unit to serve as a low-volume copier and to preview fax transmissions. For example, the Xerox Telecopier 7021, shown in Figure 11-9, doubles as a fax unit and a convenience copier. It employs thermal transfer imaging technology that produces copy on cut-sheet bond paper, such as company letterhead. Other fax models include microcomputer technologies, digital copying, and laser printing capabilities.

Faxphone. Figure 11-10 shows a faxphone—a compact desktop unit that combines a fax device and a telephone into one unit. The unit minimizes desk space and preserves fax input and output confidentiality; documents are transmitted from or received directly at the user's desk.

FIGURE 11-9 **Xerox Telecopier 7021**

Courtesy of Xerox Corporation.

FIGURE 11-10 Faxphone

Courtesy of Harris/3M Document Products, Inc., Facsimile Products Division.

Videofax. **Videofax** combines a Group 3 fax unit with a 16-mm camera, a display screen, and a telephone interface. With videofax, users may transmit or receive pictures of three-dimensional objects. Rather than using overnight delivery of the actual object, the image of the object can be transmitted in less than a minute.

Integrated Units. Also available are **integrated fax units**—units that are compatible with other office equipment. By adding an RS-232-C interface to a fax unit, the fax unit can communicate with digital equipment, such as computers and word processors. For example, an interface added to the Xerox Telecopier 7021 shown in Figure 11-9 can turn this fax unit into a printer for a microcomputer.

■ Placement of Equipment

Fax units can be assigned to a *centrally located* mailroom or reprographics (copying) room or can be *decentrally located,* such as being placed on a secretary's or an executive's desk. A decentralized location offers users the assurance of knowing that their transmitted document has been received at its destination. They do not have to worry whether a mailroom clerk has remembered to deliver the document to the intended recipient.

Companies with multiple locations use fax in their intracompany networks. One or more fully featured fax units are often installed in a company's communication center to serve as the hub of the company's network. Less powerful units are placed in the network's satellite locations. For example, a corporation in Houston with twenty-six branches uses a Murata's ImageMaster as a network hub while less sophisticated ImageMate units operate as satellites in each of the branches. The corporation's hub unit sends daily price and inventory updates to each of the satellite fax units.

■ Equipment Features

Fax units offer features that make fax transmission easier and more efficient. Fax manufacturers offer these features as either a standard or an option, depending on the model. Examples of major features are described below and in Figure 11-11.

Unattended Operation. Some fax units can operate without operator assistance, making it possible to send and receive documents automatically. For example, *automatic telephone dialing* allows the unit to dial telephone numbers in an unattended mode. When the receiving unit is busy, *automatic*

FIGURE 11-11 **Facsimile Equipment Features: Descriptions of Selected Features of Facsimile Equipment**

Automatic Answer: Allows the fax machine to receive documents 24 hours a day without an operator in attendance.

Automatic Dialing: A built-in telephone dialer remembers often-used telephone numbers.

Automatic Document Feeder: Automatically feeds documents into the fax machine, allowing the equipment to run unattended, which is especially important during nonworking hours.

Automatic Transmission Reduction: Allows the fax machine before transmission to scan an oversize document up to 11" wide, such as a computer printout, and automatically reduce the document to a width of 8½ inches.

Automatic Voice Request: Allows the sending operator to talk to the receiving operator before or after transmitting.

Downward Capability: Allows a high-speed fax machine to communicate with low-speed machines.

Duplex: Allows the fax machine to simultaneously transmit and receive.

RS-232-C Interface: Allows a fax machine to communicate with telex/TWX, encryption devices for secure transmission, microcomputers, and other digital networks.

Secure Polling: Requires that the polling fax machine use a password to identify itself to the remote station.

Unattended Transmission: Allows the fax machine, at an appointed time, to retrieve a previously dialed telephone number from its memory and transmit the appropriate document.

redialing is available. **Delayed dialing** allows documents to be sent automatically at a later time—when telephone rates are least expensive, such as after office hours, during weekends, or across national or international time zones. **Store-and-forward** allows the fax unit to store documents in its memory for transmission, without operator attendance, when telephone rates are least expensive. *Automatic answer* allows the fax machine to receive documents 24 hours a day without an operator in attendance.

Broadcasts to Multiple Locations. With **sequential broadcasting**, the fax unit automatically sends the same document—one after the other—to multiple locations. With **relay broadcasting**, the fax unit automatically sends a document to an intermediary fax unit, such as a center facsimile unit that contains memory capability and a relay transmission feature, as shown in Figure 11-12. The intermediary fax unit then relays the document to a number of nearby locations. The first document is sent at the long-distance rate, while subsequent documents are relayed at local telephone rates.

For example, a company faxes a document from its New York headquarters to its division in Dallas. The Dallas division then faxes the document to several branches located within its local area at local telephone rates. The company's headquarters saves on long-distance telephone charges to the branches.

Polling. The **polling** feature makes it possible for the fax unit to call a remote fax unit to request transmission from it. For example, a fax unit can instruct another fax unit to transmit a previously loaded document when

FIGURE 11-12 Relay Broadcasting Network

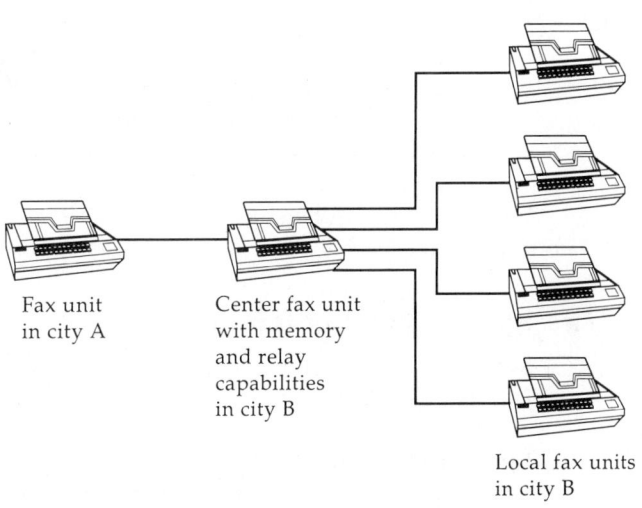

telephone costs are the lowest. This feature requires that the remote unit be able to operate in an unattended mode, although the unit making the request can be attended. **Secure polling** requires that the polling fax unit use a password to identify itself to the remote station.

Other Features. The *transmit terminal identifier* consists of a number and a name that identifies each fax unit. This information is automatically printed at the top of each page along with the date, time, and number of pages. An *activity-reporting feature* provides a record of all transmission and receptions. Other features are *automatic reduction of oversized documents* such as computer printouts, *diagnostic features*, and *notification to the sender of successful transmission*. An *automatic paper cutter* cuts copies to the exact length of the originals, while an *automatic receive reduction* automatically reduces an oversized incoming document to fit the size of paper it is equipped to handle.

Two-Color Facsimile. Two-color fax is now available in a unit that can send and receive in two colors, black and red. A new scanning technology allows two distinct light sources to be integrated into the scanning unit, making it possible to read whether a scanned area is black, red, or white. For transmission to machines that cannot print in two colors, the benefit of highlighting can still be gained; the two-color fax transmits data as a grayscale pattern in the two-color mode. A two-color fax uses special thermal recording paper, the color being printed depending on the heat energy applied from the thermal printing head. The lowest level of heat energy produces black. As the level of heat energy increases, the color changes from black to white and finally, at the highest level, to red.

Document Security. Confidential documents can be protected from security breaches, as follows:

- By coding data, *encryption devices* can protect documents from unauthorized access during transmission. Should a document be intercepted by an unauthorized third party, it cannot be read or understood. For example, Ricoh's Rapicom 200 series Private Fax Interface connects Ricoh transceivers to encryption devices to protect documents from unauthorized access during transmission.
- Documents can be stored in the fax unit's memory and printed out only when the authorized recipient uses a special password.

■ Special Fax Equipment

Examples of special fax equipment are portable fax units, virtual facsimile, and Fax-Alert.

Portable Fax Units. Portable fax units, equipped with a carrying case or an attached handle, weigh less than fifteen pounds and can be attached to any public, private, or cellular telephone. Figure 11-13 shows the OMNIFAX

FIGURE 11-13   Portable Fax Equipment

Courtesy of OMNIFAX/Telautograph Corporation.

GT portable facsimile unit, which comes with its own carrying case, and gives the business traveler fast and convenient fax communications while away from the office. Although some portables are powered by batteries, most units require a standard 115 volt VAC electrical outlet. They connect to the telephone line by using a RJ-11 jack. If the telephone is permanently wired into the wall, an acoustic coupler is essential. A special jack is available to connect a portable fax unit to a cellular car phone. A fax machine used in a car can be powered by direct connection to the car's battery. The car lighter should not be used as a power source, as it can damage the lighter's circuit.

Virtual Facsimile.   An alternative to **traditional facsimile**—one that uses a transceiver—is **virtual facsimile**, which uses a microcomputer. The configuration of virtual fax consists of three separate components: a microcomputer with a fax modem board inserted into one of its empty slots; a laser printer, and an image (OCR) scanner. A fax board, acting as a high-speed modem, turns the microcomputer into a fax unit and, with the necessary computer software, converts computer files into standard fax format. With the fax board the microcomputer can send and receive documents or other images directly from the microcomputer to a Group 3 or Group 4 fax machine or to another microcomputer equipped with a fax board. Or, if preferred, documents received via fax transmission can be printed by a laser printer.

Hard copy documents can also be entered into a microcomputer without keyboarding. By connecting the fax board to a scanner unit, information on the hard copy is scanned and faxed into the microcomputer, where it is reviewed, edited, stored, and/or faxed to another fax machine. Figure 11-14 shows a diagram of faxing using a microcomputer.

FIGURE 11-14 Virtual Facsimile

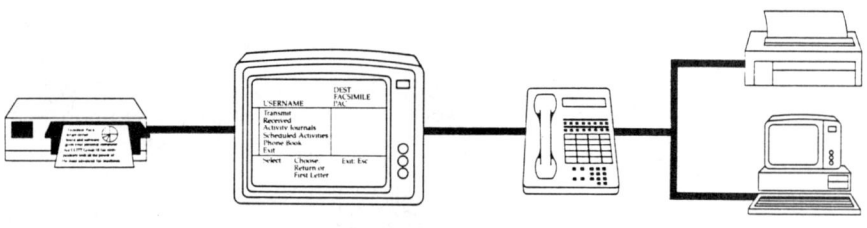

Courtesy of DEST Corporation.

Figure 11-15 shows how LAN users can share a fax. EZ-Fax LAN is a software option that enables LAN users to share EZ-Fax across the LAN. One MS-DOS workstation becomes the nondedicated background fax gateway. The EZ-Fax card and telephone line are installed in this workstation. All other workstations can perform all EZ-Fax functions by accessing that single EZ-Fax card.

FIGURE 11-15 Faxing on a LAN

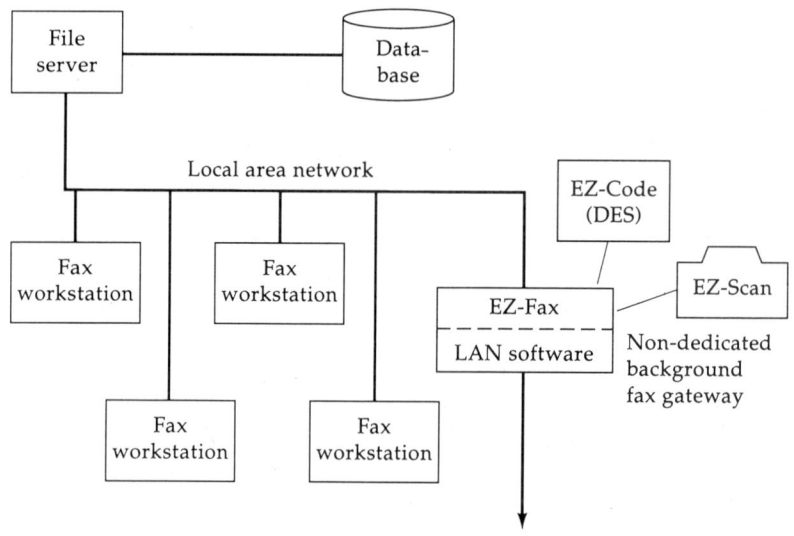

Redrawn courtesy of DEST Corporation.

Drawbacks of virtual facsimile are that the computer software might be difficult to use, the microcomputer cannot be used for other applications when it is being used for fax transmission, and the microcomputer cannot receive fax documents when it is being used for computing applications.

Fax-Alert. No longer does an employee need to be physically close to the fax machine to know when a fax document has been received. Triad Enterprises' *Fax-Alert*, shown in Figure 11-16, notifies fax users instantly when a fax document has arrived. Fax-Alert consists of a transmitter connected to the fax machine and a small, lightweight, cordless receiver powered by batteries. You can place a receiver in your pocket or on your desk or clip it to your belt.

The transmitter detects the arrival of a faxed document and signals the receiver. Each transmitter can be set to different channels for different fax machines, or multiple receivers can receive from the same transmitter signal. The receiver can receive signals from the transmitter within a building up to a distance of 500 feet, depending on the construction of the building, and outside a building up to 900 feet.

FIGURE 11-16   **Fax-Alert**

Courtesy of Triad Enterprises.

Public Facsimile Services

Public facsimile services, also called public fax operators and public access services, are offered by both private companies and government organizations. These fax services are designed for people who do not have access to fax equipment of their own for either sending or receiving documents or both. Charges are usually based on the number of pages to be transmitted and the cost of telephone transmission.

■ Users of Public Fax Services

Public fax services are used by owners and nonowners of fax units as follows:

From Privately Owned Fax Unit to Public Fax Services. As owner of fax equipment can transmit a document to a public fax service company near the recipient's location. The recipient then arranges to pick up the document or have it delivered. Fax telephone directories are available. Dial-A-Fax Directories Corporation publishes a directory listing 10,000 public facsimile service organizations located throughout the world. To identify an organization near the sender or the recipient, organizations are listed by ZIP Code. See the section on benefits and drawbacks of facsimile for more information about Dial-a-Fax Directories Corporation.

From Public Fax Services to Privately Owned Fax Unit. Users with no fax equipment of their own can use a public fax service company near them to send documents directly to a fax owner.

From Public Fax Services to Public Fax Services. If both the sender and the receiver have no fax equipment of their own, then the sender can go to the nearest public service company to fax a document to the public fax service company nearest the recipient.

For example, an advertising company located in Boulder, Colorado, must send a copy of a contract to a company in New York City for immediate approval. Neither company has a fax machine. A representative from the advertising company brings the contract to a public fax service company in Boulder to be faxed to a public fax service company in New York City. On receipt of the copy of the contract, the New York City public fax service company notifies the recipient.

■ Companies Offering Public Fax Services

Among the private and government organizations offering public fax services are the following. The cost of each of the fax serves described in this section is based on 1989 figures.

Sir Speedy, Inc. Sir Speedy, Inc., based in Laguna Hills, California, is one of the largest franchisers of printing centers in the world. The company's market is small- and medium-sized businesses without in-house printing and copying facilities. In 1988, Sir Speedy began operating FASTFAX—a public fax network—by adding fax machines to its over 800 Sir Speedy printing centers throughout North America, Great Britain, and Hong Kong. The local Sir Speedy transmits documents over standard telephone lines, either to another Sir Speedy near the intended recipient or directly to the recipient's own fax. Charges for the service include $10 for five pages and $1 for each additional page plus long-distance telephone costs. An advantage to offering fax services at a printing center is that a document to be faxed can be improved through typesetting or graphic design. At the receiving center, faxed documents can be copied onto bond paper, typeset, printed, and/or bound.

Hotelecopy, Inc. Hotelecopy, Inc., of Miami, Florida, is installing fax machines in hotels throughout the United States, the Caribbean, and Europe. Hotel guests and the general public can use these units to send and/or receive documents. Members of Hotelecopy's network—FAX MAIL—include such hotels as Holiday Inns, Hyatts, Quality Inns, Marriotts, Radissons, Ramada Inns, Sheratons, and Stouffers. FAX MAIL is available at the hotel's front desk, 24 hours a day, seven days a week. The cost to hotel guests for national and international service is $9 for the first ten pages and 60 cents for each additional page plus long-distance telephone charges. Transmission time is 30 seconds per page.

DHL International. The courier service DHL International offers Satellite Express Service, which moves documents over a satellite network. The company uses Group 4 fax machines, which support higher transmission speeds and better resolution than Group 3 fax machines. Satellite Express allows DHL to offer overnight document delivery between the United States and Bahrain, Hong Kong, and Japan. Fax owners can fax their documents to DHL's central dispatching center in Cincinnati, where the documents are printed out and refaxed over the DHL network. Charges are $30 for the first five pages and $2 for each additional page.

International Facsimile Services. In addition to private international fax service companies, the U.S. Postal Service in cooperation with the postal administration of thirty-three participating foreign countries operates a public fax service—INTELPOST. This fax service offers same-day/next-day delivery of documents overseas. INTELPOST documents are transmitted between post offices via CCITT Group 3 fax machines that can send a page to foreign destination in one minute or less over standard telephone lines.

INTELPOST is offered at 200 U.S. post offices in thirteen major cities. Fax owners with equipment that is compatible with the Postal Service's fax equipment can transmit documents from their own fax machines to one of the designated post offices, 24 hours a day, seven days a week. INTELPOST service costs $10 for the first page and $6 for each additional page.

■ Services Available to Fax Owners

Owners of Groups 2 and 3 fax units can cut their sending costs by subscribing to US Fax, Inc. of Philadelphia. The company offers US FAXSYS—a packet-switched data network—for faxing documents.

Fax documents enter and exit US FAXSYS through local nodes installed by US FAX throughout the United States. The node is a high-capacity store-and-forward switch. Nodes are linked by AT&T's Accunet packet-switching service, as shown in Figure 11-17. The node receiving a document processes it and forwards it over the packet network to the node nearest to the recipient, where it is processed and, according to the sender's instructions, sent to the addressee. Control of the network is distributed among the nodes and a central controller. Documents sent to a node can be processed, forwarded, and delivered to an addressee anywhere in the world within seconds.

Using their existing fax machines, subscribers access the US FAXSYS network by dialing a toll-free number from their own fax machine to reach

FIGURE 11-17 US FAXSYS

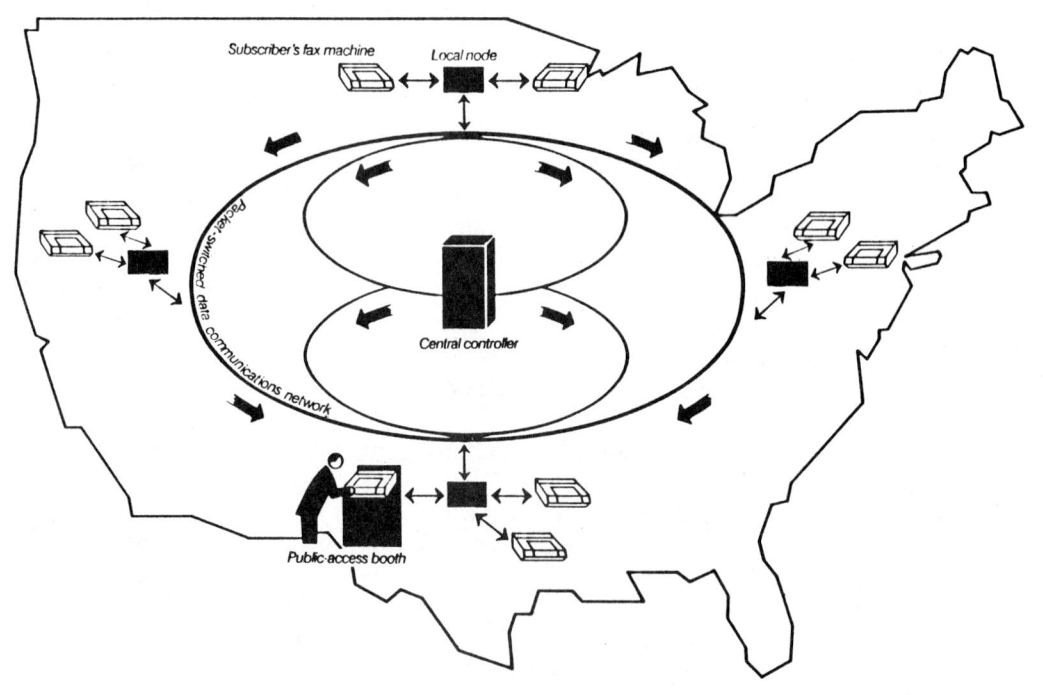

Courtesy of US FAX, Inc.

one of US FAX's network nodes. After the sender enters an identification number, a one-digit delivery code, and the destination fax telephone number, the node takes over. The node—not the sender—then dials the intended recipient's fax machine and transmits the document over AT&T's Accunet Packet Service.

Subscribers to the US FAXSYS pay a nominal monthly fee for the service plus a charge for each page faxed. US FAX estimates that an average page of text costs 8 cents to fax anywhere in the United States. For example, an average three-page document from Boston to San Francisco using US FAXSYS costs about 24 cents—54% less than the 78 cents it costs using the public switched telephone network. (The telephone day rate from Boston to San Francisco is $0.25 for the first minute and $0.25 for each additional minute. If each page takes one minute to fax using the PSTN, the cost would be $0.78 ($0.75 + $0.03 tax), 1989 costs.)

In addition to cutting the cost of sending documents, US FAXSYS offers other advantages:

- If the recipient's fax machine is busy, the service redials every five minutes for an hour. The fax owner does not have to cope with redialing. If redialing proves unsuccessful, the transmission is placed in the recipient's electronic fax mailbox to be picked up by dialing the node at some later time. If the recipient is not a subscriber, the sender is sent a notification receipt that it was not sent.
- Subscribers can buy lower-priced fax machines and use the FAXSYS to obtain a level of functionality usually available only with more expensive machines.
- Subscribers need to place only one telephone call to US FAXSYS to send, or "broadcast," documents to several recipients at once or to a stored distribution list.

To provide ready access to the system for traveling subscribers, US FAX is installing more than 2000 fax machines in hotels, airports, and printer/copier shops. These fax machines will use the US FAXSYS transmission system to communicate with any fax machine in the United States. Plans also include renting portable faxes in hotels for in-room use. Nonsubscribers can also use the machines by punching in the fax identification number of the host hotel, airport lounge, or print shop.

Facsimile Applications

In the office environment, fax is often substituted for teletype message transmission or as a faster alternative to the U.S. mail or overnight courier services. Some examples of how business uses fax are the following:

- Corporate headquarters use fax to exchange documents with their branches.

- Administrative offices use fax to transmit interoffice memos and letters for decision-making purposes.
- Sales representatives fax orders to speed processing and delivery.
- Sales departments fax notices of order actions, delivery schedules, specification sheets, proposals, drawings, and price quotes to customers.
- Banks use fax for interbranch communications, such as daily reports and loan applications, and for money and wire transfers between financial institutions. Banks also place fax units in automobile agencies to speed up the processing of loan application approvals. For example, the completed application is faxed in seconds to the bank for a bank officer's approval.
- Lawyers use fax to exchange copies of depositions, wills, agreements, settlements, and correspondence with their clients and copies of briefs, transcripts, bills of complaint, and deeds with courts.
- Hospitals fax laboratory reports and X-rays to doctors' office or to other hospitals for faster, more accurate diagnosis of patients' illnesses.

Lawson Products, Inc., of Des Plaines, Illinois, one of the country's leading distributors of parts and supplies for industrial equipment and vehicles, stocks more than 19,000 products at six highly automated distribution centers and two subsidiaries. About 1300 sales agents handle more than 160,000 accounts in the United States, Puerto Rico, and Canada, directing orders to assigned distribution centers.

Until eight years ago, sales agents sent their orders by regular mail or telephone, a procedure that is subject to verbal errors and that often resulted in an eighteen-day turnaround for customer receipt. To speed delivery and provide better service to customers, Lawson now faxes orders. By faxing orders, the company can ship an average of 99% of its line items within 24 hours. Faxing has reduced the labor hours spent handling orders as well as the person-to-person telephone orders.

Lawson uses Group 3 fax units, which transmit a single page order in less than one minute. More than 7500 of its 9700 customer orders are processed weekly by fax. The company also uses faxes for interoffice communication, including credit checking and purchasing information.

Benefits and Drawbacks of Facsimile

■ Benefits of Facsimile

The major benefit of fax is that *an exact copy of a document can be received immediately.* Exchanging information through fax transmission reduces both time and money frequently lost in waiting for information. For example, a page to be delivered within the United States by fax can be transmitted by telephone lines in less than a minute for a cost of about 25 cents or less during the day. The same page takes about two days by first-class mail for a cost of 25 cents. As of late 1989, overnight mail costs were $8.75 (U.S. Postal

Service Express Mail) or courier service, $15 (Federal Express). Figure 11-18 compares the cost of transmitting a one-page document by different types of services.

Usually each fax transmission also includes a cover sheet, which increases the cost of faxing. The one-page cover sheet, also called a telecopier transmitted form, identifies the following items:

- The sender's name, company, voice telephone number, and telephone fax number
- The receiver's name, company name, address, voice telephone number, and fax telephone number
- The total number of copies including cover page being sent

Also included on the form is a statement, such as "If you do not receive this entire document, please contact the company at (voice telephone number)" and a section reserved for the sender to add a message.

In addition to fast delivery and providing an exact replica, fax systems offer other benefits:

- *Equipment installation is easy.* A fax can be installed at any location that has available electrical power and a telephone.
- *Fax can transmit various types of documents.* Handwritten and typed text, charts, graphs, and photographs can be transmitted and received.

FIGURE 11-18 Cost of Transmitting a One-Page Document by Types of Services (Based on July 1989 Rates)

New York to	Telex[1]	Overnight Courier[2]	Express Mail[3]	Analog Fax[4] Group 1 6 minutes	Analog Fax[4] Group 2 3 minutes	Digital Fax[5] Group 3 20 seconds
Boston	1.38	15.00	8.75	1.42	.71	.24
Chicago	1.38	15.00	8.75	1.49	.74	.25
Dallas	1.38	15.00	8.75	1.55	.77	.26
Los Angeles	1.38	15.00	8.75	1.55	.77	.26
Montreal	2.92	22.00	10.75	2.98	1.51	.56

[1]Based on an 8½ × 11 inch average letter (200 word telex message at 110 baud averaging 100 wpm or 2 minutes) at rates in effect 8 A.M.–5 P.M., Monday through Friday, from a Telex II to a Telex II over telephone lines economy telex.

[2]Overnight courier is a service of the Federal Express Corporation with delivery the next day before 10:30 A.M. or 12 noon depending on the receiver's location.

[3]Express Mail is an overnight service of the United States Postal Service with delivery the next day before 3 P.M.

[4]Based on AT&T long-distance telephone rates, includes 3% federal tax.

[5]Based on one-minute minimum line charge at AT&T long-distance telephone rates, including 3% federal tax and one-minute minimum line charge. Document transmission time is typically less.

- *Fax units require only minimal training to operate.* See the section on Facsimile Technology in this chapter.
- *Fax operation is automatic.* To transmit a document, the user (1) places the original document into the unit's feeder, (2) dials the telephone number of the receiving fax unit, and (3) once the connection is made, presses the unit's transmission button.
- *No rekeying is necessary.* The document to be transmitted by fax does not need to be rekeyed by an operator, saving time and eliminating rekeying errors.

■ Drawbacks of Facsimile

A problem that tends to be overlooked is how to manage a fax. Employees, both managers and staff, often fax unnecessarily unless guidelines are developed for when to use the fax, for what purposes, and by what employees. Among the other drawbacks of fax systems are the following:

- *The sender must know the telephone number of the receiving machine.* Access to directories of fax numbers is important, especially for international communications. Dial-A-Fax Directories Corporation, 1761 West Hillsboro Boulevard, Deerfield Beach, FL 33442, telephone 1-800-FINDFAX, publishes annually (1) *FAX Phone for North America,* which lists over 100,000 names and telephone numbers of fax owners, (2) international fax directories, (3) *FAX Business Guide,* which classifies facsimile owners by products and/or services, and (4) *Public Access Service Bureaus,* which lists over 10,000 public access facsimile service organizations by ZIP Code. The company also offers Dial-a-Fax directory service, which provides a daily update of telephone numbers of fax owners. *The International Official Facsimile Users' Directory,* Second Edition, is available from fax dealers or directly from the publisher: FDP Associates, One Park Avenue, Suite 1093, New York, NY 10016. More than 80,000 listings worldwide are included.
- *Operating problems are difficult to identify.* Most manufacturers provide ways to diagnose equipment problems. Since Group 3 machines are solid state, they have fewer malfunctions than Groups 1 and 2.
- *The sender's and the receiver's equipment must be compatible.* Lack of industry standards has made fax equipment compatibility a problem for users. Manufacturers' moves toward adopting worldwide fax standards, as recommended by CCITT, are helping to reduce this problem. Incompatibility produces distorted copy and possibly total inability to communicate.
- *If the receiver requires an original copy, a fax copy becomes unacceptable.*
- *Fax units usually cannot transmit color.* However, as was previously discussed, some fax units can send and receive in two colors—black and red.
- *Photographs tend to reproduce poorly.*
- *Receipt of junk mail via fax is becoming a problem for fax owners.* Junk mail ties up machine availability and uses paper without permission. Many state

legislators are proposing bans and restrictions on unsolicited fax advertisements. Some fax owners are dealing with the problem by installing a dedicated telephone line between two locations with password protection.
- *Other delivery methods may be more cost-effective.* If the time factor for receiving a document is not important, the postal system is cheaper. If a high volume of mail is to be sent to the same address and overnight delivery is sufficient, Express Mail or courier services may be less costly. Mail or courier service is based on weight rather than on transmission speed.

Selecting a Fax System

A plan for selecting a fax consists of the following two phases: (1) evaluating your current delivery system and (2) selecting a fax system.

■ Phase 1: Evaluate Your Current Delivery System

Before selecting fax equipment you must determine the need for a fax system. The selection procedure should begin with an evaluation of your current delivery system of sending and receiving information within and outside the company. Obtain the following information:

- Record what and where materials are sent, to whom, and by what method. Is the current delivery system taking too much time? Is it too costly? Is information lost at any time?
- Identify which messages and documents are potentially faxable.
- Identify which recipients have fax equipment or have access to public access facsimile services.
- Calculate the cost of using fax for these messages.
- Compare the cost of using fax with the cost of current services.

■ Phase 2: Select a Fax System

Once the need for a fax system has been confirmed, contact at least three reliable fax vendors.

Meeting Preparation. Prepare for your meeting with these vendors by answering the questions listed in Figures 11-19, 11-20, and 11-21. The questions in Figure 11-19 seek information about documents to be sent and received by fax, those in Figure 11-20 seek information about fax users and vendors, and those in Figure 11-21 seek information about transmission requirements, including fax features to consider.

Requests of Vendors. Ask each vendor for an on-site demonstration and for a one- or two-week trial use of its fax machine. Obtain local references

FIGURE 11-19 Information About Documents to Be Sent and Received

- *How much "traffic" (pages) will each fax unit transmit each month?*
- *How much "traffic" (pages) will each fax unit receive each month*? Do not underestimate your fax machine. You have no control over the number of documents being faxed to you. With a thermal fax, select a machine that can hold a large (328 feet) paper roll.
- *What is the size of each original document to be transmitted*? All fax units handle standard 8½" by 11" documents; some can also handle larger and smaller sizes.
- *Will oversized documents be transmitted or received*? Reduction capability allows oversized documents to be reduced to letter size either before transmission or at the receiving end to fit the receiver's capability.
- *What is the required scanning width for each original document*? Although a unit handles 8½" by 11" paper, its scanning width may be only 8 inches. For example, notations written in margins might require a fax unit with a wider scanning capability.
- *What type of information, such as text, graphics, or photographs with various tones of gray, will each fax transmit and/or receive*? Price is directly proportional to image resolution. The higher the resolution, the more expensive the fax unit. For standard text printing, almost any fax unit can be used. For high image resolution a more sophisticated printing technique is required.
- *How important is the quality of the fax document? Is the received document to be of the same quality as the original or a copy of a copy*? A file copy might not require as high an image resolution as other documents. For a high-quality copy, select a receiver with sharp image resolution. Some fax machines include a "half-tone mode" that recognizes sixteen shades of gray. Most fax machines normally recognize only black and white tones.
- *What will be the average distance of fax station-to-station calls?*
- *What will be the average length of fax documents*? For example, some fax units will only transmit five pages automatically and then require redialing for additional pages. Sturdy machines allow 20 or more pages to be loaded at one time.

about each vendor from satisfied customers. Check the warranty and service policies offered by each vendor.

Compare the Costs of Selected Fax Units. A comparison of the costs of the fax units you are considering for purchase or rent should include the following items:

- Rental charge or purchase price of each fax unit
- Cost of transmission over communication lines, such as telephone lines
- Cost of supplies
- Cost of operator's time

The major expense of a slow-speed fax system is the cost of the telephone line, while the major expense of a high-speed fax system is the cost of the equipment. For example, a digital fax system has a high rental rate

FIGURE 11-20   **Information About Fax Users and Vendors**

Information about users
- *How many employees will be accessing the fax unit?*
  The number of users will help determine the number of fax units needed.
- *Where are the fax users located in the office?*
  Their location will help determine where to place the fax unit(s).
- *Where should the fax units be located to serve the greatest number of people? Should units be portable?*
- *Will fax users be able to maintain the equipment themselves?*

Information about vendors
- *What does each vendor's service plan include?*
  Compare vendors' services according to service plan options, costs, and average time for service representatives to respond to a service call. If possible, obtain a one-year on-site agreement. Although fax machines are usually reliable, repair costs can exceed the machine's original purchase price.

FIGURE 11-21   **Information About Transmission**

- *To what group(s) of fax units—Groups 1, 2, 3, and/or 4—will you be communicating?*
- *Will documents be transmitted at night and/or during the weekend when telephone rates are lower?* If so, select the store-and-forward feature so that you can store documents and preset the exact time of transmittal. Also select the automatic redial feature to enable the fax unit to redial busy numbers without operator assistance.
- *Will documents to be sent repeatedly to the same person?* If so, select the automatic dial and the automatic redial features to eliminate manual monitoring of the fax unit.
- *Will more than one document be stored at a time?* If so, determine the amount of memory that the fax unit requires.
- *Will the same document be transmitted to multiple recipients?* If so, select the sequential broadcasting feature and/or the relay broadcasting feature.
- *Will documents be received unattended during office hours or on weekends?* If so, the automatic answering feature is required.
- *Will multiple documents be sent to different locations?* If so, select the automatic document feeder to eliminate assigning an employee to the fax machine to feed each document one by one.
- *Will other fax machines be sending you messages?* If so, add the polling feature. Polling enables your equipment to dial up other fax units and query them for documents that were left for you.
- *Will you receive confidential information?* If so, your fax machine may need added memory to receive faxed documents directly into its stored memory, which acts as a mailbox. Access to this mailbox is by authorized users with the appropriate password.
- *Will you need to verify that transmitted documents have been received?* If so, add the verification feature that verifies that the same number of bits were sent and received by the sending and receiving fax unit. This feature eliminates telephone calls to check whether or not the document was received.
- *If roll paper is used, how will each page be separated?* An automatic cutter ensures that each page of a document is separated, otherwise much time must be spent separating pages.

combined with a low-transmission charge. A company sending 150 documents per month by a digital system may be paying as much as $3.86 per page in machine costs but only $0.46 in telephone line charges. The equipment cost per page may be reduced by increasing the volume of documents sent per month.

Other Key Factors. Select a facsimile unit that is as automatic as possible and that can be upgraded. Consider whether you need a RS-232-C interface, described in Figure 11-11, to allow the fax unit to communicate with computers. Order a separate telephone line for each fax unit.

Summary

"What is your fax number?" This question is now being asked nearly as often as "What is your address?" Companies are faxing documents to their destination rather than calling on Federal Express or some other overnight courier or using the mail. An important factor in fax transmission is complying with standards recommended by the CCITT. Group 3 fax units, the prevailing technology, can transmit a one-page document in less than one minute, while Group 4 fax units, now entering the market, can transmit the same page in less than 10 seconds. Public fax services, offered by both public and government organizations, are available for those who do not have an available fax unit at hand.

To determine the need for a fax system, a company should conduct an evaluation of its current delivery system of sending and receiving information within and outside the company. If a fax system is to be selected, then information about the documents to be sent and received, fax users and vendors, and fax transmission should be obtained and analyzed, and costs of selected fax units should be compared.

■ Key Terms

Analog processing method
CCITT Fax Groups 1, 2, 3, 4
CCITT Group 4: Classes 1, 2, 3
Data compression code standard:
 Modified Huffman code
 Modified Read code
Digital processing method

Facsimile (fax)
Fax features:
 Delayed dialing
 Downward capability
 Polling
 Relay broadcasting
 Secure polling
 Sequential broadcasting
 Store-and-forward
Handshake protocol
Pixels

Public fax service
Resolution
Traditional facsimile
Transceiver
Types of equipment:
 Integrated fax unit
 Multifunctional or hybrid fax unit
 Stand-alone fax unit
Videofax
Virtual facsimile

Self-Quiz

Indicate whether the statement is true or false.

1. The Japanese are the major manufacturers and users of fax.   T/F
2. Fax units that use the analog processing method transmit at faster speeds than those using the digital processing methods.   T/F
3. Packet-switched networks are more reliable than dedicated telephone lines.   T/F
4. A decrease in resolution increases the cost of fax transmission.   T/F
5. A disadvantage of fax is that an operator must rekey documents for transmission.   T/F
6. Class 1 fax units transmit more quickly than class 3 fax units.   T/F

Complete each of the following statements.

1. The first fax system was patented by _____ .
2. Fax manufacturers comply with standards recommended by _____ .
3. The exchange of preliminary information between the sending and the receiving fax units before transmission is called _____ .
4. A fax can communicate with a microcomputer by adding a(n) _____ .
5. If you wanted to transmit pictures of three-dimensional objects, you would purchase a(n) _____ .
6. Virtual facsimile requires using a(n) _____ .

Match Column A with Column B.

Column A
(a) Automatic dialing
(b) Downward capability
(c) Duplex
(d) Relay broadcasting
(e) Sequential broadcasting
(f) Store-and-forward

Column B
____ 1. Allows a fax to send a document automatically to one or more remote locations, which in turn relays the document to a number of other locations.
____ 2. Allows the fax to simultaneously transmit and receive.
____ 3. Allows the fax to store documents in its memory and then transmit them at a later time, without an operator in attendance.
____ 4. Allows a high-speed fax machine to communicate with low-speed machines.
____ 5. Allows the fax to send documents automatically—one after the other—to several locations.
____ 6. A built-in telephone dialer that remembers often-used numbers.

Review Questions

1. (a) What is fax transmission?
   (b) What kinds of documents can you fax?
2. (a) Identify the components of a fax system.
   (b) Explain what each component does.
3. (a) How are fax units classified? Who makes these classifications?
   (b) How important is this information to fax users? To prospective fax purchasers?
4. (a) What is the transmission time for sending an average business letter using Group 3 digital fax machines?
   (b) What is the cost of faxing the following documents during the day a distance of 50 miles using Group 3 fax units: a one-page letter? A ten-page report (transmission time is 8.5 minutes)? (The toll call rate is $0.43 for the first minute and $0.17 for each additional minute plus 3% federal tax.)
   (c) How do these costs compare with those of regular mail and an overnight courier such as Federal Express? Which means of delivery would you select? Why?
5. What is the difference between stand-alone, hybrid, and integrated fax equipment?
6. What feature(s) should a fax have in order to perform each of the following functions?
   (a) Documents are to be sent after regular office hours and during the weekend.
   (b) Documents are to be received unattended after regular office hours and during the weekend.
   (c) The same documents are to be sent periodically to six locations in Hong Kong.
   (d) Documents from a Group 3 facsimile machine are to be sent to Groups 1, 2, and 3 facsimile machines.
   (e) Documents are to be requested from remote fax machines when telephone costs are cheaper.
   (f) Documents received from fax senders are to be protected from access by unauthorized employees.
7. What is the difference between traditional facsimile and virtual facsimile?
8. You would like to fax documents from your company in Salt Lake City to companies in California and London. You do not have a fax machine, and you do not know whether the recipients have their own machines. What would you do?
9. Should a fax machine owner consider using the services of US FAX or similar services? Why?
10. Give examples of how a company can use a fax machine.
11. (a) Why should a company consider purchasing fax equipment for sending documents rather than using U.S. Postal Service, Federal Express, Express Mail, or telex?

(b) What are the drawbacks to using a fax system?
12. (a) Identify each of the costs you should consider when purchasing or renting fax equipment.
   (b) Which cost(s) can you control? How?

■ *Activities/Projects*

1. Visit a nearby office to see how a facsimile machine operates. Also obtain a description of the equipment, its users, and the tasks performed by the fax. Before your visit, prepare a list of questions to be answered during the demonstration. Refer to Figures 11-19, 11-20, and 11-21 for question suggestions. Summarize the information obtained from your visit in a written report. Include your question guide and any other exhibits that are helpful.
2. Develop guidelines for managing a fax machine in an organization of your choice. For example, who should use the fax? Under what circumstances should it be used? When should people use it? For what purposes should they use it?
3. Design a cover sheet to be filled out and included with each fax transmission sent from an organization of your choice. On the form, specify the name of the sending organization, address, voice and fax telephones, and the following items to be filled in at the time of the transmission: current date, sender's name, receiver's name, company, fax number, number of pages being transmitted including the cover sheet, and special instructions. Are there any other items that should be included?
4. Discuss the following issues:
   (a) Should every company own a facsimile?
   (b) Can a faxed document serve as a legal document?
   (c) What impact, if any, will fax have on other office services?
   (d) Should fax junk mail be banned or restricted?
5. You are considering purchasing a fax. You estimate that your monthly faxing will consist of the following items: 30 one-page documents, 10 two-page documents, and 10 five-page reports. Added to each transmission is a one-page identification sheet that states the sender's name, address, fax telephone number, the receiver's name, the number of pages being transmitted including the identification sheet, and other pertinent information regarding the transmission. You estimate transmission time for the first page will be 40 seconds and each succeeding page will be 30 seconds.
   The faxing of the one- and two-page documents will be within state and within a 50-mile radius of your company located in Denver, Colorado. Day rates average $0.31 for the first minute and $0.23 for each additional minute. A copy of each report will be faxed to a company in each of the following cities: Philadelphia; Chicago; Seattle, Washington; and Washington, D.C. The day rate is $0.25 for each minute plus 3% federal tax. Evening discount is 38% and night discount is 53% of the day rate.
   (a) What are your weekly and monthly faxing costs? Can these costs be reduced in any way?

(b) How do these costs compare with other means of delivery including public facsimile services?

Case: Facsimile versus Telex

As manager of communications, you have been asked to determine whether your company should be using facsimile or telex to send documents between New York City and Paris, France. You know that facsimile does not require special operators while telex requires trained operators. Facsimile requires no document preparation for transmission while telex requires document preparation, such as rekeying the document, proofing, and correcting typed output. Facsimile documents are transmitted by telephone lines, while telex documents are transmitted via leased lines from Western Union. With facsimile you can send business forms, charts, graphics, pictures, signatures, and handwritten messages, while with telex you can send only typed messages/documents. Althouh facsimile seems to have more advantages, you must still analyze the costs of each technology.

For facsimile, international direct dial from New York to Paris, France, (AT&T) is $1.77 per minute for transmission between 7 A.M. and 1 P.M. (the cheapest time at which to transmit). Fax speed is 300 words per minute. For telex, the rate is $1.90 per minute. Telex speed is 60 words per minute. Monthly cost of equipment for fax if $194; for telex it is $76.50 per month.

(a) To send 100 300-word documents a month, how much would you save by selecting the cheaper transmission method? What are the monthly savings? What are the yearly savings? *Note*: To obtain the information for your analysis, complete the computational workform below.
(b) To send 500 300-word documents a month, how much would you save by selecting the cheaper transmission method? What are the monthly savings? What are the yearly savings? Use the workform below.
(c) Which method should you select? Why?

Computational Workform: Complete the Calculations.

		Facsimile	Telex
(a)	Average words per document	300	300
(b)	Equipment speed (words per minute)	300	60
(c)	Minutes per document (a ÷ b = c)	_____	_____
(d)	Rate per minute	$1.77	$1.90
(e)	Cost per document (c × d = e)	_____	_____
(f)	Documents per month (low volume)	100	100
(g)	Documents per month (high volume)	500	500
(h)	Monthly transmission cost for low volume (e × f = h)	_____	_____
(i)	Monthly transmission cost for high volume (e × g = i)	_____	_____
(j)	Monthly equipment cost	$194	$76.50

	Facsimile	Telex
(k) Total monthly cost for low volume (h + j = k)	_____	_____
(l) Total monthly cost for high volume (i + j = l)	_____	_____
(m) Total yearly cost for low volume (12 × k)	_____	_____
(n) Total yearly cost for high volume (12 × l)	_____	_____

Notes

1. "More Fax in Your Future," *Modern Office Technology*, September 1987, p. BC4.
2. Daniel Gross, "The Emerging Trends in Facsimile Technology," *The Office*, February 1988, p. 58.

Additional Readings

"All About Facsimile," *Telecommunications* (Delran, N.J.: Datapro Research Corporation, April 1987), pp. TC 17-0020-101–TC17-0020-114.

Sally Becker, "Forging Ahead with Facsimile," *Office Systems '87* (September 1987), pp. 36–41.

Sherli Evans, "Tracking the Fax," *Modern Office Technology* (September 1989), pp. BC3–BC8.

David Greenfield, "Files by FAX," *LAN Magazine*, April 1989, pp. 45–53.

Pamela Licalzi, "Fax Makers Target Low-End Market," *High Technology Business* (March 1988), pp. 26–30.

Rick Minicucci, "Getting a Fix on Personal Fax," *Today's Office* (January 1988), pp. 21–26.

The Office Automation Report: Equipment Analysis (Natick, Mass.: Venture Development Corporation, August 15, 1987).

Donald J. Ryan, "Computers Now Speak FAX," *TPT*, February 1988, pp. 33–42.

Donald J. Ryan, "Making Sense of Today's Image Communications Alternatives," *Data Communications* (April 1987), pp. 110–115.

Facsimile Newsletters

BLI's FAXreporter is published monthly by Buyers Laboratory Inc., 20 Railroad Avenue, Hackensack, NJ 07601.

Facts Exchange is published by 3M Document Systems Division, Building 220-10W, 3M Center, St. Paul, MN 55144-1000.

FaxFacts is published quarterly by Paper Manufacturers Company, a manufacturer of a broad line of folded and rolled papers, 24 Triangle Park Drive, Cincinnati, OH 45246. Telephone number: 513-772-5057. This industry-based newsletter provides current information on new facsimile equipment and discusses unique features related to facsimile equipment and supplies.

Fax Organization

Founded in 1986, the American Facsimile Association, 110 North 17th Street, Philadelphia, PA 19103, publishes *Faxfocus*, a monthly newsletter, and *The Journal of the American Facsimile Association*, a quarterly publication, and offers access to AFA's Information Clearinghouse and a toll-free hotline. Members include fax users and telecommunications managers as well as fax manufacturers and dealers.

CHAPTER 12

Videotex and Teletext

Evolution of Videotex and Teletext

Videotex
  Videotex Defined
  How Videotex Operates
  Videotex Equipment Components
  Ways of Accessing a Videotex System

Teletext
  Teletext Defined
  How Teletext Operates
  Teletext Equipment Components

Comparison of Videotex and Teletext Systems

Videotex Standards
  Major Videotex Standards
  Other Standards

Applications—Types
  Information Retrieval
  Computation
  Transaction
  Messaging
  Downline Loading

Applications—Ways of Using Videotex
  Business Videotex
  Home or Consumer-Oriented Videotex
  Public Access Videotex

```
MONEY MATTERS/MARKETS
 1 Market Quotes/Highlights
 2 Company Information
 3 Banking/Brokerage Services
 4 Earnings/Economic Projections
 5 Micro Software Interfaces
 6 Personal Finance/Insurance
 7 Financial Forums
 8 MicroQuote II ($)
 9 Business News
10 Instructions/Fees
11 Read Before Investing
```

Courtesy of CompuServe Inc.

Commercial Videotex Systems
General-Purpose Commercial Videotex Systems
Specialized Commercial Videotex Systems
Commercial Videotex—Revenues and Fees
Selecting a Commercial Videotex System

Videotex and Teletext Issues
Standards
Information Reliability
Information Privacy and Confidentiality
Legal Issues

CHAPTER OBJECTIVES

After completing this chapter, you should be able to

1. Distinguish between videotex and teletext.
2. Explain how each system operates.
3. Specify videotex and teletext applications.
4. Select a commercial videotex system.
5. Discuss major issues of concern to the industry.

Attorneys search LEXIS on their computer terminals to tell them what courts throughout the country are saying about a specific case or legal issue.

Employees access CompuServe on their computers to bank electronically. They review their banking transactions, transfer funds, pay bills, compare current interest rates, and even exchange electronic mail with bank officers.

When managers need business information from various regions throughout the country, they can access VU/TEXT on their microcomputers. VU/TEXT, the world's largest online newspaper, provides access to leading newspapers throughout the country.

Levi Strauss and Company of San Francisco installed over 100 kiosks in select retail stores nationwide. Levi's electronic shopping terminals offer information about customizing jeans and jackets for their customers. Some kiosks provide only information; others allow customers to enter purchase orders.

In each of the above situations a videotex or a teletext system is being used to access information. In this chapter, videotex and teletext technology, equipment, applications, and issues are discussed so that the reader can select, operate, and manage these systems.

More than 300,000 executives and professionals in the United States use services provided by videotex and teletext systems. Market Intelligence Research Company of Palo Alto, California, predicts that online vendors of these information services will receive $4.12 billion in revenues by 1989—an increase of $1.31 billion over 1983.

Videotex and teletext systems can be easily operated by untrained users. For many people these systems serve as their first introduction to computers. Typical user instructions are "Press the enter key to proceed" and "Enter option number desired (1-6) or Q for quit."

The cost of operating and using these systems is generally less in comparison to other forms of electronic information available to business, government, or the general public. For example, a videotex terminal can cost as little as a videocassette recorder or as much as a microcomputer.

Evolution of Videotex and Teletext

The concept of videotex was introduced in the early 1970s as an outgrowth of research in video telephony. In 1976 the British, the pioneers in videotex technology, introduced to the public the first commercial application of teletext, called *Ceefax* ("see facts"). In 1979, British Telecommunications (formerly the British Post Office) developed *Prestel*, the first interactive two-way videotex system. The French soon followed with *Antiope*, another videotex system. In the late 1970s the Canadian Communication Research Centre of the Federal Department of Communications developed the *Telidon concept*.

The first Telidon commercial service as well as the first commercial videotex service in North America became known as project *Grassroots*.

Although much of the basic research in videotex technology was performed in the United States, the country was slow to enter the videotex industry. The governments of Britain, France, and Canada provide financial support for research and development of videotex and teletext and exercise greater control over these systems than in the United States. The U.S. government tends to let private companies handle the research and development and then to establish control through regulations.

In the United States, one of the first experiments with a videotex system was conducted in 1980 by Videotext America, a joint partnership of Knight-Ridder and AT&T. Soon after, Videotext America with Times-Mirror Videotext Services and Infomart of Toronto, Canada, conducted *Project Gateway*, a Telidon-based videotex. In 1981, AT&T and Canada's Department of Communications reached an agreement that led to the development of a compatible North American videotex system, based on Canada's Telidon, called the NAPLPS (North American Presentation Level Protocol Syntax) agreement. One of the earliest commercial videotex systems in the United States was *Dow Jones News/Retrieval system*. Today, over 2000 commercial videotex systems offer services in this country.

Videotex

■ Videotex Defined

Videotex, also called viewdata, "refers to easy-to-use interactive electronic services which allow a user to access textual or graphics information and services on a personal computer or a dedicated videotex terminal."[1] A user can retrieve information such as news and weather, calculate mortgage payments, conduct transactions such as shopping and banking, send and receive electronic messages, and downline load computer programs and data. Examples of videotex systems are Prestel (United Kingdom), Project Grassroots (Canada), Teletel (France), and CompuServe (United States).

■ How Videotex Operates

A schematic of a videotex system, shown in Figure 12-1, connects the user's computer with the host computer by telephone lines, coaxial cables, or fiber-optic lines. A user retrieves information stored in a host computer by using a telephone, a modem, and a computer (or a modified television set or a terminal). The telephone and modem connect the user to the host computer directly or through an appropriate communication network, such as Telenet.

FIGURE 12-1 Schematic of a Videotex System

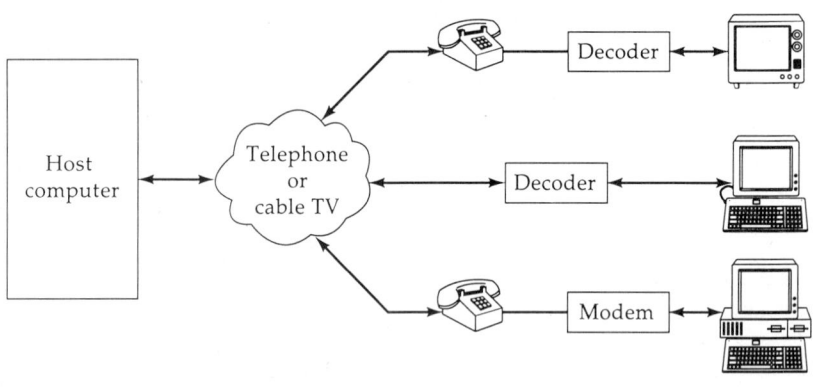

The host computer stores information in pages, which are grouped in the form of tree-structured databases, as shown in Figure 12-2. A user selects the desired information, computer interactions, or computer transactions either from directory pages called menus or indexes or by issuing appropriate commands. Menus are understood easily and require no computer skill. A user-friendly method of retrieving information is critical for these systems.

For example, suppose you want to access from your home a commercial videotex service, such as GEnie from GE Information Services. You need a microcomputer, a telephone, a modem, and communications software. You dial a local telephone number to access a communications network, such as GEnie's network or Telenet, which in turn will connect you to GEnie. Once a telephone connection has been made with GEnie, you log onto the system by keyboarding in your identification number and password and then respond to a sequence of menus, as shown in Figure 12-3.

FIGURE 12-2 Example of a Tree-Structured Database

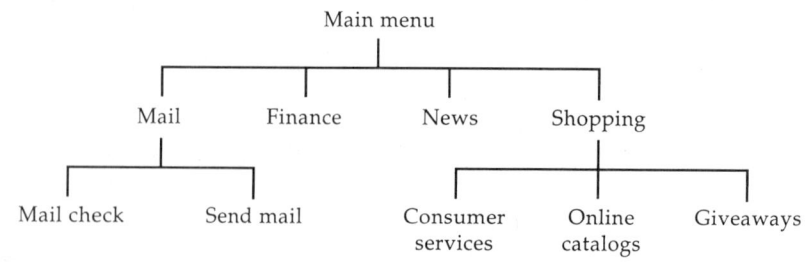

Videotex

FIGURE 12-3   Using a Videotex System

First screen

```
** Thank you for choosing GEnie **

   The Consumer Information Service
        from General Electric
          Copyright (C), 1989

GEnie Logon at: 15:45 EST on: 890222
Last Access at: 15:41 EST on: 890222


  *  Business Owners! Moonlighters!  *
     New survey underway in the "BOSB".

  *  Car Buyers: "AUTOQUOT-R" saves $  *
     GEnie Mall Auto Price Quotes: $12.
```

Second screen

```
You have 7 LETTERS WAITING.

GEnie         TOP         Page   1
       GE Information Services

  1. About GEnie...   2. New on GEnie
  3. GE Mail          4. LiveWire CB
  5. Computing        6. Travel
  7. Finance          8. Shopping
  9. News            10. Games
 11. Professional   12. Leisure
 13. Reference      14. Logoff

Enter #, or <H>elp?NEWS
```

Third screen

```
GEnie         NEWS        Page 300
         US & World News

  1. NewsGrid Headline News
  2. USA TODAY Decisionlines
  3. Press Releases
  4. Personal Computer News
  5. Home Office/Small Business RT
  6. Fight Back With David Horowitz
  7. FCC Proposal News
  8. GEnie QuikNews

Enter #, <P>revious, or <H>elp?1
```

Fourth screen

```
GEnie        NEWSGRID      Page 340
         NewsGrid Headline News

  1. About NewsGrid
  2. NewsGrid Instructions
  3. Today's News
  4. Enter the Livewire News Room

  5. Send Feedback to NewsGrid

Enter #, <P>revious, or <H>elp?1
```

Fifth screen

```
          NewsGrid Headline News
          Wednesday, February 22 1989
                 15:46EST

  1. U.S. and World News Headlines
  2. Business News Headlines
  3. Sports
  4. Features
  5. Other News
  6. Keyword Search Today's News

          Custom Clipping Service

  7. Enter Clipping Keywords
  8. Select Standing Stories
  9. View/Modify Clipping Profile
 10. Display Stories in Your Profile

Enter #, <P>revious, or <H>elp?1
```

Sixth screen

```
- NEWS HEADLINES

  1. SOVIET, ISRAELI FOREIGN MINISTERS MEET IN EGYPT
  2. SOVIET ACADEMICIAN URGES ISRAEL TO TALK WITH PLO
  3. SENATORS REVIEW FBI REPORT ON DEFENSE SECY-DESIGNATE JOHN TOW
  4. IRAN PLEDGES TO CONTINUE EXECUTION ORDER ON AUTHOR SALMAN RUS
  5. TOP U.S. AUTHORS BACK BRITISH WRITER SALMAN RUSHDIE
  6. WEST GERMANY FAVORS U.N. SECURITY COUNCIL ACTION IN RUSHDIE A
```

Courtesy of GE Information Services.

■ Videotex Equipment Components

The major components of a videotex system include the serving equipment, the receiving equipment, and communication facilities.

Serving Equipment. The host or central computer is usually a minicomputer but may be a microcomputer or a mainframe computer. The host computer maintains a variety of databases and services. The computer's capacity is determined by the following factors:

- The amount of storage required for databases and other information
- The computational power required by the types of services provided by the videotex system
- The number of users to be served at any given time
- The computer speed required to service the users

An increase in any of these factors results in the need to increase the computer's capacity. For example, the need to increase its capacity is indicated when the number of people using the system simultaneously causes the computer to respond more slowly to each person's request.

Receiving Equipment (User's Equipment)

Videotex Terminal. Videotex terminals may be a modified television set, a microcomputer, or a computer terminal. These terminals are capable of performing the following functions: input, output, processing, and communications. Output is usually by a display or CRT monitor and/or a printer for hard copy, although voice synthesizers are available to read output, such as from Telenet or CompuServe.

Decoder. A user selects pages of text from the system or communicates interactively with it by using a numeric keypad or an alphanumeric keyboard. A **decoder** then translates and assembles the digital television/video signal into a video display. A decoder can be a separate unit or included within the display screen unit, making the terminal an *integrated terminal*. Decoders can also be added to existing television sets.

Communication Software. Communication software allows the receiving computer to connect with the host computer. Software requirements include being compatible with the user's equipment and modem; being able to save, redisplay, and print information received from the videotex system; being able to set protocols for major telecommunications networks, such as Telenet; and being able to provide efficient file transfer and a utility for downloading information.

Communication Facilities. Videotex systems commonly use public switched telephone networks and packet-switching networks as communication facilities. Users can also access systems by using gateways.

FIGURE 12-4 Videotex Systems Using the Public Switched Telephone Network

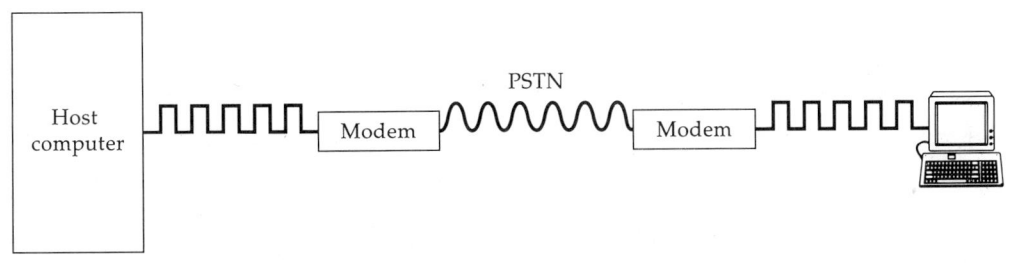

Public Switched Telephone Network (PSTN). Figure 12-4 shows a videotex system connecting to users via the PSTN. As you recall from Chapter 2, a modem converts computer data signals to analog signals for transmission over analog telephone lines and then reconverts them to digital signals at the receiving end. When a videotex system uses telephone facilities, it also requires a modem at the receiving terminal and another modem at the serving (host) computer, both of which are capable of translating from digital to analog and from analog to digital for two-way communication. The modem is either separate from the terminal or built inside the terminal housing.

Packet-Switching Network. Packet-switching networks, discussed in Chapter 6, permit messages from user terminals to be sent over long distances more efficiently and less expensively than the PSTN. An example of a packet-switching network connecting videotex systems is shown in Figure 12-5. Some videotex systems, such as CompuServe and GENie, have their own private packet-switching networks. Subscribers can elect to use these private networks at a minimal or no charge if they can access them from their local calling area; otherwise, they pay a long-distance telephone charge to the access point.

Gateway. As was discussed in Chapter 7, a gateway is a device that connects two systems, especially systems that use different protocols, and provides a communication path that enables data to be exchanged between networks. A gateway provides videotex users with real-time access to data stored in other computers, such as bank account information. The regional Bell operating companies are entering the videotex industry by serving as gateway providers. In this role the Bell companies will link services and users. For example, a gateway user with a modem-equipped personal computer at home or the office can access a range of services by using a single telephone number on a nonsubscription basis. The telephone company bills

FIGURE 12-5 Videotex Systems Using a Packet-Switching Network

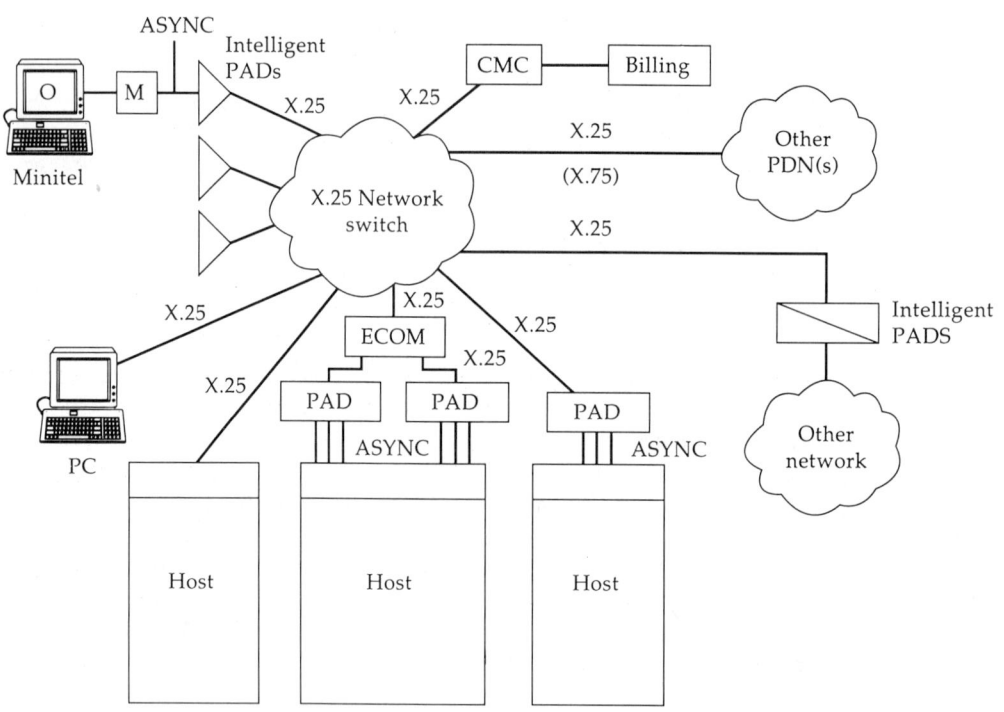

Redrawn courtesy of U.S. Videotel.

the user for online time and forwards a portion of the collected monies to the particular videotex service provider(s) accessed during the session.

■ Ways of Accessing a Videotex System

A videotex user can connect to a host computer by using one of the following telephone communication methods. The method selected depends on its availability and comparative costs.

- *The user and host computer can use the same local network if both are connected to it.* For example, suppose a customer is located within local calling distance of the videotex system. A local telephone call can connect the customer's terminal to the videotex system.
- *If the host computer and the user use different local networks, the user can access the long-distance public switched telephone network to reach the host computer.* This method tends to be an expensive method. For example, suppose a

customer is located outside of the local calling area of the supplier. Terminals can be connected by the customer placing a long-distance call to the supplier.
- *A more frequently used method is to have an access point to a packet-switching network available to the videotex user by way of a local telephone call.* For example, a customer who is located outside of the local calling area of the videotex system can place a local telephone call to the nearest Tymnet or Telenet access port rather than placing a long-distance call to a videotex system.

For example, John, a subscriber located within local distance of the videotex system, has three choices:

1. He can place a local telephone call to the videotex system's host computer.
2. If all local lines are busy, John can dial a local number to access a public packet-switching network, such as Telenet or Tymnet.
3. A third choice would be to dial long-distance to another city to reach Telenet or Tymnet.

Charges include for choice 1 the cost of the local call, for choice 2 the cost of the local call and the cost of using Telenet or Tymnet, for choice 3 the cost of using Telenet or Tymnet and the cost of the long-distance call to access it. Note that John may be charged for local calling by message units used or according to a fixed monthly rate.

Teletext

- ### **Teletext Defined**

Teletext is a pseudointeractive information retrieval system that uses a one-way television link for information transmission. The system is described as pseudointeractive because it appears to the user to be interactive when in reality it is not. The teletext user does not at any time interact with the host computer. By using a modified television set a user can retrieve information such as news highlights, weather, classified advertisements, transportation schedules, and electronic yellow pages. Examples of teletext systems are Oracle (United Kingdom), Antiope (France), and Iris (Canada).

- ### **How Teletext Operates**

In a teletext system, a host computer is linked to a standard broadcast teletext system. Information stored in a host computer is transmitted to many locations repeatedly in round-robin fashion as a fixed set of pages of text. A user may select information from this text for viewing on the screen of a modified television set, as shown in Figure 12-6.

FIGURE 12-6   Schematic of a Teletext System

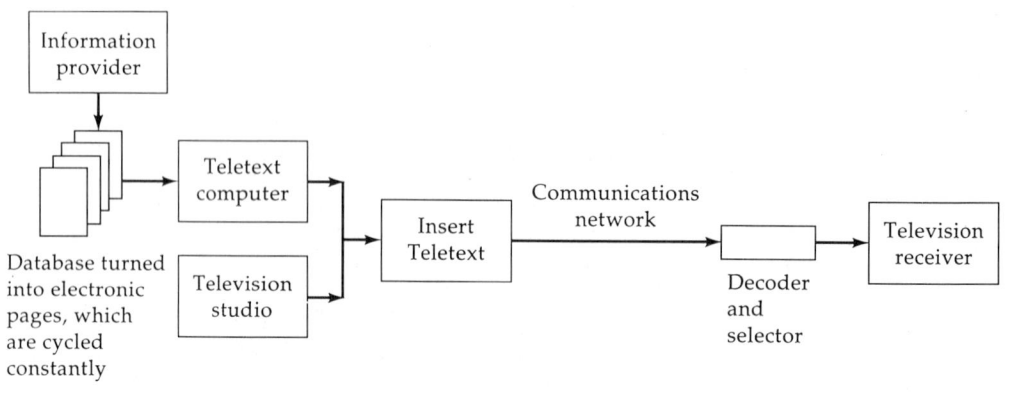

Teletext is a one-way transmission system that uses an unallocated segment of the bandwidth of a broadcast television signal, called the **vertical blanking interval**. The host computer transmits data to users by UHF, VHF, FM/SCA, MDS, or satellite channels. Although the system appears to interact with the user, no interaction between the user and the host computer occurs. Instead, the user interacts with his or her terminal.

As with videotex, teletext uses tree-structured databases with higher-level pages containing menus that guide the selection of lower-level pages. Since only a small portion of the television signal bandwidth is used, the number of pages is limited by a desire to reduce access time. By using two lines of the vertical blanking interval, 100 pages can be cycled in 25 seconds.

A number of hotels offer teletext services, commonly referred to as a "hotel magazine." The "magazine" lists hotel services, events, and city amenities. Hotel guests access the magazine by using the television set in their rooms or the terminals located throughout the hotel.

■ Teletext Equipment Components

The major components of a teletext system include serving equipment, receiving equipment, and communications facilities.

Serving Equipment.   Teletext users retrieve preformatted pages of data from the host or central computer. Because they do not interact with the users they serve, host computers for a teletext system require considerably less computational power than those for a videotext system. As a result, teletext host computers tend to be smaller and cheaper than those used for videotext systems. The number of users—whether 500 or 50,000—being

FIGURE 12-7 **Teletext Receiver**

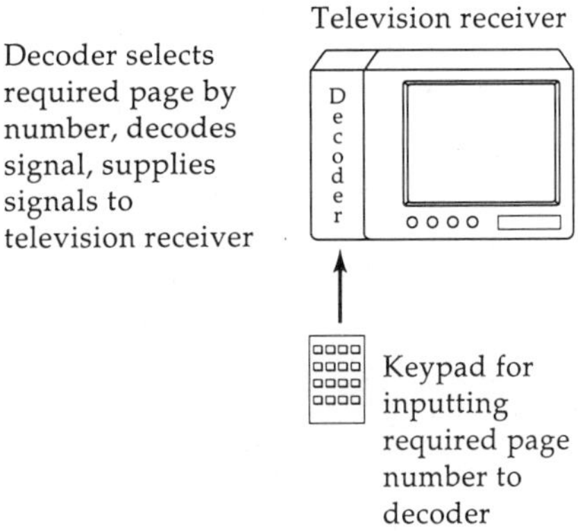

Decoder selects required page by number, decodes signal, supplies signals to television receiver

Television receiver

Keypad for inputting required page number to decoder

served by a host computer does not affect its size. Since teletext computing costs are not affected by the number of users, teletext is suitable for use as a general computer communication mass medium. The processing components that affect a teletext system's host computer are creating and loading content, obtaining content from other systems, and transmitting the output data in the appropriate form and at the right speed.

Receiving Equipment. The receiver may consist of an ordinary television set, a simple keypad for user entry, and a special decoder and storage unit, as shown in Figure 12-7. By using a keypad attached to a terminal, users can select the particular page desired for viewing. The decoder reads that page from the incoming signal, stores it, and displays it continuously until instructed to do otherwise. Some decoders can store several pages at a time, which results in faster retrieval time for users.

Communication Facilities. Teletext communication facilities are classified in two ways: (1) over-the-air or cabletext and (2) narrowband or broadband.

Over-the-Air or Cabletext. **Over-the-air teletext** includes broadcast teletext and direct broadcast satellite. **Broadcast teletext** is the transmission of teletext signals via a radio frequency transmission or broadcast. The signals are embedded in the vertical blanking interval (VBI) of a standard television broadcast. The signal is transmitted to the users with a television antenna. From the antenna the signal is sent to the decoder of the user's teletext terminal. In **direct broadcast satellite teletext** the teletext signals are transmitted to an earth station, then to a powerful satellite, and finally to a small, relatively inexpensive dish antenna. Figure 12-8 shows a diagram of such a

FIGURE 12-8   Direct Broadcast Teletext

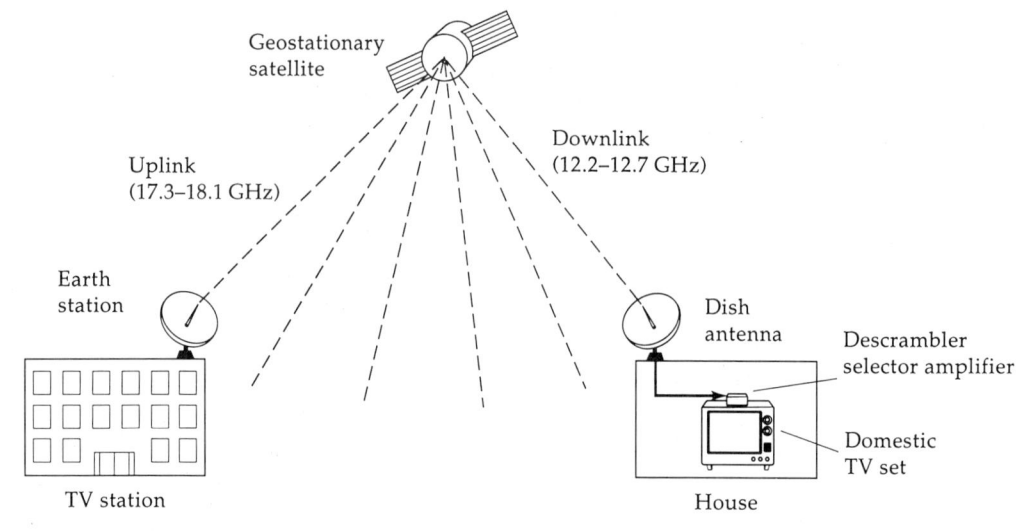

system. Both narrowband and broadband (full channel) teletext can be broadcast in this way.

Cabletext refers to the cable television network distributing teletext signals. More than 40% of the nation's cable systems offer electronic open-channel or billboard services such as news, weather, sports, and stock quotations. Cable systems use their own dedicated channels or a regular channel after it goes off the air. This means that the full video television channel is used to transmit information in the form of video signals.

Narrowband or Broadband Teletext.   Teletext is either narrowband or broadband. **Narrowband teletext** uses part of the VBI to transmit teletext signals. One VBI transmits only a small amount of data—about 100 pages in one cycle. **Broadband teletext**, or *full-channel teletext*, uses the entire active portion of the video signal to transmit teletext signals. This channel provides from 5,000 to 10,000 or more pages of full screens of information in the teletext transmission cycle.

Comparison of Videotex and Teletext Systems

Videotex and teletext are complimentary; each offers certain benefits and limitations. Figure 12-9 compares the two systems.

FIGURE 12-9 **Comparison of Videotex and Teletext Systems and Services**

Videotex	Teletext
Information is represented in pages.	Information is represented in pages.
Offers two-way transmission (from host to/from user).	Limited to one-way transmission (from host to user only).
Has large information capacity.	Information capacity depends on the bandwidth of the channel used.
Users request service from the host computer.	Users request service from a local device.
Offers information retrieval, computation, transactional services, messaging, and downline loading.	Offers only information retrieval and possibly downline loading and computation.
Systems are more costly to own and operate—costs are directly related to number of users and services offered.	Systems are less expensive to own for large number of users. Operating costs are independent of the number of users.
Operating costs are directly related to the number of users on the system.	Operating costs are not related to the number of users on the system.
Host computer size is affected by number of users.	Host computer size is not affected by number of users.
Information can be retrieved by hierarchy menus, keywords, or attributes.	Information can be retrieved only by hierarchy menus.
Connection is by telephone lines, packet-switching networks, and broadband cable lines.	Connection is by radio broadcast frequency, direct broadcast satellite, or cable television.

Videotex Standards

A computer requires means of encoding information, such as alphanumeric or graphic characters, in digital form to store in the computer's memory or to communicate to another computer or terminal. Standards developed for videotex deal with the presentation level protocol that corresponds to the sixth level of the seven-level reference model of OSI (Open Systems Interconnection) defined by the International Standards Organization (ISO). The presentation level protocol specifies rules, formats, and procedures for encoding text, graphics, and display techniques. For example, how is a page of information to be set up and formatted for display to the user?

■ Major Videotex Standards

The major videotex standards currently being used in North America are ASCII, NAPLPS, Prestel, and Antiope. Each of these standards uses different text and graphics display techniques. For example, alphanumeric characters and graphics can be displayed on the screen by one of the following three methods: alphamosaic, alphageometric, and alphaphotographic. The key difference between European and North American standards is that European standards use alphamosaic coding, while North American standards use alphageometric coding.

ASCII. Business videotex systems in North America generally use *American Standard Code for Information Interchange* (ASCII, pronounced "ask'-ee"), a standard adopted by the American Standards Association, to achieve compatibility among minicomputers and microcomputers communicating data by modem. Although ASCII is a text-only standard, it does include a special character set that allows minimal graphic capability. For users who do not require extensive graphics capability, the ASCII standard is satisfactory.

NAPLPS. *North American Presentation Level Protocol Syntax* (NAPLPS, pronounced "nap lips") is based on an alphageometric approach. This standard uses picture description instructions (PDIs) to tell the computer how to define basic shapes, such as a point, a line, an arc of a circle, a rectangular area, or a polygon, as well as color. NAPLPS produces high color graphics and is suited for applications that require high graphic resolution. NAPLPS uses ASCII alphanumerics and mosaic graphics for simple graphics and compatibility with European systems.

Prestel. *Prestel*, introduced in the early 1970s by the British Post Office (now known as British Telecom), was the first standard to be developed. This standard uses an alphamosaic approach in which shapes are generated from a series of mosaic shapes. Alphamosaic displays are of low resolution but have the advantage of low cost. Prestel uses serial coding, which prevents information from being significantly distorted. Prestel incorporates a SDCS (statistically defined character sets) coding method.

Antiope. In France the standard *Antiope* was created by the Ministère des Postes et Télécommunications (the PTT). Antiope also uses alphamosaic graphics as well as dynamically redefinable character sets (DRCS) mosaics. The addition of DRCS mosaics improves the quality of graphic mosaic images. Images are less angular and jagged in appearance than those consisting of static mosaics. Antiope uses parallel coding and asynchronous data transmission, resulting in information being transmitted in bursts rather than in a continuous stream.

■ Other Standards

Other standards are available, such as CEPT and CAPTAIN, but are not applicable to videotex systems in North America. *Consul of European Postal Telegraph* (CEPT) combines Prestel and Antiope coding schemes into one standard with rules governing switching between serial and parallel modes. This standard has been adopted by a consortium of European countries. *Character and Pattern Telephone Access Information Network* (CAPTAIN), the

Japanese videotex standard, uses alphageometrics. CAPTAIN has the ability to portray Kanji characters of the Japanese alphabet and use the alphaphotographic encoding methods.

Applications—Types

The types of videotex applications are information retrieval, computation, transaction, messaging, and downline loading. Since teletext is a one-way medium, it can perform three of these types of applications: information retrieval, computation, and downline loading. As explained below, when programs are downline-loaded to a teletext system, computing operations are then possible.

■ Information Retrieval

Information retrieval involves collecting, storing, updating, and easy access to large volumes of data. Information retrieval permits access to preformatted frames of information. Users interact with the system only by specifying the particular information that they desire to retrieve, such as bulletin boards or databases of information on a variety of subjects. Information can be either *permanent*, such as a listing of court rulings, or *perishable*—of short-term utility—such as stock market prices. For example, the Electronic Edition Travel Service of Official Airline Guides includes both types of information. On a given day a user of the service can access airline schedules (permanent information), as shown in Figure 12-10(a), as well find out whether seats for a particular flight are available (perishable information—information that is continuously being updated), as shown in Figure 12-10(b).

FIGURE 12-10 Information Retrieval Applications

```
DIRECT FLIGHTS
From: CHICAGO, IL USA/O'HARE      Departs: TUE-15 NOVEMBER, 1988
  To: SAN FRANCISCO: OAKLAND, CA, USA
                                              On-    Travel
 #   Departs     Arrives   Flight   Equip Meals Stops time  Time
No earlier direct flight service
1   754A ORD    955A   SFO UA  473  727    B    0    0    2:01
2   800A ORD   1014A   SFO UA  127  767    B    0    8    2:14
3*  845A ORD   1119A   OAK AA  483  72S    L    1    N    2:34
4*  850A ORD    226P   SFO AA  265  D10   B/S   2    V    4:36
5  1000A ORD   1220P   SFO UA  123  D10   L/S   0    U    2:20
6  1004P ORD   145A+1  OAK UA 1113  72S    L    0    1    2:41
 *Thomas Cook ticketing only for Electronic Edition bookings on this flight
PLEASE ENTER A COMMAND:           ?  = HELP
                                  X# = expand flight
 + = later flights     F# = fares offered     (# = line no.)
 – = earlier flights   A# = seats/fares available  RS = return schedules
 0 = original display  B# = book itinerary    CX = connections
```

(a) Air Travel Schedule

```
Available Seats and
Fares for UA 299 ORD/LAX               Departs: THU-15 SEP
Fares: US Dollars                  Fare Restriction Summary:
 #  One-way  Rnd-trp  Seats  Farecode  Cancel Advance Min.
                                       Penalty Purchase Stay Other
No lower fares
1            216.00            V1E7NR  : 100%   7 day  Sat.  *
2            236.00   Yes      VSE7NR  : 100%   7 day  Sat.  *
3   119.00           Gov t     VCA1    :  —      —      —
4            266.00            H1E2P25 :  25%   2 day  Sat.  *
5            286.00   Yes      QSE7NR  : 100%   7 day  Sat.  *
6            296.00   Yes      HSE7P25 :  25%   7 day  Sat.  *
7            356.00   Yes      HSE7P25 :  25%   7 day  Sat.  *
8   198.00                     H1A3    :  —     3 day   —    *
                                    *Additional Restrictions apply
PLEASE ENTER A COMMAND:
 + = higher fares   X# = expand fare          ? = HELP
                    L# = view fare restrictions  RS = return schedules
                    S# = schedules that apply (# = line number)
```

(b) Available Flight Seating

Courtesy of Official Airline Guides.

Information can be public or private. *Public information*, such as news, weather, and sports, is available to any subscriber. *Private information*, such as special business reports, may be restricted to subscribers with passwords.

■ Computation

Computation involves one or more of the following five operations: classifying, sorting, calculating, recording, and summarizing data. Computation occurs when the user accesses the host computer and sends it data to be processed. Typically, a user keys in data to the host computer, which in turn uses a program to process the data and then transmits the results to the user. An example is calculating the amount of each loan payment. In response to screen prompts, a user enters parameters, such as the amount of the loan, the length of the repayment period, and the loan percentage rate. These parameters are then processed by a program in the host computer, and the results are transmitted to the user.

■ Transaction

Transaction is a type of computer interaction that allows videotex subscribers to use the host computer to execute online a series of predetermined steps to obtain goods or services. Examples are teleshopping and telebanking, including electronic funds transfer.

Teleshopping is using the videotex system to conduct shopping transactions online. Examples are browsing through an electronic catalog, selecting and ordering merchandise from this catalog, making travel reservations, and purchasing theater tickets. For example, CompuServe offers online discount home shopping and the services of a discount broker for the online purchase and sale of securities. Figure 12-11 shows a typical teleshopping menu.

Telebanking is a videotex service that permits its users to perform banking operations online. Users can access their bank account records, select the desired banking service, and then be connected to the particular bank that is hooked into the videotex network. Users can review their transactions, transfer funds, pay bills, compare current interest rates, and exchange electronic mail with bank officers. Privacy, confidentiality, and security of transactions are important requirements in these interactive communication services.

Electronic funds transfers (EFT) is an integral component of teleshopping and telebanking, the final step requiring the user to initiate an EFT transaction.

Teleshopping and telebanking are becoming increasingly popular throughout North America and Western Europe. For example, the U.S. mail order business has recognized the compatibility between videotex and telephone or mail-in orders. Businesses that use videotex to sell their products and services benefit from immediate receipt of payment. Advantages to

FIGURE 12-11   **Teleshopping Menus**

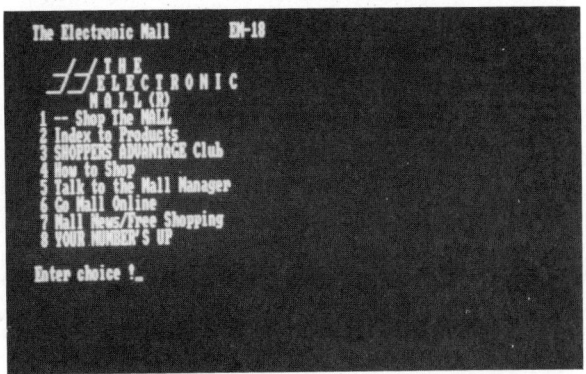

Courtesy of CompuServe Inc.

consumers include ease of ordering, increased product selection, and access to a 24-hour ordering service.

■ Messaging

Messaging, also known as electronic mail, is a computer communications service that permits a videotex system user to send information to and receive information from other users of the service. Typically, videotex message senders identify the recipient or recipients by an identification number and then create their own messages. The host computer immediately stores and forwards the message. The message service may be conversational or may store messages in mail boxes for retrieval by recipients at their convenience.

Messaging within a company may include distributing memos, maintaining meeting calendars, and circulating draft documents for communications, revision, and approval. Messaging to those outside a company includes communications with suppliers and trade news to customers.

■ Downline Loading

Downline loading refers to the host or sending computer transferring computer programs, computer-based instruction programs, videogames, and data to another computer, which allows it to operate in an off-line mode. Once the receiving computer receives the downloaded computer programs and data, its users can work with them or can transfer the data to their own word processing program to use, for example, in company reports.

When the computer memory is in the user's terminal, the computer activity can be performed more quickly. Another benefit of downloading is that the videotex user's cost of continuous communication between his or her terminal and the host computer is eliminated. In addition, when a number of users' terminals do not have to be tied into the host computer for long periods of time, the host computer's capacity is increased without capital being invested to increase its size. Both videotex and teletext systems can download programs.

Applications—Ways of Using Videotex

The main ways of using videotex are categorized as business, home or consumer-oriented, and public access videotex.

■ Business Videotex

A number of companies, ranging from Fortune 500 companies to those with 20 or fewer employees, use videotex to improve the distribution of corporate information to their employees. These companies are part of a rapidly growing business videotex market, which is expected to reach $1 billion in annual revenue by the mid-1990s.[1]

Business videotex is of two types: corporate videotex and business-to-business videotex. **Corporate videotex** refers to in-house videotex that enables a company to communicate internally with its employees. **Business-to-business videotex** is videotex that enables a company to communicate with its customers.

Corporate Videotex. Companies install their own videotex systems to reduce costs and to improve employee productivity. For example, the use of videotex for communicating internally with employees eliminates hard copy costs of paper, printing, and distribution. Employee productivity can be increased as follows:

- Employees can retrieve company information when needed. They do not have to depend on hard copy that takes more time to obtain or that requires costly and difficult-to-use data processing systems.
- Employees can communicate with each other by using electronic mail and thus eliminate the time usually spent playing telephone tag.
- Employees can conduct transactions electronically. For example, ordering supplies electronically reduces the need for multicopy order forms, shortens delivery time, and makes inventory control easier.

Typical applications of corporate videotex are identified in Figure 12-12. An in-house videotex system may also provide gateways that can access commercial videotex systems for the services they offer. These services give

FIGURE 12-12 **Typical Applications of Corporate Videotex**

- Distribute information to employees, such as policy and procedures manuals, personal benefits information, travel timetables, job postings, internal newsletters, and general company information.
- Update constantly changing documents, such as telephone directories, and distribute them immediately to employees.
- Update product and pricing information and distribute to employees and customers.
- Distribute electronic versions of product catalogs, account profiles, and customer order status reports.
- Complete customer orders by using the videotex system to place the orders, confirm them, and monitor the delivery operation. Once an order has been processed, inventory is instantly updated.
- Notify employees about training/course offerings, schedules, and cancellations.
- Conduct online course registration for employees.
- Administer online course quizzes and tests to employees wherever they are located.

users access to additional business and financial information, such as special industry reports.

Business-to-Business Videotex. As with corporate videotex, business-to-business videotex reduces costs and increases employee productivity. For example, the annual cost for a company to print and distribute mail catalogs can be reduced by using electronic versions of catalogs for both distribution and product ordering. Since videotex distributes information and processes orders faster than other methods, employee productivity also increases.

A company also uses business-to-business external videotex as a marketing tool to increase sales of its products and services and to keep customers up to date on product and service information. A company also experiences more direct contact with its customers than would otherwise be possible. Videotex also permits field sales personnel to communicate with the home office. A company may develop a business-to-business videotex system that delivers only its own product information. Other companies with related products may use a single business-to-business videotex service to combine their product information. Such a system gives its users a one-stop source of product information.

Typical applications of business-to-business videotex are identified in Figure 12-13.

Home or Consumer-Oriented Videotex

Home or consumer-oriented videotex systems offer information, products, and services to consumers through commercial systems, commonly called systems operators. A **systems operator** is a company that bundles together

FIGURE 12-13 **Typical Applications of Business-to-Business Videotex**

- Deliver up-to-date information, such as electronic product catalogs and servicing information, directly to customers.
- Provide online ordering for customers.
- Provide field sales personnel with up-to-date sales and customer information.
- Enable field personnel to file expense reports and access instantly inventory and shipment data.
- Allow customers to communicate with corporate personnel, access an electronic bulletin board on product or service information, participate in market research surveys, and contribute to product improvement suggestions.

several services offered by different companies and sells them to videotex subscribers at a fixed monthly charge and/or by usage time. The offerings of each systems operator vary, some systems operators providing more capabilities than others. Systems operators offer one or more of the following types of services: information retrieval, computing, transactions, messaging, and downline loading. Consumers may subscribe to more than one of these systems operators.

Typical applications of commercial videotex systems (system operators) are identified in Figure 12-14.

Commercial videotex systems and services (systems operators) are discussed more fully in the next section.

■ Public Access Videotex

Public access videotex (PAV), as defined by the Videotex Industry Association, differs from home or business videotex by being used in public locations by the general public. PAV services usually consist of several electronic displays (known as **kiosks** or electronic terminals) placed in high-traffic, consumer-oriented locations such as airports, shopping malls, and hotel and office building lobbies. These services deal with consumer needs and/or interests by providing information about products and services and/or transacting business with them.[2] A directory of PAVs may be obtained from the Videotex Industry Association. Figure 12-15 shows an example of such a kiosk.

Information can be displayed on screens as text-only screens, text with computer graphics, or full motion video with audio. A kiosk is easy to use, even for people who are not familiar with computers. The user selects the desired information from tables of contents or menus by touch-screen display monitors, numeric keypads, or alphanumeric keyboards. Figure 12-16 shows a typical kiosk menu. PAV services may also include one or more of the following:

- A printer to dispense coupons, product information, and/or directions

Applications—Ways of Using Videotex

FIGURE 12-14 Typical Applications of Commercial Videotex Systems

- Retrieve information such as news, weather, sports, travel schedules, and stock market information.
- Retrieve course offerings and schedules provided by universities. The user can then send a message to the host computer requesting a list of the available courses on a particular subject.
- Perform tasks related to work and/or personal business, such as calculating income tax or mortgage payments.
- Perform transactional services, such as teleshopping and telebanking. For example, some commercial systems allow users to access the electronic edition of the Official Airlines Guide for rate information and schedules and other directories for hotel and restaurant listings and make airline, hotel, and car reservations through telebanking.
- Perform electronic mail services.
- Download complete computer programs for interactive or computational activity, such as computer-based instructional programs, electronic games, and financial calculation.

FIGURE 12-15 A Levi's Shopping Kiosk

Courtesy of Levi Strauss & Company.

FIGURE 12-16 A Kiosk Menu

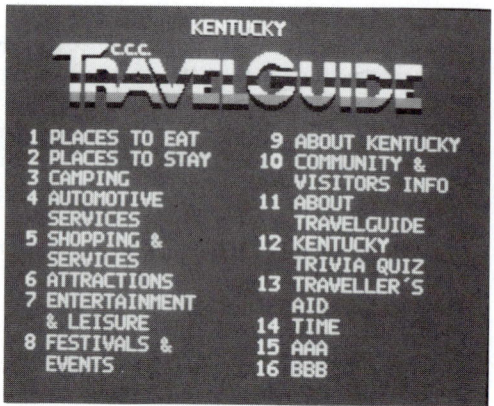

Courtesy of St. Clair VideoTex Design.

- A credit card reader to identify the consumer and allow actual purchase of products and services
- A telephone hookup to connect the user to the advertiser for making a purchase or a reservation

Growth of Kiosks. The major growth of kiosks is as terminals that offer information. Over 30,000 information terminals are in operation in supermarkets, department and hardware stores, and home improvement centers. Retailers and marketers particularly use these kiosks to demonstrate product uses and benefits. For example, Lowe's home centers, located throughout the Southeast, rely on electronic terminals to demonstrate do-it-yourself projects.

Kiosks placed in retail stores are becoming more popular with customers than kiosks installed in airports, office buildings, and other public places. One reason for their popularity in stores is that they act as an extension of the sales staff. Customers view the merchandise, touch a button for additional product information, and touch another button to place their order immediately. Kiosks in airports are often ignored because people don't know what they are for.

Advertiser-Supported PAV Services. PAV services are categorized as "advertiser-supported" or "operator-specific." **Advertiser-supported PAV services** are those in which organizations pay to have their information, product, or corporate identity displayed. This type of service permits advertisers to promote products and services by easy access to information. Users are more likely to act on the information viewed, since they initiate the request to see the advertiser's message. Advertisers can quickly change and/

FIGURE 12-17 **Typical Applications of Advertiser-Supported Public Access Videotex Services**

- Offer coupons, directions, or menus to a restaurant or store.
- Sponsor news, weather, and sports.
- Provide an electronic merchandise catalog.
- List local events (community calendar).
- Offer a messaging system at a convention.
- Provide store directories, floor plans, or maps.
- Sponsor a contest, quiz, or sweepstakes.
- Sponsor online questionnaires on related or unrelated information.
- Provide online applications for financial services.

or update information. Figure 12-17 lists typical applications of advertiser-supported PAV services.

Operator-Specific PAV Services. Operator-specific PAV services are those that are designed, operated, and funded by single organizations. They are aimed to appeal to the organization's target audience and are placed in locations convenient to this audience. This type of service can be a cost-effective alternative to existing promotion and sales methods. Costly salespeople and product displays can be replaced with kiosks. Information can be quickly changed and/or updated. Organizations can develop their own PAV services by investing in microcomputer equipment and software. For example, a department can computerize bridal and baby gift registries. Shoppers can then use a kiosk to obtain information about registrants' gifts. Figure 12-18 lists typical applications of operator-specific PAV services that are targeted directly to a particular organization.

FIGURE 12-18 **Typical Applications of Operator-Specific Public Access Videotex Services**

- Provide employee communications, bulletin boards, and announcements.
- Provide a building directory and floor plans.
- Describe employee benefits.
- Provide product demonstration and information (e.g., how to use a copier).
- Offer instructions about ordering products and services, such as health, diet, and exercise information in a health club.
- Dispense a product to the PAV user, such as a cash machine at a bank or videocassette rental machine.
- Act as a sales tool, for example, for travel agents to show customers an interactive videodisc kiosk featuring several tours or for automobile dealers to query inventory, selection, and information about automobile line.
- Act as customer service center to answer customer inquiries about products.
- Provide employee announcements.

A pioneer of kiosks is Florsheim's Express Shops. The Chicago-based shoe retailer began installing kiosks in the Chicago area in July 1987. By 1989, 2000 kiosks were operating. The kiosks offer an electronic catalog of odd-size men's shoes.

Commercial Videotex Systems

Over 2000 commercial videotex systems including teletext systems are available to users. Commercial videotex systems can be classified as general-purpose or specialized systems. **General-purpose** ("supermarket-type") **systems** offer a large variety of services ranging from general news and travel information to electronic mail. **Specialized systems** provide extensive coverage of limited areas, such as finance and banking or law or medicine. Refer to Appendix D for a list of selected commercial videotex systems/services. Also refer to the current issue of the *North American On-Line Directory*, published by R. R. Bowker Company, 245 W. 17th Street, New York, NY 10011, lists over 2000 databases and 130 information gateways in business.

■ General-Purpose Commercial Videotex Systems

A brief description of the services offered by three general-purpose commercial videotex systems are as follows:

CompuServe. CompuServe, a subsidiary of H&R Block, offers communications and information services to more than 500,000 users in more than 100 countries. At least 95% of the U.S. population can access CompuServe as a local telephone call through more than 600 U.S. cities. These services are offered through the company's CompuServe Information Service, which provides access to over 400 business, consumer, and entertainment videotex offerings. Included are electronic banking, shopping, travel services, current and historical stock quotes and commodities information, real-time communications, computer games, and up-to-the-minute news. CompuServe also offers electronic mail and value-added telecommunications services to more than 1100 major U.S. corporations and government agencies. Most services operate 24 hours a day, five days a week Monday through Friday, and 8 to 12 hours on Saturday and Sunday. A service may close for maintenance, usually between 4 A.M. and 6 A.M.

Prodigy. *Prodigy* is a consumer-oriented videotex offered by International Business Machines Corporation and Sears Roebuck & Company. The system is designed to create a subscriber base that numbers in the millions and that, together with advertising revenue and subscriber charges (a flat monthly fee), will support itself. Although Prodigy offers database-oriented services such as news, weather, and special events, its primary activity is transaction and information services in which content changes and use tends to be brief, such as home shopping and home banking. For example, users can make

Commercial Videotex Systems

FIGURE 12-19   A Prodigy Menu

Courtesy of Prodigy Services Company.

flight reservations, not just check schedules, and pay for the transactions by credit card or bank card or when they pick up their tickets. Subscribers are encouraged to make Prodigy part of their daily routine by connecting each day for five or ten minutes. Figure 12-19 shows a Prodigy menu.

■ Specialized Commercial Videotex Systems

A brief description of the services offered by four specialized commercial videotex systems are as follows.

Dow Jones News/Retrieval.   A leading videotex system that provides business and financial interactive information is Dow Jones News/Retrieval, established in 1974 as a service of Dow Jones & Company. In addition to its financial and business services, News/Retrieval offers general news, weather, and sports reports. The company currently has more than 230,000 subscribers.

DIALOG.   DIALOG has the largest collection of online databases with over 300 different types of proprietary databases published by both the government and private organizations. Topics include science, technology, business, medicine, social science, current affairs, and humanities. Among the users are businesses, industries, governments, and libraries. Examples of two proprietary databases that Dialog offers are as follows:

- ABI/INFORM includes extensive summaries of articles from top business and management journals—business practices, corporate strategies, and trends (from Data Courier Inc.).

- ARTHUR D. LITTLE/ONLINE includes management summaries from A. D. Little's market research reports—planning and industry research (from A. D. Little.)

LEXIS/NEXIS. Mead Data Central Inc., offers online, full-text databases of legal, news, business, and general information. LEXIS, the leading service for legal information, provides complete coverage of legal decisions and other subjects pertinent to the legal profession, such as patents, statutes, regulations, and administrative rulings. NEXIS, a business-information database, offers brokerage and investment data, stock reports, and other financial information.

VU/TEXT. VU/TEXT, offered by VU/TEXT Information Services, Inc., a Knight-Rider Information Retrieval Company, is the world's largest online newspaper databank with over thirty-five newspapers available in full text. Online services also include access to magazine, news wires, business and financial databases, maritime information databases, an encyclopedia, Canadian news sources, and international news sources. Business coverage is provided through the ABI/INFORM (a database also offered by Dialog) and Predicasts PROMPT databases. (PTS Prompt, a database supplied by Predicasts of Cleveland, Ohio, provides a primary source of information on product introductions, market share, corporate directions and ventures, and companies in every industry, containing detailed summaries of articles from trade and industry sources—market and strategic planning, tracking new technologies and products.)

The company also installs stand-alone electronic library systems for newspaper and other companies interested in establishing their own in-house electronic libraries. For newspapers that do not want an in-house system, VU/TEXT provides computerized storage and retrieval support.

For example, one company decided to track reactions and responses to drug testing in the workplace. A search in six VU/TEXT newspaper and wire service databases—the *L.A. Times*, the *Chicago Tribune*, the *Washington Post*, *Newsday*, the *Boston Globe*, and the *Philadelphia Inquirer*—using the phrase "drug test" in the headline or lead paragraph, identified 754 articles. The most recent article is displayed first, a portion of which is shown in Figure 12-20. The search took about 5 minutes at a cost of $8 (cost in 1989).

■ Commercial Videotex—Revenue and Fees

Commercial videotex companies, also called system operators, generate revenue both from information providers, those providing them with information, and from users of the systems.

Information Providers. Information for videotex and teletext systems can be provided by anyone. **Information providers** may pay a fee to rent space

FIGURE 12-20 **VU/TEXT: Screen Displaying Search Results on "Drug Testing"**

```
             RANK    1 OF    754,   PAGE    1 OF   6,  DB LT9, DOCUMENT  20330
                                 THE LOS ANGELES TIMES
                             Copyright Times Mirror Company 1989

  DATE: SUNDAY       February 12, 1989
  EDITION: Orange County Edition              LENGTH: MEDIUM
  PART-NAME: ONE                              PAGE: 1
  PART-NUMBER: 1                              COLUMN: 3
  DESK: Metro

  SOURCE: JIM CARLTON
          Times Staff Writer

                              EL TORO, TUSTIN BASES
                         TESTS SHOW MARINES'*DRUG*USE DECLINING

      Despite widespread perceptions of rampant*drug*use in the military, only
  four of every 1,000 servicemen stationed at Orange County's two Marine bases
  last year tested positive for marijuana, cocaine or other illegal drugs.
      *Drug*test results obtained by the Times Orange County Edition also show
  that the apparent*drug*use among servicemen in the Marine aircraft wing that
  includes El Toro and Tustin has been dropping steadily since 1986, when five
  of every 1,000 Marines tested positive for drugs. The figures correspond to a
  drop in*drug*use among Marines worldwide.

             RANK    1 OF    754,   PAGE    2 OF   6,  DB LT9, DOCUMENT  20330
      Marine officials attributed the drop to a rigorous*drug*testing*program
  instituted after nearly one-third of the nation's military admitted in a 1980
  survey that they experimented with drugs.
      ''Marines are now tested enough to be a deterrent but not so often to be
  detrimental to morale,'' said Master Sgt. Steve Merrill, a spokesman for the
  El Toro base. There are 12,000 Marines stationed at the two Orange County
  bases.

  Spotlighted by Kraft Trial
      *Drug*use among servicemen was spotlighted in testimony recently during
  Randy Steven Kraft's trial in Orange County Superior Court, where he is
  charged with killing 16 young men. There, it was suggested that Terry Lee
  Gambrel, a dead Marine found in Kraft's car when he was arrested 6 years ago,
  was heavily involved in drugs.
      A friend of Gambrel's, himself an ex-Marine, testified that half the
  Marines at the El Toro base where Gambrel was stationed were also using drugs.
      But a 1982 crackdown has effectively discouraged*drug*use in the military.
      Pentagon studies had found that military personnel were more likely to use
  drugs than civilians because of the rigors and loneliness of military life. In
  addition, the military consisted primarily of young men who are more prone to
  both*drug*and alcohol abuse.
      The military has never attracted hard-core*drug*users because the training
```

Courtesy of VU/TEXT Information Services, Inc.

on these systems. They place information on the systems that they think will be of interest to the public or business users. In other instances the commercial company pays for use of their information, such as databases. In still other instances, neither the information providers nor the system operators are charged for displaying pages of information. For example, information providers may be providing users with a social service or may be generating revenue from other sources, such as from the sales of merchandise and responses to classified advertisements.

Subscribers' Fees. The four basic types of fee systems used in the videotex industry are as follows:

- **Flat-rate pricing**, in which the user pays a monthly or annual subscription fee and is given unlimited access to the system.
- **Tiered flat-rate pricing**, in which the subscriber receives unlimited access to particular tiers or levels of information as specified in the subscription.
- **Usage-based pricing**, in which subscribers are charged only for online time.
- **Hybrid pricing**, in which two or more of the other pricing systems are combined.

Fees may vary with the time of day and the baud rate used. Daytime is considered prime time, while evening is nonpeak or standard time. Baud rates of 300 usually cost less to use than baud rates of 1200 or 2400. Other fees may include a registration fee, an annual membership fee, and service fees, such as computing online, using terminal equipment, accessing special information, creating pages, and administrative handling. A charge for using a network, such as Telenet or Tymnet may also be included. Figure 12-21 gives rates for selected commercial videotex systems offering services.

For example, a commercial videotex service that uses hybrid pricing charges an annual membership fee of $120 and a usage fee for communicating at any time. The usage fee at 300 or 1200 baud is $60/hour or $1/minute; at 2400 baud it is $90/hour or $1.50/minute. Other fees include online charges for databases, such as business newsletters.

■ Selecting a Commercial Videotex System

Before selecting a commercial videotex system, you should identify the type of applications appropriate for videotex systems. Among the questions that should be addressed are the following:

- Why do you want to use videotex?
- Which of your company applications are appropriate for videotex?
- Is videotex the most suitable technology for these applications?

Anyone involved in selecting videotex systems must be knowledgeable about videotex technology. Information can be obtained from the following sources:

- Videotex newsletters, books, conferences, and special reports
- Software and hardware vendors
- Consultants in the videotex industry
- Videotex users

Once the desired videotex services have been identified, information about the services offered by commercial videotex companies should be

FIGURE 12-21   Basic Rates of Selected Commercial Videotex Systems (July 1, 1989)

Commercial Videotex System	One-Time Registration Fee	Monthly Fee	Usage Cost			Connect Charges[1]
			300 Baud	1200 Baud	2400 Baud	
CompuServe (Columbus, Ohio)	$39.95		$ 6.30/hr	$12.80/hr	$12.80/hr	Local access
Dow Jones News/ Retrieval (Princeton, N.J.)	$29.95	$18.00[2]	$ 1.30/min	Prime time:[3] $ 2.80/min	$ 2.80/min + $0.03/1000 characters	Local access
			$ 0.80/min	Nonprime time: $ 1.76/min	$ 1.76/min + $0.06/1000 characters	
GEnie (Rockville, Md.)	$29.95		$18.00/hr	Prime time:[4] $18.00/hr	$18.00/hr	Local access
			$ 5.00/hr	Nonprime Time: $ 6.00/hr	$10.00/hr	
Prodigy (White Plains, N.Y.)	$49.95[5]	$ 9.95	None	None	None	Local access

[1] If the network cannot be accessed by a local telephone call, then long-distance telephone charges from the subscriber's location to the network apply. For example, a person living in Laconia, NH, using CompuServe pays long-distance charges from Laconia to Portland, ME, the closest CompuServe network access point. Although CompuServe has a network access point in Nashua, NH, it is cheaper to call out-of-state than within the state.
[2] Service fee begins after the first year.
[3] Prime time is from 6 A.M. to 6 P.M. Eastern Standard Time Monday through Friday; all other hours are nonprime time.
[4] Prime time is from 8 A.M. to 6 P.M. Monday through Friday; all other hours are nonprime time.
[5] This charge is for a software package that provides six passwords, for example, for six family members.
Note: These services may charge additional hour and/or per-search fees for using specific databases.

obtained. Figure 12-22 identifies the type of information that should be sought from each videotex company.

When more than one company (system operator) is to be selected, the services that each one offers should be complementary rather than identical. Before a final decision is made, the services of each company should be thoroughly tested. Employees who know how the videotex services are to be applied to the company's applications and who are computer literate should be selected to use and evaluate each system.

FIGURE 12-22 **Guide for Selecting a Commercial Videotex System/Service**

Directions: After responding to each question, test the service for a short period of time and then evaluate it.

Name of videotex system:
Company:
Address and telephone number:

1. Identify the videotex services offered:
   _____ Information retrieval
   _____ Computing
   _____ Transactions
   _____ Messaging
   _____ Downline loading
2. Specify the costs of the service:
   Registration fee:
   Monthly membership fee:
   Basic connect charges: _____ Baud rate _____ Prime time _____ Nonprime time
   _____ Baud rate _____ Prime time _____ Nonprime time
   Other charges:
3. Specify the communication surcharges:
   Carrier name: _____ _____ Prime time _____ Nonprime time
4. What type(s) of terminal equipment does the service support?
5. Does the service provide training?
   _____ Online _____ Seminars in major cities _____ Training manuals
6. Does the service provide a hotline? _____ Yes _____ No
7. Does the service provide a monthly newsletter about new services or better use of the old ones? _____ Yes _____ No
8. In what year was the service established? _____
9. Who has used the service in your area? _____
   Were they satisfied? _____ Yes _____ No
   (Contact them for information about the service.)

Comments:

Videotex and Teletext Issues

Among the major issues of videotex providers and users are the following.

■ Standards

Videotex procedures, codes, and signals vary among countries making it impossible for them to work with each other. For example, subscribers using British Prestel cannot access the Canadian Telidon system. Each system uses a different method of constructing text and graphics. International groups are trying to define standards to permit compatibility among videotex procedures, codes, and signals.

■ Information Reliability

The ability of videotex systems to make large amounts of information available may raise the issue of information reliability. Should commercial videotex systems be responsible for ensuring that the information that they provide is reliable? How can business and consumers be protected from misinformation?

■ Information Privacy and Confidentiality

Information privacy and confidentiality are key factors to businesses and other users in considering the use of videotex. Companies must be certain that transactions and information exchange within videotex systems are secure.

Information privacy refers to the right of individuals and businesses to control the processing and use of data about their business and personal activities. Videotex systems can provide information about a business or an individual's activities. For example, a business's or an individual's financial status can be obtained from telebanking and their buying habits from teleshopping. If information were collected and integrated with other electronically stored information, a fairly complete profile of their business and personal matters could be obtained.

Information confidentiality refers to protecting information and limiting its use to authorized people for authorized purposes. Information entered into a computer and accessed from it should be controlled by authorized means. Governments have begun to address the public's concern regarding information privacy and confidentiality in computer databases. Proposed privacy guidelines have been issued by the Videotex Industry Association. But even if the videotex industry establishes privacy guidelines, who will be responsible for enforcing them?

■ Legal Issues

Among the legal issues that are significant are copyright protection and regulatory controls.

Copyright protection involves the storage and retransmission of pages. Any videotex terminal equipped with the capability of printing and storing pages can record and, if desired, retransmit copyrighted pages without the permission of the copyright holder.

Regulatory issues include the following:

Who should set policy for videotex? Should representatives from government, business, and/or other organizations, individually or collectively, set the policies?

Who should regulate the communication networks? The Federal Communications Commission, a regulatory body that is independent of both Congress and the President, provides telecommunications guidelines and regulations to videotex systems owned and operated by private corporations. Should the government closely regulate communications networks? Should the current private system be reorganized to become a public information utility similar to the U.S. Postal Service? If videotex is considered an essential service because it transmits information necessary to the functioning of the nation, is it appropriate that a profit be derived from this service?

Who should set rates? Should rates for videotex services in the United States be set according to market demand or according to government-approved tariffs? Government rates may result in lower access charges and promote heavier use. However, if rates do not reflect market demand, business might be reluctant to invest in the videotex industry.

Summary

Both videotex and teletext systems are used by businesses internally as well as to communicate with customers. Systems are also used in homes and in public locations such as hotels and airports. Available commercial systems either are the supermarket-type or provide extensive coverage in a particular area, such as finance or law. With a personal computer, communications software, a modem, and a telephone, today's employees can access thousands of databases covering such topics as airline schedules, stock prices, weather reports, and world events or perform such transactions as teleshopping and telebanking. Employees can download programs and data for use with their own programs. In return for these services, employees typically pay a subscription fee, an hourly connect charge, and telephone line costs. Among the major issues of videotex providers and users are defining standards for compatibility among videotex procedures, codes, and signals; determining whether or not commercial videotex systems should provide reliable information; and addressing information privacy and confidentiality. Significant legal issues concern copyright protection and regulatory controls.

■ *Key Terms*

Broadband teletext
Broadcast teletext
Business-to-business
  videotex
Cabletext
Commercial videotex
  systems:

General-purpose
  systems
Specialized systems
Corporate videotex
Decoder
Direct broadcast
  satellite teletext

Fee systems:
  Flat-rate pricing
  Hybrid pricing
  Tiered flat-rate pricing
  Usage-based pricing
Information providers
Kiosk

Narrowband teletext
Over-the-air teletext
PAV services:
   Advertiser-supported PAV services
   Operator-specific PAV services
Public access videotex
Systems operator
Teletext
Vertical blanking interval
Videotex
Videotex applications:
   Computation
   Downline loading
   Information retrieval
   Messaging
   Transaction

■ *Self-Quiz*

Indicate whether the statement is true or false.

1. When desired, a teletext user can interact with the host computer.   T/F
2. Standards developed for videotex deal with the seventh level of the OSI model.   T/F
3. Broadband teletext uses the entire portion of a video signal.   T/F
4. The size of a teletext's host computer is not affected by the number of users.   T/F
5. Public access videotex uses kiosks to offer services.   T/F
6. The costs of operating a videotex system are directly related to the number of users on the system.   T/F

Complete each of the following statements.

1. The first commercial application of teletext was called _____ .
2. The major components of a videotex system are _____ .
3. An example of a commercial videotex system is _____ .
4. The unallocated segment of the bandwidth of a broadcast television signal is called the _____ .
5. A typical application of business-to-business videotex is _____ .
6. A company that bundles together several videotex services offered by different companies and sells them for a fee is called a(n) _____ .

Match Column A with Column B.

Column A
(a) Computation
(b) Downline loading
(c) Information retrieval
(d) Messaging
(e) Transaction

Column B
___ 1. Permits access to preformatted frames of information.
___ 2. Permits goods or services to be obtained.
___ 3. Processes user's data.
___ 4. Transfers programs and data to another computer.
___ 5. Permits a user to send and receive information.

■ Review Questions

1. (a) Identify the components of a videotex system.
   (b) Describe how the system operates.
2. (a) Identify the components of a teletext system.
   (b) Describe how the system operates.
3. Describe the differences and similarities between videotex systems and teletext systems.
4. What are the various ways in which the following subscribers can access a videotex system in Columbus, Ohio?
   (a) The subscriber lives in Columbus, Ohio.
   (b) The subscriber lives in New York City.
5. (a) Describe how a company could apply each of the various types of videotex applications.
   (b) Describe how a company could apply each of the various types of teletext applications.
   (c) Why is teletex limited to certain applications?
6. (a) What is the difference between corporate videotex and business-to-business videotex?
   (b) Give an example of each.
7. What kind of services can commercial videotex systems (system operators) offer consumers?
8. (a) How can a company use public access videotex?
   (b) How can your school use public access videotex?
9. (a) Describe the services offered by a commercial videotex system (system operator) of your choice.
   (b) How do commercial videotex companies generate revenues?
   (c) What criteria should you use when selecting a commercial videotex system?

■ Activities/Projects

1. Discuss issues that are of concern to videotex suppliers and users. For suggestions, refer to the section on issues in this chapter.
2. Experiment with videotex and teletext. Visit an organization that uses these systems. *Note*: Some colleges and universities offer students and faculty access to videotex systems, particularly Dow Jones/New Retrieval, NewsNet, and Dialog. Alternatively, check large organizations and travel agencies in your area.
3. Arrange with one of the videotex companies listed in Appendix D or one of your choice for a free demonstration of its offerings. You will need a microcomputer; communication software; a modem of 300, 1200, or 2400 baud; and a telephone. Check whether you can access the system without any charge, including telephone charges.

(a) Is the system easy to use?
(b) What information does the system provide?
(c) What are the costs for a subscriber?
(d) What do you consider the system's weaknesses? Its strengths?
4. How could videotex or teletext systems be used at your school or workplace? What benefits could they offer your college community or employees?
   (a) Develop a proposal of how your school or workplace could use either or both of these systems.
   (b) What benefits would the implementation of your plan offer to the school or workplace? Would there be any drawbacks to your plan?

Case: Costing a Videotex System/Service

Donna, the manager of a company located in Boston must decide which of the videotex systems listed in Figure 12-21 to select for her company and what method(s) the employees will use to access the system. Donna wants to select the system and the method of access that will be least costly for the company. Although she knows that some employees will use the system more than others, she estimates that the average usage will be three hours a week during the day for each of the company's twenty employees. Transmission will be at 1200 baud.

Donna must calculate the cost of each videotex system, including the cost of the various ways of accessing the system. She has collected the following data for her analysis (Figure 12-21 provides rate information for each of the videotex systems): Donna's company's local calling plan is a flat-rate service that provides local calling in Boston with no additional message or measured rate charges. All four videotex services provide access to their system through their own network or through Telenet or Tymnet, all of which can be accessed by calling a local Boston telephone number. Donna also learns that some companies have special corporate rates.

CompuServe corporate rates are $44.95 registration fee for the first subscriber and $10 for each additional one. At 1200 the baud rate, the usage cost is $12.80/hour for both prime time and nonprime time for each subscriber. A $25 usage credit is applied to the first month's total bill.

Dow Jones News/Retrieval charges no registration or startup fee to corporate subscribers but gives ten hours of free online time to the company in the first month of membership. Charges include a $75 monthly charge and the following usage charges: Prime time rates at 1200 baud are $1.87/minute for news and financial information and $1.43/minute for current and history quotes and general services. Nonprime time rate rates at 1200 baud are $0.29 for news, current and history quotes, and general services and $1.17/minute for financial information.

GENie charges are the same for both individuals and corporate customers. Charges include a fee of $29.95 for each password and a usage charge at 1200 baud of $18/hour for prime time and $6/hour for nonprime time. Each password receives a usage credit of $10 that is applied to the first month's bill.

Prodigy charges are also the same for both individuals and corporate customers. Prodigy charges $49.95 for a software package that contains six passwords and a monthly charge of $9.95 for each software package. The first month is free. Prodigy does not charge for online usage.

For information concerning prime time and nonprime time hours refer to Figure 12-21.

(a) What are the monthly charges for each system?
(b) What system should Donna select? Why?
(c) How can the costs be controlled once a system is installed for a company's employees?

Notes

1. *An Executive's Guide for Understanding and Implementing Business Videotex* (Rosslyn, Va.: Videotex Industry Association, 1986), p. 5.
2. Public Access Committee, "Introduction to Public Access Videotex," (Rosslyn, Va.: Videotex Industry Association), pp. 1–6.

Additional Readings

AT&T Presentation Level Protocol (Parsippany, N.J.: AT&T, May 1981).

Paul Hurly, Matthias Laucht, and Denis Hlynka. *The Videotex and Teletext Handbook* (New York: Harper & Row, Publishers, 1985).

Graham Langley, *Telecommunications Primer* (London, England: Pitman Publishing Limited, 1984).

James Martin, *Viewdata and the Information Society* (Englewood Cliffs, N.J.: Prentice-Hall, Inc., 1982).

Charles T. Meadow and Albert S. Tedesco, *Telecommunications for Management* (New York: McGraw-Hill Book Company, 1985), Chapter 12.

Rick Minicucci, "Electronic Information Services Deliver Data to Your Desktop," *Today's Office*, June 1987, pp. 56–62.

Erick Mortenson, "Tap into Information Power," *Administrative Management*, November 1987, pp. 24–29.

Gary Power, "Videotex for Competitive Advantage," *Information Management Review*, Vol. 1, No. 3, Winter 1986, pp. 35–46.

Efrem Sigel with Joseph Roizen, Collin McIntyre, and Max Wilkinson, *Videotext: The Coming Revolution in Home/Office Information Retrieval* (White Plains, N.Y.: Knowledge Industry Publications, Inc., 1980).

Efrem Sigel with Peter Sommer, Jeffrey Silverstein, Collin McIntyre, and Blaise Downey, *The Future of Videotext* (White Plains, N.Y.: Knowledge Industry Publications, 1983).

John Tydeman, Hubert Lipinski, Richard P. Adler, Michael Nyhan, and Lawrence Zwimpfer, *Teletext and Videotex in the United States* (New York: McGraw-Hill Publications Company, 1982).

Periodicals

DataBase is published bimonthly by Online, Inc., 11 Tannery Lane, Weston, CT 06993. Publishes articles on database usage and creation.

Additional Readings

Dowline is published bimonthly by Dow Jones & Company, Inc., P.O. Box 300, Princeton, NJ 08543.

Online is published bimonthly by Online, Inc., 11 Tannery Lane, Weston, CT 06993. Covers broad areas of information management, training, and equipment and online services, database usage, and hardware (especially microcomputers).

CHAPTER 13

Teleconferencing

Teleconferencing Defined
  Types of Teleconferencing Systems
  Applications

Teleconferencing Evolution

Audio Conferencing
  Audio-Conferencing Transmission
  Audio-Conferencing Bridges
  Audio-Conferencing Equipment and Facilities
  Benefits and Drawbacks of Audio Conferencing
  Audio-Conferencing Applications

Enhanced Audio Conferencing
  Telewriters
  Facsimile
  Freeze-Frame Video
  Enhanced Audio-Conferencing Applications

Two-Way Videoconferencing
  Two-Way Videoconferencing Defined
  Videoconferencing Operation, Technology, and Equipment
  Videoconferencing Applications

Business Television
  Business Television Defined
  Business Television Operation, Technology, and Equipment
  Business Television Networks
  Business Television Applications

Courtesy of Darome, Inc.

Computer Conferencing
    Computer Conferencing Defined
    Computer Conferencing Operation
    Computer Conferencing Applications
    Administering Computer Conferencing
    A Computer Conferencing System—VAX Notes
    Benefits and Drawbacks of Computer Conferencing
    Comparison of Electronic Mail, Bulletin Boards, and Computer Conferencing

Benefits and Drawbacks of Teleconferencing

Planning, Conducting, and Evaluating a Teleconference

CHAPTER OBJECTIVES

After studying this chapter, you should be able to

1. Distinguish among the different types of teleconferencing systems.
2. Discuss how each type of teleconferencing system operates.
3. Suggest how each system can be used by an organization.
4. Plan, conduct, and evaluate a teleconference.

Sears Roebuck & Company is equipping twenty-four regional offices to send and receive live video transmission via satellite. At the same time, 800 retail stores and catalog stores are being set up to receive these video images but not transmit any. But a two-way audio component will allow them to enter into discussion with the offices. These facilities will speed management decisions, conduct staff training, and reduce employee travel between offices and retail stores.

Corporate headquarters of a national real estate company uses the telephone daily to conduct audio-only conferences to discuss immediate and future operations with its branch managers nationwide. The number of branches participating in a conference runs from as few as three to as many as forty.

The Darome Connection, another audio conferencing service, recently arranged a one-time audio conference that linked the President's Oval Office with West Germany's Chancellor and reporters assembled at U.S. embassies in six European capitals.

A national labor union uses the CompuServe's Participate, a computer conferencing service, to distribute information to its members as well as to allow them to discuss timely topics. Whenever their individual schedules permit, members use their computers to access the information as well as to enter into discussions with union officials and the other members.

A Boston law firm is using Dialcom's computer conferencing CAUCUS for internal case preparation and for staying in close communication with its clients.

In each of these scenarios a type of teleconferencing is being used. Businesspeople need to talk frequently with each other for such reasons as developing new ideas, solving problems, and making decisions. Meetings have become an everyday occurrence in business. In fact, 20 million meetings are held daily in the nation, 80% of them lasting no more than 30 minutes. Two-thirds of these meetings could be handled by voice communications only, according to Link Resources Corporation.

Teleconferencing offers alternatives to the traditional meeting but at the same time changes one of the basic activities of business—how people communicate. To understand the potential impact of teleconferencing and how to select, plan, and implement "electronic meetings," this chapter discusses the technology, benefits and drawbacks, and applications of teleconferencing.

Teleconferencing Defined

A conference implies that more than two people are involved; otherwise, it would be a conversation. **Teleconferencing** is often defined as the use of a telecommunications system for communicating with two or more groups or with three or more individuals at separate locations.

In teleconferencing, communication is often interactive and synchronous, although one-way communication can take place. A conference is referred to as a **synchronous conference**, or *real-time conference*, when all the participants are present simultaneously, regardless of location or time zone. Most teleconferences are conducted in real time. A conference in which participants can check in when they wish is an **asynchronous conference**, or *store-and-forward conference*.

Types of Teleconferencing Systems

Teleconferencing systems range from simply setting up a speakerphone and dialing a number to two-way video meetings in which participants at different locations can see and hear each other and exchange documents and graphics. The objectives of a meeting, the number and characteristics of the participants, and the facilities available are major factors in selecting the appropriate type of teleconferencing system. Teleconferencing can require an investment ranging from under $100 to over $1 million.

Organizations can choose from among five types of teleconferencing systems to transmit voice and data. Each system can operate independently or can be combined with another for multimedia exchanges. The five main types of teleconferencing are described below and illustrated in Figure 13-1.

- **Audio conferencing systems** are audio-only systems in which two or more groups or three or more individuals at separate locations exchange verbal information with each other using amplified telephone speaker devices. Participants can hear and be heard, but not see and be seen, by each other.
- **Enhanced audio conferencing systems**, also referred to as audiographic systems, supplement audio-only systems by allowing participants at two or more sites to create graphics, snap photographs, or assemble documents and transmit them in real time.
- **Two-way videoconferencing systems** provide two or more sites with interactive, two-way video, audio, and graphics capabilities.
- **Business television systems** transmit live television one way from a central site to one or more other sites. These systems are usually complemented by two-way audio transmission so that viewers may enter into a discussion with the speakers.
- **Computer conferencing** allows participants to exchange messages with each other by using computer keyboards. Computer conferencing may be synchronous, that is, interactive in real time; but more often, it is asynchronous, that is, messages are stored in a central computer until retrieved by their intended recipients.

Figure 13-2 compares the characteristics of teleconferencing systems.

Applications

Teleconferencing has practically unlimited uses. Examples of applications are listed in Figure 13-3 as well as in the discussion of each type of teleconferencing system.

FIGURE 13-1 The Five Types of Teleconferencing Systems

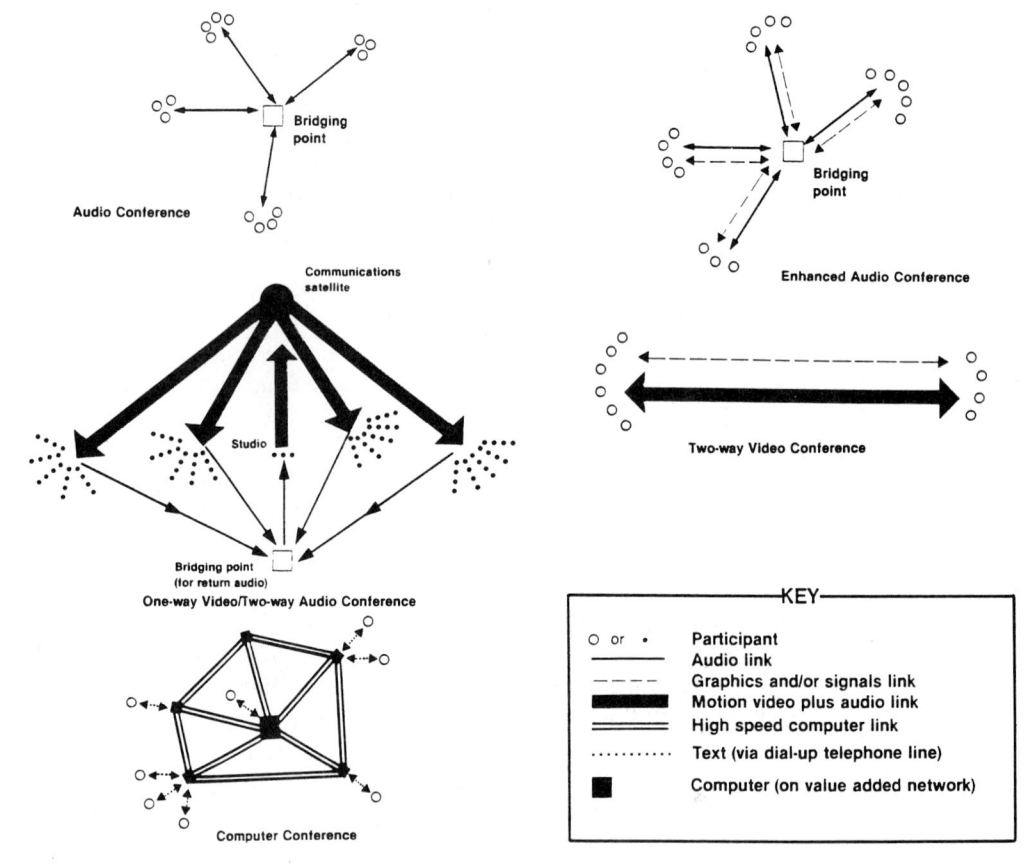

Courtesy of Knowledge Industry Publications, Inc.

Teleconferencing Evolution

The first audio conferencing system was the traditional telephone conference call that allows a three-way telephone connection. Another early system was the hands-free telephone containing a loudspeaker allowing several people to participate in a conversation. These audio systems are still being used along with more advanced technologies, such as amplifier speakers and multiple microphones. Since the 1970s, the use of audio conferencing has been increasing, particularly since its transmission time is cheap, it can be accessed on demand, and the equipment is already available.

At the 1964 New York World's Fair, AT&T introduced its Picturephone—one of the first videoconferencing systems to be developed. It was lauded as the precursor to a revolution in communications. Unfortunately, two-way

FIGURE 13-2 Comparison of Characteristics of Teleconferencing Systems

Characteristic	Basic Audio Conferencing	Enhanced Audio Conferencing	One-Way Video Conferencing	Two-Way Video Conferencing
Maximum number of locations	Usually from 16 to 50, depending on bridge	Usually from 16 to 50, depending on bridge	Usually as for basic audio conferencing	Usually only 2
Typical number of locations	From 2 to 6	From 2 to 6	Highly variable, depending on purpose	2
Maximum number of persons per location	A few hundred, if lines allowed at microphone	A few hundred, if lines allowed at microphone	A few hundred	From 6 to 12
Typical number of persons per location	Up to about 5	Up to about 5	Highly variable; usually from 20 to 200	About 5
Fully two-way transmission	Yes	Usually	No	Yes
Locations outside North America	Easy	Easy, if terminal equipment available	Very unusual and expensive	Very unusual and expensive
Number of technical/production personnel	Usually at most 1 (at bridge)	Usually 1 at bridge; maybe 1 per site	Usually at least 6 at center and 1 per remote site	Usually 1 on call at either end
Relative average cost per occasion	Low	Fairly low	High to very high	High to very high
Relative average cost per participant	Low	Fairly low	Fairly low to moderate	High to very high
Constraints on location of sites	Often only access to telephone network	Where terminal equipment is located	Large enough rooms; access to satellite dishes; availability of rooms	Usually one of a fixed set of installed rooms

Courtesy of Knowledge Industry Publications, Inc.

videoconferencing did not attract the wide audience that was predicted. The prohibitive cost of videoconferencing transmission and equipment limited its use to only a few companies, such as those in the aerospace industry.

But in 1980, advances in teleconferencing technologies began to lower the costs of transmission and equipment, thereby making videoconferencing more attractive to an increasing number of organizations. According to Link Resources Corporation, the total teleconferencing market is expected

FIGURE 13-3   Examples of Teleconferencing Applications

Exchange information.
Make decisions.
Solve problems.
Announce new products/services.
Conduct seminars for employees/customers/clients.
Access experts.
View documents/blueprints with others at different locations.
Train employees.
Hold a one-time event for employees at all locations to view simultaneously.
Respond to emergency meetings.

to grow from $279 million 1984 to $3.7 million by 1990. Although audio conferencing still represents the largest segment of the market, the most significant growth is occurring in corporate use of video, particularly business television.

Audio Conferencing

As was previously stated, audio conferencing permits voice interaction among a number of participants, usually over standard telephone lines, as shown at the beginning of the chapter. "Conference calling" is a normal part of the daily activities of many businesses, although it is often not called teleconferencing. The three basic components of audio conferencing are

- The transmission that links the participating locations
- A conference bridge that connects multiple parties together for the conference
- Terminal equipment, such as a desktop speakerphone, and facilities, such as a conference room

■ Audio-Conferencing Transmission

Audio-conferencing calls are usually transmitted over standard telephone lines, although for heavy audio conferencing between the same sites, leased telephone lines are often used. The low cost of standard telephone lines and their high availability make them especially suitable for audio conferencing.

The channel's bandwidth determines information capacity: The greater the bandwidth, the more information can be transmitted. As was discussed in Chapter 2, the bandwidth of analog lines is measured in cycles per second, which defines the range of frequencies that can be transmitted. Digital transmission line capacity is measured in bits per second (bps). Audio conferences, conducted over standard voice lines, require a bandwidth of 2700

FIGURE 13-4 Bandwidth Requirements of Teleconferencing Systems

Type of Teleconferencing	Analog Bandwidth	Digital Bit Rate (kbps)
Audio conference (telephone grade)	2700 Hz	64
Commercial radio audio broadcast conference	5000 Hz	80
Electronic blackboard	2700 Hz	1.2
Freeze-frame video (9–35 seconds per frame)	2700 Hz	—
Full-motion video (compressed)	—	1.5
Full-motion video (noncompressed)	6 MHz	

Hz, while commercial radio audio broadcast transmissions require 5000 Hz. The analog and digital requirements for audio conferences and the other types of teleconferences are shown in Figure 13-4.

■ Audio-Conferencing Bridges

Every telephone connection has a certain amount of signal loss and background noise. To minimize these problems when three or more sites are used in an audio conferencing system, an electronic device called a **conference bridge** connects the participants' telephone lines, as shown in Figure 13-5.

FIGURE 13-5 Connecting Telephone Lines to a Bridge

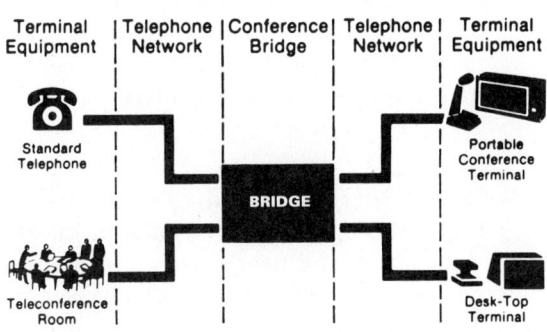

Courtesy of Darome, Inc.

A bridge performs the following functions.

- Protects participants from noise generated from locations where no one is speaking. It allows only one line to be active at any given time and quiets the output of the other lines.
- Minimizes signal loss. For example, if one line is producing a weak signal, the bridge amplifies it to enable it to be heard by all participants.
- Cancels echoes that occur internally at the bridge. An echo is a weakened version of a signal reflected back because of an obstruction.
- Provides fast switching among inputs to eliminate signal "slipping" as a person begins speaking.

Methods of Bridging. The two methods of bridging are end-point bridging and midpoint bridging. In end-point bridging, the bridge is placed at one of the end points of the network. In midpoint bridging, the bridge is located as closely as possible to the center of the network. Midpoint bridging is preferable, since signals do not have to travel as far and thus are subject to fewer loss and other transmission disturbances.

Types of Bridge Setups. A bridge can be set up by a telephone operator, by "meet-me," or by the conference originator. Traditionally, setting up a conference has required the assistance of a telephone operator. In this type of setup, the originator of the conference provides the operator with telephone numbers of the other participants; at the time of the conference the operator then calls and connects each participant. Alternatively, the conference originator can connect the participant by dialing each of the participant's telephone numbers—a lengthy and expensive process. Once everyone is online, a roll call is taken. After the roll is completed, the telephone charges begin.

"**Meet-me**" bridging, outlined in Figure 13-6, is replacing these methods. Instead of the operator or the conference originator calling each of the participants, each participant calls a predetermined telephone number from any telephone at the specified meeting time. The conference bridge automatically answers the call and adds the caller to the conference. The company offering the bridging service assigns a permanent number to companies that offer frequent conferences and a one-time conference number to other companies.

Bridge Services. Bridges are provided by AT&T, embedded in PBX and key systems, offered by conferencing services, or are stand-alone devices installed on the user's premises. Some of these bridges also allow documents, graphics, and still video pictures to be transmitted.

AT&T Audio Conferencing Services. AT&T offers two services: AT&T Conference Center and AT&T Alliance Teleconferencing Services.

FIGURE 13-6 Setting Up a Call with "Meet-Me"

TO SET UP A CALL WITH MEET-ME

1. Dial 1 800 544-6363. An operator will ask the date, time, call duration, number of locations and method of billing.*
2. You will be given two special access numbers. One you will keep, the other you will give to your fellow conferees.
3. At the meeting time, everyone calls their special access number, and is automatically connected together. Only *you* are required to use a touch-tone phone.

*You may want to accommodate those who call in early by reserving a start time five minutes prior to the time you've scheduled the meeting to begin.

FEATURES

To add locations (domestic or int'l)

Dial [#] if you have already reserved space
Dial [#][0] if you have *not* reserved space
Dial [*] if:
• Busy, no answer
• Make a mistake
• Poor connection

To screen callers

Dial [#] to speak with caller
Dial [#] to add caller
Dial [*] to disconnect caller
Dial [#] to reconnect yourself

GENERAL TIPS

Dial [#][0] to:
• Extend call time
• Request assistance

Dial [#] to:
• Leave call
• Rejoin call

Copyright, 1986, AT&T, reprinted by permission.

AT&T Conference Center is operator-assisted and is accessed by calling the AT&T telephone operator from any telephone asking to be connected to the AT&T Conference Operator. This system handles as many locations as desired for each conference call. Some conference calls include more than 300 participants and last more than eight hours. For each location the conference originator is billed a fixed amount—ranging from $3 for within state conferences to over $11 for international calls—and the station-to-station long-distance telephone rate between the originator and each participant's location for the length of the conference.

AT&T Alliance Teleconferencing Services provides all three types of bridges. The Alliance can connect a maximum of fifty-nine locations* by telephone, including the originator's location. Its bridges are physically located in White Plains, New York; Chicago; Reno, Nevada; and Dallas. The cost of a "meet-me" conference includes station-to-station long-distance

---

*A location refers to one telephone.

charges between each location and the conference's bridge location and a bridge charge of $0.25 per minute per location. If an operator sets up the conference call, an additional $3.50 per location is charged. Although more expensive than AT&T Conference Center, Alliance is preferred by business customers because it offers "meet-me" as an option. WATS, FX, and tie line circuits cannot be linked to either of the AT&T bridges.

PBX or Key System Conferencing Bridges. Conference bridges are available on PBX, Centrex, and key systems. Advantages of using these bridges include low cost and the ability to use any low-cost service, such as WATS lines or tie lines, that can be dialed on the company's PBX or key systems. These bridges are usually limited to six lines and cannot amplify weak connections. To ensure reasonable quality without amplification, PBX bridges usually restrict audio conferencing to using only two of the six lines as outside lines.

Audio-Conferencing Services. Companies such as Darome, Inc., Connex, and MultiLink Electronic Meeting Service also offer conference bridges. The conference originator is charged a linking fee by the conference service and long-distance telephone charges by the telephone company. The conference company's operator initiates and monitors each conference. If participants are cut off during the conference call, they can redial, and the conference operator will reconnect them to the conference. These companies provide both operator-assisted and "meet-me" bridges.

For example, a sales manager might use MultiLink Electronic Meeting Service to meet regularly with his or her regional salespeople. Instead of being required to travel to the company's headquarters or to one of the regional offices for the meetings, they are directed to use "meet-me"—that is, to go to the nearest telephone at the meeting time and dial a special 800 number. The MultiLink Operator greets each person and then connects each one to the conference. No special equipment is required. The conference service includes the following features:

- *Subconferencing* allows several participants to meet separately on the telephone and return to the main meeting at any time by touching zero on the telephone and asking the operator for a subconference.
- *Lecture mode* cuts off the ability of everyone to talk online except for the main speaker.
- *Operator dial out* allows a missing party to be dialed and added to the conference at any time.

Stand-Alone Audio Conference Bridges. A stand-alone audio conferencing bridge, also called an "on-premises bridge," can be purchased from such companies as Darome and AT&T and installed on the user's premises. With

FIGURE 13-7 **Stand-alone Conference Bridge**

Courtesy of Darome, Inc.

a stand-alone bridge, each user can enjoy the flexibility of being independent from an outside bridging service. Although additional lines may need to be leased, the costs should still be lower than using a service if use is high enough to defray the costs of the unit's purchase and installation. Figure 13-7 shows an example of a stand-alone bridge that includes a console that offers attendant call setup and "meet-me" conferencing.

■ Audio-Conferencing Equipment and Facilities

The simplest audio conferencing terminal is the telephone. However, for extended conferences the telephone receiver can be tiring as well as awkward to hold while taking notes. One solution is to replace the receiver with a lightweight headset that allows hands-free conversation.

Speakerphone. The speakerphone, the most popular being Type 4A, is sold by telephone companies and interconnect companies. The 4A speakerphone, shown in Figure 13-8, is a simple audio terminal that is modular: One unit contains the microphone, an on-off switch, volume control, and an indicator light; the other unit is the loudspeaker. A telephone handset must also be installed with the speakerphone.

For participants gathered around a speakerphone the maximum distance is 28 inches, making it possible for a few participants to gather around a small table, such as 4 feet by 4 feet. The quality of the speakerphone should

FIGURE 13-8 Speakerphone

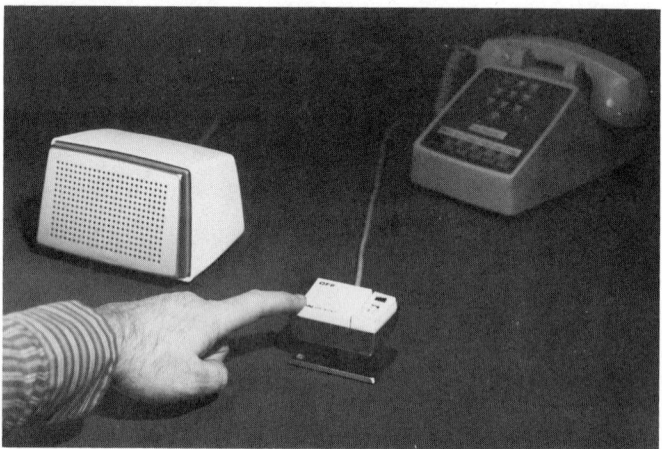

Courtesy of AT&T Archives.

be similar to that of a regular telephone handset. Before a conference you should test the speakerphone in the room where it will be used and under the same noise conditions. The major complaint about using a speakerphone is that it generates a **barrel effect**—a slight echo from the speaker's voice. Both the barrel effect and the amount of background noise in the room detracts from a speaker's intelligibility.

The barrel effect can be overcome by acoustically treating the meeting room or reducing the distance between the speaker and the microphone. You can acoustically treat a room by identifying physical materials in the room that are not absorbing the sound's energy, such as uncarpeted floors, flat walls, windowpanes, and flat plaster ceilings. These materials can be made to absorb the sound by using carpeting to cover bare floors, drapes for flat walls or windows, and an acoustic tile ceiling.

Background noise can be minimized by reducing the distance between the speaker and the microphone or by increasing the number of microphones, preferably assigning one to each speaker. Speakerphone manufacturers specify the maximum speaker distance, which also helps to determine the required number of microphones.

Conference Telephone. Conference telephones are used with groups of ten or more people. The unit, shown in Figure 13-9, is placed in the center of a conference table and uses an omnidirectional microphone. It easily accommodates ten conferees in a 16′ × 16′ room. Individual microphones can also be attached for increased ease.

Audio Conferencing 475

FIGURE 13-9 Quorum Conference Telephone

Courtesy of AT&T Archives.

These systems are designed for one person to speak at a time, to ensure that the message is sent and received. Some systems are voice-switched, which directs the system's resources to the party speaking while reducing the levels at other microphones. Other systems are manually controlled by either the conference leader operating individual microphones or each user activating a push-to-talk switch. Both manual methods work well if all participants understand and apply the rules for speaking.

Audio-Conferencing Rooms. An audio conference may be conducted with some participants in their offices, at home, or at public telephone booths while others are in specially equipped conference rooms. The type of facility selected depends on the number of participants and the need to use special terminal equipment.

The lighting, heating, air conditioning, and ventilation requirements for any teleconferencing room, including an audio conferencing room, are basically the same as those for a well-designed conventional conference room. The conference room should be zoned separately, having its thermostatic control located within the room.

Research at AT&T Bell Laboratories indicates that room appearance and comfort have an impact on participants' impressions of teleconferencing. The room should be pleasant with a decor that is superior, to that of the participants' work areas, but not overwhelming. For example, the size of the room should be appropriate to meet the needs of the participants. A 20' × 16' room with an 8'–10' ceiling will accommodate a maximum of fourteen people.

- **Benefits and Drawbacks of Audio Conferencing**

   Compared to conventional meetings, audio conferences offer these unique benefits: They can be set up more quickly, require only voice-grade telephone lines for transmission, tend to be shorter, are generally more organized, and tend to generate decisions more quickly.

   The biggest drawback is getting potential users to accept this form of meeting. One solution to overcoming user resistance is to promote the benefits of audio conferencing by such means as citing successful examples of its use. Second, audio meetings tend to be demanding and tiring for participants. Third, when the audio quality is poor, participants often have difficulty in concentrating.

- **Audio-Conferencing Applications**

   Audio conferencing is a quick way to conduct a conference. For example, some pharmaceutical companies use audio conferencing to conduct seminars for doctors, allowing them to access the conference from a telephone anywhere in the country. Schools use audio conferencing to bring into the classroom subject-matter experts whose fees the schools might not be able to afford and whose busy schedules would otherwise not permit a visit. Two other examples are described at the beginning of the chapter.

   Audio conferencing is also being offered to large groups of strangers, enabling them to listen and/or talk to each other. Teleconversant Ltd. of Cambridge, Massachusetts, offers audio conferencing on topics such as caring for the elderly. Callers pay a small fee, which is included on their monthly telephone statement, to listen to a program. Some programs allow callers to participate in a question-and-answer session following the lecture. A similar service is offered to radio stations using satellite by American Teleconferencing Services Ltd. of Kansas City, Missouri. Reporters access audio press conferences, giving sports information while concurrently audio-taping the conference for direct quotes for their broadcasts.[1]

Enhanced Audio Conferencing

Audio-only conferences can be enhanced by transmitting still images as well as automatically identifying who is speaking at any time. Three ways of transmitting images by telephone lines are by telewriter devices, facsimile equipment, and freeze-frame video equipment. These audiographic enhancements allow all participants to interact verbally and visually between sites. Still another way is to deliver copies of slides to each of the sites before the start of the meeting. Equipment is now available that allows the conference leader to use the telephone keypad to remotely operate the film projector (and even a microfiche projector) at these sites.

FIGURE 13-10 Electronic Blackboard

Interand Corporation, Chicago, Illinois.

■ Telewriters

A *telewriter* is an electromechanical device that allows participants to write or draw their contributions as they talk. Images—every mark, line, and dot—drawn or written on a transmitting board, such as the **electronic blackboard** shown in Figure 13-10, are immediately translated into signals that are communicated through the telephone network. At the receiving end, the information is displayed on a video monitor, exactly as it is drawn (or erased) on the board. The entire discussion, including the graphics, can be recorded on a standard audio cassette (two-track) recorder, one track for audio and the other for graphics. The recording can be played back at any location; the playback can also be transmitted, just as the original teleconference was. Examples of telewriting equipment include AT&T's Gemini 100 Electronic Blackboard, NEC EB-100 Electronic Writing Board System, and AT&T's Quorum.

■ Facsimile

Facsimile machines, as described in Chapter 11, provide audio conferencing meetings with immediate copies of documents, including graphics, charts, and exhibits. Since facsimile transmission and freeze-frame video transmissions, described in the next section, are delayed a number of seconds at the receiving end, they must be carefully timed to keep the discussion flowing smoothly.

FIGURE 13-11 A Freeze-Frame System

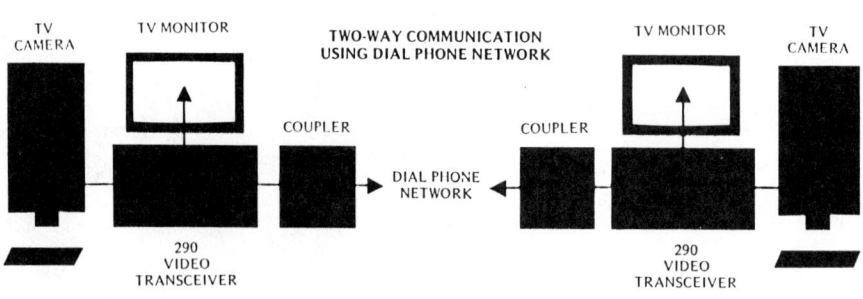

Courtesy of Colorado Video Inc.

■ Freeze-Frame Video

Freeze-frame video, also called "still frame" or "slow-scan video," allows still video images to be transmitted over regular telephone lines during a teleconference. Images can be of pictures, live people, text, graphics, or three-dimensional objects. Figure 13-11 shows a diagram of a freeze-frame system.

Freeze-Frame Operation and Technology. At the transmitting site a freeze-frame system requires a camera, a monitor, a transmitter, and a modem. At the receiving site a monitor, a modem, and a receiver are required. Equipment at each site can include a transceiver, a combination transmitter, and a receiver.

The oldest method for translating the electrical output of a television camera into a single still image is to photograph the screen of a television monitor and "freeze it." The frozen picture is converted to slow-scan signals suitable for transmission over telephone lines. At the receiving sites the slow-scan signals are reconverted to a still image on a regular television monitor. Viewers at the remote site see a complete image a number of seconds later, depending on the transmission speed. Another method is to digitize a single frame of the television image and then store it in digital memory, such as on a computer diskette or hard disk, to be transmitted to remote locations when desired.

Once the frame has been received, it can be reviewed as long as necessary on the monitor, and/or a special device can produce a hard copy of the screen image on a television monitor. Since monitors generally do not have storage capabilities, each frame that is sent erases the previous one.

Freeze-Frame Equipment. Freeze-frame equipment is relatively inexpensive. The main operating costs are the local or long-distance telephone charges for transmitting the images. Figure 13-12 shows Interland Corpora-

FIGURE 13-12 **Freeze-Frame Equipment**

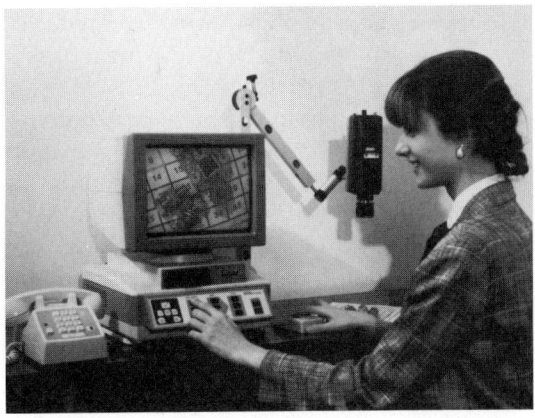

Courtesy of Interand Corporation, Chicago, Illinois.

tion's Discon Imagephone, a desktop freeze-frame unit that photographs documents, pictures, and objects and then transmits their still images using voice-grade telephone lines. The Imagephone uses a video camera to photograph objects, documents, drawings, and people and a transceiver to send them at 9.6 bps to another Imagephone in another location. Images can be stored on hard or floppy disks.

Transmission Time. Freeze-frame video images do not happen in real time as do telewriter drawings. The transmission time depends on the resolution level. The higher the resolution, the longer the transmission time. For example, a standard resolution of 256 × 240 is transmitted in 35 seconds by telephone, while a resolution of 256 × 480 takes 76 seconds.

■ Enhanced Audio-Conferencing Applications

An engineering company has installed at each of its locations in Canada and the United States an enhanced audio system, which includes a speakerphone, a telewriter, a facsimile machine, and freeze-frame video. A technician at each site operates the equipment so that participants can concentrate completely on the meeting. Daily audio discussions with freeze-frame transmission of blueprint images, telewriter transmission of participants' drawings, and faxing of documents allow easy coordination of projects and changes of plans as needed. The result is improved productivity and communications.

To increase the effectiveness of audio presentations between two or more sites, companies also use telewriters and freeze-frame video to send photographs of slides, graphics, or other hard copy. For example, video snapshots of speakers hold viewers' attention. Manufacturers reduce machine downtime by transmitting freeze-frame images of broken parts to the repair shop. A physician away from the hospital can receive a freeze-frame X-ray and respond by delivering a preliminary diagnosis, thus reducing the time required to deliver medical care.

Companies and other organizations, such as universities and hospitals, are teaching with enhanced audio conferencing. For example, the University of West Indies at Kingston, Jamaica, uses audio conferencing and freeze-frame video to teach courses from its Kingston campus to other English-speaking East Caribbean sites. New York University also uses audio-conferencing with freeze frame video for courses conducted in San Juan, Puerto Rico. Telephone charges from New York City to Puerto Rico are $15 per hour during the day and $10 per hour during the evening.[2]

Two-Way Videoconferencing

■ Two-Way Videoconferencing Defined

The most sophisticated form of teleconferencing is two-way videoconferencing. It is the closest approximation to a face-to-face meeting, providing face-to-face interaction and transmitting body language, which can enhance communication and facilitate decision making.

Two-way videoconferencing, diagrammed in Figure 13-13, is defined as a two-way, full-motion video system that permits two or more people in different locations to conduct face-to-face audio and visual communication. The sites are connected as though participants were in the same room. Because of its high equipment and transmission costs, videoconferencing was until recently used primarily by very large organizations.

■ Videoconferencing Operation, Technology, and Equipment

Operation. At each site a camera that is located on the same wall as the television monitor being watched by participants picks up and transmits their images. The result is that all participants are looking directly at one another. The speaker's voice activates camera switching, the camera automatically focusing on each new speaker while other cameras pick up and transmit overview shots of all the participants. Two or more video images can be displayed at the same time, appearing either on one monitor using a split screen format or displayed on two or more different monitors. This capability, shown in Figure 13-14, is referred to as **continuous presence video**.

FIGURE 13-13 **Two-Way Videoconferencing**

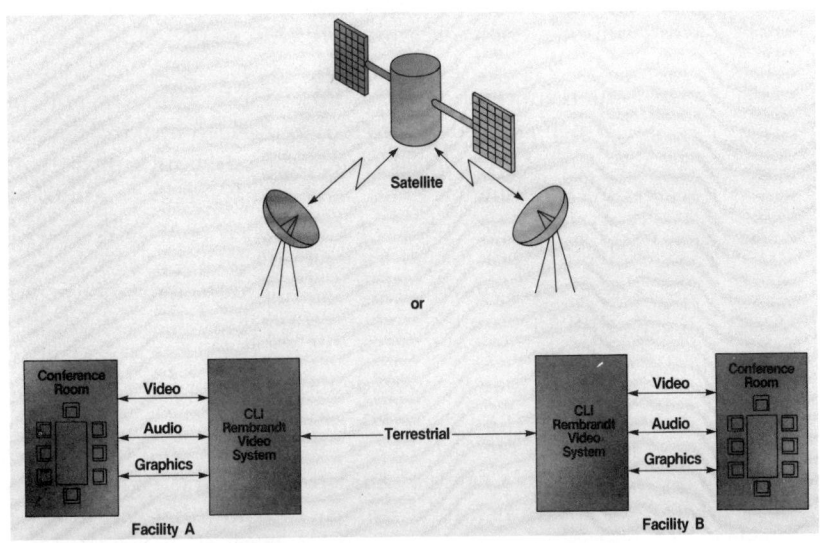

Courtesy of Compression Labs, Incorporated.

FIGURE 13-14 **Continuous Presence Video**

Courtesy of Apple Computer, Inc.

Facilities. A two-way videoconference requires a facility for users, such as a dedicated conference room, a portable or mobile conference room, or a desktop system similar to a microcomputer. An organization's needs and applications determine which type of facility is appropriate.

Permanent or built-in videoconference rooms are rooms that resemble a regular conference room but conceal cameras and other video equipment, which are manipulated by remote control from the conference table.

Portable or mobile conference systems include the same equipment as a built-in conference room but are contained in a unit that can be moved from one room to another. An example of a mobile videoconferencing system is PictureTel's V-2100 Videoconferencing System, shown in Figure 13-15. The system contains a video coder/decoder, a color monitor, a camera, and a single-port audio system. It supports two-way full-motion video using two 56 kbps circuits, one to transmit and one to receive. It also supports split-screen images; one side of the screen supports full-motion video, while the other supports still images.

Desktop systems are integrated with a personal computer that houses a monitor, a camera, a microphone, and a viewport, which shows the image being transmitted, in an enclosure that can fit on a desk. The equipment enables small groups and individuals to hold video meetings without dedicated videoconferencing rooms. When a desktop system is being used in your office, you also have the benefit of being able to immediately access documents stored in your computer for use during the video meeting. Fig-

FIGURE 13-15 PictureTel's V-2100 Portable Conferencing System

Courtesy of PictureTel Corporation.

ure 13-16 shows ways in which desktop units can communicate with each other.

Transmission. The type of transmission selected depends on the organization's budget, the distance between conference sites, and the channel bandwidth required to conduct the conference. A local area network (LAN) can be used for transmission within a building or group of buildings, while microwave transmission can be used for longer distances, such as within cities or between cities. Satellite transmission should be selected for distances of more than a couple hundred miles. Long-distance transmission services can be provided by a public carrier or by the company's private transmission network. Often, an organization's existing telecommunications systems will have surplus bandwidth that will allow it to support videoconferencing.

Analog Transmission. Because video signals contain much more information than a telephone conversation, they require a significantly wider bandwidth. A standard video signal is analog and requires 6 MHz for signal bandwidth when paired with its companion audio signal. A typical analog

FIGURE 13-16   Desktop Videoconferencing

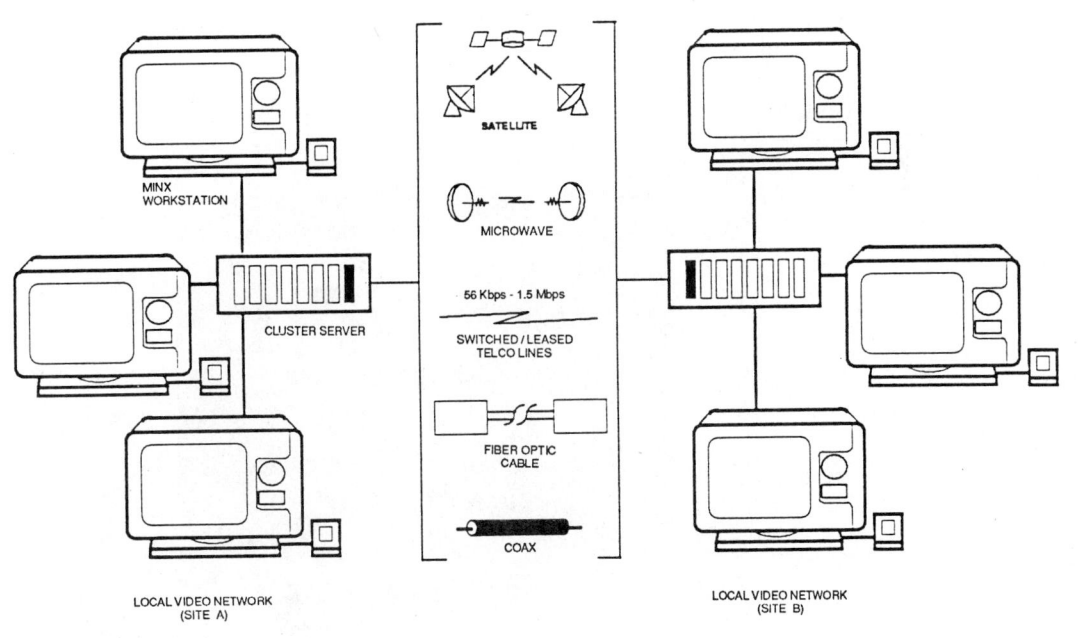

Courtesy of Datapoint Corporation.

videoconference requires 12 MHz total bandwidth to transmit both ways. Analog transmission provides high-quality transmission, although it does not use **encryption** techniques—a way of scrambling signals to ensure secure communications for sensitive information. The paired (video and audio) analog signals can be transmitted as is over selected microwave, satellite, and fiber-optic networks.

Digital Transmission. Signals in digital form can be compressed to a fraction of their original size. In **compressed digital video**, compression reduces the bandwidth required for transmission of electronic images by eliminating redundant information and thereby reducing transmission costs. Only information that changes from frame to frame is transmitted. An electronic device, called a **codec** (coder-decoder), converts analog signals to digital ones for digital transmission and then compresses the digital data. At the receiving station, another codec decodes the signals and converts them back to analog signals for display on the video monitor.

The quality of compressed digital video depends on the data speed and the compression technique used by the codec manufacturer. Although the quality evaluation of the final video picture is subjective, users tend to accept 56 kbps to 384 kbps codecs, such as the one shown in Figure 13-17, and the quality that they deliver. Codec devices offer compressed speeds from 56 kbps with high data compression to 1.5 Mbps with low data compression. Another benefit of sending digital compressed video is that encryption techniques are available on most codecs, preventing unauthorized access during transmission.

FIGURE 13-17   **Codec**

Courtesy of Compression Labs, Incorporated.

FIGURE 13-18   **The Declining Cost of Videoconferencing: 1983 and 1988**

COST FACTORS
($THOUSANDS)

	1983	1988
High Bandwidth		
Fully-Equipped Conference Facility	$500	$95
CODEC	$151	$68
Transmission (NY-SF) - 768 Kbps	$1500/Hour	$375/Hour
Low Bandwidth		
Fully-Equipped Conference Facility	N/A	$49.5
CODEC	N/A	$ 30
Transmission (NY-SF) - 56 Kbps	N/A	$45/Hour

Courtesy of Compression Labs, Incorporated.

Cost. The digitalization of video signals and developments in data compression technology are making videoconferencing less expensive and more affordable to an increasing number of businesses of all sizes. Figure 13-18 compares the 1983 and 1988 costs.

■ Videoconferencing Applications

Hambrecht and Quist (H&Q) was one of the first investment firms to use a two-way videoconferencing system. A typical H&Q video day begins at 5:30 A.M. San Francisco time (8:30 A.M. New York time) with connection of the videoconferencing facilities at the San Francisco, New York City, and Boston offices. Branches in London and Los Angeles do not have two-way video facilities but have access to the meetings by two-way audio. First, the stock traders meet for 15 minutes to discuss the coming day's market activities; then research analysts meet for 30 minutes to review long-range industry developments. Meanwhile, the conference is also broadcast throughout the company, some listeners having access to a two-way audio system. Within one hour, all employees have participated in a companywide morning meeting. At other times the facilities are used for smaller employee meetings and by other companies to give investment presentations to the H&Q's brokers.

Business Television

Television is moving from the employees' lounge to the company's teleconferencing room. According to a 1988 survey, thirty-six of the largest companies in the United States have their own business television networks with a total of over 12,000 viewing sites. These companies generate most of their own programming. Other companies, mainly banks, hospitals, law offices, automobile dealers, manufacturers, and public utilities, have one or more receiving sites on their premises to receive regularly scheduled programs from others.[3]

■ Business Television Defined

A distinction should be made between two-way videoconferencing and business television, since one is often mistaken for the other. A two-way videoconference, discussed in the previous section, is classified as **point-to-point videoconferencing** because each site can transmit and receive audio and video. These conferences involve small groups of people who are highly interactive.

Point-to-multipoint videoconferencing, commonly referred to as *business television*, is a videoconference in which all sites receive images but only one site can transmit them, as shown in Figure 13-19. In other words, business television allows a company to broadcast audio and video messages simultaneously to all or any of its geographically dispersed offices. Although the receiving sites cannot transmit video, their audio component may be bidirectional, allowing them to participate in discussion with the sending site. Business television is targeted to large groups.

■ Business Television Operation, Technology, and Equipment

Operation. The television show could be any television talk show except that the topic is on changes in *your* company's employee-benefit plan and the network is operated by *your* company. Three panelists from the company's human resources department discuss employee benefits in front of cameras at the company's teleconference studio for about 45 minutes and then take calls from viewers—actually employees watching the show on television sets nationwide.

Transmitting studios are usually on the company's premises, although some companies use public television facilities or commercial production studios. Business television programs are either broadcast live or taped and then rebroadcast from television studios, just like commercial TV shows. Viewers at the receiving locations gather around the television set and watch the program.

Business television broadcasts that are live usually have a two-way audio system that allows viewers to call in and ask questions of the people speaking. Viewers may telephone a number flashed on the screen or may give a written question to a designated person for telephoning it to the transmitting station. Live audio interaction is accomplished through either a telephone switchboard that connects one call to one operator or an audio bridge. An audio bridge, as described earlier in this chapter, links together all incom-

FIGURE 13-19 Business Television

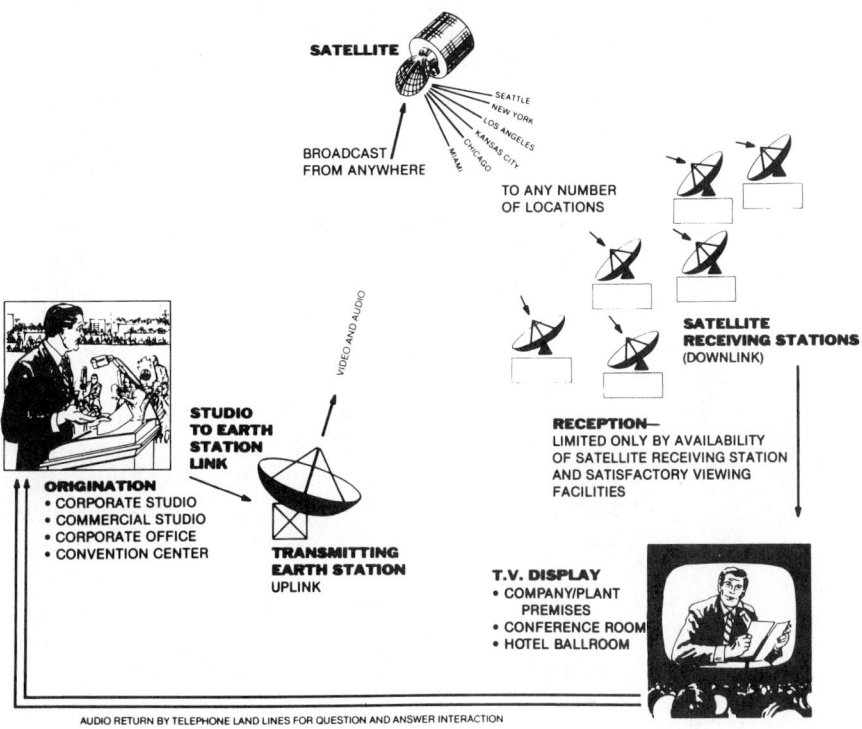

Courtesy of VideoStar Connections, Inc.

ing calls and allows callers to be connected to the presenter as well as to other callers.

Transmission. Business television programs are often encrypted before transmission to prevent unauthorized people from viewing them. Television signals are sent to receiving sites by LANs, microwave, or satellite networks. As shown in Figure 13-19, signals originating from corporate headquarters are transmitted via microwave or telephone link to an uplink earth station to a satellite and are then retransmitted to locations that are equipped with a television monitor, a decoder, a receive-only antenna, and a videocassette recorder.

■ **Business Television Networks**

Business television networks are either public or private.

Public Business Television Networks. In the 1970s, AT&T introduced facilities that offered Picturephone Meeting Services for public use. These videoconferencing facilities were not as successful as desired and were discontinued in 1985. Meanwhile, in 1980, hotels such as the Holiday Inn, Mariott, and Weston hotels began offering business television to the public. They still conduct special or single-event broadcasts, referred to as **ad hoc videoconferences**, and provide viewers with comfortable meeting facilities along with technical network support. Companies without their own networks use **public business television networks** to conduct small to medium-sized meetings. Companies with their own networks also use these facilities primarily for special events and to handle their overflow operations.

US Sprint's *The Meeting Channel* is a full-service provider of teleconferencing services that includes fully interactive audio and full-motion video. The Meeting Channel serves over 425 videoconferencing rooms in over twenty-four countries throughout the world, one-third of the rooms being available to the public at an hourly rate. For example, a company can rent a two-way audio and a two-way video or can broadcast to dozens of meeting rooms and have a two-way audio communication with every one of them. In addition, both private and public networks using different networking technologies can talk to each other by interfacing through The Meeting Channel, which is providing the kind of connectivity that is needed by teleconferencing users.

Private Business Television Networks. In the early 1980s, many companies with experience in using the public business television networks began installing their own networks. **Private business television networks** offer convenience—a few steps to the company's teleconference room is easier than a trip to the local hotel. In 1988 the cost of installing a satellite uplink was $500,000, and renting satellite time cost about $700 per hour. At the receiving end, depending on the volume of business, the cost to install a downlink to connect the satellite to an individual station was about $6000–$7000. For example, the Federal Express network includes 800 downlinks.[4] Figure 13-20 lists a few of the companies that have their own business television facilities. Figure 13-21 identifies companies that operate private satellite networks.[5]

■ Business Television Applications

Companies use business television for ad hoc events, that is, special or occasional events, such as new product introductions, press conferences, and special employee meetings. They also use business television for ongoing activities such as employee training and routine meetings. The audience may be employees, customers, investors, and others. For some companies, business television serves as an electronic newsletter.

FIGURE 13-20 Examples of Companies with Business Television Facilities

Company	Number of Sites		Satellite	Band	Satellite Time Leased from	Uplink Location	Activity in 1988	
	Active	Projected					Events/Month	Hrs/Month
A. L. Williams/ALW-TV	1000	1500	GStar	Ku	SCN	Duluth, GA	13	20
Aetna Life & Casualty	92	107	GE American K1	Ku	VideoStar	HBO, NY	3	8
AT&T	150	150	GE American K2	Ku	AT&T Skynet	New York/Golden, CO	8	24
Church of Latter Day Saints	1800	2000	Westar IV	C	Bonneville	Salt Lake City, UT	4	20
Digital Equipment Corp.	72	126	GE American K1	Ku	VideoStar	Washington, DC	0.5	4
Eastman Kodak	60+	75	GE American K1	Ku	VideoStar	Customer premises	8	20
Federal Express/FXTV	800	900	GStar 1	Ku	Self	Customer premises	27	24
Hospital Satellite Network	970	1500	SoaceNet 1/GStar 1	C/Ku	Bonneville	Los Angeles/San Diego	225	270
Howard University	95	110	GE K2/Westar IV	Ku	Conus	Howard, University, Washington, DC	5	66
J.C. Penney	715	727	GStar II	Ku	PSN	DFW Teleport	17	80
K-Mart	800	2200	GStar II	Ku	GTE Spacenet	Troy, MI	2	2
Merrill Lynch	475	475	GE American K1	Ku	PSN	NY Teleport	10	10
National Technological University	221	400	GStar I	Ku	GTE	24 Universities	—	2004
Texas Instruments/TIB-TV	59	90	GE American K1	Ku	VideoStar	DFW Teleport	8	20
Voluntary Hospitals of America	360	500	GStar 1	Ku	HSN & Others	DFW Teleport	2.5	6.25

Courtesy of Telespan BusinessTV Inc., 1989.

FIGURE 13-21 **Companies Offering Business Television Networks**

Network	Number of Networks	Number of Sites
Bonneville Satellite Communications	5	3700
Contel/ASC	1	800 (planned)
GTE/Spacenet	1	150
Private Satellite Network	16	More than 1800
Satellite Conference Network	5	1567
VideoStar Connections	14	1788

High Technology Business magazine, May 1988. Copyright 1988 by Infotechnology Publishing Corp., 270 Lafayette Street #705, New York, NY 10012.

Examples of Ad Hoc Business Television. Frequent users of ad hoc video conferences are the automobile manufacturers, such as Ford Motor Company, Chrysler, and General Motors. These companies introduce their new products to dealers and salespeople by scheduling receive sites in large meeting rooms. The meetings enable all personnel to receive the same message simultaneously, which eliminates the need for dealers to interpret and reconvey it to salespeople.

Press conferences are conducted as ad hoc conferences. A well-known example is the one held by Johnson & Johnson after the Tylenol deaths in Chicago. The company held an ad hoc conference that was transmitted throughout the country with audio feedback to network television stations. The conference helped the company to quickly regain its share of the market.

Both the Republican and Democratic parties use ad hoc conferencing for fund raising during congressional campaigns. President Reagan addressed groups outside Washington when his schedule did not permit him to travel.

Examples of Ongoing Activities. Hewlett-Packard informs its employees of policy changes, introduces new products, and trains sales employees via business television. J.C. Penney used to spend millions of dollars flying regional buyers to New York City, where they required accommodations and attention, twelve to fifteen times a year. The company now uses business television to televise its sample merchandise to buyers around the country. In the first year of the satellite network's operation the company saved more than $4 million, which more than paid for the network. Sears, K-Mart, and the May Company now conduct similar activities.

Examples of Business Television Servers. Training and retraining are provided for doctors, nurses, and rehabilitation specialists from Hospital Satellite Network, Voluntary Hospitals of America Satellite Network, The

American Rehabilitation Education Network, and the American Hospital Association.

The National Technological University (NTU), with administrative offices at Fort Collins, Colorado, makes it possible for twenty-four participating universities to offer selected graduate and undergraduate courses that lead to master's degrees in various areas of engineering. Courses originate at the campus of member universities and are broadcast directly to over 100 company sites via a satellite system. By using business television, courses are taught by faculty from the home campuses of the participating universities to students who are located at their work sites nationwide.

The NTU distribution system uses GTE Spacenet's G-STAR I Satellite. A series of satellite uplink stations located at participating universities have been installed, while a network of television receive-only terminals are at each company site of participating students. The technical operations of the network are controlled at NTU, where course schedules are prepared, satellite channels are monitored for technical quality, and return communications (student to instructor) are coordinated.

Course transmissions are often recorded on videotape at the students' site to be used at their convenience. Students and instructors interact through electronic mail by using one of the packet-switched networks, such as Telenet. Computer conferencing, to be discussed in the next section, allows all students to participate and interact with each other as well as with the instructor.

Computer Conferencing

Computer conferencing is based on digital information that is transmitted through a computer with a store-and-forward message-handling system.

■ Computer Conferencing Defined

Computer conferencing is an electronic messaging technology that allows two or more people to meet online to conduct meetings by exchanging typewritten or graphic information with each other in different geographic locations at the same or different times.

Computer conference participants use their computers to key in messages and read any that have been typed by others. They interact with each other by keying in new topics or replying to previous ones. Messages are not deleted after being read. Any participant, even one joining at a later time, can catch up with the conference, review all comments by others, and add new messages or comments.

The geographic location can be anywhere as long as each participant has access to the network leading to the company that handles the conference.

Participants can be online at the same time, or they can choose to attend the meeting at their own convenience by accessing the stored information. Entry of a message is independent of whether anyone else is entering one at the same time. Members can talk all at once, which does not block sequential reading or input by others.

Computer Conferencing Operation

Basic equipment requirements for a participant to confer are a microcomputer or computer terminal, a modem, and communications software. The service can be installed in-house or accessed through a time-sharing system.

In-House System. In an **in-house system** the participant's terminal is connected directly or over telecommunications lines to a host computer. Once a participant logs onto the host computer for conferencing, the participant can key in messages, send them to the host computer for storage and future retrieval, and read any messages that have been input by others.

Time-Sharing System. In a **time-sharing system**, participants access by telephone a commercial service, such as CompuServe's (formerly The Source) Participate. The service is accessed by a telephone call using a microcomputer, a modem, and communications software. Once CompuServe is reached, the user logs onto Participate.

Conference proceedings can be searched by a variety of criteria, such as by name of participant, subject, or keyword. Everything that is discussed online, including stray thoughts that would be eliminated in face-to-face meetings and conversations, is stored for the duration of the conference.

Computer Conferencing Applications

Computer conferencing augments or replaces traditional conference activities. For example, employees can use computer conferencing to prepare for monthly department meetings. The online conference enables employees to combine the back-and-forth discussion of a meeting, where new ideas can be addressed immediately, with research reports and other documents stored in the computer that can be accessed when desired. All department members have the opportunity to participate in the conference—sharing ideas and offering suggestions. At any time a participant can be updated by retrieving a record of all comments or selected comments. The online conference gives all employees an opportunity to add comments and suggestions to the discussion of department matters.

However, computer conferencing is not limited to traditional activities. Its applications are limited only by the imaginations of the participants. For example, the Electronic Networking Association uses Participate to publish and distribute *Netweaver*, a monthly journal, although the staff never meets in person. Another example is a college or university's use of conferencing to provide online courses for college credit.

The computer services subsidiary of a major aerospace manufacturer is using Dialcom's computer conferencing service, CAUCUS, to support a companywide technology transfer program. A CAUCUS network is being established by a committee of the California State Assembly to link policymakers with constituents, while another network is linking chiefs of police throughout the nation with criminal justice researchers and other experts in innovative police practices. Still another example is the labor union scenario at the beginning of this chapter.

■ Administering Computer Conferencing

The person responsible for managing a conference is called a *moderator*. Typical duties of a moderator include establishing the conference, specifying membership rules, determining which notes to delete, creating or terminating subconferences or committees, and terminating the conference. For example, a moderator can announce a new conference by creating an online notice that is displayed each time a participant accesses the current conference.

Conferences can be public or private. *Public conferences* are open to anyone; *private conferences* are restricted to a particular group of people.

■ A Computer Conferencing System—VAX Notes

Digital Equipment Company (DEC) offers computer conferencing software that provides users with the capability of creating and accessing online conferences or meetings. The software, available for all DEC VAX systems, can be used by a small group of people on a single MicroVAX system or by hundreds of people on a worldwide network of VAX systems. For example, a software specialist in DEC's office in Paris, France, has the ability through VAX Notes to comment on a software program written by an engineer at DEC's headquarters in Maynard, Massachusetts.

VAX Notes can be either public or private. Participants create a conference on any subject, monitoring topics and replies, and writing their own topics or replies. All functions can be accessed by easy-to-use commands, supported with online help. A conference, which consists of topics and replies, may have more than 50,000 topics, each topic having a similar number of replies. Directories can list topics by author, subject, and date as well as number of replies. All notes can be read either sequentially or at random. Each participant has an online Notebook, which lists conferences of personal interest. When a conference is accessed, the Notebook shows whether or not new entries have been made since the last time the participant accessed it. Users may choose to read only those notes that they have not yet seen. Examples of VAX Notes screens are shown in Figure 13-22.

FIGURE 13-22   **VAX Notes Screens**

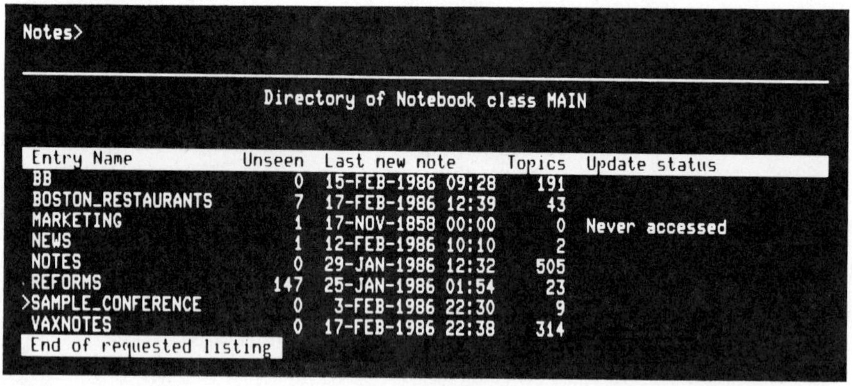

```
Notes>

              Directory of Notebook class MAIN

 Entry Name            Unseen  Last new note       Topics  Update status
 BB                       0    15-FEB-1986 09:28     191
 BOSTON_RESTAURANTS       7    17-FEB-1986 12:39      43
 MARKETING                1    17-NOV-1858 00:00       0   Never accessed
 NEWS                     1    12-FEB-1986 10:10       2
 NOTES                    0    29-JAN-1986 12:32     505
 REFORMS                147    25-JAN-1986 01:54      23
>SAMPLE_CONFERENCE        0     3-FEB-1986 22:30       9
 VAXNOTES                 0    17-FEB-1986 22:38     314
 End of requested listing
```

(a) Directory

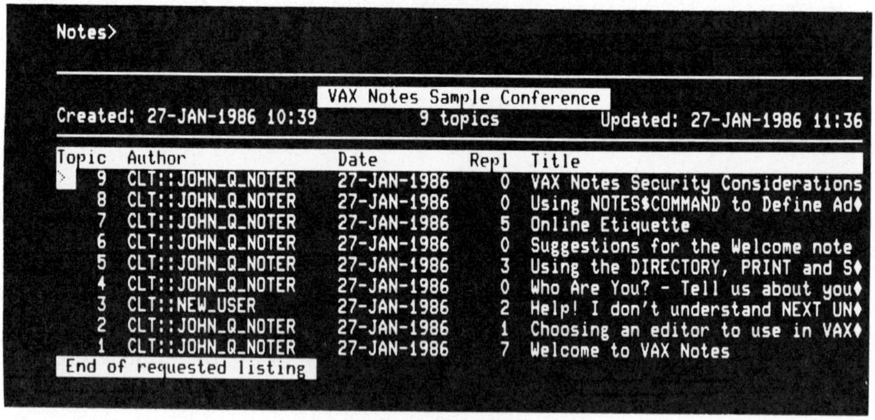

```
Notes>

                    VAX Notes Sample Conference
 Created: 27-JAN-1986 10:39     9 topics        Updated: 27-JAN-1986 11:36

 Topic  Author              Date          Repl  Title
   9    CLT::JOHN_Q_NOTER   27-JAN-1986    0    VAX Notes Security Considerations
   8    CLT::JOHN_Q_NOTER   27-JAN-1986    0    Using NOTES$COMMAND to Define Ad♦
   7    CLT::JOHN_Q_NOTER   27-JAN-1986    5    Online Etiquette
   6    CLT::JOHN_Q_NOTER   27-JAN-1986    0    Suggestions for the Welcome note
   5    CLT::JOHN_Q_NOTER   27-JAN-1986    3    Using the DIRECTORY, PRINT and S♦
   4    CLT::JOHN_Q_NOTER   27-JAN-1986    0    Who Are You? - Tell us about you♦
   3    CLT::NEW_USER       27-JAN-1986    2    Help! I don't understand NEXT UN♦
   2    CLT::JOHN_Q_NOTER   27-JAN-1986    1    Choosing an editor to use in VAX♦
   1    CLT::JOHN_Q_NOTER   27-JAN-1986    7    Welcome to VAX Notes
 End of requested listing
```

(b) Sample Conference

Courtesy of Digital Equipment Corporation.

■ Benefits and Drawbacks of Computer Conferencing

Computer conferencing has certain distinct benefits, such as the following:

- Documents, such as letters and research reports, can be imported from other electronic services and included with conference comments. For example, participants can include business reports from commercial videotex systems, such as Dialog, with their conference comments.
- Participants can easily review subjects discussed in a conference by accessing all or selected comments.

- Participants can join the conference at any time, review the comments of previous attendees, and add their own comments.
- Participants with time constraints can participate at their convenience.
- A written record of the conference proceedings can be easily output into a printed proceedings.
- The number and/or length of face-to-face meetings can be reduced by discussing issues and topic details while online.
- The online discussion of issues, details, and other matters makes it possible to concentrate on major issues in face-to-face meetings and thus helps to improve the quality of these meetings.

A major drawback of computer conferencing is the lack of personal contact. Another is that some people have difficulty expressing themselves in writing through a keyboard rather than orally or in handwritten form. Other drawbacks include the following:

- Until DEC introduced VAX Notes in 1986, computer conferencing was not marketed aggressively. DEC was the first major computer company to offer a conferencing system. Although small companies offered systems before 1986, they did not have the budget necessary for large-scale marketing.
- Equipment required for online conferences, such as modems and communications software, might not be available.
- Prospective users might not be fully aware of the benefits offered by online conferencing.
- The technology and procedures of computer conferencing might overwhelm prospective users. For example, users might have difficulty setting up the modem, telephone, and computer for online conferencing.

These barriers can be overcome by providing users with orientation and training programs and helping them to develop a commitment to using this technology.

■ Comparison of Electronic Mail, Bulletin Boards, and Computer Conferencing

To some extent, computer conferencing, electronic mail, and bulletin boards are similar. All three are a text-based means of communication by which users can communicate with others regardless of where they are by logging onto a system.

Electronic mail messages are usually sent on a one-time basis to one or more mailboxes and cannot be classified by topic for easy retrieval. The decision whether or not to save messages is the choice of the receiver. If the message is not saved, it is soon deleted from the host computer. *Computer conferencing messages* are stored in the host computer for the duration of the conference. These messages are not sent to mailboxes but are appended to topics and can be retrieved by keywords.

Although *electronic bulletin boards* store notes under topic headings, they do not identify which messages are new ones. Thus, to identify the desired messages, all messages for each topic must be reviewed. With computer conferencing, each time a user logs onto the system, the system tells the user which messages are new to each topic that he or she selects.

Benefits and Drawbacks of Teleconferencing

Among the benefits of teleconferencing are the following:

- *It controls travel costs and time.* Instead of traveling to on-premise and off-premise meetings held at remote locations, participants can meet electronically, saving both travel time and money. The cost for gathering people in meetings is high, considering transportation, lodging, meals, actual mailing expenses, and nonproductive employee time. Employees are usually unavailable during travel time—time that could be used productively. A comparison of the cost of a conventional meeting with a videoconference is shown in Figure 13-23.
- *It brings together employees/customers dispersed over a wide geographical area.* Employees and/or customers located at distant sites might not have either the time or the money to travel to a meeting. One company set up video links to communicate with its major customers, such as Westinghouse in Maryland and Edwards Air Force Base in California.
- *It improves user productivity.* A typical audio conference can accomplish all the elements of a meeting in an average of 45 minutes. Participants also need not spend time relocating to another area for the meeting.
- *It speeds the decision process.* If several managers are required to approve a decision and each one is located in a different geographical area, the decision can be made more quickly by conducting a teleconference. For example, scientists at a manufacturing company's laboratories in Texas and California found it difficult to meet regularly to discuss product design. The company set up video links between the two laboratories that resulted in work on design progressing smoothly and products being introduced ahead of schedule.
- *It solves problems quickly and efficiently.* For example, problem solving can be speeded up by immediately arranging an audio conference instead of trying to coordinate the schedules of the people involved for a conventional meeting.
- *It facilitates employee training and cuts training costs.* Employees at different sites can be trained simultaneously without moving either the employees or the instructors. For example, until recently, a manufacturing company

FIGURE 13-23 **Comparison of Costs of a Conventional Meeting with Costs of a Videoconference**

Conventional Meeting	Videoconference
Three engineers schedule a manufacturing staff meeting at their plant 870 miles away. They travel by car to the airport, where they board a plane for the two-hour trip. On arriving at their destination they rent a car and drive for 30 minutes to the plant office. After lunch they will spend two hours in meetings and then return as they arrived, by both rental car and air. They arrive back at their home office at exactly closing time.	Three engineers schedule a manufacturing staff meeting at their plant 870 miles away. The videoconference takes two hours.

Conventional Meeting Costs

One location—two-hour meeting and five hours of traveling.
Travel expense:
$600 × 3 engineers = $1800
Productivity loss:
$208 × 3 engineers = 624

Total cost $2424

Assumptions
(1) Travel expenses—$600/person including airfare, meals, and ground transportation
(2) Productivity loss—$208/person

Videoconference Costs

Two locations—two-hour meeting

Meeting costs:

	Two-Transmission Alternatives	
	56K	768K
Codecs (2)	$ 52	$ 118
Conference facility	43	82
Maintenance	12	25
Support personnel	65	65
Transmission	90	750
Total cost	$262 or	$1040

Assumptions
(1) 2 codecs at $30,000 each (56K) or $68,000 each (768K)
(2) 3-year amortization
(3) 242 working days per year (less weekends and 10 holidays)
(4) 40% usage per day

Courtesy of Compression Labs, Incorporated.

regularly conducted intensive two-week training at each branch site at a cost of $14,000. By using teleconferencing, training is conducted in four-hour segments every other day for two weeks. The results indicate that trainees absorb more information with higher retention than participants in the old program. In addition, trainers can now present all training to its

branches in the amount of time previously allotted for training at one branch and thereby reduce training costs by more than 75%.
- *It provides an opportunity to exchange information.* Teleconferencing provides participants with an opportunity to exchange verbal information as well as documents and graphics.
- *It provides an efficient way to announce new products and services.* A company can inform its employees, particularly salespeople and prospective customers, about new products or services. For example, one company introduces new machinery to customers by conducting a full-motion video conference so that customers talk to people who manufacture the machinery as well as watch them operate it.
- *It provides access to experts.* Key people who normally do not have time to travel to meetings or lecture to trainees can participate in a teleconference without moving from their desks.
- *It offers tighter control of meetings.* Participants are aware of limited meeting time because of conference transmission charges and more structured communications pattern for delivery of messages.

Among possible drawbacks of teleconferencing are these:

- It can increase nonproductive time spent in meetings because these meetings can be arranged and implemented easily.
- It can decrease freedom of operation for remote field sites as a result of too much control by management.
- It encourages overspecialization and narrowness.
- It decreases sense of interpersonal contact and morale.
- It depends on technology that can break down or be sabotaged.[6]

Planning, Conducting, and Evaluating a Teleconference

Successful use of teleconferencing depends on knowing the company's needs. Analyzing these needs identifies the areas in which teleconferencing will offer the maximum benefits and the type of teleconferencing to be implemented. A suggested plan consists of four phases: (1) conduct a needs assessment, (2) plan the teleconference, (3) conduct the teleconference, and (4) evaluate the teleconference.

Phase 1: Conduct a Needs Assessment. A needs assessment includes an analysis of the types of meetings, travel costs to these meetings, unproductive costs, and outcome. Once you have identified work groups that can benefit from teleconferencing, then the type of teleconferences, equipment, and facilities can be addressed. Refer to Figure 13-23 for an example of travel costs.

Analyze the types of meetings that are being conducted in your department or organization: What types of meetings is your department/organization conducting? What are the purposes of these meetings? Who attends these meetings? Where are the meeting participants located? How is information exchanged, such as through discussion, demonstration, and/or lecture? How often are meetings held? How are they scheduled? Also examine travel expenditures to and from meetings. Will teleconferencing reduce these expenses?

Phase 2: Plan the Teleconference. Whatever type of teleconference is used, planning the meeting is necessary. Suggestions for planning an audio conference are listed in Figure 13-24.

Phase 3: Conduct the Teleconference. By carefully planning your meeting you ensure a successful one. Figure 13-25 outlines how to conduct an audio meeting.

FIGURE 13-24   Planning an Audio Conference: A Checklist

____ What is the subject of the meeting?
____ What is the purpose of the meeting?
____ Prepare and distribute a meeting agenda. Limit the number of agenda topics to three or four.
____ Allot the amount of time for each topic.
____ Make the conference reservation. Reserve two or more rooms and equipment for the date and time period desired.
____ Notify participants of the meeting by telephone, electronic mail, interoffice mail, or postal mail.
____ Prepare and mail supporting materials, including a list of attendees and their telephone numbers.
____ Plan how to implement the agenda items. To present information, consider interviewing, reporting, or lecturing. To exchange information with participants, consider round table discussion, brainstorming, and/or case study.

FIGURE 13-25   Conducting an Audio Conference: A Checklist

____ Start on time.
____ Conduct a roll call.
____ Review the agenda, objectives, and meeting rules.
____ Ask participants to identify themselves when they speak.
____ Encourage everyone to participate.
____ Stimulate discussion by asking questions.
____ Adhere to the agenda.
____ Pause occasionally to allow others to comment.
____ Spell out unusual terms, names, and numbers.
____ Summarize key points and ask for opinions and suggestions.
____ Assign follow-up action activities.
____ Plan and schedule the next meeting.
____ Summarize decision actions and adjourn.

After the meeting you should conduct a follow-up. For example, for an audio meeting you might perform the following activities:

- Distribute minutes of the meeting to the participants.
- If the meeting was recorded, review the tapes.
- Follow up on decisions and action items.
- Arrange for future audio conferences.

Phase 4: Evaluate the Audio Conference. On completion of the audio conference you should consider distributing a questionnaire to participants to query them about the effectiveness of the meeting and to solicit suggestions for future meetings. Such information is helpful in improving conferences and enhancing their usage. Questionnaires or surveys may also be administered periodically to determine whether teleconferencing is meeting its objectives, such as reducing travel costs and time, improving decision making, and cutting other costs or increasing revenues.

Summary

Teleconferencing ranges from a three-way telephone call to a multipoint-site full-motion videoconference. Two-way videoconferencing is the closest approximation to a face-to-face meeting, each site transmitting audio and video. Business television allows a company to broadcast video messages to all or any of its geographically dispersed sites. The receiving sites cannot transmit video but may have a directional audio component, allowing them to participate in discussion with the sending site.

Because of advances in teleconferencing technologies, the cost of videoconferencing transmission and equipment is decreasing and becoming affordable to an increasing number of businesses of all sizes. An analysis of a company's types of meetings, travel costs to these meetings, unproductive costs, and outcome identifies the areas in which teleconferencing offers the maximum benefits and the type of teleconferencing to be implemented. Carefully planning the teleconference is important for its successful implementation. The potential impact of teleconferencing on the workplace can result in changing how people communicate in the workplace—one of the basic activities of the business environment.

Key Terms

Ad hoc videoconference
Audio conferencing systems
Barrel effect
Business television systems
Codec
Compressed digital video
Computer conferencing:
   In-house system
   Time-sharing system
Conference bridge
Continuous presence video

Electronic blackboard
Encryption
Enhanced audio conferencing systems
Freeze-frame video
"Meet-me"
Point-to-multipoint videoconferencing
Point-to-point videoconferencing
Private business television network
Public business television network
Teleconferencing:
Asynchronous conference
Synchronous conference
Two-way video-conferencing systems

Self-Quiz

Indicate whether the statement is true or false.

1. Computer conferencing is used only as an in-house system of communicating. T/F
2. A drawback of computer conferencing is that the user cannot tell which messages are the new ones. T/F
3. Computer conferencing does not allow participates to all "talk" at the same time. T/F
4. A videoconference between two sites, each of which can transmit and receive both video and audio, is a point-to-multipoint videoconference. T/F
5. Business television is suitable for large groups. T/F
6. A unique advantage of audio conferences is that they require only voice-grade telephone lines. T/F

Complete each of the following statements.

1. A conference in which participants can check in whenever they wish is _____ .
2. A conference in which each participant calls a predetermined number at a specified meeting time is called _____ .
3. The device that allows the creation of drawings in real time with images appearing on a receiving monitor is called a(n) _____ .
4. A conference conducted for a special or a single event is called a(n) _____ .
5. The use of a telecommunications system for communicating with three or more people located at two or more locations is called a(n) _____ .
6. A conference that combines audio transmission with facsimile is an example of _____ .

Match Column A with Column B.

Column A
(a) Barrel effect
(b) Bridge
(c) Codec

Column B
____ 1. Two or more images displayed on a monitor at the same time.
____ 2. Can minimize signal loss.

(d) Compressed digital video
(e) Continuous presence
(f) Freeze-frame video

___ 3. Allows still images to be transmitted over telephone lines.
___ 4. Data reduced to a fraction of its size.
___ 5. Converts analog signals to digital ones.
___ 6. Can be generated when using a speakerphone.

■ Review Questions

1. How could you use teleconferencing at your school or place of business? Suggest four or five applications.
2. How can a "meet-me" audio conference be helpful to the conference originator?
3. (a) How does a bridge help an audio conference?
   (b) How are bridges set up?
   (c) Who provides bridging services?
   (d) Which type of bridge service would you recommend to a prospective business user? Why?
4. (a) How do telewriter devices, facsimile equipment, and freeze-frame video differ?
   (b) Can all of this equipment be used during the same audio conference? Explain.
5. What are the costs involved in an audio conference? An enhanced audio conference?
6. When would a two-way videoconference be more appropriate to use than another type of teleconferencing?
7. What is the purpose of a codec?
8. (a) Is business television considered to be a videoconference? Why?
   (b) How does business television operate?
9. (a) How does computer conferencing differ from other types of teleconferencing?
   (b) How does computer conferencing differ from electronic mail and electronic bulletin boards?
10. What should a conference originator do to prepare for an audio conference?
11. What should a conference originator do to successfully manage an audio conference?

■ Activities/Projects

1. Assume that you would like to set up an audio conference from your town or city with three people located at the following sites: Atlanta, Dallas, and Omaha. You estimate that the conference beginning at 9:30 A.M. will last 30 minutes. You would like the conference telephone operator to call each of the participants for the calls. You are considering using one of the following

bridging services: AT&T Conference Center or AT&T Alliance Teleconferencing Service.
   (a) What would each service charge be for the conference call? Information about the costs of each bridging service can be obtained by calling your local operator and asking to be connected to the service or by calling 800-555-1212 for the toll-free number.
   (b) Which service would you select? Why?
   (c) How could you reduce conference call charges?
   (d) What would a 60-minute audio conference cost from your school or workplace to three other schools or workplaces, each located in a different state?

2. Specify the type of teleconferencing that would be most appropriate to use in each of the following situations and the reason(s) for your selection.
   (a) An investment company sends memos to employees to keep them up to date on important corporate matters.
   (b) A food supplier with manufacturing plants and sales offices throughout the country conducts training for its employees by either sending instructors to the sites or having employees attend training at the home office.
   (c) At the automobile manufacturer's expense, dealers travel to the company's plant for a presentation of its new product lines.
   (d) Electrical power research laboratories throughout the world need to keep in touch with each other on a daily basis according to their own schedules.
   (e) A pharmaceutical company briefs its sales force with a slide presentation of its new drug products.
   (f) A company's division managers, who are scattered throughout the country, must meet every two weeks to plan company strategies.

3. Select one of the following topics for discussion.
   (a) Should managers master video techniques to reach today's employees?
   (b) Should teleconferencing be used to replace the traditional classroom?
   (c) Will teleconferencing affect how employees communicate with each other in the workplace?
   (d) Will teleconferencing change how companies communicate with each other?

4. With a dozen or more people as an audience and possibly one or two others as your assistants, you are to serve as the conference originator at the main campus of your school or company and conduct a four- or five-minute role play for each of the five types of teleconferencing.
   (a) Preparation:
      (1) Select one of the topics in question 3 or a topic of your choice for the teleconferencing presentation and discussion.
      (2) Use this topic to prepare a role play for each type of teleconference.
   (b) Conduct each type of teleconference:
      (1) Divide your audience into two or three groups, each group representing a branch of your school or company located some

distance away from the main site. Assign each group to a different part of the room.

(2) When conducting an audio conference and an enhanced audio conference, no one should be able to see each other. When conducting a business television conference, you should conduct the conference with your back to the other groups so that you cannot see them.

(c) After the role plays, discuss with the audience the benefits and drawbacks of each type of teleconferencing. You might want to develop a teleconferencing evaluative form and distribute a copy to each participant on completion of the role plays. The completed evaluative forms can be used as a basis for discussion.

■ *Case:* **Traditional Training versus Teletraining**

A computer software company has just developed a new software package, which is to be introduced to the market at the end of the month. Since the new product is significantly different from previous packages, the sales staff will have to be trained in how to use the product and how to sell it.

The company estimates that training will require seven hours. The company usually conducts its training by sending an instructor to each of its ten locations. The company is currently considering conducting training from its headquarters, using audio conferencing and facsimile transmission of training documents during the conference. How do you think the company should conduct its training?

The approximate costs of an instructor to travel to each site with one overnight stay are as follows: Airfare ($200), lodging ($85), per diem expense ($35), teaching time ($30 per hour), eight hours of unproductive time ($30 per hour). Costs for an audio conference include long-distance telephone charges including facsimile transmission ($30 per hour) and connection service for the audio conference ($20 per hour).

(a) What are the costs of each training approach? Are there any other costs that you think should be added to either training approach? If so, identify each one with an approximate cost.
(b) Which approach do you recommend?
(c) What are the benefits gained from your recommendation? Are there any drawbacks?

■ *Notes*

1. "Teleconferencing for the Masses," *High Technology*, June 1988, p. 12.
2. "Teaching with Freeze-Frame Video," *Tech Trends*, January 1988.
3. "The Best Companies in the Country Use Business Television," *Business TV*, March 1988, pp. 1–2.
4. "Standing Ovations for Shoes and Socks," *New York Times*, August 21, 1988.
5. Stephen J. Shaw, "The Growth of Business Television," *Business Television*, March 1988, pp. 5–6.

6. Robert Johansen, *Teleconferences and Beyond: Communication in the Office of the Future* (New York: McGraw-Hill, 1984), p. 101.

Additional Readings

Richard Caldwell, *Installing Your Satellite Uplink* (Washington, D.C.: Public Service Satellite Consortium, 1988).

Martin C. J. Elton, *Teleconferencing: New Media for Business Meetings* (American Management Association, 1982).

Kathleen J. Hansell, *The Teleconferencing Manager's Guide* (White Plains, N.Y.: Knowledge Industry Publications, Inc., 1988).

Ellen A. Lazer, Martin C. J. Elton, James W. Johnson, et al., *The Teleconferencing Handbook: A Guide to Cost Effective Communication* (White Plains, N.Y.: Knowledge Industry Publications, Inc., 1983).

George A. Mathis, *How to Produce Your Own Videoconference* (White Plains, N.Y.: Knowledge Industry Publications, Inc., 1983).

TeleSpan's Definitive Buyer's Guide to Teleconferencing and Business Television Products and Services (Altadena, Calif.: TeleSpan Publishing Corporation). Published annually.

Doug Widner, *Teleguide* (Washington, D.C.: Public Service Satellite Consortium, 1987).

Doug Widner, *The Teleguide Interviews* (Washington, D.C.: Public Service Satellite Consortium, 1988).

Periodicals

BusinessTV is published quarterly by BusinessTV, Inc., Post Office Box 6250, Altadena, CA 91001.

Teleconference: The Business Communications Magazine is published six times a year by Applied Business Telecommunication, Box 5105, San Ramon, CA 94583.

Associations

Founded in 1983, the International Teleconferencing Association, 1299 Woodside Drive, Suite 101, McLean, VA 22102, is a nonprofit corporation that provides a clearinghouse for exchange of information in the field of teleconferencing and publishes a monthly newsletter. Members include users, providers, and consultants/researchers.

Founded in 1975, the Public Service Satellite Consortium, 600 Maryland Avenue SW, Suite 220, Washington, DC 20023, provides telecommunications services, technical assistance, training, information, and research and publishes a newsletter. Members include corporations, nonprofit organizations, vendors, and consultants that use telecommunications.

CHAPTER 14

Mobile Communications

Mobile Communication Services
  Types of Mobile Communication Services
  Evolution of Mobile Communication Services
  Channel Availability

Radio Paging
  Radio Paging Operation
  Types of Pagers
  Cost of Paging

Two-Way Radio
  Two-Way Radio Operation
  Conventional Two-Way Radio
  Trunked Radio

Mobile Telephone Service
  Conventional Mobile Telephone Service
  Cellular Mobile Telephone Service

Selecting a Cellular Telephone

CHAPTER OBJECTIVES

After studying this chapter, you should be able to

1. Describe the types of mobile communication services.
2. Identify the types of pagers and costs of using them.

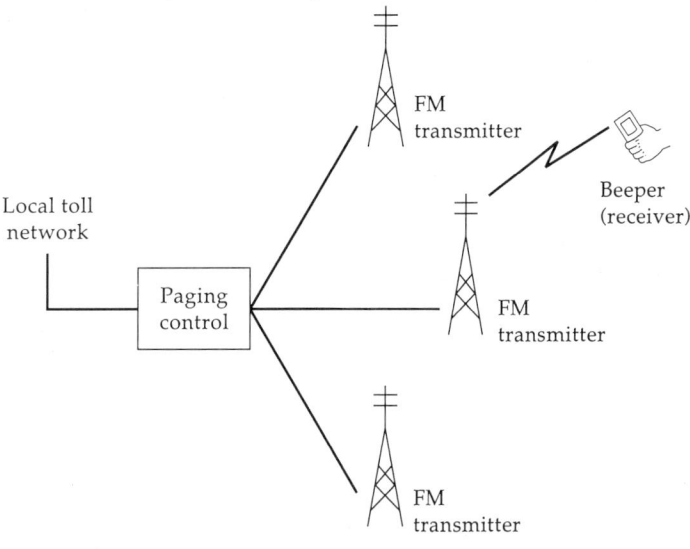

3. Distinguish between conventional and trunked two-way radios.
4. Explain the differences between conventional and cellular mobile telephone services.
5. Specify the basics of cellular mobile telephone service.
6. Select a cellular mobile telephone.

The Holiday Inn–Central Park in Orlando, Florida, rents hand-held paging devices to its guests. These pagers alert guests instantly to telephone messages, even if the guests stray 100 miles from the hotel.

A New York stockbroker, a loyal Yankees fan, has never missed a game because of work. From the middle of Yankee Stadium she uses her portable cellular telephone to advise customers on buying and selling.[1]

A lawyer in Dallas uses a cellular car telephone to communicate with clients and office staff on the way to and from his home and between trips to the courthouse. Time that used to be lost is now productive and profitable.

Cuyahoga Community College in Cleveland, Ohio, uses a 22-foot Winnebago van equipped with cellular telephones to register students for the new semester. The van travels from county fairs to shopping malls, where prospective students sign up for courses. Student information is entered into a personal computer and transmitted through the cellular telephone to a computer at the central campus.[2]

These people need to stay in contact with others without hampering their mobility. The demand for telephone service to and from moving or temporary stationary users continues to grow rapidly. It is much more than a convenience; it has become a way of doing business. This chapter discusses mobile communication services—equipment, operation, applications, and selection.

Mobile Communication Services

■ Types of Mobile Communication Services

Mobile communication services use radio transmission to provide one- and two-way communication service to people on the move. Services include land mobile communication services, air/ground service, marine radiotelephone services, and train telephone service.

Land mobile communication services include paging systems, two-way radios, cellular telephone services, and Citizens Band radios. A one-way *paging system* signals a person when someone wishes to communicate with him or her. *Two-way radio*, such as the dispatch systems used by taxi and ambulance services, uses two-way communication for short messages. *Cellular telephone service* provides mobile communications, enabling users to make and receive local and long-distance calls from any cellular telephone or regular telephone. **Citizens Band** (CB) **radio**, a system of two-way radio communication for short distances, provides a large number of broadcasters with a party line. Transmission delays, lack of privacy, and interference make CB radio most suitable for personal purposes and for some small businesses.

Air/ground service provides two-way communication between airborne telephones and the public switched telephone network. Airborne telephones are linked to a network of ground stations. Figure 14-1 demonstrates the operation of one system.

Marine radiotelephone services include very high frequency (VHF) maritime service, coastal-harbor service, and high-seas maritime radio telephone service.

High-speed train telephone service provides telephone service between a passenger train and the public switched telephone network. Travelers use the standard cellular communications network to place telephone calls from passenger trains.

■ Evolution of Mobile Communication Services

Voice transmission by radio began to become practical with the invention of the audion (the vacuum tube) in 1912. The purpose of the first radiotelephone service, like the wireless telegraph, was to provide links where wires ordinarily could not be used, primarily across bodies of water.

Land mobile radio was introduced by police departments' development

FIGURE 14-1 The GTE Airfone® Air-to-Ground Public Telephone System

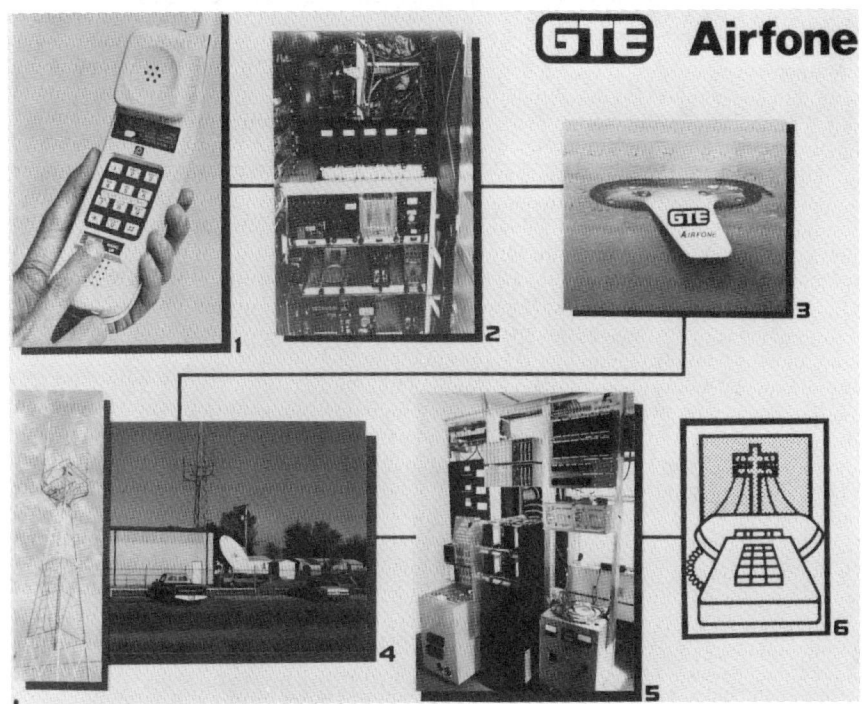

A telephone call, initiated from an aircraft, is placed on an Airfone® system handset featuring a standard keypad (#1). When a passenger introduces a valid major credit card into the system, the call is processed via an airborne computer unit (ACU) located in the aircraft's radio equipment bay (#2) and transmitted via an antenna attached to the belly of the aircraft (#3). The ACU collects the credit card validation and billing data, establishes an air-to-ground link with a computer at a ground station (#4 and #5), and "requests" a telephone line. From the ground station, the call is routed through the traditional public switched telephone network (#6) to the party called.

Courtesy of GTE Airfone Incorporated. ®Registered trademark of GTE Airfone Incorporated.

of one-way and two-way mobile radio systems. In 1921 the Detroit Police Department made significant use of mobile radio at a frequency of 2 MHz. During the 1930s the use of mobile radio spread to fire departments and other emergency services. Low-frequency channels soon became crowded with mobile radio users. As a result, in 1940 the Federal Communications Commission (FCC) made new frequencies in the 30 MHz to 40 MHz frequency spectrum available for mobile radio use. In 1943 the quality of mobile radio was improved by the development of frequency modulation (FM) techniques. FM increased reception in the presence of signal fading, electrical noise, and static on the systems.

The improvement in mobile radio technology resulted in more users—private individuals, private companies, and public agencies—operating

FIGURE 14-2 **Examples of Radio Frequencies Allocated to Mobile Communications Services**

Aviation and marine	Various frequency-band segments between 20 KHz and 1535 MHz
Land mobile	30–50 MHz, 150–162 MHz, 450–470 MHz, 825–845 MHz, 870–890 MHz

their own mobile radio systems. Examples of private companies include taxi, trucking, and construction firms. Examples of public agencies are police, fire, and emergency medical squads. The FCC responded to the increasing demand by allocating an additional 40 MHz of spectrum for land mobile service within the 30 MHz to 500 MHz band. In 1946 the first commercial mobile telephone system in the United States was established in St. Louis, Missouri.

■ Channel Availability

A major concern for any mobile communications system is the availability of radio channels. The radio spectrum is a limited but renewable source. By international agreement the radio frequency spectrum is divided into eight bands. The FCC assigns subdivisions within these bands for various radio services, as shown in Figure 14-2.

In land mobile communications the *low-frequency band* is used by organizations that require long-range mobile communications, such as county and state law enforcement units, long-haul trunk and business lines, pipeline operators, and electric and gas utilities. In flat terrain the range may reach 50 miles; in hilly terrain the range is less.

The *very high frequency band* (VHF) is used by organizations operating within an urban area, such as police, fire, forestry, and highway units. The range varies from 5 to 25 miles, although greater ranges are often experienced.

The *ultra high frequency* (UHF) band provides a clear two-way radio link, even in skyscraper canyons. Data transmission and cellular communications operate in the 800 MHz to 900 MHz frequency range.

In the next sections of this chapter, telephone services—radio paging, two-way radio, and mobile telephone service including cellular telephone—will be discussed. The largest percentage of sales in land mobile communications is currently in the area of two-way radio, followed by pagers, and then cellular telephones.

Radio Paging

A radio service that offers one-way communication is *paging*. The mobile user carries a small, pocket FM radio receiver, called a *pager* or a "*beeper*," as shown in Figure 14-3.

FIGURE 14-3   A Pager

Courtesy of Motorola Inc., Communications Sector, Schaumburg, IL.

▪ Radio Paging Operation

Radio paging operates in simplex mode. A central unit transmits a signal to a radio receiver—a pager—informing that device that someone wants to communicate. The signal received by the pager activates a tone or a light and may include a brief verbal message or display a numeric or alphanumeric message. The pager only receives signals and does not allow conversation with the sender. The pager is available in low-, high-, and UHF frequency bands. Each pager is assigned a unique number that identifies its signal.

The person initiating the paging dials a special telephone exchange to obtain access to the paging system and then dials a unique number that identifies the particular pager desired. The person paged then uses a regular telephone to retrieve the message. The person with the pager typically gives only certain people his or her pager number.

▪ Types of Pagers

The first pagers, introduced in the 1950s, were large and bulky. Today, pagers are lightweight, compact radio receivers that are available in various sizes and styles. Traditional rectangular-shaped pagers clip easily onto a belt, fit into a pocket, or affix to a purse or briefcase. The four basic types of pagers are the following.

Tone Alert Pagers.   Tone alert pagers signal with a "beep" or a continuous tone. They may also have unique alerts that allow the user to distinguish between people and locations. For example, one type of tone can be used for emergency calls and another for routine calls. Or one tone can identify calls from the office while another signifies calls from home.

Tone and Voice Pagers. Tone and voice pagers relay a voice message, allowing the user to hear the voice of the person who is paging him or her.

Numeric Display Pagers. Numeric display pagers display numeric messages, such as a telephone number, and are equipped with memory that allows numbers to be stored for later viewing, if desired.

Personal Message Receivers. Personal message receivers display both words and numeric messages. They can store in memory for future reference the equivalent of a full page of typed text—words and numbers.

Other Pager Features. Some pagers can turn off the pager's alert tone and receive messages without disturbing other people nearby. For example, pagers are available that alert by using a blinking light or a special visual pattern in the display, by permitting use of earphones, or by giving the person being paged a silent vibration (referred to as vibrate silent alert) for a few seconds. In addition to providing privacy these paging features are suited for noisy locations where a pager's alert tone might not be heard.

■ Cost of Paging

Pager Device. Pagers may be leased or purchased; 80% of all pager users lease their pagers from a paging service. Leasing offers the user the opportunity to change the style or type of pager when desired and includes maintenance services. The cost of leasing varies from company to company and depends on the type of pager leased. In 1988 the purchase prices of pagers ranged from under $100 for the basic tone and visual alert to over $400 for models with more capabilities or features. Frost & Sullivan, Inc., a New York consulting firm, estimates that prices of pagers will decrease 10% annually through 1991 as the demand for pagers increases.

Other Costs. Other costs of paging include subscription charges to a paging service for monthly airtime. These costs vary from service to service and from city to city. An example of paging costs is shown in Figure 14-4.

Two-Way Radio

Two-way radios increase the effectiveness of paging by allowing two or more parties to interact. These radios are usually designed for a specific group of users, such as police cars, ambulances, taxis, and dispatch/delivery services.

FIGURE 14-4 **Typical Cost of a Paging Service—Average Paging Service Monthly Airtime Charges for 1987**

Type of Pager	Monthly Airtime Charge If You Own Your Pager	Monthly Airtime Charge and Lease of Pager
Tone Alert	$6.00–10.00	$13.00–25.00
Tone & Voice	$12.00–20.00	$25.00–30.00
Numeric Display	$10.00–15.00	$20.00–35.00
Personal Message Receiver	$20.00–30.00	$40.00–60.00

Christine Westphal, "Keeping Close Contact Is Only a Beep Away," *Today's Chicago Woman*, November 1987. Courtesy of Today's Chicago Woman.

Calls from the public telephone network can be manually patched in. Figure 14-5 shows two-way radio equipment.

■ Two-Way Radio Operation

A two-way radio system operates in half-duplex mode by operating on different frequencies. Only one party on the call can transmit at a time, usually by holding down a button or transmit key. Unless the transmission is scrambled, any listener tuned to the channel being used can listen to the call. The FCC has allotted mobile radio communications a wide range of frequencies, from 6 MHz to 10 GMz.

FIGURE 14-5 **Two-Way Radio Equipment**

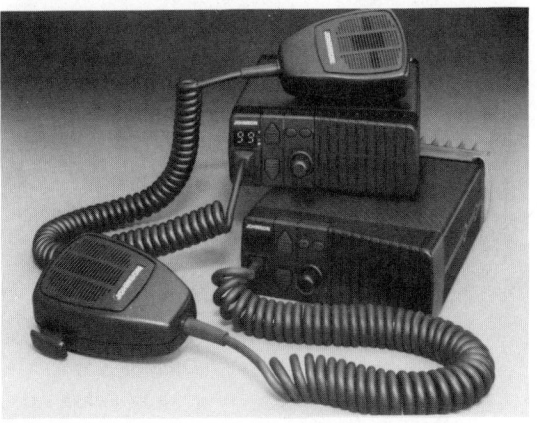

Courtesy of E. F. Johnson Company.

- **Conventional Two-Way Radio**

  Although the conventional two-way radio has improved the operations of many businesses, two-way radio channels are becoming increasingly congested. The *conventional two-way radio* limits each user to a single manually selected channel. If your assigned channel is in use, then you must wait until it is free before you can communicate. When your channel is free and you talk, you have no privacy; all others on your channel can hear your conversations.

- **Trunked Radio**

  Trunking techniques have been used in the telephone industry for quite some time but only recently in two-way radio systems. A **trunked radio system**, such as General Electric's Management and Resource Control trunked radio system, overcomes the congestion problems associated with conventional two-way radio.

  Trunking allows the automatic sharing of a small number of radio channels by a large number of users. Unlike conventional two-way radio systems, which restrict multiple users to a fixed channel, trunked systems allow multiple users automatic access to whichever channels are not being used. They also prevent unauthorized persons from interrupting and listening to conversations.

Mobile Telephone Service

Mobile telephone service operates like the regular telephone service that we use in our homes or offices. This service uses full-duplex mode, not the half-duplex mode that two-way radios use. The full-duplex mode sends two-way simultaneous transmission, each mobile telephone unit being assigned its own private telephone number. Mobile telephones are designed to interconnect with the public switched telephone network and can be directly connected to one another. Calls from a mobile telephone can be made to another mobile telephone or between a mobile telephone and a "wireless" telephone. The two types of mobile telephone services are *conventional mobile telephone service* and *cellular mobile telephone service*.

- **Conventional Mobile Telephone Service**

  In 1964, AT&T introduced its **conventional mobile telephone service**, also called *improved mobile telephone service* (IMTS). IMTS uses a single transmitter/receiver and an antenna to serve an entire metropolitan area, usually 26 miles in diameter. A single channel connects each telephone to the area's radio tower.

Each area has a set number of channels. The number of channels determines the number of subscribers allowed for the system. A channel is usually limited to 1000 subscribers.

The number of calls that can take place at the same time is limited to the number of available radio channels assigned to the IMTS in each area. For example, the system in Boston has five channels, making it possible for no more than five calls to take place concurrently. If the five channels are busy, the subscriber must wait until one is free to place or receive a call.

Although IMTS is being replaced by cellular radio, it is still used, especially in rural areas where cellular service has not yet been implemented. Each of the regional Bell operating companies offers IMTS and continues to maintain the system.

■ Cellular Mobile Telephone Service

Compared with conventional mobile telephone service, **cellular mobile telephone service** offers better-quality transmission, instant channel access, and a larger subscriber base. The transmission quality is equivalent to that of home or business telephones, and channels are immediately available to users.

Evolution. AT&T's Bell Laboratories invented cellular mobile radiotelephone. Both Bell Laboratories and Motorola contributed significantly to its development for commercial use. Cellular radio technology is primarily used to interconnect common carrier switched mobile radiotelephone service with the public switched telephone network.

On October, 13, 1983, Ameritech Mobile Communications began operating the nation's first commercial cellular system. By the end of 1984, 91,600 customers on thirty-three systems were operating in twenty-six market areas. In 1987, four years after the first commercial cellular system went online, 1 million customers on over 235 systems were operating in 144 market areas.

The Cellular Telecommunications Industry Association (CTIA) reports that cellular telephone services are currently available in forty states as well as Washington, D.C., the Gulf of Mexico, and Puerto Rico; services are available to 65% of the U.S. population. In Canada, cellular services are offered in twenty-two major cities. Services are also available in smaller cities adjacent to these cities through switches in the larger cities. Cellular telephone carriers have invested more than $1.7 billion in building their systems and expect to generate more than $1 billion in revenue in 1988. (CTIA, a national trade association, represents more than 85% of licensed cellular carriers as well as those in the business community with an interest in cellular communication. CTIA was formed in May 1984 to promote the cellular industry, address the common concerns of cellular carriers, and serve as a forum for the exchange of nonproprietary information. Members include cellular operators in the United States and Canada, most major manufacturers of cellular equipment, and people in the legal, financial, and service communities with an interest in cellular communication.)

Cellular Telephone Market Areas. Title II of the Communications Act of 1934 authorizes the FCC to regulate cellular radio providers as common carriers. In April 1981 the FCC approved a licensing plan for cellular radio markets: Each market serves a particular geographical area that is defined as one of the 305 Standard Metropolitan Statistical Areas (SMSAs). (The SMSA is the federal government definition of an urban metropolitan area. Each SMSA is numbered according to population size from 1 to 305. The largest is New York City, with a 1980 census population of 14,696,685; the smallest is Alton–Granite City, Illinois, with a population of 20,538.) The remaining areas of the country outside the SMSAs are less populated rural areas, the average population being 150,000. The FCC has divided these areas into 428 Rural Service Areas (RSAs). The SMSAs cover 77% of the United States population, and the RSAs cover the remaining 23%.

Cellular Carriers. The FCC licenses two cellular carriers in each market area or SMSA. One license goes to a telephone company providing local exchange service in the SMSA, referred to as the **wireline company** or **block B frequencies company**. The other license goes to a private company that does not provide telephone service. This company is referred to as the **nonwireline company** or **block A frequencies company**. The terms "wireline" and "nonwireline" are classifications developed by the FCC and do not indicate whether a particular cellular system uses wire, cable, or microwave. The FCC selects the nonwireline carrier by choosing from qualified applicants in a lottery. The purpose of licensing two companies in each geographical area is to serve the public's interest by promoting competition in the cellular industry.

In 1983 the FCC authorized the first commercial carrier of cellular telephone service. By 1987, 200 cellular carriers were serving almost 900,000 customers in more than 127 U.S. cities. In the next few years, cellular service will be available in about 180 additional cities and will extend to rural areas. Examples of wireline and nonwireline companies are the following: In the Boston SMSA the wireline carrier is NYNEX Mobile, and the nonwireline carrier is Cellular One; in the Atlanta SMSA the wireline carrier is BellSouth Mobility, and the nonwireline carrier is Gen-Cell; in the Akron, Ohio, SMSA the wireline carrier is GTE Mobilnet, and the nonwireline company is Akron Cellular Telephone Company.

The FCC allocates 40 MHz of spectrum (825–845 MHz and 870–890 MHz) to each geographical area for cellular telephone service. The FCC automatically sets aside one of the 20-MHz bands for the local wireline

FIGURE 14-6 The Cellular System

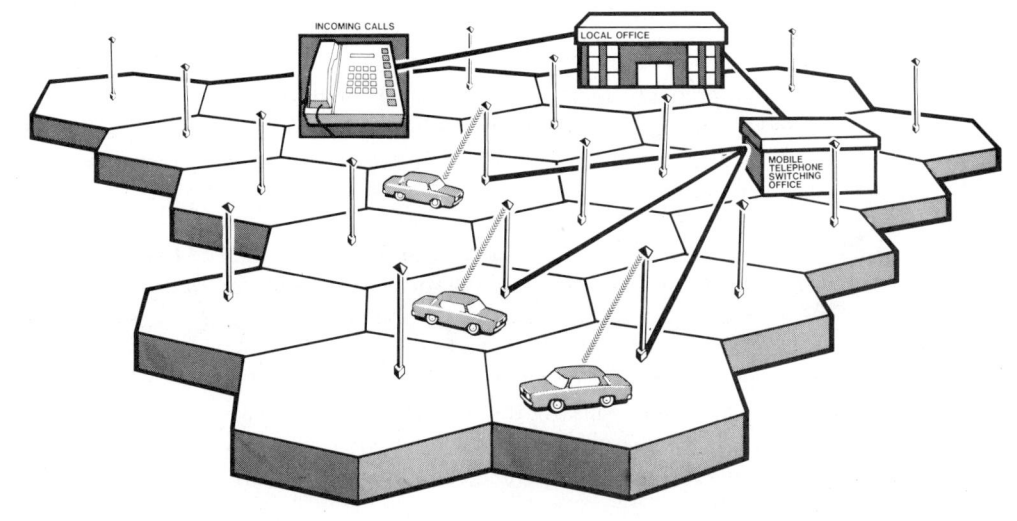

Courtesy of Southwestern Bell Mobile Systems.

company and offers the other 20 MHz band to the selected nonwireline company.

Cellular System Operation

Cellular Geographic Area. Each cellular geographic area, as defined by the FCC, is subdivided into a honeycomb of hexagonal cells as shown in Figure 14-6. Cells range from 2 to 20 miles in diameter. The number of cells per system is not defined by the FCC. Each cellular carrier sets up the cell configuration based on anticipated traffic patterns. As demand for service increases, the cellular carrier can split or combine cell groups. Such flexibility makes it possible to increase the number of cells to virtually an infinite number.

Cell Station. As shown in Figure 14-6, each cell has its own **cell station**—one radio transmitter, two receivers, and an antenna at the top of a 100- to 300-foot tower. The station, acting as an interface between the cellular telephone unit and a centrally located computer-controlled switch, connects to the area's *mobile telephone switching office* (MTSO) by leased four-wire telephone lines, microwave radio links, or fiber-optic cable. Telephone lines connect the MTSO to the local telephone company's central office.

Each cellular subscriber is assigned a unique seven-digit telephone number. The subscriber can place and receive calls directly from a car, from a building, or while just walking down the street to other telephones, either cellular or regular, without operator assistance and without having to wait for a channel as with IMTS.

Cellular users located within a cell or passing through the cell to an adjacent cell communicate with the cell station's transmitter. Each cell station receives and sends signals from and to the MTSO, which also helps to control its operations.

Hands Off. As the cellular user travels from one cell to an adjacent one, the computer at the MTSO automatically transfers or "**hands off**" the call to the new cell site and a new radio channel without noticeable interruption. Transfer or "hands off" occurs when signal strength indicates that a cellular phone is reaching the outer range of its present cell. Hands off usually takes a fifth of a second, making the break in the conversation undetectable. Since cellular systems are interconnected with the regular telephone network, cellular users, like traditional telephone users, can reach telephones anywhere in the world.

Roaming. **Roaming** allows users of a mobile or portable cellular telephone to place and receive calls in cities outside their "home" service area. Roaming is made possible through agreements between cellular service providers in the United States, Canada, and the United Kingdom. These reciprocity agreements permit one company's customers to have cellular telephoning privileges from another company's service and vice versa.

Roaming arrangements also include billing agreements. Roaming customers are billed for all calls through their home service provider, rather than being billed by each system in which they roam. Roaming costs usually include a daily usage cost plus a minute usage cost.

Radio Channels. The FCC has allocated 666 radio channels to each cell; 333 are assigned to the local wireline company and 333 to the selected nonwireline company. Of each group of 333 channels, 312 are designated for voice and data channels and 21 for control purposes. Within a cell, each channel can support one mobile telephone user at a time, any user having the possibility of being assigned to any idle channel. Adjacent cells use different groups of channels to avoid interference. Nonadjacent cells can use the same groups of channels, thus allowing a limited number of channels to be used again and again to serve many subscribers. By splitting cells, as shown in Figure 14-6, the cellular system has the capacity to accommodate everyone who wants a mobile phone for business or personal use.

Cellular Telephone Components. The components of a cellular telephone are a control unit, a transceiver (transmitter/receiver) with a logic unit, and an antenna. The *control unit* houses a handset/hangup cup and user controls and indicators, such as a twelve-button keypad and electronic buttons for making the calls. The *transceiver* uses a frequency synthesizer for tuning into a designated cellular system channel. The *logic unit* interprets both user actions and system commands and manages the transceiver and control units. The *antenna* is installed in a car's trunk, roof, or window and/or is included in a unit's carrying case or telephone component.

For example, the components of a cellular car telephone include a car telephone that is wired and installed inside an automobile's interior or trunk, a control unit that is placed on the car's dashboard or on the floor by the front seat, and a transceiver that is placed in the car trunk or under the seat and is hard-wired to the antenna, handset, and car battery. When the telephone is hard-wired to the car battery, the car telephone is provided with virtually an unlimited power service, resulting in a strong signal.

Cellular Telephone Operation. To operate a cellular telephone, dial the desired number and then press the "send" button. When your conversation has ended, press the "end" button.

Types of Cellular Telephones. Types of cellular telephones include car telephones and portable telephones. Portable telephones are classified as briefcase phones, transportable phones, and handheld phones. With the exception of the car phone, each phone is completely portable. All operating components are contained in a carrying case or within the instrument itself.

Car Phone. The car phone, shown in Figure 14-7, is the most popular of the cellular telephones. It can also be used on boats, airplanes, and trains. Refer to the discussion on cellular phone components for a discussion of car phones.

Briefcase Phone. A briefcase phone is a battery-powered telephone designed to fit into a briefcase, a coat or pants pocket, or even a women's handbag, for easy portability. Most briefcase telephones feature a rechargeable battery that will provide eight hours of normal operation between charges, including 90 minutes of conversation. The major drawback of this type of telephone is its weight, which can be as much as 22 to 24 pounds.

Transportable Phone. The transportable phone, shown in Figure 14-8, offers more versatility and convenience than the briefcase phone. The telephone is lighter, weighing between 8 and 14 pounds. It can be converted from a car phone to a field phone more easily than the car phone. Its modular design enables it to be unlatched from the car and snapped onto a portable pack component for easy carrying. When used in the car, these telephones offer high-power transmitting signal strength. They have rechargeable four-hour batteries that can handle up to 60 minutes of continuous calling.

FIGURE 14-7 Using a Cellular Car Telephone

Courtesy of Motorola Inc.

FIGURE 14-8 Transportable Phone

Courtesy of Motorola Inc.

FIGURE 14-9 **Portable Cellular Telephone**

Courtesy of Motorola Inc.

Handheld Phone. The handheld phone, shown in Figure 14-9, is the most portable, lightweight of the cellular telephones, weighing only two or three pounds. Its battery provides eight hours of normal operation between charges, including 30 minutes of conversation. A drawback is its low power, resulting in a transmitting range of only about two miles.

Applications. Cellular telephones are being used by many people to carry on their business activities when they are not in the office, as described in the scenarios at the beginning of this chapter. Cellular telephones work well with pagers. When a marketing manager is out of the office, customers contact the manager by pager. When the manager receives the paging message, the manager uses his or her cellular telephone to respond. The pager also serves as a screening device for incoming cellular telephone calls. When a paging message arrives, the manager can decide whether or not it requires his or her immediate attention.

Cellular radio transmission is ideally suited for data applications. A car or a remote workplace can be transformed into a mobile office by using a cellular telephone with a cellular modem to transmit data from a portable computer or to fax documents from a portable fax machine. For example, police cars equipped with cellular phones, modems, and computers and/or fax equipment transmit their reports to police headquarters and receive reports. When away from the office, a sales representative uses a portable computer, a cellular phone, and a modem to access computer data from the company's mainframe computer. When out in the field, equipment repair people obtain copies of technical diagrams by having the company fax these to their portable facsimile machines, which connect to cellular telephones and modems. The opening scenario of this chapter describes how Cuyahoga Community College registers students by using cellular radio technology.

Selecting a Cellular Telephone

Guidelines for selecting a cellular telephone are described below.
First, determine the need for a cellular telephone by answering the following:

- Do you spend much time commuting each day?
- Do you often use your car to attend business meetings or take brief business trips?
- Is using a car important in conducting your business activities?
- Must you be in contact with your staff and/or customers while traveling?
- Does your business require you to travel two or more times a week?
- Do you make/receive many telephone calls each day within your area?
- Would a telephone in your car increase your profits, productivity, and/or customer satisfaction?

If you answer "yes" to most of these questions, you should consider using a cellular phone. For example, if you spend more than 30 minutes a day commuting, traveling to many business meetings, and conducting a great deal of business by telephone, your travel time could be spent more productively with a cellular telephone. By keeping in touch with customers or staff you can immediately address problems or urgent business matters.

Second, choose the cellular mobile telephone. Select the type of cellular telephone needed—car phone, briefcase phone, transportable phone, or handset phone. All products must conform to standards approved by the FCC, making them usable on all of the nation's cellular systems, either wireline or nonwireline. However, features of cellular telephones may differ among manufacturers.

Standard features of most cellular telephones include *illuminated buttons* that make them easy to use at night, a *digital display* that shows the number you just dialed, *last-number recall*, and a *telephone directory memory* for storing frequently dialed numbers.

For safety the American Automobile Association recommends a *hands-free speakerphone attachment and a dialing mechanism* that allow you to make calls, talk, and listen while keeping both hands on the wheel. This feature is especially important in cars with manual transmission. Some models can be *voice activated*, which allows a telephone number to be dialed by voice command. For example, when you say "home," the cellular telephone automatically dials your house.

Each cellular telephone is programmed with an *electronic serial number*, a unique number that is embedded electronically in the cellular telephone. Because cellular service is so costly, an important feature to include is an *electronic lock*. The lock is a number code that is dialed each time the user makes a call and thus prevents unauthorized use of the telephone.

If the cellular phone is stolen and you report the number to the local cellular carrier, the carrier's switches can be programmed to reject any contact with the stolen unit. A cellular phone with a *detachable handset and antenna* that can be stored in the car's trunk or glove compartment when it is parked can also be helpful.

Another desirable feature is an **A/B switch**. Telephones with this switch can operate on either of the two frequencies available in each geographical area. The switching feature makes it possible to roam from one frequency to the other when you travel.

The typical custom calling features are offered for an additional monthly charge. *Call forwarding* allows a customer to redirect calls intended for one cellular telephone to another number. *Busy transfer* allows a user to redirect calls to another telephone number when the called cellular telephone is busy. *Call waiting* allows a customer currently engaged in one call to be alerted that another incoming call is waiting. *Three-way conference* allows a three-way conversation to be initiated from a cellular telephone. *Call answering* is an electronic voice message box that answers the cellular phone when the called person cannot or does not wish to answer.

Examples of other features to be considered include the following:

- An *auxiliary alert mode* flashes the headlights or honks the horn to notify a user of an incoming call.
- An *airtime meter* keeps a record of the actual calling time of individual calls in intervals of 6, 30, or 60 seconds.
- *Hookups* are available for facsimile and answering machines.
- *Call restriction* limits the placement and receipt of calls.
- *Horn alert* signals when you are outside the car.
- *Call duration agent* emits a beep tone at specified intervals for tracking call length.
- *Keyboard programmability* allows features such as Call Timer, Call Restriction, and Call Duration Alert to change according to needs.
- A *membrane keyboard* provides spill resistance and backlighting for nighttime viewing.
- *Call-in-progress override* permits a conversation to continue after the car ignition is turned off.
- *Call-in-absence* indicates that a call was received during your absence.

Third, evaluate the cellular service provider. Choosing the cellular service provider is as important as selecting the right cellular equipment. Cellular mobile telephone service is offered by cellular system carriers (wireline and nonwireline carriers) and by resellers. *Resellers* are companies that purchase cellular service wholesale from either the wireline carrier or the nonwireline carrier and then offer service to customers at retail rate. Many of these companies also sell telephone equipment.

The **cellular service provider**, whether it be a cellular system carrier or a reseller, is responsible for activating your cellular telephone number, handling your bill, providing cellular telephone service, and possibly installing the phone. Special services offered by the cellular service provider should be examined, including testing the service of each cellular carrier. For example, ask the cellular service provider for a road demonstration or rent a car with a cellular telephone and drive in the area where you will be using the system.

A potential subscriber to a cellular service should evaluate both networks—the wireline carrier and the nonwireline carrier—that operate in his or her selected geographical area. A comparison of cellular networks should include the following points:

- Are the places in the metropolitan area in which you frequently travel served by the cellular network?
- What are the layout and configuration of the network?

Some cellular companies install their transmitters on existing buildings to save money. The result can be spotty coverage and interference and inadequate call handling. Other companies use fewer but taller cellular towers, claiming that such towers are better. Additional cells cannot be added or more radio channels reused within the same metropolitan area without interference unless the antennas on these towers are first lowered. When changes are made to a system, tall towers often require major system redesign.

Fourth, select an equipment vendor. FCC-approved cellular telephones can be obtained from many different types of vendors, such as car dealers, two-way radio dealers, telephone sales centers, television stores, electronic equipment distributors, and cellular telephone companies. Wireline and nonwireline cellular carriers also offer cellular phones.

Consideration should be given to purchasing a telephone from a vendor that installs as well as provides repair maintenance service under warranty. The vendor's installation, maintenance, replacement, and repair warranty plans should be examined. Vendors should include equipment warranties for parts and labor. Warranties typically range from one to five years, depending on the manufacturer and model.

Fifth, select a purchase, lease, or rental equipment plan. Cellular telephones can be purchased, leased, or rented. In 1989, telephones ranged in price from under $1000 to over $4000, depending on models, features, and installation costs. Lease plans allow users to spread payments over several years.

Monthly rental plans are most commonly used, since they require no large cash outlay, no long-term commitment, and no termination fee. Some plans apply a percentage of the monthly rental payment toward the price of the equipment. Typical 1989 monthly rental fees ranged from $20 to over $100, depending on model, features, and installation costs. These fees usually include maintenance, manufacturer warranty, and insurance.

Sixth, calculate usage charges. Users might discover that cellular usage charges result in bills that are higher than expected. Carrier companies generally offer users a choice of pricing plans to match individual needs. Typical charges include the following:

- *A one-time service activation charge, usually about $30.* This charge covers the cost of programming the cellular phone number and hooking up the service.
- *A monthly access charge that can range from $10 to over $60.*
- *A per-minute usage charge* that usually includes both airtime and message unit charges, referred to as land charges. **Airtime** refers to the time a cellular subscriber uses his or her cellular phone. A customer is charged for airtime usage by the minute or fraction of a minute. Charges are usually higher during weekday business hours and lower at night and on weekends. When the phone conversation is between two cellular phones, there is no land charge.
- *Long-distance charges.* These charges are billed twice—once for the per-minute local usage and again for long-distance usage.
- *Charges for incoming calls.* Cellular carriers charge subscribers for incoming calls because they have no way of billing callers who are not their customers. You can avoid unwanted incoming call charges by requesting that your cellular phone number not be published in cellular directories or by programming your cellular phone not to accept incoming calls.
- *Charges for customer calling features.* A monthly charge is assessed for such custom calling features as call forwarding, busy transfer, call waiting, three-way conference, and call answering.

An average monthly phone bill, for example, ranges between $100 and $150. It includes the monthly access charge, a per-minute usage charge ranging from $0.05 to $0.50 for each minute on the phone for both incoming and outgoing calls, and any long-distance charges. Extra monthly charges may be imposed for itemizing the bill; for roaming, that is, for using the cellular system when outside of the subscriber's geographical area; and for optional features. Examples of optional features are automatic transfer of calls if no answer; call forwarding; three-party conferencing; call waiting; cellular answering service; call restrictions, such as incoming or outgoing calls only; and restricted long distance. Figure 14-10 shows a sample bill. Industry experts predict that within a decade, monthly cellular phone rates will approach regular phone rates.

Refer to Figure 14-11, the "Cellular Shoppers' Checklist," as a guide in selecting a cellular carrier, services, and the mobile phone.

FIGURE 14-10   Sample Monthly Bill of a Cellular Phone Subscriber

This page describes the status of your account, including previous balance, payments received, adjustments, new charges and your new balance. If your account has multiple phones, the total account status will appear on this page.

A detailed description of your charges is included on the following pages.

(a) Account Summary

1. Date of call.
2. Time of call.
3. Number called or "*Incoming*" if a call was received by your cellular phone.
4. Call destination.
5. Peak (P), Off-peak (OP) or Multiple Period (M) phone usage.
6. Duration of call.
7. Airtime charge per call.
8. Local call charge or toll charge per call if applicable.
9. Total cost of call.

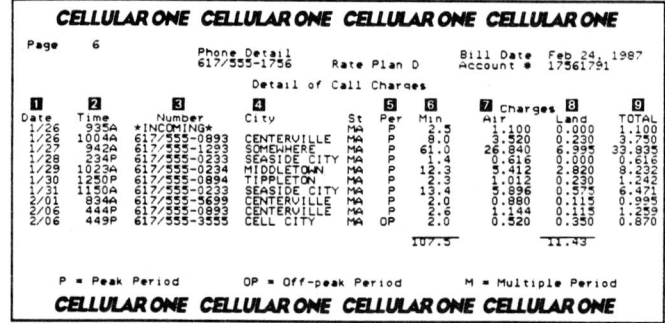

(b) Detail of Phone Charges

1. Indicates what cellular system the calls have been placed on.
2. Indicates Peak, Off-peak or Multiple Period usage, based on visited systems rates.
3. Airtime charge per call based on visited systems rates.
4. Local call charge or toll charge per call if applicable.
5. Local or state tax if applicable.
6. Total cost of call.

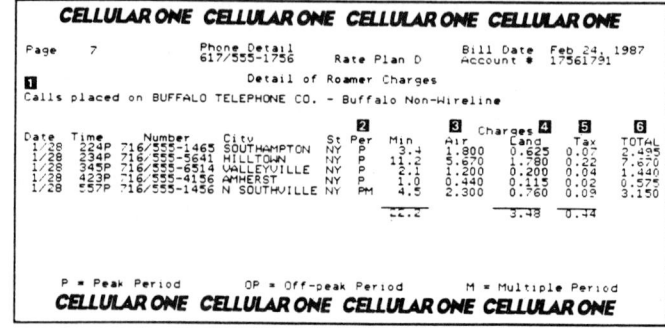

(c) Detail of Roamer Charges

Courtesy of Cellular One.

FIGURE 14-11 **Cellular Shoppers' Checklist**

Evaluating a Cellular Network
- Who built and operates the cellular network?
- What locations does the network coverage area include?
- How is the system laid out and configured?
- How dependable is the network?

Choosing a Cellular Service Provider
- Which retail outlets offer cellular service?
- Do the installation people have high standards? Certification?
- Is automatic roaming available? To which cities?
- Is free emergency dialing offered?

Figuring the Cellular Service Bill
- Is more than one pricing plan available?
- How much is the basic monthly access fee? The one-time service activation fee?
- In what increments are airtime rates calculated? Are any discount calling times available?
- Are custom calling features offered?

Selecting a Cellular Mobile Phone
- Which type is best for me: car phone or portable models?
- What features are available?
- Who sells cellular equipment? What kind of warranties are available?
- Would purchasing, leasing, or renting equipment make the most sense for me?
- Is it a genuine rental agreement or actually a long-term lease? What does the rental fee include?

Courtesy of Southwestern Bell Mobile Systems.

Summary

Mobile communication services include land mobile communication services, air/ground service, marine radiotelephone services, and train telephone service. Of particular interest to business users are radio paging, two-way radio, and mobile telephone service, with cellular mobile service taking the lead. The two cellular carriers in each market area or SMSA compete to provide cellular telephone users with service that meets their needs.

Paging, an inexpensive one-way communication system, suits people desiring immediate one-way contact. For those needing two-way communication, cellular telephones with many of the same features as a standard telephone offer a solution. Roaming agreements among cellular carriers make cellular telephones usable in cities nationwide. Pagers and cellular telephones work well together: Pagers notify cellular users about important calls to be made and/or serve as a way of screening incoming cellular calls. Cellular telephones are also used with portable computers, modems, and facsimiles for screen display or hardcopy output.

Key Terms

A/B switch
Airtime
Block A frequencies company
Block B frequencies company
Cell station
Cellular mobile telephone service
Cellular service provider
Citizens Band radio
Conventional mobile telephone service
Hands off
Land mobile communication services
Nonwireline company
Radio paging
Roaming
Trunked radio system
Wireline company

Self-Quiz

Indicate whether the statement is true or false.

1. The invention of the vacuum tube began to make voice transmission by radio practical.   T/F
2. The first commercial mobile telephone system was established in St. Louis, Missouri.   T/F
3. Radio paging operates in half-duplex mode.   T/F
4. A two-radio system operates in full-duplex mode.   T/F
5. Mobile telephones cannot connect with each other.   T/F
6. A cellular telephone service provider is either a wireline or a nonwireline company.   T/F

Complete each of the following statements.

1. By international agreement the radio frequency spectrum is divided into _____ bands.
2. Mobile telephone service that uses a single transmitter/receiver and an antenna to service an entire metropolitan area is called _____ .
3. The number of cellular carriers that the FCC licenses in each market or SMSA area is _____ .
4. The number of frequencies of spectrum that the FCC allocates to each geographic area for cellular service is _____ .
5. The number of radio channels that the FCC allocates to each cell in a cellular geographic area is _____ .
6. Authorization is given to the FCC to regulate cellular radio providers as common carriers by _____ .

Match Column A with Column B.

Column A
(a) Block A frequencies company
(b) Block B frequencies company
(c) Hands off
(d) Roaming
(e) Trunking

Column B
____ 1. Occurs when signal strength indicates that a cellular telephone is reaching the outer limits of its present cell.
____ 2. Allows multiple users automatic access to multiple channels.

_____ 3. Provides local telephone service.
_____ 4. Allows a mobile cellular telephone user to place calls while outside the home service area.
_____ 5. Provides no local telephone service.

■ *Review Questions*

1. What frequencies has the FCC assigned to land mobile communications?
2. If you decide to purchase a pager, what other charges can you expect to pay monthly for the paging service?
3. How do two-way radios and pagers differ?
4. What is the difference between a conventional two-way radio system and a trunked radio system?
5. How does mobile radio service differ from mobile telephone service?
6. How does the operation of improved mobile telephone service differ from the operation of cellular telephone service?
7. What is the difference between a wireline company and a nonwireline company?
8. (a) What can you do to prevent others from using your cellular phone?
   (b) How can you prevent your cellular phone from being stolen?
   (c) If your cellular phone is stolen, what should you do?
9. What are the responsibilities of the cellular service provider?
10. What information is helpful in selecting a cellular phone equipment vendor?
11. What types of charges can you expect to see on your monthly statement for cellular phone operation?

■ *Activities/Projects*

1. Obtain a pager, two-way radio, or cellular telephone. Demonstrate how it operates.
2. Investigate the cost of operating a cellular telephone in your town or city.
   (a) Who are the two cellular carriers? Which one is the wireline company? Which one is the nonwireline company?
   (b) Use the checklist in Figure 14-11 as a guide in your investigation of the cost of cellular telephone operation.
   (c) What other questions would you add to the checklist in Figure 14-11.
3. Examine the sample monthly bill of a cellular phone subscribe shown in Figure 14-10.
   (a) Describe each of the charges.
   (b) Suggest ways in which the subscriber could reduce phone charges.
4. Which cellular telephone (or pager or two-way radio) would you recommend for use in business?

(a) Obtain information about cellular telephones from a local distributor. Also refer to the section in this chapter on selecting a cellular telephone and to the last section of Figure 14-11 for selection guidelines.
(b) Describe the cellular telephone that you would select, including the its cost, features, and warranties.
(c) Why did you select this particular cellular telephone?
5. Brainstorm and discuss one or both of the following topics.
   (a) The danger and/or problems associated with using cellular telephones, such as while driving in traffic. Develop a safety guide.
   (b) The various ways in which pagers, two-way radios, and cellular telephones can be used in business or in other settings.

■ *Case:* **Two-Way Radio System Savings Analysis**

You would like to determine how much you would save by using a two-way radio system to communicate with five of your drivers. At present, drivers must use pay phones on the road to make phone calls. Each driver's mileage is about 100 miles per day throughout the year (240 working days). The cost per vehicle per mile is $0.50. Each driver makes five calls per day, each call averaging about 8 minutes and costing $0.50. The hourly pay of each driver is $15.

Use the Radio System Savings Analysis Form shown below to determine the answers to the following questions:
(a) What is the savings per day in mileage cost for the five vehicles?
(b) What is the savings per day in labor and phone costs for the five vehicles?
(c) What is the total savings per year in mileage, labor, and phone costs?
(d) What is the total annual cost of a two-way radio system costing $8000 if you amortize the system over a five-year period?
(e) What is the annual savings produced by the two-way radio system?

Radio System Savings Analysis Form

	Typical Savings	Your Savings
A. Daily Mileage Savings		
1. Total number of vehicles	4	_____
2. Total miles per vehicle per day	× 50	× _____
3. Total vehicle miles per day	200	_____
4. Cost per vehicle per mile (average 45 cents per mile)	× 0.45	× _____
5. Total vehicle cost per day	$90.00	$ _____
6. Approximate savings in mileage with two-way radio	× 20%	× 20%
Total Daily Savings in Daily Mileage Cost	$ 18.00	$ _____

B. Daily Labor and Phone Savings
   1. Hours per day per driver on phone
      (3 calls per day, 10 min. each)   30 min.   _____ min.
   2. Total number of drivers   × 4   × _____
   3. Total phone hours per day   2 hrs.   _____ hrs.
   4. Hourly wage per driver ($5.00 per hr.)   × $ 5.00   × $ _____
   5. Total labor savings $10.00 $ _____
   6. Money spent for calls   + $ 2.40   + $ _____
   Total Daily Labor and Phone Savings $ 12.40 $ _____

C. Total Annual Savings with Two-Way Radio
   1. Total savings per day—mileage and
      phone costs (items A + B) $30.40 $ _____
   2. Total working days per year   × 240   × 240
   Total Annual Savings $ 7296.00 $ _____

D. Total System Operating Cost of Two-Way
   Radio
   1. Radio system cost $5145.00 $ _____
   2. Amortization period of system   ÷ 5 years   ÷ 5 years
   Total Annual Cost of Radio System $ 1029.00 $ _____

E. Savings Produced by Two-Way Radio
   1. Total savings per year (from C) $7296.00 $ _____
   2. Total operating cost per year (from D)   −$1029.00 $ _____
   Annual Savings Produced by Two-Way Radio $ 6267.00 $ _____
                                                        ×   5   ×   5
   Total Five-Year Savings $31335.00 $ _____

Courtesy of GE Mobile Communications, General Electric Company.

■ *Notes*

1. "Mobile Telephones for All Occasions," *New York Times*, September 23, 1987, p. 2.
2. "Car Phones: From Toy to Valued Tool," *Los Angeles Times*, July 7, 1987.

■ *Additional Readings*

Raymond Bowers, Alfred M. Lee, and Cary Hershey, *Communications for a Mobile Society: An Assessment of New Technology* (Beverly Hills, Calif.: Sage, 1978).

Cellular Telephone (Delran, N.J.: Datapro Research Corporation, 1988).

John J. Keeler, "Hello Anywhere: The Cellular Phone Boom Will Change the Way You Live," *Business Week*, September 18, 1987, pp. 84–92.

Richard C. Notebaert, "Portable Phones for a Mobile Society," *TPT*, April 1988, pp. 31–33.

Stan Prentiss, *Introducing Cellular Communications* (Blue Ridge Summit, Pa.: TAB Books, 1984).

PART IV

Telecommunications Management

CHAPTER 15

Managing Your Telephone/ Telecommunications System

Ten Steps to Telecommunications Management
Basic Traffic Concepts
    Traffic Defined
    Traffic Engineering
    Traffic Load
Tariffs
Active Cost Control Methods
    Automatic Route Selection/Least-Cost Routing
    Calling Restrictions
    Authorized Codes and Levels of Services
    Timed Signals
Telephone Management Systems
    Telephone Management Systems Defined
    TMS Configurations
    TMS Features
    TMS Reports
    Benefits of Telephone Management Systems
Selecting a Telephone Management System
Managing Telecommunications in the Next Decade
    Technology Trends
    Regulatory Trends
    Organizational and Management Trends

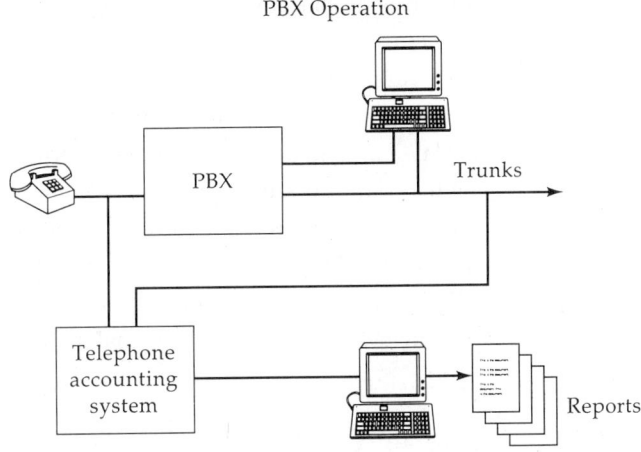

Redrawn courtesy of Bitek International Corporation.

CHAPTER OBJECTIVES

After studying this chapter, you should be able to

1. Outline a plan for managing a telecommunications system.
2. Apply basic traffic concepts.
3. Suggest ways to control telephone costs.
4. Describe applications of telephone management systems.
5. Discuss benefits of using telephone management systems.
6. Develop a plan for selecting a telephone management system.
7. Identify trends in the telecommunications industry.

A time-consuming chore for a Denver law firm was tracking the previous month's telephone calls. After eighty copies of the month's telephone bill were made, a copy was distributed to each company attorney, paralegal, and secretary for them to identify as many of their long-distance calls as they could remember. Today, the firm uses a telephone management system that provides details about each telephone call and automatically allocates costs to the proper parties, including clients. The system not only saves the firm time and money but automatically allocates 95% of the calls to clients, compared to 50% before the system was installed.

One of the ways in which LaBarge Pipe and Steel Company of St. Louis, Missouri, uses its computer telephone management system is to gauge the performance of its salespeople. A detailed call report identifies each salesperson's calling activities—who was called, the length of each call, the type of line used, and the cost. This information is compared with the number of orders placed by each salesperson and determines whether any calling was for personal reasons.

The telecommunications manager at Official Airlines, Oak Brook, Illinois, uses telecommunication systems management software to determine which trunks are overutilized or underutilized. What previously took a couple of hours to calculate now takes only a couple of minutes. In addition, the system's "what if" capability helps to make decision making more efficient.

Historically, managers relied on the local telephone company to design their telephone networks and solve network problems. Since divestiture, these services no longer exist. Instead, companies must identify their telephone network requirements and make their own decisions about what to procure and how to implement a telephone network. Although the network's increasing complexity can be managed with the aid of computerized systems, choosing the system that provides the services at the desired cost and operating it can be difficult tasks. These tasks are further complicated by the explosion of available products and services from which to choose. Each of the scenarios at the beginning of the chapter tells how one company is managing its telephone networks. This chapter outlines a basic plan for managing a telephone/telecommunications system, describes the basic concepts of traffic management and the tools available for managing telephone networks, and identifies trends occurring in the telecommunications industry.

Ten Steps to Telecommunications Management

How do you manage a telephone/telecommunications system? Where do you begin? First, you must develop a plan for managing the system. Such a plan is necessary for establishing a communications department and/or continuing the management of the system.

One approach to successfully managing a system is outlined in Figure 15-1. For a new telecommunications manager this plan identifies what the manager must do within the first few months of starting the job as well as in the months that follow.

FIGURE 15-1 **The Ten Steps to Telecommunications Management**

Step 1. *Know your company's business.*
Step 2. *Learn your present system.*
  (a) Conduct a physical survey and document the present system.
  (b) Determine which vendors and services are being used.
  (c) Survey management and key employees to determine your system's impact on the company's business.
Step 3. *Identify costs.*
  (a) Total monthly and annual costs: Recurring charges, usage charges, installation, and other service charges
  (b) Costs by department, or location
  (c) Costs by type of service: local, toll FX, WATS, etc.
  (d) Costs by vendor
Step 4. *Monitor usage of your system and determine your company's needs.*
Step 5. *Evaluate your present system.*
  (a) Trunking
  (b) Equipment
  (c) Services
  (d) Personnel
Step 6. *Evaluate alternative equipment and services.*
Step 7. *Design an optimal system to meet your company's present and future needs.*
Step 8. *Develop plans for implementation of the optimal system.*
Step 9. *Develop a corporate telecommunications policy.*
  (a) Procedures for ordering of equipment and services
  (b) Procedures for repair and maintenance
  (c) Staff training program
  (d) Procedures for use of the system and cost control
Step 10. *Continue to monitor changes in the industry.*
  (a) Rates and tariffs
  (b) New equipment
  (c) New services
  (d) Regulatory changes

Larry Arredondo, "How to Start Your Telecommunications System," *Telecommunications Management for Business & Government*, edited by Harry Newton, © 1980 Telecom Library Inc. Reprinted by permission of the publisher.

Basic Traffic Concepts

To assist in managing your telephone system, such as in evaluating the effectiveness of your present telephone system and monitoring usage of your system and company needs, this section and the two that follow discuss the basic concepts of traffic tariffs, active cost control methods, and telephone management systems.

Traffic Defined

The term **traffic** is used in telecommunications to describe the flow of information or messages through the network, as described in previous chapters. A communications network consists of transmission facilities, switching equipment, and station equipment. Information flow may be generated by telephone conversations or may be the result of providing data, audio, and video services.

Only a small percentage of the many millions of potential telephone users use the communications network at the same time. A network that can be shared by different people at different times is much more economical than one that is dedicated to each of the millions of users. But when people share equipment, they might not always be able to complete a telephone call if the equipment is already in use. The more equipment that is available for use the better, but the more costly the service will be. What exists is a tradeoff between cost and quality of service.

Traffic Engineering

A company must design a network that is a balance between costs and quality of service. **Traffic engineering** is a network planning activity that determines the number and type of communication paths required between switching points and the call-handling capacity of the switching points. Traffic engineering methods configure a telephone network—for example, determining its capacity based on its expected demand. These methods are based on a type of applied probability theory called traffic theory. They also identify existing and potential network problems and offer possible solutions to users.

Traffic Load

Characteristics of Traffic Load. To understand the concept of "traffic load," its characteristics must be defined. Traffic load can be expressed in terms of offered load or carried load. **Offered load** measures the demand that is placed on a telephone system; that is, it tells how many people were trying to place a telephone call. **Carried load** measures how well the demand that was placed on the system was actually satisfied. In other words, it tells how many people were successful in carrying on a telephone conversation.

Holding Time, Conversation Time, and Operating Time. The elements of a "telephone call" can be described according to operating time, conversation time, and holding time. **Conversation time** is the time from the start to the finish of a (voice) conversation or a data transmission. It does not include the time to establish or end the connections.

Operating time is the time necessary to establish and release a connection with the called party. Operating time includes all necessary dialing and waiting for the called party to answer. Long-distance telephone calls are usually billed only for conversations (conversation time), but some other common carriers also include the operating time.

Holding time is the length of time from the moment a facility is seized for use until the time it is released. Holding time is the sum of the operating time and the conversation time. The holding time of a voice call over a private line is equal to the operating time to establish the call, its conversation time, and the operating time to disconnect the call. Traffic monitors measure holding time—the entire time the circuit is in use—while automatic call-accounting equipment measures only conversation time. Thus the average holding time may differ when obtained from automatic call equipment.

The term **peg count** is used to refer to the number of calls actually handled during a specified time interval, such as one hour. For example, a peg count of 20 could mean that twenty telephone calls took place in one hour.

Traffic Load Defined. In the design and utilization of a network, a major concern is determining the traffic load. *Traffic load* is determined by the number of calls carried by the communication path or channel and the duration of each call or its *average holding time*. In a given hour the load on any part of the network is expressed as the product of the average holding time for a call and the number of calls carried. For example, if the average holding time for a telephone call was 5 minutes and the number of calls carried on the network was twenty, then the traffic load on that particular network would be 100 minutes of calling.

Blockage. How often have you tried to call someone but have been unable to do so because the line was busy? When you attempt to place a call and cannot complete the call, the call has probably been blocked. **Blockage** is a key factor to consider in setting up and maintaining telephone facilities.

Your telephone call could be blocked for one of the following reasons:

- All of the outgoing lines that are available for calls are in use.
- The line that you are attempting to call is busy.
- Occasionally, the telephone system does not have enough internal circuits, so you do not receive a dial tone when you pick up your telephone.
- The local or long-distance circuits might be busy on the route your call is attempting to use.

You can change the first situation and possibly the second one. The last two situations are ones over which you have little or no control.

When your telephone calls are blocked, you may do one of the following:

- Leave the system or go away and not return within the hour

- Retry or reenter the system within the hour
- Go another way or select an alternate route
- Delay or wait until a server becomes available (A server is any facility that handles traffic or the facility that carries the traffic; it may be a trunk, a link, or an attendant position.)

Grade of Service. Blocked calls can mean lost business. The relationship of blocked calls to traffic load can be expressed in terms of offered load and carried load as follows:

- Offered load = carried load + blockage
- Carried load = offered load − blockage

Since the network is being shared, some blockage of calls will occur. But how many blocked calls should you expect? To determine what is satisfactory, the concept of grade of service is used. **Grade of service** (GOS) is an index that represents the probability that a call will be blocked or delayed during the busiest hour of the day. If your call is blocked because you do not receive a dial tone or because all the outgoing lines are busy, you consider the grade of service to be a poor one.

The GOS index specifies the number of calls that get blocked per 100 calls attempted. The GOS is represented by P (for probability) followed by a decimal value to indicate the percentage of calls that are apt to be blocked out of a total number of calls placed during the *busy hour*, the hour when the largest volume of calls is handled. For example, if your telephone system provides a P.05 GOS, then 5 of every 100 calls you attempt during the busy hour will probably get blocked because the shared facilities are in use. P.05 is considered a good GOS. A P.01 GOS indicates that 1 call of every 100 will probably be blocked; P.20 GOS indicates that 20 calls of every 100 will be blocked. A GOS of P.20 or more indicates that you should consider improving your telephone service by adding more circuits or trunks.

Whether or not you add one or more trunks will depend on how much each trunk costs and how the additional trunks are to be used. For example, suppose that you have eight local telephone lines coming into your telephone system, and you learn that the current grade of service is P.12. While this grade of service is satisfactory, you still might want to add one or more local lines to improve the service, particularly if the cost for an additional line per month is only a few dollars. When customers can telephone you and reach you on the first try, you are helping your business.

But suppose you have two PBX systems, one in Boston and one in Philadelphia, that are connected by a tie line. A tie line is a private communications line connecting two PBXs. You find out that the grade of service over the tie line is P.50, which is quite unsatisfactory. To add another tie line would cost $900 per month. Since tie lines are only for internal use, you would probably decide not to incur the expense for another one. Instead, you might plan to arrange a schedule that would distribute the traffic evenly at both sites.

FIGURE 15-2 Converting Minutes and Hours to CCS and CCS to Erlangs

One CCS equals 36/60 or 1⅔ minutes.
One CC equals 100 seconds of telephone traffic.
36 CCS equals 1 erlang.

To convert minutes to CCS, multiply the number of minutes by 0.6.
  Example: 60 minutes of traffic × 60/100 = 36 CCS of traffic

To convert erlangs hours to CCS, multiply the erlang value by 36.
  Example: 1 hour of traffic × 36 = 36 CCS of traffic

To convert CCS to erlangs, divide the CCS by 36 (36 CCS = 1 erlang).
  Example: 36 CCS/36 = 1 erlang of traffic

Measuring Traffic Load. The traffic load is measured in either of the following units: hundred seconds per busy hour (CCS) or hours per busy hour (erlangs). In the United States the most frequently used traffic unit is the **hundred call seconds (CCS)** (C for hundred). Expressing traffic in CCS is preferred to using a standard 60-second minute because CCS can be divided into fractions more easily. Figure 15-2 shows how to convert minutes and hours to CCS.

Example. Suppose that during the busy hour a trunk experienced sixty sequential calls of one-minute duration or one call of 60 minutes duration. The circuit would have carried 3600 calling seconds of load (60 calls × 60 seconds). To express the same load more easily, traffic engineers divide the number of calling seconds by 100 and express the result as hundred call seconds (CCS). Thus in the example, 3600 is divided by 100 to give an answer of 36 CCS. A load of 36 CCS represents 100% occupancy of a circuit for the busy hour.

The rest of the world uses **erlangs**, named after the Danish traffic engineer and mathematician A. K. Erlang. Erlangs give an immediate indication of the percent of the busy hour the trunk was occupied during an interval, usually a busy hour. For example, if the trunk load on one trunk is 0.80 erlang, then that trunk is occupied 80% of the busy hour.

Example. Suppose a group of ten trunks to Chicago has a traffic load of 1.24 erlangs during the busy hour. Each trunk would then be occupied 0.124 erlang (1.24/10) or 12.4% of the busy hour. Or suppose a group of ten trunks to the same city has a traffic load of 5.90 erlangs. Then each trunk would be occupied 0.59 erlang or 59.4% of the busy hour. The traffic load in both examples can also be expressed in CCS, with 36 CCS equal to 1 erlang.

Example. Suppose the holding time (operating time plus conversation time) for an average call is 180 seconds. The peg count or number of telephone calls during the one-hour period is 10. What is the traffic load expressed in CCS for the period?

- First, calculate the traffic load expressed in seconds:
  Average holding time × peg count = 180 seconds × 10 calls = 1800 seconds
- Second, convert 1800 seconds to CCS:
  Number of seconds/100 = 1800/100 = 18 CCS
- Finally, convert the CCS to erlangs, dividing by 36 (1 erlang = 36 CCS):
  18/36 = 0.5 erlang

Busy Hour. The period of time that is to be measured must be selected carefully. The **busy hour** is the hour when the largest volume of communications traffic is handled during the day, the hour(s) of the day during which traffic normally peaks. In metropolitan areas the busy hour occurs some time between 9:00 and 11:00 weekday mornings. Another peak in traffic usually occurs in the afternoon, which may be the busy hour for some offices. The optimum number of lines needed for a system is determined by providing the number of lines needed for the best possible grade of service during the busy hour. Although the busy hour concept is still used, the system should still be designed to provide efficient service over the longest time period. Figure 15-3 shows one method of calculating the average busy hour.

The local telephone company will study your telephone lines to determine how frequently they are busy. The study will indicate whether you have too few or too many lines. If you have too many lines, the study will not indicate the number, which will require that you remove one or more, and repeat the study. If the telephone company charges for the studies, this process can be costly as well as time-consuming. Another way of estimating usage is to obtain data from an organization that is similar in size and purpose to yours.

FIGURE 15-3 Calculating the Busy Hour for a Specific Period of Days

1. Obtain the traffic load of the busiest hour in each day of the study.
2. Obtain the busiest hour total loading by adding the busiest hour loads of each day of the study period.
3. Obtain the busy hour average for the period by dividing the figure in Step 2 by the total study period days.

   Example:

Day	Busy Hour	CCS
Monday	9 A.M.–10 A.M.	37
Tuesday	10 A.M.–11 A.M.	41
Wednesday	10 A.M.–11 A.M.	43
Thursday	11 A.M.–12 noon	31
Friday	11 A.M.–12 noon	32
5 days	Total:	184

   Busy hour for the average day is 184/5 = 36.8 CCS

Basic Traffic Concepts

Traffic Load Applications. Once you have determined the traffic load, you can determine how many trunks you will require to handle the load at the desired GOS. This information can be obtained from traffic tables or from manufacturers for their own equipment. Figures 15-4 and 15-5 are tables based on Erlang B and are used in determining the number of trunks, switches, and other traffic facilities. Computer software, as discussed in the next section, can assist you in this job. (The *Erlang B Theory* states that arriving calls could possibly find all servers busy and thus be unable to obtain service. The calls will leave the system with no further attempts to gain service. Another theory, the *Erlang C Theory*, states that arriving calls could possibly find all servers busy and thus be unable to obtain service. These calls will encounter a delay, waiting indefinitely to be served. A third theory, the *Poisson Theory*, states that arriving calls could possibly find all servers busy and thus be unable to obtain service. The calls will then enter a "waiting pool" for a maximum duration of one holding time, at which point the calls either are severed or leave the system.)

FIGURE 15-4 **Trunk Capacity Table: Erlang B**

	P = .001		P = .01		P = .02		P = .03		P = .05		P = .10	
TRUNKS	CCS	ERLANGS	CCS	ERLANGS	CCS	ERLANGS	CCS	ERLANGS	CCS	ERLANGS	CCS	ERLANGS
1	.0	.001	.4	.01	.7	.02	1.1	.03	1.8	.05	4.0	.11
2	1.8	.05	5.4	.15	7.9	.22	10.1	.28	13.7	.38	21.6	.60
3	6.8	.19	16.6	.46	21.6	.60	26.9	.72	32.4	.90	45.7	1.27
4	15.8	.44	31.3	.87	39.2	1.09	45.4	1.26	54.7	1.52	73.8	2.05
5	27.4	.76	49.0	1.36	59.8	1.66	67.7	1.88	79.9	2.22	104	2.88
6	41.4	1.15	68.8	1.91	82.1	2.28	91.4	2.54	107	2.96	135	3.76
7	56.9	1.58	90.0	2.50	106	2.94	117	3.25	135	3.74	168	4.67
8	73.8	2.05	113	3.13	131	3.63	144	3.99	163	4.54	202	5.60
9	92.2	2.56	136	3.78	156	4.34	171	4.75	193	5.37	236	6.55
10	111	3.09	161	4.46	183	5.08	199	5.53	224	6.22	270	7.51
11	131	3.65	186	5.16	210	5.84	228	6.33	255	7.08	306	8.49
12	152	4.23	212	5.88	238	6.62	257	7.14	286	7.95	341	9.47
13	174	4.83	238	6.61	267	7.41	287	7.97	318	8.83	377	10.47
14	196	5.45	265	7.35	295	8.20	317	8.80	350	9.73	413	11.47
15	219	6.08	292	8.11	324	9.01	347	9.65	383	10.63	449	12.48
16	242	6.72	319	8.87	354	9.83	378	10.51	415	11.54	486	13.50
17	266	7.38	347	9.65	384	10.66	409	11.37	449	12.46	523	14.52
18	290	8.05	376	10.44	414	11.49	441	12.24	482	13.38	560	15.55
19	314	8.72	404	11.23	444	12.33	472	13.11	515	14.31	597	16.58
20	339	9.41	433	12.03	474	13.18	504	14.00	549	15.25	634	17.61
21	364	10.11	462	12.84	505	14.04	536	14.89	583	16.19	671	18.65
22	389	10.81	491	13.65	536	14.90	568	15.78	617	17.13	709	19.69
23	415	11.52	521	14.47	567	15.76	600	16.68	651	18.08	748	20.74
24	441	12.24	550	15.29	599	16.63	633	17.58	685	19.03	784	21.78
25	467	12.97	580	16.12	630	17.50	665	18.48	720	19.99	822	22.83

Copyright © 1968 Automatic Electric Company.

Application. Suppose that you decide the GOS for your telephone system is to be P.01, which means that 1 in every 100 calls will be blocked. How many trunks will you require for a trunk group to handle 90 CCS of traffic? To solve this problem quickly, refer to Figure 15-4 and locate the P.01 column labeled CCS. Reading down the column, locate the quantity of CCS that is closest to 90—the CCS figure can be same quantity, but cannot be less than 90. In this application you should find the number 90.0. Next read across this line to the trunks column, which will tell you how many trunks you will need for 90 CCS of traffic at P.01 GOS. Your answer is seven trunks.

Application. Let's try another example. Suppose that you decide you want fewer trunks and change the GOS to P.10, meaning that instead of 1 call in 100 probably being blocked, 10 calls in 100 would be blocked. How many trunks will you need? This time you refer to the P.10 column in Figure 15-4. Reading down the CCS column, you find that 104 CCS is the closest quantity approaching (but not less than) 90. In this situation you would need five trunks.

Application. Suppose that your analysis indicates that your group of ten trunks is giving you P.05 service. You would like to improve this service. How many trunks would you need to add for P.01 service? This time you refer to the trunks column in Figure 15-4 and read down the column to 10. You then read across to the CCS column under P.05. You note that the CCS quantity is 224. Now you go to the P.01 column. Read down the CCS column until you reach a quantity that is the closest to 224, but not less than 224. The amount is 238 CCS. Next read across this line to the trunk column, which tells you that you will need thirteen trunks for this amount of CCS of traffic at P.01 GOS. Since you already have ten trunks, you will need three more trunks to achieve P.01 GOS.

Application. Suppose that you have a group of seven trunks at a GOS of P.005. You would like to know how many CCS of traffic the seventh trunk is handling if the busy hour load is 200 CCS. For this application, refer to Figure 15-5. For 200 CCS, trunk 1 will carry 31 CCS and overflow 169 CCS to trunk 2. Trunk 2 will carry 29 CCS and overflow 140 CCS to trunk 3, and so on. The seventh trunk carries 16 CCS with an overflow of 31 CCS. In other words, the seven trunks as a group carry 200 CCS less 31 CCS or a total of 169 CCS.

Application. Suppose that the average busy hour load is 200 CCS. What is the minimum number of trunks required to carry 90 CCS? Refer to Figure 15-5. In the column labeled "CCS Offered" locate the traffic load of 200 CCS. Read across the column of trunk quantities, noting that as each trunk is added to the group it carries a little less traffic than the one before it. When you reach the fourth trunk, the cumulative CCS carried by these four trunks

FIGURE 15-5 Alternate Route Trunking for P.005 Grade of Service

TRUNK NUMBER

CCS Offered	1 Car.	1 Ofl.	2 Car.	2 Ofl.	3 Car.	3 Ofl.	4 Car.	4 Ofl.	5 Car.	5 Ofl.	6 Car.	6 Ofl.	7 Car.	7 Ofl.	8 Car.	8 Ofl.	9 Car.	9 Ofl.	10 Car.	10 Ofl.
100	26	74	23	51	19	32	14	18	9	9	5	4								
110	27	83	24	59	20	39	16	23	10	13	7	6								
120	28	92	25	67	21	46	17	29	12	17	8	9								
130	28	102	26	76	22	54	19	35	14	21	9	12								
140	29	111	26	85	23	62	20	42	16	26	11	15								
150	29	121	27	94	24	70	21	49	17	32	13	19								
160	30	130	27	103	25	78	22	56	18	38	14	24								
170	30	140	27	113	26	87	23	64	19	45	16	29								
180	30	150	29	121	26	95	24	71	20	51	17	34	12	22						
190	30	160	29	131	27	104	24	80	22	58	18	40	14	26						
200	31	169	29	140	27	113	25	88	22	66	19	47	16	31						
220	31	189	30	159	28	131	26	105	24	81	21	60	18	42	14	28	13	26		
240	31	209	30	179	29	150	28	122	25	97	22	75	20	55	16	39	15	35	12	23
260	31	229	31	198	30	168	28	140	26	114	24	90	22	68	18	50	17	45	14	31
280	32	248	31	217	30	187	29	158	27	131	25	106	23	83	21	62	19	57	16	41
300	32	268	31	237	31	206	29	177	28	149	27	122	24	98	22	76				

Copyright © 1968 Automatic Electric Company.

will be 112 (31 + 29 + 27 + 25). Thus the minimum number of trunks required to carry 90 CCS of traffic for a busy hour level of 200 CCS is four.

Application. Suppose that you have two trunk groups with a GOS P.005 and expected traffic of 280 CCS. Each trunk of the first group is to carry a *minimum of 27 CCS*. The second group of trunks is used for the remaining traffic. How many trunks will you need in the first trunk group? Refer to Figure 15-5. In the column "CCS Offered," locate 280 CCS. Read across the column of trunk quantities. In column 5, note that when the fifth trunk is added, it will carry a minimum of 27 CCS, which results in having five trunks in the first trunk group. The second group of trunks will be assigned the remainder of the load of 131 CCS.

Tariffs

Tariffs are the published rates, regulations, and descriptions governing the conditions for various telephone services. A tariff includes a description of the service, the rate that may be charged for the service, and the regulations under which that service can be provided. Tariffs must be approved by the Federal Communications Commission (FCC) or appropriate state public utilities commissions before the service can be offered. Tariff information is critical to network management. Tariffs not only provide pricing and service information, but also indicate the regulatory views that prevail at the federal and state levels. When designing and implementing telephone networks, managers must have current tariff information.

Active Cost Control Methods

Active methods of controlling telephone costs use technology, such as the telephone switch, to reduce the cost of each telephone call and to prevent unnecessary calling. These methods include automatic route selecting/least-cost routing, calling restrictions or blocking, authorization codes and levels of service, and timed signals.

■ Automatic Route Selection/Least-Cost Routing

Not too long ago, a company had only a few options for making long-distance calls. A Denver company could only communicate with its San Francisco office by using direct-distance dialing, a WATS service, or a dedicated private line.

Today, a company has various alternatives for making local and long-distance calls. For example, AT&T offers WATS lines, foreign exchange (FX) lines, and tie lines, while other common carriers provide most or all of the same services, often at lower prices than AT&T. (A foreign exchange line service uses a central office other than the one from which the service would normally be provided. FX lines are used primarily to reduce the company's cost for traffic to or from a heavily used remote location.) But which service should an employee choose when making a call? Educating employees about which service to use is a difficult task, particularly because rates vary with time of day, calling location, and the carrier's dialing plan.

Instead, you can use **automatic route selection (ARS)**, also called *least-cost routing* (LCR), which automatically connects a call to the least expensive line that is available based on the cost of the service and the time of day. ARS/LCR is a software-controlled feature that automatically selects from a given group of carriers and services the lowest-cost carrier no matter at what time of day or night a call is placed. The software must be continuously updated as tariffs and prices change.

The ARS/LCR feature is transparent to the user. After the caller dials a number, a computer program searches through a table of available lines, times, and rates to select the route that is least costly for the call. At busy times of day, when all of the cheapest routes are busy, other choices are available. In fact, some systems sound a warning tone when a call is about to be routed to an expensive service, allowing callers to hang up before the connection is completed.

The ARS/LCR feature has been available in PBX systems since the late 1970s and in Centrex systems and key systems since soon after. The ARS/LCR feature is now available as a software package from such companies as Bell operating companies, AT&T Communications, US Sprint, and TDX Communications.

To use ARS/LCR effectively, you must analyze your telephone needs to make certain that you have access to the various carriers, such as AT&T and other common carriers, and different types of facilities, such as WATS lines, leased lines, and direct distance dialing, that match your company's calling pattern.

Application of ARS/LCR. A company located in New York City uses ARS/LCR for long-distance calls and has set up a prioritized long-distance calling plan, as shown below. When a manager places a call to a company in Atlanta, Georgia, the ARS/LCR feature directs the system to go to the first route choice—the cheapest choice. If the trunk is busy, the call goes to the next cheapest choice, which is choice 2, and so on. In this example the call can finally be completed, if necessary, over direct distance dialing, which might not be the most cost-effective route. The choices available for this call are as follows:

- Choice 1: US Sprint WATS
- Choice 2: AT&T Band 3 WATS
- Choice 3: AT&T Band 5 WATS

- Choice 4: US Sprint long distance
- Choice 5: AT&T direct distance dialing

Application of ARS/LCR with Tie Lines. In this example the company has set up the following calling plan, using tie lines that connect its PBX in New York City with the PBX at its branch office in Chicago as the first choice.

- Choice 1: New York City and Chicago tie lines
- Choice 2: US Sprint WATS
- Choice 3: AT&T Band 3 WATS
- Choice 4: AT&T Band 5 WATS
- Choice 5: US Sprint long distance
- Choice 6: AT&T direct distance dialing

Tie lines represent the cheapest option, since their cost is a fixed rate and not based on usage. If callers are currently using the tie lines, then the next cheapest choice would be US Sprint WATS, followed by AT&T WATS lines. LCR can be programmed to designate only certain users to have access to one or more of the other options. Note that tie lines are cost-effective for a company to install if the lines will be used more than six hours a day.

Applications of ARS/LCR with Queuing. An ARS/LCR plan can also include queuing. Since you want to encourage use of WATS lines, you can set up a 15-second queue for each WATS line before the call overflows to the next choice. In this example you have a 30-second queue before the call overflows to the fourth choice and then to the fifth choice. A short-term queue tends to increase the use of that choice.

- Choice 1: Tie lines
- Choice 2: US Sprint WATS (15-second queue)
- Choice 3: AT&T Band 3 WATS (15-second queue)
- Choice 4: US Sprint long distance
- Choice 5: AT&T direct distance dialing

Often, users do not know which WATS line to select and will use direct distance dialing—the most expensive route. An ARS/LCR feature prevents unintentional telephone abuse. For example, a company has one trunk for AT&T Band 5 WATS and another for AT&T Band 1 WATS. An analysis shows that 35% of the calls that were placed on Band 5 WATS could have been placed on Band 1 WATS—at a much lower rate. By combining LCR with queuing this costly practice can be minimized. An LCR plan might be set up as follows:

- Choice 1: AT&T Band 1 WATS (15-minute queue)
- Choice 2: AT&T Band 5 WATS (15-minute queue)
- Choice 3: AT&T direct distance dialing

Calling Restrictions

Telephones can be programmed to restrict the type of calls made by certain telephones or certain callers. For example, the telephone switch may be programmed to prevent calls from using certain exchanges, such as 900 exchanges, or audio text calls (time, weather, dial-a-joke).

The telephones of employees that do not deal with the public can be programmed to allow only internal calls. The telephones of employees with no out-of-town business can be programmed to provide only local service. Other employees can have telephones programmed to use only the cheapest long-distance service, while others may be given telephones that allow a variety of long-distance options.

Authorization Codes and Levels of Service

Telephone systems can be programmed to require long-distance calls to be preceded by an authorization code that is known only to people authorized to make such calls. The code also allows the system to charge a call to a particular person or account.

Authorization codes can be programmed for different levels of service. An authorization code can be assigned to employees who need to make international calls. A code that allows more restricted calling can be assigned to employees who makes calls only to certain cities. Another code can permit employees to make calls but using only the cheapest service. Still another code can allow employees more costly services when low-cost services lines are busy. For example, the federal government assigns the following levels for outgoing calls:

- *Standard service* allows calling only to government telephones in the local area.
- *Commercial service* allows local government calling and commercial (dial 9) lines.
- *Government service* allows local and intercity government calling but does not allow commercial calling.
- *National service* allows full access to both government and commercial telephone networks, but no international dialing.
- *International service* allows all of the above plus international direct distance dialing.

An advantage of authorization codes is that they are independent of the individual telephone instrument. An employee with authorization to make long-distance calls can use any telephone in the system just by using the authorization code before dialing the long-distance number. Codes can also be easily changed. For example, if an employee's job requires a change in level of telephone service or if it is discovered that an unauthorized person is using the code, the old authorization code can be immediately replaced with a new one.

A drawback of authorization codes is that they require the user to dial five to seven additional digits at the beginning of each long-distance call. Dialing a code is time-consuming, especially for people who must make many long-distance calls each day. One way of reducing dialing time is to use speed dialing, in which the user stores a list of frequently called long-distance numbers in the telephone's memory and then accesses each one by a two-digit code. To call any of the stored numbers, the user still dials the authorization code in full but now only dials a two-digit code to reach the frequently called number. Since authorization codes are used to allocate calling costs, they are usually part of a call-accounting program.

■ Timed Signals

As callers converse, a timed signal can remind them of the amount of time that they are spending talking. A telephone system can be programmed to give callers a tone after a 4- or 5-minute period. Although callers are not penalized for continuing to talk beyond this time period, the signal often helps to reduce the average length of calls by serving as a reminder that long-distance calls cost money. Callers might not realize how long they have been talking; the 5-minute warning reminds them that long-distance calls should be kept as short as possible.

Telephone Management Systems

Until recently, telephone users had no accurate way of managing their telecommunications costs and improving or maintaining desired levels of service. On receipt of their telephone statements, companies typically approved payment and entered the expense in the company's ledger. Some companies, such as the one described in the first scenario at the beginning of this chapter, did try to identify which employees were making long-distance calls in order to allocate the costs to them, but the task was tedious and subject to error. Some companies even tried to reduce costs by eliminating one or more telephone extensions and/or issuing memos to employees directing them to reduce their personal telephone calls. These solutions were only temporary ones; a short time later extensions would be reconnected and personal calling would return to former calling levels.

One of the first ways for companies to reduce telephone costs was introduced in the 1960s by AT&T—the use of WATS for long-distance telephone calls. Wide-area telecommunications service (WATS) is a special bulk-rate arrangement for direct-dialed station-to-station toll telephone service. The Bell operating companies offer different bands of service at different rates.

Band 1 usually provides interstate coverage to nearby states; Band 5 provides nationwide interstate coverage, excluding Alaska, which is Band 6. Bands 2, 3, and 4 provide intermediate coverage. WATS to a higher-numbered band includes service to all lowered-numbered bands. A call beyond the specified coverage of the contracted band is charged at the regular long-distance telephone rate.

In the 1970s, other ways to reduce telephone costs became available, such as other common carriers offering their services and the introduction of telephone management systems. The early telephone management systems only monitored and stored telephone call activity, some more active systems also routing telephone calls.

Today, companies must be able to control their telephone costs as well as to configure facilities to achieve the desired grade of service. According to Market Intelligence Research Company of Palo Alto, California, the market for telephone management systems was $60 million in 1982 and $182.7 million in 1986; by 1992 it is expected to reach $1.4 billion.

■ Telephone Management Systems Defined

Telephone management systems (TMSs) perform a variety of functions from recording, storing, and processing call data, to managing telephone facilities, to engineering traffic. TMSs vary in price from under $1000 to over $100,000. A maintenance fee that includes database and tariff updates typically costs about 10–15% of the computer software purchase price.

■ TMS Configurations

A TMS may be designed for general business use or for a particular type of business, such as hotels, hospitals, and law firms. A company's needs determine which one of the following configurations is selected.

Stand-Alone or Turnkey System. A basic stand-alone system is a microprocessor-based device that is connected to the station message detail recording (SMDR) output port of the telephone system via an RS-232-C interface, such as the system shown in Figure 15-6. (A microprocessor is a silicon chip containing the necessary circuitry to perform a variety of computer operations in accordance with a set of instructions.) The system is dedicated to collecting, storing, and processing call records. Whenever a telephone goes off-hook, the TMS begins collecting specific details about the call based on the SMDR data output of the telephone system. These systems can store a maximum of 6500 call records and can print reports on demand or be programmed to print automatically at designated intervals. Prices range from $2,000 to $10,000 (1988 prices).

FIGURE 15-6 **A Stand-Alone Telephone Management System**

Courtesy of The Abacus Group.

Microcomputer, Minicomputer, and Mainframe Computer-Based TMSs. Each of these three choices has advantages and disadvantages as identified in Figure 15-7. A mainframe TMS allows the company to centrally control and manage its telephone activities. Compared to the other TMS choices, mainframe TMSs offer more processing power, higher speeds, and unlimited capacity and can run more sophisticated applications. However, mainframe TMS software and the system's operation are more costly, and users are subject to slower responses to change requests.

Minicomputer TMSs are commonly used on the department level, providing more user control over the system. These systems offer advantages similar to those of the mainframe systems, such as allowing for multiple applications and a high-volume capability, which makes the distinction between these two choices less clear. Drawbacks of minicomputer TMSs include possible limits on its capacity and a higher capital investment than is needed for a microcomputer-based system.

Of the three choices, a microcomputer-based system requires the least capital investment, operates most easily, and provides the most direct control over report and request turnaround times. With the use of powerful microcomputer chips, previous limitations on capacity and processing power are being removed. For example, a microcomputer, such as an IBM or compatible personal computer, can be fitted with a microprocessor card and connected to the telephone switching equipment via an RS-232-C interface to turn the microcomputer into a TMS (see Figure 15-8). These machines can store more than 100,000 call records, depending on storage capability. With a low-cost buffer added to the microcomputer, TMS software can run simultaneously with other programs, such as spreadsheets and word processing

FIGURE 15-7 Microcomputer, Minicomputer, and Mainframe Computer Telephone Management Systems: Advantages, Disadvantages, and Political Profile

	Mainframe	Minicomputer	Microcomputer	Service Bureau
Advantages	Maximum capacity limits Multiple users Processing power and speed Less telecommunications support responsibility System partitioning Experienced mainframe support and system backup	High capacity levels Multiple users Dedicated departmental processor System partitioning	Less capital expense and maintenance expense than mainframe or minicomputer Dedicated departmental processor Full system autonomy User-friendly Most common DOS interfaces	Unlimited capacity High level of telemanagement system expertise Off-load telemanagement system responsibility No capital expense
Disadvantages	Less direct system control MIS less responsive to change requests Less MIS familiarity with telemanagement Higher purchase and support costs Higher operational expertise necessary	Requires more operational expertise from telecommunications staff Limits on system capacity Minicomputer market challenged by new microcomputer capabilities Higher capital expense than microcomputer or service bureau	Number of users limited by system configuration Limits on system capacity Slower processing and printing More critical backup procedures necessary	Report lag times User rarely has on-line capability Applications generally limited Data security hampered
Political profile	Mainframe telemanagement system requires a strong level of interdepartmental cooperation, more technical expertise and financial investment	Departmental system control still requires sophisticated computer and software support Cost varies with both hardware and software	Direct telecommunications control over telemanagement system at the microcomputer level. Telecommunications will have full system responsibility. Most responsive to price-sensitive market	Users have no control over system administration and are totally dependent on vendor for service. Recurring costs

Copyright 1989 by NWW Publishing Inc., Framingham, MA 01701—Reprinted from *Network World*.

FIGURE 15-8 **Microcomputer Telephone Management Systems**

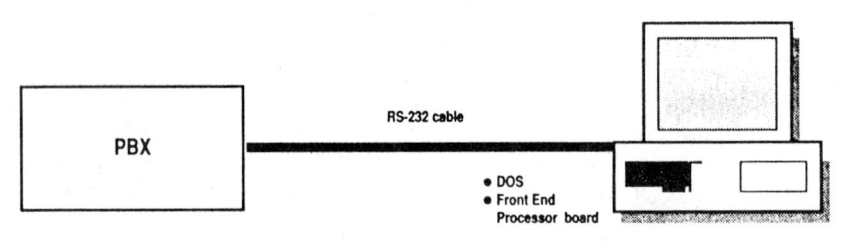

Courtesy of Infortext Systems Inc.

programs. This feature, "multitasking," makes this configuration cost-effective except when certain microcomputers must be dedicated to perform certain TMS applications such as call accounting. In these situations, stand-alone or turnkey systems might be more cost-effective. Call-accounting packages can be purchased for under $1000 for a small business to over $100,000 for a local-area network.

Integrated with PBX, Centrex, and Key Systems. PBXs may contain a traffic usage register that measures the number of calls and line usage. Some PBX systems require the vendor to remotely poll for the information and mail a report to the company. Other PBXs, Centrex, and key systems have an SMDR feature that allows each telephone call to be logged, typically by time and charges. Data can be retrieved by connecting a TMS in the form of a microprocessor device to the system's SMDR output port via an RS-232-C interface. This setup permits telephone calls to be charged to the appropriate departments.

Service Bureau. Instead of using its own TMS, a company can rely on a service bureau for reports on its telephone system. The service bureau collects its data by connecting an onsite device to a company's telephone system or by processing magnetic data tapes produced by the company. This service tends to be expensive and usually cannot generate information as quickly as the other configurations. A benefit of service bureaus is that no one in the company has the responsibility for maintaining the system's software and hardware, including its maintenance and repairs.

One of the largest service bureaus is Aristonics Corporation, based in New England with 170 processing locations throughout the United States. The bureau collects, stores, retrieves, and processes a company's call detail records and print and delivers reports. The cost is based on the number of stations in the client company's system.

■ TMS Features

A TMS performs the basic functions of collecting and recording call data and producing reports on screen or in hard copy form. Data that is collected includes

- Extension number originating the call
- Time the call originated
- Date of the call
- Telephone number dialed
- The length of time of the call
- The type of outside line used to complete the call

More advanced systems perform other management functions, record additional data, and generate more comprehensive reports. Some companies implement a TMS by beginning with the basic functions and then adding other functions when needed.

Features that are available on telephone management systems deal with

- Call accounting
- Traffic engineering and network design optimization
- Inventory management, including equipment inventory, cable management, and work order preparation and tracking

A TMS can contain one feature or as many as the company desires, the complexity and sophistication of each feature varying widely with the TMS manufacturer. A 1986 survey conducted by Datapro Research Corporation of 315 TMS users reported that over two thirds used TMS for call accounting, cost allocation, and generating detail and summary reports, while about one third used network and facility optimization packages.

The **call-accounting** feature collects and analyzes call records from the telephone system, allocates monthly call costs, and generates reports. Call record data from a PBX, Centrex, or key system usually includes data on extension dialing, when the call started, the duration of the call, and the trunk/line used, such as direct distance dialing or WATS (see Figure 15-9). The call-accounting feature of a TMS processes the data to show actual usage and costs. If desired, a TMS can mark up the cost of a call by a fixed percentage. Detail or summary call information can be generated for individual extensions and/or grouped by department or division and directly charged to each user's budget. The information enables a company to prepare budgets and allocate its telecommunications dollars.

Monthly reports monitor calling patterns and identify abuse from within and outside the company. For example, "exception reports," those that list the most expensive calls, the longest calls, the most frequent numbers called, can be produced.

The *directory* feature is a database that provides information about its users, such as name, telephone number, title, and department. Information

FIGURE 15-9 **Call-Accounting Station Extension Detail Screen Report**

```
Jan 12, 19    16:55              OS Plus 1000                       Page   1
                                 ABC Customer, Inc.
                                 Extension  Detail Report

From: 11/19/      To: 12/12/

Ext: 330
Name : Lewis, Charles                    Division:         1 Corporate G&A
Title: Appraiser                         Department:       127 Main Leasing
Loc: 2nd Floor West                      Cost Center:      231 Special Accounts


Date   Time   Duration  Facil.   Cost    Digits Dialed     City           St
-----  -----  --------  ------   ------  ----------------  -------------  --
11/20  14:57  0:00:30   WATS-5   0.16    617-267-0099      BOSTON         MA
11/20  15:02  0:04:42   WATS-5   0.70    203-794-1228      DANBURY        CT
11/21  09:08  0:00:06   C/O      0.31    617-720-0880      BOSTON         MA
11/21  09:44  0:00:42   WATS-5   0.31    617-720-0880      BOSTON         MA
11/21  11:01  0:16:54   WATS-5   4.63    617-720-0880      BOSTON         MA
12/06  10:42  0:11:09   WATS-5   3.28    617-976-6868      Dial a ????
12/06  15:39  0:00:45   WATS-5   0.31    617-726-2225      BOSTON         MA
12/06  15:52  0:01:03   WATS-4   0.58    516-360-0622      SMITHTOWN      NY
12/06  17:28  0:10:21   WATS-4   1.96    516-360-0872      SMITHTOWN      NY
12/07  09:34  0:01:03   WATS-5   0.58    617-742-9110      BOSTON         MA
12/07  10:57  0:00:27   WATS-4   0.31    516-360-0932      SMITHTOWN      NY
12/07  11:11  0:00:21   WATS-4   0.31    516-360-0312      SMITHTOWN      NY
12/07  13:05  0:10:15   WATS-5   3.01    203-794-1728      DANBURY        CT
12/07  15:28  0:02:57   WATS-5   0.85    516-360-0172      SMITHTOWN      NY
12/07  17:25  0:04:45   C/O      2.46    516-360-0712      SMITHTOWN      NY
12/07  17:26  0:00:15   C/O      0.60    312-411           Information
12/08  11:17  0:00:27   C/O      0.60    312-411           Information
12/08  14:16  0:11:45   WATS-5   3.28    617-742-9570      BOSTON         MA
12/08  16:55  0:00:33   WATS-4   0.31    516-360-0592      SMITHTOWN      NY
12/11  09:10  0:00:15   WATS-4   0.16    516-360-0082      SMITHTOWN      NY
12/11  10:09  0:04:21   WATS-5   0.70    516-360-0172      SMITHTOWN      NY
12/11  11:42  0:00:27   WATS-5   0.16    203-794-1238      DANBURY        CT
12/11  11:45  0:02:45   WATS-5   0.43    203-791-2445      DANBURY        CT
12/11  17:54  0:06:21   WATS-4   1.26    516-360-0172      SMITHTOWN      NY
              --------           ------
              1:33:09          $  27.26
Fixed Cost                     $   7.50
                                 ------
Total Cost                     $  34.76
```

Courtesy of Infortext Systems Inc.

is instantly available online, making it easier for both internal and external callers to locate people. Search commands enable employees to be located by name, department, or extension. A system can be programmed so that changes cannot be made to the directory database or unauthorized users cannot access the authorization code list. Some TMSs can print directories from the databases, while others provide copy ready for a printer. The reports generated from the directory feature can serve as replacements for the service and equipment records that used to be provided by the local telephone company. Figure 15-10 shows an example of a directory screen printout.

Traffic statistics provides information about the telephone system's traffic activities. For example, the TMS provided by Telecommunications Systems Management, Inc. collects and processes traffic information from the peg count traffic data output of the PBX's maintenance ports.

Figure 15-11 shows an online screen of traffic statistics about trunk usage. This screen tells how many trunks are equipped and enabled in each trunk group. Note that the screen shows that one trunk is not working. The screen also shows how many times the trunks were busy at the same time—in this case, none, even though one trunk was not working. Do you think there are too many trunks? The amount of traffic that actually occurred over

FIGURE 15-10 Directory Screen

```
                    THE  ABC  COMPANY,  INC.  (NT)
                          EXTENSION  LISTING
                   SORT KEY: EXTENSION NUMBER / FILTER: ALL

         Period: 6                                08/15/  - 13:54:10
         ---------------------------------------------------------------

                      Last              First         Dept
                Ext   Name              Name          Code
                ----  ----------------  ------------  --------
                2250  Baron             Bill          ADMIN
                2345  Coleman           Bob           ADMIN
                2445  Fisher            Gloria        ADMIN
                2778  Ryan              Fred          ADMIN
                3201  Coyne             Harold        FIN
                3215  Freeman           Shirley       FIN
                3306  Hall              Mitchell      FIN
                3512  Stevens           Michael       FIN
                4211  Cardwell          Tracy         HR
                4234  Fenton            Scott         HR
                4356  Larson            William       HR
                4677  Maxwell           Thelma        HR
                4888  Sternola          Susan         HR
                4921  Verbeck           James         HR
                5012  Adams             Tracy         MIS
                5144  Curtis            Mark          MIS
                5334  Richards          Dan           MIS
                5998  Riley             Pam           MIS
                6110  Alexander         Pauline       PURCH
                6224  Carter            Cecil         PURCH
                6318  James             Janus         PURCH
                6420  Pitchford         Teri          PURCH
                7101  Goodman, Dr.      James         R&D
                7223  Gordon            Jerrold       R&D
                7445  Hambrecht         Mickey        R&D
                7446  Hillary, Dr.      Daniel        R&D
                7512  Norman            Lee           R&D
                8111  Frye              Celeste       SALES
                8116  Hunter            Roxanne       SALES
                8119  Krueger           Joan          SALES
                8223  Stevens           Jill          SALES
                8776  Simpson           Sally         SALES
```

Courtesy of Infortext Systems Inc.

FIGURE 15-11 Traffic Statistics Trunk Usage Inquiry Screen

```
        ----TRF111B-------         THE TSM TOTAL SOLUTION      ---02/02/    2:21---
        ------------------          TRAFFIC STATISTICS INQUIRY    ------------------
        ------------------                 TRUNK USAGE            ------------------
                              CUSTOMER NUMBER        0
           INTERVAL    2      TRUNK GROUP NUMBER     1      LOCAL OUT TRUNKS
        HOURLY  = 1                   DATE & TIME           EQUIPPED          32
        DAILY   = 2           FROM   1/31/  6:00:00         ENABLED           31
        WEEKLY  = 3           TO     2/01/  6:00:02         ALL BUSY           0
        MONTHLY = 4           RANGE  1 DAYS 0:00:02         TOLL/LOC LINE    312
        ------------------------------------------------------------------------
                              # CALLS   LENGTH MINS   LENGTH HRS   AVG LENGTH MINS

          INBOUND TRUNKS         0          0.0           0.0            0.0

          OUTBOUND TRUNKS     1844       4275.0          71.3            2.3

          COMBINED TRUNKS     1844       4275.0          71.3            2.3
```

Courtesy of Telecommunications Systems Management, Inc., St. Charles, MO.

this group is indicated at the bottom of the screen by the number of calls, total minutes, and total hours for the interval (see upper left) desired. The information is available on an hourly, daily, weekly, or monthly basis.

Traffic engineering uses traffic statistics data to determine how many trunks a company needs to carry its volume of calls to optimize utilization of the network. For example, traffic engineering provides trunk usage information to help users decide the number of central office trunks needed to support traffic loads and also determine routing strategies when using a combination WATS services, FX services, and other common carrier services for long-distance calling.

With a **traffic modeling** feature you can perform "what if" analyses based on various desired GOS requirements. You can try out changes to the system and find out how these changes would affect the overall performance of the system. Such information helps in planning and/or improving a telephone system.

For example, traffic modeling allows you to eliminate unneeded trunks, one at a time if necessary, and learn your real GOS for both inbound and outbound traffic. Line configurations, queuing requirements, route optimization, and direct distance dialing can be simulated with "what if" scenarios to help in planning.

Suppose that to the input screen in Figure 15-12(a) you key in numbers from actual usage and then press [ENTER]. The system will automatically calculate the data into trunk requirements, as shown in Figure 15-12(b). The information at the top portion of this screen details the data that you input. The center of the screen shows the required trunks based on desired blockage and the actual GOS attained. The bottom of the screen tells how much traffic occurs over each individual line. You can print this information and then return to your input screen (Figure 15-12(a)) to simulate and do "what if" scenarios. You might decide to change the desired blockage to 5%, as shown in Figure 15-12(c). The result of your "what if" is shown in Figure 15-12(d).

The *common carrier pricing* feature allows users to price the services of AT&T and other common carriers in seconds instead of talking hours by manual calculation. Updates are included in the maintenance agreement, or users can input the rate changes themselves. Once a user knows the type and number of lines to be used, the user can calculate how much telephone service will cost. For example, a user can determine whether or not MCI is really less expensive than AT&T or check monthly telephone bills for accuracy. This feature provides traffic statistics and/or traffic engineering features with cost information.

Figure 15-13 shows your input screen requesting carrier pricing for AT&T WATS. All you input is the originating state, direction identifier, number of hours of traffic by band, and percentage of network traffic for that carrier, and the TMS does the rest. The prices for the WATs service are displayed on the next screen (Figure 15-14). The screen displays the result of your common carrier pricing calculation. Total cost by band is calculated by

Telephone Management Systems

FIGURE 15-12   Traffic Engineering

```
-----TSM220A--------   THE TSM TOTAL SOLUTION   ---02/02/   2:15---
---------------------              TRAFFIC ENGINEERING
---------------------              TRAFFIC MODELING
                                            OUTBOUND       INBOUND
TOTAL NUMBER OF CALLS                         25000           0
AVERAGE CALL LENGTH IN MINUTES                  3.2           0.0
CALL PROCESSING TIME IN SECONDS                 20            0
TRUNKS REQUIRED                                 
WORKING DAYS IN THE MONTH                       21
PERCENT OF TRAFFIC IN THE BUSY HOUR             15.0
BLOCKAGE DESIRED                                 2.0
PERCENT OF BLOCKED CALLS FOR RETRIAL           100.0
```

(a) Input Screen

```
-----TSM220B--------   THE TSM TOTAL SOLUTION   ---02/02/   2:18---
---------------------              TRAFFIC ENGINEERING
---------------------              TRAFFIC MODELING

OUTBOUND TRAFFIC IN HOURS       1333.3    RING TIME IN SECONDS      12
INBOUND TRAFFIC IN HOURS           0.0    WORKING DAYS IN MTH       21
AVERAGE OUTBOUND CALL LENGTH       3.2    % TRAFFIC IN BUSY HR    15.0
AVERAGE INBOUND CALL LENGTH        0.0    BLOCKAGE DESIRED         2.0
CALL PROCESSING TIME IN SECONDS   20      RETRIAL DESIRED        100.0

TRUNKS REQUIRED                    18     GRADE OF SERVICE         1.8
DDD OVERFLOW USAGE                 0.0    INBOUND LOST CALLS         0

LINE   USAGE     LINE   USAGE     LINE   USAGE
001   115.275    006   102.636    011   71.597
002   113.603    007    98.319    012   62.499
003   111.593    008    93.140    013   52.785
004   109.159    009    86.985    014   42.892
005   106.207    010    79.805    015   33.337
```

(b) Analysis Screen

```
-----TSM220A--------   THE TSM TOTAL SOLUTION"   ---05/17/   --8:00---
---------------------              TRAFFIC ENGINEERING
---------------------              TRAFFIC MODELING
                                            OUTBOUND       INBOUND
TOTAL NUMBER OF CALLS                         25000           0
AVERAGE CALL LENGTH IN MINUTES                  3.0           0.0
CALL PROCESSING TIME IN SECONDS                 20            0
WORKING DAYS IN THE MONTH                       21
PERCENT OF TRAFFIC IN THE BUSY HOUR             20.0
BLOCKAGE DESIRED                                 5.0
PERCENT OF BLOCKED CALLS FOR RETRIAL           100.0
```

(c) "What If" Screen

```
-----TSM220B--------   THE TSM TOTAL SOLUTION"   ---05/17/   --8:00---
---------------------              TRAFFIC ENGINEERING
---------------------              TRAFFIC MODELING

OUTBOUND TRAFFIC IN HOURS       1250.0    RING TIME IN SECONDS      12
INBOUND TRAFFIC IN HOURS           0.0    WORKING DAYS IN MTH       21
AVERAGE OUTBOUND CALL LENGTH       3.0    % TRAFFIC IN BUSY HR    20.0
AVERAGE INBOUND CALL LENGTH        0.0    BLOCKAGE DESIRED         5.0
CALL PROCESSING TIME IN SECONDS   20      RETRIAL DESIRED        100.0

TRUNKS REQUIRED                    19     GRADE OF SERVICE         4.2
DDD OVERFLOW USAGE                 0.0    INBOUND LOST CALLS         0

LINE   USAGE     LINE   USAGE     LINE   USAGE
001    26.870    007    84.507    013   63.624
002    91.424    008    82.258    014   58.015
003    90.440    009    79.612    015   51.897
004    89.291    010    76.449    016   45.277
005    87.949    011    72.820    017   38.344
006    86.369    012    68.502    018   31.464
                                  019   24.888
```

(d) "What If" Analysis Screen

Courtesy of Telecommunications Systems Management, Inc., St. Charles, MO.

FIGURE 15-13   Carrier Pricing Input Screen

```
-----TSM510B---------   THE TSM TOTAL SOLUTION   ---02/02/   2:34---
---------------------              CARRIER PRICING
---------------------              NETWORK PRICING
                                      AT&T WATS
        ORIGINATING STATE    MO     STATE DIRECTION       SELECT BAND 1
                         TOTAL MONTHLY TRAFFIC BY BAND

              DAY        EVENING    NIGHT     TRUNKS    % ON NET
BAND #0      0.00          0.00      0.00        0        0.0
BAND #1    600.00         50.00     18.00        7      100.0
BAND #2      0.00          0.00      0.00        0        0.0
BAND #3    750.00         85.00     20.00       10      100.0
BAND #4      0.00          0.00      0.00        0        0.0
BAND #5   1500.00        100.00     20.00       19      100.0
BAND #6      0.00          0.00      0.00        0        0.0
BAND #7      0.00          0.00      0.00        0        0.0
BAND #8      0.00          0.00      0.00        0        0.0
```

Courtesy of Telecommunications Systems Management, Inc., St. Charles, MO.

FIGURE 15-14 **Carrier Pricing Total Cost Screen**

```
----TSM510B---------          THE TSM TOTAL SOLUTION        ---02/02/   2:37---
--------------------              CARRIER PRICING          --------------------
--------------------          TOTAL MONTHLY COST BY BAND   --------------------
                                     AT&T WATS
                    USAGE           LINE       SURCHARGE       TAX       TOTAL COST
         BAND #0     0.00           0.00          0.00         0.00         0.00
         BAND #1  9334.43         221.55         42.00       290.29      9888.27
         BAND #2     0.00           0.00          0.00           0           0.00
         BAND #3 12723.50         316.50         60.00       396.36     13496.36
         BAND #4     0.00           0.00          0.00           0           0.00
         BAND #5 26423.11         601.35        114.00       820.53     27958.99
         BAND #6     0.00           0.00          0.00           0           0.00
         BAND #7     0.00           0.00          0.00           0           0.00
         BAND #8     0.00           0.00          0.00           0           0.00

         TOTALS  48481.04        1139.40        216.50      1507.18     51543.62
```

Courtesy of Telecommunications Systems Management, Inc., St. Charles, MO.

summarizing usage charges, line charges, the applicable FCC surcharge, and any applicable taxes. A total cost for all bands is then provided. After you print the screen, you can obtain similar screens for other carriers and then compare them.

Economics and Technology, Inc. offers a computer software package, the ETI Private Line Pricer, updated monthly, that calculates monthly and nonrecurring charges for both interstate and intrastate private lines. When the user enters the type of service (analog voice/data, digital data, or high-capacity digital data—T-1) and circuit end points, the Private Line Pricer automatically selects the correct tariff(s) and routing. Figure 15-15 shows an interstate multipoint circuit configuration using AT&T tariffs. This multipoint circuit connects two customer premises to AT&T's Boston, Massachusetts, POP (101–283) and two customer premises to AT&T's Providence, Rhode Island, POP (101–303) and converts the two POPs using one interexchange channel. (POP refers to point of presence, an interstate carrier's facility in a LATA.) Figure 15-16 shows the total charges for the multipoint circuit configuration. One central office connection (COC) charge applies per local channel and bridging charges apply to LEC-provided local chan-

FIGURE 15-15 **Configuration of Multipoint Circuit**

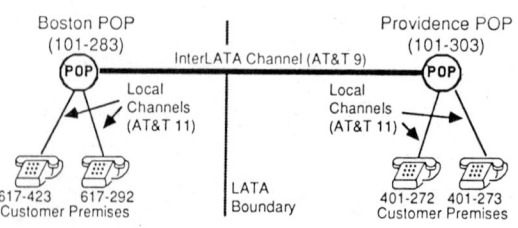

Courtesy of Economics and Technology, Inc.

FIGURE 15-16   **Pricing a Multipoint Circuit Configuration**

```
                    ETI PRIVATE LINE PRICER
                  MULTIPOINT CIRCUIT DESCRIPTION
ANALOG VOICE   2 WIRE    INTERSTATE
CIRCUIT ID:    POP HUBBING
                                              COC      BRIDGE
LEG QTY  ORIGIN  DESTIN  TYPE  TARIFF  CHG(#)  CHG(#)

 1   1   101283  617423  LOC   ATT11     1        0
 2   1   101283  617292  LOC   ATT11     1        0
 3   1   101283  101303  IXC   ATT9      0        0
 4   1   101303  401272  LOC   ATT11     1        0
 5   1   101303  401273  LOC   ATT11     1        0
```

(a) Screen for Circuit End Point and Tariff Entry

```
                    ETI PRIVATE LINE PRICER
                     CIRCUIT PRICE SUMMARY
CIRCUIT ID:      POP HUBBING
SERVICE:         VOICE         PRICEOUT DATE: AUG 01 1986
CIRCUIT FILE:    TEMPOT

                              EFFECT
LEG QTY ORIGIN DEST  TARIFF   DATE    MONTHLY    NRC
 1   1  101283 617423 ATT11  070186   $100.13  $508.10
 2   1  101283 617292 ATT11  070186   $100.13  $508.10
 3   1  101283 101303 ATT9   041986   $153.09  $  0.00
 4   1  101303 401272 ATT11  070186   $100.13  $510.36
 5   1  101303 401273 ATT11  070186   $100.13  $510.36

TOTAL CHARGES:                        $553.61  $2036.92
```

(b) Circuit Price Summary Screen

Courtesy of Economics and Technology, Inc.

nels. (LEC refers to the local exchange carrier, the telephone company providing local exchange services to specific exchanges.) Figure 15-16(b) displays monthly and nonrecurring charges by leg for the circuit.

The *trouble reporting and tracking* feature allows users to monitor and control maintenance problems. A log is kept of troubles and the corrective actions performed by vendors, even including how long it takes a vendor to respond to a call. The feature tracks repairs and generates reports on the system's performance. A typical feature can log the date and time when trouble was reported and the date and time when it was resolved, the type of trouble, whether or not hardware is involved, whether the call is billable, the names of the employees and repair people involved, the amount of time each one spent on the problem, a description of the problem, and the solution to the problem. Figure 15-17 shows a sample trouble log screen.

For example, a trouble call is entered into the system with the user's name and telephone number to recall the file and where the user can be reached. The feature allows the system to issue a trouble ticket for the problem and assigns the problem to the appropriate group of technicians on the basis of decision criteria provided by the software program. Vendor response and problem resolution can be monitored and graphically presented. A report can also show which technicians perform effectively and which ones need more training.

FIGURE 15-17   Trouble Reporting Log Screen

```
----- RM910A ------------ REMOTE SERVICE CENTER ----- 7/19/    12:53 -----
---------------------- CUSTOMER TROUBLE LOG MAINT ----------------------
              CUST #     7- 0           NAME    SAMPLE COMPANY

   TROUBLE DATE   3/29/   TIME   10:30   RESOLUTION DATE  4/04/    TIME 10:00
   TYPE    60- 0    SOFTWARE ERROR         HDWOREQ   (Y/N)    CHARGE    0.00
   C.S.R.    GREG TOUHY                    TIME SPENT  (H:M)   0:00  BILL  (Y/N)
   TECH.                                   TIME SPENT  (H:M)   0:00  BILL  (Y/N)

   PROBLEM   PAT-LOCAL 1 + TOOL CALLS PRICING AT 0.

   SOLUTION  GREG-NEED TO HAVE CDRGRP.DAT RESTORED FROM TBL BACKUP'S MADE
             THE DAY BEFORE SYS WAS UPGRADED.  HAD PAT RESTORE CDDRGRP.DAT
             TO GET PRICING BACK TO ORIGINAL PRICING.
```

Courtesy of Telecommunications Systems Management, Inc., St. Charles, MO.

The **work order preparation and tracking** feature adds, moves, and changes equipment in voice and data networks. It provides the capability of entering new service orders, tracking service activity, and completing orders. Figure 15-18 shows a work order screen that displays the work order number, the date received, the date due, an account order number, a purchase order number, the requested date, and a local contact and telephone number. The work is assigned to a service company and technician for completion. At the bottom of the screen you can specify the work to be done, such as the type of station set to be worked on.

Work order data can be transferred to permanent station files or used for updating inventory records and scheduling installation workload. After labor and material charges have been determined for each work order, shown in Figure 15-19, the charges can be entered into a billing system. The work order charges can then be automatically allocated to the appropriate user, such as a department.

FIGURE 15-18   Work Order Information Screen

```
    -----W0110A----------         THE TSM TOTAL SOLUTION      ---02/02/   1:26---
    ---------------------         WORK ORDER MANAGEMENT       --------------------
    ---------------------         INFORMATION/MAINTENANCE     --------------------

    ACCT #              1- 0- 0     ACCT NM      PIONEER CORPORATION
    SYSTEM    SL-1                  RELEASE      11
    LIASON    DAVID CROCKETT        PHONE #         214-434-1200
    WO #                       1    DAY RCD                       2-02-
    DAY DUE                2-15-    ACCT OR      16450
    PO #              223           DAY REQ                       2-15-
    LOC CON   STAN FORD             PHONE #         314-569-8760
    SER CO#                    1    CO NAME      ACME SERVICE
    DAY ASN                2-15-    PER ASN      MICHAEL DAVIDSON
    ITEM #                     4    TYP SET                           1
    NAME      TEN BUTTON KEY SET    TERM #
    OLD ID#              —    —    NEW ID#            —    —    —
    FNA TO                          FBT
    HUNT TO                         PKUP GP
    COS                        2    COS...             —    —    —
    COS...           —    —    —   NCOS
```

Courtesy of Telecommunications Systems Management, Inc., St. Charles, MO.

FIGURE 15-19   **Work Order Billing Data Screen**

```
----W0112A----------         THE TSM TOTAL SOLUTION        ---02/02/    2:53---
--------------------         WORK ORDER MANAGEMENT         -------------------
--------------------              BILLING DATA             -------------------

     ACCOUNT NUMBER                    1- 0- 0      BALANCE      908.91+
     ACCOUNT NAME       PIONEER CORPORATION         W/O NUMBER        1
     LINE NUMBER        1

     IND  P/S#  LOC    AMOUNT      QTY     EXT AMOUNT     DESCRIPTION       BIL
      P    1     0      75.00 *    2.0 =      150.00   HOURLY RATE            N
      S    1     1      82.50 *    1.0 =       82.50   TEN BUTTON KEY SET     N
           0     0       0.00 *    0.0 =        0.00
           0     0       0.00 *    0.0 =        0.00
           0     0       0.00 *    0.0 =        0.00
           0     0       0.00 *    0.0 =        0.00
           0     0       0.00 *    0.0 =        0.00
           0     0       0.00 *    0.0 =        0.00
           0     0       0.00 *    0.0 =        0.00

                     TODAY'S CHARGES          232.50
```

Courtesy of Telecommunications Systems Management, Inc., St. Charles, MO.

Some TMS systems can automatically schedule work orders and update the equipment and cable inventory databases on completion of the work. These systems also produce reports that flag overdue orders or identify jobs experiencing work order problems.

Since divestiture, companies are now responsible for the cable inside their offices. They need to know what cable exists, its location, and how much is available for new stations. A *cable management* feature keeps track of a building's telephone wiring and thereby reduces the technician's time when installing new station equipment, working with equipment already in place, and knowing what is available for use at a later date. A database, for example, can provide records of the entire circuit for any location.

The *vendor bill reconciliation* feature compares vendor invoices with your inventory databases and produces an exceptional report that lists discrepancies.

Alarms monitoring and reporting feature monitors the operation of voice and data networks as well as notifies and documents system failures. Some alarm systems prioritize the seriousness of the problem, and some automatically issue a trouble ticket. Reports provide performance statistics on hardware and software components.

Equipment inventory is a database that keeps track of equipment and can be automatically updated. Each item can be described according to its age, type, purchase or lease price, location, and users it serves. For example, when a location is targeted for additional equipment, the database provides information to ensure that only compatible equipment is ordered. When a user reports equipment trouble or requests an equipment move or change, a list of all of the user's equipment can be generated. When the accounting department needs information about equipment, the database provides such information as the age, type, and purchase or lease cost.

Figure 15-20 shows a station inventory screen in which station equipment is identified, priced, and assigned a monthly allocation amount to be

FIGURE 15-20   **Equipment Inventory Screen**

```
----INV110A---------        THE TSM TOTAL SOLUTION      ---02/02/   2:48---
--------------------        INVENTORY MANAGEMENT        --------------------
--------------------        INVENTORY MAINTENANCE       --------------------

    STOCK NUMBER         1       DESCRIPTION    TEN BUTTON KEY SET
    PRIMARY LOC          1       NAME           MAIN STOCK
    VENDOR NUMBER        1       NAME           TELECOM SUPPLY CO.
    VENDOR PART NUMBER           RJ4-743849
--------------------------------------------------------------------------------
       QUANTITIES                    COSTS                  LOCATION/STATUS
    ON HAND         30       UNIT             0.00     AISLE            12
    ON ORDER         0       DISCOUNT         0.00     SIDE (L/R)        R
    MIN ORDER       10       PRICE           82.50     BIN NUMBER        3
    PRICE BREAK     10       QTY PRICE       75.00     REORDER PT.      10
    DISCOUNT         0       MTHLY ALLOC      3.44     STOCK PEND.       0
```

Courtesy of Telecommunications Systems Management, Inc., St. Charles, MO.

charged to the user. The allocation charge is added to the user's cost of calls provided in the call detail recording feature. The telephone directory provides identification information about the user. Thus the three features—equipment inventory, call detail recording, and directory—work together.

■ TMS Reports

Reports produced by TMSs, such as the example identified in Figure 15-21, are important tools for managing telecommunications operations. A TMS reporting feature should be able to provide realtime online reports and/or produce hard copies whenever desired. The advantage of real-time online reports is that sudden changes in telephone operations can be easily spotted and problems can be solved immediately instead of waiting for month-end reports, by which time minor problems might have blossomed into major ones. Examples of reports are shown in Figure 15-22.

■ Benefits of Telephone Management Systems

The major reason for installing a TMS is to manage telephone usage. When current data is continuously available, problems can be identified and corrected before they become major ones. Among the benefits of TMS are the following:

- *It provides a record of calls made by each individual.* Each call is usually described according to number called, length of call, cost, and type of line used.
- *It summarizes telephone usage by departments, which is helpful in preparing budgets.*
- *It allocates telephone costs to departments or divisions.* An account code is assigned to each telephone extension and/or project. Because the appropriate code is entered each time a telephone call is made, report summaries

FIGURE 15-21 **Examples of Types of Reports Generated by Telephone Management Systems**

Call-Accounting Reports
Details of calling by station
Details of calling by department
Details of calling by exception
Summary reports of area codes, extensions, exceptions
Trunk usage reports
Company total by department

Traffic Analysis Reports
WATS activity by bands, state, area code
Non-WATS activity by band, state, area code
Non-WATS activity by exchange code (FX determination)
Busy hour reports
Carrier company information
Common carrier pricing
Traffic modeling

FIGURE 15-22 **Sample Reports**

NAME	STATION	BLDG	FL	LOC	MAIL	DEPARTMENT
AGARN, RANDOLPH B	3001	4	-001	-39	3001	160-EMPLOYEE RELATIONS
CLAMPETT, JED A	3041	1	-001	-33	3041	160-EMPLOYEE RELATIONS
CUNNINGHAM, RICHARD P	3102	1	-001	-35	3102	120-PLANNING RESEARCH & ANAL.
DOUGLAS, OLIVER W	3211	2	-005	-211	3212	140-LEGAL
DRAKE, PAUL	3212	2	-005	-533	3211	150-SYSTEMS & DATA PROCESSING
FEVER, JOHNNY	3313	7	-009	-219	3313	160-EMPLOYEE RELATIONS
FRIDAY, JOSEPH	3319	7	-009	-221	3319	190-CUSTOMER SERVICE
GANNON, WILLIAM P	3333	7	-009	-230	3333	170-FACILITIES MANAGEMENT
GRANT, GINGER R	3357	7	-009	-241	3357	160-EMPLOYEE RELATIONS
HANEY, PATRICK F	3367	2	-002	-440	3367	110-CONTROLLER
HOWELL, THURSTON	3380	11	-002	-221	3380	190-CUSTOMER SERVICE
KIRK, JAMES T	3489	11	-002	-443	3489	150-SYSTEMS & DATA PROCESSING
KOTTER, GABE	3545	1	-023	-231	3545B	150-SYSTEMS & DATA PROCESSING
MASON, PERRY	3545	1	-023	-231	3545	150-SYSTEMS & DATA PROCESSING
MCCOY, LEONARD F	3651	4	-002	-2	3651	160-EMPLOYEE RELATIONS
MERTZ, FRED E	3765	2	-004	-47	3765	160-EMPLOYEE RELATIONS
STEVENS, DARRIN N	3767	2	-004	-44	3767	130-MARKETING & PRODUCT DEV.
TATE, LARRY M	3819	1	-004	-449	3819	110-CONTROLLER
WAYNE, JOHN	3890	1	-004	-456	3890	120-PLANNING RESEARCH & ANAL.

(a) Directory Report

```
COMPANY       :   1 SAMPLE COMPANY              STATION NUMBER  :  3890
LEVEL ONE     :   100 CORPORATE/ADMINISTRATIVE  STATION NAME(S) :  ALICE B INKERTON
LEVEL TWO     :   120 PLANNING RESEARCH & ANAL.
LEVEL THREE   :
LEVEL FOUR    :   122 MODELING/FORECASTING      CLASS OF SERVICE : 2
```

DATE	TIME	DURATION	COST	GROUP	ACCESS	NUMBER DIALED	CITY / STATE	NUMBER IDENTIFICATION	EXCESS
01/23/87	11:49	0.9	$ .00	LOCO3		8226800	KIRKWOOD MI		
01/23/87	11:54	0.5	.00	LOCO2		8317600	FLORISSANT MI		
01/23/87	12:11	15.9	.00	INWAT				* INCOMING CALL *	D
01/23/87	12:12	0.3	.00	INWAT				* INCOMING CALL *	
01/23/87	12:22	8.6	.00	LOCO1		8226800	KIRKWOOD MI		
01/23/87	12:28	0.7	.00	LOCO2		8226800	KIRKWOOD MI		
01/23/87	12:30	0.6	.56	WATS5		8187801587	VAN NUYS CA		
01/23/87	12:31	0.9	.56	WATS5		8187801387	VAN NUYS CA		
01/23/87	12:38	7.1	.00	WATHO				* INCOMING CALL *	
01/23/87	12:44	0.3	.00	LOCO1		0324416100			
01/23/87	12:51	5.6	.00	INWAT				* INCOMING CALL *	
01/23/87	13:03	0.7	.55	WATS5		5123456480	AUSTIN TX		
01/23/87	13:13	3.2	.00	WATHO				* INCOMING CALL *	
01/23/87	13:28	5.1	.00	INWAT				* INCOMING CALL *	
01/23/87	13:57	8.7	.00	INWAT				* INCOMING CALL *	
01/23/87	14:49	12.0	.00	INWAT				* INCOMING CALL *	D
01/23/87	14:58	2.4	.00	WATHO				* INCOMING CALL *	
01/23/87	15:13	1.8	.00	WATS5		5013780863	LITTLEROCK AR		
01/23/87	16:02	14.5	4.32	INWAT				* INCOMING CALL *	D
01/23/87	16:14	2.8	.81	INWAT				* INCOMING CALL *	

(b) Call Detail Recording

(continued next page)

FIGURE 15-22 Continued

```
                                          AVG CALL                 MODELING INPUTS
    TYPE TRAFFIC     CALLS    MINUTES  HOURS  LENGTH
TRUNK GROUP 00000  DID                                  OUTBOUND TRAFFIC IN HOURS          1000.0
  34 TRUNKS EQUIPPED                                    INBOUND TRAFFIC IN HOURS            625.0
   0 TIMES ALL TRUNKS BUSY          34 TRUNKS ENABLED   OUTBOUND CALL LENGTH IN MINUTES       3.0
    INBOUND         1,751  5,231.7    0 TOLL CALLS ON LOCAL LINES
                                       87.2       3.0   INBOUND CALL LENGTH IN BUSY HOUR      2.5
    OUTBOUND            0      .0        0        .0    PERCENT OF TRAFFIC IN BUSY HOUR     15.0%
    COMBINED        1,751  5,231.7    87.2       3.0    RING TIME IN SECONDS                  18
                                                        WORKING DAYS IN THE MONTH             15
TRUNK GROUP 00001  LOCAL OUT                            DESIRED BLOCKAGE                      21
  32 TRUNKS EQUIPPED                 31 TRUNKS ENABLED  PERCENT OF CALLS FOR RETRIAL        70.0
   0 TIMES ALL TRUNKS BUSY        354 TOLL CALLS ON LOCAL LINES
    INBOUND             0      .0       .0        .0             MODELING STATISTICS
    OUTBOUND        2,177  4,851.7    80.9       2.2
    COMBINED        2,177  4,851.7    80.9       2.2    TRUNKS REQUIRED                       20
                                                        GRADE OF SERVICE                     1.6%
TRUNK GROUP 00002  BAND 5 OUT                           DDD OVERFLOW USAGE                   4.8
  10 TRUNKS EQUIPPED                 10 TRUNKS ENABLED  TOTAL INBOUND LOST CALLS              72
 156 TIMES ALL TRUNKS BUSY          0 TOLL CALLS ON LOCAL LINES
    INBOUND             1      .0       .0        .0
    OUTBOUND        1,033  2,813.3    46.9       2.7         LINE            USAGE
    COMBINED        1,034  2,813.3    46.9       2.7           1            118.309
                                                                2            117.092
TRUNK GROUP 00003  BAND 5 IN                                    3            115.654
  22 TRUNKS EQUIPPED                 16 TRUNKS ENABLED          4            113.953
   0 TIMES ALL TRUNKS BUSY          0 TOLL CALLS ON LOCAL LINES 5            111.930
    INBOUND           318  1,661.7    27.7       5.2            6            109.517
    OUTBOUND            0      .0       .0        .0            7            106.645
    COMBINED          318  1,661.7    27.7       5.2            8            103.215
                                                                9             99.143
TRUNK GROUP 00004  MCI                                         10             94.328
  18 TRUNKS EQUIPPED                 13 TRUNKS ENABLED         11             88.686
   0 TIMES ALL TRUNKS BUSY          0 TOLL CALLS ON LOCAL LINES 12             82.162
    INBOUND             0      .0       .0        .0           13             74.752
    OUTBOUND          674  1,906.7    31.8       2.8           14             66.530
    COMBINED          674  1,906.7    31.8       2.8           15             57.674
                                                               16             48.480
TRUNK GROUP 00005  DDD OVERFLOW                                17             39.332
  01 TRUNKS EQUIPPED                 01 TRUNKS ENABLED         18             30.669
   0 TIMES ALL TRUNKS BUSY          0 TOLL CALLS ON LOCAL LINES 19             22.901
    INBOUND             0      .0       .0        .0           20             16.328
    OUTBOUND            2      .0       .0        .0
    COMBINED            2      .0       .0        .0

TOTALS
    INBOUND         2,070  6,893.4   114.9       3.3
    OUTBOUND        3,886  9,571.7   159.6       2.5
    COMBINED        5,956 16,465.1   274.5       2.8
```

(c) **Traffic Statistics**   (d) **Traffic Engineering**

Courtesy of Summa Four, Inc.

of telephone costs can be generated for each department or project. These reports allow companies to budget telephone expenses on a department basis.

- *It allocates telephone costs to clients.* Because a client's account code is entered when a call is dialed that pertains to the client, a report can be generated that shows the cost of each telephone call incurred on the client's behalf. The total cost of telephone usage is then added to the client's bill.
- *It verifies telephone bills.* A TMS calculates the cost of each call, including separate rates for different trunk lines and for different times of day. These costs can be compared with the actual telephone bills to identify any discrepancies.
- *It identifies telephone misuse or abuse.* Analyzing TMS reports helps to identify misuse of telephone services. Incorrect usage of specific telephone services can be identified and corrected by blocking employee calls to prevent access to these services. A frequently dialed number report, such as the one shown in Figure 15-23, identifies calling patterns, including identification of telephone usage.

FIGURE 15-23 **Frequently Dialed Number Report**

```
                          OS Plus 1000
                       ABC Customer, Inc.
                        Frequency Reports

From: 10/02/   To: 10/25/

Digits Dialed     City        St    Frequency    Cost
-------------     ------------      ---------    ------
619-931-9000      CARLSBAD    CA       59        78.49
703-321-3515      D.C. Office          39        63.45
813-875-0776      TAMPA       FL       32        42.69
415-539-4716      OAKLAND     CA       29         9.06
617-236-9880      BOSTON      MA       27         8.31
609-429-0104      HADDONFLD   NJ       27        63.24
803-232-9336      GREENVILLE  SC       26        14.54
612-687-1883      ST PAUL     MN       26        20.55
617-482-3117      BOSTON      MA       25        44.20
714-951-8229      SADLEBKVLY  CA       21        35.30
                                      -------   ------
                                        311     379.83
```

Courtesy of Infortext Systems Inc.

- *It helps to reduce the average length and the number of call that are made.* Each employee becomes accountable for every call placed on his or her extension. Employees typically reduce the length and quantity of their calls when shown that they talk frequently and for long periods of time. In fact, just the existence of a call-accounting system can have a deterrent effect on personal use, even if management makes little use of the reports.
- *It reduces the number of calls that employees make to directory assistance.* If the report shows that a large number of calls are being made to the same directory assistance area code, then hard copy directories of these areas can be obtained. Directories become a must for companies with large telemarketing departments to reduce the thousands of dollars spent each month on directory assistance calls.
- *It provides traffic data that can be used to analyze companywide telephone usage.* The amount of calling activity to specific cities is reported. Data traffic can be analyzed to determine whether special services are required and whether they are cost-justified. For example, trunk reports specify how much each trunk is being used, which indicates whether the trunk is cost-justified. Data about daily traffic usage helps in scheduling proper telephone coverage during peak hours. A comparison of monthly summaries might indicate that more local lines will soon be needed.
- *It serves as a management tool for employee evaluation and training.* Calling patterns can be analyzed in terms of call frequency and duration to determine sales effectiveness and to set calling quotas. For example, the calling patterns of successful salespeople can be compared with the patterns of marginal salespeople to obtain possible reasons for differences in performance and to determine whether some salespeople need additional training. Calling patterns of other employees can be compared to provide useful information for personal time management.
- *It generates revenue.* Since TMSs allow a surcharge and a margin of profit to be added to each call, a company can add revenue by reselling its

telephone services to others. These services may be offered to employees for personal use or to neighboring companies that cannot afford their own telephone system. Institutions such as hospitals and hotels receive extra revenue by reselling some of their telephone services. Hotels and motels also add a commission to local and long-distance calls when billing guests.

Selecting a Telephone Management System

What kind of telephone management system does your company need? When does your company need it?

A suggested telephone management plan consists of four phases: (1) describe your present telephone system including its traffic characteristics, (2) determine the features that the new system should offer, (3) prepare a request for a proposal, and (4) evaluate and select a telephone management system.

Phase 1: Describe your present telephone system including its traffic characteristics. Answers to the following questions help to determine the type of telephone management system that will best serve your needs.

- How many working extensions does your present system have? How many of these are touch-tone telephones? How many are rotary dial telephones?
- How many employees use the present telephones?
- What type of telephone system, such as PBX, Centrex, or key system, are you currently using?
- What features does your present telephone system offer? Examples are station message detail recording, automatic route selection, trunk queuing, speed dialing, and restricted extension lines.
- What is the name of your local telephone company?
- How many local lines do you currently have? How many hours of traffic is the system in use? What is the cost?
- How many direct dialing lines, WATS line, tie lines, and foreign exchange lines does your present system have?
- How does your present system allow you to make overseas telephone calls?

Phase 2: Determine the features that the new system should offer. Answers to the following questions help to determine these features.

- Should the new system be able to allocate expenses to individuals, departments, clients, etc.?
- Should the system be able to track local calls?
- What type of reports should the system generate?
- What traffic information do you need?

- What restrictions must you be able to place on certain extensions?
- Will users need to access the system from outside the company?

Phase 3: Prepare a request for proposal (RFP). Vendors typically tailor boilerplate proposals that outline their products and services to fit a company's request for proposal. To be certain that you receive the information that you need, your RFP should include a request for the following information and any other information required by your company.

- Request a description of the vendor's company, its background, business, current status, objectives, and financial data to determine its soundness.
- Describe your telephone management requirements. (See Phase 1.)
- Describe the current devices or services being used to collect telephone data.
- Describe the types of reports that the new system must generate.
- Specify the date that you require installation or indicate if no date has been scheduled.
- Request the following information from the vendor. What are the initial and recurring costs? Does the vendor provide training? Does the vendor provide maintenance? Are tariff updates provided? What are the costs of training, maintenance, and tariff updates? Can the system be expanded as the company grows? Can the system be customized if desired? What else does the company provide?

Phase 4: Evaluate and select a telephone management system. From your evaluations of the vendors' responses to your REP, select three or four vendors as finalists. Ask them for demonstrations and talk with their customers.

Today, companies can manage their telephone activities with the assistance of telephone management software. A company may even obtain a competitive advantage by managing its telephone resources carefully.

Managing Telecommunications in the Next Decade

Telecommunications has become the infrastructure of the Information Age and is vital to the successful operating of a company. (Infrastructure is the essential elements of a structure or a system, such as a communications facility.) However, telecommunications in the next decade will be even more complex than it is today and not an easy task to manage.

■ Technology Trends

According to research by A. T. Kearney, by the year 2001 the speed and processing capabilities of networks will increase considerably. For example, technology will make possible widespread use of fiber optics, a transmission medium that will be capable of transmitting at a speed of 1 billion bytes per second in both long-haul and local connections to the customer. Increased intelligence will be built into networks, providing them with more capabilities, such as advanced diagnostic features. Switching systems will be developed to handle increased transmission speeds, and appropriate hardware and software interfaces will be developed for workstations, mainframe computers, and other devices to access high-speed networks efficiently.

Telecommunications applications will be greatly enhanced in going beyond the integrated services digital network (ISDN). For example, the ability to integrate speech into communications for controlling computation and describing processes will be possible. The issues of security and privacy of information in telecommunications networks will continue to be important, especially if networks are to be used to their fullest potential.

A continuing challenge will be identifying profitable ways to introduce new telecommunications technology. The conversion of what is technologically possible into what is commercially viable is no easy task.

■ Regulatory Trends

Although government regulations in the United States will continue to decrease, including the role of the FCC, they will still be important. The extent of deregulation and when it happens will significantly affect the manufacture, distribution, and use of telecommunications products and services. Most important, the decrease in traditional regulations will subject telecommunications to competitive market forces.

■ Organizational and Management Trends

Telecommunications technologies and applications will continue to change how people perform their work and work with each other in the office. For example, desktop videoconferencing makes it possible for people to work as a team on a project in real time but separated by distance. For organizations to succeed in the changing telecommunications environment, organizations will need to develop structures that will

- Include fewer vertical levels and less horizontal specialization
- Assign more responsibility and authority to lower levels of the organization
- Stress managerial discretion with less reliance on detailed methods and procedures
- Develop strategies that the organization can execute effectively[1]

The changing functions of telecommunications management are illustrated in Figure 15-24.

FIGURE 15-24 The Evolving Management Structure

Technology	Industry	Telecom Management
1970		
Voiceband data	Monopoly	Facilities management
SNA	IBM-driven DP	Cost containment
Async networks	Beginning of deregula-	Bell system liaison
Stored-program PBX	tion	Separate voice and data
Centrex	Capital intensive	Voice emphasis
Specialized networks (OA, CAD)	Mainframe oriented	Engineering oriented
1980		
SNA	Divestiture	Voice/data integration
DECnet	Deregulation	Cost management
Packet	Moving to software	Network planning/oper-
Satellite	driven	ations
Fiber	ISDN trials	Applications dependent
Store-and-forward voice	Customer decentraliza-	Multivendor liaison
Digital transmission	tion	Planning oriented
T-1 (user based)		
LANs		
1990		
SNA	Re-segmentation	Systems integration
DECnet/ISO	Globalization	Profit motivation
ISDN	Standardization	Applications planning
LANs	Customer driven	Network management
T-1 (T-2, T-3, T-4)		Multivendor consoli-
Digitized voice		dation
Graphics		High visibility
Integrated facilities		

John Gantz, "The Network of 1998," *TPT/Network Management*, January 1988, p. 32. Courtesy of *TPT/Networking Management*.

To carry out their changing role, telecommunications managers in the next decade will need to

- Be constantly aware of relevant technological developments
- Integrate technology strategy with business strategy
- Appreciate the financial, operational, and regulatory implications of technology
- Understand the competitive dynamics created by technology-related structural changes in the industry
- Identify customer needs and develop application-oriented products and services

Telecom managers can begin adjusting to change by carefully analyzing the present environment to determine the ways in which it is changing and which of these changes are important. Such an analysis then makes it possible to devote time and resources to the areas that are most critical to succeeding in this environment.[2]

Accelerating technological change, the continuing decline of traditional regulation, and the introduction of competition are making it increasingly difficult to control the pace and timing of change. How quickly the organization and its people adjust to an uncertain and changing external environment will become critical. Detailed written procedures will no longer be able to address all contingencies. To meet changing market demands, managers must focus on results, informed decision making, and flexibility and innovation.[2]

Summary

Some managers have yet to realize that many of the tasks formerly performed by the telephone company are now not being done by anyone. Since divestiture, companies are on their own in selecting, setting up, and maintaining their telephone systems. Instead of the one-stop shopping provided by the Bell systems, companies must now do business with multiple providers for their telephone needs. Even selecting the appropriate telephone management system is not an easy task. These computer-based systems monitor a network, identify and diagnose problems, help correct them quickly, and generate management reports on network activities; some can also plan and improve network traffic and operations. As telecommunications moves into the next decade, the telecommunications environment will continue to be characterized by change, such as accelerating technological change, the continuing decline of traditional regulations, and the introduction of competition.

■ *Key Terms*

Automatic route selection (ARS)
Blockage
Busy hour
Call accounting
Carried load
Conversation time
Erlang
Grade of service
Holding time
Hundred call seconds (CCS)
Offered load
Operating time
Peg count
Tariffs
Telephone management system
Traffic
Traffic engineering
Traffic modeling
Trouble reporting and tracking
Work order preparation and tracking

Self-Quiz

Indicate whether the statement is true or false.

1. Operating time includes the time for dialing and ringing, conversation, and ending the connection.   T/F
2. A grade of telephone service of P.90 is considered satisfactory.   T/F
3. An authorization code can be programmed for different levels of service.   T/F
4. Least-cost routing can be programmed to automatically queue a call and signal the user when a line is free.   T/F
5. A manager can solve a blocking problem that is caused by all of the available outgoing lines being in use.   T/F
6. A telephone management system can serve as a tool for evaluating employees.   T/F

Complete each of the following statements.

1. Average holding time is 150 seconds per call. Peg count is 10. The traffic load expressed in CCS is _____ .
2. A traffic load of 18 CCS expressed in erlangs would be _____ .
3. A traffic load of 20 calls, each with a holding time of 2 minutes, expressed in erlangs is _____ .
4. Traffic that refers to all the people who tried to make calls is called _____ .
5. Traffic that refers to the people who succeed in making calls by carrying on conversations is called _____ .
6. The hour during the day when the largest volume of telephone calls is handled is called the _____ .

Match Column A with Column B.

Column A
(a) Call accounting
(b) Traffic engineering
(c) Traffic modeling
(d) Traffic statistics
(e) Trouble reporting and tracking
(f) Work order preparation and tracking

Column B
____ 1. Determines number of trunks for a network.
____ 2. Manages, adds, moves, and changes of voice equipment.
____ 3. Controls maintenance problems.
____ 4. Collects information on trunk usage.
____ 5. Shows actual call usage and costs.
____ 6. Performs "what if" analysis.

Applications

1. How many trunks will your telephone system require to handle 314 CCS of traffic at P.02 GOS? Refer to Figure 15-4.

2. If you change the GOS in question 1 to P.10, how many more or fewer trunks would you need? Refer to Figure 15-4.
3. Your present GOS is 0.10 for nine trunks. You would like to change the GOS to 0.01. How many trunks would you need to add or delete to obtain the new GOS? Refer to Figure 15-4.
4. If the GOS is 0.005 and the busy hour load is 220 CCS, how many CCS will the fourth trunk handle? Refer to Figure 15-5.
5. If the GOS is 0.005, what is the minimum number of trunks required to handle 125 CCS of traffic if the average busy hour load is 300 CCS? Refer to Figure 15-5.
6. You have a P.005 GOS and expect a total of 180 CCS. (a) How many trunks will you need if you limit the capacity of the first group to a traffic load of 75 CCS? (b) How many CCS will be routed on the second group of trunks? Refer to Figure 15-5.

■ Review Questions

1. What is the difference between an erlang and a CCS? Give an example.
2. (a) Convert the following traffic loads to CCS:
   (1) 50 minutes of traffic
   (2) 80 minutes of traffic
   (3) 3 hours of traffic
   (4) 8.8 hours of traffic
   (b) Convert the following traffic loads to erlangs:
   (1) 432 CCS of traffic
   (2) 31.5 CCS of traffic
   (3) 900 CCS of traffic
   (4) 72 CCS of traffic
3. A report shows that the average holding time for a telephone call is 225 seconds. The peg count (number of telephone calls) for the period is 50. What is the traffic load in erlangs for the period? (*Note*: First express the traffic load in CCS and then convert to erlangs.)
4. How does traffic at supermarket checkout counters resemble traffic in a telephone environment?
5. Refer to Figures 15-4 and 15-5 to answer the following questions.
   (a) How many trunks would you need for 12 erlangs at P.03 GOS?
   (b) Your group of six trunks is giving you P.10 GOS. How many trunks would you need to add for P.02 GOS?
   (c) For a group of five trunks, how many CCS is the fifth trunk estimated to handle if the busy hour load is 170 CCS?
   (d) What is the minimum number of trunks required to carry 150 CCS if the average busy hour load is 240 CCS?
6. (a) What does P.01 grade of service mean?
   (b) How would you interpret a grade of service of P.30? P.05?

7. (a) Why should a company consider using least-cost routing?
   (b) Set up a least-cost routing plan that includes three alternatives for calling between your school or office and neighboring states.
   (c) How could queuing be included with your plan?
8. (a) What is the difference between telephones with calling restrictions and employees using authorized codes?
   (b) Give examples of each.
9. How can "timed signals" be of help to a company?
10. (a) Which type of telephone management configuration would you recommend for a large company? Why?
    (b) When would you consider using the other configuration?
11. What is(are) the difference(s) between call accounting features and traffic engineering features offered in telephone management systems?
12. As a manager, which telephone management system feature(s) would you need in order to answer each of the following questions:
    (a) When were the telephones that are installed in the advertising department purchased?
    (b) What type of telephones are we using in the marketing department?
    (c) What kinds of repair problems have we had with our telephones over the past two years?
    (d) How much unused cable is available on the second floor?
    (e) Which employees make more than ten personal calls a month?
    (f) What is the telephone extension number of the company's treasurer?
    (g) Should the number of long-distance trunks be increased?
    (h) How much is the sales department spending on long-distance calls each week?
    (i) How could employees be encouraged to use WATS instead of direct distance dialing?
13. How can a telephone management system benefit your school or office?
14. What are some of the changes in the telecommunications environment that you can expect in the next decade?

■ Activities/Projects

1. Prepare to discuss the following issues.
   (a) Does call-accounting software impinge on the privacy of the people using the telephone?
   (b) Should a company with fewer than twelve employees install a telephone management system?
   (c) How will the telecommunications environment in the year 2001 affect how employees perform their work? Affect how the telecommunications manager manages?
2. Visit the telecommunications or business manager of a school or organization that uses a telephone management system. In a written or an

oral report, include the following information: the name of the system, a description of its features, the types of reports generated, and how the organization uses the information.
3. Obtain a sample printout of a department's call-accounting records from your school or office or any organization of your choice. (Replace user names with fictitious ones.) Describe the data provided and how the data can be used in managing the telephone system.
4. How could a telephone management system be used to improve each of the following situations?
   (a) Operators must spend time searching through hard copy personnel directories before transferring incoming calls to the correct extensions.
   (b) Callers hang up because of constant busy signals or no answer from the switchboard.
   (c) Managers' requests for telephone additions, moves, and changes are processed by completing various paper forms.
   (d) Responses to managers' requests for telephone installations and users' requests for telephone repairs take several weeks. No user or system records are maintained.
   (e) The company verifies its monthly telephone bills by sending copies to users and asking them to identify which calls they made.
   (f) The company is unable to allocate line and equipment costs to users.
   (g) Employees use their telephone for local and long-distance personal calls whenever they wish.
   (h) The company's maintenance staff uses the telephones when working in the evenings.
   (i) The company provides long-distance calling over AT&T and MCI with both carriers providing direct distance dialing and WATS lines. Employees usually use AT&T direct distance dialing when placing long-distance calls.

■ *Case:* Analyzing a Company's Telephone Usage

An increasing number of companies are managing their telephone operations with the assistance of telephone management systems. You have been asked to examine the reports shown in Figures 15-25 and 15-26 and explain them to employees and, if possible, to make suggestions for improving the company's telephone operations.

■ *Notes*

1. David E. Harper, "The Future of Telecommunications: Part II," *Telecommunications*, February 1989, p. 49.
2. David E. Harper, "The Future of Telecommunications: Part II," *Telecommunications*, January 1989, pp. 27–33.

FIGURE 15-25 Sample Staffing Requirements Report

```
                        STAFFING PARAMETERS

        AVERAGE TALK TIME (MIN)      3.0    PERCENTAGE OF RETRIAL       70.0
        AVERAGE POST TALK (SEC)       20    DESIRED BLOCKAGE             2.0
        AVG OPERATOR EFFICIENCY     80.0    NUMBER OF TRUNKS REQUIRED      5
        NUMBER OF RINGS DESIRED      3.0    GRADE OF SERVICE               1
        DELAY LENGTH DESIRED (MIN)   2.0    INBOUND LOST CALLS             0
                                            TOTAL HOLD TIME IN HOURS    1.05
```

STAFFING STATISTICS	SUN	MON	TUES	WED	THURS	FRI	SAT
TIME = 8:00 am							
TOTAL NUMBER OF CALLS	0.0	20.0	20.0	20.0	20.0	20.0	0.0
NBR OF OPERATORS REQUIRED	0.0	3.0	3.0	3.0	3.0	3.0	0.0
PROBABILITY OF DELAY	0.0	19.8	19.8	19.8	19.8	19.8	0.0
AVG DELAY, DELAYED CALLS	0.0	1.3	1.3	1.3	1.3	1.3	0.0
TOTAL HOLD TIME (MINUTES)	0.0	6.0	6.0	6.0	6.0	6.0	0.0
TIME = 9:00 am							
TOTAL NUMBER OF CALLS	0.0	30.0	30.0	30.0	30.0	30.0	0.0
NBR OF OPERATORS REQUIRED	0.0	4.0	4.0	4.0	4.0	4.0	0.0
PROBABILITY OF DELAY	0.0	19.5	19.5	19.5	19.5	19.5	0.0
AVG DELAY, DELAYED CALLS	0.0	1.2	1.2	1.2	1.2	1.2	0.0
TOTAL HOLD TIME (MINUTES)	0.0	7.0	7.0	7.0	7.0	7.0	0.0

The TSM Total Solution™, copyright 1988 Telecommunications Systems Management.
™Registered trademark of Telecommunications Systems Management.

FIGURE 15-26 Sample Inbound/Outbound Summary Report

```
                         MODELING INPUTS
                         ---------------
        OUTBOUND TRAFFIC IN HOURS                   1000.0
        INBOUND TRAFFIC IN HOURS                     625.0
        OUTBOUND CALL LENGTH IN MINUTES                3.0
        INBOUND CALL LENGTH IN BUSY HOUR               2.5
        PERCENT OF TRAFFIC IN BUSY HOUR              15.0%
        RING TIME IN SECONDS                            18
        WORKING DAYS IN THE MONTH                       15
        DESIRED BLOCKAGE                                21
        PERCENT OF CALLS FOR RETRIAL                  70.0

                        MODELING STATISTICS

        TRUNKS REQUIRED                                 20
        GRADE OF SERVICE                              1.6%
        DDD OVERFLOW USAGE                             4.8
        TOTAL INBOUND LOST CALLS                        72
```

LINE	USAGE
1	118.309
2	117.092
3	115.654
4	113.953
5	111.930
6	109.517
7	106.645
8	103.215
9	99.143
10	94.328
11	88.686
12	82.162
13	74.752
14	66.530
15	57.674
16	48.480
17	39.332
18	30.669
19	22.901
20	16.328

The TSM Total Solution™, copyright 1988 Telecommunications Systems Management.
™Registered trademark of Telecommunications Systems Management.

■ *Additional Readings*

Larry A. Arredondo, *Telecommunications Management for Business and Government*, edited by Harry Newton (New York: The Telecom Library, 1981).

T. Frankel, *ABC of the Telephone: Tables for Traffic Management and Design, Book 1—Trunking* (Geneva, Ill.: abc TeleTraining, Inc., 1976).

Lillion Goleniewski and Andrea Wells, "The Telemanagement Symphony," *Network World*, February 20, 1989, pp. 32–35, 42.

Steven C. Grant, *A Management Guide to Automatic Call Distributors* (New York: The Telecom Library, 1981).

Howard J. Gunn, *ABC of the Telephone: Principles of Traffic and Network Design* (Geneva, Ill.: abc TeleTraining, Inc., 1986).

John Hunter, "Integration Is a Long Way Off," *Network World*, June 27, 1988, pp. 45–48.

James E. Jewett and Jacqueline B. Shrago, *Traffic Engineering Tables: The Complete Practical Encyclopedia* (Chicago, Ill.: Telephony Publishing, 1980).

James E. Jewett, Jacqueline B. Shrago, and Bernard D. Yomtov, *Designing Optimal Voice Networks for Businesses, Government, and Telephone Companies* (Chicago, Ill.: Telephony Publishing, 1980).

Robert Kaufman, *Cost-Effective Telecommunications Management: Turning Telephone Costs into Profits* (Boston, Mass.: CBI Publishing Company, 1983).

"The Roundup: What the Makers Want You to Know," *Teleconnect*, June 1988, pp. 106–128.

Robert L. Self, *Long Distance for Less: How to Choose Between Ma Bell and Those "Other" Carriers* (New York: The Telecom Library, 1982).

Tom Smith, *Anatomy of Telecommunications* (Geneva, Ill.: abc TeleTraining, Inc., 1987).

Daniel I. Stusser and Rosanne S. Passafro, "Evaluating Telemanagement Systems," *TPT*, July 1988, pp. 32–38.

APPENDIX A

The Evolution of Telecommunications: A Brief Review

A look backward in time can add a sense of perspective to present and future developments in telecommunications. There are abundant records of human and technical achievement in communications before electrical communications. Communication techniques have evolved from the Egyptian hieroglyphics to the satellites of today.

The human need to communicate is obvious. People go to great lengths to share news or warn others of danger when voice alone is not possible. For thousands of years before electrical communications, messages were transmitted by such means as signal fires, intricate drum codes, runners, horses, ships, and even pigeons. One of the first attempts at colonial military "broadcasting" was Paul Revere's ride. News of the shot heard around the world at the Battle of Lexington took four days to reach New York and eleven more to arrive at Charleston, South Carolina. Horsepower, such as the Pony Express, was the foundation for the early postal system. Sailing vessels were the prime communications links for transoceanic messages.

Today, these modes of communication have been replaced by electronic methods, but the purpose is still the same—to send messages, make connections, and communicate. Electronic signals are sent by such means as telephone links, private cables snaked through hidden spaces in buildings, and microwave radio transmission relayed by communications satellites or by land-based repeater stations.

■ Telegraph

The first, and for over 20 years the most important, system of electrical telecommunications was the telegraph. The purpose of the telegraph, as of other electrical media such as the telephone, is the instantaneous transfer by electrical means of intelligence over distance. Telegraphy differs from other electrical systems in transmitting messages as a sequence of codified letters, numerals, punctuation, and symbols and recording them on paper.

Samuel Morse invented the telegraph in 1855. The first public telegram was sent over a 40-mile line between Washington and Baltimore on May 24, 1844, with the message "What hath God wrought?" For 35 years, from 1845 until telephones became generally available in 1880, the telegraph was the standard means of communicating. Within the next 20 years, telegraph companies were opened everywhere. In 1856, Hiram Sibley and Ezra Cornell consolidated many of them into the Western Union Telegraph Company. By 1866 the company owned 2250 offices using 100,000 miles of lines. An important impetus was the development of a telegraphic news service, led by the Associated Press.

■ Telephone

At least 30 years before Alexander Graham Bell's patent was granted in March 1876, the essential elements for the telephone were available. The concept of sound as a vibration was understood at the beginning of the nineteenth century as was the fact that vibrations could be transferred to solid bodies. Michael Faraday in 1831 showed how the vibration of a piece of iron or steel could be converted into electrical pulses.

On March 7, 1876, Alexander Graham Bell was issued a patent, No. 174,465, on his telephone invention. At that time, Bell had not used his invention to transmit speech. Bell did so on March 10, 1876, when he uttered and transmitted the famous words to his assistant, "Mr. Watson, come here, I want you."

The invention of the telephone was followed almost immediately by the construction of manual switchboards to interconnect telephone lines. The first switchboard, installed in Hartford, Connecticut, in July 1877, was used to connect telephones between doctors and drug stores. In 1891 the first patent for an "automatic" switch, one that required no operators, was granted to A. B. Strowger, and the first system was installed in La Porte, Indiana, in 1892 by the Automatic Electric Company.

Bell was the first to recognize the commercial potential of the telephone. By March 1889 there were 138 exchanges in operation in the United States and 30,000 subscribers. By 1887, only a decade after the commercial introduction of the telephone, there were 743 main and 44 branch exchanges connecting over 150,000 subscribers with 146,000 miles of wire. The telephone gradually supplanted telegraphy as the principal system of telecommunications.

In 1883 the linking of New York and Boston marked the beginning of a national network. By 1911, Philadelphia, Washington, D.C., Albany, and Denver had been added to the network. The telephone signal became too weak for the network to be extended beyond Denver. What was needed was a method to amplify the signal. Lee De Forest's invention of the triode vacuum tube in 1906 and its improvement by others in 1916 made it possible to increase signal strength with amplifiers and thus extend the network. On January 25, 1915, the first official transcontinental call was made between Alexander Graham Bell in New York City and Thomas Watson in San Francisco. Bell said, "Mr. Watson, come here. I want you!" In addition to the vacuum tube the invention of the electrical wave filter in 1917 by George Campbell, then of Bell Laboratories, made it possible to send more than one message over a single telephone circuit at the same time (called multiplexing).

Another important invention was the transistor, invented at Bell Laboratories in 1947 by John Bardeen, Walter Brattain, and William Shockley. The transistor replaced the vacuum tube in communication circuits and took over many functions that had been performed by electromechanical relays and other mechanical devices.

■ Wireless Telegraphy

In 1898, Guglielmo Marconi installed the world's first commercial radio service. He promoted his wireless telegraphy initially as a means of communicating with ships at sea rather than as a competitor against the wire and cable telegraph industries. Wireless telegraphy, the forerunner of modern radio, used electromagnetic waves to send and receive information over long distances in the form of Morse code. Messages could now be sent to mobile receivers on ships and other remote locations. In 1907, Marconi established the first regular commercial transatlantic wireless telegraph service.

■ Microwave Radio

The introduction of microwave carrier systems greatly increased the number of voice channels per circuit. Microwave radio relay links were introduced shortly after World War II. Instead of using coaxial cable, microwaves were transmitted through the air over a line-of-sight path from one station to another. It was used for both coast-to-coast television and telephone communications.

■ Satellite

Although the telephone network has been extended overseas by cable and radio, the advent of communications satellites also makes transoceanic communications possible. Telstar, a low-orbit nonsynchronous relay station was placed in orbit in 1962. When the synchronous satellite Syncom II was positioned over the Atlantic Ocean in 1963, regular commercial service began. A synchronous satellite is one whose period of rotation is the same as that of the Earth. If the satellite is positioned above the equator, it appears to be stationary. A nonsynchronous satellite moves with respect to the earth's surface.

■ Computer Communication

Communicating with computers uses ordinary telephone circuits—the same network that makes it possible for anyone throughout the world with a telephone to speak with anyone else possessing an instrument. The incompatibility between computer data and the network has been resolved by using a transducer, a translating device inserted between a computer and the telephone system at the origin of transmission.

■ Telecommunications Network

The telecommunications network has evolved from manual to automatic, from mechanical to electronic, from wire to laser beam, and from voice only to voice, digital, and video. Noisy telephone switching units have been replaced by microchips. Each new system has improved on the one before it. Today's network of transmission and switching technology offers more capacity and speed as well as more and smarter services, such as information networks, mobile communications, even burglar and fire alarms, and appliance and heating controls. A new digital standard of global communications, the integrated services digital network (ISDN), represents a major milestone in telecommunications.

APPENDIX B

History of Telecommunications Regulations

	Regulatory Actions
The Constitution, Article 1, Section 8	"The commerce clause," which grants Congress the power to "regulate Commerce with foreign Nations, and among the several States. . . ."
The Constitution, Tenth Amendment	The powers to regulate commerce "not delegated to the United States by the Constitution, nor prohibited by it to the States, are reserved to the States respectively, or the people."
	Early Regulations
1866 Post Roads Act	Authorized the U.S. Postmaster General to fix rates for government telegrams and granted telegraphy the right of way over public lands.
1910 Mann-Elkins Act	Extended the authority of the Interstate Commerce Commission (ICC) to telegraph and telephone lines.
1912 Radio Act	Allocated specific communicating frequencies for government use, set rules for the transmission of distress signals from ships at sea, and provided for the licensing of the first radio stations.
1913 Kingsbury Commitment	AT&T negotiated an agreement with the Department of Justice to relinquish its controlling interest in the Western Union Telegraph Company, to cease purchasing independent telephone companies without consent of the ICC, and to allow these companies to interconnect with Bell system companies.
	Regulations of the 1920s and 1930s
1921 Graham-Willis Act	Exempted telephone companies from the Sherman Antitrust Act regarding the acquisition of competing companies, giving AT&T the opportunity of resuming expansion of its territory.
1923 and 1924 National Radio Conferences	Resulted in the U.S. Department of Commerce establishing the present AM broadcast band.
1929 Radio Act	Created a five-member Federal Conference Radio Commission with the power to issue licenses, allocate frequency bands for certain uses, and assign specific frequencies and power limits to individual stations.
Communications Act of 1934	First comprehensive U.S. legislation to establish a regulatory system for national telecommunication services; created the

Federal Communications Commission (FCC) with responsibility for regulating the rates and conditions of interstate, international, and marine communications.

Antitrust Actions of the Justice Department

1956 Consent Decree	AT&T agreed (1) to limit its manufacturing operations to the type of equipment purchased by its company and (2) to license patents for its technology to competitors. The agreement left AT&T intact but prohibited AT&T from entering new, nonregulated areas, such as data processing and computer services.
1982 Consent Decree	Required the breakup of AT&T.

Equipment Regulations

1968 Carterfone decision	Allowed non-Bell equipment to be connected to the public telephone switched network (marked the birth of the interconnect industry).
1971 Computer Inquiry I	FCC's final decision: Telecommunications services would be regulated, while computer service would remain unregulated and allowed to flourish in a competitive market.
1980 Computer Inquiry II	FCC's final decision, II: (1) The FCC was no longer to define data processing separately from data communications but instead was to establish two classes of services—basic and enhanced. *Basic* services, providing only for the movement of information, would remain subject to FCC regulation and would continue to be tariffed. *Enhanced* services, providing anything beyond basic transportation, such as services requiring subscriber interaction, were detariffed and no longer subject to FCC regulation; (2) the FCC removed controls on rates for all customer premises equipment, such as telephones and switches. The FCC required AT&T to offer all of its deregulated competitive services through a subsidiary, whose activities would still be subject to regulation (to comply with the 1956 Consent Decree) but would not be subject to tariffing.
1980 AT&T's Response to Computer Inquiry II	AT&T established American Bell, Inc., to provide services and equipment.
1986 Computer Inquiry II	FCC's Phase 1: AT&T and the Bell operating companies would no longer be required to offer enhanced services only through a fully separate subsidiary. The FCC imposed new rules requiring AT&T and the Bell operating companies to offer enhanced services based on the Open Network Architecture (ONA) standard; to offer basic services supporting enhanced services on an unbundled basis to outside enhanced service vendors under the same terms and conditions as their own operations.

APPENDIX C

Major Standard-Setting Organizations

Standards or sets of procedures govern the interaction of equipment and networks allowing diverse equipment to communicate. Standards are usually established through the efforts of a standards committee formed specifically to examine and evaluate recommendations made by private and public organizations and to select the set of each recommendation to create the standard. Such a committee is usually an authorized body within a larger organization, such as a technical organization, a government agency, or an international consortium.

■ International Standard Setting

Standards in telecommunications are provided by national and international organizations. Throughout the book, standard-setting organizations are identified and major standards are described as they relate to the technologies being discussed. International standards include voluntary standards that meet most international requirements and treaty-based standards. Two major organizations are the *International Standards Organization* (ISO) and the *International Electrotechnical Commission* (IEC). Both are considered voluntary organizations. A third major organization is the *International Telecommunication Union* (ITU), an intergovernmental body established by treaty.

Within the ITU are the *Consultative Committee on International Radio* (CCIR) and the *Consultative Committee on International Telephone and Telegraph* (CCITT). For each committee the U.S. government maintains an active advisory body that prepares the nation's positions and submissions on a variety of issues including international standards. For example, the CCIR addresses issues related to broadcasting, radio spectrum allocation, and the geostationary orbit. Within the United States the Indepartmental Radio Advisory Committee manages the federal government's use of the electromagnetic spectrum (explained in Chapter 2), the FCC manages the private sector's use of the spectrum, and the State Department attempts to coordinate it when dealing with other countries. Radio spectrum planning deals with issues that set or do not set standards by which technology will be developed. The nation's domestic decisions and policy goals cannot prevail in isolation.

The CCITT charts the rules for international common carriers. Because of the emerging technologies, computers and other enhanced services are now included. The CCITT addresses equipment standards, service definitions, and tariff principles. Its actions affect commerce in many ways. For example, in 1987 a treaty was negotiated for a basic protocol for international credit card calls. With a stroke of a pen a savings of $100 million resulted for the U.S. telephone industry. The convenience of international credit card calling is now available.*

■ U.S. Standard Setting

Whenever possible, the U.S. government wants standard setting to be generated by industry, rather than by government on a consensus basis. For the United States a standard must be specific enough to allow an industry to develop and technologies to grow but not so detailed as to impede innovation or competition. In other countries, standard setting is usually controlled by government monopolies. Industry participation is usually limited to a favored domestic company that has preferred status. As a result, the standard setting favors preserving the status quo of a government monopoly rather than emphasizing competition, low prices, and customer choice as in the United States.

ANSI. The *American National Standards Institute* (ANSI) is the standards group that represents the United States in its dealings with ISO and ITU. ANSI is a nongovernmental, nonprofit organization comprising 300 standards committees. Both consumers and manufacturers are represented on ANSI committees. The *Institute of Electrical and Electronic Engineers* (IEEE) and the *Electronic Industries Association* (EIA) are two prominent organizations that promulgate standards through ANSI.

■ Major Organizations

- American National Standards Institute (ANSI), 1430 Broadway, New York, NY 10018
- Consultative Committee on International Telegraph and Telephone (CCITT), General Secretariat, International Telecommunications Union, Place de Nations, 1211 Geneva 20, Switzerland.**
- Electronic Industries Association (EIA), 2001 I Street NW, Washington, DC 20006
- European Computer Manufacturers Association (ECMA), 114, rue de Rhone CH-1204 Geneva, Switzerland 41 22 35-36-34

---

*Diana Lady Dougan, "The High Stakes Game of International Standard Setting," an address given before a symposium on standards sponsored by the National Bureau of Standards, Washington, D.C., May 5, 1987.

**To order copies of CCITT standards in the United States, contact the U.S. Department of Commerce, National Technical Information Service 5285 Port Royal Road, Springfield, VA 22161.

- Federal Information Processing Standards (FIPS), Department of Commerce National Technical Information Service, 5285 Port Royal Road, Springfield, VA 22161
- Federal Telecommunications Standards Committee (FTSC), General Service Administration Specification Distribution Branch, Building 197, Washington Navy Yard, Washington, DC 20407
- Institute of Electrical and Electronics Engineers (IEEE), IEEE Computer Society Suite 608, 111 19th Street NW, Washington, DC 20036
- International Organization for Standardization (ISO), Central Secretariat 1, rue de Varembe, CH-1211 Geneva, Switzerland 41 22 34-12-40

APPENDIX D

Selected Commercial Videotex Systems/Services—System Operators

- **ADP Network Services**, Division of Automatic Data Processing
  175 Jackson Plaza, Ann Arbor, MI 48106   (313) 769-6800

  Founded in 1969, ADP Network Services specializes in online computer services and databases for corporations, banks, investment and brokerage firms, insurance companies, and government agencies.

- **BRS/Search Service**, BRS Information Technologies
  1200 Route 7, Latham, NY 12110   (800) 468-0908

  Established in 1976, BRS/Search Service, a service of BRS Information Technologies, provides access to databases covering current and historical information from journal articles, books, dissertations, and government reports in areas of health, medicine, pharmacology, the biosciences, science and technology, education, business, and finance.

- **CompuServe**
  5000 Arlington Centre Blvd., P.O. Box 20212, Columbus, OH 43220   (800) 848-8199

  Founded in 1969, CompuServe, a division of H&R Block, is a comprehensive general information service. CompuServe provides online communications and bulletin boards (electronic mail, online conferencing, electronic bulletin boards, forums); personal computing support (microcomputer forums, software forums, computing publications—online editions of magazines and newsletters); news, weather, and sports; electronic shopping; financial transaction services; travel; entertainment and games; home, health, and family; money matters and markets; education and reference; business and other interests.

- **DRI (Data Resources Inc.)**
  24 Hartwell Avenue, Lexington, MA 02173   (617) 863-5100

  Founded in 1968, DRI, a division of McGraw-Hill, specializes in online business, financial, and economic databases. DRI offers over 75 financial databases, including DRI's Financial and Credit Statistics and DRI's Bank Analysis Service.

- **Delphi**
  3 Blackstone Street, Cambridge, MA 02139   (617) 491-3393

  General Videotext Corporation, founded in 1980, offers Delphi, which provides online information on business, finance, travel, news, weather, sports, entertainment, shopping on merchant's row (buy and sell, swap items and services), and job search (U.S. Employment Opportunities).

- **Dialog Information Services, Inc.**
  3460 Hillview Avenue, Palo Alto, CA 94304   (800) 334-2564

Established in 1965 as an information-retrieval research and development project. Dialog Information Services went commercial in 1972 and is now a subsidiary of Knight-Ridder, Inc. Dialog offers over 300 databases for information retrieval on topics such as business, industry, corporate; chemistry; medicine, biosciences; law, government, intellectual property; science and technology; news; energy, environment agriculture; education; humanities and social science; and people.

- **Dow Jones News/Retrieval**
  P.O. Box 300, Princeton, NJ 08540   (800) 522-3567

Established in 1974, Dow Jones News/Retrieval, a service of Dow Jones Information Services, is an online business information resource. The service includes more than 40 databases that focus on business and financial information, general news, weather, and sports.

- **GEnie**, GE Consumer Services
  Department 02B, 401 North Washington Street, Rockville, MD 20850   (800) 638-9639

Founded in 1985, GEnie, operated by General Electric Information Services as a consumer-oriented videotex service, offers bulletin boards, software libraries, special interest groups, entertainment, communication, and shopping services, as well as electronic newsletters and magazines. The accent is on communications-related services, not on information.

- **Human Resources Information Network (HRIN)**
  College Park North, 9585 Valparaiso Court, Indianapolis, IN 46268   (800) 421-8884

Human Resources Information Network, a subsidiary of the Bureau of National Affairs, Inc., offers online databases on administration and tax legislation and court rulings, affirmative action, benefits and compensation, employment and recruiting, labor relations, safety and health legislation and regulations, training and development, legal-oriented human-resource information, and general executive information.

- **LEXIS/NEXIS**, Mead Data General
  9333 Springboro Pike, Post Office Box 933, Dayton, OH 45401 (800) 227-4908

Established in 1973, Mead Data Central Inc., a division of the Mead Corporation, offers online, full-text databases of legal, news, business, and general information. The LEXIS database provides comprehensive legal information on such topics as legal decisions, patents, statutes, regulations, and administrative rulings. NEXIS, a business information database contains brokerage and investment data, stock reports, and other financial information.

- **NewsNet, Inc.**
  945 Haverford Road, Bryn Mawr, PA 19019   (800) 345-1301
Founded in 1982, NewsNet, Inc., an online database of timely business information, offers over 320 newsletters, 11 worldwide newswires, TRW business profiles, stock and commodity quotes, and its Investext company and industry reports.

- **Predicasts Terminal System (PTS)**
  Predicasts, 1101 Cedar Avenue, Cleveland, OH 44106   (800) 321-6388
Founded in 1972, PTS offers online databases on overviews of markets and technology, business and industry news, marketing and advertising reference service, aerospace/defense markets and technology new product announcements, annual corporate reports (corporate review of plans and performance), and forecasts and time series. Also offers online national and international trade and business journals, local newspapers, annual reports, bank letters, investment analysts' reports, news releases, and government publications in 15 languages.

- **Telescan Inc.**
  2900 Wilcrest, Suite 400, Houston, TX 77042   (713) 952-1060
Founded in 1983, Telescan Inc. is an online investment analysis service that provides stock price, volume, earnings and other corporation information on over 8000 stocks and 2000 mutual funds. The subscriber base includes security analysts, stockbrokers, money managers, and private investors.

- **VU/TEXT**, VU/TEXT Information Services, Inc.
  325 Chestnut Street, 1300 Mall Building, Philadelphia, PA 19106
  (800) 258-8080

VU/Text Information Services, Inc., a Knight-Ridder, Inc., information retrieval company, is the world's largest newspaper databank providing full-text archives. VU/TEXT provides online access to newspaper, magazine, newswire, maritime, and business information. The company will install SAVE, a stand-alone electronic library system, for newspapers and other publications that are interested in establishing their own in-house electronic libraries or provide computerized storage and retrieval support for newspapers that do not want an in-house system.

APPENDIX E

Answers to Chapter Self-Quizzes

Chapter 1: Telecommunications Overview

True/False: (1) T; (2) T; (3) F (a type of teleconferencing); (4) F (proprietary standards are company standards); (5) T; (6) F (would have resulted in wasted resources and user confusion).

Completion: (1) the sender, the receiver, and the transmission link over which information flows; (2) integrated services digital network (ISDN); (3) electronic data interchange (EDI); (4) Justice Department's 1982 Consent Decree; (5) Communications Act of 1934; (6) the Federal Communications Commission (FCC) and the public utility commissions (PUCs) in each of the fifty states.

Matching: (1) c; (2) b; (3) a; (4) d; (5) e; (6) f.

Chapter 2: Transmission Basics

True/False: (1) F (Transmission includes frequencies from 20 to 20,000 Hz.); (2) T; (3) T; (4) T; (5) F (radio is omnidirectional; microwave is focused); (6) T.

Completion: (1) Federal Communications Commission; (2) 3.3 kHz; (3) simplex transmission; (4) carrier waves; (5) multiplexing; (6) 0.50 percent.

Matching: (1) f; (2) d; (3) b; (4) c; (5) a; (6) e.

Chapter 3: Telephone Basics

True/False: (1) T; (2) F (a condition known as going "off-hook" occurs); (3) F (the measured-rate service is preferred); (4) T; (5) T; (6) T.

Completion: (1) switchhook; (2) local loop; (3) tandem; (4) the central office switch of the number you are calling; (5) a reorder tone, also called a fast busy tone; (6) traffic.

Matching: (1) a; (2) c; (3) d; (4) f; (5) e; (6) b.

Chapter 4: The Public Telephone System

True/False: (1) T; (2) T; (3) T; (4) T; (5) F (a class 5 office is also called an end office or central office); (6) F (bypass occurs when a company buys or leases lines to complete its transmission without going through a central office).

Completion: (1) Other common carriers; (2) nine; (3) LATA; (4) the local telephone network; (5) resellers; (6) class 2 toll office.

Matching: (1) a; (2) c; (3) d; (4) f; (5) b; (6) e.

Chapter 5: Business Telephone Systems

True/False: (1) T; (2) T; (3) T; (4) F (optional features require additional equipment and/or software); (5) F (is usually located at one of the telephone company's central offices); (6) F (Centrex offers its customers the potential of virtually an unlimited number of stations).

Completion: (1) Carterfone Decision; (2) nine central office lines and a maximum of 18 telephone stations; (3) trunks; (4) a foreign exchange trunk; (5) tie trunks; (6) an RS-232-C interface.

Matching: (1) h; (2) d; (3) a; (4) f; (5) c; (6) i; (7) b; (8) e; (9) g.

Chapter 6: Data Communication Networks and Hardware

True/False: (1) T; (2) F (modems that handle higher speeds are synchronous); (3) T; (4) F (the wider the bandwidth, the faster the possible transmission speed); (5) F (they use data compression techniques); (6) T.

Completion: (1) the mainframe or host computer, data terminal equipment, data communications equipment, and medium; (2) microcomputer or personal computer; (3) wideband modems; (4) an acoustic modem or an acoustic coupler; (5) a multipoint network; (6) a stand-alone multiplexer.

Matching: (1) d; (2) a; (3) f; (4) e; (5) b; (6) c.

Redesign the following network:
1.

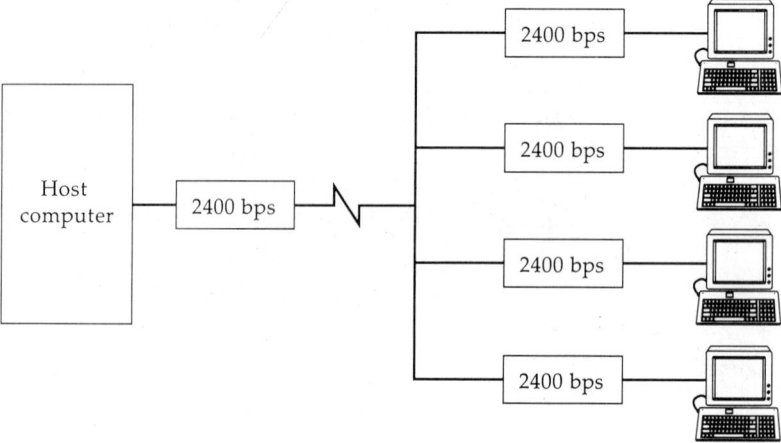

2.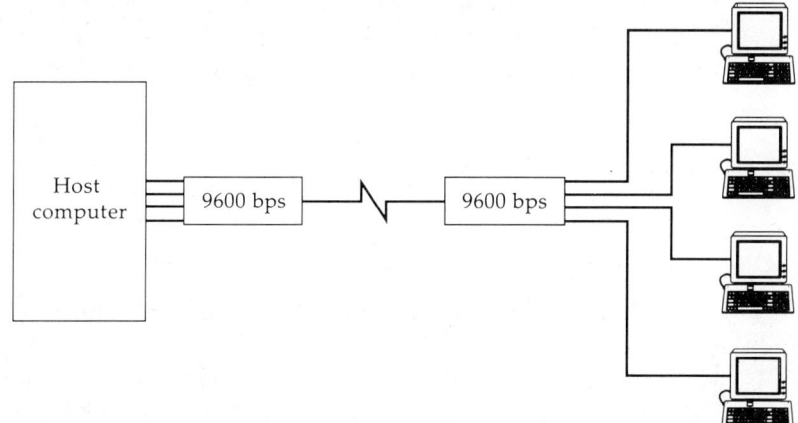

3.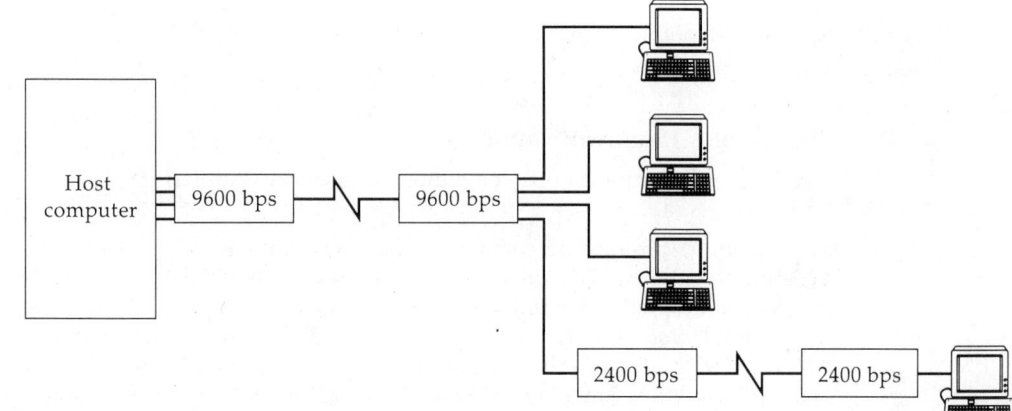

4.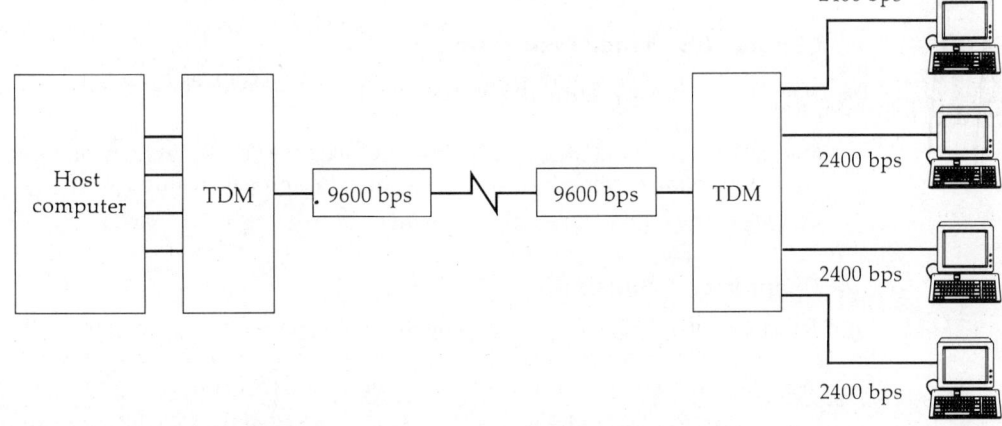

Chapter 7: Networks: Local- and Wide-Area Networks

True/False: (1) F; (2) T; (3) T; (4) T; (5) T; (6) F (the spanner is a gateway); (7) T.

Completion: (1) baseband; (2) fiber-optic cable; (3) unshielded twisted-pair wire; (4) peer-to-peer network; (5) a network interface card is installed; (6) interoperability.

Matching: (1) e; (2) g; (3) b; (4) f; (5) c; (6) a; (7) d.

Specify the level of the OSI model that deals with each of the following functions: (1) 1; (2) 3; (3) 4; (4) 2; (5) 5; (6) 6; (7) 7.

Chapter 8: Microwave and Satellite Communications

True/False: (1) F; (2) T; (3) T; (4) T; (5) F (COMSAT is a government-regulated private organization and the U.S. member of INTELSAT); (6) F (majority of the nation's teleports are facility-based; majority of the international teleports are real-estate-based).

Completion: (1) 18 GHz and 23 GHz; (2) fiber-optic network; (3) microwave radio network; (4) footprint; (5) multiplexing; (6) teleport.

Matching: (1) b; (2) f; (3) e; (4) a; (5) c; (6) d.

Chapter 9: Electronic Mail

True/False: (1) F (a third-party communications service is preferred); (2) F; (3) T; (4) T; (6) F.

Completion: (1) a computer, communications software, a modem, a telephone, and a computer with a hard disk to direct the operations of the CBMS or a computer terminal hard-wired to a mainframe computer or a minicomputer; (2) protocols; (3) Western Union's EasyLink, US Sprint's Telemail, Dialcom's Dialcom Services, AT&T's AT&T Mail, and others; (4) Digital's All-In-One, IBM's PROFS, Data General's CEO, or Wang Laboratories' Wang Office; (5) the X.400 standard; (6) an upload text feature.

Matching: (1) c; (2) b; (3) a; (4) e; (5) d; (6) f.

Chapter 10: Voice Processing

True/False: (1) T; (2) T; (3) F (converted to digital signals for storage); (4) T; (5) T; (6) T.

Completion: (1) phonemes; (2) Digital's DECtalk; (3) voice recognition; (4) desktop voice processing system; (5) broadcast feature; (6) annotate feature.

Matching: (1) c; (2) b; (3) d; (4) a; (5) e; (6) f.

Chapter 11: Facsimile

True/False: (1) T; (2) F (fax units using the analog processing method transmit at slower speeds than those using the digital processing method); (3) T; (4) F (decrease in resolution decreases the cost of fax transmission); (5) F; (6) F.

Completion: (1) Alexander Bain; (2) Study Group XIV of the CCITT; (3) electronic handshaking or the handshake protocol; (4) RS-232-C interface to a fax unit; (5) videofax; (6) a microcomputer with a fax modem board.

Answers to Chapter Self-Quizzes

Matching: (1) d; (2) c; (3) f; (4) b; (5) e; (6) a.

Chapter 12: Videotex and Teletext

True/False: (1) F; (2) F (standards for videotex deal with the sixth level of the OSI model); (3) T; (4) T; (5) T; (6) T.

Completion: (1) Ceefax; (2) a host computer, a computer, and possibly a telephone and a modem; (3) CompuServe (see Appendix D for others); (4) vertical blanking interval; (5) providing online ordering for customers (applications enable a company to communicate with its customers); (6) systems operator.

Matching: (1) c; (2) e; (3) a; (4) b; (5) d.

Chapter 13: Teleconferencing

True/False: (1) F; (2) F; (3) F; (4) F (a videoconference is point-to-point); (5) T; (6) T.

Completion: (1) asynchronous or store-and-forward; (2) "meet-me" or "meet-me-bridging"; (3) telewriter; (4) ad hoc videoconference; (5) telecommunications system; (6) an enhanced audio conference (audiographic).

Matching: (1) e; (2) b; (3) f; (4) d; (5) c; (6) a.

Chapter 14: Mobile Communications

True/False: (1) T; (2) T; (3) F (operates in simplex mode); (4) F (operates in half-duplex mode); (5) F; (6) F (can also be a reseller).

Completion: (1) eight; (2) improved mobile telephone service (IMTS); (3) two; (4) 40 MHz (20 MHz for the local wireline company and 20 MHz for the selected nonwireline company); (5) 666; (6) Title II of the Communications Act of 1934.

Matching: (1) c; (2) e; (3) b; (4) d; (5) a.

Chapter 15: Managing Your Telephone/Telecommunications System

True/False: (1) F (does not include conversation time); (2) F (considered extremely unsatisfactory); (3) T; (4) F (lease-cost routing automatically connects a call to the least expensive line that is available based on the cost of the service and the time of day); (5) T; (6) T.

Completion: (1) 15 (150 seconds $\times$ 10 calls = 1500 seconds; 1500 seconds/100 = 15 CCS); (2) 0.50 erlang (18/36 = 0.50); (3) 0.67 (20 calls $\times$ 2 minutes = 40 minutes; 40 minutes $\times$ 60 seconds = 2400 seconds; 2400/3600 = 0.67 erlang); (4) offered load; (5) carried load; (6) busy hour.

Matching: (1) b; (2) f; (3) e; (4) d; (5) a; (6) c.

Applications: (1) 15 trunks; (2) need 3 fewer trunks for a total of 12 trunks; (3) add 4 trunks; (4) 26 CCS; (5) 5 trunks; (6a) 3 trunks; (6b) 95 CCS.

GLOSSARY

Words within a definition that are capitalized are defined elsewhere in the glossary. Some of the definitions are based on the sources listed below, with permission. A letter abbreviation that corresponds to the particular source is included at the end of each of these definitions.

Datapro Research Corporation (DRC), Delran, N.J.

Engineering and Operations in the Bell System (EOBS), AT&T Bell Laboratories, Murray Hill, N.J. 1986. Copyright © 1977, 1983, Bell Telephone Laboratories, Inc.

Graham Langley, *Telephony's Dictionary, Second Ed.* (TD), Telephony, Chicago, 1986.

IEEE Standard Dictionary of Electrical and Electronics Terms, 3rd ed. (IEEE), Institute of Electrical and Electronics Engineers, New York, 1984.

- **A/B switch.** Allows a cellular telephone to operate on either of the two frequencies available in each geographical area.
- **Acoustic modem.** Converts electrical data signals to and from tones for transmission over a telephone line using a conventional telephone handset. Instead of being hard-wired directly to a dial telephone line, it has built-in rubber cups that fit a standard telephone handset; also called acoustic coupler.
- **Ad hoc videoconference.** A one-time or occasional use of videoconferencing facilities for a specific meeting or event, such as one-way video and two-way audio (BUSINESS TELEVISION), rather than on a regular basis. Also called special-event videoconferencing or TELECONFERENCING.
- **Advertiser-supported PAV services.** Public access VIDEOTEX services in which organizations pay to have their information, product, or corporate identity displayed.
- **Alternative LANs.** Include DATA SWITCH, SUBLAN, DATA PBX, MULTIUSER SYSTEM, and CENTRAL OFFICE LAN.
- **Amplitude modulation (AM).** A method of modifying the amplitude of a SINE WAVE to make it carry information.
- **Analog channel.** A TRANSMISSION path that accepts a band of frequencies and is compatible with the transmission of ANALOG SIGNALS. (EOBS)
- **Analog processing method.** Associated with FACSIMILE units that transmit at speeds ranging from two to six minutes. Scan every part of an original, such as the characters, the spaces between characters, the spaces between lines, and the margins.
- **Analog signal.** A continuously varying electromagnetic wave whose pattern varies to represent the message being transmitted. An analog signal may be contrasted with a DIGITAL SIGNAL, which represents only discrete states.

Glossary

- **ANSI X.12 standard.** ANSI standard that describes the generic standards for electronic data interchange.
- **Antenna.** In a microwave system the function of the antenna is to radiate transmit signals and capture receive signals.
- **Asynchronous conference.** A teleconference in which participants check into when they wish. Also called a STORE-AND-FORWARD conference.
- **Asynchronous transmission.** Transmission in which each information character is individually synchronized by using start and stop elements; also called start-stop transmission.
- **Attendant console.** Centralized operator position, either desktop or floor-mounted, that uses pushbutton keys for all control and call connecting functions. (DRC)
- **Attenuation.** A transmission impairment that is a decrease in signal amplitude during TRANSMISSION from one point to another, usually expressed in DECIBELS(dB). (EOBS)
- **Audio conference.** An audio-only conference in which two or more groups or three or more individuals at separate locations exchange verbal information with each other using amplified telephone speaker devices.
- **Audiotex.** See *Information Providing*.
- **Automatic call distributor.** A computerized switching system that distributes a large volume of incoming calls in sequence to available operators, referred to as operators.
- **Automatic route selection (ARS).** Automatically connects a telephone call to the least expensive line that is available on the basis of the cost of the service and the time of day. Also called least-cost routing (LCR).
- **Band.** (1) A portion of the ELECTROMAGNETIC SPECTRUM. (2) Range of frequencies between two defined limits. (3) In a WATS service the specific geographical area that the subscriber is allowed to telephone.
- **Bandwidth.** The difference, expressed in HERTZ (Hz), between the upper and lower limits or between the highest and lowest frequencies of a transmission CHANNEL or a BAND of FREQUENCIES.
- **"Barrel effect."** The listener receives a slight echo from the speaker's voice, such as that generated by a speakerphone.
- **Baseband network.** Devotes its entire BANDWIDTH to a single CHANNEL in order to carry one signal at a time.
- **Basic exchange services.** Services, which include local calling, operator assistance, and usually directory assistance, provided to a subscriber within his or her geographic area.
- **Baud.** Measures transmission speed, which is equal to the number of signal changes per second. When a signal change represents one BIT, the baud's rate is equivalent to BITS PER SECOND (bps). When a signal change represents groups of more than one bit, baud and bps are not always identical.
- **Bell operating company (BOC).** One of 22 divested operating companies in the United States, such as New Jersey Bell and Southern Bell.
- **Bell standards for modems.** Standards established by AT&T for MODEMS, such as Bell 103, Bell 212, and Bell 212A.
- **Binary.** A numbering system that uses only the digits 1 and 0. Used internally by computers and digital electronic equipment.
- **Bit.** The smallest unit of information in a binary system, represented by either 1 ("on") or 0 ("off").

- **Bits per second (bps).** A TRANSMISSION rate expressed as the number of binary digits (BITS) transmitted per second from one point to another. To measure bps by the thousand, the abbreviation kbps is often used; to measure bps by the million, Mbps is used; to measure bps by the billion, Gbps is used. A transmission rate of 2 million bits per second can be stated as 2,000,000 bps; 2000 kbps; 2 Mbps, and 0.002 Gbps.
- **Block A frequencies company.** A telephone company licensed by the FEDERAL COMMUNICATIONS COMMISSION to provide CELLULAR MOBILE TELEPHONE SERVICE in a particular market or SMSA area.
- **Blockage.** Occurs when an attempted call cannot be completed.
- **Block B frequencies company.** A private company that does not provide telephone services licensed by the FEDERAL COMMUNICATIONS COMMISSION to provide CELLULAR MOBILE TELEPHONE SERVICE in a particular market or SMSA area.
- **Blocking PBX.** A PRIVATE BRANCH EXCHANGE switch that can handle only a limited number of calls simultaneously. See also NONBLOCKING PBX.
- **Bridge.** A device that operates at layer 2 of the OSI MODEL. Can connect two LANS of the same topology, such as token ring to token ring or ETHERNET to ETHERNET, and operates at layer 2 of the OSI MODEL. *Local bridges* link LANS within the same building, while *remote bridges* connect remote LANS into WANS.
- **Broadband network.** Divides its BANDWIDTH into subchannels so that multiple applications including voice, data, and video can be sent simultaneously.
- **Broadband or full-channel teletext.** Uses the entire active portion of the video signal to transmit TELETEXT signals. Contrasted with NARROWBAND teletext.
- **Broadcast.** A feature in a VOICE PROCESSING system that allows a subscriber to automatically send the same voice message to multiple mailboxes with one command.
- **Broadcast teletext.** The transmission of TELETEXT signals via a radio frequency transmission or broadcast.
- **Buffer.** A storage area added to a host computer and/or terminal to compensate for the differences in transmitting rates.
- **Business television.** Transmits live television one way from a central site to one or more other sites. These systems are usually complemented by two-way audio transmission to allow viewers to enter into a discussion with the speakers.
- **Business-to-business videotex.** VIDEOTEX that enables a company to communicate with other companies, such as its customers.
- **Bus topology.** Connects all NODES to one cable running the length of the network.
- **Busy hour.** The hour when the largest volume of communications TRAFFIC, such as telephone calls, is handled during the day.
- **Bypass.** An arrangement of circuits that establishes communications directly between two organizations without using the switching facilities of the local telephone company.
- **Byte.** A group of 8 bits makes a byte, the smallest addressable unit of information in computer memory.
- **Cabletext.** The transmission of TELETEXT signals by cable television network.
- **Call accounting.** A telephone management system feature that collects and analyzes call records from the telephone system, allocates monthly call costs, and generates reports.
- **Call Block.** A CLASS CALLING SERVICE that allows the subscriber to block certain telephone numbers from calling his or her telephone number.
- **Caller routing.** In a VOICE PROCESSING system this function manages the system by

answering calls and allowing callers to route themselves to the desired extension by keying the appropriate button on a touch-tone telephone. Also called automated attendant.

- **Call Forwarding.** A CUSTOM CALLING SERVICE in which a call can be rerouted from one line to another by dialing a special code sequence.
- **Call Trace.** A CLASS CALLING SERVICE that allows the subscriber to initiate a trace of the number of the last call received.
- **Call Waiting.** A CUSTOM CALLING SERVICE in which a subscriber engaged in a telephone conversation receives a beep indicating that another party is trying to reach the subscriber.
- **Carried load.** Measures how many people were successful in carrying on a telephone call. Carried load = OFFERED LOAD − BLOCKAGE.
- **Carrier Sense Multiple Access with Collision Detection (CSMA/CD).** A contention method for accessing a LAN that is used with BUS TOPOLOGIES.
- **Carrier system.** A transmission system in which one or more CHANNELS of information are processed and converted to a form suitable for the transmission medium used by the system. Common types of carrier systems are FREQUENCY-DIVISION, in which each information channel occupies an assigned portion of the frequency spectrum, and TIME-DIVISION, in which each information channel uses the transmission medium for periodic, assigned time intervals. (EOBS).
- **Carterfone Decision.** Landmark 1968 FCC decision that permitted interconnection of customer-owned devices to interconnect with the telephone network. The decision also launched the INTERCONNECT INDUSTRY by permitting subscribers to rent, buy, or lease equipment from companies other than the Bell System.
- **C-band.** Frequency band used for uplinks to satellites (6 GHz) and downlinks from satellites (4 GHz).
- **CCITT.** Consultative Committee on the International Telephone and Telegraph, an international body that sets universal standards for INTEGRATED SERVICES DIGITAL NETWORKS. Its members are worldwide telephone companies, with input from national and international standards bodies.
- **CCITT Fax Groups 1, 2, 3, 4.** Defines the classifications of FASCIMILE transmissions. Groups 1 and 2 are analog devices; Groups 3 and 4 are digital devices.
- **CCITT X.400 standard.** CCITT standard that defines the basic structure of an electronic mail message.
- **CCITT X.500 standard.** CCITT standard that defines how electronic directories of users should be developed.
- **Cellular cell.** The geographical area designated for a CELLULAR MOBILE TELEPHONE SERVICE is divided into cells, each ranging from 2 to 20 miles in diameter.
- **Cellular mobile telephone service.** Provides common carrier switched mobile radiotelephone service interconnecting with the PUBLIC SWITCHED TELEPHONE NETWORK. The FEDERAL COMMUNICATIONS COMMISSION's licensing plan includes two cellular carriers in each market or SMSA area.
- **Cellular service provider.** Responsible for activating a user's cellular telephone number, installing the telephone, handling charges, and providing service.
- **Central office.** Usually refers to a SWITCHING SYSTEM that connects lines to lines and lines to trunks. The term sometimes refers to a telephone company building that contains switching equipment.
- **Central office LAN (CO LAN).** Operates by the local telephone company's CENTRAL OFFICE connecting a company's computers to its switching equipment by twisted-pair wire.

Glossary

- **Centrex service (CENTRAL EXCHANGE).** A CENTRAL OFFICE–based business telephone system with switching equipment located at a telephone company's central office. Although the central office controls the switching functions for the subscriber's telephone system, the system offers PBX-type features, including DIRECT INWARD DIALING.
- **Channel.** A TRANSMISSION path between two points. Usually the smallest subdivision of a CIRCUIT, such as a voice channel or a data channel.
- **Circuit.** A TRANSMISSION path between two or more points. Also called a LINK or CHANNEL.
- **Circuit-switched network.** A communications path is established between the sender and the receiver and held for the duration of the transmission.
- **Citizens Band (CB) radio.** A system of two-way radio communications for short distances available for public use. The 27 MHz band is most commonly used for CB in most countries.
- **Class Calling Services.** Services offered in addition to BASIC EXCHANGE SERVICES and CUSTOM CALLING SERVICES by some BOC's CENTRAL OFFICES. Examples include SPECIAL RING, CALL BLOCK, SELECTED CALL FORWARDING, RETURN CALL, REPEAT CALL, and CALL TRACE.
- **Class of service.** Classifies telephone users according to specific type of telephone use, such as access to SPEED CALLING or automatic Call Back.
- **Coaxial cable.** A type of GUIDED MEDIUM made up of tubes, each cable containing from 4 to 22 coaxial tubes.
- **Codec (coder-DECoder).** (1) A device that converts ANALOG SIGNALS, such as voice or video, into digital form and then compresses the digital data for transmission over a DIGITAL CIRCUIT. At the receiving end, another codec decodes the signals into their original analog form. (2) a TRANSDUCER that transforms ANALOG SIGNALS to DIGITAL SIGNALS at the sending end and returns them to their original form at the receiving end.
- **Common carrier.** An organization that provides telecommunications facilities to the public. In the United States, common carriers are regulated by the FEDERAL COMMUNICATIONS COMMISSION if interstate and by the state public service or PUBLIC UTILITIES COMMISSION if intrastate.
- **Communications Act of 1934.** Established the U.S. FEDERAL COMMUNICATIONS COMMISSION (FCC) for regulating national and international communications.
- **Communications Satellite Corporation (COMSAT).** A government-regulated private organization, the U.S. member of INTELSAT.
- **Compressed digital video.** To reduce the BANDWIDTH required for transmission over a DIGITAL CIRCUIT, videoconferencing signals in digital form are compressed to a fraction of their original state by eliminating redundant information and are then transmitted.
- **Computer-based message system (CBMS).** A form of ELECTRONIC MAIL that allows computers and/or TERMINALS to communicate with each other for the purpose of sending and receiving text and data messages—short messages, memos, and other documents. Commonly referred to as ELECTRONIC MAIL or *E-mail*. The two types are IN-HOUSE CBMS and PUBLIC ELECTRONIC MAIL.
- **Computer conference—in-house system.** The participant's TERMINAL is connected directly or over telecommunication lines to a host computer.
- **Computer conference—time-sharing system.** Participants access a commercial service, such as CompuServe's Participate, by using a telephone call, a microcomputer, a MODEM, and communications software.

- **Computer conferencing.** Allows participants to exchange messages with each other by using computer keyboards. May be *synchronous*, that is, interactive in real time, or *asynchronous*, that is, messages are stored in a central computer until retrieved by their intended recipients.
- **Conference bridge.** An electronic device for interconnecting three or more circuits, such as telephone lines.
- **Connectivity.** The ability to tie devices together physically, such as linking microcomputers and interconnecting heterogeneous hardware systems and components to pass data.
- **Contention.** Method of line control in which the terminals request to transmit. If the CHANNEL in question is free, transmission proceeds; if it is not free, the TERMINAL has to wait until it becomes free. (DRC)
- **Contention-oriented methods.** LAN access methods that anticipate conflicts or collisions and use them to allocate the common channel. A popular method is CARRIER SENSE MULTIPLE ACCESS WITH COLLISION DETECTION (CSMA/CD).
- **Continuous presence video.** Two or more images in a videoconference are displayed at the same time, appearing either on one monitor using a split screen format or on two or more different monitors.
- **Conventional mobile telephone service.** Operates like the regular telephone service by interconnecting with the PUBLIC SWITCHED TELEPHONE NETWORK. Uses a transmitter/receiver and an ANTENNA to service an entire metropolitan area. Also called improved mobile telephone service (IMTS). Is being replaced by CELLULAR MOBILE TELEPHONE SERVICE.
- **Conversation time.** The time from the start to the finish of a (voice) conversation or a data transmission.
- **Corporate videotex.** Refers to in-house VIDEOTEX that enables a company to communicate internally with its employees.
- **Crossover data switch.** A switch that allows two computers to share two PERIPHERALS, such as a printer and a MODEM.
- **Crosstalk.** A transmission impairment that is an interference in a communications CHANNEL resulting from a signal traveling in an adjacent CHANNEL. Telephone crosstalk may be intelligible or unintelligible to the parties engaged in conversation. (EOBS)
- **Custom Calling Services.** Services offered in addition to BASIC EXCHANGE SERVICES. Included are CALL WAITING, CALL FORWARDING, THREE-WAY CALLING, and SPEED CALLING.
- **Data communications equipment.** Includes any device, such as a MODEM, attached to the transmission or communications lines that manipulates the transmitted signal or data.
- **Data compression.** Basic data compression increases throughput by as much as a factor of 2. Advanced data compression increases throughput by a factor of 3.
- **Data PBX.** A switch that handles data traffic and that can perform LAN functions, such as connecting devices so that they can communicate. Uses CIRCUIT SWITCHING, while a LAN uses PACKET SWITCHING.
- **Data service unit (DSU).** A device required to connect a terminal or computer to a digital communication line. Since it does not convert DIGITAL SIGNALS to ANALOG SIGNALS for transmission, it is not classified as a MODEM.
- **Data switch.** A switch that allows as many as 20 microcomputers to share a PERIPHERAL.

Glossary

- **Data terminal equipment (DTE).** Includes any digital device, such as TERMINALS, printers, or computers that transmit data.
- **Decibel (dB).** Measures the loss or gain of signal strength between two TRANSMISSION points by expressing the difference between power input and power output in the form of a ratio.
- **Decoder.** A device that translates and assembles the digital television/video signal into a video display.
- **Dedicated access line.** A CIRCUIT assigned to a subscriber for exclusive use between the subscriber's telephone equipment and the CENTRAL OFFICE.
- **Dedicated network server.** A computer designed exclusively to serve the LAN.
- **De facto standard.** A standard, generally developed by a company, that is used where an official standard has not been fully defined or widely implemented.
- **Delay dialing.** Allows the FASCIMILE unit to send documents at a later time when telephone rates are lowest or to overcome time zone problems.
- **Delay distortion.** A TRANSMISSION impairment that results in unequal signal delays at different frequencies.
- **Demodulation.** The process of restoring a signal to its original form at the receiving end of the TRANSMISSION system. (EOBS)
- **Dial tone.** An audible tone sent from an automatic SWITCHING SYSTEM to a customer to indicate that the equipment is ready to receive dial signals. (EOBS)
- **Dial-tone multifrequency (DTMF).** A means of signaling that uses a simultaneous combination of two frequencies to represent each digit or character.
- **Digital channel.** A TRANSMISSION CHANNEL that carries signals in digital form. (EOBS)
- **Digital processing method.** Associated with FACSIMILE units that transmit at speeds under one minute. Analyzes a document in terms of its actual picture elements and converts them into BINARY codes of 1's (black) and 0's (white).
- **Digital signal.** A series of discrete, discontinuous voltage pulses—a stream of on-off pulses. A digital signal may be contrasted with an ANALOG SIGNAL.
- **Digitized speech.** Refers to human speech recorded and digitized onto a computer disk for storage and then reconverted to human speech for playback. Also referred to as "digital recording."
- **Direct broadcast satellite teletext.** The transmission of TELETEXT signals via satellite.
- **Direct-connect modem.** Modem that is physically wired to the telephone line.
- **Direct distance dialing (DDD).** (1) The automatic establishment of toll calls in response to signals from the dialing device of the originating customer. (EOBS) (2) A telephone exchange service that enables users to dial long distance without operator assistance. (DRC)
- **Direct inward dialing (DID).** A feature that permits incoming calls to stations served by a PRIVATE BRANCH EXCHANGE or a CENTREX SYSTEM to be dialed directly and thus bypassing the system's attendant.
- **Divestiture.** The breakup of AT&T in 1984. See also MODIFIED FINAL JUDGMENT.
- **Downline loading.** Refers to the host or sending computer transferring computer programs, computer-based instruction programs, videogames, and data to another computer, which allows it to operate in an off-line mode.
- **Downward capability.** Allows a high-speed FASCIMILE unit to communicate with low-speed units.
- **Dynamic nonhierarchical routing (DNHR).** Computer-controlled routing of long-

distance telephone calls dependent on actual traffic flow at the time; i.e., calls are not automatically passed right up the hierarchic structure to a Class 1 office for routing on a final choice circuit if high usage circuits are busy. The availability of relatively inexpensive digital switching centers enables through-circuits to be established on routes passing through several such centers in tandem without degrading the transmission quality of the overall circuit. (TD)

- **Earth station.** The physical equipment used to transmit to a satellite (referred to as the UPLINK) and/or receive from a satellite (called the DOWNLINK).
- **Echo.** A TRANSMISSION impairment causing the reflection of signals back to their source.
- **EDI service provider.** A third-party that handles the transmission of ELECTRONIC DATA INTERCHANGE for the sending and receiving organizations.
- **Effective isotropic radiated power (EIRP).** A measure, expressed in DECIBELS, of the power levels reaching the earth that is included on FOOTPRINT maps.
- **Electromagnetic spectrum.** Includes the entire range of available signal frequencies.
- **Electronic blackboard.** Images drawn or written on a transmitting board are immediately translated into signals, transmitted through the telephone network, and displayed on video monitor(s) exactly as written at the receiving end.
- **Electronic data interchange (EDI).** A computer-to-computer exchange of intercompany and intracompany business documents in a public standard format. (McDonnell Douglas Corporation)
- **Electronic key telephone system (EKS).** Uses microprocessors and integrated circuit chips. Includes pushbuttons to access electronically CALL FORWARDING, CALL TRANSFER, and SPEED CALLING.
- **Electronic mail.** The generic name for "the noninteractive communication of text, data, images, or voice messages between a sender and designated recipient(s) by systems utilizing telecommunication links." Includes all types of noninteractive communication, such as COMPUTER-BASED MESSAGE SYSTEMS, VOICE MAIL, and FACSIMILE.
- **Electronic switching system.** Connects communication paths. Includes the SWITCHING network that contains individual switching devices to connect the communications paths and the control mechanism that directs the operation of the switching devices.
- **End office.** A local office where all call originate and terminate in the HIERARCHY OF SWITCHING CENTERS. Also called the CENTRAL OFFICE or the class 5 office.
- **Enhanced audio conferencing.** Supplements audio-only systems by allowing participants at two or more sites to create graphics, snap photographs, or assemble documents and transmit them in real time. Also called an audiographic system.
- **Equal access.** The Department of Justice ruling (9/86) requires OTHER COMMON CARRIERS besides AT&T be offered the same quality of connection at the same rates. Enables customers to choose the long-distance network for routing their calls.
- **Erlang.** Measures TRAFFIC LOAD in hours per BUSY HOUR. Named for A. K. Erlang.
- **Ethernet.** A LOCAL AREA NETWORK communication system developed by Xerox, Digital Equipment Corporation, and Intel Corporation.
- **Facility-based teleport.** A TELEPORT whose users are not physically located at the teleport site.
- **Facsimile (fax).** The sending and/or receiving of an exact replica—a facsimile—of the original document from one location to another by using communication lines. The term "fax" can be used as a noun, an adjective, or a verb.

- **Fax copier.** Equipment that functions as either a FACSIMILE unit or a copier.
- **Faxphone.** A compact desktop unit that combines a FACSIMILE unit and telephone into one unit.
- **Federal Communications Commission (FCC).** A board of commissioners, appointed by the President of the United States under the COMMUNICATIONS ACT OF 1934, that is charged with regulating interstate and foreign communications originating in the United States by wire and radio.
- **Fiber-optic cable.** Also called lightguide cable, a type of GUIDED MEDIUM that replaces electricity with light and copper wires with hair-thin strands of glass.
- **Flat-rate service.** A fixed payment for service for local calling that is independent of use.
- **Footprint.** The area of the earth's surface to which a satellite can transmit. Some parts of the footprint need more powerful or larger EARTH STATION facilities to achieve satisfactory signal strength.
- **Foreign exchange (FX) service.** Connects a subscriber's location to a remote CENTRAL OFFICE, which provides the equivalent of local service from the long-distance exchange.
- **Free space path loss.** The weakening of power as a signal travels from the satellite's downlink ANTENNA to earth.
- **Freeze-frame video.** A device that transmit and/or receives still video images over telephone lines. Also called still frame or slow-scan video.
- **Frequency.** Rate at which a current alternates, measured in HERTZ kilohertz, etc.
- **Frequency-division multiple access.** A FREQUENCY-DIVISION MULTIPLEXING method used in SATELLITE COMMUNICATIONS transmission.
- **Frequency-division multiplexing (FDM).** A MULTIPLEXING system that divides the available transmission frequency band into narrower bands, each used as a separate CHANNEL. Some of the BANDWIDTH must be reserved for GUARDBANDS between the channels.
- **Frequency modulation (FM).** A method of modifying the frequency of a SINE WAVE to make it carry information.
- **Frequency-shift keying method (FSK).** A MODULATION method used to change DIGITAL SIGNALS to correspond with ANALOG SIGNAL characteristics for transmission over an ANALOG CIRCUIT.
- **Fresnel zones.** A series of concentric ellipsoid surfaces that surround the LINE-OF-SIGHT path between the two ANTENNAS. Expresses the amount of clearance required for obstacles in a MICROWAVE system.
- **Front-end processor (FEP).** A dedicated computer or system of computers that has the task of controlling and scheduling message traffic to and from multiple communication lines and terminals.
- **Full-duplex transmission.** Signals can be transmitted in both directions simultaneously.
- **Gateway.** A device designed to interface two dissimilar networks by translating the PROTOCOLS of one network to those of another network like a language interpreter.
- **Grade of service.** An index that represents the probability that a call will be BLOCKED or delayed during the busiest hour of the day.
- **Guardbands.** A reserved portion of a BANDWIDTH that separates each CHANNEL or pair of FREQUENCIES.
- **Guided medium.** A TRANSMISSION medium, such as OPEN WIRE, twisted-pair wire (PAIRED-WIRE CABLE), COAXIAL CABLE, and FIBER-OPTIC CABLE, that physically constrains and guides signals.

- **Half-duplex transmission.** Allows signals to be sent in both directions but in only one direction at a time.
- **Handshake protocol.** Describes the exchange of predetermined signals between two communicating devices. Allows one device to determine whether another is ready to receive or transmit data.
- **Hands off.** As a cellular telephone user travels from one CELLULAR CELL to an adjacent one, the call is automatically transferred to the new cell site and a new radio channel without noticeable interruption.
- **Hayes compatibility for modems.** A type of compatibility common to MODEMS. Includes the Hayes command structure, a DE FACTO STANDARD.
- **Hertz (Hz).** Unit of FREQUENCY: one cycle per second.
- **Hierarchical network.** Designated NODES control access to the LAN, all data transfer taking place through the "control" nodes.
- **Hierarchy of switching centers.** The AT&T switching hierarchy for making long-distance calls. Consists of five levels: regional centers, sectional center, primary centers, toll centers, and class 5 offices.
- **Holding time.** The length of time from the moment a facility is seized for use until the time it is released, including both CONVERSATION TIME and OPERATING TIME.
- **Hundred call seconds (CCS).** (1) A unit of traffic used to express the average number of calls in progress or the average number of devices in use. Measures TRAFFIC LOAD in hundred seconds per BUSY HOUR. (2) Numerically, it is 36 times the traffic expressed in ERLANGS.
- **Hybrid facsimile equipment.** Combines the FACSIMILE function with other office technologies, such as a facsimile copier.
- **Hybrid key telephone system (HKTS).** Combines the low cost and easy-to-use features of the KEY TELEPHONE SYSTEM with the cost-maintenance and advanced system features commonly associated with PRIVATE BRANCH EXCHANGES.
- **IEEE 800 Standards.** LAN standards produced by the Institute of Electrical and Electronics Engineers that deal with the first and second layers of the OSI MODEL.
- **Impulse noise.** A type of noise that causes voice TRANSMISSION to be corrupted by short clicks or crackles but without the loss of intelligibility.
- **Information providers.** Provide information for VIDEOTEX and TELETEXT systems.
- **Information providing.** In a VOICE PROCESSING system this function is a voice bulletin board that gives a caller access to prerecorded information in a "listen-only" mode. Also called audiotex.
- **In-house CBMS.** A type of COMPUTER-BASED MESSAGE SYSTEM that a company operates on its premises for its own benefit.
- **Integrated facsimile equipment.** By adding a RS-232-C INTERFACE to a FACSIMILE unit, the facsimile can become compatible with other office equipment.
- **Integrated services digital network (ISDN).** An end-to-end digital network that moves voice, data, telemetry, slow-motion video, signaling, and FACSIMILE separately or simultaneously over the same pair of copper wires or FIBER-OPTIC CABLE in the PUBLIC SWITCHED TELEPHONE NETWORK.
- **Integrated voice processing system.** A VOICE PROCESSING system integrated with a PRIVATE BRANCH EXCHANGE or a CENTREX system by using a special communications link between the two systems to allow each to give commands to each other.
- **Interactive messaging.** See VOICE MAIL.
- **Interconnect industry.** Nontelephone company manufacturers and distributors who supply telephone equipment by sale, rental, or leasing directly to customers.

Glossary

- **Interexchange carrier.** AT&T and OTHER COMMON CARRIERS that handle calls between LATAS.
- **Interface.** A common boundary between two systems or pieces of equipment where they are joined. (EOBS)
- **InterLATA call.** Long-distance calls between LATAS, within a state or across state lines, that are handled by an INTEREXCHANGE CARRIER, such as AT&T or one of the OTHER COMMON CARRIERS.
- **International number.** The number to be dialed that follows the international prefix. Includes the country code and the national number of the party being called.
- **International Numbering Plan.** A plan developed by CCITT that consists of a combination of digits to be dialed to obtain access to the international network.
- **International Telecommunications Satellite Organization (INTELSAT).** An international satellite organization that owns and operates commercial communication satellite systems that are used by countries worldwide for international communications and domestic communications.
- **Interoperability.** Goes beyond connectivity by allowing users from diverse environments to correctly interpret and respond to the data received.
- **Intraexchange carrier.** BELL OPERATING COMPANIES that handle INTRALATA CALLS.
- **IntraLATA calls.** Local calls within a LATA or toll calls that originate and terminate within the LATA and are handled by INTRAEXCHANGE CARRIERS, the BELL OPERATING COMPANIES.
- **In-WATS.** Allows calls to be placed to a location from anywhere in the continental United States at no cost to the calling party. Also referred to as an 800-number service. See also WATS and OUT-WATS.
- **Ka-band.** MICROWAVE frequencies approximately in the 12 GHz to 30 GHz range.
- **kpbs (kilobits per second).** A rate of data TRANSMISSION equal to 1000 bps (BITS PER SECOND).
- **Key telephone system (KTS).** An arrangement of key telephone sets and associated circuitry, located on a subscriber's premises, with the capability of performing other desired functions, such as call hold and call pickup, and interconnecting with on-premise stations without connecting through the CENTRAL OFFICE or a PRIVATE BRANCH EXCHANGE.
- **Kiosks.** Electronic displays for public access that are placed in high-traffic, consumer-oriented locations such as airports, shopping malls, and hotel and office building lobbies. Also called electronic terminals.
- **Ku-band.** MICROWAVE frequencies approximately in the 10 GHz to 12 GHz range.
- **Land mobile communication service.** Radio communication service to and from mobile stations. Includes paging systems, two-way radios, cellular telephone services, and CITIZENS BAND RADIO.
- **Line conditioning.** To bring to standard, such as bringing ATTENUATION, impedance, and delay characteristics to within set limits.
- **Line-of-sight.** An open-air TRANSMISSION path, between the sending and the receiving locations that is required in a MICROWAVE system.
- **Link.** A communication path between two NODES.
- **Local access and transport area (LATA).** A geographic area within which a BELL OPERATING COMPANY is responsible for handling local customers' calls as well as any toll calls that both originate and terminate within this area.
- **Local-area network (LAN).** A privately owned network that offers reliable high-speed communication CHANNELS for connecting information processing equipment, such as microcomputers, in a limited geographical area.

- **Local loop.** The path between the subscriber's equipment and the equipment in the serving CENTRAL OFFICE. A loop may also be called a line.
- **Logical topology.** Describes how signals flow between NODES and how they interact on a LAN.
- **Long-haul microwave system.** A MICROWAVE system that uses frequencies between 1 GHz and 12 GHz and can travel a distance of 30 miles.
- **Mbps (Megabits per second).** A rate of data TRANSMISSION equal to 1 million bps (BITS PER SECOND).
- **Measured rate service.** A telephone service for which charges are made for local calling based on the number and length of the calls.
- **Meet-me bridge.** A CONFERENCE BRIDGE that can be accessed directly by the participants calling a predetermined telephone number.
- **Metropolitan Area Network (MAN).** A type of WIDE-AREA NETWORK that links together LANs at different sites within a city.
- **Microwave.** (1) Usually refers to radio frequency wavelengths between 1 GHz and 30 GHz. (2) A form of radio TRANSMISSION that consists of a narrow beam that can be separated in space by FREQUENCY-DIVISION MULTIPLEXING to form several channels.
- **Microwave communications.** Includes radio signals used by terrestrial MICROWAVE systems and by EARTH STATIONS via satellite, although the term is often used to refer only to terrestrial microwave radio systems.
- **Modem (MODulator-DEModulator).** (1) A TRANSDUCER that transforms DIGITAL SIGNALS into ANALOG SIGNALS at the sending end and returns them to their original form at the receiving end. (2) an electronic device that converts computer or terminal electrical DIGITAL SIGNALS to ANALOG SIGNALS so that data can be transmitted over an ANALOG CIRCUIT.
- **Modified Final Judgment (MFJ).** Terminated a 1974 Department of Justice antitrust suit against AT&T and ordered the breakup (DIVESTITURE) of AT&T Bell Telephone System, with January 1984 set as the target date for its completion.
- **Modified Huffmann (MH).** The data compression code standard for CCITT Group 3 FACSIMILE units. As an option, the manufacturer may use *Modified Read (MR)*, a data compression code that transmits at a faster rate than MH for Group 3 FACSIMILE units or their own code, a *Proprietary Code*, that transmits at even a faster rate.
- **Modulation.** The process by which an electrical signal is converted from one form to another more appropriate form for TRANSMISSION over a CIRCUIT between two locations.
- **Multiplexing.** A method of providing a transmission CIRCUIT with the capability of handing several separate, individual signals simultaneously. Methods include FREQUENCY-DIVISION MULTIPLEXING, TIME-DIVISION MULTIPLEXING, and STATISTICAL MULTIPLEXING.
- **Multipoint network.** Consists of two or more TERMINALS sharing the same communications link, which is normally a private or leased line.
- **Multiuser system.** A mainframe computer that interfaces with attached dumb TERMINALS, sometimes with intelligent terminals and microcomputers.
- **Narrowband.** Uses part of the VERTICAL BLANKING INTERVAL (VBI) to transmit TELETEXT signals. Contrasted with BROADBAND or FULL-CHANNEL TELETEXT.
- **Narrowband modems.** Operates over the lowest end (300 bps) of the voice-grade CHANNEL. Used with slow-speed TERMINALS, such as teletype terminals.
- **Network.** (1) A system of interconnected elements represented by NODES (switches)

Glossary

and by LINKS that interconnect the nodes. (2) A communications system that allows attached devices, such as computers, to communicate with one another.

- **Network interface card.** A circuit board that plugs into an expansion slot of a microcomputer to make the physical connection between the WORKSTATION and the network cable of a LAN. Serves a major component of a LAN.
- **Network server.** A special-purpose computer whose main function is to serve the needs of the WORKSTATION users on a LAN.
- **911 Emergency Service.** Allows direct access to a variety of emergency agencies, such as police, fire, or emergency medical services.
- **Node.** An intelligent device, such as a WORKSTATION, a DEDICATED NETWORK SERVER, or an interconnecting equipment facility, that is attached to a network.
- **Noise.** Any unwanted signal in a TRANSMISSION path.
- **Nonblocking PBX.** A PRIVATE BRANCH EXCHANGE switch that can handle simultaneously conversations among all users by having enough pathways to carry all the TRAFFIC. See also BLOCKING PBX.
- **Noncontention-oriented method.** LAN access methods that determine the order in which NODES can take turns accessing the NETWORK so that message-sending nodes do not collide with each other and thus do not require retransmission. Two common methods are roll-call POLLING and TOKEN PASSING.
- **Nondedicated network server.** A microcomputer that functions as both a NETWORK SERVER and a WORKSTATION on a LAN.
- **Nonimpact printer.** A form of ELECTRONIC MAIL that can accept digital input from computers and other nonimpact printers at local and remote sites and can act as communication terminal to transmit text, data, and graphics from one site to another at high speeds.
- **Number Identification.** Allows the number calling the subscriber's telephone to be displayed on the subscriber's telephone screen to view before answering the telephone.
- **Numbering Plan Area (NPA).** The familiar area code that defines a geographic division within which telephone directory numbers are subgrouped.
- **Offered load.** Measures the demand that is placed on a telephone system, such as telling how many people were trying to place a telephone call. Offered load = CARRIED LOAD + BLOCKAGE.
- **Off-hook.** The condition existing when the receiver or handset is removed from its switch, indicating the in-use or request-service state.
- **1A2 KTS.** The standard KEY TELEPHONE SYSTEM in the electromechanical key telephone industry, commonly known as "the one with the six built-in buttons."
- **On-hook.** The condition existing when the receiver or handset is resting on the switch, indicating the equipment-idle state.
- **Open Systems Interconnection (OSI) reference model.** The purpose of the OSI model is to allow computers worldwide to exchange data with each other, independent of manufacturer or implementation of technology. Divides the total data communications tasks into seven separate functions or layers, each layer having its own PROTOCOLS and STANDARDS.
- **Open-wire lines.** A type of GUIDED MEDIUM in which copper, copper-clad steel, or galvanized steel wires are strung between telephone poles.
- **Operating time.** The time necessary to establish and release a connection with the called party.
- **Operator-specific PAV services.** PUBLIC ACCESS VIDEOTEX services that are

designed, operated, and funded by single organizations, in which organizations pay to have their information, product, or corporate identity displayed. Examples are providing employee announcements and demonstrating a product.

- **Other common carrier (OCC).** A long-distance carrier other than AT&T that is licensed by the FEDERAL COMMUNICATIONS COMMISSION to provide long-distance services.
- **Out-WATS.** Allows a subscriber to make an unlimited number of calls within a given area from a particular telephone station without registering individual call charges. A single access line permits inward or outward services but not both. See also WATS and IN-WATS.
- **Packet.** A group of BITS that is switched as an integral unit. Typically, a packet contains data, destination, origination information, and control information arranged in a particular format. (EOBS)
- **Packet-switched network.** A NETWORK that is designed to transport and switch data in PACKET form.
- **Packet switching.** (1) Describes a system whereby messages are broken down into smaller units called PACKETS, which are then individually addressed and routed through the NETWORK. (2) The process of routing and transferring data by means of addressed packets so that a CHANNEL is occupied only during the transmission of the packet. On completion of the transmission the channel becomes available for the transfer of other TRAFFIC.
- **Paired-wire cable.** A type of two-wire or four-wire GUIDED MEDIUM. Also referred to as twisted-pair wire.
- **Peer-to-peer network.** Allows every NODE to have equal access to the LAN.
- **Peg count.** Refers to the number of calls actually handled during a specified time interval, such as one hour.
- **Peripheral equipment.** Equipment that works in conjunction with a communications system or a computer system but is not part of it.
- **Phonemes.** Basic units of sound that make up words, such as vowels, consonants, and diphthongs.
- **Physical topology.** Determines the way cables run and the way the NODES are physically connected to each other on a LAN.
- **Pixel.** The smallest element of a computer display surface that can be independently assigned color or intensity (picture element).
- **Point-to-multipoint videoconferencing.** A videoconference in which all sites receive images but only one site can transmit them. The audio component is bidirectional. Commonly referred to as BUSINESS TELEVISION.
- **Point-to-point network.** Two TERMINALS or NODES connected by a single communication link.
- **Point-to-point videoconferencing.** A TWO-WAY VIDEOCONFERENCE, each site transmitting and receiving audio and video.
- **Polling.** (1) An equipment feature that allows the FACSIMILE unit to call a remote FACSIMILE unit to request TRANSMISSION from it. (2) Means of controlling communications lines. When many stations are connected to the same circuit, polling from the center is used to ensure an orderly flow of data to the central location. An alternative is CONTENTION, which makes sure that no terminal is kept waiting for a long time. (DRC)
- **Port.** (1) Point of access into a communications switch, a NETWORK, or other electronic device. (2) Physical or electrical interface through which one gains access. (3) INTERFACE between a process and a communications or TRANSMISSION facility. (DRC)

Glossary

- **Primary Center.** A class 3 office in the HIERARCHY OF SWITCHING CENTERS.
- **Private Branch Exchange (PBX).** A telephone communications system serving a specific location as an office or a building. Includes a switch, a specialized minicomputer performing telephone switching within an organization's private network. Provides for switching calls internally and to and from the PUBLIC SWITCHED TELEPHONE NETWORK.
- **Private business television.** A BUSINESS TELEVISION network installed, operated, and maintained by a company for its own use.
- **Propagation.** (1) The traveling of electrical waves along a TRANSMISSION medium. (2) The movement of MICROWAVES from their source.
- **Protocol.** A set of agreed-on rules and conventions governing the formats and procedures used in communications.
- **Public access videotex (PAV).** VIDEOTEX used in public locations by the general public. See also KIOSKS.
- **Public business television.** BUSINESS TELEVISION network facilities to be used by the public for a fee.
- **Public Electronic Mail Service.** A type of COMPUTER-BASED MESSAGE system that allows users to share the use of a third party's off-site computer to obtain specific data or perform text processing operations without investing in the installation of a similar type of computer.
- **Public facsimile services.** Services offered by both private companies and government organizations. Also called public fax operators and public access services.
- **Public switched telephone network (PSTN).** Refers to the ordinary dialup telephone system, which consists of the local network and the long-distance network. Also called the public switched network, the public telephone network, and the direct distance dialing (DDD) network.
- **Public utility.** A legal monopoly consisting of a privately owned company that provides an essential public service and is subject to government regulation.
- **Public utilities commission (PUC).** An agency charged with regulating communications services and other PUBLIC UTILITY services within a state.
- **Pulse-amplitude modulation (PAM).** A modulation technique in which the amplitude of each pulse is related to the amplitude of an ANALOG SIGNAL. (EOBS)
- **Pulse-code modulation (PCM).** Conversion of an ANALOG SIGNAL, such as voice, to a digital format, usually in terms of BINARY-coded pulses representing the quantized amplitude samples of the ANALOG SIGNAL. (EOBS)
- **Pulse rate.** The number of pulses transmitted per unit of time. May also be called the BAUD rate. When the pulses or symbols have only two possible values (BINARY), the pulse rate is also called the BIT rate. (EOBS)
- **Rack-mount modem.** Can hold a number of MODEM cards; tailored for central computers and LANS.
- **Radio paging service.** Service that transmits a signal, such as a beep or a continuous tone, via radio from any telephone in the PUBLIC SWITCHED TELEPHONE NETWORK to a small, portable radio receiver. Some pagers offer VOICE MESSAGING or visual displays.
- **Real-estate-based teleport.** A TELEPORT located in an office park that offers shared TELECOMMUNICATIONS services to tenants located at the teleport office park as well as to others.
- **Regional Bell operating companies (RBOC).** One of seven holding companies formed by the DIVESTITURE of AT&T to provide both regulated and nonregulated

telephone services. The seven RBOCs include the twenty-two BOCs. Also called regional companies and regional holding operating companies.
- **Regional center.** A class 1 office in the HIERARCHY OF SWITCHING CENTERS; the highest level toll office.
- **Regulatory commission.** An agency, such as the FEDERAL COMMUNICATIONS COMMISSION and the state PUBLIC UTILITIES COMMISSIONS, endowed by law with legislative, executive, and judicial powers.
- **Relay broadcasting.** Allows a FACSIMILE unit to automatically send a document to an intermediary facsimile unit, which in turn relays the document to a number of nearby locations.
- **Remote call forwarding.** Allows a company with customers located in another city to call the company as a local call.
- **Repeat Call.** A CLASS CALLING SERVICE that redials the last number the subscriber dialed, even if it was busy.
- **Repeater.** (1) A device that serves as an interface between two circuits, receiving signals from one circuit and transmitting them to the other. (2) A device that amplifies an input signal or—in the case of pulses—amplifies, reshapes, retimes, or performs a combination of any of these functions on an input signal for retransmission. It may be either a one-way or a two-way type. (TD) (3) LAN device that operates at the first level of the OSI MODEL. Extends the length of cable by repeating all electrical signals from one segment to the next.
- **Return Call.** A CLASS CALLING SERVICE that allows the subscriber to call back the last number received, whether or not the ring was answered.
- **Ringer.** Operated by electric current, alerting a person that someone is calling on the telephone.
- **Ring topology.** Connects all NODES in a closed loop.
- **Roaming.** Allows a user to use his or her mobile or portable cellular telephone to place and receive calls in cities outside his or her home service area.
- **Router.** A device that connects LANs at the NETWORK layer, layer 3 of the OSI MODEL. Can connect only two LANs using the same network operating systems.
- **RS-232 standard.** An Electronic Industry Association (EIA) standard that defines the electrical characteristics of the signals in the cables that connect a TERMINAL to communications equipment.
- **RS-232-C interface.** Identifies a specification defined by the Electronic Industries Association (EIA) detailing the physical configuration of the connector to interface between DATA COMMUNICATION EQUIPMENT and DATA TERMINAL EQUIPMENT. For example, the interface allows a FACSIMILE unit to communicate with TELEX/TWX.
- **Satellite communications.** (1) A type of UNGUIDED MEDIUM in which MICROWAVE signals are transmitted between EARTH STATIONS via a geosynchronous satellite. (2) The use of orbiting satellites to relay transmissions from one EARTH STATION to another or to several other earth stations by means of MICROWAVE.
- **Sectional center.** A class 2 office, the next to highest rank, in the HIERARCHY OF SWITCHING CENTERS.
- **Secure polling.** Requires that the polling FACSIMILE unit use a password to identify itself to the remote station.
- **Sequential broadcasting.** The FACSIMILE unit automatically sends the same document, one after the other, to multiple locations.
- **Selected Call Forwarding.** A CLASS CALLING SERVICE that is the same as CALL FORWARDING except that the subscriber determines which calls he or she wants forwarded by entering up to six callers' numbers.

- **Short-haul microwave system.** A MICROWAVE system that uses frequencies of 18 GHz and 23 GHz and can travel a distance from several hundred feet to about 15 miles and possibly more.
- **Short-haul modems.** Used for transmissions ranging from one to about twenty miles, require metallic (copper) lines, generally used to transmit data within company facilities at speeds usually ranging from 9600 to 19.2 kbps, some units reaching 1.5 Mbps.
- **Signal loss.** The drop in signal level between the sending and receiving points on a CIRCUIT.
- **Signal-to-noise ratio.** The ratio of the average signal power at any point in a TRANSMISSION path to the average noise power at that same point. The ratio is often expressed in DECIBELS. (EOBS)
- **Simplex transmission.** Signals are transmitted in only one direction.
- **Sine wave.** Represents the basic shape of an electrical wave.
- **Spanner.** Devices that expand the size of a LAN or connect a LAN with other LANs or WANs. Examples are REPEATERS, BRIDGES, ROUTERS, and GATEWAYS.
- **Special area codes (SACs).** Area codes designed for special purposes, such as 800 toll-free service numbers, 900 Dial-IT, and Western Union TWX service (510, 710, or 910).
- **Specialized server.** A computer designed exclusively to handle specific network services. Examples are database servers, print servers, and communication servers.
- **Special Ring.** Allows a distinct ring to be assigned to a maximum of six callers.
- **Speech synthesis.** A text-to-speech system in which the computer reads text and creates synthesized speech from the text. The computer converts textual information stored in ASCII into a computer-generated voice that synthesizes human speech.
- **Speed Calling.** Allows a user to call frequently called numbers by dialing only one or two digits.
- **Stand-alone fax equipment.** A unit that performs only the FACSIMILE function.
- **Stand-alone voice processing system.** Connects to a telephone system through a single-line extension and performs the basic VOICE PROCESSING functions: telephone answering, message STORE-AND-FORWARD, and call routing. Also called free-standing systems.
- **Standards.** (1) Communications standards are formally adopted and widely accepted rules that describe an agreed-on way for computers to communicate. (2) Sets of procedures that govern the interaction of equipment and networks allowing diverse equipment to communicate.
- **Star topology.** Connects all NODES (stations) to a central node, which routes data to the appropriate place.
- **Station.** One of the input or output points in a communications system, such as a STATION TERMINAL.
- **Station equipment.** Equipment that allows a customer to access the network and the available services. The most common station equipment being the ordinary single-line telephone set. (EOBS)
- **Station terminal.** The interface between the user and the system, such as a voice terminal (telephone sets) or a data terminal.
- **Statistical multiplexing (statmux).** A form of TIME-DIVISION MULTIPLEXING that makes use of the idle times in a TDM circuit by allocating BANDWIDTH to active terminals only.
- **Store-and-forward.** Allows the FACSIMILE machine to store documents in its memory and then transmit them at a later time and without an operator in attendance.

- **SubLAN.** Connect microcomputers by using their standard RS-232 serial PORTS instead of LAN NETWORK INTERFACE CARDS. Also called low-cost LANS or zero-slot LANS.
- **Subscriber.** An individual station set user.
- **Switchhook.** A plunger beneath the telephone handset that is an electrical make-and-break connection that turns the telephone on and off.
- **Switching.** Refers to the process of connecting appropriate lines and trunks to form a desired communication path between two station sets. Included are all kinds of related functions, such as sending and receiving signals, monitoring the status of CIRCUITS, translating addresses to routing instructions, alternate routing, testing circuits for busy condition, and detecting and recording troubles. (EOBS)
- **Switching center.** A location where an incoming call/message is automatically or manually directed to one or more outgoing CIRCUITS.
- **Switching matrix.** Switches telephone calls by creating and maintaining a path for signals to travel between the calling party and the called party. Space-division switching requires a physically separate pathway for each call; time-division switching shares a single high-speed pathway for all calls.
- **Switching system.** An electromechanical or electronic system for connecting lines to lines, lines to trunks, or trunks to trunks.
- **Synchronous conference.** All participants in a TELECONFERENCE are present simultaneously, regardless of location or time zone.
- **Synchronous transmission.** Transmission process whereby the information and control characters are transmitted at a fixed rate with the transmitter and receiver synchronized.
- **System access terminal (SAT).** Attaches directly to a PRIVATE BRANCH EXCHANGE'S control processor to allow the manager to administer the system's features and services.
- **Systems operator.** A company that bundles together several services offered by different companies and sells them at a fixed monthly charge and/or by usage time.
- **Tariffs.** A schedule published by a communication carrier filed (in the United States) with a state PUBLIC UTILITIES COMMISSION for intraservice or the FCC if interstate. A tariff includes the published rates, regulations, and descriptions governing the conditions under which the telephone services are available.
- **Telecommunications.** Any process that permits the passage of information from a sender to one or more receivers in any usable form (printed copy, fixed or moving pictures, visible or audible signals by means of electromagnetic system—electrical transmission by wire, radio, optical transmission, waveguides, etc.) Includes telegraphy, telephony, video-telephony, data transmission, etc. (DRC)
- **Teleconferencing.** The use of a TELECOMMUNICATIONS system for communicating with two or more groups or three or more individuals who are in separate locations. Communication is via audio, audiographics, video, and/or computer.
- **Telephone management system (TMS).** A computerized system that performs a variety of functions from recording, storing, and processing call data, to managing telephone facilities, to engineering its TRAFFIC.
- **Teleport.** A communication distribution center that allows its customers to share access to receiving and transmitting voice, data, and video information via satellite, FIBER-OPTIC CABLE, and MICROWAVE without directly incurring the large expense of their construction.
- **Teletext.** A pseudointeractive information retrieval system that uses a one-way television link for information transmission.

Glossary

- **Telewriter.** An electromechanical device that allows participants to write or draw their contributions as they talk.
- **Telex I and II.** A form of ELECTRONIC MAIL that uses a keyboard-oriented message system.
- **Terminals.** A *dumb terminal* is a low-speed terminal that transmits in asynchronous mode (by character). A *smart terminal* is a synchronous device that transmits at high speed entire blocks of data, can perform specific functions, such as editing and storing data, and can be POLLED. In addition to having the characteristics of a smart terminal, an *intelligent terminal* can accept programs written by the user and process data with little assistance from the host computer; some can operate as stand-alone computers.
- **Terrestrial microwave radio.** (1) A point-to-point medium with MICROWAVE ANTENNAS usually located at substantial heights above the ground and spaced 20–30 miles apart. (2) Also can be defined in terms of their frequencies at which they operate, such as between 1 and 23 GHz. (3) Or defined as a radio operating between two points via a focused beam of high-frequency radio signals. (4) A type of UNGUIDED MEDIUM in which signals are broadcast through the air to the receiving ANTENNA, which in turn retransmits them to the next antenna.
- **Three-Way Calling.** A CUSTOM CALLING SERVICE that allows a talking subscriber to add a third party to the conversation without operator assistance.
- **Throughput.** The number of bits, characters, or blocks which can pass through a data communications system, or portion thereof, when the system is working at saturation. The throughput, which is expressed in data units per period of time, will vary greatly from its theoretical maximum. For telephone systems throughput is measured in terms of the number of telephone call attempts satisfactorily processed per second. (TD)
- **T-1 line.** A basic 24-channel TIME-DIVISION MULTIPLEXED digital transmission facility, operating at 1.544 Mbps and above; usually provided by AT&T or BELL OPERATING COMPANIES.
- **Tie line.** (1) A leased or private dedicated telephone line provided by common carriers that links two points together without using the PUBLIC SWITCHED TELEPHONE NETWORK; (2) A telephone line directly connecting two PRIVATE BRANCH EXCHANGES.
- **Time-division multiple access.** A TIME-DIVISION MULTIPLEXING method used in SATELLITE COMMUNICATIONS transmission.
- **Time-division multiplexing (TDM).** (1) A multiplexing or channel-sharing technique in which each station has access to transmit at certain times under rules enforced by a network controller. (2) A MULTIPLEXING system in which the original ANALOG SIGNALS are converted into digital form. The DIGITAL SIGNALS for several CHANNELS are then transmitted sequentially at discrete time intervals.
- **Tip and ring leads.** The two conductors associated with a two-wire cable pair that connects each telephone to a CENTRAL OFFICE switch.
- **Token passing.** A NONCONTENTION-ORIENTED METHOD for accessing a LAN that is primarily used with RING TOPOLOGIES.
- **Toll center.** A class 4 office in the HIERARCHY OF SWITCHING CENTERS; the lowest level toll office.
- **Traffic.** Describes the flow of information or messages through the network. This information flow may be generated by telephone conversations or may be the result of providing data, audio, and video services. (EOBS)
- **Traffic engineering.** A network planning activity that determines the number and

type of channels or communication paths required between switching points and the call-handling capacity of the switching points.
- **Traffic load.** Determined by the number of calls carried by the communication path or CHANNEL and the duration of each call or its average HOLDING TIME.
- **Traffic modeling.** A TELEPHONE MANAGEMENT SYSTEM feature that allows users to perform "what if" analyses based on various desired GRADE-OF-SERVICE requirements.
- **Transaction processing.** In a VOICE PROCESSING system, provides a telephone interface into an external computer for access to its database or other information, such as order entry. Also called voice response.
- **Transceiver.** Combines the FACSIMILE transmitter and receiver into one unit.
- **Transducer.** Any device that converts energy from one form to another, such as a CODEC or a MODEM.
- **Translator software.** Computer software that translates documents from a sender's internal format to an accepted ELECTRONIC DATA INTERCHANGE format.
- **Transmission.** The process of sending information in the form of electrical signals over a NETWORK or facility from one point to another.
- **Transponder.** A MICROWAVE REPEATER onboard the satellite, amplifies the UPLINK signals and then retransmits them to the satellite's ANTENNA, which sends them to their destination EARTH STATION(s) within the particular satellite's FOOTPRINT. Today, satellites generally have 24 transponders.
- **Trouble reporting and tracking.** A TELEPHONE MANAGEMENT SYSTEM feature that allows users to monitor and control maintenance problems.
- **Trunk.** The transmission CIRCUIT or LINK that carries telephone calls between two SWITCHING SYSTEMS, such as CENTRAL OFFICES, toll switching systems, PRIVATE BRANCH EXCHANGES, and KEY TELEPHONE SYSTEMS.
- **Trunked radio.** A two-way radio system that allows automatic sharing of a small number of radio CHANNELS by a large number of users.
- **Two-way videoconferencing.** Provides two or more sites with interactive, two-way video, audio, and graphics capabilities.
- **Unguided medium.** A TRANSMISSION medium, such as terrestrial MICROWAVE radio and satellite communications, that uses the atmosphere and outer space.
- **Uplink/downlink.** In SATELLITE COMMUNICATIONS, separate frequencies used for the two directions of TRANSMISSION are expressed in frequency pairs, such as 6/4 GHz band pair. The higher figure represents the uplink, while the lower represents the downlink.
- **Value-added network.** A COMMON CARRIER that provides services in addition to transmitting unaltered data streams.
- **Vertical blanking interval.** An unallocated segment of the BANDWIDTH of a broadcast television signal used for TELETEXT, a one-way transmission system.
- **Very small aperture terminal (VSAT).** A small EARTH STATION with an ANTENNA (dish) only 2–6 feet in diameter.
- **Videofax.** Combines a Group 3 FACSIMILE unit with a 16mm camera, a display screen, and a telephone INTERFACE. Allows users to receive pictures of three-dimensional objects.
- **Videotex.** Easy-to-use interactive electronic services that allow a user to access textual or graphics information and services on a personal or a dedicated videotex terminal.
- **Videotex fees.** *Flat-rate pricing* charges the user a monthly or annual subscription for unlimited access to the system. *Tiered flat-rate pricing* charges the subscriber for

Glossary

particular tiers or levels of information. *Usage-based pricing* charges subscribers only for online time. *Hybrid pricing* combines two or more of the pricing systems.

- **Virtual fax.** Transmits FACSIMILE by using a microcomputer compared to "traditional" facsimile, which uses a TRANSCEIVER.
- **Voiceband modems.** Range from low-speed MODEMS (up to 1200 bps), to medium-speed modems (up to 4800 bps), to high-speed modems (9600 bps and above). Also called long-haul modems.
- **Voice mail.** This function in a VOICE PROCESSING system provides for "nonsimultaneous" conversations that allow a subscriber to send messages to one or more subscribers or groups of subscribers as well as to reply to these messages. Also called voice store-and-forward or interactive messaging.
- **Voice messaging.** In an automated office system, allows a user to retrieve, create, reply to, or forward voice messages by following the display prompts and pressing the appropriate keys on the system. Telephone conversations can also be recorded by using this feature.
- **Voice processing.** The umbrella terms for the various voice functions, such as telephone answering, CALLER ROUTING, INTERACTIVE MESSAGING, INFORMATION PROVIDING, and TRANSACTION PROCESSING.
- **Voice recognition.** The ability of the computer to transform the wavelengths of the human voice into computer text.
- **Voice response.** See TRANSACTION PROCESSING.
- **Voice store-and-forward.** See VOICE MAIL.
- **VSAT network.** Includes a master EARTH STATION that acts as the hub for a number of small earth stations to form a star network. See also STAR TOPOLOGY.
- **White noise.** Also called thermal noise, the familiar background hiss or static on radio and telephone.
- **Wide-area network (WAN).** Connects computers that are geographically separated, such as across a city, a country, or countries.
- **Wide-Area Telephone Service (WATS).** A service that allows customers to make (OUT-WATS) or receive (IN-WATS) long-distance calls and to have them billed on a bulk basis rather than individually. (EOBS)
- **Wideband modem.** Similar to VOICEBAND MODEMS except that it operates in a different part of the frequency spectrum and uses more BANDWIDTH to transmit more information or transmit it faster. Also called broadband modem.
- **Work order preparation and tracking.** A TELEPHONE MANAGEMENT SYSTEM feature for managing work orders, such as entering new service orders, tracking service activity, and recording order completion.
- **Workstation.** A microcomputer with an installed NETWORK INTERFACE CARD that serves as a major component of a LAN.

INDEX

Acoustic modem (acoustic coupler), 179
Add-on conference, 126, 146
Ad/hoc videoconference, 488, 490
ADP Network Services, 588
Advertiser-supported public access videotex services, 446–47
Altitude control apparatus, 288
American National Standards Institute (ANSI), 277, 586
American Standard Code for Information Interchange (ASCII) Code
 definition, 30–33, 319
 telex, 319
 videotex, 437–38
 voice processing, 370
American Telephone and Telegraph Company (AT&T), 10–12, 94–98, 127, 317, 318, 427, 466, 470–72, 475, 583–84. *See also* Bell System
Analog bridge, 188–89
Analog transmission, 483–84
 signals and circuits, 29
Antiope, 426, 433, 437–38
Arpanet, 321
Asynchronous conference, 465
Asynchronous transmission, 32, 175–76
AT&T Bell Laboratories, 95, 98, 475, 515, 580–81
AT&T long-distance network
 bypassing the PSTN, 108–09
 competitors, 99–100
 equal access, 106
 hierarchy of switching, 100–03
 interLATA calls, 103–05
 long-distance services, 109–12
 resellers, 107–08
 selecting, 116–17
AT&T Long Lines, 94–95
AT&T Mail, 323, 329, 331
Audio conferencing, 465–67, 468–76
 applications, 464, 476
 benefits, 476
 bridges, 469–73
 bridge services, 470–73
 drawbacks, 476
 equipment and facilities, 473–75
 transmission, 468–69
Audio conferencing bridges, 469–73

Audiotex. *See* Information providing
Automated attendant. *See* Caller routing
Automated (comprehensive) office systems, 375–76. *See also* Comprehensive office systems
Automatic call distribution (ACD), 80, 145, 148–50
Automatic callback, 126, 146
Automatic Electric Company, 580
Automatic routing of calls (ARS), 136, 147–48, 546–48

Bain, Alexander, 390
Bandwidth, 24–27
 circuit capacity, 27
 electromagnetic spectrum, 24–26
 satellite, 290
 voice bandwidth, 26–28
Bardeen, John, 581
Barrel effect, 474
Baseband network, 230
Baudot code, 319
Bell, Alexander Graham, 580
Bell Communications Research, Inc. (BELLCORE), 98
Bell operating companies, 95–96, 98, 103–05, 107, 108–09, 126
Bell System
 after divestiture, 96–100
 in 1982, 94–96
Binary system, 31–36, 326, 395
Blocked calls, 539–40, 544
Blocking PBX, 141
Brattain, Walter, 581
Bridge, 239–43
Broadband network, 230–31
BRS/Search Service, 588
Buffer, 169–70, 250
Business telephone system(s), 124–60
 selecting, 157–60
Business television, 485–91
 applications, 9, 463–64, 465–67, 488–91
 definition, 486
 networks, 487–89
 operation, technology, and equipment, 486–87
Bus topology, 221–25
Busy hour, 365–67, 540–45
Bypassing the PSTN, 4, 108–09

 carrier bypass, 108
 private (complete) bypass, 108

Cable management, 563
Call accounting, 539, 555
Call block, 63–64, 79–80
Caller routing, 377–78
Call forwarding, 63–64, 78–79, 126, 146
Call hold, 135
Call park, 146
Call pickup, 126, 135, 146
Call restriction, 147, 549
Call trace, 79–80
Call waiting, 63–64, 78, 146
Campbell, George, 580
Camp-on, 146
Carried load, 538–40
Carrier system, 37
Carrier wave, 39
Carterfone decision, 126–27, 390, 584
C-band, 290–91
Cellular mobile telephone service
 carriers, 516–17
 evolution, 515
 market areas, 516
 system operation, 517–18
Cellular system operation
 cell station, 517–18
 geographic area, 517
 hands off, 518
 mobile telephone switching office (MTSO), 517–18
 radio channels, 518
 roaming, 518
Cellular Telecommunications Industry Association, 515
Cellular telephone
 applications, 10, 507, 521–22
 components, 518–19
 features, 522–24
 operation, 519
 selecting, 522–27
 types, 519–21
Central office, 68–73, 100
 dial tone, 70
 dialing pulsing, 70
 dual tone multi-frequency, 70–71
 local telephone calls, 71–73
 switching, 68–69
Central office LAN, 256

618

Index

Centrex services, 126, 151–56
　comparison with PBX systems, 155–56
　evolution, 153
　features, 126, 154–55
　market, 155
　operation, 80–81, 153–54
　rates, 155
Channel, 37. *See also* Circuit
　definition, 37
Circuit, 37–38
　four-wire circuit, 38
　two-wire circuit, 38
Citizens Band (CB) radio, 508
Clarke, Arthur C., 282
Class calling services, 79–80
Class of service, 145
Coaxial cable, 4, 49, 50–52, 229
Codec, 21, 34, 139, 171, 484
Common carrier pricing, 558–61
Common ring, 136
Communications Act of 1934, 12, 516, 583–84
Communication Satellite Corporation (COMSAT), 292
Communications system
　basic elements, 21, 22
Comprehensive office systems, 327–28. *See also* Automated office systems
Compressed digital video, 484
CompuServe, 329, 333, 334, 426, 427, 431, 440–41, 448, 453, 464, 492, 588
Computer conferencing, 465–67, 491–96
　administering, 493
　applications, 9–10, 464, 492–93
　benefits, 494–98
　comparison with E-mail and bulletin boards, 495–96
　definition, 491–92
　drawbacks, 495
　operation, 492
　VAX Notes, 493–94
Computer Inquiry I, 584
Computer Inquiry II, 96, 127, 584
Computer-based message system(s), 321–32
　applications, 5, 7, 315–17
　benefits, 332
　comparison with voice processing system, 355
　definition, 321–22
　drawbacks, 321–22
　features, 324, 326–37
　operation, 322–35
　selecting, 345–47
　types of systems, 327–31
Conference telephone, 474–75
Connectivity, 231

Consent Decree (1956), 584
Consent Decree (1982), 11, 584
Consultation hold, 146
Consultative Committee on International Radio (CCIR), 299, 585
Consultative Committee on International Telephone and Telegraph (CCITT), 585–87
　International numbering plan, 73
　ISDN, 257
　See also Standards
Contention-oriented methods, 227–28
Continuous presence video, 480
Conversation time, 538–39
Cornell, Ezra, 580
Corporation for Open Systems (COS) International, 232
Custom calling services, 78–79

Data communications equipment (DCE), 166
Data General
　Comprehensive Electronic Office, 323, 324, 327–28, 375–76
Data network, 165–66
Data PBX, 252–54
DRI (Data Resources Inc.), 588
Data service unit, 171
Data switches, 248–50
Data terminal equipment (DTE), 166
Decibel (dB), 45–49
　signal-to-noise ratio, 48–49
Decoder, 430, 435
DECtalk, 370–71
DECvoice response system, 353, 373
DeForest, Lee, 580
Delphi, 588–89
Dialcom, Inc., 329, 330, 333, 464
　CAUCAS, 493
　Dialcom Message Service, 323–25
Dialog, 449–50, 451, 589
Differential phase-shift keying method, 36
Digital Equipment Corporation, 235–37
　All-In-One, 324, 328, 330, 371, 375
　DECtalk, 370–71
　DECvoice response system, 353, 373
　VAX Notes, 493–95
Digital-sharing device, 189–90, 198–99
Digital transmission, 483–85
　benefits, 33
　signals and circuits, 29–33
　signal conversion, 34–36
Digitized speech, 360–69, 373
Direct-connect modem, 178

Direct inward dialing (DID), 141, 153
Direct outward dialing (DOD), 146, 153
Distinctive ringing, 146
Divestiture agreement of 1982, 94
Dow Jones News/Retrieval, 427, 429, 453, 589
Downlink, 287, 290–91
Dynamic nonhierarchical routing (DNHR), 103, 104

Earth station, 287, 293–98
　definition, 56, 285
　receive only, 293
　transmit, 294
EasyLink, 319, 331, 326, 329. *See also* Western Union Corporation
Effective isotropic radiated power (EIRP), 287–88
EIA RS-232, 172–75
Electrical waves, 24, 25
Electromagnetic spectrum, 24–27
Electronic Data Interchange, 327, 337–46
　applications, 7, 316, 337
　benefits, 344–45
　definition, 337–38, 339
　drawbacks, 345
　operation, 338–42
　selecting, 345–46
　standards, 340, 342–44
Electronic Industries Association (EIA), 586
Electronic Mail, 314–48
　applications, 5, 7–8, 315–16
　computer-based message system(s), 321–22
　definition, 316–17
　electronic data interchange, 337–45
　evolution, 317
　facsimile, 388–418
　selecting, 345–47
　standards, 326, 332–37, 342–44
　telex, 317–20
　voice processing, 352–84
Electronic Mail Association (EMA), 316
Electronic switch (ESS), 85–87
　1AESS, 153
　5AESS, 85–87, 153
Enhanced audio conferencing, 465–67, 476–80
　applications, 479–80
　facsimile, 477
　freeze-frame video, 478–79
　telewriters, 477
Erlang, A. K., 541
Erlang B theory, 543
Erlang C theory, 543

Erlangs, 541–46
Ethernet, 237, 240, 245
European Computer Manufacturers Association (ECMA), 586
Executive override, 146

Facility-based teleport, 303–04
Facsimile, 388–418
 applications, 7–8, 10, 389–90, 411–12
 benefits, 412–14
 data compression, 399
 definition, 390
 drawbacks, 414–15
 evolution, 390–92
 public fax services, 408–11
 selecting a fax system, 415–18
 technology, 392–96
Facsimile equipment
 Fax-Alert, 407
 features, 402–04
 placement, 401–02
 portable fax, 404–05
 types of, 399–401
 virtual fax, 405–06
Facsimile equipment standards, 396–99
 classification, 396–97
 machine protocol and transmission, 397–99
Faraday, Michael, 580
Federal Communications Association (FCC), 584, 585
 Carterfone decision, 126–27, 390, 584
 Computer Inquiry II, 96, 127
 definition, 12
 electromagnetic spectrum, 24–27
 interLATA calls, 105
 key telephone system, 134–35
 microwave, 272, 282
 mobile, 509, 510, 513, 516, 518, 524
 regulatory trends, 570
 satellite, 299
 tariffs, 546
 videotex, 456
Federal Information Processing Standards (FIPS), 587
Federal Telecommunications Standards (FTSC), 587
Feedhorn (feed), 293, 294, 295
Fiber-optic cable, 4, 49, 52–54, 229
Fiber-optic data distribution interface (FDDI), 229–30
Floppy-disk exchange, 247
Footprint, 287
Foreign exchange, 107, 113–15
Free space path loss, 288
Freeze-frame video, 476, 478–80
Frequency-division multiple access (FDMA), 295

Frequency-division multiplexing, 40–42, 43, 44, 193–94
Frequency-shift keying method, 35–36
Fresnel zones, 273, 281
Front-end processor, 197–99
Full-duplex transmission, 37, 38, 175

Gateway, 239–40, 245–47, 431–32
GE Information Services Quik-Comm, 329, 330, 332. *See also* GEnie
GEnie, 428–29, 431, 453, 589
Grade of service, 366–67, 540–46, 558–59
Graham-Willis Act (1921), 583
Greene, Judge Harold H., 98
Guardband, 27

Half-duplex transmission mode, 37, 175
Hands-free answer, 146
Hands off, 518
Hierarchy of switching, 100–03
Holding time, 538–39, 542–43
Human Resources Information Network (HRIN), 389
Hundred call seconds (CCS), 541–46
 applications, 543–46

IBM Corporation, 236–37, 246, 301
 PROFS, 324, 328, 330, 375
 DISOSS, 324
Independent telephone companies, 96, 99, 105–06
Information provider, 450–51
Information providing, 354, 378
Institute of Electrical and Electronic Engineers (IEEE), 586–87
Integrated Services Digital Network, 257–60
 applications, 5, 6, 570, 582
 benefits, 260
 comparison with LANs, 260
 definition, 257
 tariffs, 578
 technology and operation, 258–60
 teleports, 307
Integrated terminal, 430
INTELSAT, 292–93
INTELSAT VI, 285, 292, 293
Interactive messaging, 378
Interconnect industry, 126–27
Interexchange carriers, 105
InterLATA calls, 103–05
International Electrotechnical Commission (IEC), 585
International numbering plan, 73
International Organization for Standardization (ISO), 231–32, 437, 585

International service carriers, 320
International Telecommunication Union (ITU), 299, 585
International Teleconferencing Association, 505
Interoffice call, 71
Interoperability, 231
Intraexchange carriers, 105
IntraLATA calls, 103–05
Intraoffice call, 71
Inward WATS, 110–12

Ka-band, 291–92
Key behind PBX, 143
Key telephone system(s) (KTS), 126, 127–36
 applications, 127–28, 134
 capacity, 133
 components and operation, 128, 133
 electronic KTS, 127–28, 132–33, 136
 evolution, 129
 hybrid KTS, 133–35, 136
 KTS costs, 136
 KTS functions/features, 126, 135–36
 KTS market, 136
 1A telephone system, 127, 129, 130–32
Kingsbury Commitment (1913), 583
Kiosks, 8, 444–48
Ku-band, 291, 292
Kurzweil Voice Works, 371–72. *See also* VoiceEM

Land mobile communication services, 508
Last number dialed, 146
Least-cost routing (LCR). *See* Automatic routing of calls
Lexis/Nexis, 450, 589
Lightguide cable. *See* Fiber-optic cable
Line conditioning, 177–80
Line-of-sight transmission, 54, 272–73
Local access and transport areas (LATAs), 103–06
Local area network (LAN), 212–47
 access methods, 225–28
 applications, 4–5, 214, 242–43, 305, 483, 487
 business television, 487
 bus topology, 221–25
 CBMS, 321, 323, 327, 334
 comparison with ISDN, 260
 components, 218–19
 definition, 214–15
 faxing, 406

Index

Local area network (*continued*)
  hardware components, 217–19, 237
  hierarchy, 237–39
  hybrid topology, 224
  logical topology, 221–22
  managing, 256, 258
  microwave, 280
  physical topology, 221
  reasons for networking, 216–17
  ring topology, 221, 223–24
  selecting, 256–57
  software components, 219–21
  span technology, 239–47
  standards, 231–35
  star topology, 221–24
  transmission media, 228–30
  transmission methods, 230–31
  videoconferencing, 483
Local area network alternatives
  central office LAN, 256
  data PBX, 252–54
  data switches, 248–50
  floppy-disk exchange, 247
  multiuser systems, 254–55
  subLANs, 250–52
Local loop (line), 68–73, 76, 82–83
Logical topology, 222–23
Long-distance carriers. *See* AT&T long-distance network; Other common carriers
Long-distance competitors, 99–100, 105
Long-distance services, 107–12
  AT&T Communications, 109–11
  MCI Communications, 110–11
  Wide Area/Bulk-Rate Services, 110–12
Long-haul microwave system, 272
Louisiana Public Service Commission v. FCC, 12

Mann-Elkins Act (1910), 583
Marconi, Guglielmo, 581
Market service areas (MSAs), 103–06
MCI Mail, 326, 329, 331, 333, 334
Meet-me bridging, 470
Message transfer agents (MTAs), 334–36
Microwave communication, 271
Microwave hop, 275
Microwave radio, 268–79
  advantages/drawbacks, 54–55
  applications, 4, 55–56, 109, 278–80, 269, 270–271, 483, 487
  comparison with fiber-optic and leased lines, 280, 281
  cost, 277
  definition, 54–56, 271–72
  evolution, 272, 581
  licensing, 277, 282

line-of-sight, 54, 272–73
planning, 280–82, 283
technology and operation, 272–75
videoconferencing, 483
Microwave repeaters, 276–77, 289
  active, 277
  passive, 277
Mobile communications, 506–27
Mobile communications services
  channel availability, 510
  evolution, 508–10
  types, 508
Mobile telephone service, 514–22
  cellular mobile telephone service, 515–22
  conventional mobile telephone service, 514–15
Mobile telephone switching office (MTSO), 517–18
Modem, 21, 35, 169–85
  configuration, 172–75
  data compression, 180–81
  definition, 21, 35, 170–71
  line conditioning, 179–80
  microwave radio, 275
  selecting, 183, 185
  standards, 181–82
  types, 175–78
Modem equipment
  basic components, 172
  dumb modem, 172
  equipment interface, 173–75
  features, 183–84
  smart modem, 172–73
Modem standards, 181–82
  Bell, 181
  CCITT, 181–82
  Hayes compatibility, 182
Modified Final Judgment (MFJ), 96, 98, 106
Modulation
  amplitude modulation, 39, 40
  definition, 39
  frequency modulation, 39, 41
Morse, Samuel, 317, 579
Multiplexing, 39–45
  frequency-division multiplexing, 40–42, 44, 193–94
  statistical multiplexing, 193, 195–97
  time-division multiplexing, 40, 42–43, 45, 193–94
  T-1 multiplexing, 193, 195, 277
Multiuser systems, 254–55
Music on hold, 147

National Radio Conferences (1923 and 1924), 583
Newsnet, Inc., 590
Network, 214
  applications, 164

multiplexing, 190–93
multipoint, 187–91
point-to-point, 185–86
Network interface card (NIC), 218
Network server, 218–19
Night answer, 147
Night class of service, 145
Nonblocking PBX, 141
Noncontention-oriented methods, 225–27
Nonwireline company, 516
North American Presentation Level Protocol Syntax (NAPLPS), 427, 437–38
Number identification, 63–64, 79–80
Numbering plan
  international numbering plan, 73–76
  numbering plan area code, 73–75
  special area codes, 73
Nutt, Emma M., 83
Nyquist interval, 34

Octel Communications Corporation, 361–69
Offered load, 538–40
Official Airline Guides, 439, 445
Off-hook, 69
On-hook, 69
Open systems interconnection (OSI) reference model, 336, 437
  benefits, 234
  description, 232–34
Operating time, 538–39
Operator-specific public access videotex services, 447–48
Other common carriers
  bypassing the PSTN, 108–09
  defined, 99–100
  equal access, 106
  interLATA calls, 103–05
  long-distance services, 110–11, 117
  operation, 106–07
  resellers, 107–08
  selecting, 116–17
Outward WATS, 110–12

Packet-switching network, 200–05, 396, 431–32
  advantages, 204–05
  definition, 200–02
  routes, 202
  selecting, 205
  types, 202–04
  X.25 standard, 204
Pagers, 10, 512–13. *See also* Radio paging
Pan American Satellite Corporation, 292
Parity, 31–32

Peg count, 539, 542, 556
Perishable information, 439
Permanent information, 439
Permanent virtual circuit, 202
Phonemes, 369–70
Physical topology, 221
Point-to-multipoint videoconferencing, 486
Point-to-point videoconferencing, 486
Poisson theory, 543
Polling, 168
Post Roads Act (1866), 583
Predicasts Terminal System (PTS), 590
Prestel, 426, 437–38, 454
Priority ring (special ring), 63–64, 79–80
Private branch exchange (PBX), 137–51
  architecture, 150–51
  comparison with Centrex services, 155–56
  components and operation, 80–81, 139–42
  evolution, 138–39
  features, 126, 144–50
  market, 151
  peripheral equipment, 142–44
Private business television network, 488, 489
Private information, 440
Private lines, 107, 113–15, 146, 396
  foreign exchange, 114–15
  remote call forwarding, 114–15
  T-1 lines, 113, 115, 258–59
  tie lines, 113, 141
Private VSAT network, 295
Prodigy, 448–49, 453
Program evaluation and review technique, 280–82
Programmable buttons, 136
Propagation, 47–48, 273
Protocol, 232
Public business television network, 488
Public electronic mail services, 328–31
Public fax service, 408–11
Public information, 440
Public Service Satellite Consortium, 505
Public switched telephone network, 100–04, 431
  definition, 100
  dynamic nonhierarchical routing, 103
  hierarchy of switching, 100–03
Public utility, 11
Public utility commission (PUC), 12
Public VSAT network, 296

Radio Act (1912), 583
Radio Act (1929), 583
Radio paging, 510–13
  applications, 10, 507
  cost, 512, 513
  operation, 511
  types of pagers, 512–13
Radome, 276
Real-estate based teleport, 303–04
Regional Bell operating companies, 12, 98–99, 126, 153–55
Regulatory agencies, 105–06
Regulatory commissions
  Federal Communications Commission (FCC), 12
  Public utility commission (PUC), 12
Remote call forwarding, 113–15
Remote location access, 148
Repeat call, 63–64, 79–80
Repeater, 239–40, 245–47, 276–77, 289
Resellers, 107–08
Return call, 63–64, 79–80
Ring topology, 221, 223–24
Roaming, 518
Rolm Corporation, 356
Router, 239–40, 244

Satellite, 288–90
Satellite communications, 56–57, 268–70, 282–301
  advantages/drawbacks, 56–67
  application, 4, 109, 269, 282–84, 296–99, 463–64, 483, 487
  comparison with fiber-optic networks, 299–300
  definition, 285
  earth stations, 285, 293
  evolution, 285, 581
  standards and licensing, 299
  technology and operation, 56–57, 286–99
  videoconferencing, 403
  VSAT technology, 294–97
Selected call forwarding, 79–80
Shockley, William, 581
Short-haul microwave system, 272
Sibley, Hiram, 580
Signal conversion, 27–34
  analog signals and circuits, 29
  binary system, 30–31
  converting from analog to digital, 34
  converting from digital to analog, 34–36
  digital signals and circuits, 29–30, 31
Signal direction, 37–38
Signal loss, 273
  absorption, 274
  fading, 274
  free space attenuation, 273
Signal-to-noise ratio, 48–49
Simplex transmission, 37, 175
Sine wave, 24–25, 39
Sound waves, 22–23
Space-division network, 87
Space-division switching, 138
Span technology, 239–47
Speakerphone, 473–74
Special area codes (SACs), 73
Special ring, 79–80
Speech synthesis. *See* Text-to-speech
Speed calling (speed dialing), 63–64, 79, 146
Standards
  advantages/drawbacks, 13
  ANSI X.12, 339–41, 342–48
  ANSI X379.5, 229
  Audio Message Interchange Standard (AMIS), 381
  CCITT V.35, 235
  CCITT X.20, 235
  CCITT X.21, 235
  CCITT X.25, 204, 235, 247
  CCITT X.225, 235
  CCITT X.400, 326, 332–35, 336, 344
  CCITT X.500, 334–37
  CCITT fax standards, 396–99
  DECnet, 235–37, 245, 247
  de facto standards, 235–37
  definition, 12–13
  DNA, 237
  EIA RS-232, 172–75, 235, 370
  IEEE 800, 234–35
  over-the-air teletext, 435
  SNA, 236–37, 246
  standard-setting organizations, 585–87
  TCP/IP, 235–37, 244–45
  videotex, 437–39, 454–55
  XNS, 235, 237
  See also Modem standards
Star topology, 221–24
Station hunting, 146
Station message detail recording, 126, 143, 147
Statistical multiplexing, 193, 195–97
Store-and-forward conference, 465
Strowger, A. B., 84, 580
SubLANs, 250–52
Supervisory signals, 135
Switch, 68–72, 100–03, 153
Switching matrix
  space-division, 138, 140
  time-division, 138, 140
Switching system, 68–69, 83–87
  function, 83
  types of switches, 83–87
Switch virtual circuit, 202

Index

Synchronous conference, 465
Synchronous transmission, 32–33, 166–68, 175–76, 185–86
  asynchronous mode, 32
  synchronous mode, 33
Systems operator, 443–44

Tandem office switch, 71–72, 100, 107
Tariff, 127, 546
Telecommunications
  definition, 4
  evolution, 579–82
  history of regulations, 583–84
  introduction to, 3–16
  issues, 10–14
Telecommunications management, 536–37
  organizational and management trends, 570–72
  regulatory trends, 570
  technology trends, 569–70
Telecommunications manager, 14–16
Telecommunications network
  definition, 82
  physical facilities, 82–87
Teleconferencing, 462–500
  applications, 8–10, 463–64, 465, 468
  audio conferencing, 465–67, 468–76
  bandwidth, 468–69
  benefits, 496–98
  business television, 465–67, 485–91
  computer conferencing, 465–67, 491–96
  definition, 464–65
  drawbacks, 498
  enhanced audio conferencing, 465–67, 476–80
  evolution, 466–68
  planning, conducting, evaluating, 498–500
  two-way videoconferencing, 465–67, 480–85
Telegraph, evaluation of, 579–81
Telenet, 329
Telephone basics, 62–87
Telephone components, 64–68
  dual tone multi-frequency signaling, 67, 70, 71
  pushbutton keypad, 67, 70
  ringer, 67
  ring leads, 67, 68, 72
  rotary dial, 67, 70
  switchhook, 67
  tip leads, 67, 68, 72
  transmitter and receiver, 65–67
Telephone cost control methods, 546–50
  authorized codes and levels of service, 549–50
  automatic route selection/least-cost routing, 546–48
  calling restrictions, 549
  timed signals, 550
Telephone, evolution of, 580–81
Telephone exchange services, 76
  basic exchange services, 76–77
  Centrex services, 80–81
  class calling services, 79–80
  custom calling services, 78–79
  local calling plan, 77
  911 emergency service, 77–78
Telephone management system (TMS), 550–69
  applications, 535–36
  benefits, 564–68
  configurations, 551–54
  definition, 551
  reports, 564, 565, 566, 567
  selecting, 568–69
Telephone management system (TMS) features, 555–63
  alarm monitoring and reporting, 563
  cable management, 563
  call accounting, 539, 555
  common carrier pricing, 558–61
  directory, 555–56, 557
  equipment inventory, 563
  traffic engineering, 558–59
  traffic modeling, 558–59
  traffic statistics, 556–59
  trouble reporting and tracking, 561–62
  vendor bill reconciliation, 563
  work order preparation and tracking, 562–63
Telephone operation, 68–73
  central office, 68–73
  local telephone calling, 71–73
  long-distance calling, 73–76
  numbering plans, 73–76
  switching, 68–69
  tandem office, 71–72
Telephony, 4n
Teleports, 4, 270, 302–08
  applications, 270, 305–07
  customers, 304
  definition, 302–03
  issues and trends, 307–08
  regulatory constraints, 304
  services offered, 304–05
  types of, 303–04
Telescan Inc., 590
Teletext, 424–27, 433–37, 439–56
  comparison with videotex, 436–37
  definition, 433
  equipment components, 434–36
  evolution, 426–27
  operation, 433–34
Teletext applications, 439–42
  computation, 440
  downline loading, 441–42
  information retrieval, 439–40
Teletext communication facilities
  broadband teletext, 436
  broadcast teletext, 435–36
  cabletext, 436
  narrowband teletext, 436
Telewriter, 476–77, 479
Telex, 317–20, 324
  benefits, 320
  domestic, 319–20
  drawbacks, 320
  international, 320
  operation, 318–19
  origin, 317
Telstar, 290, 581
Terminals, 166–69
  dumb, 166–68
  intelligent, 166–68
  selecting, 169
  smart, 166–68
Text-to-speech, 355, 360, 369–71, 373
Three-way calling, 63–64, 79
Tie line (Tie trunk), 113, 141, 540–41
Time-division multiple access (TDMA), 295
Time-division multiplexing, 40, 42–43, 45, 87, 193–94
T-1 lines, 113, 115, 258–59
T-1 multiplexing, 193, 195, 277
Traffic, 537–46
  defined, 82, 538
Traffic engineering, 538, 558–59
Traffic load, 538–46
  applications, 543–46
  blockage, 539–40, 544
  busy hour, 540–45
  characteristics, 538–39
  definition, 539
  grade of service, 540–46, 558–59
  measuring, 541–46
Traffic statistics, 556–59
Transaction processing, 379
Transducer, 22, 34–35
Translator software, 338
Transmission basics, 20–57
Transmission impairments, 43–49
  attenuation, 45–47
  crosstalk, 49
  delay distortion, 47–48
  echo, 21, 49
  noise, 48–49
Transmission media, 4, 43–44, 49–50
  coaxial cable, 4, 49–52, 229
  fiber-optic cable, 4, 49, 52–54, 229–30
  guided media, 49–50
  microwave radio, 4, 50, 54–56, 268–79
  open-wire lines, 49–50

Transmission media (*continued*)
  satellite communication, 4, 56–57, 268–70, 282–301
  twisted-pair wire, 4, 49–50, 228–29
  unguided media, 50
Transponder, 289–90, 291
Transport protocol, 232
Trunked radio, 514
Trunks, 71–73, 82–83, 100–03, 141–42
Twisted-pair wire, 4, 49–50, 228
Two-way radio, 508–10, 512–14
  conventional two-way radio, 514
  operation, 513–14
  trunked radio, 514
Two-way videoconferencing, 480–85
  applications, 9, 485
  cost, 485
  defined, 480
  operation, technology, equipment, 480–85
Tymnet, 305, 329

United States Sprint-Telenet, 54, 204, 317, 329, 333, 488, 491
Uplink, 287, 290–91
User agents (UAs), 334–36

Value added network (VAN), 202–05, 329, 339–40, 341, 396
VAX Notes, 493–95
Vertical blanking interval, 434
Very small aperture terminal (VSAT) system(s), 285, 294–301
  application, 298–99
  benefits, 296–98
  drawbacks, 298
  planning, 300–01
  selecting, 301
  standards and licensing, 299
  technology, 294–97
Videotex, 424–33, 436–50
  comparison with teletext, 436–37
  definition, 427
  equipment components, 430–33
  evolution, 426–27

  gateway, 431–32
  information privacy and confidentiality, 455
  information reliability, 455
  legal, 455–56
  operation, 427–29
  packet switching, 430–31
  PSTN, 430–31
  revenues and fees, 450–53
  selected commercial systems, 588–90
  selecting a system, 452–54
  standards, 454–55
  types of systems, 448–50
  ways of accessing, 432–33
Videotex applications, 8, 439–48
  business videotex, 442–43
  computation, 440
  downline loading, 441–42
  home or consumer-oriented videotex, 443–44
  information retrieval, 439–40
  messaging, 441
  public access videotex (PAV), 444–48
  transaction, 440–41
Videotex Industry Association, 444, 455, 460
VoiceEM, 354, 372, 382. *See also* Kurzweil Voice Works
Voice mail. *See* Interactive messaging
Voice Message Exchange (VMX), 355–56
Voice processing
  benefits, 379–81
  Centrex, 374–75
  comparison with CBMS, 355
  definition, 355
  drawbacks, 381–82
  evolution, 355–56
  functions and applications, 353–54, 376–79
  operating a system, 356–58
  PBX, 374–75
  selecting a system, 382
  system features, 358–60, 361, 362
  technology, 360–73

  types of systems, 373–76
Voice processing functions and applications, 7, 353–54, 376–79
  caller routing, 377–78
  information providing, 354, 378
  interactive messaging, 378
  telephone answering, 376–77
  transaction processing, 379
Voice recognition, 360, 371–73. *See also* Voice-to-text conversion
Voice response. *See* Transaction processing
Voice store-and-forward. *See* Interactive messaging
Voice-to-text conversion, 355, 360, 371–73
Voice transmission, 22–28
  bandwidth, 24–28
  electrical waves, 22, 24, 25
  sound waves, 22–28
VU/TEXT, 426, 450–51, 590

Wang Laboratories
  Integrated Office Solution (WIOS), 375
  Wang Office, 328
Watson, Thomas, 580
Waveguide, 276
Western Electric, 94–95
Western Union Corporation, 317–20, 328, 329. *See also* Easylink
Western Union Telegraph Company, 580
Wide area network (WAN)
  definition, 215
  reasons for networking, 216–17
Wide Area Telecommunications services (WATS), 109–12, 395
  application, 117
  definition, 110
  inward WATS, 110–12
  outward WATS, 110–12
Wireline company, 516
Workstation, 218, 219
World Teleport Association, The, 302